MW01670927

Topic relevant selected content from the highest rated entries, typeset, printed and shipped.

Combine the advantages of up-to-date and in-depth knowledge with the convenience of printed books.

A portion of the proceeds of each book will be donated to the Wikimedia Foundation to support their mission: to empower and engage people around the world to collect and develop educational content under a free license or in the public domain, and to disseminate it effectively and globally.

The content within this book was generated collaboratively by volunteers. Please be advised that nothing found here has necessarily been reviewed by people with the expertise required to provide you with complete, accurate or reliable information. Some information in this book maybe misleading or simply wrong. The publisher does not guarantee the validity of the information found here. If you need specific advice (for example, medical, legal, financial, or risk management) please seek a professional who is licensed or knowledgeable in that area.

Sources, licenses and contributors of the articles and images are listed in the section entitled "References". Parts of the books may be licensed under the GNU Free Documentation License. A copy of this license is included in the section entitled "GNU Free Documentation License"

Contents

Articles

References

Article Licenses

Robin Williams

Robin Williams	
 At "Stand Up for Heroes", a benefit organized by the Bob Woodruff Family Fund to raise money for injured U.S. servicemen (2007)	
Birth name	Robin McLaurin Williams
Born	July 21, 1951 Chicago, Illinois, United States
Medium	Stand-up, film, television
Nationality	American
Years active	1972–present
Genres	Character comedy, physical comedy, improvisational comedy, satire/political satire, observational comedy, blue comedy
Influences	Peter Sellers, Richard Pryor, Jonathan Winters, George Carlin, Chuck Jones
Influenced	Conan O'Brien, Frank Caliendo,[1] Dat Phan, Jo Koy
Spouse	Valerie Velardi (1978–1988; 1 child) Marsha Garces Williams (1989–2008; 2 children) Susan Schneider (2011–present)
Website	RobinWilliams.com [2]
Academy Awards	
Best Supporting Actor 1997 *Good Will Hunting* – Sean Maguire	
Emmy Awards	
Individual Performance in a Variety or Music Program 1987 *Carol and Carl and Whoopi and Robin* **Individual Performance in a Variety or Music Program** 1988 *ABC Presents A Royal Gala*	
Golden Globe Awards	

Best Actor – Television Series Musical or Comedy
1978 *Mork & Mindy* – Mork
Best Actor – Motion Picture Musical or Comedy
1987 *Good Morning, Vietnam* – Adrian Cronauer
Best Actor – Motion Picture Musical or Comedy
1991 *The Fisher King* – Parry
Best Actor – Motion Picture Musical or Comedy
1993 *Mrs. Doubtfire* – Daniel Hillard ("Euphegenia Doubtfire")
Cecil B. DeMille Award
2005
Screen Actors Guild Awards
Outstanding Performance by a Cast in a Motion Picture
1996 *The Birdcage* – Armand Goldman
Outstanding Performance by a Male Actor in a Supporting Role
1997 *Good Will Hunting* – Sean Maguire
American Comedy Awards
Funniest Actor in a Motion Picture (Leading Role)
1994 *Mrs. Doubtfire* – Daniel Hillard ("Euphegenia Doubtfire")

Robin McLaurin Williams[3] [4] (born July 21, 1951)[5] is an American actor and comedian. Rising to fame with his role as the alien Mork in the TV series *Mork and Mindy*, and later stand-up comedy work, Williams has performed in many feature films since 1980. He won the Academy Award for Best Supporting Actor for his performance in the 1997 film *Good Will Hunting*. He has also won two Emmy Awards, four Golden Globes, two Screen Actors Guild Awards and five Grammy Awards.[6] [7]

Early life

Williams was born in Chicago, Illinois. His mother, Laura McLaurin (née Smith, 1922–2001), was a former model from New Orleans, Louisiana.[8] His father, Robert Fitzgerald Williams (September 10, 1906 – October 18, 1987), was a senior executive at Ford Motor Company in charge of the Midwest region. His maternal great-great-grandfather was senator and Mississippi governor Anselm J. McLaurin.[9] Williams is of English, Welsh, Irish, and French ancestry.[10] He was raised in the Episcopal Church (his mother practiced Christian Science).[11] [12] He grew up in Bloomfield Hills, Michigan, where he was a student at the Detroit Country Day School,[13] and later moved to Woodacre, Marin County, California, where he attended the public Redwood High School. Williams studied at Claremont McKenna College (then called Claremont Men's College) for four years.[14] He has two half-brothers: Todd (who died August 14, 2007) and McLaurin.[15]

Williams has described himself as a quiet child whose first imitation was of his grandmother to his mother. He did not overcome his shyness until he became involved with his high-school drama department.[16]

In 1973, Williams was one of only 20 students accepted into the freshman class at the Juilliard School, and one of only two students to be accepted by John Houseman into the Advanced Program at the school that year, the other being Christopher Reeve.[17] In his dialects class, Williams had no trouble mastering all dialects quickly. Williams left Juilliard in 1976.

Television career

After appearing in the cast of the short-lived *The Richard Pryor Show* on NBC, Williams was cast by Garry Marshall as the alien Mork in the hit TV series *Happy Days*.[18] As Mork, Williams improvised much of his dialogue and physical comedy, speaking in a high, nasal voice. Mork's appearance was so popular with viewers that it led to a spin-off hit television sitcom, *Mork and Mindy*, which ran from 1978 to 1982; the show was written to accommodate Williams' improvisations. Although playing the same character as in his appearance in *Happy Days*, the show was set in the present day, in Boulder, Colorado, instead of the late '50s in Milwaukee. Mork was an extremely popular character, featured on posters, coloring books, lunchboxes, and other merchandise.

Starting in the late 1970s and throughout the 1980s, Williams began to reach a wider audience with his standup comedy, including three HBO comedy specials, *Off The Wall* (1978), *An Evening with Robin Williams* (1982), and *Robin Williams: Live at the Met* (1986). Also in 1986, Williams reached an ever wider audience to exhibit his style at the 58th Academy Awards show.

His stand-up work has been a consistent thread through his career, as is seen by the success of his one-man show (and subsequent DVD) *Robin Williams: Live on Broadway* (2002). He was voted 13th on Comedy Central's list "100 Greatest Stand-ups of All Time" in 2004.[19]

After some encouragement from his friend Whoopi Goldberg, he was set to make a guest appearance in the 1991 *Star Trek: The Next Generation* episode, "A Matter of Time", but he had to cancel due to a scheduling conflict;[20] Matt Frewer took his place as a time-traveling con man, Professor Berlingoff Rasmussen. Williams, along with Billy Crystal, appeared in a cameo together at the beginning of an episode of the third season of *Friends*. Both Williams and Crystal's parts weren't originally in the script. They were apparently in the building where the show was shooting and were asked to improvise their lines.[21]

Williams appeared on an episode of the American version of *Whose Line Is It Anyway?* (Season 3, Episode 9: November 16, 2000). During a game of "Scenes from a Hat", the scene "What Robin Williams is thinking right now" was drawn, and Williams stated "I have a career. What the hell am I doing here?"[22] On December 4, 2010, he appeared with Robert De Niro on SNL in the sketch *What Up with That*.

Movie roles

Most of Williams' acting career has been in film, although he has given some performances on stage as well (notably as Estragon in a production of *Waiting for Godot* with Steve Martin). His performance in *Good Morning, Vietnam* (1987) resulted in Williams being nominated for an Academy Award.[18] Many of his roles have been comedies tinged with pathos.

His role as the Genie in the animated film *Aladdin* (1992) was instrumental in establishing the importance of star power in voice actor casting. Williams also used his voice talents in *Fern Gully*, as the holographic Dr. Know in the 2001 film *A.I. Artificial Intelligence*, in the 2005 animated film *Robots*, the 2006 Academy Award-winning *Happy Feet*, and an uncredited vocal performance in the film *Everyone's Hero*. Furthermore, he was the voice of The Timekeeper, a former attraction at the Walt Disney World Resort about a time-traveling robot who encounters Jules Verne and brings him to the future.

In 1998, he won an Oscar as Best Supporting Actor for his role as a psychologist in *Good Will Hunting*.[18] Williams has also starred in dramatic films, which earned him two subsequent Academy Award nominations: First for playing an English teacher in *Dead Poets Society* (1989), and later for playing a troubled homeless man in *The Fisher King* (1991);[18] that same year, he played an adult Peter Pan in the movie *Hook*. Other acclaimed dramatic films include *Awakenings* (1990) and *What Dreams May Come* (1998). In the 2002 film *Insomnia*, Williams portrays a writer/killer on the run from a sleep-deprived Los Angeles policeman (played by Al Pacino) in rural Alaska. And also in 2002, in the psychological thriller *One Hour Photo*, Williams played an emotionally disturbed photo development technician who becomes obsessed with a family for whom he has developed pictures for a long time. In 2006 Williams starred in *The Night Listener*, a thriller about a radio show host who realizes he has developed a friendship with a child who may or may not exist.

He is known for his improvisational skills and impersonations. His performances frequently involve impromptu humor designed and delivered in rapid-fire succession while on stage. According to the *Aladdin* DVD commentary, most of his dialogue as the Genie was improvised.

In 2006, he starred in five movies including *Man of the Year* and was the Surprise Guest at the 2006 Nickelodeon Kids' Choice Awards. He appeared on an episode of *Extreme Makeover: Home Edition* that aired on January 30, 2006.

At one point, he was in the running to play the Riddler in *Batman Forever* until director Tim Burton dropped the project. Earlier, Williams had been a strong contender to play the Joker in *Batman*. He had expressed interest in assuming the role in *The Dark Knight*, the sequel to 2005's *Batman Begins*,[23] although the part of the Joker was played by Heath Ledger, who went on to win, posthumously, the Academy Award for Best Supporting Actor.

He was portrayed by Chris Diamantopoulos in the made-for-TV biopic *Behind the Camera: The Unauthorized Story of Mork & Mindy* (2005), documenting the actor's arrival in Hollywood as a struggling comedian.

Disputes with Disney

In gratitude for his success with the Disney/Touchstone film *Good Morning, Vietnam*, Robin Williams voiced the Genie in the Disney animated film *Aladdin* for SAG scale pay ($75,000), on condition that his name or image not be used for marketing, and his (supporting) character not take more than 25% of space on advertising artwork, since *Toys* was scheduled for release one month after *Aladdin*'s debut. The studio went back on the deal on both counts, especially in poster art by having the Genie in 25% of the image, but having other major and supporting characters portrayed considerably smaller. Disney's Hyperion book, *Aladdin: The Making Of An Animated Film*, listed both of Williams' characters "The Peddler" and "The Genie" ahead of main characters, but was forced to refer to him only as "the actor signed to play the Genie".[24]

Williams and Disney had a bitter falling-out, and as a result Dan Castellaneta voiced the Genie in *The Return of Jafar*, the *Aladdin* animated television series, and had recorded his voice for *Aladdin and the King of Thieves*. When Jeffrey Katzenberg was fired from Disney and replaced by former 20th Century Fox production head Joe Roth (whose last act for Fox was greenlighting Williams' film *Mrs. Doubtfire*), Roth arranged for a public apology to Williams by Disney. Williams agreed to perform in Hollywood Pictures' *Jack*, directed by Francis Ford Coppola, and even agreed to voice the Genie again for the *King Of Thieves* sequel (for considerably more than scale), replacing all of Castellaneta's dialogue.[25]

When Williams re-teamed with *Doubtfire* director Chris Columbus for 1999's *Bicentennial Man*, Disney asked that the budget be cut by approximately $20 million, and when the film was released on Christmas Day, it flopped at the box office. Williams blamed Disney's marketing and the loss of content the film had suffered due to the budget cuts. As a result, Williams was again on bad terms with Disney, and Castellaneta was once again recruited to replace him as Genie in the *Kingdom Hearts* video game series and the *House of Mouse* TV series. The DVD release for *Aladdin* has no involvement whatsoever from Williams in the bonus materials, although some of his original recording sessions can be seen.

Robin Williams has recently made peace with the Walt Disney Company and in 2009 agreed to be inducted into the Disney Hall of Fame, designated as a Disney Legend.[26]

Stand-up career

Williams has done a number of stand-up comedy tours since the early 1970s. Some of his most notable tours include *An Evening With Robin Williams* (1982), *Robin Williams: At The Met* (1986) and *Robin Williams LIVE on Broadway* (2002). The latter broke many long-held records for a comedy show. In some cases, tickets were sold out within thirty minutes of going on sale.

After a six year break, in August 2008 Williams announced a brand new 26-city tour titled "Weapons of Self Destruction". He was quoted as saying that this was his last chance to make cracks at the expense of the current Bush Administration, but by the time the show was staged only a few minutes covered that subject. The tour started at the end of September 2009, finishing in New York on December 3, and was the subject of an HBO special on December 8, 2009.[27]

Accusations of plagiarism

Williams was accused of stealing material from other comics to the extent that David Brenner claims that he confronted Williams personally and threatened him with bodily harm if he heard Williams utter another one of his jokes.[28]

Theater career

In theatre, Williams has headed his own one-man show, *Robin Williams: Live on Broadway*, that played at The Broadway Theatre in July 2002.[29] He made his Broadway acting debut in Rajiv Joseph's *Bengal Tiger at the Baghdad Zoo*, which opened on Broadway at the Richard Rodgers Theatre on March 31, 2011.[30] [31] [32] He previously appeared opposite Steve Martin at Lincoln Center in an Off-Broadway production of *Waiting for Godot*.[33]

Personal life

Marriages and children

Robin Williams' first marriage was to Valerie Velardi on June 4, 1978. They have one child, Zachary Pym (Zak) (born April 11, 1983). During Williams' first marriage, he was involved in an extramarital relationship with Michelle Tish Carter, a cocktail waitress whom he met in 1984. She sued him in 1986, claiming that he did not tell her he was infected with the herpes simplex virus before he embarked on a sexual relationship with her in the mid-1980s, during which, she said, he transmitted the virus to her. The case was settled out of court. Williams and Velardi divorced in 1988.[34]

On April 30, 1989, he married Marsha Garces, his son's nanny who was already several months pregnant with his child. They have two children, Zelda Rae (born July 31, 1989) and Cody Alan (born November 25, 1991). However, in March 2008, Garces filed for divorce from Williams, citing irreconcilable differences.[35]

Williams married his third wife, graphic designer Susan Schneider, on October 23, 2011 in St. Helena, California.[36]

Family and friends

While studying at Juilliard, Williams befriended Christopher Reeve. They had several classes together in which they were the only students, and they remained good friends for the rest of Reeve's life. Williams visited Reeve after the horse riding accident that rendered him a quadriplegic, and cheered him up by pretending to be an eccentric Russian doctor (similar to his role in *Nine Months*). Williams claimed that he was there to perform a colonoscopy. Reeve stated that he laughed for the first time since the accident and knew that life was going to be okay.[17]

On August 20, 2007, Williams' elder brother, Robert Todd Williams, died of complications from heart surgery performed a month earlier.[37]

Addiction and health problems

During the late 1970s and early 1980s, Williams had an addiction to cocaine; he has stated that he has since quit. Williams was a close friend of and frequent partier alongside John Belushi. He says the death of his friend and the birth of his son prompted him to quit drugs: "Was it a wake-up call? Oh yeah, on a huge level. The grand jury helped too."[18]

On August 9, 2006, Williams checked himself in to a substance-abuse rehabilitation center (located in Newberg, Oregon), later admitting that he was an alcoholic.[38] His publicist delivered the announcement:

> After 20 years of sobriety, Robin Williams found himself drinking again and has decided to take proactive measures to deal with this for his own well-being and the well-being of his family. He asks that you respect him and his family's privacy during this time. He looks forward to returning to work this fall to support his upcoming film releases.[39]

Williams was hospitalized in March 2009 due to heart problems. He postponed his one-man tour in order to undergo surgery to replace his aortic valve.[40] [41] The surgery was successfully completed on March 13, 2009, at the Cleveland Clinic.[42] [43]

Other interests

Williams is a member of the Episcopal Church. He has described his denomination in a comedy routine as "Catholic Lite – same rituals, half the guilt."[44]

Williams is an avid enthusiast of games, even naming both his children after game characters. He named his daughter after Princess Zelda from *The Legend of Zelda* action-adventure game series.[45] [46] [47] They both have even been featured in an advert for the Nintendo 3DS remake of The Legend of Zelda: Ocarina of Time.[48] On this note, his son may have been named after Cody from the beat 'em up game *Final Fight*.[49] He also enjoys pen-and-paper role-playing games and online video games, recently playing *Warcraft 3*, *Day of Defeat*, *Half-Life*,[50] and the first-person shooter *Battlefield 2* as a sniper.[51] He was also previously a fan of the *Wizardry* series of role-playing video games.[52]

Williams speaking at the 2008 BBC World Debate.

On January 6, 2006, he performed live at Consumer Electronics Show during Google's keynote.[53] In the 2006 E3, on the invitation of Will Wright, he demonstrated the creature editor of *Spore* while simultaneously commenting on the creature's look: "This will actually make a platypus look good."[54] He also complimented the game's versatility, comparing it to *Populous* and *Black & White*. Later that year, he was one of several celebrities to participate in the Worldwide Dungeons & Dragons Game Day.[55]

A fan of professional road cycling, he was a regular on the US Postal and Discovery Channel Pro Cycling team bus and hotels during the years Lance Armstrong dominated the Tour de France.[56] He owns over 50 bicycles.[57]

He also enjoys rugby union and is a big fan of former All Black, Jonah Lomu.[58]

Williams is a supporter of eco-friendly vehicles. He currently drives a Toyota Prius,[59] and is on the waiting list for an Aptera 2 Series electric vehicle.[60]

Williams has recently announced that he would love to play The Riddler in the next installment to the *Batman* films by director Christopher Nolan, though Nolan has stated that The Riddler will not be featured in the film.[61]

Charity work

Williams performing at Camp Victory for the USO on December 13, 2010.

Williams and his former wife, Marsha, founded the Windfall Foundation, a philanthropic organization to raise money for many different charities. Williams devotes much of his energy to charity work, including the *Comic Relief* fundraising efforts (the program is hosted by himself, Billy Crystal, and Whoopi Goldberg).[18] In December 1999, he sang in French on the BBC-inspired music video of international celebrities doing a cover of the Rolling Stones' "It's Only Rock & Roll" for the charity Children's Promise.[62]

In response to the 2010 Canterbury Earthquake, Williams donated all proceeds of his "Weapons of Self Destruction" Christchurch performance to helping rebuild the New Zealand city. Half the proceeds were donated to the Red Cross and half to the mayoral building fund with the words "I hope this donation will go some way to helping the extensive rebuilding effort in the city."[63] Williams has performed with the USO for U.S. troops stationed in Iraq and Afghanistan.[64]

Filmography

Film credits

Year	Title	Role	Notes
1977	*Can I Do It 'Till I Need Glasses?*	Himself	
1980	*Popeye*	Popeye	
1982	*The World According to Garp*	T.S. Garp	
1983	*The Survivors*	Donald Quinelle	
1984	*Moscow on the Hudson*	Vladimir Ivanov	Nominated—Golden Globe Award for Best Actor – Motion Picture Musical or Comedy
1986	*Seize the Day*	Tommy Wilhelm	
1986	*Club Paradise*	Jack Moniker	
1986	*The Best of Times*	Jack Dundee	
1987	*Good Morning, Vietnam*	Adrian Cronauer	• Golden Globe Award for Best Actor – Motion Picture Musical or Comedy • Nominated—Academy Award for Best Actor • Nominated—BAFTA Award for Best Actor in a Leading Role • Nominated—American Comedy Award for Funniest Actor in a Motion Picture (Leading Role)
1988	*The Adventures of Baron Munchausen*	King of the Moon	• Credited as Ray D. Tutto • Nominated—American Comedy Award for Funniest Supporting Actor in a Motion Picture
1988	*Portrait of a White Marriage*	Air Conditioning Salesman	Uncredited
1988	*Rabbit Ears: Pecos Bill*	Narrator	Voice

1989	*Dead Poets Society*	John Keating	• Nominated—Academy Award for Best Actor • Nominated—BAFTA Award for Best Actor in a Leading Role • Nominated—Golden Globe Award for Best Actor – Motion Picture Drama
1989	*I'm from Hollywood*	Himself	
1990	*Cadillac Man*	Joey O'Brien	
1990	*Awakenings*	Dr. Malcolm Sayer	• Nominated—Golden Globe Award for Best Actor – Motion Picture Drama • National Board of Review Award for Best Actor (Tied with Robert DeNiro for *Awakenings*)
1990	*Back to Neverland*	Himself	
1991	*Dead Again*	Doctor Cozy Carlisle	
1991	*The Fisher King*	Parry	• Golden Globe Award for Best Actor - Motion Picture Musical or Comedy • Nominated—Academy Award for Best Actor • Nominated—Saturn Award for Best Actor
1991	*Hook*	Peter Banning/Peter Pan	
1991	*Rabbit Ears: The Fool and the Flying Ship*	Narrator	Voice
1992	*Toys*	Leslie Zevo	Nominated—Saturn Award for Best Actor
1992	*Aladdin*	Genie, merchant	• Voice • Saturn Award for Best Supporting Actor • Special Golden Globe Award (for his vocal work) • MTV Movie Award for Best Comedic Performance
1992	*The Timekeeper*	The Timekeeper	
1992	*FernGully: The Last Rainforest*	Batty Koda	Voice
1992	*Shakes the Clown*	Mime Class Instructor	
1993	*Mrs. Doubtfire*	Daniel Hillard/Mrs. Doubtfire	• Golden Globe Award for Best Actor - Motion Picture Musical or Comedy • American Comedy Award for Funniest Actor in a Motion Picture (Leading Role) • MTV Movie Award for Best Comedic Performance • Nominated—MTV Movie Award for Best Male Performance
1993	*Being Human*	Hector	
1994	*In Search of Dr. Seuss*	Father	
1995	*Jumanji*	Alan Parrish	• Nominated—Saturn Award for Best Actor • Nominated—Blimp Award for Favorite Movie Actor
1995	*To Wong Foo, Thanks for Everything! Julie Newmar*	John Jacob Jingleheimer Schmidt	
1995	*Nine Months*	Dr. Kosevich	Nominated—American Comedy Award for Funniest Supporting Actor in a Motion Picture
1996	*Aladdin and the King of Thieves*	Genie	Voice
1996	*Hamlet*	Osric	
1996	*The Secret Agent*	The Professor	
1996	*Jack*	Jack Powell	Nominated—Blimp Award for Favorite Movie Actor

1996	*The Birdcage*	Armand Goldman	• Screen Actors Guild Award for Outstanding Performance by a Cast in a Motion Picture • Nominated—MTV Movie Award for Best Comedic Performance • Nominated—MTV Movie Award for Best On-Screen Duo (Shared with Nathan Lane)
1997	*Good Will Hunting*	Sean Maguire	• Academy Award for Best Supporting Actor • Screen Actors Guild Award for Outstanding Performance by a Male Actor in a Supporting Role • Nominated—Golden Globe Award for Best Supporting Actor – Motion Picture • Nominated—Screen Actors Guild Award for Outstanding Performance by a Cast in a Motion Picture • Nominated—Satellite Award for Best Supporting Actor – Motion Picture
1997	*Flubber*	Professor Philip Brainard	• Blockbuster Entertainment Award for Favorite Actor/Actress – Family • Nominated—Blimp Award for Favorite Movie Actor
1997	*Deconstructing Harry*	Mel/Harry's Character	
1997	*Fathers' Day*	Dale Putley	
1998	*Patch Adams*	Hunter "Patch" Adams	• Nominated—Golden Globe Award for Best Actor – Motion Picture Musical or Comedy • Nominated—American Comedy Award for Funniest Actor in a Motion Picture (Leading Role) • Nominated—Satellite Award for Best Actor – Motion Picture Musical or Comedy
1998	*Junket Whore*	Himself	
1998	*What Dreams May Come*	Chris Nielsen	
1999	*Bicentennial Man*	Andrew Martin	• Nominated—Blockbuster Entertainment Award for Favorite Actor – Comedy • Nominated—Blimp Award for Favorite Movie Actor
1999	*Jakob the Liar*	Jakob Heym/Narrator	
1999	*Get Bruce*	Himself	
2000	*Model Behavior*	Faremain	
2001	*A.I. Artificial Intelligence*	Dr. Know	Voice
2002	*The Rutles 2: Can't Buy Me Lunch*	Hans Hänkie	
2002	*Insomnia*	Walter Finch	Nominated—Saturn Award for Best Supporting Actor
2002	*Death to Smoochy*	'Rainbow' Randolph Smiley	
2002	*One Hour Photo*	Seymour 'Sy' Parrish	• Saturn Award for Best Actor • Nominated—Broadcast Film Critics Association Award for Best Actor • Nominated—Online Film Critics Society Award for Best Actor • Nominated—Satellite Award for Best Actor – Motion Picture Drama
2004	*Noel*	Charlie Boyd/The Priest	
2004	*House of D*	Pappass	
2004	*The Final Cut*	Alan W. Hakman	
2005	*The Big White*	Paul Barnell	

2005	*Robots*	Fender	• Voice • Nominated—Blimp Award for Favorite Voice from an Animated Feature
2005	*The Aristocrats*	Himself	
2006	*Man of the Year*	Tom Dobbs	
2006	*Night at the Museum*	Theodore Roosevelt	
2006	*Happy Feet*	Ramon/Lovelace	Voice
2006	*Everyone's Hero*	Napoleon Cross	Voice
2006	*RV*	Bob Munro	
2006	*The Night Listener*	Gabriel Noone	
2007	*License to Wed*	Reverend Frank	
2007	*August Rush*	Maxwell "Wizard" Wallace	
2009	*Shrink*	Holden	
2009	*World's Greatest Dad*	Lance Clayton	
2009	*Night at the Museum: Battle of the Smithsonian*	Theodore Roosevelt	
2009	*Old Dogs*	Dan Rayburn	
2011	*Happy Feet 2*	Ramon, Lovelace	Voice

Television credits

Year	Title	Role	Notes
1977	*The Richard Pryor Show*	Himself	• Writer • "Man with Bad Arm", "John Brownstein, Defense Attorney/Archeologist/Shopper", "Himself", "Himself/Titanic Survivor/Voice of Gun"
1977	*Laugh-In*		
1977	*Eight is Enough*		Episode: "The Return of Auntie V"
1978	*Happy Days*	Mork	Episode: "My Favorite Orkan" (There are two versions of this episode. One with the original ending where events were all a dream of Richie Cunningham's and another that sets up the Mork and Mindy spin-off series. Williams appears in both versions.)
1978	*America 2-Night*	Jason Shine	Episodes: "Jason Shine" and "Olfactory Distosis Telethon"
1978–1982	*Mork & Mindy*	Mork	• Appeared in 92 episodes • Golden Globe Award for Best Actor – Television Series Musical or Comedy (Won in 1979, Nominated in 1980) • Nominated—Primetime Emmy Award for Outstanding Lead Actor – Comedy Series
1979	*Happy Days*	Mork	Episode: "Mork Returns"
1979	*Out of the Blue*		Episode: "Random's Arrival"
1981	*Saturday Night Live*	Himself	Host/Various
1982	*The Billy Crystal Comedy Hour*	Himself	Episode: #1.1
1982	*Faerie Tale Theatre*	Frog/Prince Robin	Episode: "Tale of the Frog Prince"

1982	*SCTV Network 90*	Various	Episode: "Jane Eyrehead"
1984	*Saturday Night Live*	Himself	Host/Various
1984	*Pryor's Place*	Gaby	Episode: "Sax Education"
1986	*Saturday Night Live*	Himself	Host/Various
1986	*The Max Headroom Show*	Himself	Episode: "Max Headroom's Giant Christmas Turkey"
1988	*Saturday Night Live*	Himself	Host/Various
1988	*Wogan*	Himself	
1991	*Wogan*	Himself	
1991	*A Wish For Wings That Work*	The Kiwi	Voice (Credited as Sudy Nim)
1992	*The Larry Sanders Show*	Himself	Episode: "Hank's Contract"
1994	*Homicide: Life on the Streets*	Robert Ellison	• Episode: "Bop Gun" • Nominated—Primetime Emmy Award for Outstanding Guest Actor – Drama Series
1994	*Live & Kicking*	Himself	
1994	*The Larry Sanders Show*	Himself	Episode: "Montana"
1994	*Nyhetsmorgon*	Himself	Episode: "Filmen 'Mrs. Doubtfire' svensk premiär"
1994	*In the Wild*	Himself	Episode: "In the Wild: Dolphins with Robin Williams"
1995	*Primer Plano*	Himself	
1996	*American Masters*	Himself	Episode: "Take Two: Mike Nichols and Elaine May"
1996	*Primer Plano*		
1996	*HBO First Look*	Himself	Episode: "Fathers Day"
1997	*Friends*	Tomas	Uncredited
1998	*Nyhetsmorgon*	Himself/Sean Maguire	Episode: "Filmen 'Good Will Hunting'"
1998	*Hollywood Squares*	Himself	Guest appearance
1998	*Noel's House Party*	Himself	Episode: #8.10
1999	*L.A. Doctors*	Hugo Kinsley	Episode: "Just Duet"
2000	*Whose Line Is It Anyway?*	Himself	Episode: #3.9
2002	*Comedy Central Canned Ham*	Himself	Episode: "Death to Smoochy"
2002	*Leute heute*	Himself	
2002	*Supermarket Sweep*	Himself	
2003	*Player$*	Himself	Episodes: "E3 03, Playa", "Players Halloweenie Televizzie"
2003	*Freedom: A History of Us*	Josiah Quincy/Ulysses S. Grant/Missouri Farmer/Wilbur Wright/Orville Wright	Episodes: "Wake Up America", "A War to End Slavery", "Liberty for All", and "Safe for Democracy"
2003	*Life With Bonnie*	Kevin Powalski	Episode: "Psychic"

2004	*This Hour Has 22 Minutes*	Himself	
2005	*Just For Laughs*	Himself	
2006	*Extreme Makeover: Home Edition*	Himself	
2006	*Mind of Mencia*	Himself	Episode: "That's F**king Historical"
2006	*Getaway*	Himself	Episode: #15.15
2008	*American Idol: The Search for a New Superstar*	Ivan "Bob" Poppanoff the "Russian Idol"/Himself	Episodes: "Idol Gives Back" and "Live Results Show: One Contestant Eliminated"
2008	*Law & Order: Special Victims Unit*	Merrit Rook	• Episode: "Authority" • Nominated—Primetime Emmy Award for Outstanding Guest Actor – Drama Series
2009	*SpongeBob SquarePants*	Himself	Episode: "Truth or Square"
2009	*TV Land Moguls*	Himself	Episode: "The 80s"
2010	*Alan Carr Chatty Man*	Himself	
2010	*Pentagon Channel*	Himself	"Promotional Advertisement for the Pentagon Channel"
2011	*Curiosity*	Himself	Episode: "What Drugs Do To Our Bodies?"

Discography

- *Reality...What a Concept* (1979)
- *Throbbing Python of Love* (1983)
- *A Night at The Met* (1986)
- *Pecos Bill* (1988)
- *Live 2002* (2002)
- *Weapons of Self Destruction* (2010)

Williams appeared in the music video of Bobby McFerrin's hit 1988 song "Don't Worry, Be Happy".[65] He teamed with McFerrin again to record a cover of The Beatles' "Come Together" for the 1998 George Martin album *In My life*.

He made a cameo in Cobra Starship's video "You Make Me Feel..." along with his daughter, Zelda Williams.[66]

References

[1] Pantagraph.com | Free Time | Caliendo hopes 'Frank TV' makes good first impression (http://www.pantagraph.com/articles/2007/11/24/freetime/doc47471a3d6fc50366297886.txt)

[2] http://www.robinwilliams.com/

[3] According to the Nevada Marriage Index, 1956-2005; at http://www.ancestry.com/

[4] The official Michigan social register, 1967, Virginia F. Searcy

[5] Sources conflict. The print biographies *The Life and Humor of Robin Williams: A Biography* and *Robin Williams: A Biography* give his birth year as 1952. *The Robin Williams Scrapbook* also gives a birth year as 1952, as does *Encyclopædia Britannica*. Williams refers to himself as being "55" in an interview published July 4, 2007. Monk, Katherine (2007-07-04). "Marriage 101 with Robin Williams" (http://www.canada.com/saskatoonstarphoenix/news/lifestyle/news/lifestyle/story.html?id=8b777192-8e77-464d-b8da-0cb90be40901&k=1045). *StarPhoenix*. . He also verifies his date of birth as July 21, 1951 in a fansite interview: Stuurman, Linda. RWF talks with Robin Williams: Proost! (http://www.robin-williams.net/interviews/RWF/rwfinterview.php), May 25, 2008.

[6] Thomas, Mike (2002-02-24). "A nose for laughs" (http://nl.newsbank.com/nl-search/we/Archives?p_product=CSTB&p_theme=cstb&p_action=search&p_maxdocs=200&p_topdoc=1&p_text_direct-0=0F360C3C1592F9AE&p_field_direct-0=document_id&

p_perpage=10&p_sort=YMD_date:D&s_trackval=GooglePM). *Chicago Sun-Times*. . Retrieved 2009-12-14.
[7] McMullen, Marion (2002-10-05). "Article: Weekend TV: Star profile. (Features)" (http://www.highbeam.com/doc/1G1-92577025.html). Coventry Evening Telegraph. . Retrieved 2009-12-14.
[8] "If Robin Williams' comedies are inspired by his life no wonder he's been in therapy" (http://pqasb.pqarchiver.com/smgpubs/access/70123882.html?dids=70123882:70123882&FMT=ABS&FMTS=ABS:FT&type=current&date=Mar+14,+1999&author=&pub=Sunday+Herald&desc=If+Robin+Williams'+comedies+are+inspired+by+his+life+no+wonder+he's+been+in+therapy&pqatl=google). Sunday Herald. 1999-03-14. . Retrieved 2009-12-14.
[9] Rubenstein, Steve (2001-09-08). "Laurie Williams - comedian's mother - SFGate" (http://articles.sfgate.com/2001-09-08/news/17615883_1_christian-science-elvis-impersonator-modeling). Articles.sfgate.com. . Retrieved 2011-11-25.
[10] "People News" (http://www.monstersandcritics.com/people/news/article_1206619.php/Robin_Williams_talks_about_rehab_and_alcoholism). *monstersandcritics.com*. .
[11] Gristwood, Sarah (1998-06-18). "Bobbin' Robin" (http://web.archive.org/web/20061004023437/http://www.chico.mweb.co.za/mg/art/film/9806/980618-robin.html). Mail & Guardian Online. Archived from the original (http://www.chico.mweb.co.za/mg/art/film/9806/980618-robin.html) on October 4, 2006. . Retrieved 2007-12-26.
[12] Topel, Fred (2007-07-03). "Robin Williams on License to Wed" (http://www.canmag.com/nw/8218-license-to-wed-robin-williams). CanMag. . Retrieved 2007-12-26.
[13] "Detroit Country Day: Frequently Asked Questions" (http://www.dcds.edu/page.cfm?p=843). Dcds.edu. . Retrieved 2010-08-29.
[14] October 1982 Playboy Magazine
[15] McLellan, Dennis (2007-08-18). "R. Todd Williams, 69; winery founder, comic's brother" (http://www.toadhollow.com/pdf/memorial/ToddLATimesObit.pdf) (PDF). *Los Angeles Times*. . Retrieved 2008-02-10.
[16] " Robin Williams: 'The Night Listener' (http://www.npr.org/templates/story/story.php?storyId=5602441)". Terry Gross (host). *Fresh Air from WHYY*. National Public Radio. 2006-08-03.
[17] Reeve, Christopher (1998). *Still Me*. New York: Random House. pp. 167–172. ISBN 978-067945235-5.
[18] " Robin Williams (http://www.bravotv.com/Inside_the_Actors_Studio/guest/Robin_Williams)". James Lipton (host). *Inside the Actors Studio*. Bravo. 2001-06-10. No. 710, season 7.
[19] "Comedy Central Presents: 100 Greatest Stand-Ups of All Time" (http://us.imdb.com/title/tt0429332/). Internet Movie Database. . Retrieved 2007-12-26.
[20] "Biography for Robin Williams" (http://www.imdb.com/name/nm0000245/bio). Internet Movie Database. . Retrieved 2008-04-13.
[21] "Episode 24 | series: Friends" (http://www.imdb.com/title/tt0583657/combined). Internet Movie Database. .
[22] "Episode 9". *Whose Line Is It Anyway?*. 2000-11-16.
[23] Otto, Jeff (2006-06-26). "Robin Williams, Joker?" (http://au.movies.ign.com/articles/714/714752p1.html). IGN. . Retrieved 2007-12-26.
[24] "Disney's got a brand-new Baghdad" (http://www.ew.com/ew/article/0,,312562,00.html). *Entertainment Weekly*. 1992-09-04. . Retrieved 2007-03-16.
[25] Hill, Jim (April 2000). "Be Careful What You Wish For" (http://jimhillmedia.com/blogs/jim_hill/archive/2000/12/31/312.aspx). Jim Hill Media. . Retrieved 2008-03-15.
[26] "2009 Disney Legends Award Recipients to Be Honored During D23 Expo in Anaheim" (http://news.prnewswire.com/ViewContent.aspx?ACCT=109&STORY=/www/story/09-01-2009/0005086237). PR Newswire. 2009-09-01. . Retrieved 2009-09-01.
[27] robinwilliams.com
[28] Richard Zoglin (2008). *Comedy at the Edge*. Bloomsbury USA. ISBN 978-1-58234-624-3.
[29] The Broadway League. "Robin Williams: Live on Broadway" (http://www.ibdb.com/production.php?id=13427). *IBDB: The Official Source for Broadway Information*.
[30] "Bengal Tiger to Roar at the Richard Rodgers Theatre March 11 Starring Robin Williams" (http://www.broadway.com/shows/bengal-tiger-baghdad-zoo/buzz/154265/bengal-tiger-to-roar-at-the-richard-rodgers-theatre-march-11-starring-robin-williams/). Broadway.com, November 12, 2010.
[31] "Culture Monster". "Robin Williams to star in 'Bengal Tiger at the Baghdad Zoo' on Broadway" (http://latimesblogs.latimes.com/culturemonster/2010/10/robin-williams-to-star-in-bengal-tiger-at-the-baghdad-zoo-on-broadway.html). *Los Angeles Times*. October 21, 2010.
[32] "Tickets for Broadway's Bengal Tiger, Starring Robin Williams, Now on Sale" (http://www.playbill.com/news/article/145030-Tickets-for-Broadways-Bengal-Tiger-Starring-Robin-Williams-Now-on-Sale) playbill.com, November 17, 2010.
[33] "Review/Theater; 'Godot': The Timeless Relationship of 2 Interdependent Souls" (http://theater.nytimes.com/mem/theater/treview.html?res=940DE4DE1231F934A35752C1A96E948260). *The New York Times*, November 7, 1988. Accessed May 4, 2011.
[34] Hoffman, Jan (1992-08-09). "THE SEXES; Pillow Talk" (http://query.nytimes.com/gst/fullpage.html?res=9E0CE2DF153FF93AA3575BC0A964958260). *The New York Times*. . Retrieved 2007-12-26.
[35] Garchik, Leah (2008-03-27). "Robin Williams' wife files for divorce after nearly 19 years" (http://www.sfgate.com/cgi-bin/article.cgi?f=/c/a/2008/03/26/DD7AVQHPA.DTL&tsp=1). *The San Francisco Chronicle*. .
[36] Ravitz, Justin (2011-10-24). "Robin Williams Weds!" (http://www.usmagazine.com/celebritynews/news/robin-williams-weds-20112410). *Us Weekly*. .
[37] Newsdaily.com (http://www.newsdaily.com/stories/tre5247lm-us-williams/)

[38] "Robin Williams Comes Clean on 'GMA' – ABC News" (http://abcnews.go.com/GMA/story?id=2515796). Abcnews.go.com. 2006-10-02. . Retrieved 2010-08-29.

[39] "Robin Williams Enters Rehab for Alcohol" (http://www.people.com/people/article/0,26334,1224730,00.html). People. August 9, 2005. . Retrieved 2007-04-28.

[40] "Robin Williams in South Florida hospital" (http://www.miamiherald.com/news/breaking-news/story/933065.html). The Miami Herald. 2009-03-04. . Retrieved 2009-03-04.

[41] Jones, Kenneth. "Robin Williams' Spring Broadway Bow Postponed Due to Heart Surgery" (http://www.playbill.com/news/article/126985.html), playbill.com, March 5, 2009

[42] "Robin Williams's Heart Surgery Called a Success" (http://www.peop/le.com/people/article/0,,20267281,00.html). .

[43] "Robin Williams' heart surgery goes 'extremely well'" (http://edition.cnn.com/2009/SHOWBIZ/Movies/03/23/robin.williams.health/). CNN. 2009-03-23. . Retrieved 2010-05-22.

[44] Johnson, Caitlin A. (2007-07-03). "A "License" to Laugh" (http://www.cbsnews.com/stories/2007/07/03/earlyshow/leisure/boxoffice/main3011495.shtml). CBS News. . Retrieved 2009-03-27.

[45] "Robin Williams named his daughter after Princess Zelda" (http://www.destructoid.com/robin-williams-named-his-daughter-after-princess-zelda-156315.phtml). Destructoid. . Retrieved 2011-11-25.

[46] "Robin Williams Zelda Commercial: Actor Lends Voice, Daughter For Newest Game" (http://www.huffingtonpost.com/2011/06/15/robin-williams-zelda-video_n_877835.html). *The New York Times*. 2011-06-15. . Retrieved 2011-06-16.

[47] "Robin Williams Jokes About Playing Call of Duty Online" (http://www.1up.com/do/newsStory?cId=3177150). 1up.com. . Retrieved 2010-08-29.

[48] John Funk (2011-06-15). "The Escapist : News : New Zelda Ad Stars Robin Williams and his Daughter Zelda" (http://www.escapistmagazine.com/news/view/111044-New-Zelda-Ad-Stars-Robin-Williams-and-his-Daughter-Zelda). Escapistmagazine.com. . Retrieved 2011-11-25.

[49] Glenn M. (November 29, 2009). "Even Robin Williams loves him some Call of Duty" (http://www.qj.net/qjnet/wii/even-robin-williams-loves-him-some-call-of-duty.html). *QuickJump Gaming Network*. . Retrieved 18 September 2011.

[50] Interview at Pro-HL.com (http://www.pro-hl.com/interviews/robin_williams.php)

[51] "Mork & Me" (http://thearchies.blogspot.com/2005/12/mork-me.html). *The Archies*. 2005-12-05. .

[52] Rusel DeMaria; Johnny L. Wilson (2003). *High score! : The illustrated history of electronic games* (http://books.google.co.uk/books?id=HJNvZLvpCEQC&pg=PA154) (2nd ed.). New York: McGraw-Hill. p. 154. ISBN 0072231726. . Retrieved 18 September 2011.

[53] "Engadget.com" (http://www.engadget.com/2006/01/06/live-coverage-of-the-google-keynote/). Engadget.com. . Retrieved 2010-08-29.

[54] "Robin Williams plays Spore" (http://video.google.com/videoplay?docid=1734727723734486891). Google. . Retrieved 2010-08-29.

[55] "Dungeons and Dragons Game Day at London Dungeon" (http://www.viewlondon.co.uk/whatson/dungeons-and-dragons-game-day-article-5339.html). Viewlondon.co.uk. . Retrieved 2010-08-29.

[56] Murphy, Brian. "Tour de Lance: 100 percent pure" (http://espn.go.com/page2/s/murphy/020729.html). ESPN. . Retrieved 2007-06-29.

[57] "Robin Williams Archive" (http://www.bikeforums.net/archive/index.php/t-10161.html). Bike Forums. 2002-06-17. . Retrieved 2010-08-29.

[58] "Robin Williams Tickets" (http://www.ticketsnow.com/Robin-Williams-Tickets.html). Ticketsnow.com. . Retrieved 2010-08-29.

[59] (http://www.granvilleonline.ca/gr/features/2008/11/12/toyota-prius-hybrid-2009)

[60] "Exclusive: Aptera 2e – Article" (http://www.roadandtrack.com/article.asp?section_id=10&article_id=7651). RoadandTrack.com. 2009-02-11. . Retrieved 2010-08-29.

[61] "Robin Williams Wants To Be The Riddler in *Batman 3*" (http://screencrave.com/2010-06-29/robin-williams-wants-to-be-the-riddler-in-batman-3/). Screencrave.com. 2010-06-29. . Retrieved 2010-08-29.

[62] "Stones cover enters festive race" (http://news.bbc.co.uk/1/hi/entertainment/558252.stm). BBC NEWS. 1999-12-10. .

[63] "Robin Williams donates proceeds to Canterbury quake" (http://tvnz.co.nz/national-news/robin-williams-donates-proceeds-canterbury-quake-3898905). 2010-11-16. . Retrieved 2010-11-11.

[64] Bronstein, Phil (2005-02-09). "Good Morning, Iraq" (http://www.sfgate.com/cgi-bin/article.cgi?f=/c/a/2005/02/09/DDG5AB3TBJ38.DTL). *San Francisco Chronicle*. . Retrieved 2009-09-04.

[65] "Bobby McFerrin Homepage" (http://www.bobbymcferrin.com/dont_worry.php). Bobbymcferrin.com. . Retrieved 2010-08-29.

[66] "Cobra Starship's 'You Make Me Feel ...' On the set of the new clip, Gabe Saporta explains how a magic photo booth tells a universal story." (http://www.mtv.com/news/articles/1666505/cobra-starship-you-make-me-feel-video.jhtml). MTV.com. . Retrieved 2011-06-28.

- "Road Trip with Robin" (http://franklovece.com/newsday2.html#robin)
- "Robin Williams mimic ends 'fraud'" (http://news.bbc.co.uk/2/hi/entertainment/4553999.stm) (BBC News)
- "Robin Williams' impersonator stopped" (http://www.askmen.com/gossip/robin-williams/robin-williams-impersonator-stopped.html) (AskMen.com)
- "Robin Williams Enters Rehab" (http://www.accesshollywood.com/news/ah1169.shtml), August 9, 2006 (Access Hollywood)
- Lovece, Frank, *New York Newsday* (April 27, 2006)

Bibliography

- Jay David (1999). *The Life and Humor of Robin Williams: A Biography*. New York: Quill. ISBN 978-068815245-1.
- Andy Dougan (1999). *Robin Williams: A Biography*. Thunder's Mouth Press. ISBN 978-156025213-9.
- Stephen J. Spignesi (1997). *The Robin Williams Scrapbook*. Secaucus, NJ: Carol Pub.. ISBN 978-080651891-6.

External links

- Robin Williams (http://www.robinwilliams.com) – official website
- Robin Williams (http://www.ibdb.com/person.asp?ID=88190) at the Internet Broadway Database
- Robin Williams (http://www.imdb.com/name/nm245/) at the Internet Movie Database
- Robin Williams (http://tcmdb.com/participant/participant.jsp?participantId=206858) at the TCM Movie Database
- Robin Williams (http://movies.yahoo.com/movie/contributor/1800013042) at Yahoo! Movies

Popeye (film)

Popeye	
Theatrical release poster	
Directed by	Robert Altman
Produced by	Robert Evans
Screenplay by	Jules Feiffer
Story by	Robert Altman
Based on	**Comic Strip:** E.C. Segar
Starring	Robin Williams Shelley Duvall Ray Walston Paul L. Smith Paul Dooley Richard Libertini
Music by	Harry Nilsson Tom Pierson (additional music)
Cinematography	Giuseppe Rotunno
Editing by	John W. Holmes David A. Simmons
Studio	Paramount Pictures Walt Disney Productions
Distributed by	Paramount Pictures (U.S.) Buena Vista International (Foreign)
Release date(s)	December 12, 1980
Running time	114 minutes
Country	United States
Language	English

Budget	$20,000,000
Box office	**United States**: US$49,823,017[1] **Worldwide**: US$60,000,000[2] :88

Popeye is a 1980 live-action film adaptation directed by Robert Altman and adapted from E. C. Segar's *Thimble Theatre* aka *Popeye* comic strip.

Marketed with the tagline, "The sailor man with the spinach can!", the film is a musical. It stars Robin Williams as Popeye and Shelley Duvall as Olive Oyl.

Plot

The film begins with an animated cartoon slide of Popeye on his ship with the words "MAX FLEISCHER presents" at the top; the cartoon is "Blow Me Down" (1933). When the doors open, he is quick to say, "Hey! What is this, one of Bluto's tricks?! I'm in the wrong movie!"

One night, Popeye (Robin Williams) rows his dinghy into the harbor of the Sweethaven. When he arrives there everyone seems to fear him. He rents a room at the Oyls' boarding house, where he falls for their daughter, Olive (Shelley Duvall). Olive's hand has been promised to Captain Bluto (Paul L. Smith), a bully and ruffian who is in charge of collecting taxes for the mysterious Commodore. Popeye and Bluto are quick to dislike each other and fight.

Popeye, who was orphaned at an early age, is searching for his missing father. Along the way he encounters George W. Geezil (Richard Libertini), J. Wellington Wimpy (Paul Dooley), "Oxblood Oxheart" (Peter Bray), and a greedy, unnamed taxman (Donald Moffat). Popeye and Olive are brought together when they find Swee'Pea (Wesley Ivan Hurt), a foundling. Swee'Pea can predict the future, whistling when he hears the right answer to a question.

Popeye allows Wimpy to take Swee'Pea on a walk, but Wimpy takes him to the horse race. Wimpy uses Swee'Pea's power to find out which horse will win. Popeye and Olive Oyl are mad at Wimpy. Popeye then throws the tax collector into the sea, making the entire town happy. While the town is celebrating Popeye's victory, Wimpy steals Swee'Pea and gives him to Bluto. Popeye hurries to find Swee'Pea, but it is too late.

When Swee'Pea is kidnapped, Popeye and Olive Oyl go looking for him. Olive and Wimpy learn that Swee'Pea was taken on the Commodore's ship, and it turns out that the Commodore is Popeye's father, Poopdeck Pappy (Ray Walston). Bluto has tied up Pappy, and is going to use Swee'Pea to find Pappy's treasure. When Olive and Wimpy tell Popeye what they have discovered, Popeye thinks it is a joke and goes to the Commodore's ship to prove them wrong. He finds the Commodore and sees the family resemblance. He learns from his father the secret to gaining great strength by eating spinach, but states his dislike of it, infuriating Pappy.

Bluto kidnaps Swee'Pea and Olive Oyl, then sails to an island on which the Commodore has said his treasure is located. He tries using Swee'Pea's predictive ability to locate the treasure. Popeye, Pappy, Wimpy and their friends chase Bluto to Pirate's Cove. Using a cannon, Pappy tries to sink Bluto's ship, but, in the end, has to ram it. Olive is trapped in a tube that is tossed in the water, and Pappy manages to get up on the cove with Swee'Pea and Popeye's friends.

Bluto and Popeye get into a sword fight. Bluto, being bigger and stronger, knocks Popeye into the water. A giant octopus tries to eat Olive. Pappy calls to Popeye and tells him that if he ate spinach he would not be losing. Bluto attempts to add insult to injury by forcing Popeye to eat a can of spinach, then wrapping him in chains and dropping him into the water. Popeye, now with extraordinary strength, shoots up from the water and defeats Bluto with a mighty punch. He then rescues Olive using a "Twisker Punch", sending the octopus flying into the air. Now beaten, Bluto turns yellow (literally) and swims out to sea, never to be heard from again.

Pappy finds his treasure, containing items from Popeye's infancy, including a picture of "Me Son". The characters sing "Popeye The Sailor Man", while Popeye dances and falls back in the water, only to pop back up smiling. The credits then play through a scene of the cove showing Bluto still swimming out to sea.

Cast

- Robin Williams as Popeye the Sailor
- Shelley Duvall as Olive Oyl
- Ray Walston as Poopdeck Pappy
- Paul Dooley as J. Wellington Wimpy
- Paul L. Smith as Bluto
- Richard Libertini as George W. Geezil
- Donald Moffat as The Taxman
- MacIntyre Dixon as Cole Oyl
- Roberta Maxwell as Nana Oyl
- Donovan Scott as Castor Oyl
- Allan F. Nicholls as Rough House
- Wesley Ivan Hurt as Swee'Pea
- Bill Irwin as Ham Gravy
- Robert Fortier as Bill Barnacle
- David McCharen as Harry Hotcash
- Sharon Kinney as Cherry
- Peter Bray as Oxblood Oxheart
- Linda Hunt as Mrs. Oxheart
- Geoff Hoyle as Scoop
- Wayne Robson as Chizzelflint
- Larry Pisoni as Chico
- Carlo Pellegrini as Swifty
- Klaus Voormann as Von Schnitzel (the conductor)
- Dennis Franz as Spike (a bully)
- Alan Autry (credited as Carlos Brown) as Slug (a bully)
- Jack Mercer as Popeye the Sailor (Animated prologue only)

Release

Popeye premiered on December 6, 1980 at the Mann's Chinese Theater in Los Angeles.[3] :123

Reception

The film grossed US$6,000,000 on its opening weekend in the U.S., and made US$32,000,000 after 32 days.[3] :123–124 The film earned $49,823,037[1] at the United States box office—more than double the film's budget—and a worldwide total of US$60,000,000.[2] :88 It received overall mixed reviews: some favorable, from critics such as Vincent Canby and Roger Ebert; others unfavorable, from critics such as Leonard Maltin, who described the picture as "...Astonishingly boring. The beloved sailorman boards a sinking ship. A game cast does its best with an unfunny script and cluttered staging. Tune in a few hours' worth of Max Fleischer cartoons instead; you'll be much better off."[4] Rotten Tomatoes gave the film a 57% "Rotten" rating with the critical consensus stating [that] "Altman's take on the iconic cartoon is messy and wildly uneven, but its robust humor and manic charm are hard to resist."

Soundtrack

Popeye (Soundtrack)		
Soundtrack album by Harry Nilsson		
Released	1981	
Recorded	1980	
Genre	Pop Music	
Label	Boardwalk	
Producer	Bruce Robb	
Professional reviews		
Allmusic ★★★★★ link [5]		
Harry Nilsson chronology		
Flash Harry (1980)	***Popeye (soundtrack)*** (1981)	*Papa's Got a Brown New Robe* (Unreleased)

Popeye is a soundtrack composed by Harry Nilsson for the movie *Popeye*. Harry Nilsson took a break in the middle of production of his album *Flash Harry* to create the music for this movie. He wrote all the original songs and co-produced the music with producer Bruce Robb at Cherokee Studios. Harry Nilsson took his band of musicians to the island of Malta where they had a purpose-built studio constructed for them. In general, the soundtrack was unusual in that the actors sang some of the songs "live". For that reason, the studio-recorded soundtrack album did not quite match the tracks heard in the film. On the end credits, Van Dyke Parks is credited as music arranger. He also acted in the movie in role of a piano player.

(All songs written by Harry Nilsson except "I'm Popeye the Sailor Man," which was composed by Sammy Lerner for the original Max Fleischer *Popeye* animated cartoon.)

1. "I Yam What I Yam" - (2:16)
2. "He Needs Me" - (3:33)
3. "Swee' Pea's Lullaby" - (2:06)
4. "Din' We" - (3:06)
5. "Sweethaven - An Anthem" - (2:56)
6. "Blow Me Down" - (4:07)
7. "Sailin'" - (2:48)
8. "It's Not Easy Being Me" - (2:20)
9. "He's Large" - (4:19)
10. "I'm Mean" - (2:33)
11. "Kids" - (4:23)
12. "I'm Popeye the Sailor Man" - (1:19)

- The song "Everything Is Food" was not included on the soundtrack album, while the song "Din' We" (which was cut from the film) was.
- The song "He Needs Me" was featured in the film, *Punch-Drunk Love*. Coincidentally, *Punch-Drunk Love* was originally released on DVD the same day as the DVD release of *Popeye*.
- The song "Sweethaven - An Anthem" is the only song heard twice in the film.

The soundtrack is now available either as a digital download from music retailers such as iTunes and Amazon MP3 or as a CD-R through Amazon.com. Again, "Everything is Food" has not been included on the soundtrack.

References

[1] "Box office statistics for *Popeye* (1980)" (http://www.the-numbers.com/movies/1980/0PPY.php). The Numbers. . Retrieved 2010-05-11.
[2] O'Brien, Daniel (1995). *Robert Altman: Hollywood Survivor*. New York: Continuum. ISBN 0-8264-0791-9.
[3] Plecki, Gerard (1985). *Robert Altman*. Boston: Twayne Publishers (G.K. Hall & Company/ITT). ISBN 0-8057-9303-8.
[4] Martin, Leonard (2006). *Leonard Maltin's Movie Guide*. Signet Books. pp. 1017. ISBN 0-451-21265-7.
[5] http://www.allmusic.com/album/r582346

Further reading

- Parish, James Robert (2006). *Fiasco - A History of Hollywood's Iconic Flops*. Hoboken, New Jersey: John Wiley & Sons. pp. 359 pages.. ISBN 978-0-471-69159-4.

External links

- *Popeye* (http://www.imdb.com/title/tt0081353/) at the Internet Movie Database
- *Popeye* (http://www.allrovi.com/movies/movie/v65569) at AllRovi
- *Popeye* (http://www.boxofficemojo.com/movies/?id=popeye.htm) at Box Office Mojo
- *Popeye* (http://www.rottentomatoes.com/m/1016534/) at Rotten Tomatoes
- Popeye at The Harry Nilsson Web Pages (http://www.harrynilsson.com/page-popeye.html)

The World According to Garp (film)

The World According to Garp	
Theatrical release poster	
Directed by	George Roy Hill
Produced by	George Roy Hill
Written by	John Irving Steve Tesich
Starring	Robin Williams Mary Beth Hurt Glenn Close John Lithgow Mark Soper
Cinematography	Miroslav Ondricek
Editing by	Stephen A. Rotter
Distributed by	Warner Bros.
Release date(s)	July 23, 1982
Running time	136 minutes
Country	United States
Language	English
Budget	$17 million
Box office	$29,712,172

The World According to Garp is 1982 American comedy drama film directed by George Roy Hill, based on the novel of the same title by John Irving, who also wrote the script together with Steve Tesich. For their roles, John Lithgow and Glenn Close were respectively nominated for Best Actor in a Supporting Role and Best Actress in a Supporting Role at the 55th Academy Awards.

Plot

The story chronicles the life of T. S. Garp (Robin Williams), the illegitimate son of a feminist mother, Jenny Fields (Glenn Close, in her feature film debut). Jenny wanted a child but not a husband. A nurse during the closing months of World War II, she encounters a dying ball turret gunner known only as Technical Sergeant Garp who was severely brain damaged in combat. Jenny nurses Garp, observing his infantile state and almost perpetual autonomic sexual arousal. Unconstrained by convention and driven by practicality and her desire for a child, Jenny uses Garp's sexual response to impregnate herself, and names the resultant son after him "T. S." (standing only for "Technical Sergeant"). Jenny raises young Garp alone.

Garp grows up, becoming interested in wrestling and writing fiction, topics his mother has little interest in. However, his writing piques the interest of the daughter of the school's wrestling coach, Helen Holm (Mary Beth Hurt). She is wary of him, however, because Garp is quite promiscuous at school. Jenny also observes Garp's behavior in this regard and is intellectually curious about it, having little more than clinical interest in sex herself. She offers to procure a prostitute for Garp, and engaging the two of them in conversation on the subject, decides to write a book on her observations of lust and human sexuality.

Her book is a partial autobiography called *A Sexual Suspect*, and is an overnight sensation. The title refers to the general assessment of her as a woman who does not care to bind herself to a man, and who chooses to raise a child on her own. The book is a best-seller and Jenny becomes a feminist icon. She uses the proceeds from the book to found a center at her home for troubled and abused women and transexuals. Meanwhile, Garp's first novel is published, which impresses Helen. The two marry and eventually have two children, Duncan and Walt.

Garp becomes a devoted parent and successful fiction writer. However, he and his wife both struggle with fidelity. He spends a lot of time visiting his mother and the people who live at her center, including transsexual ex-football player Roberta Muldoon (John Lithgow). He learns much about the intolerance and brutality directed toward the center's residents. He also first hears the story of Ellen James, a girl who was gang raped and then had her tongue cut out so that she could not easily identify her attackers. Some of the women at Jenny's center are "Ellen Jamesians", women who voluntarily cut out their own tongues as a show of solidarity. Garp is horrified by the practice and learns that the Jamesians have received a letter from Ellen James herself begging them to stop the practice, but that they have voted to refuse.

Having learned about his wife infidelity with one of her students, Garp gets in a car accident while his children are riding in the back seat of his car. The person he crashed into was his wife, who was performing fellatio on the man with whom she was having an affair. One of the sons is killed and the other experiences an eye injury as a result. Garp's jaw was wired-shut in order to heal from the injury and Helen also experienced an unspecified injury to her jaw. The man on whom she was performing fellatio apparently had his penis severed as a result of the accident. This turns into a time of emotional healing when Garp, through the aid of his mother, learns to forgive himself and his wife for his fidelity problems. The couple reconcile and they have a baby daughter named Jenny after her grandmother.

Jenny encounters intolerance, including violent men in the lives of the women that she helps. Because of both her center and her book, she has been receiving credible death threats. To Garp's dismay, she is dismissive of physical danger, and in fact, decides to endorse a politician who supports her message. Garp writes a book about the life of Ellen James. The book is very successful and well-regarded, but is highly critical of the Jamesians. Garp begins receiving death threats of his own from them.

During a political rally, Jenny is shot and killed by a fanatic male anti-feminist. The women of Jenny's center hold a memorial for her, but forbid any man from attending. Garp, dressed as a woman, is secreted into the memorial by Muldoon. However, he is identified by Pooh, a Jamesian he had known when they both were in school. A commotion breaks out and Garp is in danger of being hurt until a woman leads him out of the memorial, away from danger, and to a taxi. The woman is Ellen James (Amanda Plummer, in an early cameo role), who thanks Garp for his book about her. The Jamesians are further outraged that Garp attended the memorial.

Garp returns to his old school to semi-retirement as the wrestling coach. One day during practice, Pooh, the Jamesian that identified him at his mother's memorial, enters the gymnasium and shoots him at close range with a pistol. She is tackled by the wrestlers, and Garp is airlifted away from the school by helicopter. He lapses into delirium, flashing back to an earlier time when his mother would toss him into the air. The movie is left open-ended on whether he survives or not.

Cast

- Robin Williams as T.S. Garp
- James "J.B." McCall as young Garp
- Mary Beth Hurt as Helen Holm
- Glenn Close as Jenny Fields
- John Lithgow as Roberta Muldoon
- Hume Cronyn as Mr. Fields
- Jessica Tandy as Mrs. Fields
- Swoosie Kurtz as The Hooker
- Peter Michael Goetz as John Wolf
- Mark Soper as Michael Milton

Reception

The World According to Garp was well-received by the majority of critics and currently holds a 79% 'Fresh' rating on Rotten Tomatoes.[1] Film critic Roger Ebert of the *Chicago Sun-Times* gave the movie a positive review, despite being critical of the film's "palatable" interpretation of the novel, stating, "John Irving's best-selling novel, *The World According to Garp*, was cruel, annoying, and smug. I kept wanting to give it to my cats. But it was wonderfully well-written and was probably intended to inspire some of those negative reactions in the reader. The movie version of *Garp*, however, left me entertained but unmoved, and perhaps the movie's basic failing is that it did not inspire me to walk out on it." However, he still gave the film three out of a possible four stars, concluding, "While I watched *GARP*, I enjoyed it. I thought the acting was unconventional and absorbing (especially by Williams, by Glenn Close as his mother, and by John Lithgow as a transsexual). I thought the visualization of the events, by director George Roy Hill, was fresh and consistently interesting. But when the movie was over, my immediate response was not at all what it should have been. All I could find to ask myself was: What the hell was that all about?"[2]

References

[1] "The World According to Garp" (http://www.rottentomatoes.com/m/world_according_to_garp/). *Rotten Tomatoes*. . Retrieved 2011-10-03.

[2] Ebert, Roger. "The World According to Garp" (http://rogerebert.suntimes.com/apps/pbcs.dll/article?AID=/19820101/REVIEWS/201010355). *Chicago Sun-Times*. . Retrieved 3 October 2011.

External links

- *The World According to Garp* (http://www.imdb.com/title/tt0084917/) at the Internet Movie Database
- *The World According to Garp* (http://www.rottentomatoes.com/m/world_according_to_garp/) at Rotten Tomatoes
- *The World According to Garp* (http://www.boxofficemojo.com/movies/?id=worldaccordingtogarp.htm) at Box Office Mojo

The World According to Garp

The World According to Garp	
First edition	
Author(s)	John Irving
Country	United States
Language	English
Publisher	E. P. Dutton, NY
Publication date	1978
Media type	Print (hardback and paperback)
Pages	newest edition is 609 pgs.
ISBN	0-525-23770-4
OCLC Number	3345460 [1]
Dewey Decimal	813/.5/4
LC Classification	PZ4.I714 Wo 1978 PS3559.R8
Preceded by	*The 158-Pound Marriage*
Followed by	*Hotel New Hampshire*

The World According to Garp is John Irving's fourth novel. Published in 1978, the book was a bestseller for several years.

A movie adaptation of the novel starring Robin Williams was released in 1982, with a screenplay written by Steve Tesich.

Plot

The story deals with the life of **T. S. Garp**. His mother, Jenny Fields, is a strong-willed nurse who wants a child but not a husband. She encounters a dying ball turret gunner known only as Technical Sergeant Garp who was severely brain damaged in combat. Jenny nurses Garp, observing his infantile state and almost perpetual autonomic sexual arousal. As a matter of practicality and kindness in making his passing as comfortable as possible and reducing his agitation, she manually gratifies him several times. Unconstrained by convention and driven by practicality and her desire for a child, Jenny uses Garp's sexual response to impregnate herself, and names the resultant son after him "T. S." (standing only for "Technical Sergeant"). Jenny raises young Garp alone, taking a position at an all-boys school.

Garp grows up, becoming interested in sex, wrestling, and writing fiction—three topics in which his mother has little interest. He launches his writing career, courts and marries the wrestling coach's daughter, and fathers three children. Meanwhile, his mother suddenly becomes a feminist icon after publishing a best-selling autobiography called *A Sexual Suspect* (referring to the general assessment of her as a woman who does not care to bind herself to a man, and who chooses to raise a child on her own).

Garp becomes a devoted parent, wrestling with anxiety for the safety of his children and a desire to keep them safe from the dangers of the world. He and his family inevitably experience dark and violent events through which the characters change and grow. Garp learns (often painfully) from the women in his life (including transsexual ex-football player Roberta Muldoon) struggling to become more tolerant in the face of intolerance. The story is decidedly rich with (in the words of the fictional Garp's teacher) "lunacy and sorrow," and the sometimes ridiculous chains of events the characters experience still resonate with painful truth.

The novel contains several framed narratives: Garp's first novella, *The Pension Grillparzer*; a short story; and a portion of one of his novels, *The World According to Bensenhaver*. As well, the book contains some motifs that appear in almost all John Irving novels: bears, wrestling, Vienna, New England, people who are uninterested in having sex, and a complex Dickensian plot that spans the protagonist's whole life. Adultery (another common Irving motif) also plays a large part, culminating in one of the novel's most harrowing and memorable scenes. There is also a tincture of another familiar Irving trope, castration anxiety, most obvious in the lamentable fate of Michael Milton.

Background

John Irving's mother, Frances Winslow, had not been married at the time of his conception,[2] and Irving never met his biological father. As a child, he was not even told anything about his father, and he baited his mother that unless she gave him some information about his biological father, in his writing he would invent the father and the circumstances of how she got pregnant. Winslow would reply, "Go ahead, dear."[3] When *The World According to Garp* was written, with the protagonist's biological father a comatose but aroused Second World War veteran, Irving was unaware that his own biological father had been in the military.

In 1981, Time magazine quoted the novelist's mother as saying, "There are parts of *Garp* that are too explicit for me."[4]

The original title of the novel was "Lunacy and Sorrow".

Cultural references

- Garp's school is based on the Phillips Exeter Academy in Exeter, New Hampshire, of which Irving is an alumnus. His stepfather was a faculty member.
- T.S. Garp's writing career resembles John Irving's own early career. Garp's first novel is about freeing animals from the Vienna Zoo, similar to *Setting Free the Bears*. Garp's second novel is about wife-swapping, similar to *The 158-Pound Marriage*, with some similarities to *The Water-Method Man*. Garp's third novel is called *The World According to Bensenhaver*, the novel's protagonist, and is about "lust" (according to Jenny). Coincidentally, Garp's third novel is a best-seller, like *The World According to Garp* itself. However, Garp (presumably speaking for Irving) ridicules the idea that his third novel is autobiographical.
- Ellen James Society, a rock band from Atlanta, took their name from a women's group in the novel.

Discussion of main themes

Death

Irving concludes the novel by stating, "In the world according to Garp, we are all terminal cases." Indeed, throughout the book, Garp seems to be obsessed with death, both in his writing and in his personal life. Garp remarks in a reading that his novella, *The Pension Grillparzer*, features the death of seven of his nine characters. His third novel, *The World According to Bensenhaver*, features multiple scenes of death and mutilation. However, Garp's writing merely reflects the broader nature of his obsession with necrosis. Garp irrationally fantasizes about ways his loved ones might die. At one point, Garp rants about his hatred of late-night phone calls—which undoubtedly bring news of a loved one's death. Ironically, several of the people closest to him do die—often in outlandish, even comical ways. In a Wildesian sense, Garp's art imitates life, and vice-versa, and his writing drives home the absurdity of a fear of death, as well as the absurdity of death itself.

Gender roles

Unavoidable in *The World According to Garp* and in Garp's own writing itself is the treatment of extreme feminism. Garp's mother Jenny Fields finds herself amidst elements of the women's rights movement, and, rejecting almost any interaction with men, is the focus of Irving's feminist overtones. Driven home by her adoption of radical feminists and her absurd New England feminist enclave at Dog's Head Harbor, Irving paints a complicated view of the women's movement. Indeed, Irving oscillates a decidedly unsympathetic view of the overzealous Ellen Jamesians, while vesting in the character of Roberta Muldoon a sanguine portrayal of a transsexual—one who ends up becoming Garp's best friend. Garp's relationship to the feminist movement is also muddled. Garp becomes a reluctant representative of the movement with his third—and most widely read—novel. At the same time, however, he is rejected outright by many feminists and Ellen Jamesians for his work's misogynistic tone.

Sexuality

Garp's world is one where sexuality—replaced in the book with the nomenclature "lust"—is basically a source of trouble and heartache. Garp's earliest feelings of lust, namely those for a girl, Cushie, result in what are ultimately negative feelings for Garp. Garp's second encounter with lust is with an Austrian prostitute, a relationship his mother used as material for national rebuke in her successful autobiography, *A Sexual Suspect*. In fact, the only character Irving creates without any symptoms of lust is Garp's mother, Jenny Fields, an asexual nurse whose repulsion from sex is highlighted by her conception of Garp himself. As a result, Garp's mother appears as one of the few steady, morally justified characters in the novel, in spite of her having committed rape. Although she does have non-consensual sex with the sergeant, that seems to be the only time when Jenny engages in sexual activity. Irving also disorients Garp's sexual moral compass by having him engage in numerous lurid affairs, by presenting Garp's marriage through an odd sexual quadrangle with another married couple (a similar quadrangle was the primary focus of Irving's previous novel, *The 158-Pound Marriage*), and especially by his depiction of Garp's wife, Helen, who also has illicit sexual liaisons. Indeed, undoubtedly the most horrifying event in the novel occurs during a scene in which Garp's son is killed because Helen, while attempting to break off her affair with one of her students, agrees to fellatio as a sort of going-away present.

References

- New York Times book review, by Christopher Lehmann-Haupt, April 13, 1978 [5]

[1] http://worldcat.org/oclc/3345460

[2] Nicholas Wroe (2005-08-13). "Grappling with life" (http://www.guardian.co.uk/books/2005/aug/13/fiction.johnirving). *The Observer*. . Retrieved 2009-11-05. "his parents had married six months before his birth"

[3] Ariel Leve (2009-10-18). "The world according to John Irving" (http://entertainment.timesonline.co.uk/tol/arts_and_entertainment/books/fiction/article6877022.ece). *The Times*. . Retrieved 2009-11-04.

[4] R.Z. Sheppard (1981-08-31). "Life into Art: Novelist John Irving" (http://www.time.com/time/magazine/article/0,9171,954955-9,00.html). *Time*. . Retrieved 2009-11-04.

[5] http://www.nytimes.com/1978/04/13/books/irving-garp.html

External links

- John Irving discusses *The World According to Garp* (http://www.bbc.co.uk/worldservice/specials/133_wbc_archive_new/page3.shtml) on the BBC *World Book Club*
- *The World According to Garp*: Reading Group Guides (http://www.readinggroupguides.com/guides/world_according_to_garp.asp#about)
- Photos of the first edition of The World According to Garp (http://www.mansionbooks.com/BookDetail.php?bk=214)

The Survivors (1983 film)

The Survivors	
Theatrical release poster	
Directed by	Michael Ritchie
Produced by	William Sackheim
Written by	Michael Leeson Jonathan Reynolds (uncredited)
Starring	Walter Matthau Robin Williams Jerry Reed
Music by	Paul Chihara
Cinematography	Billy Williams
Editing by	Richard A. Harris
Distributed by	Columbia Pictures
Release date(s)	June 22, 1983 (New York City)
Running time	102 minutes
Country	United States
Language	English

The Survivors is a 1983 comedy film directed by Michael Ritchie. It stars Walter Matthau and Robin Williams.

Plot

Donald Quinelle (Williams) is a simple employee who gets fired from his job. Sonny Paluso (Matthau) is a gas station owner whose station is accidentally blown up by Donald. The two men meet up at a restaurant when it is robbed by a man in a ski mask (Jerry Reed). Donald is shot, but Sonny gets a good look at the man. Then Donald goes on the news to explain the incident and the robber learns Sonny's identity. That night the robber visits Sonny to kill him and his teenage daughter Candice, but is saved by Donald. Afterwards Sonny and Donald take Jack Locke, the robber, to the police at gun point.

On the way back they stop at a gun store and Donald buys a huge amount, even though Sonny can't stand them. Donald goes to a survival camp taught by a man named Wes. Jack, fresh from jail, finds Sonny again. The two make a deal that Jack won't kill them if he and Donald agree to say nothing to the police. Sonny and his daughter go to try to talk to Donald. After Donald insults Jack on the phone Jack decides to come up there to settle it himself.

Donald has now become a killing machine thanks to Wes' teachings. After a quick battle with Jack, Donald runs away and the rest of the camp gets wind of what's going on. Jack hides in Donald's cabin and Sonny tries to reason with rest of the camp. Jack and Donald come out and Donald is yelling about how they are going to kill him. However, it is a ruse and Sonny, Candice, Jack, and Donald escape in Sonny's car. After exposing Wes as a fraud to the rest of the camp the group heads home. Donald gets out of the car and has a moment of reflection in the snow and Sonny tries to comfort him. The two walk back to the car as friends.

Cast

- Walter Matthau as Sonny Paluso
- Robin Williams as Donald Quinelle
- Jerry Reed as Jack Locke
- John Goodman as Commando
- James Wainwright as Wes Huntley
- Kristin Vigard as Candice Paluso
- Annie McEnroe as Doreen
- Mariah Hailey as Jack's Wife
- Joseph Carberry as Detective Matt Burke
- Skipp Lynch as Wiley

Reception

The film did not garner many good reviews, scoring only a 17% fresh rating on Rotten Tomatoes, based on 6 reviews.[1] Many felt that Robin Williams and Walter Matthau's style of humor did not mesh well together. An exception to the negative critical tide was the review that Pauline Kael gave the film in *The New Yorker*:

> The banner line on the ad says ' Once they declare war on each other, watch out. You could die laughing.' *The Survivors* isn't about two men declaring war on each other; it's about two New Yorkers without anything in common who become friends. The advertisers probably didn't know what to do with it because it's a comedy for grownups. There's a lot of unconventional humour in the writing by Michael Leeson - (he won awards for his work on the TV series Taxi.) Robin Williams' work transcends the film's flaws. He acts with an emotional purity that I can't pretend to understand. A lot of the comedy comes from his being a grownup with this ranting little kid inside him. Walter Matthau gives a quiet, old pro's performance.[2]

References

[1] "The Survivors (1983)" (http://www.rottentomatoes.com/m/survivors/). *Rotten Tomatoes*. Flixster. . Retrieved September 28, 2010.
[2] Pauline Kael p.15-18 State of the Art ISBN 0-7145-2869-2

External links

- *The Survivors* (http://www.imdb.com/title/tt0086397/) at the Internet Movie Database
- *The Survivors* (http://www.allrovi.com/movies/movie/v1:48010) at AllRovi

Moscow on the Hudson

Moscow on the Hudson	
Theatrical release poster	
Directed by	Paul Mazursky
Produced by	Paul Mazursky
Written by	Paul Mazursky Leon Capetanos
Starring	Robin Williams María Conchita Alonso Cleavant Derricks
Music by	David McHugh
Cinematography	Donald M. McAlpine
Editing by	Richard Halsey
Studio	Delphi Premier
Distributed by	Columbia Pictures
Release date(s)	April 6, 1984
Running time	115 minutes
Country	United States
Language	English
Budget	$13 million
Box office	$25,068,724

Moscow on the Hudson is a 1984 comedy-drama film starring Robin Williams, and directed by Paul Mazursky. Williams plays a Soviet circus musician who defects from the Soviet Union while on a visit to the United States. The film was released on April 3, 1984.

Williams' co-stars in this film were María Conchita Alonso (in her film debut), Elya Baskin, Savely Kramarov, Alejandro Rey, and Cleavant Derricks.

Plot

Set against the backdrop of the Cold War early 1980s prior to the perestroika years of the later 80s, Vladimir Ivanov (Robin Williams), a saxophonist with the Moscow circus, lives in a crowded apartment with his extended family. He sucks up to the apparatchik assigned to the circus, standing in line for hours to buy shoes to obtain his favor. He cruises the streets, scrounging for black market gasoline for his friend's car. He buffers between his crazy grandfather and the KGB, who want to arrest him for shouting anti-Soviet slogans out the window.

As a rare treat, the circus troupe is sent to perform in New York City. Ivanov's clown friend, Anatoly (Elya Baskin), who has talked of little else but defecting, is intimidated into canceling his plan, and Vladimir, who had opposed the scheme as reckless and foolhardy suddenly decides to do it. He runs from his Soviet controllers, and hides behind a perfume counter at Bloomingdale's, where he originally met the clerk, Lucia Lomardo (María Conchita Alonso). When local police arrive, Ivanov stands up to his controllers and defects in what later becomes a newsworthy spectacle.

With the help of sympathetic Orlando Ramirez (Alejandro Rey), a naturalized citizen from Cuba and attorney who witnessed Ivanov's defection, Ivanov tries adapting to living in America. Ivanov attempts to find work despite speaking very little English and fearing the threat of his former countrymen. Aside from living in poor neighborhoods and taking low-paying jobs, he becomes friends with Lionel Witherspoon (Cleavant Derricks), a security guard who helped him at Bloomingdale's, and starts a relationship with Lucia. However, after Ivanov's romance with Lucia ends, Lionel decides to move back to Alabama to see his young son, and Vladimir learns that his beloved grandfather back home has died. Grieving, Ivanov goes to a Russian nightclub to ease his mind. He later walks back to his apartment building drunk, only to be mugged by two teenagers. He later reports the incident to the police with Orlando present and the two go to a diner where Ivanov rants about his misfortunes. A nearby Russian immigrant overhears the conversation, and interrupts Ivanov to disagree, leading the two into a tense confrontation that is settled after Ivanov realizes his fortunes of living in America. Soon after, Lucia comes back to him, Lionel moves back from Alabama, and Vladimir gets a job as a saxophonist in a wedding band, with time to play the music he loves during the day. He encounters the former apparatchik operating a hot dog stand, having lost his status back in the Soviet Union after Ivanov's defection. Ironically, the apparatchik is grateful to see Ivan and gives him a hot dog for free, showing his appreciation for the life he now has in America.

Cast

- Robin Williams as Vladimir Ivanoff
- María Conchita Alonso as Lucia Lombardo
- Cleavant Derricks as Lionel Witherspoon
- Alejandro Rey as Orlando Ramirez
- Saveli Kramarov as Boris
- Elya Baskin as Anatoly
- Yakov Smirnoff as Lev

The film features the late Soviet comedic actor Saveliy Kramarov, as a KGB officer, in one of his first Western film roles. Ironically, Kramarov was a Russian comedian who gave up a successful film career in his homeland for religious freedom and bit parts in films in the United States. He made 42 films in the former Soviet Union before he was allowed to leave in the early 1980s. This reality seems to mirror Vladimir's defection to the U.S. in the film.

The three Russian actors; Kramarov, Oleg Rudnik, and Elya Baskin also appear together in the film *2010* as cosmonauts. Kramarov and Rudnik play the two KGB agents always shadowing Vladimir and Baskin plays Vladimir's friend the circus clown. Stand up comedian Yakov Smirnoff also has a minor role in the film.

Reception

The film garnered positive reviews around the time of its release, and was moderately successful at the box office, bringing in $25 million in ticket sales. It currently holds an 89% on Rotten Tomatoes.

Litigation

The poster, depicting a bird's eye view of New York with Moscow and Russia beyond, prompted a lawsuit by Saul Steinberg, the famous artist whose work frequently appeared in *The New Yorker* magazine. Steinberg alleged that the movie poster infringed the copyright in Steinberg's seminal depiction "*View of the World from Ninth Avenue*". The district court agreed and awarded summary judgment to Steinberg in Steinberg v. Columbia Pictures Industries, Inc., 663 F. Supp. 706 (S.D.N.Y. 1987).

External links

- *Moscow on the Hudson* [1] at the Internet Movie Database
- *Moscow on the Hudson* [2] at Box Office Mojo
- *Moscow on the Hudson* [3] at Rotten Tomatoes

References

[1] http://www.imdb.com/title/tt0087747/
[2] http://www.boxofficemojo.com/movies/?id=moscowonthehudson.htm
[3] http://www.rottentomatoes.com/m/moscow_on_the_hudson/

Seize the Day (film)

Seize the Day	
Directed by	Fielder Cook
Starring	Robin Williams
Release date(s)	1986
Running time	93 min.
Country	United States
Language	English

Seize the Day is a 1986 film directed by Fielder Cook. It stars Robin Williams and Jerry Stiller.[1] It is based on the novel of the same name by Saul Bellow.

Plot Summary

After losing his job, his girlfriend, and his sanity, Salesman Tommy Wilhelm (Williams) packs up for New York City to try to repair the pieces of his broken life. His skill as a salesman comes naturally, but his strained relationship with his father (Joseph Wiseman) certainly does not. Tommy must face the father he never really knew while trying to balance the new life that he attempts to carve out for himself.

Cast

- Robin Williams as Tommy Wilhelm
- Jerry Stiller as Dr. Tamkin
- Joseph Wiseman as Dr. Adler
- Richard B. Shull as Rojax
- David Bickford as Son-in-law
- Glenne Headly as Olive
- Stephen Strimpell as Stockbroker

References

[1] http://allmovie.com/work/seize-the-day-43628

External links

- *Seize the Day* (http://www.imdb.com/title/tt0091920/) at the Internet Movie Database

Club Paradise

Club Paradise	
Theatrical poster	
Directed by	Harold Ramis
Produced by	Michael Shamberg
Screenplay by	• Harold Ramis • Brian Doyle-Murray
Story by	• Ed Roboto • Tom Leopold • Chris Miller • David Standish
Starring	• Robin Williams Peter O'Toole Rick Moranis Jimmy Cliff Twiggy Adolph Caesar Eugene Levy Joanna Cassidy Andrea Martin Brian Doyle-Murray
Music by	• David Mansfield • Van Dyke Parks
Cinematography	Peter Hannan
Editing by	Marion Rothman
Distributed by	Warner Bros.
Release date(s)	July 11, 1986
Running time	95 minutes
Country	United States
Language	English
Budget	$21 million
Box office	$12,308,521 (domestic)

Club Paradise is a 1986 American comedy film directed by Harold Ramis starring Robin Williams, Peter O'Toole, and Jimmy Cliff. The film reunites director/co-writer Ramis with most of his SCTV co-stars -- *SCTV* cast members Andrea Martin, Eugene Levy, Rick Moranis, Joe Flaherty, and Robin Duke play supporting roles in the film, as does co-writer Brian Doyle-Murray, a former *SCTV* staff writer.

Plot details

Jack Moniker (Robin Williams) is a Chicago firefighter who gets injured on the job. Using his disability money, he decides to retire and live the good life in a small Caribbean island named Saint Nicholas. He buys a small amount of property there and lives among other washed-up personalities such as Anthony Cloyden Hayes (Peter O'Toole). Appointed by the British crown as governor of St. Nicholas, Hayes is more concerned with vacationing than governing.

Jack befriends financially troubled reggae musician Ernest Reed (Jimmy Cliff), and they together form "Club Paradise," which they market as a Club Med-style resort. This attracts a handful of tourists, including Barry and Barry (Rick Moranis and Eugene Levy), who are there for the pot and the women. Much of the film involves the tourists' comic misadventures adjusting to island life and the low-rent facilities of Club Paradise.

(Brian Doyle-Murray) plays a key role, as a developer who wants to run Jack and Ernest off their property so he can build a massive high-end casino on the beach. To do that, he uses the help of the local prime minister (Adolph Caesar) and the prime minister's men to cause trouble and get Club Paradise to close "legally." When this doesn't work, the prime minister orders a military takeover of the island. Ernest builds up a resistance force, and St. Nicholas is soon threatened with the possibility of civil war.

Cast

- Robin Williams .... Jack Moniker
- Peter O'Toole .... Governor Anthony Cloyden Hayes
- Rick Moranis .... Barry Nye
- Jimmy Cliff .... Ernest Reed
- Twiggy .... Phillipa Lloyd
- Adolph Caesar .... Prime Minister Solomon Gundy
- Eugene Levy .... Barry Steinberg
- Joanna Cassidy .... Terry Hamlin
- Andrea Martin .... Linda White
- Brian Doyle-Murray .... Voit Zerbe
- Joe Flaherty .... Pilot
- Steven Kampmann .... Randy White
- Robin Duke .... Mary Lou
- Mary Gross .... Jackie
- Simon Jones ... Toby Prooth
- Louise Bennett ... Portia
- Ansel "Double Barrel" Collins ... Flamboyant (Ernest Reed's band)
- Earl "Chinna" Smith ... Flamboyant (Ernest Reed's band)
- Carey Lowell ... Fashion Model
- Louis Zorich ... Swiss Businessman
- Bruce McGill ... Dave, Jack's fireman buddy
- Anne Ramis, wife of director Harold Ramis ... Travel Agent

Production

Shooting for *Club Paradise* took place from April[1] to July 1985.[2] Production company Warner Bros. planned to release it in early 1986,[3] but held it back until July.

During development, Bill Murray turned down the film's lead role; his brother, Brian Doyle-Murray, ended up in the cast instead.[4] British actor John Cleese was also slated to star.[5]

"Ed Roboto" is a pseudonym for Harry Shearer, who was asked to do a rewrite with Tom Leopold. Only two words of what they wrote ended up in the film (the title) and Shearer was "so appalled by the movie" that he removed his name from the credits.[6]

Adolph Caesar died of a heart attack four months before the film's release.[3] It was his last completed role.

Although there is an extended sequence involving Robin Williams' character, in correspondence to the lyrics, "taking off his clothes and living in the jungle", the song Apeman by The Kinks was not included on the official soundtrack.

Reception

The film was given mostly negative reviews from critics with Rotten Tomatoes maintaing *Club Paradise* an 8% rating. Peter O'Toole's performance in the film earned him a Razzie Award nomination for Worst Supporting Actor.

References

[1] Maples, Tina (April 5, 1985). "Offstage: Tropical capers" (http://news.google.com/newspapers?id=ZGgaAAAAIBAJ&sjid=RioEAAAAIBAJ&pg=5738,3921333&dq=club-paradise&hl=en). *The Milwaukee Journal* (Journal Communications): p. 3 (Accent; Weekend). . Retrieved December 31, 2010.

[2] Associated Press (AP) (July 18, 1986). "Harold Ramis Directs Robin Williams" (http://news.google.com/newspapers?id=wIg_AAAAIBAJ&sjid=8VQMAAAAIBAJ&pg=5995,6472074&hl=en). *The Mount Airy News TV Plus*: p. 8. . Retrieved December 31, 2010.

[3] Associated Press (AP) (March 8, 1986). "Death ends late-blooming career of 'Purple' actor Caesar" (http://news.google.com/newspapers?id=-ElOAAAAIBAJ&sjid=EhQEAAAAIBAJ&pg=1698,2030043&hl=en). *Wilmington Morning Star* (The New York Times Company): p. 1D. . Retrieved December 31, 2010.

[4] Pollock, Dale (October 23, 1984). "Bill Murray had reluctant backing for 'Razor's Edge'" (http://news.google.com/newspapers?id=VJIpAAAAIBAJ&sjid=ZcAEAAAAIBAJ&pg=1344,4117343&dq=club-paradise+bill+murray&hl=en). *Anchorage Daily News*. Los Angeles Times **39** (297): p. D-6. . Retrieved January 3, 2011.

[5] Sun wire reports (September 28, 1984). "Actor cleaning up his act" (http://news.google.com/newspapers?id=RLQRAAAAIBAJ&sjid=uOkDAAAAIBAJ&pg=5542,4241458&dq=club-paradise+cleese&hl=en). *Gainesville Sun*: p. 2A. . Retrieved January 3, 2011.

[6] Gurwitch, Annabelle (2006). *Fired!: Tales of the Canned, Canceled, Downsized, and Dismissed* (http://books.google.com/books?id=egvbc_I7nNUC&pg=PA65&vq=Tom+Leopold&source=gbs_search_s&cad=0J). New York: Simon and Schuster. p. 65. ISBN 0-7432-9760-1. . Retrieved January 3, 2011.

External links

- *Club Paradise* (http://www.imdb.com/title/tt0090856/) at the Internet Movie Database
- *Club Paradise* (http://www.allrovi.com/movies/movie/v10078) at AllRovi
- *Club Paradise* (http://www.rottentomatoes.com/m/club_paradise/) at Rotten Tomatoes

The Best of Times (film)

The Best of Times	
Theatrical release poster	
Directed by	Roger Spottiswoode
Produced by	Gordon Carroll
Written by	Ron Shelton
Starring	Robin Williams Kurt Russell Pamela Reed Holly Palance Donald Moffat M. Emmet Walsh R.G. Armstrong
Music by	Arthur B. Rubinstein
Cinematography	Charles F. Wheeler
Editing by	Garth Craven
Distributed by	Universal Studios
Release date(s)	January 31, 1986 (USA)
Running time	104 min.
Country	United States
Language	English
Budget	Unknown
Box office	$7,790,931 (USA)

The Best of Times is a 1986 American film. It starred Robin Williams and Kurt Russell.

Overview

Robin Williams plays Jack Dundee, a banker obsessed with what he considers the most shameful moment in his life: The moment that he dropped a perfectly thrown pass in the final seconds of the 1972 high school football game between Taft and their arch-nemesis, Bakersfield.

Since that game, Jack has found it impossible to forget his drop. He works in a bank for his father-in-law, a.k.a. The Colonel, Bakersfield's biggest supporter, and is reminded by him almost daily, that it was *his* clumsiness and inability to catch a football that lost Taft its one chance for glory by finally beating Bakersfield, and how Taft would never do it again.

Thirteen years later, Jack coerces Reno (Kurt Russell), star quarterback of the fateful game and now a financially struggling garage owner in debt to Jack's bank, into helping him replay the game. He convinces supporters in both towns to re-stage the game and in the process revitalizes Taft, as well as his and Reno's marriages. The game is replayed and at the critical moment Reno throws another perfect pass to Jack. He catches it, and Taft defeats Bakersfield.

Much of the film was shot in and around Taft. The football scenes took place at Pierce Junior College in the San Fernando Valley. The night game was filmed at Moorpark Memorial High School, in Moorpark, CA.

Music in the film - "Pomp and Circumstance Marches", by Edward Elgar; and "The First Time Ever I Saw Your Face"' by Roberta Flack.

In so far as the film is 'a small town comedy where the whole population is caught up in some glorious foolishness'[1] it can trace its lineage to such films as Hail the Conquering Hero and The Miracle of Morgan's Creek, both Preston Sturges, and Jonathan Demme's Handle with Care.

Cast

- Robin Williams as Jack Dundee
- Kurt Russell as Reno Hightower
- Pamela Reed as Gigi Hightower
- Holly Palance as Elly Dundee
- Donald Moffat as The Colonel
- Margaret Whitton as Darla
- M. Emmet Walsh as Charlie
- Donovan Scott as Eddie
- R.G. Armstrong as Schutte
- Dub Taylor as Mac
- Carl Ballantine as Arturo
- Kathleen Freeman as Rosie
- Tony Plana as Chico
- Kirk Cameron as Teddy
- Robyn Lively as Jacki
- Jeff Doucette as Olin
- Anne Haney as Marcy
- Linda Hart as Blender #1
- Tracey Gold as Jaki's friend (uncredited)

References

[1] Pauline Kael 'Hooked' p.110 ISBN0-7145-2903-6

External links

- *The Best of Times* (http://www.imdb.com/title/tt0090713/) at the Internet Movie Database

Good Morning, Vietnam

Good Morning, Vietnam	
Theatrical release poster	
Directed by	Barry Levinson
Produced by	Larry Brezner Mark Johnson
Written by	Mitch Markowitz
Starring	Robin Williams Forest Whitaker Bruno Kirby J. T. Walsh
Music by	Alex North
Cinematography	Peter Sova
Editing by	Stu Linder
Distributed by	Touchstone Pictures
Release date(s)	December 23, 1987
Running time	120 minutes
Country	United States
Language	English
Budget	$13 million
Box office	$123,922,370 (USA)

Good Morning, Vietnam is a 1987 American comedy-drama film set in Saigon during the Vietnam War, based on the career of Adrian Cronauer, a disc jockey on Armed Forces Radio Service (AFRS), who proves hugely popular with the troops serving in South Vietnam, but infuriates his superiors with what they call his "irreverent tendency." The film was written by Mitch Markowitz and directed by Barry Levinson.

Most of Williams' humorous radio broadcasts were improvised.[1] Williams was nominated for an Academy Award for Best Actor in a Leading Role. The film is number 100 on "AFI's 100 Years...100 Laughs."

Plot

In 1965, Airman Second Class Adrian Cronauer (Robin Williams), of the United States Air Force, arrives in Saigon from Crete to work as a DJ for the Armed Forces Radio Service. Cronauer's irreverence contrasts sharply with many staff members and soon rouses the ire of two of his superiors, Second Lieutenant Steven Hauk (Bruno Kirby) and Sergeant Major Dickerson (J. T. Walsh). Hauk adheres to strict Army guidelines in terms of humor and music programming, while Dickerson is annoyed by Cronauer's behavior in general. However, Brigadier General Taylor (Noble Willingham) and the other DJs quickly grow to like the new man and his brand of comedy. Cronauer is also befriended by Private Edward Garlick (Forest Whitaker). Cronauer's show consists of unpredictable humor segments mixed with news updates (vetted by the station censors) and rock and roll records that are frowned upon by his superiors. Hauk finds nothing funny about any of it and tries, without success, to get him to change his approach.

Cronauer meets Trinh (Chintara Sukapatana), a Vietnamese girl, and follows her to an English class. Bribing the teacher to let him take over the job, Cronauer starts instructing the students in the use of American slang. Once class is dismissed, he tries to talk to Trinh but is stopped by her brother Tuan, who tells him to leave her alone. Instead, Cronauer befriends Tuan and takes him to Jimmy Wah's, the local G.I. bar, to have drinks with Garlick and the station staff. Two other soldiers, angered at Tuan's presence, start a fight with the group that rapidly escalates into a full-scale brawl.

Dickerson reprimands Cronauer for this incident, but the broadcasts and unorthodox English classes go on as usual. Impressed with the DJ's behavior, Tuan sets him up on a date with Trinh, with the rest of the family chaperoning them. While relaxing in Jimmy Wah's one afternoon, he is pulled outside by Tuan moments before the building explodes, killing two soldiers and leaving Cronauer badly shaken. The cause of the explosion is determined to be a bomb planted inside; the news is censored, but he locks himself in the studio and reports it anyway. Dickerson cuts off the broadcast signal in mid-report and Cronauer is suspended. Hauk takes over his time slots, but his poor attempts at comedy and insistence on playing polka music, instead of rock and roll, lead to a flood of letters and phone calls from servicemen who demand that Hauk be removed and that Cronauer be put back on the air.

In the meantime, Cronauer spends most of his time drinking and trying to pursue a relationship with Trinh, only to be rebuffed at every attempt. At the radio station Taylor intervenes on his behalf, ordering Hauk to reinstate him, but Cronauer refuses to go back to work when Garlick brings him the news. He now fears that Dickerson will send him to the front lines if he does anything else wrong. During a traffic jam, Garlick and Cronauer's vehicle is stopped by a convoy of soldiers; the GIs persuade him to do an impromptu "broadcast" for them, giving them a good laugh before they go off to fight. The performance for the troops – many of whom Cronauer realizes won't come back alive – renews his sense of purpose and reminds him why his job is important during the war, and he is soon back on the air.

Dickerson devises a ploy to get rid of Cronauer by sending him and Garlick to interview soldiers in the field – knowing that the only road into this particular area, An Lộc, is controlled by the Viet Cong (VC). Their jeep is blown off the road by a mine and they are forced to hide in the jungle from the VC patrols. Back in Saigon, Tuan learns of their trip after Cronauer fails to show up for English class, then steals a van and drives off after them. He finds them, but the van breaks down and they must flag down an Army helicopter to take them back to the city.

At the station, a gleeful Dickerson confronts Cronauer, declaring he is now off the air for good. His friend "Tuan" is actually Phan Duc To, a VC operative responsible for the bombing of Jimmy Wah's. He will be killed if the Army catches up to him. Dickerson has arranged for an honorable discharge, provided Cronauer leaves "quietly." Brigadier General Taylor arrives, and informs Cronauer that he cannot help this time; a US Armed Forces member being friends with a Vietcong could be a serious PR problem for the Army. Once Cronauer has left, however, Taylor informs Dickerson that he is being transferred to Guam as punishment for his vindictive attitude.

Cronauer finds Trinh and angrily persuades her to take him to her brother. Calling out his real name, he chases him into a back lot, where the boy angrily accuses Cronauer and the American forces of being the real enemy in this war and killing most of his family. He then slips away.

The next day, on his way to the airport, Cronauer sets up a quick softball game with the students from his English class. As he boards the plane, he gives Garlick a taped farewell message; Garlick – taking Cronauer's place as DJ – plays the tape on the air the next morning. It begins with a yell of *"Goooooooooooooooodbye, Vietnam!"* and runs through a few of Cronauer's impressions before ending with his wish that everyone will get home safely.

Cast

- Robin Williams as Airman Second Class Adrian Cronauer
- Forest Whitaker as Private Edward Garlick
- Tung Thanh Tran as Tuan
- Chintara Sukapatana as Trinh
- Bruno Kirby as Second Lieutenant Steven Hauk
- Robert Wuhl as Staff Sergeant Marty Lee Dreiwitz
- J. T. Walsh as Sergeant Major Dickerson
- Noble Willingham as Brigadier General Taylor
- Richard Edson as Private Abersold
- Richard Portnow as Sergeant Dan 'The Man' Levitan
- Floyd Vivino as Private Eddie Kirk
- Juney Smith as Sergeant Phil McPherson

Production

In 1979, Adrian Cronauer pitched a sitcom based on his experiences as an AFRS DJ. TV networks were not interested, because they did not see war as comedy material, despite the fact that one of the most popular shows at the time was *M*A*S*H*. Cronauer then revamped his sitcom into a script for a movie of the week, which eventually got the attention of Robin Williams. Very little of Cronauer's original treatment remained after writer Mitch Markowitz was brought in.[2] The film was shot in Bangkok, Thailand.

Awards and honors

American Film Institute recognition

- 2000: AFI's 100 Years... 100 Laughs #100

Robin Williams was nominated for an Academy Award, and was awarded a Golden Globe.

Soundtrack

Song	Artist
"Around the World in 80 Days"	Lawrence Welk
"Baby, Please Don't Go"	Them*
"Ballad of a Thin Man"	The Grass Roots
"Beach Blanket Bingo"	Frankie Avalon
"California Sun"	The Rivieras*
"Cast Your Fate To The Wind"	Sounds Orchestral
"Danger! Heartbreak Dead Ahead"	The Marvelettes*
"Don't Worry Baby"	The Beach Boys
"Dream On Little Dreamer"	Perry Como
"Five O'Clock World"	The Vogues*
"Game of Love"	Wayne Fontana & The Mindbenders*
"There'll Be a Hot Time in the Old Town Tonight"	Lawrence Welk & Myron Floren
"I Get Around"	The Beach Boys*

"I Got You (I Feel Good)"	James Brown*
"I'll Never Smile Again"	Lawrence Welk
"In the Midnight Hour"	Wilson Pickett
"It's Alright"	Adam Faith
"Kit Kat Polka"	Lawrence Welk & Myron Floren
"Liar, Liar"	The Castaways*
"Acapulco"	Herb Alpert & The Tijuana Brass
"Lollipops and Roses"	Jack Jones
"Nowhere to Run"	Martha and the Vandellas*
"Smoke Gets in Your Eyes"	Ray Conniff
"Sugar and Spice"	The Searchers*
"The Warmth of the Sun"	The Beach Boys*
"What a Wonderful World"	Louis Armstrong*
"Yeh Yeh"	Georgie Fame & The Blue Flames
"My Boyfriend's Back"	The Angels
"Puff, the Magic Dragon"	Peter Yarrow & Leonard Lipton
"Rawhide"	Dimitri Tiomkin & Ned Washington
"You Keep Me Hangin' On"	The Supremes
"Like Tweet"	Joe Puma & Eddie Hall
"Get a Job"	The Silhouettes

The soundtrack album included only the songs indicated with an asterisk above. It was certified platinum in the US.[3] The Louis Armstrong song was released as a single and became a top 40 hit twenty years after its original release.

References

[1] DVD extras

[2] Adrian Cronauer interview (http://www.harrisonline.com/audio/listings/2006/04/adrian-cronauer.htm) by Paul Harris, *The Paul Harris Show*, KMOX, April 28, 2006

[3] Joel Whitburn, Top Pop Albums 1955–2001 (Menomonee Falls, WI: Record Research, 2001), 1016.

External links

- *Good Morning, Vietnam* (http://www.imdb.com/title/tt0093105/) at the Internet Movie Database
- *Good Morning, Vietnam* (http://www.allrovi.com/movies/movie/v20309) at AllRovi
- *Good Morning, Vietnam* (http://www.rottentomatoes.com/m/good_morning_vietnam/) at Rotten Tomatoes
- *Good Morning, Vietnam* (http://www.boxofficemojo.com/movies/?id=goodmorningvietnam.htm) at Box Office Mojo
- Good Morning Vietnam (http://www.the-numbers.com/movies/1987/0GMVN.php) at The Numbers

Awakenings

Awakenings	
Theatrical release poster	
Directed by	Penny Marshall
Produced by	Penny Marshall Lawrence Lasker Walter F. Parkes
Written by	Steven Zaillian
Based on	*Awakenings* by Oliver Sacks
Starring	Robert De Niro Robin Williams
Music by	Randy Newman
Cinematography	Miroslav Ondrícek
Editing by	Battle Davis Gerald B. Greenberg
Distributed by	Columbia Pictures
Release date(s)	December 22, 1990
Running time	121 minutes
Country	United States
Language	English
Box office	$52,096,475[1]

Awakenings is a 1990 American drama film based on Oliver Sacks's 1973 memoir *Awakenings*. It tells the true story of British neurologist Oliver Sacks, fictionalized as American Malcolm Sayer and portrayed by Robin Williams who, in 1969, discovers beneficial effects of the then-new drug L-Dopa. He administered it to catatonic patients who survived the 1917–28 epidemic of encephalitis lethargica. Leonard Lowe (played by Robert De Niro) and the rest of the patients were awakened after decades of catatonic state and have to deal with a new life in a new time. The film was nominated for three Academy Awards.

Directed by Penny Marshall, the film was produced by Walter Parkes and Lawrence Lasker, who first encountered Sacks's book as undergraduates at Yale University and optioned it a few years later. *Awakenings* stars Robert De Niro, Robin Williams, John Heard, Ruth Nelson, Julie Kavner, Penelope Ann Miller, and Max Von Sydow. The film features a non-speaking cameo from jazz legend Dexter Gordon (who died before the film's release) who appears as a patient and then-unknowns Bradley Whitford, Peter Stormare, Vin Diesel, and Vincent Pastore play a doctor, neurochemist, hospital orderly and a psych-ward patient, respectively.

Plot

In 1969, Dr. Malcolm Sayer (Robin Williams) is a dedicated and caring physician at a local hospital in the New York City borough of The Bronx. After working extensively with the catatonic patients who survived the 1917-1928 epidemic of encephalitis lethargica, Sayer discovers certain stimuli will reach beyond the patients' respective catatonic states; actions such as catching a ball thrown at them, hearing familiar music, and experiencing human touch all have unique effects on particular patients and offer a glimpse into their worlds. Leonard Lowe (Robert De Niro) proves elusive in this regard, but Sayer soon discovers that Leonard is able to communicate with him by using a Ouija board.

After attending a lecture at a conference on the subject of the L-Dopa drug and its success with patients suffering from Parkinson's Disease, Sayer believes the drug may offer a breakthrough for his own group of patients. A trial run with Leonard Lowe yields astounding results as Leonard completely "awakens" from his catatonic state; this success inspires Sayer to ask for funding from donors so that all the catatonic patients can receive the L-Dopa medication and experience "awakenings" back to reality.

Meanwhile, Leonard is adjusting to his new life and becomes romantically interested in Paula (Penelope Ann Miller), the daughter of another hospital patient and begins spending time with her when she comes to the hospital to visit her father. Leonard also begins to chafe at the restrictions placed upon him as a patient of the hospital, desiring the freedom to come and go as he pleases and stirs up a bit of a revolt in the process of arguing his case repeatedly to Sayer and the hospital administration. Sayer notices that as Leonard grows more agitated battling administrators and staff about his perceived confinement, a number of facial and body tics are starting to manifest and Leonard has difficulty controlling them.

While Sayer and the hospital staff continue to delight in the success of L-Dopa with this group of patients, they soon find that it is a temporary measure. As the first to "awaken", Leonard is also the first to demonstrate the limited duration of this period of "awakening". Leonard's tics grow more and more prominent and he starts to shuffle more as he walks, and all of the patients are forced to witness what will eventually happen to them. He soon begins to suffer full body spasms and can hardly move. Leonard, however, puts up well with the pain, and asks Sayer to film him, in hopes that he would some day contribute to research that may eventually help others. Leonard acknowledges sadly what is happening to him and has a last lunch with Paula where he tells her he cannot see her anymore. Leonard and Dr. Sayer reconcile their differences, but Leonard returns to his catatonic state soon after. The other patients' fears are similarly realized as each eventually returns to catatonia no matter how much their L-Dopa dosages are increased.

Sayer tells a group of grant donors to the hospital that although the "awakening" did not last, another kind — one of learning to appreciate and live life — took place. The film ends with Sayer standing over the once again-catatonic Leonard behind a Ouija board, with his hands on Leonard's hands which man the planchette. "Let's begin." Sayer says.

Cast

- Robert De Niro as Leonard Lowe
- Robin Williams as Dr. Malcolm Sayer
- John Heard as Dr. Kaufman
- Ruth Nelson as Mrs. Lowe
- Julie Kavner as Eleanor Costello
- Penelope Ann Miller as Paula
- Max Von Sydow as Dr. Peter Ingham
- Alice Drummond as Lucy
- Judith Malina as Rose

- Richard Libertini as Sidney
- Keith Diamond as Anthony
- Peter Stormare as Neurochemist
- Bradley Whitford as Dr. Tyler
- Dexter Gordon as Rolando
- Vincent Pastore as Ward patient (as Vinny Pastore)
- Vin Diesel (*uncredited*) as Hospital orderly

Release and reception

Awakenings opened in limited release on December 22, 1990 with $417,076, then released on January 11, 1991 in wide release at #2 with $8,306,532 behind *Home Alone*'s ninth weekend.[2] The film is "Certified Fresh" on Rotten Tomatoes, with 90% of critics giving the film a positive review, with an average score of 6.8 out of 10 from 29 reviews.[3]

Academy Award nominations

The film received three Academy Award nominations:

- Academy Award for Best Picture
- Academy Award for Best Adapted Screenplay
- Academy Award for Best Actor for Robert De Niro

References

[1] http://www.boxofficemojo.com/movies/?id=awakenings.htm

[2] "Home Alone in 9th Week as No. 1 Film : Movies: 'Godfather Part III' takes dramatic slide from second to sixth place in its third week out. 'Awakenings' is in second." (http://articles.latimes.com/1991-01-14/entertainment/ca-310_1_godfather-part-iii). The Los Angeles Times. . Retrieved 2011-01-01.

[3] "Awakenings Movie Reviews, Pictures" (http://www.rottentomatoes.com/m/1032970-awakenings/). *Rotten Tomatoes*. . Retrieved January 18, 2011.

External links

- *Awakenings* (http://www.imdb.com/title/tt0099077/) at the Internet Movie Database
- *Awakenings* (http://www.allrovi.com/movies/movie/v3464) at AllRovi
- *Awakenings* (http://www.boxofficemojo.com/movies/?id=awakenings.htm) at Box Office Mojo
- *Awakenings* (http://www.rottentomatoes.com/m/1032970-awakenings/) at Rotten Tomatoes
- *Other Places* (http://www.haroldpinter.org/plays/plays_otherplaces.shtml) – Listed in "Plays" section of haroldpinter.org. [Includes photograph of playbill, production details, and retyped performance review by Alan Jenkins, originally published in TLS entitled "The Withering of Love", reproduced with permission.]

Dead Poets Society

Dead Poets Society	
Theatrical release poster	
Directed by	Peter Weir
Produced by	Steven Haft Paul Junger Witt Tony Thomas
Written by	Tom Schulman
Starring	Robin Williams Robert Sean Leonard Ethan Hawke Josh Charles Gale Hansen
Music by	Maurice Jarre
Cinematography	John Seale
Editing by	William M. Anderson
Studio	Silver Screen Partners IV
Distributed by	Touchstone Pictures
Release date(s)	June 2, 1989
Running time	128 minutes 142 minutes (USA TV cut)
Country	United States
Language	English
Budget	$16.4 million
Box office	$235,860,116[1]

Dead Poets Society is a 1989 American drama film directed by Peter Weir and starring Robin Williams. Set at the conservative and aristocratic Welton Academy in Vermont in 1959,[2] it tells the story of an English teacher who inspires his students through his teaching of poetry.

The script was written by Tom Schulman, based on his life at the Montgomery Bell Academy in Nashville, Tennessee. Filming took place at St. Andrew's School in Middletown, Delaware.

Plot

Neil Perry (Robert Sean Leonard), Todd Anderson (Ethan Hawke), Knox Overstreet (Josh Charles), Charlie Dalton (Gale Hansen), Richard Cameron (Dylan Kussman), Steven Meeks (Allelon Ruggiero), and Gerard Pitts (James Waterston) are senior students of the Welton Academy prep school, whose ethos is defined by the headmaster Gale Nolan (Norman Lloyd) as "tradition, honor, discipline and excellence". Both Neil and Todd are under harsh parental pressure to become a doctor and a lawyer respectively, but Todd wants to be a writer, and Neil discovers a passion for acting.

The teaching methods of their new English teacher, John Keating (Robin Williams), are unorthodox by Welton standards, whistling the *1812 Overture* and taking them out of the classroom to focus on the idea of *carpe diem*. He tells the students that they may call him "O Captain! My Captain!," in reference to a Walt Whitman poem, if they feel daring. In another class, Keating has Neil read the introduction to their poetry textbook, prescribing a mathematical formula to rate the quality of poetry which Keating finds ridiculous, and he instructs his pupils to rip the introduction out of their books, to the amazement of one of his colleagues. Later he has the students stand on his desk in order to look at the world in a different way. Inspired by Keating, the boys secretly revive a school literary club, the eponymous "Dead Poets Society," to which Keating had belonged, meeting in a cave off the school grounds.

Due to self-consciousness, Todd fails to complete a writing assignment and Keating takes him through an exercise in self-expression, realizing the potential he possesses. Charlie publishes an unauthorized article in the school newspaper, asserting that girls should be admitted to Welton. At the resulting school inquiry, he offers a phone call from God in support, incurring the headmaster's wrath. After being lectured by Headmaster Nolan about his teaching methods, Keating tells the boys to "be wise, not stupid" about protesting against the system.

Knox meets and falls in love with a girl named Chris, using his new-found love of poetry to woo her. He presents one of these poems in class, and is applauded by Keating for writing a heartfelt poem on love. Knox travels to Chris's public school and recites his poem to her, later convincing her to go to a play with him. Neil wants to be an actor but knows his father (Kurtwood Smith) will disapprove. Without his father's knowledge, he auditions for the role of Puck in a production of *A Midsummer Night's Dream*. His father finds out and orders Neil to withdraw. Neil asks Keating for advice and is advised to talk to his father and make him understand how he feels, but Neil cannot muster the courage to do so. Instead he goes against his father's wishes. His father shows up at the end of the play, furious. He takes Neil home and tells him that he intends to enroll him in a military school to prepare him for Harvard University and a career in medicine. Unable to cope with the future that awaits him or to make his father understand his feelings, Neil commits suicide.

At the request of Neil's parents, the headmaster launches an investigation. Richard meets the school governors and board of regents. Later, confronted by Charlie, Richard admits that he squealed on them and made Keating the scapegoat, and urges the rest of them to let Keating take the fall. Charlie punches Richard and is later expelled. Todd is called to Nolan's office, where his parents are waiting. Nolan forces Todd to admit to being a member of the Dead Poets Society, and makes him sign a document blaming Keating for abusing his authority, inciting the boys to restart the club, and encouraging Neil to flout his father's wishes. Todd sees the other boys' signatures already on the document, and is threatened by his father to sign it. Keating is subsequently fired.

The boys return to English class, now being taught by Nolan, who has the boys read the introductory essay only to find that they had all ripped it out. Keating enters the room to retrieve a few belongings. Todd reveals that the boys were intimidated into signing the denunciation. Nolan orders Todd to be quiet and demands that Keating leave. As Keating is about to exit, Todd for the first time breaks his reserve, calls out "O Captain! My Captain!" and stands on his desk. Nolan warns Todd to sit down or face expulsion. Much of the class climb onto their desks and look to Keating, ignoring Nolan's orders until he gives up. Keating leaves happily.

Cast

- Robin Williams as John Keating
- Robert Sean Leonard as Neil Perry
- Ethan Hawke as Todd Anderson
- Josh Charles as Knox Overstreet
- Gale Hansen as Charlie Dalton
- Norman Lloyd as Headmaster Gale Nolan
- Kurtwood Smith as Mr. Perry
- Dylan Kussman as Richard Cameron
- Allelon Ruggiero as Steven Meeks
- James Waterston as Gerard Pitts

- Alexandra Powers as Chris Noel

Reception

The critical reaction to this film has been extremely favorable; it received positive reviews from 86% of critics cited by Rotten Tomatoes,[3] as well as a weighted average score of 79 out of 100 from 14 mainstream critics registered on Metacritic.[4]

The Washington Post reviewer called it "solid, smart entertainment", and praised Robin Williams for giving a "nicely restrained acting performance".[5] Vincent Canby of *The New York Times* also praised Williams' "exceptionally fine performance", while noting that "*Dead Poets Society*... is far less about Keating than about a handful of impressionable boys".[2]

Roger Ebert's review was mixed, two out of four stars, criticizing Williams for spoiling a creditable dramatic performance by occasionally veering into his onstage comedian's persona, and additionally describing the movie as an often poorly constructed "collection of pious platitudes [...] The movie pays lip service to qualities and values that, on the evidence of the screenplay itself, it is cheerfully willing to abandon."[6]

Awards and nominations

Dead Poets Society won the Academy Award for Best Original Screenplay (Tom Schulman). Peter Weir received a nomination for Best Director and the film itself was nominated for Best Picture of 1989. Robin Williams received his second Best Actor in a Leading Role nomination and it has since been widely recognized as one of the actor/comedian's best roles. It also won the BAFTA Award for Best Film (the first Touchstone Pictures release to receive a best picture nomination).

The film's line "Carpe diem. Seize the day, boys. Make your lives extraordinary." was voted as the 95th greatest movie quote by the American Film Institute.[7] Also, the film was voted one of the 100 Most Inspiring Films of All Time by the AFI.[8]

- **Academy Awards** (USA)[9]
  - **Won**: Best Original Screenplay (Tom Schulman)
  - Nominated: Best Actor in a Leading Role (Robin Williams)
  - Nominated: Director (Peter Weir)
  - Nominated: Best Picture (Steven Haft, Paul Junger Witt and Tony Thomas, Producers)
- **BAFTA Awards** (UK) 1989[10]
  - **Won**: Best Film
  - **Won**: Best Original Film Score (Maurice Jarre)
  - Nominated: Best Actor in a Leading Role (Robin Williams)
  - Nominated: Best Achievement in Direction (Peter Weir)
  - Nominated: Best Editing (William Anderson)
  - Nominated: Best Original Screenplay (Tom Schulman)
- **César Awards** (France)[11]
  - **Won**: Best Foreign Film
- **David di Donatello Awards** (Italy)[12]
  - **Won**: Best Foreign Film
- **Directors Guild of America** (USA)[13]
  - Nominated: Outstanding Directorial Achievement in Motion Pictures (Peter Weir)
- **Golden Globe Awards** (USA)[14]

- Nominated: Best Performance by an Actor in a Motion Picture – Drama (Robin Williams)
- Nominated: Best Director – Motion Picture (Peter Weir)
- Nominated: Best Motion Picture – Drama
- Nominated: Best Screenplay – Motion Picture (Tom Schulman)

- **Writers Guild of America** (USA)[15]
  - Nominated: Best Screenplay – Original (Tom Schulman)

Soundtrack

All tracks composed by Maurice Jarre.

1. "Carpe Diem"
2. "Neil"
3. "To the Cave"
4. "Keating's Triumph"

References

[1] "Dead Poets Society (1989) – Box Office Mojo" (http://www.boxofficemojo.com/movies/?id=deadpoetssociety.htm). *Box Office Mojo*. . Retrieved 2010-10-17.

[2] Canby, Vincent (June 2, 1989). "Dead Poets Society (1989) June 2, 1989 Review/Film; Shaking Up a Boys' School With Poetry" (http://movies.nytimes.com/movie/review?res=950DE0DE1F31F931A35755C0A96F948260). *The New York Times*. New York City: The New York Times Company. . Retrieved 8 November 2011.

[3] "Dead Poets Society Movie Reviews, Pictures – Rotten Tomatoes" (http://www.rottentomatoes.com/m/dead_poets_society). Rotten Tomatoes. . Retrieved 2010-01-25.

[4] "Dead Poets Society reviews at Metacritic.com" (http://www.metacritic.com/movie/dead-poets-society). Metacritic. . Retrieved 2010-01-25.

[5] Howe, Desson (June 9, 1989). "'Dead Poets Society'" (http://www.washingtonpost.com/wp-srv/style/longterm/movies/videos/deadpoetssocietypghowe_a0b21e.htm). *The Washington Post*. . Retrieved 2010-10-17.

[6] Ebert, Roger (June 9, 1989). "Dead Poets Society" (http://rogerebert.suntimes.com/apps/pbcs.dll/article?AID=/19890609/REVIEWS/906090301/1023). *Chicago Sun-Times*. . Retrieved 2010-10-17.

[7] AFI's 100 YEARS...100 MOVIE QUOTES (http://www.afi.com/100years/quotes.aspx)

[8] AFI's 100 YEARS...100 CHEERS (http://www.afi.com/100Years/cheers.aspx)

[9] "Nominees & Winners for the 62nd Academy Awards" (http://www.oscars.org/awards/academyawards/oscarlegacy/1990-1999/62nominees.html). Oscars.org. . Retrieved 2010-11-17.

[10] "Awards Database" (http://www.bafta.org/awards-database.html?year=1989&category=false&award=false). Bafta.org. . Retrieved 2010-11-27.

[11] Dead Poets Society (http://www.peterweircave.com/dps/)

[12] Ente David di Donatello – Accademia del Cinema Italiano (http://www.daviddidonatello.it/english/schedaanno.php)

[13] "Welcome to the Directors Guild of America" (http://www.dga.org/index2.php3). Dga.org. . Retrieved 2010-11-27.

[14] HFPA – Awards Search (http://www.goldenglobes.org/browse/film/23935)

[15] Mathews, Jack; Easton, Nina J. (February 9, 1990). "Some Surprises in WGA Nominees, Shutouts : Film: 'Baker Boys,' 'My Left Foot' are dark-horse nominees for Writers Guild awards; non-union 'Do the Right Thing,' 'Drugstore Cowb..." (http://articles.latimes.com/1990-02-09/entertainment/ca-404_1_drugstore-cowboy). *Los Angeles Times*. .

Further reading

- Munaretto, Stefan (2005). *Erläuterungen zu Nancy H. Kleinbaum/Peter Weir, 'Der Club der toten Dichter'*. Hollfeld: Bange. ISBN 3-8044-1817-1.

External links

- *Dead Poets Society* (http://www.imdb.com/title/tt0097165/) at the Internet Movie Database
- *Dead Poets Society* (http://www.boxofficemojo.com/movies/?id=deadpoetssociety.htm) at Box Office Mojo
- *Dead Poets Society* (http://www.rottentomatoes.com/m/dead_poets_society/) at Rotten Tomatoes
- *Dead Poets Society* (http://www.metacritic.com/movie/dead-poets-society) at Metacritic
- "To the Virgins, to Make Much of Time" (http://www.poets.org/viewmedia.php/prmMID/15923) by Robert Herrick, a poem quoted in the film

Cadillac Man

Cadillac Man	
Theatrical release poster	
Directed by	Roger Donaldson
Produced by	Roger Donaldson and Charles Roven
Written by	Ken Friedman
Starring	Robin Williams Tim Robbins Pamela Reed Fran Drescher Lauren Tom
Music by	J. Peter Robinson
Cinematography	David Gribble
Editing by	Richard Francis-Bruce
Distributed by	Orion Pictures
Release date(s)	May 18, 1990 (USA)
Running time	97 minutes
Country	United States
Language	English
Budget	Unknown
Box office	$27,627,310 (USA)

Cadillac Man is a 1990 comedy film starring Robin Williams and Tim Robbins.

Plot

Brooklyn car salesman Joey O'Brien (Robin Williams) must deal with the ever-increasing pressures in his life: he has an ex-wife demanding alimony, a daughter who's missing, a married mistress (Fran Drescher) and a single mistress (Lori Petty) who are both desperately in love with him, and a two-day deadline to either sell twelve cars or lose his job. In addition, he has an outstanding loan to a Mafia Don which he must either quickly repay, or lose his life.

On the day of the big dealership car sale (and the final day of O'Brien's deadline), the car dealership is taken hostage by an AK-47-toting motorcyclist (Tim Robbins) (on a Kawasaki H2) who believes his wife (Annabella Sciorra) is cheating on him. Joey manages to talk the man out of doing any harm to the other hostages, as police surround the dealership. After most of the hostages are released, the police wound the assailant due to belief that his gun was still loaded. Joey promises to stick with him while he recovers. In the end, he gets back together with his wife and drives off as the hero of the day.

Cast

- Robin Williams as Joey O'Brien
- Tim Robbins as Larry
- Pamela Reed as Tina
- Annabella Sciorra as Donna, Larry's wife
- Fran Drescher as Joy Munchack, Joey's married mistress
- Zack Norman as Harry Munchack
- Lori Petty as Lila, Joey's single mistress
- Paul Guilfoyle as Little Jack Turgeon
- Judith Hoag as Molly
- Lauren Tom as Helen the dim sum girl
- Elżbieta Czyżewska as Soviet wife

Box office

The film was not a box office success.[1]

References

[1] "`Recall' Totally Outdistances `Future' in Box-Office Race Movies" (http://articles.latimes.com/1990-06-05/entertainment/ca-641_1_box-office). The Los Angeles Times. . Retrieved 2010-11-30.

External links

- *Cadillac Man* (http://www.imdb.com/title/tt0099204/) at the Internet Movie Database
- *Cadillac Man* (http://www.allrovi.com/movies/movie/v7802) at AllRovi

Dead Again

Dead Again	
Theatrical Release Poster	
Directed by	Kenneth Branagh
Produced by	Lindsay Doran
Written by	Scott Frank
Starring	Kenneth Branagh Andy García Emma Thompson Lois Hall Richard Easton Jo Anderson Derek Jacobi Robin Williams
Music by	Patrick Doyle
Editing by	Peter E. Berger
Distributed by	Paramount Pictures
Release date(s)	August 23, 1991
Running time	107 minutes
Country	United States
Language	English
Box office	$38,016,380

Dead Again is a 1991 psychological thriller/neo-noir directed by Kenneth Branagh, starring Branagh and his then-wife Emma Thompson. Andy García, Derek Jacobi and Robin Williams are also featured.

Plot summary

The film begins with opening credits intercut with pans across newspaper clippings about a society murder committed by conductor-composer Roman Strauss (Kenneth Branagh). Most of the articles were written by Gray Baker (Andy García), who visited Strauss on the day of his execution. The gates of a mansion in the past fade into the same gates in the present day, now the grounds of a Catholic orphanage. As the main narrative begins, we meet Mike Church (also Branagh), a smart-alecky Los Angeles private investigator whose jobs usually involve running down deadbeats and finding missing persons. He's called in by Father Timothy (Richard Easton), the priest in charge of the orphanage where Mike was raised, to help identify a woman (Emma Thompson) who showed up in a state of shock, unable to speak, and with amnesia.

Mike takes the woman, whom he calls Grace, to stay at his apartment, where he discovers she is terrified of scissors. The two uncover clues to her identity but nothing concrete. Grace regains her voice during a hypnotic session with Franklyn (Derek Jacobi), an antique dealer who claims she is having a "past-life" experience. Under hypnosis, she recalls a couple who lived during the 1940s, a famous composer and his pianist wife, as if she were part of their history. Franklyn finds a *LIFE* magazine identifying the couple as actual people, Roman and Margaret. Margaret was brutally murdered, and Roman was executed for her murder.

As Mike and Grace fall in love, Grace is upset by the similarities of their courtship to that of Roman and Margaret. Grace becomes afraid of Mike and is unconvinced by his assertions that he's "not Roman." Franklyn hypnotizes Mike, leading to the revelation that Mike is not the reincarnation of Roman, but of Margaret. Now, Mike becomes afraid of Grace. Mike consults with Cozy Carlisle (Robin Williams), a disgraced psychiatrist who lost his license and now works in a butcher shop. Grace consults with Franklyn; each is advised to kill the other. Meanwhile, Mike's friend at the newspaper, Pete (Wayne Knight), uncovers Grace's true identity: Amanda Sharpe, an artist. He takes Amanda and Franklyn to her apartment, where she discovers she is an artist who is obsessed with scissors. Franklyn gives Amanda an antique gun from his shop.

Mike finds Baker, old and decrepit, at a nursing home. Baker says he no longer thinks Roman killed Margaret and says that the housekeeper, Inga, would know. After the murder, the housekeeper moved out and opened an antiques shop run by her son, Frankie, a disturbed boy who was accused of stealing by Margaret. Mike visits Inga (Hanna Schygulla), who explains it was Frankie who killed Margaret. Inga had always been in love with Roman, after she saved his life while they fled war-torn Europe. After Margaret married Roman, Inga was treated coldly. Baker, who was attracted to Margaret, instilled suspicions in Margaret that Roman had indeed killed his first wife and that he was having a sexual affair with Inga. But Roman refused to fire Inga, despite Margaret's pleading, which made her more suspicious. Inga was unhappy about her treatment and told Frankie. Frankie killed Margaret with scissors. After having heard Inga's story, Mike (realizing that Franklyn is Frankie) races to Amanda's apartment; Frankie in the meantime arrives at the shop and smothers his mother.

Mike breaks into Amanda's apartment. She shoots him as he is trying to explain to her the truth about Roman and Margaret. Frankie shows up. Amanda tries to shoot him but the gun misfires. Frankie slaps Amanda unconscious and prepares to shoot her (in the mouth, so it looks like suicide), but Mike rouses himself and stabs Frankie with the scissors (placed in his hand by Frankie to incriminate him). Pete shows up with a pizza and tries to prevent Mike from what he thinks he's doing — killing Amanda — but he quickly realizes it is Frankie who intends to do the killing (who now has got hold of Mike's gun). After a brief standoff, Amanda stabs Frankie in the back with the scissors. Enraged, Frankie (whose stutter has returned) removes the scissors and lunges at her and Mike, but Mike moves a giant sculpture made of scissors directly into his path to impale him. Roman and Margaret kiss, and the scene fills with color as the shot fades to Mike and Amanda kissing.

Cast

- Kenneth Branagh as Mike Church/Roman Strauss
- Emma Thompson as Amanda Sharp/"Grace"/Margaret Strauss
- Andy García as Gray Baker
- Derek Jacobi as Franklyn Madson
- Wayne Knight as "Piccolo" Pete Dugan
- Robin Williams as Dr. Cozy Carlisle
- Hanna Schygulla as Inga
- Campbell Scott as Doug
- Jo Anderson as Sister Madeleine
- Richard Easton as Father Timothy

Production

The movie was filmed entirely in color. After test screenings, it was decided to use black and white for the "past" sequences to help clear up audience confusion. The final frame, once the mystery is solved, fades from black and white to color. The negative of the final frame was flipped to match the present day lovers to the doomed 1940s newlyweds they embodied; i.e., Margaret dissolves into Mike, and Roman dissolves into Grace.

When the audience first meets Mike Church, he's seated in his car, which is parked on the wrong side of the street. While it may seem that this is because Branagh is from the United Kingdom (where cars are driven on the left-hand side of the road), it is actually because behind him are a number of skyscrapers that he, as the director, wanted included in the background.

In addition to the dual roles played by Branagh and Thompson, actress Jo Anderson and the film's composer Patrick Doyle both play small dual parts, appearing in the present-day and 1940s sequences.

Branagh has said that at the time he made this film (and still, to some extent) he was very interested in the technique of uninterrupted takes, and several can be seen throughout the movie. Also note sequences such as the first hypnosis sequence at the Laughing Duke, which features an extremely complicated camera shot in 360 degrees, which involved a great deal of precise timing and technical faculty. Branagh noted that this relatively short scene was shot perhaps fifteen times, taking all day.

According to the director's commentary on the DVD edition of the movie, the film has numerous in-jokes. For instance, a date seen in one of the newspaper clippings is actually Branagh's birthday, and Roman Strauss' prisoner number is the date of the Battle of Agincourt. (Branagh's previous film, which launched his career, was *Henry V*.)

Reception

The movie was released on August 23, 1991 and was #1 at the U.S. box office for three weeks. It has an overall rating of 82% on Rotten Tomatoes with a 75% rating from the top critics.[1]

Patrick Doyle was nominated for a Golden Globe for his score. The film was entered into the 42nd Berlin International Film Festival.[2]

References

[1] "Dead Again" (http://www.rottentomatoes.com/m/dead_again/). *Rotten Tomatoes*. . Retrieved 2011-10-03.

[2] "Berlinale: 1992 Programme" (http://www.berlinale.de/en/archiv/jahresarchive/1992/02_programm_1992/02_Programm_1992.html). *berlinale.de*. . Retrieved 2011-05-24.

External links

- *Dead Again* (http://www.imdb.com/title/tt0101669/) at the Internet Movie Database

The Fisher King (film)

The Fisher King	
Theatrical release poster	
Directed by	Terry Gilliam
Produced by	Debra Hill Lynda Obst Tony Mark (associate)
Written by	Richard LaGravenese
Starring	Jeff Bridges Robin Williams
Music by	George Fenton
Editing by	Lesley Walker
Distributed by	TriStar Pictures
Release date(s)	September 20, 1991
Running time	137 minutes
Country	United States
Language	English
Budget	$24 million
Box office	$42 million[1]

The Fisher King is a 1991 American comedy-drama film written by Richard LaGravenese and directed by Terry Gilliam. It stars Jeff Bridges, Robin Williams, Mercedes Ruehl, Amanda Plummer and Michael Jeter. The film is about a radio shock-jock who tries to find redemption by helping a homeless man whose life he inadvertently shattered.

Plot

Jack Lucas (Jeff Bridges), a cynical, arrogant talk radio host, becomes suicidally despondent after his insensitive on-air comments inadvertently prompt a depressed caller to commit a mass murder at a popular Manhattan bar. Three years later, while heavily intoxicated and depressed, he attempts suicide. Before he can do so, he is mistaken for a homeless person and is attacked and nearly set on fire by thugs. He is rescued by Parry (Robin Williams), a deluded homeless man who is on a mission to find the Holy Grail, and tries to convince Jack to help him. Jack is initially reluctant, but comes to feel responsible for Parry when he learns that the man's condition is a result of witnessing his wife's horrific murder at the hands of Jack's psychotic caller. Parry is also continually haunted by a hallucinatory Red Knight, who terrifies him whenever he shows any confidence.

Jack learns that Parry had slipped into a catatonic state following his wife's death and had remained there for a few years. When he emerged he seemed obsessed with the legend of the Fisher King, a form of which Parry recounts to Jack. The legend varies, but all iterations possess three elements: the Fisher King was charged by God with guarding the Holy Grail, but later incurred some form of incapacitating physical punishment for his sin of pride, and had to wait for someone to deliver him from his suffering. A simpleminded knight named Percival, referred to in the movie as "The Fool," healed the wounds with kindness to the king, asking him why he suffers and giving him a cup of water to drink. The king realizes the cup is the Grail and is baffled that the boy found it, as demonstrated in the closing exchange: "I've sent my brightest and bravest men to search for this. How did *you* find it?" The Fool laughed and said "I don't know. I only knew that you were thirsty."

Jack seeks to redeem himself and help Parry find the Grail and find love again. Jack sets Parry up with a woman Parry has been smitten with from afar, Lydia, a shy woman who works as an accountant for a Manhattan publishing house. Jack successfully introduces them to each other and sets up an equally successful dinner date (Jack and his strong-willed girlfriend, Anne, join them). Following dinner, Parry declares his love for Lydia but is once again haunted by the Red Knight. Parry tries to escape his hallucinatory tormentor but is attacked by the same thugs who had earlier attacked Jack. The beating is not fatal but causes Parry to become catatonic again.

Jack infiltrates the Upper West Side castle of a famous architect and retrieves the "Grail," a simple trophy. When he brings it to Parry, the catatonia is broken and Parry regains consciousness. While he and Jack lead the patients of the mental ward in a rousing rendition of "How About You?," Parry is reunited with Lydia. Later, Jack, who had earlier broken up with Anne, is reunited with her.

Production

According to Gilliam's episode of *The Directors* (which is available on the 2-Disc DVD for Gilliam's film *Time Bandits*), he wanted to do the film because he was tired of doing big budget special effects films, such as his previous film *The Adventures of Baron Munchausen*, which went over budget and cost over $45 million, nearly twice as much as *King*'s budget of $24 million. This was the first film Terry Gilliam directed in which he was not involved in writing the screenplay, as well as Gilliam's first film not to feature any other members of Monty Python. However, it is Gilliam's second film involving the Holy Grail, the first being *Monty Python and the Holy Grail*.

Also, according to the *Directors* episode, Gilliam came up with the scene where Robin Williams and Amanda Plummer meet during a huge waltz in the middle of Grand Central Terminal, because he felt the scene LaGravenese had written (which had a large group of people in a crowded subway listen to a homeless black woman sing with a beautiful voice) wasn't working. He was at first hesitant about this because his original intentions were to just shoot the script and that the waltz would make it "a Terry Gilliam film." The scene was shot in one night with some professional extras and others just passengers getting off the train.

Reception

The Fisher King was a critical success, earning an 85% approval rating on Rotten Tomatoes.[2] Peter Travers of *Rolling Stone* wrote that the film "sweeps you up on waves of humor, heartbreak and ravishing romance."
The movie did moderate business at the box office,[3] [4] with revenue of approximately $42 million.[1]

Awards

Mercedes Ruehl won the Academy Award for Best Supporting Actress for her role, and Robin Williams was nominated for Best Actor. Other awards were Best Art Direction-Set Decoration (Mel Bourne, Cindy Carr), Best Music, Original Score (George Fenton) and Best Writing, Screenplay Written Directly for the Screen (Richard LaGravenese).[5]

Mercedes Ruehl also won the Academy of Science Fiction, Fantasy and Horror Films Award for Best Supporting Actress, the American Comedy Award for Funniest Supporting Actress in a Motion Picture, the Boston Society of Film Critics Award for Best Supporting Actress, the Los Angeles Film Critics Association Award for Best Supporting Actress and a Golden Globe for Best Supporting Actress.

Robin Williams won a Golden Globe for Best Performance by an Actor in a Motion Picture in a Comedy/Musical.

Terry Gilliam won the People's Choice Award from the Toronto International Film Festival and the Silver Lion in the Venice Film Festival (the latter tied with Zhang Yimou and Philippe Garrel).

Jane Jenkins and Janet Hirshenson won an Artios Award from the Casting Society of America for Best Casting in a Feature Film (Comedy).

References

[1] "The Fisher King > Overview" (http://allmovie.com/work/77235). *AllMovie.com*. Rovi Corporation. . Retrieved 2010-10-22.

[2] "The Fisher King Movie Reviews, Pictures" (http://www.rottentomatoes.com/m/fisher_king/). Rotten Tomatoes. . Retrieved 2011-10-29.

[3] "Weekend Box Office `House Party 2' Takes Top Spot" (http://articles.latimes.com/1991-10-29/entertainment/ca-481_1_house-party). *The Los Angeles Times*. . Retrieved 2011-01-01.

[4] "Terminator 2 About to Hit $200-Million Mark : Movies: While fall releases are in box-office slump, the summer smash climbs to 13th on all-time domestic ticket sales list." (http://articles.latimes.com/1991-10-31/entertainment/ca-816_1_box-offices/2). *The Los Angeles Times*. . Retrieved 2011-01-01.

[5] "The 64th Academy Awards (1992) Nominees and Winners" (http://www.oscars.org/awards/academyawards/legacy/ceremony/64th-winners.html). *oscars.org*. . Retrieved 2011-08-02.

External links

- *The Fisher King* (http://www.imdb.com/title/tt0101889/) at the Internet Movie Database
- *The Fisher King* (http://www.allrovi.com/movies/movie/v77235) at AllRovi
- Dreams: *The Fisher King* (http://www.smart.co.uk/dreams/fkprod1.htm)

Hook (film)

Hook	
Theatrical release poster by Drew Struzan	
Directed by	Steven Spielberg
Produced by	Frank Marshall Kathleen Kennedy Gerald R. Molen
Screenplay by	James V. Hart Malia Scotch Marmo
Story by	James V. Hart Nick Castle
Based on	*Peter Pan* by J. M. Barrie
Starring	Robin Williams Dustin Hoffman Julia Roberts Bob Hoskins Charlie Korsmo Amber Scott Dante Basco
Music by	John Williams
Cinematography	Dean Cundey
Editing by	Michael Kahn
Studio	Amblin Entertainment
Distributed by	TriStar Pictures

Release date(s)	December 11, 1991
Running time	144 minutes
Country	United States
Language	English
Budget	$70 million[1]
Box office	$300,854,823

Hook is a 1991 American fantasy film directed by Steven Spielberg. The film stars Robin Williams, Dustin Hoffman, Julia Roberts, Bob Hoskins, and features Maggie Smith, Caroline Goodall, Charlie Korsmo, Amber Scott, and Dante Basco. *Hook* acts as a sequel to Peter Pan's original adventures, focusing on a grown-up Peter who has forgotten his childhood. Now known as "Peter Banning", he is a successful corporate lawyer with a wife and two children. Captain Hook kidnaps his two children, and he must return to Neverland and reclaim his youthful spirit as Peter Pan in order to challenge his old enemy.

Spielberg began developing the film in the early-1980s with Walt Disney Productions and Paramount Pictures, which would have followed the storyline seen in the 1953 animated film and 1924 silent film. *Peter Pan* entered pre-production in 1985, but Spielberg abandoned the project. James V. Hart developed the script with director Nick Castle and TriStar Pictures before Spielberg decided to direct in 1989. *Hook* was shot entirely on sound stages at Sony Pictures Studios in Culver City, California. Although receiving negative reviews by critics at the time of its release, it was a success with audiences, grossing over $300 million worldwide, and was nominated for multiple categories at the 64th Academy Awards. It also spawned merchandise, including video games and comic book adaptations.

Plot

Peter Banning (Robin Williams) is a mild-mannered corporate attorney whose relationship with his family, especially his two young children Jack (Charlie Korsmo) and Maggie (Amber Scott), is strained by continuous absences and broken promises. His wife, Moira, (Caroline Goodall) struggles to keep them together and grows frustrated at Peter for his callous behavior. The family flies to London to visit Moira's grandmother, Wendy Darling (Maggie Smith), who helped Peter find a family when he was a young orphan.

Upon arrival, they meet Tootles (Arthur Malet), Wendy's first orphan, now an elderly gentleman who has "lost his marbles". Peter, Moira, and Wendy attend a ceremony for the expansion of Wendy's orphanage. While they are out, the children are abducted and a note is left for Peter by a James Hook. Wendy attempts to explain to Peter that he is in fact Peter Pan, who left Neverland years ago after falling in love with Moira, and that his old nemesis, Captain Hook (Dustin Hoffman), has returned and taken his children for revenge, but he denies it and attempts to drink the idea away in his bed.

Tinker Bell (Julia Roberts) appears before Peter that night and knocks him unconscious and flies him to a pirate port in Neverland. There, he awakens in disbelief, and is discovered by Hook and his second in command Smee (Bob Hoskins), who threaten to harm the children unless he accepts Hook's challenge to a duel. However, Peter's failure to reach expectations disheartens Hook, who commands the crew to kill them all. Tinker Bell intervenes and is granted three days in which to prepare Peter for a proper duel. Peter is accidentally knocked overboard and eventually finds his way to the Lost Boys' hideout, now led by Peter's successor, Rufio (Dante Basco). The Lost Boys at first dismiss him as an old man who has no hope of regaining his former glory, but through their rigorous training and his own sparks of inspiration he begins to relearn the magic of Neverland.

Meanwhile, Hook gets an idea from Smee to persuade Peter's children to love him more than Peter, so Hook makes a ploy for Maggie and Jack called "Why Parents ***Hate*** Their Children". Maggie does not fall for the ploy, but Jack does when Hook uses Jack's frustration over his father's continuous broken promises to steal his affection. Peter is heartbroken when he sees Hook treating Jack like a son, and becomes determined to win his family back. Stumbling upon his childhood home in a tree (destroyed by Hook), he finally remembers his past, learning how to fly by recalling his "happy thought": being a father. Peter regains the leadership of the Lost Boys and they challenge Hook and his pirates in an all-out battle. Peter tries to take Jack back from Hook, but Jack refuses as he now has come to look towards Hook as if he was his father, and Hook challenges Peter to a fight. However, Peter soon regains Jack's love when Jack realizes what Hook is really like, after Hook kills Rufio in a fair duel. Peter then saves Maggie from Hook's pirates. Peter and Hook engage in a climactic sword fight, and Hook is apparently killed when the Crocodile, which Hook has built into a massive clock tower, falls on him. Jack and Maggie return home as Peter designates the largest member of the Lost Boys, Thud Butt (Raushan Hammond), the only other lost boy besides Rufio whom Peter grew a connection to, as the new leader of the Lost Boys, and tells them to take care of everybody smaller than them, adding "Thank you for believing," as he leaves Neverland.

Returning home, Peter finally realizes the love he has for his family and the importance of having a youthful heart. Tootles is dismayed at missing the adventure, but discovers pixie dust in his bag of lost marbles and uses it to go flying around London and back to Neverland. Wendy remarks to Peter that his adventures are now over, but Peter says, "To live would be an awfully big adventure."

Cast

- Robin Williams as Peter Banning / Peter Pan: Peter has forgotten his childhood in Neverland and then being adopted by an American couple, Hank and Jane Banning. He has become a successful corporate lawyer with a wife and two kids. After Captain Hook kidnaps his two children, Peter Banning must reclaim his youthful spirit as Peter Pan in order to challenge Hook.
  - Ryan Francis as young Peter Pan in flashbacks, and Max Hoffman as the younger Peter.
- Dustin Hoffman as Captain Hook: A villainous pirate who has had a long enemy relationship with Peter Pan. After escaping from his death, Hook seeks revenge against Peter by kidnapping his two children.
- Julia Roberts as Tinker Bell: A fairy who helps Peter gain memory of his childhood and "happy thoughts". She is in love with Peter, but understands why he must continue his relationship with his family.
  - Lisa Wilhoit as the young Tinker Bell.
- Charlie Korsmo as Jack Banning: Peter and Moira's son who begins to rebel against his father and looks towards Captain Hook as a father figure when Hook uses Jack's frustration of his father's broken promises to turn him against Peter.
- Amber Scott as Maggie Banning: Peter and Moira's daughter and Jack's younger sister who, after the kidnapping, does not fall for Hook's ploy of "why parents hate their children". A *Peter Pan* enthusiast, after Maggie discovers her father and the hero she idolizes are one and the same, she is proud to be his daughter.
- Bob Hoskins as Smee: Hook's henchman who devises the plan to persuade Peter's children to "love" Hook. Hoskins also portrays a garbage sweeper in Kensington Gardens.
- Caroline Goodall as Moira Banning: Wendy's granddaughter, Peter's loving wife, mother to Jack and Maggie and sister to the unseen Margaret. After realized that he missed his chance with Wendy, young Peter decides to leave Neverland for Moira to prevent his history with her grandmother repeats itself after falling in love with her at first sight.
- Maggie Smith as Wendy Darling: A former neighbor of J. M. Barrie, who was credited as the author of *Peter Pan*. After Wendy's adventures with Peter Pan, she becomes well-known for helping orphans. After Peter decided to leave Neverland to find love with Moira, the adult Wendy taught young Peter how to read and arranged for him to be adopted by the Bannings. As a young girl, she was in love with Peter Pan, but young Peter realized too late his own feelings for Wendy after seeing her as a married older woman.
  - Gwyneth Paltrow appears as young Wendy Darling in flashbacks.

- Dante Basco as Rufio: Leader of the Lost Boys since Peter's departure from Neverland. Rufio is initially resentful of him but soon wishes he had a father like Peter. He is killed by Captain Hook during a duel.
- Arthur Malet as Tootles: A senile old man living with Wendy. A former Lost Boy, Tootles is also Wendy's "first orphan". Peter helps giving him the ability to fly by finding his lost marbles, which he left in Neverland.
- Jasen Fisher and James Madio portray Lost Boys. Kelly Rowan makes a cameo appearance as Peter Pan's mother and Genesis vocalist Phil Collins appears briefly as an English police inspector. More cameos include singers David Crosby and Jimmy Buffett as members of Hook's pirate crew, Nick Tate as a pirate who fights Peter Pan while taking away Maggie, and Glenn Close similarly appears as a male pirate who is punished by Hook. Filmmaker George Lucas and actress Carrie Fisher appear as the couple accidentally sprinkled with fairy dust as Tinker Bell brings Peter to Neverland.

Production

J. M. Barrie considered writing a story in which Peter Pan grew up; his 1920 notes for the latest stage revival of *Peter Pan* included possible titles for another play: *The Man Who Couldn't Grow Up* or *The Old Age of Peter Pan*.[2] The genesis of *Hook* started when director Steven Spielberg's mother often read him *Peter and Wendy* as a bedtime story. Spielberg explained in 1985, "When I was eleven years old I actually directed the story during a school production. I have always felt like Peter Pan. I still feel like Peter Pan. It has been very hard for me to grow up, I'm a victim of the Peter Pan syndrome."[3]

In the early 1980s, with Walt Disney Pictures, Spielberg began to develop the film which would have closely followed the storyline of the 1953 animated film and 1924 silent film.[4] He also considered directing *Peter Pan* as a musical with Michael Jackson in the lead.[5] The project was taken to Paramount Pictures, where James V. Hart wrote the first script with Dustin Hoffman already cast as Captain Hook.[5] *Peter Pan* entered pre-production in 1985 for filming to begin at sound stages in England. Elliot Scott had been hired as production designer.[4] With the birth of his first son, Max, in 1985, Spielberg decided to drop out. "I decided not to make *Peter Pan* when I had my first child," Spielberg commented. "I didn't want to go to London and have seven kids on wires in front of blue screens. I wanted to be home as a dad."[5] Around this time, Spielberg considered directing *Big*, which carried similar motifs and themes with Peter Pan.[5] In 1987, Spielberg "permanently abandoned" *Peter Pan*, feeling he expressed his childhood and adult themes in *Empire of the Sun*.[6]

Meanwhile, Paramount and Hart moved forward on production with Nick Castle as director. Hart began to work on a new storyline when his son, Jake, showed his family a drawing. "We asked Jake what it was and he said it was a crocodile eating Captain Hook, but that the crocodile really didn't eat him, he got away," Hart reflected. "As it happens, I had been trying to crack *Peter Pan* for years, but I didn't just want to do a remake. So I went, 'Wow. Hook is not dead. The crocodile is. We've all been fooled'. In 1986 our family was having dinner and Jake said, 'Daddy, did Peter Pan ever grow up?' My immediate response was, 'No, of course not'. And Jake said, 'But what if he did?' I realized that Peter did grow up, just like all of us baby boomers who are now in our forties. I patterned him after several of my friends on Wall Street, where the pirates wear three-piece suits and ride in limos."[7]

By 1989, Hart and Castle changed the title of *Peter Pan* to *Hook*, and took it from Paramount to TriStar Pictures, headed by Mike Medavoy, who was Spielberg's first talent agent. Robin Williams signed on, but Williams and Hoffman had creative differences with Castle. Medavoy saw *Hook* as a vehicle for Spielberg and Castle was fired, but paid a $500,000 settlement.[7] Spielberg briefly worked together with Hart to rewrite the script[4] before hiring Malia Scotch Marmo to rewrite Captain Hook's dialog and Carrie Fisher for Tinker Bell's dialog. The Writers Guild of America gave Hart and Marmo screenplay credit, while Hart and Castle were credited with story. Fisher went uncredited. Filming started on February 19, 1991, occupying nine sound stages at Sony Pictures Studios in Culver City, California.[1] Stage 30 housed the Neverland Lost Boys playground, while Stage 10 supplied Captain Hook's ship cabin. Hidden hydraulics were installed to rock the setpiece to simulate a swaying ship, but the filmmakers found the movement distracted the dialogue, so the idea was dropped.[8]

Stage 27 housed the full-sized pirate ship *Jolly Roger* and the surrounding Pirate Wharf.[8] Industrial Light & Magic provided the visual effects sequences. *Hook* was financed by Amblin Entertainment and TriStar Pictures, with TriStar distributing the film. Impressed with his work on *Cats*, Spielberg brought John Napier as a "visual consultant". The original production budget was set at $48 million, but ended up between $60–80 million.[1] [9] This was also largely contributed by the shooting schedule, which ran 40 days over its original 76 day schedule. Spielberg explained, "It was all my fault. I began to work at a slower pace than I usually do."[9] He also found it difficult to work with Julia Roberts, who was suffering from a mental disorder after her breakup with Dylan McDermott.[4]

Themes

Spielberg found close personal connection to the film. The troubled relationship between Peter and his son echoed Spielberg's relationship with his father. Previous films of Spielberg that explored a diminishing father-son relationship included *E.T. the Extra-Terrestrial* and *Indiana Jones and the Last Crusade*. Peter Banning's "quest for success" paralleled Spielberg starting out as a film director and transforming into a Hollywood business magnate. This led to Spielberg's divorce from Amy Irving, which would possibly lead to Banning's relationship with his family.[10] "I think a lot of people today are losing their imagination because they are work-driven. They are so self-involved with work and success and arriving at the next plateau that children and family almost become incidental. I have even experienced it myself when I have been on a very tough shoot and I've not seen my kids except on weekends. They ask for my time and I can't give it to them because I'm working."[4] Similar to Peter Banning at the beginning of *Hook*, Spielberg also has a fear of flying. He feels that Peter Pan's "enduring quality" in the storyline is simply to fly. "Anytime anything flies, whether it's Superman, Batman, or E.T., it's got to be a tip of the hat to Peter Pan," Spielberg reflected. "*Peter Pan* was the first time I saw anybody fly. Before I saw *Superman*, before I saw *Batman*, and of course before I saw any superheroes, my first memory of anybody flying is in *Peter Pan*."[4]

Soundtrack

Hook: Original Motion Picture Soundtrack	
Film score by John Williams	
Released	November 26, 1991
Label	Epic Records

The film score was composed by John Williams. The lyrics for tracks "We Don't Wanna Grow Up" and "When You're Alone" were written by Leslie Bricusse.

Hook: Original Motion Picture Soundtrack[11]		
No.	**Title**	**Length**
1.	"Prologue"	1:30
2.	"We Don't Wanna Grow Up"	1:50
3.	"Banning Back Home"	2:22
4.	"Granny Wendy"	2:57
5.	"Hook-Napped"	3:56
6.	"The Arrival of Tink and the Flight to Neverland"	5:55
7.	"Presenting the Hook"	2:58

8.	"From Mermaids to Lost Boys"	4:24
9.	"The Lost Boy Chase"	3:31
10.	"Smee's Plan"	1:44
11.	"The Banquet"	3:07
12.	"The Never-Feast"	4:39
13.	"Remembering Childhood"	11:02
14.	"You are the Pan"	3:59
15.	"When You're Alone"	3:13
16.	"The Ultimate War"	7:53
17.	"Farewell Neverland"	10:16
Total length:		**75:19**

Commercial songs from film, but not on soundtrack

- *Pick'em Up* - Music by John Williams and lyrics by Leslie Bricusse
- *Take Me Out to the Ball Game* - Written by Jack Norworth & Albert Von Tilzer

Reception

Spielberg, Williams and Hoffman did not take salaries for the film. Their deal called for the trio to split 40% of TriStar Pictures' gross revenues. They were to receive $20 million from the first $50 million in gross theatrical film rentals, with TriStar keeping the next $70 million in rentals before the three resumed receiving their percentage.[1] *Hook* was released in North America on December 11, 1991, earning $13.52 million in its opening weekend. The film went on gross $119.65 million in North America and $181.2 million in foreign countries, accumulating a worldwide total of $300.85 million. *Hook* was declared a financial success,[12] and is the fifth-highest grossing "pirate-themed" film, behind all four films in the *Pirates of the Caribbean* film series.[13] In North America totals, *Hook* was the sixth-highest grossing film in 1991,[14] and fourth-highest worldwide.[15]

Film critics gave *Hook* generally negative reviews. As of December 2011, review aggregator Rotten Tomatoes reports that 29% of critics have given the film a positive review, based on 38 reviews, certifying it "Rotten", with an average rating of 4.4/10.[16] At the same time, the film receives a 72% positive audience rating. Roger Ebert wrote that the "failure in *Hook* was its inability to re-imagine the material, to find something new, fresh or urgent to do with the Peter Pan myth. Lacking that, Spielberg should simply have remade the original story, straight, for the '90s generation."[17] Peter Travers of *Rolling Stone* felt *Hook* would "only appeal to the baby boomer generation" and highly criticized the sword-fighting choreography.[18] Vincent Canby of *The New York Times* felt the story structure was not well balanced, feeling Spielberg depended too much on art direction.[19] Hal Hinson of *The Washington Post* was one of few who gave the film a positive review. Hinson elaborated on crucial themes of children, adulthood and loss of innocence. However, he observed that Spielberg "was stuck too much in a theme park world".[20]

Despite some negative reviews, *Hook* was nominated for five categories at the 64th Academy Awards. This included Art Direction (Norman Garwood, Garrett Lewis) (lost to *Bugsy*), Costume Design (lost to *Bugsy*), Visual Effects (lost to *Terminator 2: Judgment Day*), Makeup (lost to *Terminator 2: Judgment Day*) and Original Song ("When You're Alone", lost to *Beauty and the Beast*).[21] *Hook* lost the Saturn Award for Best Fantasy Film to *Aladdin*, in which Robin Williams co-starred,[22] while cinematographer Dean Cundey was nominated for his work by the American Society of Cinematographers.[23] Dustin Hoffman was nominated the Golden Globe Award for Best Actor (Musical or Comedy).[24] John Williams was given a Grammy Award nomination;[25] Julia Roberts received a Golden Raspberry Award nomination for Worst Supporting Actress.[26]

References

[1] Joseph McBride (1997). *Steven Spielberg: A Biography*. New York City: Faber and Faber. pp. 411. ISBN 0-571-19177-0.

[2] Andrew Birkin (2003). *J.M. Barrie and the Lost Boys*. New Haven, Connecticut: Yale University Press. ISBN 978-0300098228.

[3] McBride, p.42—43

[4] Ana Maria Bahiana (March 1992). "*Hook*", *Cinema Papers*, pp. 67—69.

[5] McBride, p. 409.

[6] Myra Forsberg (1988-01-10). "Spielberg at 40: The Man and the Child". *The New York Times*.

[7] McBride, p. 410.

[8] DVD production notes

[9] McBride, p. 412.

[10] McBride, p. 413.

[11] [www.allmusic.com/album/hook-r123471 "*Hook* - John Williams"]. *Allmusic*. www.allmusic.com/album/hook-r123471. Retrieved August 26, 2010.

[12] "Hook" (http://boxofficemojo.com/movies/?id=hook.htm). *Box Office Mojo*. . Retrieved 2008-09-19.

[13] "Pirate Movies" (http://boxofficemojo.com/genres/chart/?id=pirate.htm). *Box Office Mojo*. . Retrieved 2011-06-03.

[14] "1991 Domestic Totals" (http://boxofficemojo.com/yearly/chart/?yr=1991&p=.htm). *Box Office Mojo*. . Retrieved 2008-09-19.

[15] "1991 Worldwide Grosses" (http://boxofficemojo.com/yearly/chart/?view2=worldwide&yr=1991&p=.htm). *Box Office Mojo*. . Retrieved 2008-09-19.

[16] "Hook" (http://www.rottentomatoes.com/m/hook/). *Rotten Tomatoes*. Flixster. . Retrieved 2011-07-12.

[17] "Hook" (http://rogerebert.suntimes.com/apps/pbcs.dll/article?AID=/19911211/REVIEWS/112110301/1023). *Roger Ebert.com*. 1991-12-11. . Retrieved 2008-09-19.

[18] Peter Travers (1991-12-11). "Hook" (http://www.rollingstone.com/reviews/movie/5947391/review/5947392/hook). *Rolling Stone*. . Retrieved 2008-09-19.

[19] Vincent Canby (1991-12-11). "Hook". *The New York Times*.

[20] Hal Hinson (1991-12-11). "Hook". *The Washington Post*.

[21] "Hook" (http://awardsdatabase.oscars.org/ampas_awards/DisplayMain.jsp?curTime=1222224401661). *Academy of Motion Picture Arts and Sciences*. . Retrieved 2008-09-20.

[22] "Past Saturn Awards" (http://www.saturnawards.org/past.html). *Saturn Awards.com*. . Retrieved 2008-09-20.

[23] "7th Annual Awards" (http://web.archive.org/web/20061109113918/http://www.theasc.com/awards/history/1992.htm). *American Society of Cinematographers*. Archived from the original (http://www.theasc.com/awards/history/1992.htm) on November 9, 2006. . Retrieved 2008-09-20.

[24] "49th Golden Globe Awards" (http://www.imdb.com/Sections/Awards/Golden_Globes_USA/1992). *Internet Movie Database*. . Retrieved 2008-09-20.

[25] "Grammy Awards of 1991" (http://www.imdb.com/Sections/Awards/Grammy_Awards/1993). *Internet Movie Database*. . Retrieved 2008-09-20.

[26] "Twelfth Annual RAZZIE Awards" (http://www.razzies.com/forum/forum_posts.asp?TID=341&PN=2). *Golden Raspberry Award*. . Retrieved 2008-10-15.

Further reading

- Terry Brooks (17 December 1991) (Hardcover). *Hook*. novelization of the film. Ballantine Books. ISBN 0449907074.
- Charles L.P. Silet (2002). *The Films of Steven Spielberg*. Scarecrow Press. ISBN 0-8108-4182-7.

External links

- *Hook* (http://www.imdb.com/title/tt0102057/) at the Internet Movie Database
- *Hook* (http://www.allrovi.com/movies/movie/v23072) at AllRovi
- *Hook* (http://www.rottentomatoes.com/m/hook/) at Rotten Tomatoes
- *Hook* (http://www.boxofficemojo.com/movies/?id=hook.htm) at Box Office Mojo

Toys (film)

Toys	
Theatrical release poster	
Directed by	Barry Levinson
Produced by	Mark Johnson Barry Levinson
Written by	Valerie Curtin & Barry Levinson
Starring	Robin Williams Michael Gambon Joan Cusack Robin Wright LL Cool J Donald O'Connor Arthur Malet Jamie Foxx Jack Warden Debi Mazar
Music by	Hans Zimmer Trevor Horn
Cinematography	Adam Greenberg
Editing by	Stu Linder
Studio	Baltimore Pictures
Distributed by	20th Century Fox
Release date(s)	December 18, 1992 (USA)
Running time	121 minutes
Country	United States
Language	English
Budget	$43 million
Box office	$21,452,082 (USA)

Toys is a 1992 comedy film directed by Barry Levinson and starring Robin Williams, Michael Gambon, Joan Cusack, Robin Wright, LL Cool J, and introducing Jamie Foxx as Baker. The film failed at the box office at the time of its release, despite its impressive cast and lavish filmmaking. Levinson was criticized for a lack of plot focus. The magnitude of perceived directorial failure was such that Levinson was consequently nominated for (but did not win) a Razzie Award for Worst Director. The film did, however, receive Oscar nominations for art direction (Ferdinando Scarfiotti, Linda DeScenna) and costume design.[1] It was also entered into the 43rd Berlin International Film Festival.[2]

René Magritte's art, particularly *The Son of Man*, is obvious in its influence on the set design, and in part the costume design, of the film. The poster for the film distributed to movie theaters features Robin Williams in a red bowler hat against a blue, cloud-lined background. *Golconda* is also featured during a sequence where Robin Williams and Joan Cusack's characters perform in a music video sequence rife with surreal imagery, much of it Magritte-inspired.

Plot

At the Zevo Toys factory in a lovely field of green, owner Kenneth Zevo (Donald O'Connor) is dying. He expresses to his assistant Owens (Arthur Malet) that he wants control of the business to go to his brother, a retired military man, and not to his son Leslie (Robin Williams), whom he deems to be too immature.

After Zevo dies, his brother Lt. General Leland Zevo (Michael Gambon) takes over. At first he has no interest in anything at the factory until he hears of possible leaks and corporate espionage. The General brings in his son Patrick (LL Cool J), a soldier and expert in covert military operations, to oversee security. He soon decides to make a series of war toys to the dismay of Leslie as Zevo has never made war toys because his father, Kenneth, did not like them.

After a confrontation with Leslie, Leland halts the development of the war toys. He asks Leslie for some space to work alone to develop some toys of his own and states he doesn't want Leslie to see them because they might not be good enough. Leland's continued demands for more space, rigid security and top-secret projects dismay the childlike Leslie, his innocent and child-like sister Alsatia (Joan Cusack), a factory worker Leslie has developed a crush on, Gwen (Robin Wright) and Owens.

Leslie becomes more suspicious when Owens shows him children arriving at the factory and ushered into the restricted area. He breaks into a research area and discovers kids playing realistic war video games. After setting off the alarm he runs through a door and falls into a well-like water tank where he sees and seems to be drowned by another toy of the Leland's, the "Sea Swine" (an amphibious drone with more autonomy than the other toys).

Patrick decides to go against his father after he discovers that his mother did not die of appendicitis but disappeared when his father sent her on a covert mission(reconnaissance) . After revealing his father's true plans of using dangerous weaponry in the form of toys, Patrick, Leslie, Alsatia, Gwen and Owen launch an attack on the General's labs to shut down his war projects.

The increasingly demented General sees this as his greatest war opportunity and attempts to destroy them all. First he sends out weapons disguised as toys, then he sends his "Tommy Tanks" and "Whirly Burly Helicopters".

An intense battle takes place between the General's toys and the original Zevo toys.

Leslie manages to win the battle and along with Patrick is very angry with the General for attempting to kill them all. Suddenly Alsatia is attacked by the General's secret weapon the Sea Swine, revealing that she is a gynoid built by Leslie's father as a play-mate for Leslie. While they are seeing to Leslie's sister, Leland tries to make his escape, but the malfunctioning Sea Swine tracks him down and attacks him as well resulting in his defeat.

In the end, Leslie is the new head of Zevo Toys, Alsatia is fixed, Gwen becomes Leslie's girlfriend, Leland is hospitalized, and Patrick decides to move on to other missions. As peace is restored to the toy factory in lush green pasture, a large toy elephant floats by overhead.

Cast

Character	Actor
Leslie Zevo	Robin Williams
Lt. General Leland Zevo	Michael Gambon
Alsatia Zevo	Joan Cusack
Gwen Tyler	Robin Wright
Capt. Patrick Zevo	LL Cool J
Kenneth Zevo	Donald O'Connor
Owen Owens	Arthur Malet
Baker	Jamie Foxx

Cortez	Julio Oscar Mechoso
Hagenstern	Blake Clark
Researcher Miss Drum	Yeardley Smith
Choir Soloist	Wendy Melvoin
Old General Zevo	Jack Warden
Nurse Debbie	Debi Mazar
Little Boy	Jack Levinson

Trailer

The film was publicized with a trailer, which featured Williams walking through a large undulating field of green grass and breaking the fourth wall, while talking to the audience. This trailer[3] was parodied in on the TV show *The Simpsons* in the episode "Burns' Heir", substituting Mr. Burns for Williams.

Soundtrack

No.	Title	Writer(s)	Performer	Length
1.	"Winter Reveries" (Excerpt from Tchaikovsky's Symphony No. 1)	Pyotr Ilyich Tchaikovsky, arranged by Trevor Horn	Shirley Walker Orchestra	2:03
2.	"The Closing of the Year" (Main Theme)	Trevor Horn, Hans Zimmer	The Musical Cast of Toys featuring Wendy & Lisa	3:28
3.	"Ebudae"	Enya, Roma Ryan	Enya	1:49
4.	"The Happy Worker"	Horn, Bruce Woolley	Tori Amos	4:19
5.	"Alsatia's Lullaby"	Zimmer	Julia Migenes & Hans Zimmer	4:16
6.	"Workers"	Horn, Woolley	The Musical Cast of Toys	1:11
7.	"Let Joy and Innocence Prevail" (Instrumental)	Horn, Zimmer	Pat Metheny	4:59
8.	"The General"	Zimmer	Michael Gambon & Hans Zimmer	2:21
9.	"The Mirror Song"	Horn, Woolley, Dolby	Thomas Dolby with Robin Williams & Joan Cusack	4:35
10.	"Battle Introduction"	Zimmer	Robin Williams	2:45
11.	"Welcome to the Pleasuredome" (Into Battle Mix)	Peter Gill, Holly Johnson, Brian Nash, Mark O'Toole	Frankie Goes To Hollywood	4:59
12.	"Let Joy and Innocence Prevail"	Horn, Zimmer	Grace Jones	5:01
13.	"The Closing of the Year / Happy Workers" (Reprise)	Horn, Woolley	The Musical Cast of Toys (including Wendy & Lisa and Seal)	5:28
Total length:				**47:14**

Video game

A video game based on the film, *Toys: Let the Toy Wars Begin!*, was released in 1993 for the Super Nintendo and Sega Genesis systems by Absolute Entertainment.[4] The game is played from an overhead perspective, and involves the player, as Leslie Zevo, attempting to destroy the elephant-head security cameras in the factory, cafeteria, and warehouse levels in order to shut down those defenses. Once the player gets to the Manhattan model, the game switches to a side-scrolling *Gradius*-style level, where the player must fly all the way to the General's control center, shut down the production of the war toys, and save the good name of Zevo Toys.

Reception

Despite prophesying new military systems such as Global Hawk and Predator drones, *Toys* received a generally negative reaction from critics and failed commercially.[5] [6]

References

[1] "The 65th Academy Awards (1993) Nominees and Winners" (http://www.oscars.org/awards/academyawards/legacy/ceremony/65th-winners.html). *oscars.org*. . Retrieved 2011-08-03.

[2] "Berlinale: 1993 Programme" (http://www.berlinale.de/en/archiv/jahresarchive/1993/02_programm_1993/02_Programm_1993.html). *berlinale.de*. . Retrieved 2011-05-30.

[3] "Toys Trailer" (http://www.youtube.com/watch?v=jqa2G9J0Bqw). TrailerMaddness. . Retrieved September 27, 2009.

[4] Toys on Gamespot (http://www.gamespot.com/snes/action/toys/index.html?tag=result;title;1)

[5] "MOVIE REVIEWS Overstuffed `Toys'" (http://articles.latimes.com/1992-12-18/entertainment/ca-1966_1_zevo-toys). *The Los Angeles Times*. . Retrieved 2010-10-26.

[6] "`Ishtar,' anyone? Box-office flops, recent and not-so, get second chance in video stores" (http://articles.chicagotribune.com/1993-06-01/features/9306010009_1_video-stores-film-costume-design). Chicago Tribune. . Retrieved 2010-12-27.

External links

- *Toys* (http://www.imdb.com/title/tt0105629/) at the Internet Movie Database
- *Toys* (http://www.allrovi.com/movies/movie/v79921) at AllRovi
- *Toys* (http://www.rottentomatoes.com/m/toys/) at Rotten Tomatoes
- A review of *Toys* (http://www.rollingstone.com/movies/reviews/toys-19921218) from *Rolling Stone*
- Toys (VG) (http://uk.gamespot.com/snes/action/toys/index.html?tag=result;title;1) from *Gamespot*

Aladdin (1992 Disney film)

Aladdin	
Original theatrical poster; art by John Alvin	
Directed by	Ron Clements John Musker
Produced by	Ron Clements John Musker
Written by	Ron Clements John Musker Ted Elliott Terry Rossio
Narrated by	Robin Williams
Starring	Scott Weinger Jonathan Freeman Robin Williams Linda Larkin Frank Welker Gilbert Gottfried Douglas Seale
Music by	Alan Menken Howard Ashman Tim Rice
Editing by	Mark A. Hester H. Lee Peterson
Studio	Walt Disney Feature Animation
Distributed by	Walt Disney Pictures
Release date(s)	November 25, 1992
Running time	90 minutes
Country	United States
Language	English
Budget	$28 million
Box office	$504,050,219

Aladdin is a 1992 American animated family film produced by Walt Disney Feature Animation and released by Walt Disney Pictures. *Aladdin* was the 31st animated feature in the Walt Disney Animated Classics series, and was part of the Disney film era known as the Disney Renaissance. The film was directed by John Musker and Ron Clements, and is based on the Arab folktale of Aladdin and the magic lamp from *One Thousand and One Nights*. The voice cast features Scott Weinger, Jonathan Freeman, Robin Williams, Linda Larkin, Frank Welker, Gilbert Gottfried, and Douglas Seale.

Lyricist Howard Ashman first pitched the idea, and the screenplay went through three drafts before Disney president Jeffrey Katzenberg greenlighted the production. The animators based their designs on the work of caricaturist Al Hirschfeld, and computers were used for both colouring and creating some animated elements. The musical score was written by Alan Menken and features six songs with lyrics written by both Ashman and Tim Rice, who took over after the former's death.

Aladdin was released on November 25, 1992 to positive reviews, despite some criticism from Arabs who considered the film racist, and was the most successful film of 1992, earning over $217 million in revenue in the United States, and over $504 million worldwide. The film also won many awards, most of them for its soundtrack. *Aladdin*'s success led to many material inspired by the film such as two direct-to-video sequels, *The Return of Jafar* and *Aladdin and the King of Thieves*, an animated television series, toys, video games, spin-offs, and merchandise.

Plot

Jafar, Grand Vizier to the Sultan of Agrabah, is attempting to retrieve a magical oil lamp containing a genie from the Cave of Wonders. After seeing a petty thief's failed attempt to enter the cave, Jafar and his parrot, Iago, learn that only a "Diamond in the Rough" can enter the cave.

Jasmine, the Sultan's daughter, frustrated with her life in the palace, flees to Agrabah's marketplace. There she meets street rat Aladdin and his monkey, Abu. The two discover they have a lot in common. When Aladdin is detained for thievery, Jasmine orders him released, but Jafar lies to her that Aladdin has been executed.

Disguised as an elder, Jafar releases Aladdin and Abu from prison and lead them to the Cave of Wonders. The tiger-shaped head of the cave says to touch nothing but the lamp. Aladdin and Abu enter the cave, where a magic carpet guides them to the lamp. Abu's attempt to steal a ruby causes the cave to start collapsing, but the carpet flies them to the entrance. As Aladdin delivers the lamp, Jafar tries to kill him, but Abu bites Jafar and gets the lamp back as he, the carpet, and Aladdin fall back into the cave just as it closes.

In the collapsed cave, Aladdin rubs the lamp, unleashing the Genie, who reveals he will grant Aladdin three wishes—with the exception of killing anyone, making anyone fall in love, or bringing back the dead. Aladdin tricks the Genie into freeing them from the cave without using a wish. While contemplating his wishes, Genie admits he would wish for freedom, since he is a prisoner to his lamp. Aladdin promises to free the Genie for his last wish. After talking about Jasmine with the Genie, Aladdin decides to use his first wish to become a prince so he can woo Jasmine.

Aladdin returns to Agrabah just as Jafar tries to trick the Sultan into arranging a marriage between himself and Jasmine. When Aladdin parades into the Sultan's palace as "Prince Ali", Jasmine rejects Ali as a suitor. Despite the Genie's suggestion that Aladdin to tell the princess who he really is, Aladdin remains the suave prince, and takes Jasmine around the world on the magic carpet. During the trip, Jasmine exposes Ali as the Aladdin, and demands the truth from him. Aladdin instead fabricates a story that he sometimes dresses as a commoner to escape palace life. The couple kisses as Aladdin returns her home.

Afterwards, Aladdin is captured by Jafar and thrown into the ocean, but the Genie rescues Aladdin as his second wish. Aladdin returns to the palace and exposes Jafar's plot; and Jafar flees after noticing the lamp in Aladdin's possession, realizing who Aladdin is. As Aladdin gets doubtful about revealing who really is, Iago steals Genie's lamp and brings it to Jafar, who becomes Genie's new master. Jafar uses his first two wishes to become Sultan and the most powerful sorcerer in the world. Using his new powers, Jafar forces Jasmine and her father to bow, exposes Aladdin as a street rat, then exiles him and Abu to a frozen wasteland.

Aladdin uses the magic carpet to return to Agrabah, where Jafar has imprisoned both Jasmine and the Sultan as his slaves. Jasmine distracts Jafar with a seductive act as Aladdin tries to steal back the lamp, but Jafar confronts him. He imprisons Jasmine in a large hourglass and turns himself into an enormous cobra. As Jafar traps Aladdin in his coils, he boasts to be "the most powerful being on Earth", which causes Aladdin to shout out that the Genie is more powerful. Faced with this realization, Jafar uses his final wish to become a genie. However, Jafar discovers that genies are not free entities as he is sucked into a black lamp, dragging Iago with him. The Genie flicks the lamp into the Cave of Wonders.

After Aladdin realizes that he cannot keep pretending to be something he is not, he decides to keep his promise and wish for the Genie's freedom. Seeing Jasmine's love for Aladdin, the Sultan changes the law to allow her to marry whomever she deems worthy. The newly free Genie leaves to explore the world while Aladdin and Jasmine celebrate their engagement.

Cast and characters

- Scott Weinger as Aladdin: A poor but kind-hearted Agrabah thief. Brad Kane supplies the character's singing voice. Weinger sent in a homemade audition tape with his mother playing the Genie,[1] and after several call backs he found six months later that he had the part.[2]
- Robin Williams as The Genie/The Narrator: A comedic genie, with nigh omnipotent power that can only be exercised when his master wishes it. Clements and Musker wrote the part of the Genie for Williams, and when met with resistance created a reel of Williams' standup to animation of the Genie. When Williams watched the video, he "laughed his ass off" and agreed to do the project.[3]
- Jonathan Freeman as Jafar: The power-hungry Grand Vizier of Agrabah and the main antagonist of the film. Jafar was originally envisioned as an irritable character, but the directors decided that a calm villain would be scarier.[4] Animator Andreas Deja tried to incorporate Freeman's facial expressions into the character.[5]
- Linda Larkin as Princess Jasmine: The princess of Agrabah, who is tired of life in the royal palace. Lea Salonga supplies the character's singing voice. Larkin was chosen nine months after her audition, and had to adjust her pitch to reach the voice the filmmakers were looking for the character.[4]
- Frank Welker as Abu: Aladdin's kleptomaniac pet monkey with a high-pitched voice. The animators filmed monkeys at the San Francisco Zoo to study the movements Abu would have.[4] In the three years it took to record the film, Welker did not meet Weinger or Williams.[6] Welker also voiced Jasmine's tiger Rajah, and the Cave of Wonders.[7]
- Gilbert Gottfried as Iago: Jafar's sarcastic, foul-mouthed pet parrot sidekick. Iago's animator Will Finn tried to incorporate some aspects of Gottfried's appearance into Iago's design, specially his semi-closed eyes and the always-appearing teeth.[4]
- Douglas Seale as The Sultan: The pompous but kind ruler of Agrabah, who desperately tries to find a suitor for his daughter Jasmine. Some aspects of the character were inspired in the Wizard of Oz, to create a bumbling authority figure.[4]
- Jim Cummings as Razoul: The Captain of the Guard. He was named after layout supervisor Rasoul Azadani.[4]
- The Magic Carpet is a sentient carpet who is able to fly. Animator Randy Cartwright described working on the Carpet as challenging, since it is just a square shape, who expresses himself through pantomime – "It's sort of like acting by origami".[8] Cartwright kept folding a piece of cloth while animating to see how to position the Carpet.[8] After the character animation was done, the carpet's surface design was applied digitally.[5]

Production

Script and development

In 1988, lyricist Howard Ashman pitched to Disney the idea of an animated musical adaptation of Aladdin. After Ashman wrote some songs with partner Alan Menken and a film treatment,[9] a screenplay was written by Linda Woolverton, who had worked on *Beauty and the Beast*.[10] Then directors John Musker and Ron Clements joined the production, picking *Aladdin* out of three projects offered, which also included an adaptation of *Swan Lake* and *King of the Jungle* – that eventually became *The Lion King*.[11] Musker and Clements wrote a draft of the screenplay, and delivered it to studio chief Jeffrey Katzenberg in 1991. Katzenberg thought the script "didn't engage", and only approved it after the screenwriting duo Ted Elliott and Terry Rossio rewrote it.[9] Among the changes, the character of Aladdin's mother was removed, Princess Jasmine was made into a stronger character, Aladdin's personality was rewritten to be "a little rougher, like a young Harrison Ford,"[9] [12] and the parrot Iago, originally conceived as a

"British" calm and serious character, was reworked into a comic role after the filmmakers saw Gilbert Gottfried in *Beverly Hills Cop II*. Gottfried was cast to provide Iago's voice.[13] Several characters and plot elements are also based on the 1940 version of *The Thief of Bagdad*,[14] [15] and many aspects of the traditional story were changed for the film – for instance, the setting is changed from "China" to a fictional Arabian city, Agrabah.[16]

Design and animation

One of the first issues that the animators faced during production of *Aladdin* was the depiction of Aladdin himself.[17] Director and producer John Musker explains:

> In early screenings, we played with him being a little bit younger, and he had a mother in the story. [...] In design he became more athletic-looking, more filled out, more of a young leading man, more of a teen-hunk version than before.[17]

He was initially going to be as young as 13, but that eventually changed to eighteen.[17] Aladdin was designed by a team led by supervising animator Glen Keane, and was originally made to resemble actor Michael J. Fox. During production, it was decided that the design was too boyish and wasn't "appealing enough," so the character was redesigned to add elements derived from actor Tom Cruise and Calvin Klein models.[3]

The design for most characters was based on the work of caricaturist Al Hirschfeld,[5] which production designer Richard Vander Wende also considered appropriate to the theme, due to similarities to the swooping lines of Persian miniatures and Arabic calligraphy.[8] Jafar's design was not based on Hirschfeld's work because Jafar's supervising animator, Andreas Deja, wanted the character to be contrasting.[18] Each character was animated alone, with the animators consulting each other to make scenes with interrelating characters. Since Aladdin's animator Glen Keane was working in the California branch of Walt Disney Feature Animation, and Jasmine's animator Mark Henn was in the Florida one at Disney-MGM Studios, they had to frequently phone, fax or send designs and discs to each other.[8]

For the scenery design, layout supervisor Rasoul Azadani took many pictures of his hometown of Isfahan, Iran for guidance.[4] Other inspirations for design were Disney's animated films from the 1940s and 50s and the 1940 film *The Thief of Bagdad*.[8] The coloring was done with the computerized CAPS process, and the color motifs were chosen according to the personality – the protagonists use light colors such as blue, the antagonists darker ones such as red and black, and Agrabah and its palace use the neutral color yellow.[4] [5] Computer animation was used for some elements of the film, such as the tiger entrance of the Cave of Wonders and the scene where Aladdin tries to escape the collapsing cave.[5]

Musker and Clements created the Genie with Robin Williams in mind; even though Katzenberg suggested actors such as John Candy, Steve Martin, and Eddie Murphy, Williams was approached and eventually accepted the role. Williams came for voice recording sessions during breaks in the shooting of two other films he was starring in at the time, *Hook* and *Toys*. Unusually for an animated film, much of Williams' dialogue was ad-libbed: for some scenes, Williams was given topics and dialogue suggestions, but allowed to improvise his lines.[5] It was estimated that Williams improvised 52 characters.[19] Eric Goldberg, the supervising animator for the Genie, then reviewed Williams' recorded dialogue and selected the best gags and lines that his crew would create character animation to match.[5]

The producers added many in-jokes and references to Disney's previous works in the film, such as a "cameo appearance" from directors Clements and Musker and drawing some characters based on Disney workers.[7] Beast, Sebastian from *The Little Mermaid*, and Pinocchio make brief appearances,[4] and the wardrobe of the Genie at the end of the film—Goofy hat, Hawaiian shirt, and sandals—are a reference to a short film that Robin Williams did for the Disney/MGM Studios tour in the late 80s.[7]

Robin Williams' conflicts with the studio

In gratitude for his success with the Disney/Touchstone film *Good Morning, Vietnam*, Robin Williams voiced the Genie for SAG scale pay ($75,000), on condition that his name or image not be used for marketing, and his (supporting) character not take more than 25% of space on advertising artwork, since *Toys* was scheduled for release one month after *Aladdin*'s debut. For financial reasons, the studio went back on the deal on both counts, especially in poster art by having the Genie in 25% of the image, but having other major and supporting characters portrayed considerably smaller. The Disney Hyperion book *Aladdin: The Making Of An Animated Film*, listed both of Williams' characters "The Peddler" and "The Genie" ahead of main characters, but was forced to refer to him only as "the actor signed to play the Genie".[3]

Williams and Disney had a bitter falling-out, and as a result, Dan Castellaneta voiced the Genie in *The Return of Jafar*, the *Aladdin* animated television series, and had recorded his voice for *Aladdin and the King of Thieves.* When Jeffrey Katzenberg was fired from Disney and replaced by former 20th Century Fox production head Joe Roth (whose last act for Fox was greenlighting Williams' film *Mrs. Doubtfire*), Roth arranged for a public apology to Williams by Disney. Williams agreed to perform in Hollywood Pictures' *Jack*, directed by Francis Ford Coppola, and even agreed to voice the Genie again for the *King Of Thieves* sequel (for considerably more than scale), replacing all of Castellaneta's dialogue.[20]

Music

Composer Alan Menken and songwriters Howard Ashman and Tim Rice were praised for creating a soundtrack that is "consistently good, rivaling the best of Disney's other animated musicals from the '90s."[21] Menken and Ashman began work on the film together, with Rice taking over as lyricist after Ashman died of AIDS-related complications in early 1991.[22] Although fourteen songs were written for *Aladdin*, only six are featured in the movie, three by each lyricist.[23] The DVD Special Edition released in 2004 includes four songs in early animations tests, and a music video of one, "Proud of Your Boy", performed by Clay Aiken,[24] which also appears on the album *DisneyMania 3*.[25]

Themes

"The original story was sort of a winning the lottery kind of thing. When we got into it, particularly coming in at the end of 1980s, it seemed like an Eighties 'greed is good' movie. (...) Like having anything you could wish for would be the greatest thing in the world and having it taken away from you is bad, but having it back is great. We didn't really want that to be the message of the movie"

Ron Clements[8]

The filmmakers thought the moral message of the original tale was not appropriate, and decided to "put a spin on it", by making the fulfillment of wishes seem like a great thing, but eventually becoming a problem.[8] Another major theme was not trying to be what the person is not – both Aladdin and Jasmine get into trouble faking to be different people,[4] and the Prince Ali persona fails to impress Jasmine, who only falls for Aladdin when she finds out who he truly is.[26] Being "imprisoned" is also discussed, a fate that occurs to most of the characters – Aladdin and Jasmine are stuck to their lifestyles, Genie is attached to his lamp and Jafar, to the Sultan – and is represented visually by the prison-like walls and bars of the Agrabah palace, and the scene involving caged birds which Jasmine later frees.[4] Jasmine is also depicted as a different Disney Princess, being rebellious to the royal life and the social structure,[27] and trying to make her own way, unlike the princesses who just wait for rescue.[8]

Release and reception

Theatrical run

A large promotion campaign preceded *Aladdin*'s debut in theaters, with the film's trailer being attached to most Disney VHS releases, and numerous tie-ins and licensees being released.[28] After a limited release on November 13, 1992,[29] *Aladdin* debuted in 1,131 theaters on November 25, 1992, grossing $19.2 million in its opening weekend – number two at the box office, behind *Home Alone 2: Lost in New York*.[30] It took eight weeks for the film to reach number one at the US box office, breaking the record for the week between Christmas and New Year's Eve with $32.2 million.[31] The film held the top spot five times during its 22-week run.[32] *Aladdin* was the most successful film of 1992 grossing $217 million in the United States and over $504 million worldwide.[33] It was the biggest gross for an animated film until *The Lion King* two years later.[34] As of 2010, it is the eighteenth highest grossing animated film and the third highest grossing traditionally animated feature worldwide, behind *The Lion King* and *The Simpsons Movie*.[35]

Critical reception

Aladdin was well received by critics. The review aggregator website Rotten Tomatoes reported that 92% of critics gave the film a positive review based on a sample of 49 reviews, with an average score of 7.9/10.[36] Among the "Top Critics", it has a 100% positive review rating from eight critics.[37]

Most critics' praise went to Robin Williams' performance as Genie,[36] with Janet Maslin of *The New York Times* declaring that children "needn't know precisely what Mr. Williams is evoking to understand how funny he is".[38] Warner Bros. animator Chuck Jones even called the film "the funniest feature ever made."[9] James Berardinelli gave it 3.5 out of 4 stars, praising the "crisp visuals and wonderful song-and-dance numbers".[39] Peter Travers of *Rolling Stone* said the comedy made the film accessible to both children and adults,[40] a vision shared with Desson Howe of *The Washington Post*, who also said "kids are still going to be entranced by the magic and adventure."[41] Brian Lowry of *Variety* praised the cast of characters, describing the expressive magic carpet as "its most remarkable accomplishment" and considered that "*Aladdin* overcomes most story flaws thanks to sheer technical virtuosity".[42]

Some aspects of the film were widely criticized. Ed Gonzalez of *Slant Magazine* wrote a negative review, describing the film as racist, ridiculous, and a "narcissistic circus act" for Robin Williams.[43] IGN's review considered that besides the Genie and the cave-in scene, *Aladdin* was "totally by the numbers (...). You know how it will all turn out, it contains no surprises, and for that matter, very little that's truly special," and described the cast, particularly the protagonists, as "cookie-cutter characters".[24] Roger Ebert, who generally praised the film in his review, considered the music inferior to its predecessors *The Little Mermaid* and *Beauty and the Beast*, and claimed Aladdin and Jasmine were "pale and routine".[44]

Awards

Aladdin also received many award nominations, mostly for its music. It won two Academy Awards, Best Music, Original Score and Best Music, Original Song for "A Whole New World" and receiving nominations for Best Song ("Friend Like Me"), Best Sound Editing, and Best Sound (Terry Porter, Mel Metcalfe, David J. Hudson and Doc Kane).[45] At the Golden Globes, *Aladdin* won Best Original Song ("A Whole New World") and Best Original Score, as well as a Special Achievement Award for Robin Williams, with a nomination for Best Motion Picture – Musical or Comedy.[46] Other awards included the Annie Award for Best Animated Feature,[47] a MTV Movie Award for Best Comedic Performance to Robin Williams,[48] Saturn Awards for Best Fantasy Film, Performance by a Younger Actor to Scott Weinger and Supporting Actor to Robin Williams,[49] the Best Animated Feature by the Los Angeles Film Critics Association,[50] and four Grammy Awards, Best Soundtrack Album, and Song of the Year, Best Pop Performance by a Duo or Group with Vocal and Best Song Written for a Motion Picture, Television or Other Visual Media for "A Whole New World".[51] *Aladdin* was among the nominees for the American Film Institute's listed lists of best comedies,[52] musicals[53] and animated films in American film,[54] while both "Friend Like Me" and "A Whole New World" were considered for AFI's 100 Years...100 Songs.[55]

Home media

The film was first released in VHS on October 1, 1993, as part of the "Walt Disney Classics" line. In its first week of availability, *Aladdin* sold over 10.8 million copies,[56] and went on to sell over 25 million in total (a record only broken by the later release of *The Lion King*).[57] It entered moratorium on April 30, 1994.[58]

On October 5, 2004, *Aladdin* was released on DVD, as part of Disney's Platinum Edition line. The DVD release featured retouched and cleaned-up animation, prepared for *Aladdin's* planned but ultimately cancelled IMAX reissue in 2003,[59] and a second disc with bonus features. Accompanied by a $19 million marketing campaign,[60] the DVD sold about 3 million units, but it was less than any of the other *Platinum Edition* released before it.[61] The film's soundtrack was available in its original Dolby 5.1 track or in a new Disney Enhanced Home Theater Mix.[24] The DVD went into moratorium on January 2008, along with its sequels.[62]

Controversies

One of the verses of the opening song "Arabian Nights" was altered following protests from the American-Arab Anti-Discrimination Committee (ADC). The lyrics were changed in July 1993 from *"Where they cut off your ear if they don't like your face,"* in the original release to *"Where it's flat and immense and the heat is intense."* The change first appeared on the 1993 video release.[63] The original lyric was intact on the initial CD soundtrack release, but the re-release uses the edited lyric. The rerecording has the original voice on all other lines and then a noticeably deeper voice says the edited line. *Entertainment Weekly* ranked *Aladdin* in a list of the most controversial films in history, due to this incident.[64] The ADC also complained about the portrayal of the lead characters Aladdin and Jasmine. They criticized the characters' Anglicized features and Anglo-American accents, in contrast to the other characters in the film, which are dark-skinned, have Arab accents and grotesque facial features, and appear villainous or greedy.[63]

Protests were also raised to another scene. When Aladdin is attacked by the tiger Rajah on the palace balcony, Aladdin quietly says *"Good kitty, take off and go..."* and the word "kitty" is overlapped by Rajah's snarl. Some people reported hearing *"Good teenagers, take off your clothes,"*[65] which they considered a subliminal reference to promiscuity. Because of the controversy, Disney replaced the phrase with *"Down, kitty"* on the DVD release.[66]

Animation enthusiasts have noticed similarities between *Aladdin* and Richard Williams's unfinished film *The Thief and the Cobbler* (also known as *Arabian Knight* under Miramax Films and *The Princess and the Cobbler* under Majestic Films International). These similarities include a similar plot, similar characters, scenes and background designs, and the antagonist Zig-Zag's resemblance in character design and mannerisms to Genie and Jafar.[67] [68] Though *Aladdin* was released prior to *The Thief and the Cobbler*, *The Thief and the Cobbler* was started much earlier in the 1960s, its production being mired in difficulties including financial problems, copyright issues, and late production times caused by separate studios trying to finish the film after Richard Williams was fired from the project for lack of finished work.[69] The late release coupled with Miramax (a Disney-owned studio) purchasing and re-editing the film, has sometimes resulted in *The Thief and the Cobbler* being labeled a copy of *Aladdin*.[68]

Legacy

Sequels and spin-offs

Aladdin was followed by Disney's first direct-to-video sequel, *The Return of Jafar* in 1994. The film saw the debut of a new character, Abis Mal, voiced by Jason Alexander, and all of the original cast, except for Robin Williams, replaced by Dan Castellaneta, and Douglas Seale, replaced by Val Bettin. The plot mainly focused on Jafar seeking revenge on Aladdin. However, this time, with Iago on Aladdin's side, Abis Mal becomes Jafar's new henchman.[70] Shortly after *The Return of Jafar*, the *Aladdin* TV Series was aired on television. The episodes focused on Aladdin's adventures after the events of the second film.[71] In 1996, the final sequel to *Aladdin*, *Aladdin and the King of Thieves* was released on video. The story concludes as Aladdin and Jasmine are about to be married and Aladdin discovers that his father is still alive, but is the king of all thieves in Agrabah.[70]

The *Aladdin* characters later made a crossover with *Hercules: The Animated Series*,[72] and were featured as guests in the television series *House of Mouse* and related works to those series—Jafar was the leader of the villains in *Mickey's House of Villains*.[73]

The film also inspired a Disney On Ice presentation,[74] and two attractions in Disney's theme parks: "The Magic Carpets of Aladdin", a Dumbo the Flying Elephant-like ride at both Magic Kingdom at Walt Disney World Resort and Walt Disney Studios Park at Disneyland Resort Paris;[75] [76] and the show *Disney's Aladdin: A Musical Spectacular* at Disney California Adventure Park.[77]

Video games

Along with the film release, three different video games based on *Aladdin* were released. A coproduction between Virgin Games and Walt Disney Feature Animation for the Sega Genesis was released in late 1993 and later ported to Nintendo Entertainment System, PC, Game Boy and Game Boy Color.[78] That same year, Capcom released a Super Nintendo game, which was ported to the Game Boy Advance in 2002.[79] [80] In 1994, SIMS released an *Aladdin* game for the Sega Game Gear and Sega Master System.[81]

The television series inspired another game by Argonaut Games, entitled *Aladdin: Nasira's Revenge* and released in 2000 for the PlayStation and PC.[82] Also, in 2004 Vivendi Universal released *Disney's Aladdin Chess Adventures*, a chess computer game with the Aladdin license.[83]

The *Kingdom Hearts* series features a playable *Aladdin* world known as Agrabah.[84] In *Kingdom Hearts* and *Kingdom Hearts: Chain of Memories*, the plotline is loosely related to the storyline of the original film.[84] [85] In *Kingdom Hearts II*, it is a mixture of *Aladdin* and *The Return of Jafar*.[86] Genie is also a recurring summon in the series.[84]

Musical adaptation

In November 2010 Alan Menken confirmed that a musical theatre adaptation of the show is in the works with a book written by Chad Beguelin.[87] The show premiered at the 5th Avenue Theatre from July 7–31, 2011.[88] Jonathan Freeman, who voiced Jafar in the film, played the role in the stage adaptation.[89] Adam Jacobs and Courtney Reed played Aladdin and Jasmine. Additional included Seán G. Griffin as the Sultan; Don Darryl Rivera as Iago; and, playing Omar, Babkak, and Kassim – a trio of characters originally conceived by the film's creators but not used – Andrew Keenan-Bolger, Brian Gonzales, and Brandon O'Neill. The show was also directed and choreographed by Casey Nicholaw.[90]

References

[1] Abbott, Jim (January 5, 1993). "As Genie, mom helped grant son's wish for 'Aladdin' role" (http://www.scottweinger.net/article13.html). *St. Paul Pioneer Press*. . Retrieved 2009-05-26.

[2] Caporaso, Jenna; Trucks, Leigh; Pompa, Andrew (February 27, 1994). "Aladdin's Voice Speaks" (http://www.scottweinger.net/article15.html). *The Charlotte Observer*. . Retrieved 2009-05-26.

[3] "Disney's Got A Brand-New Baghdad" (http://www.ew.com/ew/article/0,,312562,00.html). *Entertainment Weekly*. 1992-09-04. . Retrieved 2007-03-16.

[4] *Pop Up Fun Facts* (DVD). *Aladdin* Platinum Edition Disc 1: Walt Disney Home Video. 2004.

[5] *Diamond in the Rough: The Making of Aladdin* (DVD). *Aladdin* Platinum Edition, Disc 2: Walt Disney Home Video. 2004.

[6] Kalidor (September 22, 2006). "The Allspark Interviews Legend Frank Welker" (http://www.allspark.com/index.php?option=com_content&task=view&id=1&Itemid=3). *allspark.com*. . Retrieved 2009-05-26.

[7] Ron Clements, John Musker, Amy Pell.*Aladdin* audio commentary – *The Filmmaker's*

[8] Culhane, John (1993-08-15). *Disney's Aladdin The Making Of An Animated Film*. Disney Editions. ISBN 978-1-56282-757-1.

[9] Richard Corliss; Patrick E. Cole; Martha Smilgis (1992-11-09). "Aladdin's Magic" (http://www.time.com/time/printout/0,8816,976941,00.html). *Time*. . Retrieved 2007-03-16. "Chuck Jones' verdict is judicious: Aladdin is "the funniest feature ever made." It's a movie for adults – if they can keep up with its careering pace – and, yes, you can take the kids. It juggles a '90s impudence with the old Disney swank and heart."

[10] "Aladdin: Crew Reunion" (http://animatedviews.com/2005/aladdin-crew-reunion/). Animated Views. . Retrieved 2009-05-31.

[11] "Show 009 – Ron and John, Part Three" (http://animationpodcast.com/ronandjohn-part-three/). The Animation Podcast. 2005-11-01. . Retrieved 2009-05-31.

[12] "Aladdin DVD review" (http://www.dvdizzy.com/aladdin.html). DVDizzy.com. . Retrieved 2007-03-20.

[13] John Musker, Ron Clements (2004). *Aladdin: Platinum Edition (Disc 2)* (DVD). Walt Disney Home Video.

[14] "Fantasy: The Thief of Bagdad" (http://www.fosteronfilm.com/fantasy/thiefbagdad.htm). Foster On Film. . Retrieved 2009-05-31.

[15] Bernstein, Matthew; Studlar, Gaylyn (1997). *Visions of the East* (http://books.google.com/books?id=q2_E_gl9BbYC). I.B.Tauris. ISBN 978-1-86064-305-7. .

[16] Dr. Ali Behdad (2004). *Aladdin: Platinum Edition (Disc 2)* (DVD). Walt Disney Home Video.

[17] Thomas, Bob: "Chapter 9: A New Tradition", pages 133–135. *Disney's Art of Animation: From Mickey Mouse to Hercules*, 1997

[18] "Aladdin animator used subtlety to design strong villain" (http://tech.mit.edu/V112/N64/aladdin.64a.html). The Tech. 1992-11-20. .

[19] James Lipton (host) (2001). *Inside the Actors Studio: Robin Williams* (Documentary). Bravo.

[20] Hill, Jim (April 2000). "Be Careful What You Wish For" (http://jimhillmedia.com/blogs/jim_hill/archive/2000/12/31/312.aspx). Jim Hill Media. . Retrieved 2008-03-15.

[21] Phares, Heather. "Aladdin soundtrack review" (http://www.allmusic.com/album/r110157). Allmusic. . Retrieved 2007-03-18.

[22] *Alan Menken: Musical Renaissance Man* (DVD). *Aladdin* Platinum Edition, Disc 2: Walt Disney Home Video. 2004.

[23] Daly, Steve (1992-12-04). "Unsettled score" (http://www.ew.com/ew/article/0,,312563,00.html). *Entertainment Weekly*. . Retrieved 2009-06-12.

[24] "Aladdin: Ultimate DVD review" (http://dvd.ign.com/articles/549/549036p1.html). IGN. 2004-09-17. . Retrieved 2007-03-16.

[25] "DisneyMania 3" (http://disneymusic.disney.go.com/albums/disneymania3.html). Disney. . Retrieved 2009-05-25.

[26] Smith, Dave (1996-08-15). *Disney A to Z: The Official Encyclopedia*. Disney Editions. ISBN 978-0-7868-6223-8.

[27] Marzolph, Ulrich (2006). *The Arabian Nights reader* (http://books.google.com.br/books?id=AKd6mZSGsVUC&pg=PA276&lpg=PA276). Wayne State University Press. ISBN 978-0-8143-3259-7. .

[28] Daly, Steve; Ascher-Walsh, Rebecca (1993-03-12). "Arabian Sheikdown" (http://www.ew.com/ew/article/0,,305817,00.html). *Entertainment Weekly*. . Retrieved 2009-08-30.

[29] "Weekend Box Office Results for November 13–15, 1992" (http://www.boxofficemojo.com/weekend/chart/?yr=1992&wknd=46&p=.htm). Box Office Mojo. . Retrieved 2009-05-26.

[30] Natale, Richard (1992-11-30). "Holiday B.O. gobbles up big bucks" (http://www.variety.com/article/VR101610.html). *Variety*. . Retrieved 2009-06-12.

[31] Fox, David J. (1993-01-26). "'Aladdin' Finally Hits No. 1 and a Record in Sales Too" (http://articles.latimes.com/1993-01-26/entertainment/ca-2081_1_weekend-box-office). *Los Angeles Times*. . Retrieved 2009-06-12.

[32] "Aladdin (1992) – Weekend Box Office Results" (http://www.boxofficemojo.com/movies/?page=weekend&id=aladdin.htm). Box Office Mojo. . Retrieved 2009-06-12.

[33] "Aladdin box office info" (http://www.boxofficemojo.com/movies/?id=aladdin.htm). Box Office Mojo. . Retrieved March 17, 2009.

[34] "The Lion King (1994)" (http://www.boxofficemojo.com/movies/?id=lionking.htm). Box Office Mojo. . Retrieved 2009-05-25.

[35] "The Simpsons Movie (2007)" (http://www.boxofficemojo.com/movies/?id=simpsons.htm). Box Office Mojo. . Retrieved 2009-05-25.

[36] "Aladdin at Rottentomatoes.com" (http://www.rottentomatoes.com/m/1042582-aladdin/). Rotten Tomatoes. . Retrieved 2009-05-27.

[37] "Aladdin: Cream of the Crop" (http://www.rottentomatoes.com/m/1042582-aladdin/?critic=creamcrop). Rotten Tomatoes. . Retrieved 2009-05-27.

[38] Maslin, Janet (1992-11-11). "Disney Puts Its Magic Touch on 'Aladdin'" (http://movies.nytimes.com/movie/review?res=9E0CE7DC1138F932A25752C1A964958260). *The New York Times*. . Retrieved 2009-06-12.

[39] Berardinelli, James (1992). "Aladdin" (http://www.reelviews.net/php_review_template.php?identifier=41). Reelviews. . Retrieved 2009-05-26.

[40] Travers, Peter (November 1992). "Aladdin" (http://web.archive.org/web/20080618163432/http://www.rollingstone.com/reviews/movie/5947957/review/5947958/aladdin). *Rolling Stone* (644). Archived from the original (http://www.rollingstone.com/reviews/movie/5947957/review/5947958/aladdin) on 2008-06-18. . Retrieved 2009-05-26.

[41] Howe, Desson (1992-11-27). "'Aladdin'" (http://www.washingtonpost.com/wp-srv/style/longterm/movies/videos/aladdinghowe_a0af3c.htm). *The Washington Post*. . Retrieved 2009-05-26.

[42] Lowry, Brian (1992-11-04). "Aladdin" (http://www.variety.com/review/VE1117900071.html?categoryid=31&cs=1). *Variety*. . Retrieved 2009-05-26.

[43] Gonzalez, Ed (2004-09-24). "Aladdin" (http://www.slantmagazine.com/film/review/aladdin/1172). *Slant Magazine*. . Retrieved 2009-05-26.

[44] Ebert, Roger (1992-11-25). "Aladdin review" (http://rogerebert.suntimes.com/apps/pbcs.dll/article?AID=/19921125/REVIEWS/211250301/1023). *Chicago Sun-Times*. . Retrieved 2007-03-17.

[45] "The 65th Academy Awards (1993) Nominees and Winners" (http://www.oscars.org/awards/academyawards/legacy/ceremony/65th-winners.html). *oscars.org*. . Retrieved 2011-10-22.

[46] "SEARCH – Aladdin" (http://www.goldenglobes.org/browse/film/23558). Hollywood Foreign Press Association. . Retrieved 2008-05-25.

[47] "Legacy: 21st Annual Annie Award Nominees and Winners (1993)" (http://annieawards.org/21stwinners.html). Annie Awards. . Retrieved 2009-05-25.

[48] "1993 MTV Movie Awards" (http://www.mtv.com/ontv/movieawards/1993/). MTV. . Retrieved 2008-05-25.

[49] "Past Saturn Award Winners" (http://www.saturnawards.org/past.html). Academy of Science Fiction, Fantasy & Horror Films. . Retrieved 2008-05-25.

[50] "18TH Annual Los Angeles Film Critics Association Awards" (http://www.lafca.net/years/1992.html). LAFCA. . Retrieved 2009-05-25.

[51] Pareles, Jon (1994-03-02). "Top Grammy to Houston; 5 for 'Aladdin'" (http://www.nytimes.com/1994/03/02/movies/top-grammy-to-houston-5-for-aladdin.html). *The New York Times*. . Retrieved 2009-05-25.

[52] AFI's 100 Years...100 Laughs Nominees (http://www.afi.com/Docs/100Years/laughs500.pdf)

[53] AFI's Greatest Movie Musicals Nominees (http://www.afi.com/Docs/100Years/musicals_ballot.pdf)

[54] AFI's 10 Top 10 Ballot (http://www.afi.com/drop/ballot.pdf)

[55] AFI's 100 Years...100 Songs Nominees (http://www.afi.com/Docs/100Years/songs400.pdf)

[56] "Arabian Might" (http://www.ew.com/ew/article/0,,308423,00.html). *Entertainment Weekly*. 1993-10-15. . Retrieved 2009-05-25.

[57] "Disney Rubs Aladdin's Lamp" (http://www.movieweb.com/news/NEkGOqpnt2XAok). Movie Web. . Retrieved 2007-03-20.

[58] Nichols, Peter M. (1994-05-20). "Home Video" (http://www.nytimes.com/1994/05/20/arts/home-video-149802.html). *The New York Times*. . Retrieved 2007-03-20.

[59] Hill, Jim (2004-10-12). ""Aladdin" Platinum Edition sets the gold standard for Disney DVD" (http://jimhillmedia.com/blogs/jim_hill/archive/2004/10/11/478.aspx). . Retrieved 2007-04-05.

[60] Arnold, Thomas K. (2005-08-09). "Best sellers" (http://www.hollywoodreporter.com/hr/search/article_display.jsp?vnu_content_id=1001011344). *The Hollywood Reporter*. . Retrieved 2009-05-27.

[61] McCourt, Judith (2004-12-02). "DVD Player Penetration Drives October Sales Growth" (http://www.homemediamagazine.com/news/dvd-player-penetration-drives-october-sales-growth-6917). . Retrieved 2007-09-19.

[62] "Out of Print Disney DVDs" (http://www.dvdizzy.com/disneyvault.html). *DVDizzy.com*. . Retrieved 24 September 2006.

[63] "Arab Stereotypes and American Educators" (http://www.adc.org/index.php?id=283). American-Arab Anti-Discrimination Committee. . Retrieved 2007-03-16.

[64] "The 25 Most Controversial Movies Ever" (http://www.ew.com/ew/article/0,,1202224,00.html). *Entertainment Weekly*. . Retrieved 2007-03-16.

[65] "How a Rumor Spread About Subliminal Sex In Disney's 'Aladdin'" (http://www.snopes.com/disney/info/aladwsj.htm). *The Wall Street Journal*. 1995-10-25. . Retrieved 2009-05-26.

[66] "Disney (Take Off Your Clothes!)" (http://www.snopes.com/disney/films/aladdin.asp). Snopes. . Retrieved 2007-03-24.. The source compiles and cites four major newspaper references.

[67] "The Thief and the Cobbler review" (http://www.dvdsnapshot.com/January07Review/ThiefAndCobbler.html). DVD snapshot. .

[68] James, Caryn (1995-08-26). "A Late Finisher About Old Araby" (http://www.nytimes.com/1995/08/26/movies/film-review-a-late-finisher-about-old-araby.html). *The New York Times*. .

[69] "The Best Animated Movie You've Never Heard Of" (http://web.archive.org/web/20080113004732rn_1/community.tvguide.com/blog-entry/TVGuide-Editors-Blog/Ask-Flickchick/Best-Animated-Movie/700013169). TV Guide. 2006-11-28. . Retrieved 2009-03-17.

[70] "Aladdin II & III Collection DVD Review" (http://www.ultimatedisney.com/aladdinsequels.html). Ultimate Disney. . Retrieved 2009-05-25.

[71] "Screen Test" (http://www.ew.com/ew/article/0,,304602,00.html). *Entertainment Weekly*. 1994-11-25. . Retrieved 2009-05-25.

[72] "Hercules and the Arabian Night". *Hercules: The Animated Series*. ABC. 1998–1999. Transcript (http://www.aladdincentral.org/transcripts/hatan/index.html).

[73] "Mickey's House of Villains DVD Review" (http://www.ultimatedisney.com/houseofvillains.html). Ultimate Disney. . Retrieved 2009-05-25.

[74] Deknock, Jan (1998-03-06). "'Aladdin' Takes Fans On An Icy 'Magic-Carpet Ride'" (http://community.seattletimes.nwsource.com/archive/?date=19980306&slug=2738043). *The Seattle Times*. . Retrieved 2009-06-04.

[75] "The Magic Carpets of Aladdin" (http://disneyworld.disney.go.com/parks/magic-kingdom/attractions/magic-carpets-of-aladdin/). Walt Disney World. . Retrieved 2009-05-26.

[76] "Les Tapis Volants – Toon Studio – Disneyland Resort Paris" (http://web.archive.org/web/20080822130155/http://parks.disneylandparis.co.uk/walt-disney-studios-park/lots/toon-studio/attractions/les-tapis-volants.xhtml). Disneyland Resort Paris. Archived from the original (http://parks.disneylandparis.co.uk/walt-disney-studios-park/lots/toon-studio/attractions/les-tapis-volants.xhtml) on 2008-08-22. . Retrieved 2009-05-26.

[77] "Disney's Aladdin – A Musical Spectacular" (http://disneyland.disney.go.com/disneyland/en_US/parks/entertainment/detail?name=AladdinEntertainmentPage). Disney's California Adventure Park. . Retrieved 2009-05-26.

[78] *Disney's Aladdin* for Genesis (http://www.mobygames.com/game/genesis/disneys-aladdin) at MobyGames. Retrieved October 6, 2010.

[79] *Disney's Aladdin* for SNES (http://www.mobygames.com/game/snes/disneys-aladdin__) at MobyGames. Retrieved October 6, 2010.

[80] "Disney's Aladdin Company Line" (http://www.gamespot.com/gba/action/disneysaladdin/news.html?sid=6097907). GameSpot. 2004-05-12. . Retrieved 2009-05-25.

[81] *Disney's Aladdin* for Master System and Game Gear (http://www.mobygames.com/game/disneys-aladdin_) at MobyGames. Retrieved October 6, 2010.

[82] "Aladdin Nasira's Revenge gamespace" (http://www.gamespot.com/ps/action/aladdinnasirasrevenge/index.html). GameSpot. . Retrieved 2007-03-16.

[83] "Disney's Aladdin Chess Adventures gamespace" (http://pc.ign.com/objects/683/683949.html). IGN. . Retrieved 2007-03-17.

[84] Birlew, Dan (2003). *Kingdom Hearts Official Strategy Guide*. BradyGames. ISBN 978-0-7440-0198-3.

[85] Hollinger, Elizabeth (2004). *Kingdom Hearts: Chain of Memories Official Strategy Guide*. BradyGames Publishing. ISBN 978-0-7440-0473-1.

[86] Hollinger, Elizabeth (2006). *Kingdom Hearts II Official Strategy Guide*. BradyGames Publishing. ISBN 978-0-7440-0526-4.

[87] BWW EXCLUSIVE: Alan Menken Talks TANGLED, SISTER ACT, LEAP OF FAITH, HUNCHBACK, ALADDIN & More (http://broadwayworld.com/article/BWW_EXCLUSIVE_Alan_Menken_Talks_TANGLED_SISTER_ACT_LEAP_HUNCHBACK_ALADDIN_More_201115_page1)

[88] Seattle's 5th Avenue Theatre Premieres ALADDIN, 7/7-31 (http://broadwayworld.com/article/Seattles_5th_Avenue_Theatre_Premieres_ALADDIN_7731_20110113), Broadway World

[89] Jonathan Freeman Will Bring Jafar from Screen to Stage in Disney's Aladdin at 5th Avenue (http://www.playbill.com/news/article/150626-Jonathan-Freeman-Will-Bring-Jafar-from-Screen-to-Stage-in-Disneys-Aladdin-at-5th-Avenue-), *Playbill*

[90] Memphis Star James Monroe Iglehart Is Genie in Disney's Aladdin; Adam Jacobs Is Title Hero (http://www.playbill.com/news/article/151393-Memphis-Star-James-Monroe-Iglehart-Is-Genie-in-Disneys-Aladdin-Adam-Jacobs-Is-Title-Hero), *Playbill*

External links

- *Aladdin* (http://www.imdb.com/title/tt0103639/) at the Internet Movie Database
- *Aladdin* (http://www.allrovi.com/movies/movie/v1338) at AllRovi
- *Aladdin* (http://www.boxofficemojo.com/movies/?id=aladdin.htm) at Box Office Mojo
- *Aladdin* (http://www.rottentomatoes.com/m/1042582/) at Rotten Tomatoes
- *Aladdin* (http://www.bcdb.com/cartoons/4-Aladdin) at the Big Cartoon DataBase

The Timekeeper

Le Visionarium	
Attraction poster	
Disneyland Park (Paris)	
Land	Discoveryland
Designer	Walt Disney Imagineering
Attraction type	Circle-Vision Theater
Theme	Time Travel
Opening date	April 12, 1992
Closing date	September 5, 2004
Hosted by	Timekeeper
Music	Bruce Broughton
Audio-animatronics	2
Replaced by	Buzz Lightyear Laser Blast
Sponsored by	Renault (1992-2002)
♿ Wheelchair accessible	

Visionarium	
Tokyo Disneyland	
Land	Tomorrowland
Designer	Walt Disney Imagineering
Attraction type	Circle-Vision Theater
Theme	Time Travel
Opening date	April 15, 1993
Closing date	September 1, 2002
Hosted by	Timekeeper
Music	Bruce Broughton
Audio-animatronics	2
Replaced by	Buzz Lightyear's Astro Blasters
♿ Wheelchair accessible	

The Timekeeper	
Magic Kingdom	
Land	Tomorrowland
Designer	Walt Disney Imagineering
Attraction type	Circle-Vision Theater
Theme	Time Travel
Opening date	November 21, 1994
Closing date	February 26, 2006
Hosted by	Timekeeper
Music	Bruce Broughton
Audio-animatronics	2
Replaced by	Monsters, Inc. Laugh Floor
♿ Wheelchair accessible	

The Timekeeper (also known as ***From Time to Time*** and ***Un Voyage à Travers le Temps***) was a 1992 Circle-Vision 360° film that was presented at three Disney parks around the world. It was the first Circle-Vision show that was arranged and filmed with an actual plot and not just visions of landscapes, and the first to utilize Audio-Animatronics. The film features a cast of European film actors of France, Italy, Belgium, Russia and England. The film was shown in highly stylized circular theaters, and featured historic and futuristic details both on the interior and exterior.

The Timekeeper and its original European counterpart *Le Visionarium* marked the first time that the Circle-Vision film process was used to deliver a narrative story line. This required a concept to explain the unusual visual characteristics of the Theater, hence the character 9-Eyes. 9-Eyes is sent through Time by The Timekeeper, so that she can send back the surrounding images as she records them in whichever era she finds herself in.[1]

The European attraction was also known by its film name as *Un Voyage à Travers le Temps*, while the Japanese version was simply named "Visionarium", with the caption *From Time to Time* on the poster. The American Film Theater was known as "Transportarium" for a period of six months after it debuted, but the name was later dropped in lieu of "Tomorrowland Metropolis Science Center", or formally "The Timekeeper".

History

Le Visionarium (the original title) was not just an ordinary Circle-Vision 360° film, but was important in that, for the first time in a Circle-Vision film, Imagineers wanted to tell an immersive story and attempt a light-hearted dialog without just switching between scenes of landscapes, as had been done in all of the previous Circle-Vision films.

The original concept for the film had included Jules Verne and the culture of past and present European history and events, and new inventions. Along with the previous elements, the story had to do with the idea of Time Travel with one concept including a child that explored the story of the great European scientists of the past on an intelligent computer. However, to keep the audience focused and use imagination to depict situations and places that do not cater to the average person, the number of visions of the past and extreme situations of the plot kept increasing all the time for the project.[2]

The film first premiered in Discoveryland at Disneyland Paris on April 12, 1992 as *Le Visionarium*. It was an extravagant attraction, and was touted by then-Disney CEO Michael Eisner as the showcase attraction of the land at the time. However, TIME Magazine derided the film as a "flop" of a "wan drama" in its review of Disneyland Paris.[3] The next year, the third incarnation of the ride opened at Tokyo Disneyland, as part of that park's 10th Anniversary Celebration.[4]

The attraction had long been on the *Discoveryland USA* proposal for the Magic Kingdom at the Walt Disney World Resort. However, when financial difficulties arose because of the EuroDisney Project, this Discoveryland project was canceled.[5] [6] At one point, the attraction was to be extended into a restaurant featured next door to the attraction. The Plaza Pavilion was to receive a makeover as the "Astronomer's Club", where a stage would have featured actors portraying famed scientists such as Leonardo Da Vinci, Isaac Newton or Galileo, who would appear in the restaurant, and then be called back to the past by either 9-Eyes or Timekeeper.

However, the film was named *From Time to Time* and opened in the Magic Kingdom's Circle-Vision Theater, rechristened "Transportarium" on November 21, 1994 as part of the New Tomorrowland expansion. Six months later, the attraction underwent some name changes. The Theater was renamed "Tomorrowland Metropolis Science Center", and the film was formally known as *The Timekeeper*.

In 2001, the attraction was moved to the seasonal list of attractions along with Walt Disney's Carousel of Progress. In February 2006, the Walt Disney World Resort reported that *The Timekeeper* was to be closed on February 26, 2006. Walt Disney World's version was the last version of the attraction to be closed. Both the Tokyo Disneyland and Disneyland Paris *Visionarium* films had closed in 2002 and 2004, respectively.

Pre-show synopsis

European pre-show

Guests are ushered into a dimly-lit library-like chamber, complete with several artifacts, such as models of Jules Verne's *Nautilus* from *20,000 Leagues Under the Sea* and *Albatross* from *The Clipper of the Clouds*, Da Vinci's Flying Machine, or the first balloon ever created. A short movie about the history of Renault making cars is shown (until this company dropped sponsorship in 2002). Guests are introduced to Timekeeper, who tells them they are about to join him in an experimentation by viewing his last and greatest invention : his extraordinary Machine to explore Time. Before he introduces it, he gives a short speech on how his Machine will change the world just as the ones that surround guests in the pre-show room. He even delivers a song about visionaries. After that, he introduces the crowd to "9-Eyes", and explains how she will travel through Time first, and let guests see this through her eyes.

Japanese pre-show

This pre-show scene is similar to the European version, however with some differences. First, the area is different. Instead of the dark circular enclave as in the Paris location, a bright open area is present. The wall that separates the building from the Tomorrowland corridor is a large stained-glass mural featuring 22 famous inventors and visionaries. Also featured is the Timekeeper's study, library and laboratory. The pre-show area also features a 20-foot model of Da Vinci's Heliocentric Solar System, the *Nautilus* from Verne's *20,000 Leagues Under the Sea*, the *Albatross* from Verne's *The Clipper of the Clouds*, a real 1920s film projector from Walt Disney Pictures, and an actual copy of Verne's novel, *20,000 Leagues Under the Sea*.[4] The film focuses on Verne and Wells, explaining how their work changed history. Then, 9-Eyes is introduced to guests.

American pre-show

Before the actual show, guests are introduced to the invention of the show, "Circumvisual PhotoDroid", more frequently referred to as "9-Eye". The nine eyes she has represents the nine cameras used in filming the show in the round, thus showing the view from one of her "eyes" on each of the nine movie screens. She is the latest development by The Timekeeper, the inventor of the Time Machine. Guests are invited to be witnesses of the first use ever of the newly invented Machine. Guests also watch 9-Eye's training videos, which include : a plunge over

Niagara Falls, a flight into a barn full of dynamite in Topeka, Kansas, a swirling ride aboard a centrifugator, and lastly, hitching a ride on a space shuttle.

Attraction synopsis

The Movie

After guests enter the Theater, Timekeeper comes to life and has 9-Eyes prepared for the journey through Time. Timekeeper then turns on the Machine for its first use, then watches from his control panel as 9-Eyes is thrust back to the Jurassic age period in Earth's history. She narrowly escapes a hungry Allosaurus as Timekeeper sends her to the last great ice age about 12,000 years ago. As she starts freezing up, Timekeeper sends her to 1450, for what should be a demonstration of Johannes Gutenberg's Printing Press.

However, Timekeeper has yet again messed up and sent her to a Scottish battlefield in which one warrior comes after her. Finally working the kinks out of the Time Machine, Timekeeper sends 9-Eye to the year 1503, at the height of the Renaissance. The Machine is placed right in the middle of Leonardo Da Vinci's workshop, where he is painting the *Mona Lisa* and working on a model of his Flying Machine. 9-Eye, being curious, picks up an item close to her, and is quickly noticed by Leonardo, who becomes fascinated by the strange machine, and starts drawing it on paper.

However, the meeting between 9-Eyes and Da Vinci is cut short. Her next stop in Time is 1763 in a French Castle, where a child named Wolfgang Amadeus Mozart is giving a performance to a crowd, which includes King Louis XV and Madame de Pompadour. The meeting is again short as she is noticed by the people, who start chasing her through the hallways. Timekeeper decides to send her to the 1878 Exposition Universelle, but the Machine is stuck on fast forward, so she witnesses a Paris skyline in such a motion that the progress of the Eiffel Tower, symbol of the 1889 Exposition Universelle, is shown in the background. Finally Timekeeper has the Machine stopped in 1900, just in time for the 1900 Exposition Universelle.

Timekeeper announces that guests are in time for a meeting between H.G. Wells and Jules Verne. 9-Eyes hides from the fair-goers but not so that Verne and Wells are hidden. After a brief conversation about their conflicting visions of the Future, Wells walks away, leaving Verne with a model of his Time Machine, which Verne has just criticized as impossible. After a sarcastic comment about Time Travel from Verne, 9-Eyes rebuts his claim and appears to the author. Jules Verne decides to take a closer look at her and tries to grab her. Timekeeper seeing this tries to bring her back to the present, but he also takes Verne.

Timekeeper and 9-Eyes, realizing their mistake, try to send him back, but he refuses after discovering he has finally arrived in the future he had always dreamed of. He begs for them to show him the world of today in 10 minutes or less, so he can return to 1900 and deliver his speech at the Exhibition (which makes Timekeeper ironically reply that he did it in 80 days). They agree, and Timekeeper sets the Machine for today. He sends Verne and 9-Eyes to a dark tunnel, which Verne believes to be a "dark future". They are unaware they are standing in a railroad tunnel. The next thing to happen is a collision between Jules Verne and a French TGV train, with Verne becoming a new hood ornament.

From the train, Jules Verne and 9-Eyes explore the modern streets of Paris (with Verne walking among the traffic, nearly causing an accident), which leads Verne, curious, to try driving. As such, Timekeeper puts him in the front seat of a race car, and Verne takes off, albeit in the wrong direction. From race car driving, Verne then enjoys a bobsled run. After this bobsled run, Timekeeper sends Verne and 9-Eyes to the bottom of the sea, to show Verne how his novel *Twenty Thousand Leagues Under the Sea* has come to life.

The scene changes and goes from underwater to flying. Jules Verne now stands in a balloon soaring over Red Square in Moscow, sharing it with a Russian couple on their honeymoon. Since Verne's presence is inconvenient, Timekeeper sends him to Roissy airport near Paris. The two Russian lovers are accidentally taken to Paris as well, where they could start their honeymoon. As Verne witnesses planes (the "flying wagons" as he calls them), he begs for Timekeeper to let him fly. An employee soon arrives, discovers 9-Eyes and start talking to her. However, Verne, who ventured far from there, is arrested by policemen. With the help of the employee and Timekeeper's grip on time, Verne is finally freed (these two scenes were not part of Orlando's version).

The screen then shows a flight through the air above the European countrysides featuring Castles and Mountains. Verne is shown in a helicopter, sitting dangerously close to its open door. After flying over Mont St Michel, Neuschwanstein Castle, English countrysides and New York skyline (only in Orlando's version), Verne requests to go even higher. They take him to Space, in order to show that another dream of his, space travel, has come true from his book *From the Earth to the Moon*.

Time is running out, so Timekeeper and 9-Eyes return Verne to the site of the Grand Palais of the 1900 Exposition Universelle. However, Timekeeper makes one mistake in the wrong year, and Verne is in the right place, but at the wrong time (in the 1990s). When they finally return Verne to his right time, H.G. Wells happens to go back to the site of his discussion with Verne, and therefore sees all that is going on with the Timekeeper. Wells is flabbergasted, and Verne and 9-Eyes exchange goodbyes as Wells tries to understand what is happening. 9-Eyes returns to the present time, and now that guests have witnessed a "flawless" demonstration of his Time Machine, Timekeeper decides to see the Future.

Timekeeper sends 9-Eyes and selected guests to 2189, 300 years after the Exposition Universelle of 1889 and the completion of the Eiffel Tower (both evidenced by the Timekeeper's clock, and by the appearance of the number "300" on the Eiffel Tower). As they explore a futuristic Paris aboard a flying car named *Reinastella*, they see Jules Verne and H.G. Wells appearing in what looks like Wells' Time Machine from 1900. A stunned 9-Eyes questions how they got there, to which Verne replies "In the future, anything is possible!". The show ends as they jet off, and Timekeeper wishes everyone well. As guests leave, Timekeeper makes plans to see other important events during History and in the Future with his Machine and 9-Eyes.

Voice cast

Character	Voice actor (American)	Voice actor (French)	Voice actor (Japanese)
Timekeeper	Robin Williams	Michel Leeb	George Tokoro
9-Eyes	Rhea Perlman	Myriam Boyer	Yuki Saito

Film cast

Character	Actor
Jules Verne	Michel Piccoli
H.G. Wells	Jeremy Irons
Leonardo Da Vinci	Franco Nero
Mona Lisa	Anna Pernicci
Louis XV	Jean Rochefort
Madame de Pompadour	Nathalie Baye
Roissy Employee	Gérard Depardieu
Mr. Verne's Translator	Patrick Bauchau

Filming locations

Palm Pavilion in Schönbrunn Palace, where 9-Eyes meets Jules Verne

- Alnwick Castle, Northumberland County, England, United Kingdom
  - Site of Scottish Battle scene
- Castello Orsini-Odescalchi, Bracciano, Italy
  - Set of Leonardo Da Vinci's workshop
- Château de Chantilly, Chantilly, France
  - Site of Mozart's performance before Louis XV
- Palm Pavilion, Schloss Schönbrunn, Hietzing, Vienna, Austria
  - Site for exterior shots for the Exposition Universelle of 1900
- Rouffach, Haut-Rhin, Alsace, France
  - Location of the scene featuring the TGV
- Paris, Île-de-France, Val-d'Oise, France
  - Site for the location of Parisian traffic jam scene
- Knittelfeld, Steiermark, Austria
  - The Renault Grand Prix Scene took place at the Österreichring
- Olympic Bobsleigh Run, Innsbruck, Tyrol, Austria
  - Site for shots for the Bobsleigh Run
- Lyford Cay, New Providence Island, Commonwealth of The Bahamas, West Indies
  - Site of deep-sea dive scene
- Red Square, Central Federal District, Moscow, Russian Federation
  - Location of hot air balloon from the European and Japanese versions
- Roissy-en-France, Île-de-France, Val-d'Oise, France
  - Location of Charles de Gaulle Airport scene from the European and Japanese versions
- Mont Saint-Michel, Normandy, Manche, France
  - Fly over Mont Saint-Michel
- Neuschwanstein Castle, Bavaria, Germany
  - Fly over Neuschwanstein Castle
- Calais, Pas-de-Calais, France
  - Fly over the European coastline
- New York City, New York, United States of America
  - Fly over New York City from the American version

Film variations

The original European version of the film was different from the American version. A certain number of scenes were cut including the hot air balloon scene, some European coastline scenes, and a dialogue between Jules Verne and an employee of Paris' Charles de Gaulle International Airport. The only addition in the American version was a New York City skyline scene. The hot air balloon scene was filmed over Red Square in Moscow, and as such taken under intense conditions by Walt Disney Productions in the then-Soviet Union.

European and Japanese scene order	American scene order
Jurassic Period	Same
Ice Age	Same
The Anglo-Scot Wars	Same
Da Vinci's Workshop	Same
Mozart's Concert in 1763)	Same
The Construction of the Eiffel Tower	Same
Exposition Universelle of 1900	Same
Jules Verne in the present day	Same
Verne's Collision with TGV	Same
Traffic scene near Arc de Triumph	Same
Bobsled Run	Same
Deep-sea exploration scene	Same
Up in the air from Red Square	Omitted
Charles De Gaulle Airport	Omitted
Flying over European countriesides	Same, although Orlando's version goes from underwater to flying
Omitted	New York skyline
Outer Space	Same
Return to Paris, today	Same
Return to Paris in 1900)	Same
Paris in 2189	Same
End	Same

Aftermath and the effects of September 11, 2001

After being placed on a seasonal schedule in April 2001, *The Timekeeper* at Walt Disney World was open on a sporadic schedule during the busy seasons. Some attribute it to the following criticisms, which the overseas versions of the attraction had not been faced with:

- Obese or elderly guests may have found it hard to stand or strainful on the eyes
- The lack of familiar Disney characters
- The building's entrance was very inconspicuous and did not feature a large rotating globe icon or full title.

After the events of September 11, 2001, the attraction faced even harder times. With a decrease in tourism due to the terrorist acts in the United States, and the fact the film featured a scene of New York that still included the now-destroyed World Trade Center Towers, the attraction's demise was certain. To preserve the memory of those events, The Timekeeper's clock registered the current year as 2000, placing him in a time prior to the attacks.

However, it managed to last five more years. During the time when construction was occurring on Stitch's Great Escape!, it was open more frequently along with Walt Disney's Carousel of Progress. On days when the show was not opened, the queue was a meet-and-greet for Disney characters such as Stitch and Pixar characters Buzz Lightyear, and Mr. Incredible, Elastigirl, and Frozone from *The Incredibles*.

Until December 2005, *The Timekeeper* in Walt Disney World Resort was the last *Timekeeper* still entertaining guests, as the Tokyo Disneyland version closed in 2002 and was replaced with Buzz Lightyear's Astro Blasters in 2004, and the Disneyland Paris version closed in 2004 and was replaced by Buzz Lightyear Laser Blast in 2006, although the Disneyland Paris version closed mainly because it lost its sponsor, Renault.

In early 2007, the former location of *The Timekeeper* became home to *Monsters, Inc. Laugh Floor*. The attraction building still retains most of the elements of the previous tenant, including the water columns in the queue and the basic Circle-Vision theater. However, the Theater floor has been modified to include seating and several of the screens are now covered by other elements. The building, theoretically, is still able to revert to a Circle-Vision Theater, although the likelihood of this occurring is low.

Failed proposal for the Disneyland Resort

During the early 1990s, then Disney-Executive, Michael Eisner released ambitious plans for changes to the parks. "Tomorrowland 2055" was planned for a remake of Tomorrowland and the Disneyland Resort in California. *The Timekeeper* was to be a showcase attraction, along with ExtraTERRORestrial Alien Encounter and Plectu's Fantastic Intergalactic Revue. One promotional brochure had Delta Air Lines[7] sponsoring the film. But these plans were later scrapped due to financial difficulties within the Parks & Resorts division, most stemming from the billion dollar losses incurred with the EuroDisney project. However, some clips of *The Timekeeper* could be seen in the queue for *Rocket Rods*, which utilized the Circle-Vision 360° Theater.

Other information placed Visionarium as an opening-day attraction at the unbuilt park next to Disneyland, WestCOT. The show would have been housed in a European Renaissance building in a European section of the WestCOT version of World Showcase. However, like the "Tomorrowland 2055" plan, this did not occur either.[8] [9]

Technical aspects

- Film negative format (mm/video inches)
  - 9 x 35 mm
- Cinematographic process
  - Circle-Vision 360
- Printed film format
  - 9 x 35 mm
- Aspect ratio
  - 12.00 : 1

Soundtrack notes

Audio dialogue

The three versions of the attraction featured a soundtrack of dialogue in each park's country's native tongue (French, Japanese, and English).

Both the Tokyo Disneyland and Disneyland Paris versions featured guest-selectable translations on headset, which included :

- For Paris :
  - English
  - German
  - Spanish
  - Italian
  - Nederlands
- For Tokyo :
  - English

- Mandarin Chinese

Since both the European and Japanese versions opened before Orlando's version was created, the voicecast and dialogue are completely different. The American-style dialogue was not present in these versions, and it was a close translation of the French dialog.

Featured music

- While the American version received a different soundtrack from the other versions, they were both scored by Bruce Broughton.[10]
- During the scene of the conversation between Verne and Wells at the Exposition Universelle, the song heard in the background is called Estudiantina, or *Band of Students Waltz*. It was composed in 1883 by Émile Waldteufel.
- When Verne returns to the Exhibition building in the 1990s, "Motownphilly" by Boyz II Men can be heard in the background. It was meant to represent popular music at the time of filming. The song can be found on their 1991 debut album *Cooleyhighharmony*.

Foreign language titles

- French: *Le Visionarium*
- Japanese: ビジョナリアム - *Visionarium*

Renault's involvement with the film

The French automobile company Renault is heavily featured throughout the attraction, since it sponsored it in Europe between 1992 and 2002.

- In the film :
  - In the scene where Jules Verne steps off the curb into a busy street in front of the Arc de Triomphe, the car that almost hits him is a five-door hatchback, Renault Clio, at the time of filming the newest model in Renault's fleet of cars.
  - In the Formula 1 scene, where Jules Verne drives a race car, he is seated and drives the Renault F1 vehicle.
  - The flying car carrying a family in the scene of Paris in the future was imagined by Renault and is called a "Reinastella".
- In front of the building in Paris :
  - A Reinastella model was displayed near the entrance, but it was removed in 2002, when Renault dropped sponsorship. However it remained in the final scene of the film. The prototype car was then seen around Europe in auto shows, most recently on display at Renault's showroom on the Champs-Élysées.
  - When the prop sat outside the theater, a plaque beneath it read :

    Blast into the Future by checking out the Renault Reinastella ! The Reinastella's futuristic design features a vocal command system that makes steering wheels and accelerators a thing of the past. With a cruising height that ranges from 15cm to 150m above surfaces, the Reinastella flies up to 300km/h. The next time you're traveling through time, stop into the 24th Century and test drive a Renault Reinastella !

References

[1] Imagineers, The (2005-09-01). *The Imagineering Field Guide to the Magic Kingdom at Walt Disney World.* Disney Editions. pp. 124–5. ISBN 0786855533.

[2] Jean de Lutèce. "Hidden Views of Le Visionarium" (http://www.jimhillmedia.com/article.php?id=639). . Retrieved December 18, 2006.

[3] Richard Corliss (April 20, 1992). "Voila! Disney Invades Europe. Will the French Resist?" (http://www.time.com/time/magazine/article/0,9171,975357-3,00.html). *Time*. . Retrieved December 1, 2007.

[4] JT Cent. "Visionarium - Tomorrowland - Tokyo Disneyland" (http://web.archive.org/web/20040416004214/jtcent.com/disneyland/tomorrow/tomvis.html). Archived from the original (http://jtcent.com/disneyland/tomorrow/tomvis.html) on April 16, 2004. . Retrieved December 26, 2006.

[5] Jim Hill. "Discoveryland U.S.A. -- Part 1" (http://jimhillmedia.com/blogs/jim_hill/archive/2002/08/18/265.aspx). . Retrieved December 18, 2006.

[6] Jim Hill. "Discoveryland U.S.A. -- Part 2" (http://jimhillmedia.com/blogs/jim_hill/archive/2002/08/18/266.aspx). . Retrieved December 18, 2006.

[7] Jim Hill. "A Special Weekend Edition of Why For?" (http://jimhillmedia.com/blogs/jim_hill/archive/2004/11/04/490.aspx). . Retrieved December 18, 2006.

[8] Tony Baxter. "Tony Baxter...on WestCOT" (http://members.tripod.com/~savehorizons/westcot1.htm). . Retrieved December 18, 2006.

[9] Shaun Finnie. "CALIFORNIA DREAMING Part 1 – WESTCOT'S World Showcase" (http://web.archive.org/web/20061217150830/http://www.mickeynews.com/Columns/DisplayColumn.asp_Q_id_E_536). Archived from the original (http://www.mickeynews.com/Columns/DisplayColumn.asp_Q_id_E_536) on December 17, 2006. . Retrieved December 18, 2006.

[10] "Timekeeper (USA) – Disney Theme Parks / Circle-vision" & "From Time to Time (Euro Disney / Japan) – Disney Theme Parks / Circle-Vision" http://www.brucebroughton.com/filmography/filmography.html

External links

English information

- *The Timekeeper* (http://www.imdb.com/title/tt0104307/) at the Internet Movie Database

Attraction history

- PatMagic - *Le Visionarium* History (http://www.patmagic.net/levis.htm)
- AllEars - *The Timekeeper* History (http://www.allearsnet.com/tp/mk/time.htm)
- Archive.org - Tokyo Disneyland *Visionarium* Informations (http://web.archive.org/web/20040416004214/jtcent.com/disneyland/tomorrow/tomvis.html)

Editorials

- Jim Hill Media - Hidden Views of *Le Visionarium* (http://jimhillmedia.com/blogs/jean_de_lutce/archive/2004/01/22/1403.aspx)

Photos

- **Disneyland Paris**
  - Photos Magiques - *Le Visionarium* (http://www.photosmagiques.com/gallery/disneyland_park/discoveryland/closed/le_visionarium.php) / *Constellations* (http://www.photosmagiques.com/gallery/disneyland_park/discoveryland/closed/old_constellations.php) / *Bureau Passeports Annuels* (formerly *Le Café des Visionnaires)* (http://www.photosmagiques.com/gallery/disneyland_park/discoveryland/bureau_passeport_annuel.php)

Media

- Making of *Le Visionarium* - Part 1 (http://www.youtube.com/watch?v=nQJkSrUwq6A&feature=related) Part 2 (http://www.youtube.com/watch?v=IE9e30IMPho&feature=related) Part 3 (http://www.youtube.com/watch?v=xgQ9sMuCZgA&feature=related)

French information

Note: All of the following links are in French.

- Imagineering Files - Histoire et conception du *Visionarium* (http://www.imagineeringfiles.com/lesdisparus/visionarium.html)
- Le Visionarium - Un hommage intemporel pour une attraction atemporelle (http://webcot.free.fr/dlp/discoveryland/visionarium.htm)
- ADCP DisneyFan - Le Visionarium (http://www.adcp-disneyfan.com/loupe/visio/loupevisio.html)
- DLRP Synopsis - Le Visionarium (http://dlrpsynopsis.free.fr/attraction.php?attraction_id=89)

FernGully: The Last Rainforest

FernGully: The Last Rainforest	
Theatrical release poster	
Directed by	Bill Kroyer
Produced by	Peter Faiman Wayne Young
Screenplay by	Jim Cox
Starring	Jonathan Ward Samantha Mathis Tim Curry Christian Slater Robin Williams
Music by	Alan Silvestri **Orchestrator/Conductor:** William Ross
Studio	Kroyer Films FAI Films
Distributed by	20th Century Fox
Release date(s)	April 10, 1992 (North America) September 17, 1992 (Australia)
Running time	75 min.
Country	Australia United States
Language	English
Box office	$32,710,894

FernGully: The Last Rainforest is a 1992 Australian-American animated film directed by Bill Kroyer, produced by Peter Faiman and Wayne Young, and written by Jim Cox based on a book of the same name by Diana Young. It is a film with a strong environmental theme. The film features the voice talents of Jonathan Ward as Zak, Samantha Mathis as Crysta, Tim Curry as Hexxus, Robin Williams as Batty Koda, and Christian Slater as Pips.

The film was released in the United States on April 10, 1992 and in Australia on September 17, 1992, and received mixed to positive reviews. In 1998, the film was followed by the direct-to-video sequel, *FernGully 2: The Magical Rescue*.

Plot

A curious fairy girl named Crysta sees a part of the world she has never seen before beyond FernGully, a rainforest near Mount Warning, Australia. She believes humans dwell on Mount Warning; however, the wise sprite of the forest and Crysta's motherly figure, Magi Lune, says humans are now extinct. She says that they fled, driven away by an attack by Hexxus, the spirit of destruction and all that is toxic to nature, never to return and presumed dead; Hexxus was defeated by the fairies and imprisoned inside a tree. Crysta mentions a black cloud that she saw rising near the mountain, and Magi identifies it as smoke, but dismisses her speculation that the smoke might be Hexxus.

Befriending a mentally unstable yet comical fruit bat named Batty Koda who has been experimented on by humans and now has wires and antennas fused into his head, Crysta heads to Mount Warning where she finds dead trees all marked with red aerosol paint crosses, which mark them for cutting. The camera then pans through the trees to reveal the source of the smoke, which turns out to be the exhaust from a huge tree leveler. She finds male humans, and accidentally shrinks one named Zak in trying to prevent him from being crushed by a tree. He gets stuck on a spiderweb on the tree that's just about to go through a tree shredder. She tries to get him off but can't when Batty swoops in, grabs them both off of the spider web and blames Crysta for her almost getting killed, because she did not listen to him.

Zak goes on a wild adventure with Crysta and Batty, nearly getting eaten by a hungry Goanna lizard named Lou, and unexpectedly falls in love with Crysta. Meanwhile, Zak's superiors cut down an enchanted baobab tree that Zak had inadvertently painted an X mark on while trying to spray a fly that was buzzing around him, discovering too late that Hexxus has been released from the tree. Seeking revenge upon the fairies of FernGully for imprisoning him, Hexxus apparently gains power from the pollution, specifically the energy and smoke produced by the Leveler, as he can be seen "drinking" from it like a liquid. He manipulates the lumberjacks and their tree leveler into tearing down the rainforest in the direction of the fairies by the next morning.

Eventually, Zak tells the truth about who he his and how the humans are destroying Fern Gully join forces and fuse their powers together, creating a protective tree cage. Magi sacrifices herself, giving her power to the fairies and Zak, and it is up to Crysta and the other fairies to defeat Hexxus. Zak turns off the leveler, causing Hexxus to lose all the energy he was gaining from it and disappear, but he soon rips out of the machine as a giant demonic skeleton creature made of oil that breathes fire. Crysta seemingly sacrifices herself like Magi did by allowing Hexxus to devour her in one bite, and uses her powers from inside him to grow a seed she had with her, imprisoning both Hexxus and the leveler inside a new tree with help from the fairies led by Pips. However, she emerges, unharmed and alive, from a flower soon after. Crysta sadly resizes Zak to normal size and he sets off with his fellow lumberjacks, Tony and Ralph, to try to stop the destruction of the rainforests. Meanwhile, Crysta takes Magi's place after learning finally how to control her powers.

Cast

- Jonathan Ward as Zak Young
- Samantha Mathis as Crysta
- Tim Curry as Hexxus
- Christian Slater as Pips
- Robin Williams as Batty Koda
- Grace Zabriskie as Magi Lune
- Geoffrey Blake as Ralph
- Robert Pastorelli as Tony
- Cheech Marin as Stump
- Tommy Chong as Root
- Tone Lōc as Goanna
- Townsend Coleman as Knotty
- Neil Ross as the Elder

Production

Production time was greatly reduced by the use of computer animation to create elements such as flocks of birds that would have taken much longer to animate traditionally.[1]

Soundtrack

The score of *FernGully* was composed by Alan Silvestri.[2] The soundtrack album was released by MCA Records with the following songs:

1. "Life Is a Magic Thing", Johnny Clegg (written by Thomas Dolby)
2. "Batty Rap", Robin Williams (written by Thomas Dolby)[3]
3. "If I'm Gonna Eat Somebody (It Might as Well Be You)", Tone Lōc[3]
4. "Toxic Love", Tim Curry (written by Thomas Dolby)[3]
5. "Raining Like Magic", Raffi
6. "Land of a Thousand Dances", Guy
7. "Dream Worth Keeping", Sheena Easton
8. "Some Other World", Elton John (written by Elton John and Bruce Roberts)

Reception

The response for the film from both critics and the public was mixed to positive. Rotten Tomatoes gave the film an approval rating of 69% based on 13 reviews (9 positive, 4 negative).[4] Film critic Roger Ebert gave it three out of four stars, saying the film was visually "very pleasing," told a "useful lesson", "and although the movie is not a masterpiece it's pleasant to watch for its humor and sweetness."[5] *The Austin Chronicle* added that the film was "funny, pretty, touching, scary, magical stuff."[6] Janet Maslin of *The New York Times* had an unfavourable impression of the film, describing it as "[a]n uncertain blend of sanctimonious principles and Saturday-morning cartoon aesthetics".[2] *FernGully* grossed $32,710,894 worldwide, including $24,650,296 from the United States.[7]

Some reviewers have commented that the 2009 film *Avatar* used thematic and plot elements from *FernGully: The Last Rainforest*.[8] [9]

References

[1] Rickitt, Richard (2000). *Special Effects: The History and Technique*. Billboard Books. p. 147. ISBN 0-8230-7733-0.

[2] Maslin, Janet (10 April 1992). "Ferngully: the Last Rainforest (1992)" (http://movies.nytimes.com/movie/review?res=9E0CEFD91338F933A25757C0A964958260). *The New York Times*. . Retrieved 2010-04-15.

[3] *Los Angeles Daily News* (13 April 1992). "Animated kiddie film beams ecology message" (http://news.google.ca/newspapers?id=8jUfAAAAIBAJ&pg=4722,5328585). *Spartanburg Herald-Journal*. p. B5. . Retrieved 2010-04-15.

[4] "Ferngully: The Last Rainforest (1992)" (http://au.rottentomatoes.com/m/ferngully_the_last_rainforest/). *Rotten Tomatoes*. . Retrieved May 12, 2010.

[5] Ebert, Roger (1992-04-10). "Ferngully: The Last Rainforest" (http://rogerebert.suntimes.com/apps/pbcs.dll/article?AID=/19920410/REVIEWS/204100301/1023). *Chicago Sun-Times*. . Retrieved 2010-01-14.

[6] Chacona, Hollis (1992-04-17). "Ferngully: The Last Rainforest" (http://www.austinchronicle.com/gyrobase/Calendar/Film?Film=oid:138826). *Austin Chronicle*. . Retrieved 2010-01-14.

[7] "Ferngully: The Last Rainforest" (http://boxofficemojo.com/movies/?id=ferngullythelastrainforest.htm). *Box Office Mojo*. . Retrieved May 11, 2010.

[8] Schwartzberg, Joel (4 January 2010). "What Did 'Avatar' Borrow from 'FernGully'?" (http://www.ivillage.com/what-did-avatar-borrow-ferngully/1-e-71746). IVillage. . Retrieved 2010-04-15.

[9] Quinn, Karl (17 December 2009). "Don't just watch Avatar, see it" (http://www.theage.com.au/opinion/blogs/the-vulture/dont-just-watch-avatar-see-it/20091216-kx47.html). *The Age*. . Retrieved 2010-04-15.

External links

- *FernGully: The Last Rainforest* (http://www.imdb.com/title/tt0104254/) at the Internet Movie Database
- *FernGully: The Last Rainforest* (http://www.allrovi.com/movies/movie/v17073) at AllRovi
- *FernGully: The Last Rainforest* (http://www.rottentomatoes.com/m/ferngully_the_last_rainforest/) at Rotten Tomatoes
- *FernGully: The Last Rainforest* (http://www.boxofficemojo.com/movies/?id=ferngullythelastrainforest.htm) at Box Office Mojo

Shakes the Clown

Shakes the Clown	
Theatrical poster	
Directed by	Bobcat Goldthwait
Produced by	Paul Colichman Ann Luly-Goldthwait
Written by	Bobcat Goldthwait
Starring	Bobcat Goldthwait Julie Brown Tom Kenny Blake Clark Adam Sandler Robin Williams
Music by	Tom Scott
Cinematography	Bobby Bukowski Elliot Davis
Editing by	J. Kathleen Gibson
Distributed by	IRS Media (Theatrical) Columbia-Tristar Home Video (Home Video)
Release date(s)	March 13, 1992
Running time	87 min
Country	USA
Language	English
Budget	$1,400,000 (estimated)

Shakes the Clown is a 1992 American movie directed and written by Bobcat Goldthwait, who performs the title role. It also features Julie Brown, Blake Clark, Paul Dooley, Kathy Griffin, Florence Henderson, Tom Kenny, Adam Sandler, Scott Herriott, LaWanda Page, Jack Gallagher, and a cameo by Robin Williams as Mime Jerry (using the pseudonym Marty Fromage).

The movie is a dark comedy about a birthday-party clown (Goldthwait) in the grip of depression and alcoholism, who is framed for murder. Different communities of clowns, mimes and other performers are depicted as clannish, rivalrous subcultures obsessed with precedence and status. This was Goldthwait's bitter satire of the dysfunctional standup comedy circuit he knew as a performer.

Cast

- Bobcat Goldthwait as Shakes the Clown
- Julie Brown as Judy
- Blake Clark as Stenchy the Clown
- Paul Dooley as Owen Cheese
- Kathy Griffin as Lucy
- Tom Kenny as Blinky the Clown
- Adam Sandler as Dink the Clown
- Jack Gallagher as Officer Crony
- Florence Henderson as The Unknown Woman
- Scott Herriott as Floor Director
- LaWanda Page as Female Clown Barfly
- Robin Williams as Mime Jerry

Reception

Shakes the Clown was not a financial success, earning only about $115,000 in ticket sales against an estimated budget of $1.4 million.[1]

Critical reaction to the movie was decidedly mixed: Leonard Maltin gave it his lowest rating, while Betsy Sherman of *The Boston Globe* called it "the *Citizen Kane* of alcoholic clown movies".[2] Roger Ebert gave *Shakes* 2-out-of-4 stars, writing that some isolated scenes are "very funny" but the plot was scattered and the performances often under-rehearsed.[3] As of mid-2011, the movie has a 37% rating on Rotten Tomatoes, based on 19 reviews.[4]

In an interview with Conan O'Brien, Goldthwait revealed that no less than Martin Scorsese had defended the movie from detractors. When a film critic derided the movie in order to make a point about good and bad movies, Scorsese revealed, "I like *Shakes the Clown*. Haven't you heard? It's the *Citizen Kane* of Alcoholic Clown Movies!"[5]

References

[1] http://www.imdb.com/title/tt0102898/business

[2] Blowen, Michael (December 2, 1997). "Rigors of family life are taming Bobcat Goldthwait" (http://pqasb.pqarchiver.com/boston/access/23351092.html?dids=23351092:23351092&FMT=ABS&FMTS=ABS:FT&type=current&date=Dec+02,+1997&author=Michael+Blowen,+Globe+Staff&pub=Boston+Globe&desc=Rigors+of+family+life+are+taming+Bobcat+Goldthwait&pqatl=google). *The Boston Globe* (The New York Times Company). . Retrieved 1 February 2011.

[3] "Shakes The Clown" (http://rogerebert.suntimes.com/apps/pbcs.dll/article?AID=/19920313/REVIEWS/203130306/1023). *Chicago Sun-Times*. .

[4] http://www.rottentomatoes.com/m/shakes_the_clown/

[5] http://www.scorsesefilms.com/quote8.htm

External links

- *Shakes the Clown* (http://www.imdb.com/title/tt0102898/) at the Internet Movie Database
- *Shakes the Clown* (http://www.allrovi.com/movies/movie/v44047) at AllRovi

Mrs. Doubtfire

Mrs. Doubtfire	
Theatrical release poster	
Directed by	Chris Columbus
Produced by	Marsha Garces Williams Robin Williams Mark Radcliffe
Screenplay by	Randi Mayem Singer Leslie Dixon
Based on	*Madame Doubtfire* by Anne Fine
Starring	Robin Williams Sally Field Lisa Jakub Matthew Lawrence Mara Wilson Pierce Brosnan Harvey Fierstein
Music by	Howard Shore
Cinematography	Donald McAlpine
Editing by	Raja Gosnell
Distributed by	20th Century Fox
Release date(s)	November 24, 1993
Running time	125 mins.
Country	United States
Language	English
Budget	$25,000,000
Box office	$441,286,195

Mrs. Doubtfire is a 1993 American comedy film starring Robin Williams and Sally Field and based on the novel *Madame Doubtfire* by Anne Fine. It was directed by Chris Columbus and distributed by 20th Century Fox. It won the Academy Award for Best Makeup.[1] The film was placed 67th in the American Film Institute's *100 Years, 100 Laughs: America's Funniest Movies* (see the 100 Years Series), a list of the 100 funniest movies of the 20th century, and was also rated #40 on Bravo's *100 Funniest Movies of All Time*. The original music score was composed by Howard Shore.

Plot

Daniel Hillard (Robin Williams) is a recently-unemployed voice actor, and a good father loved by his three children. However, he also suffers from an increasingly strained marriage to his wife Miranda (Sally Field), an interior designer who has grown to dislike her husband's child-like antics. On the day of their son's twelfth birthday, Daniel hires a local petting zoo to throw a large birthday party for his son. After receiving a complaint at work from their neighbor Gloria Chaney, Miranda discovers that Daniel has thrown the party without her consent, because their son had a bad report card. This is the last straw for Miranda, who subsequently divorces her husband. Since Daniel has no steady source of income, Miranda gets primary custody of their three children, twelve-year-old Chris (Matthew Lawrence), fourteen-year-old Lydia (Lisa Jakub), and five-year-old Natalie (Mara Wilson). Daniel has visitation rights limited to Saturday evenings. The judge, acknowledging this, agrees to consider a joint custody arrangement if Daniel can get a job and create a suitable home within three months.

When Daniel learns that Miranda intends to place an advertisement for a housekeeper, he adopts the persona of a sixty-year-old Scottish caretaker named Euphegenia Doubtfire, and applies for the job himself. When Miranda accepts, Daniel recruits his brother Frank (Harvey Fierstein), a makeup artist, and his partner Jack (Scott Capurro), to design a costume for Mrs. Doubtfire. Though the children are initially hostile toward their new nanny, as Mrs. Doubtfire, Daniel is able to see his children every day, giving him the opportunity to be the firm father figure he wasn't before. Eventually the children begin to respond favorably to Mrs. Doubtfire's methods, and Miranda is able to heal her relationship with them and with Daniel as well, who begins to improve himself through his alter ego by learning gourmet cooking and refurnishing his new apartment.

For a while, Daniel is able to keep up the charade, despite nearly being discovered by his caseworker Mrs. Sellner (Anne Haney), and attempting to stop his ex-wife's relationship with Stuart Dunmire (Pierce Brosnan), her new boyfriend, who is not particularly fond of Daniel.

Ultimately, Daniel's cover is blown when Chris walks in on him in the bathroom by accident. He explains to Lydia and Chris what he has done, and tells them that they cannot tell Miranda, because Miranda would put Daniel in jail, or Natalie, as she is too young to understand and would possibly tell Miranda. Both children are happy to have their father back in their lives, and agree to help maintain the pretense. Meanwhile, at the TV station where Daniel works as a shipping clerk, the station's CEO Jonathan Lundy (Robert Prosky) sees him clowning with toy dinosaurs on the set of a children's program and is impressed enough to schedule a dinner meeting to hear his ideas. Stuart plans to celebrate Miranda's birthday by taking the family out to the same restaurant at the same time, and everyone expects Mrs. Doubtfire to join them. Daniel tries to postpone his dinner with Lundy, but Lundy is booked for two months, and Lundy's secretary advises him not to cancel the appointment.

At the restaurant, Daniel attempts to rotate back and forth between Lundy and his family, using the restroom to change back and forth from himself to Doubtfire. At one point, Daniel dumps cayenne pepper on Stuart's order of jambalaya, an ingredient that he is allergic to, not realizing the potential consequences of this action. He also becomes increasingly intoxicated throughout the evening and forgets to remove his costume before returning to Lundy's table. He covers for the mistake by explaining to Lundy that his alter ego is merely his idea for a new TV persona. Lundy is once again impressed, and agrees to develop the character into a possible television program.

At that moment, Daniel notices that Stuart is choking on the pepper and administers the Heimlich maneuver. However, part of his mask peels off, revealing part of his real face in the process, and Miranda is horrified to discover his identity. As a result, Miranda receives full custody of the children. Despite his impassioned plea that the motive was solely for the love of his children, the judge, believing his actions to be the result of insanity, restricts Daniel's visitation rights by ordering him to undergo supervised visits, only once a week. Miranda is equally appalled by this, but says nothing. Meanwhile, as Mrs. Doubtfire, he becomes the star of Lundy's new television program, "*Euphegenia's House*". It quickly becomes the highest-rated program in its timeslot, creating the possibility that the show will be aired nationwide.

Upon seeing how unhappy she and the children are without Mrs. Doubtfire in their lives, Miranda pays Daniel a visit on the set and tells him that she doesn't want to keep hurting the children over the custody issues, and, as a surprise for the kids, invites him back as their caretaker. Daniel picks the kids up to spend an afternoon with them, while Miranda, smiling, watches an episode of Daniel's show in which Mrs. Doubtfire answers a letter from another child of divorce asking for advice. She explains that no matter what type of living arrangement such children may have, love will maintain the bond of the family.

Cast

- Robin Williams as Daniel Hillard/Mrs. Euphegenia Doubtfire
- Sally Field as Miranda Hillard
- Lisa Jakub as Lydia Hillard
- Matthew Lawrence as Christopher Hillard
- Mara Wilson as Natalie Hillard
- Pierce Brosnan as Stuart Dunmire
- Harvey Fierstein as Uncle Frank Hillard
- Scott Capurro as Jack Hillard
- Robert Prosky as Jonathan Lundy
- Polly Holliday as Gloria Chaney
- Anne Haney as Mrs. Sellner
- William Newman as Mr. Sprinkles the Postman / Boring Dinosaur Show Host
- Martin Mull as Miranda's partner at work
- Todd Williams as Todd the Bartender
- Ashley Harris as Female Swimmer
- James Rankin as Matthew
- Stuart Fredrick Hillard as Arnold Alden
- Roscoe Lee Browne as Buck

Soundtrack

The score was composed, orchestrated, and conducted by Howard Shore. The song Robin Williams sings at the cartoon voiceover in the beginning is "Largo al factotum". Other songs featured often were chosen referencing the identity of Mrs. Doubtfire. These songs include:

- "Dude (Looks Like a Lady)" performed by Aerosmith
- "Walk Like a Man" performed by The Four Seasons
- "Luck Be A Lady" performed by Frank Sinatra
- "Papa's Got A Brand New Bag" performed by James Brown

Additionally, these songs were featured:

- "Jump Around" performed by House of Pain (but some lines were cut to keep the image family-friendly)
- "Stormy Monday Blues" performed by B. B. King and Albert Collins

Locations

Chicago was the studio's first choice for filming. However, two new television shows (*ER* and *Chicago Hope*) had a lease with the city around the same time period, and the production team eventually went with San Francisco. Various locations in San Francisco were used for filming. Parts were shot at the studios of television station KTVU in Oakland. The street signs for the intersection near the "Painted Lady" home, Steiner and Broadway, were visible on-screen. The exact address, 2640 Steiner Street 37°47′38.07″N 122°26′10.78″W, became a tourist attraction for some time after the film's release.[2] Though the film's home exteriors were impressive, its interiors were all shot in a warehouse in the Bay area that was turned into a soundstage. Robin Williams' divorced father character 'Daniel' lived upstairs from Danilo Bakery at 516 Green St., and his children attended a school at Filbert and Taylor.

The restaurant scene was filmed in an actual upscale restaurant, Bridges Restaurant & Bar, in downtown Danville, California, which is still in operation.

Release

Box office

The film was a huge box office success. It became the second biggest film of 1993, behind only *Jurassic Park.*[3] [4]

Critical Reception

The film received mixed to positive reviews. At the time of its release, several critics compared *Mrs. Doubtfire* unfavorably with *Some Like It Hot* (1959), and others who viewed the movie favorably noted its similarity to *Tootsie* (1982).[5]

Mrs. Doubtfire has a "fresh" rating of 69% with an average score of 5.8 out of 10 on Rotten Tomatoes.[6] [7]

Accolades

- 66th Academy Awards[1]
  - Best Makeup (Won)
- 51st Golden Globe Awards
  - Best Picture (Musical/Comedy) (Won)
  - Best Actor (Musical/Comedy) - Robin Williams (Won)

BAFTA Awards

- 1994
  - Best Makeup & Hair (nominee)

American Film Institute Lists

- AFI's 100 Years... 100 Laughs - #67
- AFI's 100 Years... 100 Songs:
  - Dude (Looks Like A Lady) - Nominated[8]

Sequel

Writing of a sequel, *Mrs. Doubtfire 2*, began in 2003 by actress Bonnie Hunt (*Beethoven*, *Cheaper by the Dozen*, *Jerry Maguire*). Robin Williams was set to return in disguise as an old nanny, similar to the first movie. Due to problems with the script, re-writing began in early 2006 as Robin Williams was allegedly unhappy with the plot. The film was expected to be released in late 2007, but following further script problems the sequel was declared "scrapped" in mid-2006.[9]

The sequel's story involved Williams as Mrs. Doubtfire moving close to his daughter's college so he could keep an eye on her. Recently in an interview for *Newsday*, Williams said the movie's sequel was indefinitely scrapped. Stating his reasons, he said, "The script they had just didn't work."[10]

On December 5, 2006, during an interview with BBC Radio 1 by DJ Edith Bowman, Williams said that if it is not going to be done right, then it is not worth doing and that there will not be a sequel with him in it. However, the character might return in some form some day in the future. The interview does not seem to have been recorded but was posted online almost immediately.[10]

In August 2010, Robin Williams was featured on *Alan Carr's Chatty Man*, and again brought up the topic of another *Mrs. Doubtfire* movie. He blamed the script not being right as the reason another movie was not shot. He claimed the script had been written three times and failed, and there was no mention of any ongoing work on the project.

Comparisons with book

During the conversion to film, most of the characters were modified heavily. In the book, all the main characters, apart from Natalie, tend to act in self-interest and expect a large amount of credit whenever they do otherwise. While Natalie is the only child left out of the loop in the film, she is the first to find out in the novel. The divorce of Miranda and Daniel in the book is also much more bitter. The scene at dinner where Daniel becomes angry at Miranda's early arrival is present in the book but takes place prior to Daniel becoming Mrs Doubtfire, while the references to Miranda getting diseases and Lydia telling him to stop it are present in both the book and film. Daniel does not swear in that scene in the book although he is reluctant to let the kids leave straight away as in the movie.

Notes

[1] Awards for Mrs. Doubtfire (http://www.imdb.com/title/tt0107614/awards). Internet Movie Database. Retrieved 2010-11-12.
[2] *Shot on This Site*, William A. Gordon, Citadel, 1995, p.39.
[3] "Mrs. Doubtfire' Still the Champ" (http://articles.latimes.com/1994-02-01/entertainment/ca-17700_1_weekend-gross). *The Los Angeles Times*. . Retrieved 2010-10-26.
[4] "Mrs. Doubtfire Takes the Holiday" (http://articles.latimes.com/1994-01-04/entertainment/ca-8201_1_weekend-mrs-doubtfire). *The Los Angeles Times*. . Retrieved 2010-11-14.
[5] "Papa's Got A Brand New Drag" (http://www.newsweek.com/1993/11/28/papa-s-got-a-brand-new-drag.html). *Newsweek*. . Retrieved 2010-11-14.
[6] Review at Rotten Tomatoes (http://www.rottentomatoes.com/m/mrs_doubtfire/?name_order=asc)
[7] "Go behind the scenes with 'Mrs. Doubtfire'" (http://articles.latimes.com/2008/mar/03/entertainment/et-weekdvd3). *The Los Angeles Times*. Retrieved 2010-11-14.
[8] AFI's 100 Years...100 Songs Nominees (http://www.afi.com/Docs/100Years/songs400.pdf)
[9] http://www.worstpreviews.com/headline.php?id=1664&count=0
[10] Brunton, Richard (2006-12-05). "Williams says no Mrs Doubtfire 2" (http://www.filmstalker.co.uk/archives/2006/12/williams_says_no_mrs_doubtfire.html). Filmstalker. . Retrieved 2007-06-02.

External links

- *Mrs. Doubtfire* (http://www.imdb.com/title/tt0107614/) at the Internet Movie Database
- *Mrs. Doubtfire* (http://tcmdb.com/title/title.jsp?stid=84089) at the TCM Movie Database
- *Mrs. Doubtfire* (http://www.allrovi.com/movies/movie/v119900) at AllRovi
- *Mrs. Doubtfire* (http://www.boxofficemojo.com/movies/?id=mrsdoubtfire.htm) at Box Office Mojo
- Movie stills (http://film.virtual-history.com/film.php?filmid=4974)

Being Human (film)

Being Human	
Theatrical release poster	
Directed by	Bill Forsyth
Produced by	Robert F. Colesberry
Written by	Bill Forsyth
Narrated by	Theresa Russell
Starring	Robin Williams John Turturro Bill Nighy
Music by	Michael Gibbs
Cinematography	Michael Coulter
Editing by	Michael Ellis
Distributed by	Warner Bros.
Release date(s)	May 6, 1994
Running time	122 minutes
Country	United Kingdom Japan
Language	English Gaelic Friulian
Budget	$40,000,000
Box office	$1,519,366

Being Human is a 1994 comedy-drama film starring Robin Williams.

Plot

The film portrays the experience of a single human soul, portrayed by Williams, through various incarnations. Williams is the only common actor throughout the stories that span man's history on Earth.

An attempt on director-screenwriter Bill Forsyth's part to depict by visual means the ordinariness of life throughout the ages, *Being Human* is deliberately slow in its pace in order to emphasize how slow life often is. The structure is one of vignette-like character studies of one man (actually at least four distinct men, all with the same soul) who keeps making the same relationships and mistakes throughout his lifetimes.

In the first incarnation, which he appears to be an ancient Celt, his family is taken from him by raiders due to his cowardice and hesitation. Before his wife is taken away she says "Don't lose the children!" The next incarnation is in Ancient Rome in which he, Hector, is a slave to a "foolish master" who loses his fortune and is compelled to commit suicide by his debtors and orders Hector to join him. Hector longed to be free to find the children and wife he had before he became a slave but he has fallen in love with another slave and forgets his waiting family. The third incarnation he is a Scottish crusader on his way home to his children. The master from his life in Rome as a slave is now a crusader trying to decide to be a priest or not in this incarnation and they travel together until Hector finds his soul mate from the life in Rome. She is a widow in this incarnation and wishes Hector to join her family but his duties to the children in Scotland pull at him. In his fourth incarnation, Hector is finally forced to confront his capacity for cowardly indecision that recurs in his lives. He is a Portuguese man in the renaissance shipwrecked on the coast of Africa. He is the master in this life, his wife from the first incarnation is shipwrecked with him as his spurned lover and the raider who spirited her away is her steadfast friend. In the fifth incarnation he is a modern man in New York paying the consequences of cowardly indecision and gaining the strength to address the children he lost lifetimes ago. He is joined in this life by his master/slave/friend, soul mate, and former wife/lover and her husband/raider from life times past support him but are people who are trying to find their own way through in this life just as in the past lives.

Production

After poor test screenings, Warner Bros. instructed Bill Forsyth to trim 40 minutes from the film, as well as add narration and a happy ending. Forsyth subsequently disowned the film.

Cast

- Hector: Robin Williams.
- Lucinnius: John Turturro.
- Julian: Bill Nighy.
- The Priest: Vincent D'Onofrio.
- The Pre-Historic Shaman: Robert Carlyle.
- Hermes: Simon McBurney.
- Dom Paulo: Hector Elizondo.
- Boris: William H. Macy.
- Beatrice: Anna Galiena.
- Francisco: Jonathan Hyde.
- The Storyteller: Theresa Russell.
- Alvarez: Ewan McGregor

References

External links

- *Being Human* (http://www.imdb.com/title/tt0106379/) at the Internet Movie Database
- *Being Human* (http://www.boxofficemojo.com/movies/?id=beinghuman.htm) at Box Office Mojo

In Search of Dr. Seuss

In Search of Dr. Seuss	
Directed by	Vincent Paterson
Produced by	Keith R. Clarke Joni Levin Thomas A. Walsh
Written by	Keith R. Clarke
Starring	Kathy Najimy Matt Frewer Christopher Lloyd Graham Jarvis Brady Bluhm
Music by	Steve Goldstein
Cinematography	Michael Lonzo
Editing by	Michael Kelly
Distributed by	TNT Warner Home Video
Release date(s)	November 6, 1994
Running time	90 min.
Country	USA
Language	English

In Search of Dr. Seuss is a feature film chronicling the adventures of a news reporter (Kathy Najimy) who enters the world of Dr. Seuss by opening a magical book. It came to DVD in 2003 and again in 2008 as a bonus feature for the TV movie *Horton Hears a Who!*.

Plot

A reporter named Kathy Lane comes to Theodor Geisel's home in order to do a report on the famous Dr. Seuss, where she meets a strange character. When Kathy asks to use him as a source, he reveals himself to be the Cat in the Hat. Curiosity allows her to open a magical book labeled "Open a book, open your imagination", which takes her on an amazing adventure through the world of Dr. Seuss. As she explores the house, she takes part in some of Dr. Seuss's well-known stories. She also learns a lot about Theodor Geisel's life.

Cast

- Kathy Najimy as Kathy
- Matt Frewer as The Cat in the Hat
- Robin Williams as Father
- Christopher Lloyd as Mr. Hunch
- Graham Jarvis as The Farmer
- Brady Bluhm as Marco
- Paul Winchell voiced some of the Sneetches
- Frank Welker dubbed the voices of Horton, Maysie, the elephant bird, Grandfather Yook, Chief Yookeroo, and VanItch

- David Paymer as Ad Man
- Andrea Martin as Ad Woman
- J. D. Daniels as Marco
- Patrick Stewart as Sgt. Mulvaney
- Eileen Brennan as Who-Villain
- Andraé Crouch as Yertle The Turtle
- Bright Eyes as Mack
- Billy Crystal as Radio Voice (The Voice of America)
- Howie Mandel as Sam I Am Voice-Over
- Zelda Williams as Daughter
- Terry Lindholm as Once-ler
- Bob Holt voiced the Once-ler, the Lorax, Sylvester McMonkey McBean, and some of The Sneetches
- Eleanor Columbus as Daughter

Stories featured

The movie features many of Dr. Seuss's stories, though they are edits of older adaptations, while some of the adaptations are newly created live-action versions. It also includes some of his political work, including excerpts of his short subject *Hitler Lives*.

- *The Sneetches* (originally from DePatie-Freleng Enterprises's special, *Dr. Seuss on the Loose* and was edited; 1973)
- *Hunches in Bunches* (live-action)
- *McElligot's Pool* (live-action)
- *Horton Hatches the Egg* (originally created by Warner Bros. in 1942 and directed by Bob Clampett; this cartoon is not only edited, but re-dubbed by Frank Welker)
- *And to Think That I Saw It on Mulberry Street* (originally created by George Pal in 1944; and the story is re-told by J. D. Daniels)
- *Yertle the Turtle* (live-action)
- *The Cat in the Hat* (live-action)
- *Green Eggs and Ham* (live-action)
- *How the Grinch Stole Christmas!* (originally the famous Chuck Jones television special created in 1966; this cartoon is not only edited, but the story is re-told by Eileen Brennan, while Boris Karloff and June Foray remain their voices of The Grinch and Cindy Lou Who.)
- *The Lorax* (originally created by DePatie-Freleng Enterprises in 1972; the present day scenes of the Once-ler are re-created in live-action.)
- *The Butter Battle Book* (originally created by Ralph Bakshi in 1989; some of the verses that weren't in the special, or weren't said the correct way for the telling of the book, are added in this version and voiced by Frank Welker.)
- *Oh, the Places You'll Go!* (live-action)

References

External links

- *In Search of Dr. Seuss* (http://www.imdb.com/title/tt0110121/) at the Internet Movie Database

Jumanji

Jumanji	
Theatrical release poster	
Directed by	Joe Johnston
Produced by	Robert W. Cort Ted Field Larry J. Franco
Screenplay by	Greg Taylor Jonathan Hensleigh Jim Strain
Based on	*Jumanji* by Chris Van Allsburg
Starring	Robin Williams Bonnie Hunt Kirsten Dunst Bradley Pierce David Alan Grier Jonathan Hyde Bebe Neuwirth Adam Hann-Byrd Laura Bell Bundy
Music by	James Horner
Cinematography	Thomas Ackerman
Editing by	Robert Dalva
Studio	Interscope Communications Teitler Film
Distributed by	TriStar Pictures
Release date(s)	December 15, 1995
Running time	104 minutes
Country	United States
Language	English
Budget	$65 million
Box office	$262,797,249

Jumanji is a 1995 American fantasy–comedy film about a supernatural board game that makes wild animals and other jungle hazards materialize upon each player's move. It was directed by Joe Johnston and is based on Chris Van Allsburg's popular 1981 picture book of the same name.[1] Industrial Light & Magic provided computer graphics and animatronics for the special effects.

The film stars Robin Williams as Alan, a man who emerges from the game's unseen jungle world, along with Kirsten Dunst as a girl who plays the game with her brother, David Alan Grier as a hapless shoemaker-turned-police officer, Adam Hann-Byrd as Alan when he was a boy, Bonnie Hunt as the woman who played the game with Alan when they were children, and Jonathan Hyde in a dual role as both Alan's father and a hunter intent on killing Alan. The cast also features Bradley Pierce as the girl's brother and Bebe Neuwirth as her aunt. It was shot in Keene, New

Hampshire, where the story is set, North Berwick, Maine (the Parrish Shoes factory) and Vancouver, British Columbia.

Plot

In 1869, two boys bury a chest containing something dangerous and terrifying in the woods near Brantford, New Hampshire. When one of them asks if someone digs it up, the other replies "May God have mercy on his soul". The sound of tribal drums is heard as the boys ride away. A century later, 12-year-old Alan Parrish (Adam Hann-Byrd) flees on his bicycle from a gang of bullies, then runs into the shoe factory owned by his father, Sam (Jonathan Hyde), where he meets his friend Carl Bentley (David Alan Grier), one of Sam's employees. When Alan accidentally damages a machine and ruins a new design for a shoe, Carl accepts the blame and loses his job. Outside the factory, after the bullies beat him up and steal his bike, Alan follows the sound of tribal drumbeats to a construction site and finds a buried chest, which contains a board game called "Jumanji".

Alan takes the game home and has an argument with Sam, who insists on sending him to a boarding school. Alan prepares to run away from home, but his friend Sarah Whittle (Laura Bell Bundy), who is the lead bully's ex-girlfriend, arrives with Alan's bicycle. Alan and Sarah begin a game of Jumanji, which acts strangely: When a player rolls the dice, the player's piece moves itself and a message appears on the board. When Alan makes his first move, a vortex sucks him into the board and traps him in an unseen jungle. He will be freed when a player rolls a five or an eight, but Sarah quits the game after being attacked by African bats.

Twenty-six years later, eight year old Judy and four year old Peter Shepherd (Kirsten Dunst and Bradley Pierce) move into the Parrish house with their aunt Nora (Bebe Neuwirth) after losing their parents in an accident. By this time, it has been rumored that Alan was murdered by his father, hacked to pieces and hidden inside the walls of the house which is now believes to be haunted. Judy and Peter hear Jumanji's drumbeats and find the game in the attic. When they begin playing, they are attacked by giant mosquitoes and crazed monkeys. The instructions say things will return to normal when someone wins, so they proceed. Peter rolls a five, releasing both a lion and Alan (Robin Williams), who is now an adult. Alan locks the lion in a bedroom, then goes to the shoe factory, which is now shut down. On the way, he meets Carl, who works unhappily as a police officer, and discovers that the town's economy was devastated by the factory's closure. In the factory, a man reveals that Sam had abandoned the business to search for his son until his death in 1991.

When rolling the dice has no effect on the board, Alan realizes they are continuing the game he and Sarah started in 1969. The next move is Sarah's. They find Sarah (Bonnie Hunt) at home, a reclusive outcast traumatized by the game and its aftermath. Alan tricks her into rejoining the game, and the following moves release man-eating vines from a giant flower, a hunter named Van Pelt (Jonathan Hyde), a stampede of rhinos, elephants and zebras, and a pelican that steals the game. Increasingly reckless havoc ensues throughout the town. Among other things, Peter turns into a monkey after trying to cheat; Peter, Sarah and Judy battle Van Pelt in a local department store; a monsoon floods the house and a crocodile attack; an earthquake breaks the house in two, Alan is sucked into the floor by quicksand, and Judy is shot in the neck by a poisonous barb from a plant. Finally, Alan wins the game just in time when Van Pelt is about to shoot him. Van Pelt and the other jungle elements are sucked back into the board.

With the game over, Alan and Sarah find themselves as children in 1969 again, but they both remember the game. Alan admits his guilt to his father for damaging the shoe, Carl gets his job back, and Sam allows Alan to attend a local school. Alan and Sarah throw the Jumanji board into a river where Sarah and Alan kiss before leaving.

Twenty-six years later, Alan's and Sarah's knowledge of their experiences during the game has changed the future for the better: Alan and Sarah are now happily married and expecting a child, Alan has taken over the shoe business, Carl still works there and Alan's father is still alive. When Judy, Peter, and their parents meet with Alan and Sarah at a Christmas party, they offer Judy and Peter's father a job in the shoe company and frantically discourage the parents from going on a skiing trip that would eventually lead to their deaths.

Sometime later, two French-speaking girls hear drumbeats as they walk along a beach, where the Jumanji board is half buried in the sand.

Cast

- Robin Williams as Alan Parrish
  - Adam Hann-Byrd as young Alan Parrish
- Bonnie Hunt as Sarah Whittle
  - Laura Bell Bundy as young Sarah Whittle
- Kirsten Dunst as Judy Shepherd
- Bradley Pierce as Peter Shepherd
- David Alan Grier as Carl Bentley
- Bebe Neuwirth as Nora Shepherd
- Jonathan Hyde as Sam Parrish/Van Pelt
- Patricia Clarkson as Carol-Anne Parrish
- James Handy as Exterminator

Soundtrack

Jumanji: Complete Motion Picture Score	
Film score (Digital download)/Audio CD by James Horner	
Released	November 21, 1995
Length	51:04
Label	Epic Soundtrax

All music composed by James Horner.

Track listing		
No.	**Title**	**Length**
1.	"Prologue And Main TItle"	3:42
2.	"First Move"	2:20
3.	"Monkey Mayhem"	4:42
4.	"A New World"	2:40
5.	""It's Sarah's Move""	2:36
6.	"The Hunter"	1:56
7.	"Rampage Through Town"	2:28
8.	"Alan Parrish"	4:18
9.	"Stampede!"	2:12
10.	"A Pelican Steals The Game"	1:40
11.	"The Monsoon"	4:48
12.	""Jumanji""	11:47
13.	"End Titles"	5:55
Total length:		**51:04**

Commercial songs from film, but not on soundtrack

- *Una Voce Poco Fa*
  - Written by Gioacchino Rossini
  - Performed by Agnes Baltsa and the Vienna Symphony
  - Orchestra and Chorus conducted by Ian Marin
- *Night & Day*
  - Written by Cole Porter
- *Serenade in D, Op. 44*
  - Composed by Antonin Dvořák
  - Performed by Academy of St. Martin-in-the-Fields
  - Conducted by Neville Marriner
- *Locomotive Breath*
  - Written by Ian Anderson
  - Performed by Jethro Tull
- *The Ballad of Gilligan's Isle (Theme from Gilligan's Island)*
  - Written by Sherwood Schwartz & George Wyle

Reception

Jumanji did well in the box office; it took in $100,475,249 in the United States and Canada and $162,322,000 overseas, totaling to $262,797,249.[2] [3] The film earned mixed reviews from critics, with review aggregator Rotten Tomatoes reporting that 47% of 30 professional critics have given the film a positive review, with a rating average of 5.6 out of 10.[4] Metacritic posts an average rating of 39%, based on 18 reviews.[5]

Legacy

- The Jumanji animated series ran from 1996 through 1999. In 1996 it was carried by the UPN network, but later seasons were syndicated by BKN. While it followed the film's plot, there were a few changes, such as the exclusion of Bonnie Hunt's character and some changes to the age and relationship of David Alan Grier's character. On each turn, the player was given a "game clue" and then sucked into the jungle until they solved their clue. Alan Parrish (Robin Williams' character) had missed his clue and was continually searching for it in order to escape the board game. At the end, the kids ultimately succeed in helping to free him from the game by finding out what his clue was.
- Milton Bradley released a Jumanji board game that was equipped with not only the game clues from the film, but also some new ones. The elephant, zebras, pelican, crocodile, man-eating pod, and barb-shooting plants have their own clues. The board game has a doomsday grid where a card would go if the other players don't roll the required rescue item in time. If the grid fills up, the game will end if a card lands on this space: "A card placed here brings dreadful news: The game is done, all players lose."
- *Zathura* is a spiritual sequel that was based on one of the author's later children's books of the same name.
- For several years after Jumanji was filmed, tire marks from the car crash into the "Sav-a-lot" could be seen on the ground in the Liquidation World in Tsawwassen, BC, until the building was subsequently demolished for a new development. They served as a constant reminder for Tsawwassen residents about the hype the filming of the movie meant to the town.
- In 2007, Fuji Trading Co., Ltd. produced an exclusive Pachinko amusement-game only released in Japan. Most of the characters had Anime looks in the game, along with unique 3D-Anime designs and it featured many pictures & clips from the movie. There are several various missions and mini games that can be played throughout the

game.

- Additionally, a party video game based on the film was made.
- The late South African musician "Umanji" Maruti Johannes Nkuna got his nickname after watching Jumanji with some friends.
- Keene, New Hampshire still has a sign from Parrish Shoes in their downtown area.
- The *Alavudeente Albhuthavilakku* TV series running on Asianet, has a story arc based on Juamanji.
- The film is dedicated to the memory of Stephen L. Price, an ILM visual effects supervisor who was involved with it.

Clues from the game

- *At night they fly, you'd better run. These winged things are not much fun* (Rolled by Sarah in 1969). —said to be African fruit bats, but portrayed as smaller, common bats.
- *In the jungle you must wait until the dice read five or eight* (Rolled by Alan in 1969). —The player (Alan) is sucked into the game board and trapped in an unseen jungle until a player rolls either 5 or 8.
- *A tiny bite can make you itch, make you sneeze, make you twitch* (Rolled by Judy). —Giant mosquitoes.
- *This will not be an easy mission. Monkeys slow the expedition* (Rolled by Peter). —Spider monkeys, portrayed in the film as small chimp-like monkeys.
- *His fangs are sharp, he likes your taste. Your party better move poste-haste* (Rolled by Peter from a 5). —An African lion. This is also the roll that frees Alan from the game.
- *They grow much faster than bamboo. Take care or they'll come after you* (Rolled by Sarah). —Crawling, man-eating vines.
- *A hunter from the darkest wild makes you feel just like a child* (Rolled by Alan). —Van Pelt.
- *Don't be fooled, it isn't thunder. Staying put would be a blunder* (Rolled by Judy). —A stampede of rhinos, elephants, zebras, and pelicans.
- *A law of Jumanji having been broken, you'll be set back even more than your token* (Rolled by Peter). —As a penalty for cheating (Peter tried to drop the dice so they would land on 12), the player (Peter) gradually turns into a monkey. "Set back" refers to devolution.
- *Every month at the quarter moon, there'll be a monsoon in your lagoon* (Rolled by Sarah). —A monsoon and a crocodile.
- *Beware the ground on which you stand. The floor is quicker than the sand* (Rolled by Alan). —The floor beneath the player (Alan) becomes quicksand which traps him.
- *There is a lesson you will learn. Sometimes you must go back a turn* (Rolled by Judy). —The effects of the previous move (quicksand) are undone, causing it to harden.
- *Need a hand? Well you just wait. We'll help you out, we each have eight* (Rolled by Peter) —Large spiders.
- *You're almost there with much at stake, but now the ground begins to quake* (Rolled by Sarah) —An earthquake.
- *Jumanji* (Rolled by Alan) -The final spot on the board. The adventure to reach Jumanji and call out its name wins. This reverses all effects of the game and returns all aspects into the board from where it came. Also the time returns to when it was played, which is 1969.

References

[1] "Jumanji Author Getting Aboard Hollywood Express : Movies: Chris Van Allsburg says the film version of his book is like a Christmas gift. It's just not the one he was expecting." (http://articles.latimes.com/1995-12-12/entertainment/ca-13163_1_van-allsburg). *The Los Angeles Times*. . Retrieved 2010-12-23.
[2] "Field Marshal" (http://www.newsweek.com/1997/02/09/field-marshal.html). *Newsweek*. . Retrieved 2010-12-22.
[3] "Jumanji (1995)" (http://www.boxofficemojo.com/movies/?id=jumanji.htm). Box Office Mojo. . Retrieved 2009-07-03.
[4] "Jumanji" (http://www.rottentomatoes.com/m/1068044-jumanji/?name_order=asc). *Rotten Tomatoes*. .
[5] "Jumanji" (http://www.metacritic.com/video/titles/jumanji?q=Jumanji). *Metacritic*. .

External links

- *Jumanji* (http://www.imdb.com/title/tt0113497/) at the Internet Movie Database
- *Jumanji* (http://www.boxofficemojo.com/movies/?id=jumanji.htm) at Box Office Mojo
- *Jumanji* (http://www.rottentomatoes.com/m/1068044/) at Rotten Tomatoes

Nickelodeon Kids' Choice Awards

Nickelodeon Kids' Choice Awards	
2011 Kids' Choice Awards	
 The Jonas Brothers performing at the 2009 show	
Presented by	Nickelodeon
Country	United States
Reward	KCA Blimp
First awarded	April 18, 1988
Official website	[1]
Television coverage	
Network	Nickelodeon
Runtime	Approx. 90-120 min. including commercials

The **Nickelodeon Kids' Choice Awards**, also known as the **KCAs** or **Kids Choice Awards**, is an annual awards show that airs on the Nickelodeon cable channel, which airs live and is usually held and telecast live (though with a three-hour time delay for those watching in the Pacific Time Zone or on the Nick 2 feed on digital cable that simulcasts the Pacific time zone feed) on a Saturday night in late March or early April, that honors the year's biggest television, movie, and music acts, as voted by Nickelodeon viewers. Winners receive a hollow orange blimp figurine, a logo outline for much of the network's 1984-2009 era, which also functions as a kaleidoscope.[2]

The show features numerous celebrity guests and musical acts. In recent years, slime stunts have been incorporated into the show. The KCAs also host live entertainment. It has also been known to overwhelmingly cover people with the network's trademark green slime. SpongeBob SquarePants has won the most KCA awards (8), followed by Will Smith (7), Miley Cyrus (6), Britney Spears (5) and Hilary Duff (4).[3] Whoopi Goldberg is the only person to have won a Kids' Choice Award, an Emmy, a Grammy, an Oscar, and a Tony. Rosie O'Donnell (8) and Jack Black (3) have hosted the most KCAs.

History

Alan Goodman, Albie Hecht and Fred Seibert started the awards show as *The Big Ballot*[4] [5] [6] [7] [8] in 1986, named for the ballots kids voted with. To vote, the viewers would send in ballots and then before the show, the ballots would be counted and the winners would tape a thank you video that would be shown during the program.

The award was configured into the current blimp shape/kaleidoscope in 1990. The only change to the award since that time has been to change the embossed logotype on the side of the trophy for 2010 to fit the network's new logo typeface.

As the Internet came into widespread use, the voting eventually moved from a combination of 900 number telephone voting and ballots either mailed or completed at Pizza Hut locations, to moving exclusively online to the network's website and by 2007, text messaging. Early years of Internet voting had the early adoption complications of ballot stuffing and even adults voting before a new system where only one vote per Nick.com account became the procedure for voting on the awards (although it is probable adults still cast votes via the texting option, which is connected to a phone number only rather than a screenname, or by creating an account with a false age or having their children vote for a chosen subject instead). In 2010, an iPhone application and mobile browser voting was also added.[9]

The 2009 KCAs featured a new award called "The Big Green Help Award" which goes to the celebrity who goes above and beyond to help the Earth. The inaugural award was presented to Leonardo DiCaprio. For the 2010 awards, the "The Big Green Help" award was renamed "The Big Help" award, with First Lady Michelle Obama winning the first award under the rename.

Unlike traditional awards shows, the Kids' Choice Awards uses other items to announce an award winner rather than a traditional envelope. The show sometimes uses balloons, T-shirts, models, giant letters, stickers (1999, where Amanda put a "Kick Me!" sticky on the model's back and somebody else put a sticker showing the winner's name). and even a foot (2008). In contrast to the trend of declining ratings for awards shows, the Kids' Choice Awards has gone from strength to strength, setting new ratings records each of the past four years (2005–2009).

Voting for Canadians became available for the 2010 ceremony with the inauguration of Nickelodeon Canada in November 2009.

In June 2011, Nickelodeon Latin America announced a Kids' Choice Awards for Mexico.[10] Other countries with their own Kids' Choice Awards: Brazil, United Kingdom, Australia, and Indonesia.

Awards

This table shows the awards from the past.

	1980s		1990s										2000s										2010s	
	1988	1989	1990	1991	1992	1993	1994	1995	1996	1997	1998	1999	2000	2001	2002	2003	2004	2005	2006	2007	2008	2009	2010	2011
Favorite Movie	Yes	Yes	Yes	Yes	No	No	No	Yes	Yes	Yes	Yes	Yes	Yes	Yes	Yes	Yes	Yes	Yes	Yes	Yes	Yes	Yes	Yes	Yes
Favorite Movie Actor	Yes	Yes	Yes	Yes	No	Yes	No	Yes	Yes	Yes	Yes	Yes	Yes	Yes	Yes	Yes	Yes	Yes	Yes	Yes	Yes	Yes	Yes	Yes
Favorite Movie Actress	Yes	Yes	Yes	Yes	Yes	Yes	No	Yes	Yes	Yes	Yes	Yes	Yes	Yes	Yes	Yes	Yes	Yes	Yes	Yes	Yes	Yes	Yes	Yes
Favorite TV Show	Yes	Yes	Yes	Yes	Yes	Yes	Yes	Yes	Yes	Yes	Yes	Yes	Yes	Yes	Yes	Yes	Yes	Yes	Yes	Yes	Yes	Yes	Yes	Yes

Favorite TV Actor	No	Yes	Yes	Yes	Yes	Yes	Yes	Yes	Yes	Yes	Yes	Yes	Yes	Yes	Yes	Yes	Yes	Yes	Yes	Yes	Yes	Yes	Yes	Yes
Favorite TV Actress	No	Yes	Yes	Yes	Yes	No	Yes	Yes	Yes	Yes	Yes	Yes	Yes	Yes	Yes	Yes	Yes	Yes	Yes	Yes	Yes	Yes	Yes	Yes
Favorite Music Group	No	No	No	No	No	No	No	No	No	Yes	No	Yes	Yes	Yes	Yes	Yes	Yes	Yes	Yes	Yes	Yes	Yes	Yes	Yes
Favorite Male Athlete	No	Yes	No	Yes	No	No	No	No	No	No	No	Yes	Yes	No	No	Yes	Yes	Yes	Yes	Yes	Yes	Yes	Yes	Yes
Favorite Female Athlete	No	Yes	No	No	No	No	No	No	No	No	No	Yes	Yes	No	No	Yes	Yes	Yes	Yes	Yes	Yes	Yes	Yes	Yes
Favorite Video Game	No	No	No	No	No	No	No	Yes	Yes	Yes	Yes	Yes	Yes	Yes	Yes	Yes	Yes	Yes	Yes	Yes	Yes	Yes	Yes	Yes
Favorite Sports Team	No	Yes	No	No	No	Yes	No	No	No	No	No	Yes	Yes	No	Yes	Yes	Yes	No	No	No	No	No	No	No
Hall of Fame Award	No	No	No	Yes	Yes	Yes	Yes	Yes	Yes	Yes	Yes	Yes	Yes	No	No	No	No	No	No	No	No	No	No	No
Wannabe Award	No	No	No	No	No	No	No	No	No	No	No	No	No	Yes	Yes	Yes	Yes	Yes	Yes	Yes	Yes	No	No	No
Big Help/Big Green Help Award	No	No	No	No	No	No	No	No	No	No	No	No	No	No	No	No	No	No	No	No	No	Yes	Yes	Yes
Favorite Animal Star	Yes	No	No	No	No	Yes	Yes	Yes	Yes	Yes	No	Yes	Yes	No	No	Yes	No	No	No	No	No	No	No	No
Cutest Couple	No	No	No	No	No	No	No	No	No	No	No	No	No	No	No	No	No	No	No	No	No	No	Yes	No
Favorite Book	No	No	No	No	No	No	No	No	No	No	Yes	Yes	Yes	No	Yes	Yes	Yes	Yes	Yes	Yes	Yes	Yes	Yes	Yes
Favorite Reality Show	No	No	No	No	No	No	No	No	No	No	No	No	No	No	No	No	No	No	No	No	No	Yes	Yes	Yes
Favorite TV Sidekick	No	No	No	No	No	No	No	No	No	No	No	No	No	No	No	No	No	No	No	No	No	No	No	Yes
Favorite Cartoon	Yes	Yes	No	Yes	No	Yes	Yes	Yes	Yes	Yes	Yes	Yes	Yes	Yes	Yes	Yes	Yes	Yes	Yes	Yes	Yes	Yes	Yes	Yes
Favorite Animated Movie	No	No	No	No	No	No	No	No	No	No	No	No	No	No	No	No	No	Yes	Yes	Yes	Yes	Yes	Yes	Yes

Favorite Voice from an Animated Movie	No	No	No	No	No	No	No	No	No	No	No	No	Yes	Yes	Yes	Yes	Yes	Yes	Yes	Yes	Yes	Yes	Yes	Yes
Favorite Buttkicker	No	No	No	No	No	No	No	No	No	No	No	No	No	No	Yes	Yes	No	No	No	No	No	No	No	Yes
Favorite Male Singer	No	No	No	No	No	No	No	No	No	No	No	No	Yes	Yes	Yes	Yes	Yes	Yes	Yes	Yes	Yes	Yes	Yes	Yes
Favorite Female Singer	No	No	No	No	No	No	No	No	No	No	No	No	Yes	Yes	Yes	Yes	Yes	Yes	Yes	Yes	Yes	Yes	Yes	Yes
Favorite Song	Yes	No	No	No	No	No	No	No	No	Yes	No	Yes	Yes	Yes	Yes	Yes	Yes	Yes	Yes	Yes	Yes	Yes	Yes	Yes

Locations

The Kids' Choice Awards are typically held in Los Angeles, California. They have been held at the Barker Hangar in Santa Monica, California, the Hollywood Bowl, the Grand Olympic Auditorium in Los Angeles, and Universal Studios in Universal City, California, but mostly at Pauley Pavilion on the UCLA campus. Due to renovations at Pauley, in 2011, the show was held at the Galen Center at USC on April 2.[11]

Finishing up with the "Orange Carpet" for the Kids' Choice Awards outside of Pauley Pavilion, UCLA campus

Timeslot and use to launch new series

Typically the program airs for 90 minutes from 8:00 PM (ET/PT) to 9:30 PM. Since 1996, either a high-profile program or series premiere takes place after the KCA broadcast (9:30 PM (ET/PT)), the network's equivalent to the post-Super Bowl time slot. Both *SpongeBob SquarePants* and *Victorious* are the only series to air on this timeslot twice. *Victorious* is the only series to air on this timeslot for two consecutive years.

The following are list of programs that have aired at this timeslot:

Year	Program
1996	*All That* (rerun)
1997	*The Angry Beavers* (series premiere)
1998	*CatDog* (series premiere)
1999	*SpongeBob SquarePants* (series premiere)
2000	*Caitlin's Way* (new episode)
2001	*The Brothers García* (new episode)
2002	*The Nick Cannon Show* (new episode)
2003	*All Grown Up!* (series premiere)
2004	*Danny Phantom* (series premiere)
2005	*Drake & Josh* (season premiere)
2006	*Romeo!* (season premiere)
2007	*SpongeBob SquarePants* (season premiere)
2008	*Dance on Sunset* (series premiere)
2009	*The Penguins of Madagascar* (new episode)
2010	*Victorious* (series premiere)
2011	*Victorious* (season premiere)

Hosts

There was no host in 1987 because by this time, it was The Big Ballot.

Year	Host(s)
1988[12]	Tony Danza Debbie Gibson Brian Robbins Dan Schneider
1989[13]	Nicole Eggert Wil Wheaton[14]
1990[15]	Dave Coulier Candace Cameron[16] David Faustino
1991[17]	Corin Nemec
1992[18]	Paula Abdul
1993	Brian Austin Green Holly Robinson Tori Spelling[19]
1994	Joey Lawrence Candace Cameron[20] Marc Weiner

1995	Whitney Houston Rick Adams
1996	Whitney Houston Rosie O' Donnell
1997	Rosie O' Donnell
1998	Rosie O' Donnell
1999[21]	Rosie O' Donnell
2000[22]	Rosie O' Donnell David Arquette LL Cool J Mandy Moore Frankie Muniz
2001[23]	Rosie O' Donnell
2002[24]	Rosie O' Donnell
2003[25]	Rosie O' Donnell
2004[26]	Cameron Diaz Mike Myers
2005[27]	Ben Stiller
2006[28]	Jack Black
2007[29]	Justin Timberlake
2008[30]	Jack Black
2009[31] [32]	Dwayne Johnson
2010[32] [33]	Kevin James[34]
2011[35]	Jack Black[36]

Hosts after 2003

After Rosie O' Donnell's final show as host in 2003, Nickelodeon started picking other celebrities to host, mainly based on child appeal and upcoming film projects targeted at a younger audience. Mike Myers and Cameron Diaz hosted the show in 2004, coinciding with their upcoming film, *Shrek 2*. In 2005, Ben Stiller was the host, as *Madagascar* was released a month later. Justin Timberlake hosted in 2007 to promote *Shrek the Third*. In 2006, Jack Black hosted the show to promote *Nacho Libre* and once again in 2008 to tie in with *Kung Fu Panda*, then in 2011 for the latter film's sequel. Dwayne Johnson hosted the 2009 ceremony, ahead of the release of *Race to Witch Mountain*. Kevin James hosted the 2010 show to promote *Grown Ups*.

To host twice or more

Jack Black hosted in 2006, 2008, and the 2011 shows and so far the first host after Rosie O'Donnell to host the show at least twice. Candace Cameron and Whitney Houston were the first hosts before O'Donnell to host at least twice (Cameron 1990 and 1994, Houston 1995 and 1996).

Special colored awards

These blimps are not orange like the regular blimps and the winners are chosen by the Nickelodeon staff. There is the gold Hall of Fame Award (1991–2000), the silver Wannabe Award (2001–2008), the green Big Green Help Award (2009) and the silver glitter Big Help Award (2010–present). The blimps sported a new Nickelodeon logo, which was shown to viewers late 2009.

The Hall of Fame Award

The Hall of Fame Award (a gold version of the Blimp award) was presented to those whose accomplishments, fame and popularity set them above everyone else. Initially, the award was chosen by the kids from a slate of nominees. Actors, athletes and singers were all eligible for the award, with ballots containing nominees from multiple categories.

Hall of Fame Award winners

Year	Winner(s)
1991	Paula Abdul
1992	Arnold Schwarzenegger
1993	Robin Williams
1994	Boyz II Men
1995	Whitney Houston
1996	Tim Allen
1997	Will Smith
1998	Tia & Tamera Mowry
1999	Jonathan Taylor Thomas
2000	Rosie O'Donnell

The Wannabe Award

The Wannabe Award (a silver version of the Blimp award) is presented to the best celebrity role model or inspiration (or the person whom the kids ***want to be*** like). The winner is determined prior to the awards, and is not voted upon by the kids. As of 2009, the only person to have won the Wannabe award and the Hall of Fame award is Will Smith. These awards replaced the Hall of Fame awards following the show in 2000.

Wannabe Award winners

Year	Winner
2001	Tom Cruise
2002	Janet Jackson
2003	Will Smith
2004	Adam Sandler
2005	Queen Latifah
2006	Chris Rock
2007	Ben Stiller
2008	Cameron Diaz

The Big Help Award

The Big Green Help (The Big Help) Award (a green version of the Blimp award) is presented to the celebrity who goes above and beyond to help the environment. This blimp was first featured on a KCA update promo with Lily Collins announcing the new award.[37] Originally, Cameron Diaz's award was supposed to be a Big Green Help award because she was to have received hers for helping the environment. Instead it was postponed until the following year when this award replaced it and Diaz presented the first award to Leonardo DiCaprio.

Big Green Help (The Big Help) Award winners

Year	Winner
2009	Leonardo Dicaprio
2010	Michelle Obama, First Lady
2011	Justin Timberlake

Slimed celebrities

During a Kids' Choice Awards, sometimes a celebrity might not know when they are going to be slimed onstage or offstage. Hosts have also been slimed, mostly in the finale of the show. Below is a list of all the celebrities that have been slimed over the past years at the Kids' Choice Awards. It does not mention any celebrities in 1992 because the audience was slimed instead. Regardless, "Sliming Is An Honor" and never used as a penalty.

The final slime at the 2010 Kids' Choice Awards

Year	Slimed Celebrity (ies)
1988	Les Lye
1989	Bill Kirchenbauer
1990	Dave Coulier Wil Wheaton
1991	Corin Nemec Bart Simpson
1993	Jonathan Taylor Thomas Zachary Ty Bryan Taran Noah Smith
1994	James Earl Jones
1995	Mark Curry
1996	Queen Latifah
1997	Rosie O'Donnell
1998	Sean "Diddy" Combs
1999	Randy Savage Chilli
2000	Will Smith
2001	Tom Cruise *NSYNC Melissa Joan Hart Rosie O'Donnell
2002	Adam Sandler Pink Ashanti
2003	Jim Carrey Rosie O'Donnell
2004	Mike Myers Mary-Kate & Ashley Olsen
2005	Will Ferrell Johnny Depp Ben Stiller
2006	Robin Williams Jack Black
2007	Chris Tucker Jackie Chan Mandy Moore Nicole Kidman Steve Carell Tobey Maguire Vince Vaughn Justin Timberlake
2008	Orlando Bloom Brendan Fraser Harrison Ford Jack Black

2009	Jesse McCartney Hugh Jackman Sandra Bullock Dwayne "The Rock" Johnson Jonas Brothers
2010	Jackson Rathbone Jerry Trainor Katy Perry Fred Figglehorn Tina Fey Steve Carell Kevin James
2011	Russell Brand Rico Rodriguez Snoop Dogg Kaley Cuoco Heidi Klum Jason Segel Josh Duhamel Jim Carrey Jack Black

Slime stunts

Started in 2002, the show began its annual ***World Record Slime Stunts***. Olympians, extreme sports superstars and daredevils participate in special stunts performed live on national television—often involving landing into the trademark green slime.

Year	Celebrity (ies)	Stunt synopsis
2002	Dave Mirra	The BMX pro-biker broke his own record for a double back flip on a BMX bike and landed in a 5,000 gallon tank of green slime.
2003	Tony Hawk	The skateboarding champion skateboarded into an 11,000 gallon tank of green slime.
2004	Mat Hoffman	The BMX pro performed the "World Record Skydiving Bike Jump" landing in a lakefull of green slime.
2005	Donald Trump	The billionaire at the time enjoying a resurgence of popularity with his TV series *The Apprentice* "fired" a human cannonball into the air, landing in a net laced with green slime.
2006	Ryan St. Onge	In a live remote from the Utah Olympic Park in Park City, Utah, the U.S. Olympic Freestyle Aerial Skier skied into 10,000 gallons of green slime.
2007	Ron Jones	Bungee jumping into a pool of slime.

2008	Jack Black Orlando Bloom	*Kids Choice 2008* had many slime stunts all hosted by professional boxer Laila Ali. Depending on the outcome of the stunt, a certain amount of green slime was added to a slime vat backstage which was called throughout as the "Slime Meter". The slime was used later on at the end of the show, in supposedly the "World's Longest Celebrity Sliming," in which Orlando Bloom joined host Jack Black to be slimed for one solid minute. Host Black even remarked about how 27 tons of slime (the grand total) could fit in a vat that only held 25 tons.
	Akon	In the first stunt, affectionately called the "Slime-o-Lition Derby", the pop star had 45 seconds to ride the Kids' Choice Bobble Head Kart. The choices were the shark-themed "Jaws Jalopy", a hot dog-shaped "Weiner Wagon" and the winner, the Jack Black Bobble Head Kart which was essentially a go-kart with a giant Jack Black head on the top. Akon successfully completed the course adding 10 tons of slime to the vat, "plus 5 for finishing" bringing the total to 15 tons.
	Usher	The famous R&B singer performed the second stunt manning a "slime hose," firing at a sumo wrestler and propelling the poor guy in the costume along a long platform. The amount of slime added to the vat was determined by how far the "human target" was propelled by the spray of slime. Viewers voting online picked the sumo wrestler over his competitor, the Scuba diver. The "human target" was launched all the way to the 5-ton mark bringing the total of slime in the vat to 20 tons.
	Heidi Klum	The last stunt was performed by the German supermodel or as host Black called her "Heidi the Human Dart". Klum was attached by a harness to a long cable, allowing her to swing freely in which she did. Armed with a pad of spikes, she swung between her platform and what was a trampoline-like wall covered in slime balloons. For every slime balloon Klum popped in 30 seconds, one more ton of slime was added to the vat. Kids voted online to determine exactly what type of spike pad Klum would use to pop the balloons. The choices were the hand-worn "mittens" and the winner the "butt pad" which unanimously beat out the mittens. Klum popped 7 balloons on the wall, adding 7 more tons of slime to the vat and bringing the total of slime in the vat to 27 tons.
2009	Will Ferrell	The comedian-actor slid down a slime-covered slide that was placed on top of Janss Steps on the UCLA campus, on a luge head first into a pool of slime.
2010	Apolo Anton Ohno	Two stunts were featured at the 2010 awards. First, eight-time Olympic medalist Ohno was catapulted into slime by sling shot with the help of WWE Superstar John Cena.
	Jerry Trainor Jackson Rathbone Nicola Peltz	For the second stunt, to promote *The Last Airbender* stars Peltz and Rathbone along with *iCarly* star Trainor were featured in a bending-slime event. Since Peltz's character can bend water, she decided to bend slime and slimed Trainor and Rathbone.
2011	Kelvin Ramer	Ramer's monster truck, rebodied and relivered for the event, jumps over a 50-foot Nickelodeon blimp award into a pool of slime. It was hosted by Paul "The Big Show" Wight who said that it was the most dangerous Kids' Choice slime stunt ever.[38]

References

[1] http://www.nick.com/kids-choice-awards

[2] Larsen, Peter (30 March 2007). "Kids' Choice Awards grow up; The Nickelodeon celebration of burps and slime has become a star-studded affair." (http://www.ocregister.com/entertainment/kids-17366-awards-says.html). *Orange County Register*. . Retrieved 25 September 2011.

[3] Miley Cyrus Passes Britney Spears for Second-Most KCAs Ever Won (http://thedisneyflame.blogspot.com/2011/04/miley-cyrus-passes-britney-spears-to.html), The Disney Flame, April 2, 2011

[4] "Nickelodeon lowering the voting age". *Atlanta Journal; Atlanta Constitution*: p. T/30. March 8, 1987.

[5] "KIDS VOTE FOR `KARATE KID II'". *Los Angeles Times*: p. 10. March 28, 1987.

[6] Painter, Virginia (April 6, 1987). "KIDS LIKE COS". *USA Today*: p. 01.D.

[7] "STAMBERG NEVER RESTS ON SUNDAY". *Philadelphia Daily News*. April 7, 1987.

[8] Wong Briggs, Tracey (April 13, 1987). "MONKEE BUSINESS". *USA Today*: p. 01.D.

[9] Nickelodeon Kids' Choice Awards 2010 Press Kit | Releases (http://www.nickkcapress.com/2010KCA/releases/hostnoms/)

[10] kicks Choice Awards Mexico 2010 (http://www.mundonick.com/concursos/mis_premios_mx/)

[11] Associated Press, UCLA to renovate famous court (http://sports.espn.go.com/ncb/news/story?id=4159898), *ESPN*, May 11, 2010

[12] Werts, Granville, Kaufman, Diane, Kari, Bill (April 17, 1988). "SCREENING ROOM And Now For a Word From Our Sponsor". *Newsday*: p. 06.

[13] "Life provides fodder for Martin's odd world". *AUSTIN AMERICAN-STATESMAN*. June 25, 1989.

[14] Kubasik, Ben (June 23, 1989). "TV SPOTS". *Newsday*: p. 05.

[15] "LOOK WHO' WINNING WITH KIDS". *Dayton Daily News*: p. 4. April 27, 1990.

[16] Jon, Burlingame (April 23, 1990). "PRIME-TIME PICK Series: PRIME-TIME PICK". *St. Petersburg Times*: p. 7.D.

[17] Lipton, Laura (April 21, 1991). "Nickelodeon gives kids a choice". *Austin American-Statesman*: p. 11.

[18] Klied, Beth (November 16, 1992). "AWARDS". *Los Angeles Times*: p. 2.

[19] "SATURDAY'S TV TIPS". *Atlanta Journal; Atlanta Constitution*: p. E/4. November 14, 1992.

[20] Mendoza, N.F. (May 1, 1994). "SHOWS FOR YOUNGSTERS AND THEIR PARENTS TOO Lamb Chop, Shari and pals `Play-Along' for third season on PBS". *Los Angeles Times*: p. 7.

[21] Nickelodeon Kids' Choice Awards '99 (1999) (TV) (http://www.imdb.com/title/tt0472150/)

[22] Nickelodeon Kids' Choice Awards 2000 (2000) (TV) (http://www.imdb.com/title/tt0475992/)

[23] Nickelodeon Kids' Choice Awards (2001) (TV) (http://www.imdb.com/title/tt1504283/)

[24] Nickelodeon Kids' Choice Awards '02 (2002) (TV) (http://www.imdb.com/title/tt0318493/)

[25] Nickelodeon Kids' Choice Awards '03 (2003) (TV) (http://www.imdb.com/title/tt0450062/)

[26] Nickelodeon Kids' Choice Awards '04 (2004) (TV) (http://www.imdb.com/title/tt0413045/)

[27] Nickelodeon Kids' Choice Awards '05 (2005) (TV) (http://www.imdb.com/title/tt0459659/)

[28] Nickelodeon Kids' Choice Awards '06 (2006) (TV) (http://www.imdb.com/title/tt0787497/)

[29] Nickelodeon Kids' Choice Awards '07 (2007) (TV) (http://www.imdb.com/title/tt1002691/)

[30] Nickelodeon Kids Choice Awards '08 (2008) (TV) (http://www.imdb.com/title/tt1212906/)

[31] Nickelodeon Kids' Choice Awards 2009 (2009) (TV) (http://www.imdb.com/title/tt1409118/)

[32] Kids' Choice Awards (http://www.nick.com/kids-choice-awards), *Nick.com*

[33] Nickelodeon Kids' Choice Awards 2010 (2010) (TV) (http://www.imdb.com/title/tt1606644/)

[34] Monica Rizzo, Kevin James to Host Kids' Choice Awards (http://www.people.com/people/article/0,,20344222,00.html), *People*, February 15, 2010

[35] Nickelodeon's Kids Choice Awards 2011 (2011) (TV) (http://www.imdb.com/title/tt1839570/combined)

[36] Posted 02/10/2011 by Corinne Heller. "Kids' Choice Awards 2011 to be hosted by Jack Black - see nominations - February 10, 2011 10:14:25 AM PST | Entertainment News from" (http://www.ontheredcarpet.com/Jack-Black-to-host-2011-Kids-Choice-Awards---see-list-of-nominations/7951194). OnTheRedCarpet.com. . Retrieved 2011-02-11.

[37] Leonardo DiCaprio to Receive Big Green Award (http://www.people.com/people/article/0,,20267754,00.html), *People*, March 25, 2009

[38] (https://www.facebook.com/kelvin.ramer#!/kelvin.ramer?sk=wall) Ramer confirmed on his Facebook page that the monster truck was his and he drove the stunt.

External links

- Nickelodeon Kids' Choice Awards – Official Site (http://www.nick.com/kids-choice-awards/kca.jhtml)
- KCA Fun Facts (http://www.nickkcapress.com/2005KCA/kcafunfacts.php)
- Indonesian Kids' Choice Awards – Official Site (http://www.globaltv.co.id/kca/)
- *Nickelodeon Kids' Choice Awards* (http://www.imdb.com/title/tt1212906/) at the Internet Movie Database
- *Nickelodeon Kids' Choice Awards* (http://www.tv.com/show/71458/summary.html) at TV.com

To Wong Foo, Thanks for Everything! Julie Newmar

To Wong Foo, Thanks for Everything! Julie Newmar	
Theatrical release poster	
Directed by	Beeban Kidron
Produced by	Walter F. Parkes Bruce Cohen
Written by	Douglas Beane
Starring	Wesley Snipes Patrick Swayze John Leguizamo Stockard Channing
Music by	Rachel Portman
Cinematography	Steve Mason
Editing by	Andrew Mondshein
Studio	Amblin Entertainment
Distributed by	Universal Pictures
Release date(s)	September 8, 1995
Running time	109 min.
Country	United States
Language	English
Box office	$47,774,193

To Wong Foo, Thanks for Everything! Julie Newmar is a 1995 American comedy film, starring Wesley Snipes, Patrick Swayze, and John Leguizamo as three New York drag queens who embark on a road trip. The film's title refers to a totemic autographed photo of Julie Newmar that the trio carries with them on their journey.

Plot

After entering a local "drag queen of the year" contest in New York City, Noxeema Jackson (Wesley Snipes) and Vida Boheme (Patrick Swayze) win a trip to Hollywood to take part in an even bigger, national drag queen contest. Before they depart, Vida persuades Noxeema to take along the inexperienced 'drag princess' Chi-Chi Rodriguez (John Leguizamo) as their protégé (the duo initially refer to Chi-Chi simply as a "boy in a dress" rather than as a fully-fledged drag queen). To do this, they trade in their airplane tickets for cash and buy a stylish but old Cadillac convertible with money given to them by John Jacob Jingleheimer Schmidt (Robin Williams) and the three of them set off for Los Angeles by car, carrying with them an iconic photo of Julie Newmar (signed, *"To Wong Foo, thanks for everything! Julie Newmar"*) that Vida purloined from a restaurant wall.

While on the road they are pulled over by the racist, homophobic Sheriff Dollard (Chris Penn), who tries to force himself onto Vida. He discovers Vida is not female and, in the commotion, Dollard falls backwards and is knocked unconscious. The trio think he is dead, and they hurry off and leave him behind. While recovering from the incident at a rest stop, their car breaks down. A young man, Bobby Ray (Jason London), from the nearby small town of

Snydersville happens by and gives them a ride, where they take refuge in a bed and breakfast owned by Carol Ann (Stockard Channing) and her abusive car repairman husband, Virgil (Arliss Howard).

The drag queens become stranded in the town for the weekend as they wait for the replacement spare part for their car to arrive. Whilst there, they are confronted by the town's small-mindedness, though it does not focus on their transgender identities but rather, their status as females, which exposes to them and the audience the difficulties faced by anyone deviating from the "default" gender status (white heterosexual male). Chi-Chi is harassed by a group of roughnecks, but is saved by Bobby Ray. The drag queens are ecstatic to find vintage fashions from the 1960s in the town's clothing store and give the town's female residents (and themselves) a make-over.

Following their make-over, the group is abused by the same roughnecks that attempted to attack Chi-Chi. Fed up, Noxeema handles the situation in a typically New York manner and teaches their ringleader a lesson in manners. Vida, Noxeema, and Chi-Chi do what they can to be positive and they set out to improve the lives of the townspeople, including offering assistance in organizing the annual "Strawberry Social" event.

Meanwhile, Sheriff Dollard is ridiculed by his colleagues, who believe he was beat up by a girl. He goes in search of the drag queens and makes a list of places to look (entitled "Places for Homos"), which reads:

- flower shops
- ballet schools
- flight attendants' lounges
- restaurants for brunch
- antique stores

Vida, meanwhile, becomes acutely aware of Carol Ann's abuse at the hands of her husband Virgil and, shortly thereafter, the three queens overhear Virgil giving Carol Ann another beating. Vida decides to intervene and beats up Virgil before throwing him out of the house. The next day Virgil runs into Sheriff Dollard at a bar and the two realize that the newcomers to town are the same people Dollard has been searching for. They head back to Snydersville and Dollard insists the townspeople turn over the drag queens.

However, the townspeople, who now realize the true gender of their new friends, begin to protect them. One by one they step up and confront Dollard, each one claiming to be a drag queen, à la *Spartacus*. Dollard is humiliated and flees. The Strawberry Social commences with everybody dressed in vibrant red outfits for the party. Shortly after, Carol Ann repairs their car and the three queens are finally able to leave Snydersville, though they are now slightly saddened to leave behind their new friends. Carol Ann reveals to Vida that she knew Vida was a man all along due to his Adam's Apple, which women do not have.

They eventually make it to Los Angeles where Chi-Chi, after having received many tips from Vida and Noxeema during their ordeal, wins the title of Drag Queen of the Year. Fittingly, the crown is presented by Julie Newmar herself.

Cast

- Wesley Snipes as Noxeema Jackson
- Patrick Swayze as Vida Boheme
- John Leguizamo as Chi-Chi Rodriguez
- Stockard Channing as Carol Ann
- Blythe Danner as Beatrice
- Arliss Howard as Virgil
- Jason London as Bobby Ray
- Chris Penn as Sheriff Dollard
- Melinda Dillon as Merna
- Beth Grant as Loretta

- Alice Drummond as Clara
- Michael Vartan as Tommy
- Jennifer Milmore as Bobbie Lee

Cameo appearances

- Julie Newmar as Herself
- Naomi Campbell as Girl at China Bowl restaurant
- Joseph Arias as Joey Arias
- Lady Bunny as Pageant Hostess
- Lady Catiria as Herself
- Laritza Dumont as Herself
- Alexander Heimberg as Herself
- Brendan McDanniel as Candis Cayne
- Clinton Leupp as Miss Coco Peru
- Quentin Crisp as NY pageant judge
- Flotilla DeBarge as NY pageant judge
- RuPaul as Rachel Tensions
- Robin Williams as John Jacob Jingleheimer Schmidt
- Christine Baranski as Woman in Red dress with leaves at Los Angeles Pageant

Awards

Swayze and Leguizamo earned Golden Globe Award nominations for "Best Actor in a Motion Picture - Comedy/Musical" and "Best Supporting Actor" respectively.

Production

The opening and closing scenes were filmed in New York City featuring dozens of New York's local drag performers and underground stars in small roles or as featured extras. Included in the mix were RuPaul, Joey Arias, Lady Bunny, Miss Understood, Candis Cayne, Flotilla DeBarge, Clinton Leupp a.k.a. Miss Coco Peru, and Quentin Crisp. The three stars had previously spent some time in the local drag scene while researching their roles. The ending scene of the movie, the anticipated Miss Drag Queen USA contest, was filmed at The John S. Phipps Estate in Old Westbury, New York, now colloquially known as Old Westbury Gardens. Much of the rest of the film was shot on location in Montclair, New Jersey,[1] Loma, Nebraska, as well as nearby Lincoln and Omaha. Though greatly faded, the coca-cola billboard painted with Chi-Chi's name still stands in Loma.

Robin Williams also has a cameo early in the film as the queens' friend John Jacob Jingleheimer Schmidt. Julie Newmar, an iconic figure to the main characters, also makes a cameo appearance as does supermodel Naomi Campbell, although it is not clear whether the latter is playing herself or not.

Champions Tour professional Chi Chi Rodriguez sued the production company and distributor over the use of his name in the movie. [2]

This American film is a parallel story/plot idea of the earlier 1994 Australian comedy-drama, *The Adventures of Priscilla, Queen of the Desert* which stars Hugo Weaving, Terrance Stamp, and Guy Pearce in the roles of the three cross-country cabaret drag queens.

Soundtrack

1. "I Am the Body Beautiful" - Salt-N-Pepa
2. "Free Yourself - Chaka Khan
3. "Turn It Out" - Labelle
4. "Who Taught You How" - Crystal Waters
5. "She's a Lady" - Tom Jones
6. "Brick House" - The Commodores
7. "Nobody's Body" - Monifah
8. "Do What You Wanna Do" - Charisse Arrington
9. "Girls Just Want to Have Fun (Hey Now)" - Cyndi Lauper
10. "Over the Rainbow" - Patti LaBelle
11. "To Wong Foo" Suite - Rachel Portman

DVD

A DVD is available with several deleted scenes.

External links

- *To Wong Foo, Thanks for Everything! Julie Newmar* [3] at the Internet Movie Database
- *To Wong Foo, Thanks for Everything! Julie Newmar* [4] at AllRovi
- *To Wong Foo, Thanks for Everything! Julie Newmar* [5] at the TCM Movie Database
- *To Wong Foo, Thanks for Everything! Julie Newmar* [6] at Box Office Mojo

References

[1] Read, Philip (May 13, 2008). "Montclair on screens big and small" (http://www.nj.com/montclairguide/index.ssf/2008/05/ready_for_its_closeup.html). *The Star-Ledger*. . Retrieved 2011-04-28.

[2] "Chi Chi to Universal Pictures: Thanks for Nothing, I'm Suing - Los Angeles Times" (http://articles.latimes.com/1995-09-16/sports/sp-46566_1_chi-chi-rodriguez). Articles.latimes.com. 1995-09-16. . Retrieved 2011-06-30.

[3] http://www.imdb.com/title/tt0114682/

[4] http://www.allrovi.com/movies/movie/v135022

[5] http://tcmdb.com/title/title.jsp?stid=93485

[6] http://www.boxofficemojo.com/movies/?id=towongfoo.htm

Wong Foo, Thanks for Everything! Julie Newmar/ *To Wong Foo, Thanks for Everything! Julie Newmar* (http://www.rottentomatoes.com/m/To) at Rotten Tomatoes

Nine Months

Nine Months	
Directed by	Chris Columbus
Produced by	Michael Barnathan Anne François Mark Radcliffe Chris Columbus
Screenplay by	Patrick Braoudé Chris Columbus
Story by	Patrick Braoudé Daniel Russo
Starring	Hugh Grant Julianne Moore Tom Arnold Joan Cusack Jeff Goldblum Robin Williams
Music by	Hans Zimmer
Cinematography	Donald McAlpine
Editing by	Raja Gosnell Stephen E. Rivkin
Studio	1492 Pictures
Distributed by	20th Century Fox
Release date(s)	July 14, 1995
Running time	103 minutes
Country	United States
Language	English
Box office	$138,510,230[1]

Nine Months is a 1995 romantic comedy film directed by Chris Columbus. It stars Hugh Grant, Julianne Moore, Tom Arnold, Joan Cusack, Jeff Goldblum, and Robin Williams. The movie is a US remake of the French movie *Neuf mois* and served as Grant's first US starring role. It was filmed on location in the San Francisco Bay Area. The original music score was composed by Hans Zimmer.

Plot

Child psychologist Samuel Faulkner's (Hugh Grant) ideal romance with ballet teacher Rebecca Taylor (Julianne Moore) is turned upside-down when Rebecca gets pregnant. His fears mount due to his encounters with overbearing couple Marty (Tom Arnold) & Gail (Joan Cusack) and their unruly daughters, as well as the confusing advice he gets from his perpetually single artist friend (Jeff Goldblum). Too uninvolved with Rebecca's needs, Samuel parts company with her and takes a last stab at playing the field, but when he sees an ultrasound of his soon-to-be-born son, he decides that it's time to take responsibility before it's too late. Robin Williams, as Rebecca's Russian OB-GYN, adds much of the comic relief in the film.

Cast

- Hugh Grant as Samuel Faulkner
- Julianne Moore as Rebecca Taylor-Faulkner
- Tom Arnold as Marty Dwyer
- Joan Cusack as Gail Dwyer
- Jeff Goldblum as Sean Fletcher
- Robin Williams as Dr. Kosevich
- Mia Cottet as Lili
- Joey Simmrin as Truman
- Ashley Johnson as Shannon Dwyer
- Alexa Vega as Molly Dwyer
- Aislin Roche as Patsy Dwyer

Reception

The film was poorly received by critics, and currently holds a 25% score on Rotten Tomatoes. Roger Ebert gave this film two stars, saying, "*Nine Months* is one of those movies where the outcome is abundantly clear to everyone but the hero, who remains in the hapless position of playing dumb because, if he didn't, there wouldn't be a plot."[2]

Box Office

The movie debuted at #3 at the box office.[3]

References

[1] "Nine Months at Box Office Mojo" (http://www.boxofficemojo.com/movies/?id=ninemonths.htm). . Retrieved 2010-09-29.
[2] Ebert, Roger (1995-07-12). "Review: Nine Months" (http://rogerebert.suntimes.com/apps/pbcs.dll/article?AID=/19950712/REVIEWS/507120301/1023). *Chicago Sun-Times*. . Retrieved 2010-11-11.
[3] "Weekend Box Office : 'Under Siege' Opens in No. 2 Spot" (http://articles.latimes.com/1995-07-18/entertainment/ca-25014_1_weekend-gross). The Los Angeles Times. . Retrieved 2011-01-13.

External links

- *Nine Months* (http://www.imdb.com/title/tt0113986/) at the Internet Movie Database
- *Nine Months* (http://www.allrovi.com/movies/movie/v134917) at AllRovi

Aladdin and the King of Thieves

Aladdin and the King of Thieves	
DVD cover	
Directed by	Tad Stones
Produced by	Jeannine Roussel Tad Stones
Written by	Mark McCorkle Robert Schooley
Starring	Scott Weinger Robin Williams John Rhys-Davies Gilbert Gottfried Linda Larkin Jerry Orbach Frank Welker
Distributed by	Walt Disney Home Video
Release date(s)	August 13, 1996 (VHS) January 18, 2005 (DVD re-release)
Running time	80 minutes
Country	United States
Language	English

Aladdin and the King of Thieves is a 1996 animated film that is the second direct-to-video sequel to the Disney animated feature *Aladdin*. *Aladdin and the King of Thieves* serves as the final chapter of the *Arabian Nights*-inspired Disney stories that began with the theatrical feature *Aladdin* (1992) and continued with its first direct-to-video sequel *The Return of Jafar* (1994) and the *Aladdin* animated TV series (1994-1995).

Robin Williams returned to voice the Genie after Disney apologized for the use of his likeness in the promotion of the original *Aladdin* film (Williams believed Disney had broken the terms of his contract). Dan Castellaneta had actually recorded all the dialogue of the Genie for this film, as he did with the previous sequel due to Disney's differences with Williams, but his recording session was not used when Robin Williams agreed to reprise his role.

This film grossed $186 million, making it the fourth-highest-grossing direct-to-video animated feature film of all time. In 2005, the film was re-released as a Special Edition DVD, with digitally restored picture and remastered sound. The DVD went back into the Disney Vault along with the other two films in the series in January 2008.[1]

The film is inspired by the tale *Ali Baba and the Forty Thieves* from the *1001 Arabian Nights*, replacing Ali Baba with Aladdin, and for the first time since the original *Aladdin*, the film has a completely new soundtrack instead of the rearranged music from the original film for *The Return of Jafar* and the TV series.

Plot

Aladdin (Scott Weinger) and Princess Jasmine (Linda Larkin) prepare for their marriage. Aladdin recovers a dagger, his only memento of his lost father, who had abandoned his family when Aladdin had been a small child. During the ceremony, they and the assembled guests find themselves the targets of a raid by the infamous Forty Thieves, led by a man named Cassim (John Rhys-Davies), who is after a particular piece of treasure: a staff which is the receptacle of a powerful oracle. Aladdin, Abu, Jasmine and the Genie fight back against the thieves, driving them off. They discover the Oracle, who has the power to answer a single question about absolutely anything to any individual. When Iago accidentally asks her why the thieves want the staff so badly, she says that they were looking for the "ultimate treasure". Learning of the Oracle's power, Aladdin become curious about his past. She hints to him that those questions can be answered by his father, who is still alive much to Aladdin's shock. After some encouragement from Jasmine, Aladdin asks the oracle about his father; the oracle reveals that his father is with the Forty Thieves, "trapped within their world".

Aladdin, along with Abu, Iago and Carpet, tracks them down and stows away into their hideout, Mount Sesame. He is shocked to find that Cassim is the thieves' leader. Sa'luk (Jerry Orbach), Cassim's subordinate tries to punish Aladdin from entering. Cassim, however, slyly suggests that Aladdin instead face "the Challenge"—an initiation ritual—where he must defeat another one of the Forty Thieves and take his place. Sa'luk fights Aladdin, but the latter just barely manages to prevail by throwing his opponent off a cliff into the sea. He is welcomed into the band, and Cassim reveals to Aladdin why he had left his wife and son: to find the Hand of Midas, a powerful artifact that can transform anything it touches into gold. Cassim believed that, with the Hand, he could return to his family and give them the life they deserved instead of one living out in the streets, and had instigated the raid so he could capture the oracle's staff and question the seer as to the precise whereabouts of the artifact.

Aladdin convinces Cassim to come back with him to the Palace as his guest and, for a while, Cassim is happy to spend quality time with his son. Cassim meets with Jasmine and the Sultan, and they immediately take a liking to Aladdin's father. Cassim decides to carry on his original scheme with Iago as his new henchman. Meanwhile, Sa'luk makes his way to Agrabah. He reveals himself to Razoul and sells out his fellow thieves by telling Razoul the password to their hideout in exchange for immunity from prosecution. After 31 of the thieves are captured, Sa'luk tells them that Aladdin is one of the forty, and his father Cassim is the King himself.

While attempting to steal the Oracle from the palace treasure chamber, Cassim and Iago are captured by the royal guards and Razoul reveals to the Sultan that Cassim is the King of Thieves. The Sultan has Razoul detain Cassim and Iago in the dungeon for life. Aladdin frees Cassim, but is discovered by Razoul. Despite being a criminal, Aladdin returns to the palace to take responsibility for his actions. The Sultan prepares to punish Aladdin, but Genie and Jasmine come to his defense, stating that all he wanted was to give his father a second chance. The Sultan accepts his apology, much to Razoul's dismay.

With the oracle in hand, Cassim and Iago return to Mount Sesame, only to be captured by Sa'luk and the remaining Thieves. Cassim is forced to use the stolen oracle in order to find the location of the Hand of Midas and then lead his men there. The Oracle directs them to The Vanishing Isle, a great marble fortress built on the back of a gigantic undersea turtle that periodically dives to the bottom of the ocean, where the Hand is hidden. Iago flees from the group, and goes off to lead Aladdin and Jasmine, Abu and Carpet to his imprisoned father.

Aladdin manages to free and reconcile with his father. Working together, they retrieve the Hand just as the turtle is beginning to submerge, when they are attacked by Sa'luk. While trying to flee from the flood Sa'luk takes Aladdin hostage, demanding that Cassim surrender the Hand. Cassim throws the Hand of Midas to Sa'luk, but Sa'luk turns into a gold statue after grabbing the Hand and Cassim and Aladdin flee. Having discovered that his obsession with the Hand can cause destruction, Cassim decides to toss it into the sea, realizing that his ultimate treasure is actually Aladdin. The Hand of Midas lands on the ship with the remaining thieves aboard, turning it into gold and sinking it.

Aladdin and Jasmine finally get married, with Cassim attending in the shadows, as he is still wanted for his crimes. Also among the guests are several cameos from characters from the TV series. Iago decides to join Cassim as a traveling companion, and they both go off once again to see the world.

A reprise of Arabian Nights is then sung; the Peddler makes an appearance at the end of this film to mark the end of the legend of Aladdin (originally planned for the end of the first film) as Aladdin and Jasmine fly past him and wave good-bye to Cassim and Iago.

Cast

- Scott Weinger as Aladdin (Brad Kane singing)
- Robin Williams as Genie
- John Rhys-Davies as Cassim
- Linda Larkin as Princess Jasmine (Liz Callaway singing)
- Gilbert Gottfried as Iago
- Jerry Orbach as Sa'luk
- Frank Welker as Abu and Rajah
- Val Bettin as Sultan
- C. C. H. Pounder as The Oracle
- Jim Cummings as Razoul
- Robin Williams as The Narrator - the mysterious merchant who appears at the beginning of the first film, returns for the end of the film. In doing so, the film suggests that the story of Aladdin, spanning three films and a TV series, were told by him, and gives the feeling of things coming full circle. His singing voice is supplied by Bruce Adler.

Reception

The film received a 30% rating from critics on Rotten Tomatoes. It also received 58% from the RT community.[2]

Soundtrack

- There's a Party Here in Agrabah: Sung by mostly Genie, partly by Iago, some of the Forty Thieves, Aladdin, and Jasmine. There was a brief pause in the song which showed Aladdin taking out his father's dagger. It tells about what Genie does during the beginning of the wedding.
- Out of Thin Air: Sung by Aladdin and Jasmine. Aladdin reminisces about his childhood and Jasmine urges him to find his father, saying their wedding can wait until he returns.
- Welcome to the Forty Thieves: Sung by the Forty Thieves after the defeat of Sa'luk and Aladdin's acceptance into the team.
- Father and Son: Sung mostly by Genie after Cassim arrived at the palace in Agrabah and Genie says how Aladdin and Cassim are together again.
- Are You In or Out?: Sung by Sa'luk and those who remained of the Forty Thieves, where Sa'luk turned them against Cassim. During the song, the Forty Thieves make several attempts to kill Sa'luk, but he easily defeats them even when they gang up on him in groups.
- Arabian Nights Reprise: Sung by the peddler seen in the beginning of *Aladdin* (which was originally meant for the first movie) which was created to give the feeling of the tale coming full circle.

Adaptation

Two comic adaptations of the movie were on sale September 1996.

- The first was in *Marvel Comics Disney Comic Hits* #12.
- The second was in *Disney Adventures* Volume 6 #12.

Genie's Guises

- Williams' many impersonations included a live-action character he portrayed: The title character of the 1993 comedy film Mrs. Doubtfire.
- At the very end of the credits, the Genie appears in front of the black screen and says, *"Game Over, man! Game Over!"* This is a spoof of an identical line by the character Private William Hudson in the movie *Aliens*.
- The "security system" set up by the Genie has the classic Cylon "sweep eye" found in Battlestar Galactica.
- During the first song, the Genie turns into Rocky.
- Ali Baba and the forty thieves are mentioned at the beginning of the song Friend Like Me from the first Aladdin movie.
- During the song "Father and Son", Genie references The Jetsons.
- Various references included Pocahontas, Pumbaa from *The Lion King*, Rocky Balboa, ED-209 from RoboCop, and Mickey Mouse from Steamboat Willie, all of which Genie turned into or made with magic.
- Genie transforms into a parody of Forrest Gump during the wedding fight scene and says "Mama always said, 'Magic is magic does.'"
- Genie also turns into various things in the film: a ninja, an old man, a baby, Tinker Bell, a construction worker, Rainman, Elvis Presley, the White Rabbit from Alice in Wonderland, Copernicus, Sagittarius, Castor and Pollux, Walter Cronkite, Albert Einstein, The Godfather, Shaquille O'Neal, Mickey Mouse's dog Pluto, a fat farmer, a wrestler, The Sorcerer's Apprentice, Donald Duck, Baloo the Bear, Ozzie Nelson, Woody Allen, and simultaneously, the Marx Brothers Bob Hope and Bing Crosby.
- There is a scene where he turns Jasmine's wedding dresses into that of Cinderella's and Snow White's. He also contemplates what she would look like as Ariel, Minnie Mouse, and Jessica Rabbit. During these scenes, Bambi and Roger Rabbit make brief appearances.

References

[1] "Out of Print Disney DVDs" (http://www.ultimatedisney.com/OOP.htm). *UltimateDisney.com*. . Retrieved 24 September 2006.

[2] Aladdin and the King of Thieves (1999) (http://www.rottentomatoes.com/m/aladdin_and_the_king_of_thieves/?name_order=asc)

External links

- *Aladdin and the King of Thieves* (http://www.bcdb.com/bcdb/cartoon.cgi?film=7274) at the Big Cartoon DataBase
- *Aladdin and the King of Thieves* (http://www.imdb.com/title/tt0115491/) at the Internet Movie Database
- *Aladdin and the King of Thieves* (http://www.rottentomatoes.com/m/aladdin_and_the_king_of_thieves/) at Rotten Tomatoes

Hamlet (1996 film)

Hamlet	
Film poster	
Directed by	Kenneth Branagh
Produced by	David Barron
Written by	William Shakespeare
Starring	Kenneth Branagh Julie Christie Billy Crystal Charlton Heston Derek Jacobi Jack Lemmon Rufus Sewell Robin Williams Kate Winslet
Music by	Patrick Doyle
Cinematography	Alex Thomson
Editing by	Neil Farrell
Studio	Castle Rock Entertainment
Distributed by	Columbia Pictures
Release date(s)	December 25, 1996
Running time	242 minutes
Country	United Kingdom United States
Language	English
Budget	$18 million
Box office	$4,708,156

Hamlet is a 1996 film version of William Shakespeare's classic play of the same name, adapted and directed by Kenneth Branagh, who also stars in the title role as Prince Hamlet. It co-stars Derek Jacobi as King Claudius, Julie Christie as Queen Gertrude, Kate Winslet as Ophelia, Michael Maloney as Laertes, Richard Briers as Polonius, and Nicholas Farrell as Horatio.

The film is notable as the first unabridged theatrical film version of the play. The complete film runs just over four hours. The longest version of the play prior to the 1996 film was the 1980 BBC made-for-television version starring Derek Jacobi, which runs three-and-a-half hours. A shorter edit of the Branagh film, approximately two-and-a-half hours long, was shown in some markets.

Although the dialogue is unchanged, the play's setting is updated to the 19th century. Blenheim Palace is the setting used for the exterior and the grounds of Elsinore Castle. Interiors were all photographed at Shepperton Studios and blended with the footage shot at Blenheim.[1]

Hamlet also has the distinction of being the last major dramatic film to be filmed entirely in 70 mm film as of 2010.

Cast

- Kenneth Branagh as Hamlet
- Derek Jacobi as Claudius
- Julie Christie as Gertrude
- Richard Briers as Polonius
- Kate Winslet as Ophelia
- Nicholas Farrell as Horatio
- Michael Maloney as Laertes
- Robin Williams as Osric
- Gérard Depardieu as Reynaldo
- Timothy Spall as Rosencrantz
- Reece Dinsdale as Guildenstern
- Jack Lemmon as Marcellus
- Brian Blessed as the Ghost of Hamlet's Father
- Rufus Sewell as Fortinbras
- Billy Crystal as the First Gravedigger
- Simon Russell Beale as the Second Gravedigger
- Charlton Heston as the Player King
- Rosemary Harris as the Player Queen
- Richard Attenborough as the English Ambassador
- Judi Dench as Hecuba
- John Gielgud as Priam
- John Mills as Old Norway
- Ken Dodd as Yorick
- Ian McElhinney as Barnardo

Production

The film's budget was $18 million. *Hamlet* was filmed in Panavision Super 70 by Alex Thomson. As of 2010, it was the last feature film shot entirely in the 70mm film format.[2]

Interpretation

Aspects of the film's staging are based on Adrian Noble's recent Royal Shakespeare Company production of the play, in which Branagh had played the title role.[3]

In a radical departure from previous *Hamlet* films, Branagh set the internal scenes in a vibrantly colourful setting, featuring a throne room dominated by mirrored doors; film scholar Samuel Crowl calls the setting "*film noir* with all the lights on."[4] Branagh chose Victorian era costuming and furnishings, using Blenheim Palace, built in the early 18th century, as Elsinore Castle for the external scenes. Harry Keyishan has suggested that the film is structured as an epic, courting comparison with *Ben Hur*, *The Ten Commandments* and *Doctor Zhivago*.[5] As J. Lawrence Guntner points out, comparisons with the latter film are heightened by the presence of Julie Christie (*Zhivago's* Lara) as Gertrude.[6]

Despite using a full text, Branagh's film is also very visual; it makes frequent use of flashbacks to depict scenes that are either only described but not performed in Shakespeare's text, such as Hamlet's childhood friendship with Yorick, or scenes only implied by the play's text, such as Hamlet's sexual relationship with Kate Winslet's Ophelia.[7] The film also uses very long single takes for numerous scenes.

Branagh's own interpretation of the title role, by his own admission, was considerably less "neurotic" than others; gone completely was the Oedipal fixation so prominently featured in Olivier's 1948 film. However, some critics, such as Leonard Maltin, felt that Branagh's performance was at times too "over-the top" (in the scenes in which Hamlet pretends to be insane, Branagh portrayed the Prince as manic; other members of the court are visibly exasperated by his behavior).

Reception

Hamlet was screened out of competition at the 1997 Cannes Film Festival.[8]

Hamlet received largely positive reviews. It has a 95% rating at Rotten Tomatoes.[9] Roger Ebert awarded the film four stars, comparing it to Laurence Olivier's lauded 1948 version while Janet Maslin praised both the film and Branagh's performance.[10] [11]

Some critics, notably Stanley Kauffmann, declared the film to be the finest motion picture version of *Hamlet* yet made, and online film critic James Berardinelli has gone so far as to declare the Branagh *Hamlet* the finest Shakespeare adaptation ever, rating it as the fourth best film of the 90s and one of his top 101 favourite films of all time. Berardinelli writes, "I have seen dozens of versions of this play (either on screen or on stage), and none has ever held me in such a grip of awe." [12] The *New York Review of Books* praised the attention given to Shakespeare's language, "giving the meter of the verse a musician's respect,";[13] Branagh himself says his aim is "telling the story with utmost clarity and simplicity.".[14]

The film did have its detractors however, with Lloyd Rose of *The Washington Post* calling it "the film equivalent of a lushly illustrated coffee-table book"[15] and Desson Howe writing of Branagh's performance "...the choices he makes are usually overextended. When it's time to be funny, he skitters over the top. When he's sad or touched, he makes a mechanical, catching noise in his throat."[16] The notoriously severe John Simon completely skewered the film, praising only the performances of Derek Jacobi, Julie Christie, and Rufus Sewell (who played Fortinbras).[17]

Hamlet was not a success at the box office, playing on fewer than 100 screens in the U.S. and earning only $5 million in its limited American run.

Awards

The film was nominated for four Academy Awards; Tim Harvey for Best Art Direction, Alex Byrne for Best Costume Design, Patrick Doyle for Best Original Score, and Kenneth Branagh for Best Writing (Adapted Screenplay).

Home media release

A 2-Disc DVD was released in the U.S. and Canada on the 14th of August 2007. It includes a full-length commentary by Branagh and Shakespeare scholar Russell Jackson.[18] A Blu-ray Disc was released on the 17th of August 2010 in the U.S. and Canada, with similar additional features.[19]

References

[1] Alternate versions (http://www.imdb.com/title/tt0116477/alternateversions)

[2] http://www.widescreenmuseum.com/widescreen/splist.htm

[3] Crowl, Samuel "Flamboyant Realist: Kenneth Branagh" in Jackson, Russell *The Cambridge Companion to Shakespeare on Film* (Cambridge University Press, 2000)

[4] Crowl, p.227

[5] Keyishian, p.78

[6] Guntner, pp.122-123.

[7] Keyishian, p.79

[8] "Festival de Cannes: Hamlet" (http://www.festival-cannes.com/en/archives/ficheFilm/id/4801/year/1997.html). *festival-cannes.com*. . Retrieved 2009-09-27.

[9] "Hamlet (1996)" (http://www.rottentomatoes.com/m/1075422-hamlet/). *Rotten Tomatoes*. IGN Entertainment, Inc. . Retrieved 2008-08-09.

[10] "Roger Ebert's Review" (http://rogerebert.suntimes.com/apps/pbcs.dll/article?AID=/19970124/REVIEWS/701240303/1023). *Chicago Sun-Times*. .

[11] "Janet Maslin's Review" (http://www.nytimes.com/library/film/hamlet.html). *The New York Times*. . Retrieved 2010-05-04.

[12] "James Berardinelli's Review" (http://www.reelviews.net/movies/h/hamlet.html). .

[13] O'Brien, Geoffrey *New York Review of Books* 6 February 1997, cited by Samuel Crowl, "Framboyant Realist: Kenneth Branagh" in Jackson, Russell *The Cambridge Companion to Shakespeare on Film* (Cambridge University Press, 2000) p.228

[14] Branagh, Kenneth *Introduction and Notes* to *Much Ado About Nothing: Screenplay* p.ix cited by Crowl, p.228

[15] "'Hamlet': Kenneth Branagh's Inaction Flick" (http://www.washingtonpost.com/wp-srv/style/longterm/movies/review97/hamletrose.htm). *The Washington Post*. 1997-07-22. . Retrieved 2010-05-04.

[16] "Branagh's 'Hamlet': Not to Be" (http://www.washingtonpost.com/wp-srv/style/longterm/movies/review97/hamlethowe.htm). *The Washington Post*. 1997-07-22. . Retrieved 2010-05-04.

[17] http://www.amazon.com/John-Simon-Film-Criticism-1982-2001/dp/1557835071/ref=sr_1_1?s=books&ie=UTF8&qid=1291258178&sr=1-1#reader_1557835071

[18] Kenneth Branagh's Hamlet (http://www.kenbranagh.com/news.htm)

[19] (http://www.wbshop.com/Hamlet-Bluray-Book/1000122740,default,pd.html?cgid=&adid=0810HamEml)

External links

- *Hamlet* (http://www.imdb.com/title/tt0116477/) at the Internet Movie Database
- *Hamlet* (http://www.allrovi.com/movies/movie/v136644) at AllRovi
- *Hamlet* (http://www.rottentomatoes.com/m/1075422-hamlet/) at Rotten Tomatoes
- 101+ reasons to watch Kenneth Branagh's Hamlet (http://www.ocf.berkeley.edu/~ngoc/101.htm)

Jack (1996 film)

Jack	
Theatrical release poster	
Directed by	Francis Ford Coppola
Produced by	Francis Ford Coppola Fred Fuchs
Written by	James DeMonaco Gary Nadeau
Starring	Robin Williams Diane Lane Jennifer Lopez Bill Cosby Fran Drescher Brian Kerwin
Music by	Michael Kamen Bryan Adams Robert Lange
Cinematography	John Toll
Editing by	Barry Malkin
Studio	American Zoetrope Highschool Sweethearts
Distributed by	Hollywood Pictures
Release date(s)	August 9, 1996
Running time	113 minutes
Country	United States
Language	English
Budget	$45 million
Box office	$58,586,889

Jack is a 1996 ensemble cast comedy-drama film starring Robin Williams, Diane Lane, Jennifer Lopez, Fran Drescher, Bill Cosby, and Brian Kerwin. It was directed by Francis Ford Coppola. Williams plays the role of Jack Powell, a boy who ages four times faster than normal as a result of a disease similar to progeria.

Plot

The movie begins with Karen Powell (Diane Lane) going into labor during a Halloween party and being rushed to the hospital by her husband, Brian (Brian Kerwin), and their friends. Although the delivery is successful, the baby is premature, born after only ten weeks of pregnancy, and is diagnosed with an exaggerated form of Werner syndrome (an aging disease) as stated by Dr. Benfante (Allan Rich) and Dr. Lin (Keone Young). According to them, as this very rare autosomal recessive disorder progresses, Jack Powell will age at a rate four times faster than normal children due to his internal clock that seems to be developing faster.

Ten years later, Jack (Robin Williams) is next seen as a 10-year-old boy in the body of a 40-year-old man, with a group of four boys telling possible stories of a "monstrosity" of a boy their age that cannot go to school. He scares them away by dipping a fake eye into slime and throwing it at them from his window. He is extremely childish as a consequence of his secluded life. He has only had contact with his parents and tutor, Lawrence Woodruff (Bill Cosby), who introduces the idea that he should go to public school. His parents initially balk at the idea of their son going there because he could be emotionally hurt.

When he first attends school, he is exploited by the other kids to win at basketball against bullies, and eventually to get adult magazines and other such items. As time goes by, he is accepted by them, beginning with Louis, as they discover that they like him. He attempts to be normal there, for example, when he deals with his first crush and heartbreak, and the relationship with his teacher, Miss Marquez (Jennifer Lopez). When he goes through a fall while attempting to leave school, he is rushed over to the hospital, where his doctor explains that he suffered a shocking severe strain (which could've been a rare form of angina), and also because of his Werner Syndrome condition, his internal clock is starting to run out. Realizing the dangers it might entail for his health, his parents decide to withdraw him from school, which upsets him.

He sneaks out of the house and goes to a bar where he gets drunk and befriends a man named Paulie (Michael McKean). Jack gets into a fight with an angry man (Edward Lynch) and gets arrested. Yet he is bailed out by Dolores, Louis' mother (Fran Drescher). When he returns home, he locks himself in his room and doesn't go out for weeks. His mother speculates that perhaps he realized the fragility of his life and is now scared of facing the outside world again. He also doubts the need to study as he realizes that he wouldn't have the time to use any of the knowledge.

Meanwhile, his friends continue coming to his house, hoping that he will come out and play, but he refuses. Finally, Louis has an idea: he brings the entire class to Jack's house as they take turns yelling "Can Jack come out and play?" and participate in various games and fun activities right in front of the house. The next day he decides to go back to school.

Seven years later, an elderly looking Jack and his four best friends are at their high school graduation. He delivers the valedictory speech, in which he reminds his classmates that life is short, and urges them to "make your life spectacular". The film ends as the five drive away down the road and into their future lives.

Cast

- Robin Williams as Jack Powell
- Brian Kerwin as Brian Powell
- Diane Lane as Karen Powell
- Jennifer Lopez as Miss Marquez
- Bill Cosby as Lawrence Woodruff
- Fran Drescher as Dolores "D.D." Durante
- Adam Zolotin as Louie Durante
- Todd Bosley as Eddie
- Seth Smith as John-John
- Ryan Kennedy as George
- Michael McKean as Paulie
- Allan Rich as Dr. Benfante
- Keone Young as Dr. Lin
- Allison Whitbeck as Lucy
- Dwight Hicks as High School Principal
- Marc Coppola as Radio Personality (voice)

Reception

The film received mostly negative reviews from critics. It holds a 17% "rotten" rating on Rotten Tomatoes. [1] However, the film debuted at #1 and it was moderately successful at the box office, grossing roughly $58.6 million on a budget of $45 million.

Music

The film theme is "Star", performed by Canadian rocker Bryan Adams.

References

[1] http://uk.rottentomatoes.com/m/1072875-jack/#

External links

- *Jack* (http://www.imdb.com/title/tt0116669/) at the Internet Movie Database
- *Jack* (http://www.allrovi.com/movies/movie/v136486) at AllRovi
- *Jack* (http://www.rottentomatoes.com/m/1072875-jack/) at Rotten Tomatoes

The Birdcage

The Birdcage	
Theatrical release poster	
Directed by	Mike Nichols
Produced by	Mike Nichols Neil A. Machlis Marcello Danon
Screenplay by	Elaine May
Based on	*La Cage aux Folles* by Jean Poiret Francis Veber Edouard Molinaro Marcello Danon
Starring	Robin Williams Nathan Lane Gene Hackman Dianne Wiest Dan Futterman Calista Flockhart Hank Azaria Christine Baranski
Music by	Stephen Sondheim
Cinematography	Emmanuel Lubezki
Editing by	Arthur Schmidt
Studio	Nichols Film Company
Distributed by	United Artists
Release date(s)	March 8, 1996
Running time	118 minutes
Country	United States
Language	English
Box office	$185,260,553

The Birdcage is a 1996 American comedy film directed by Mike Nichols, and stars Robin Williams, Nathan Lane, Gene Hackman, Dianne Wiest, Dan Futterman, Calista Flockhart, Hank Azaria, and Christine Baranski. The script was written by Elaine May. It is an American remake of the 1978 Franco-Italian film, *La Cage aux Folles*, by Jean Poiret and Francis Veber, starring Michel Serrault and Ugo Tognazzi.

Plot

Val Goldman and Barbara Keeley are engaged to be married, and wish to have their families meet. Val's father, Armand, owns The Birdcage, a South Beach drag club. His domestic partner is Albert, who appears regularly as "Starina," the show's star drag queen. Barbara's father is ultraconservative Republican Ohio Senator Kevin Keeley, who is seeking re-election as the co-founder of the "Coalition for Moral Order". Fearing their reaction if they learn the truth about Val's parents, Barbara tells her parents that Armand is a cultural attaché to Greece, that Albert is a housewife, and that they divide their time between Greece and Florida; she also changes the family's last name from Goldman to Coleman to hide their Jewish background.

Kevin receives a phone call: Senator Jackson, Kevin's colleague and co-founder of the Coalition for Moral Order, has been found dead in the bed of an underage African-American prostitute; the event receives a large amount of coverage in the media. Louise Keeley proposes a visit to meet their new in-laws as a diversion to save Kevin's political career, and Barbara's marriage into a white, "traditional, wholesome" all-American family will give the Senator excellent PR material. Barbara phones Val in South Beach about the lies she has told her parents. Val convinces Armand to go along with the farce. Armand has the house redecorated in an austere manner, and begins remaking himself as an unassuming, conventional, heterosexual American male. He contacts Val's biological mother, Katherine Archer, and she agrees to join in the charade he is planning.

Despite the changes to the house and Katherine's help, Armand realizes that Albert's outlandish, effeminate mannerisms will reveal the true nature of the Goldman household. Armand asks Albert not to be present for the dinner party that evening; Albert is offended and threatens to leave Armand. A compromise is reached where Albert will act as Val's uncle, but this soon falls apart when Albert cannot effectively pretend to be heterosexual. Another argument ensues and Albert locks himself in his bedroom.

As the evening draws nearer, Agador, the Goldman's flamboyant gay housekeeper, has been made into a butler and chef for the evening, despite the fact that he cannot cook and never wears shoes. The Keeleys arrive at Armand's residence, but Katherine, who is to play Val's mother, ("Mrs. Coleman") is stuck in traffic. Kevin and Louise are worried that Armand's nervousness is because he has heard about the Jackson scandal and is uncomfortable having the Keeleys in his house. Suddenly, Albert emerges dressed as a middle-aged mother. Armand and Val are horrified, fearing that Katherine's arrival will destroy the illusion. Agador has prepared nothing for dinner but a bizarre soup containing shrimp and hard-boiled eggs. Despite the many challenges facing them, Armand, Val and Barbara all act the part and interact with Albert as "Mrs. Coleman".

Before dinner, Louise notices that the soup bowls depict men in homoerotic poses in a classical Greek style. Armand insists that she is mistaken and promptly fills everyone's bowl with the soup before the Keeleys can take a closer look. The primary topic of conversation is politics and, despite many potential pitfalls, Albert wins over the Senator with a very right-wing tirade on the moral collapse of American society. Louise is still suspicious: the dinner was terrible and Armand kept leaving the table. Kevin defends Albert as a true lady and remarks that Armand is just a "pretentious European". Val leaves a note for Katherine on the front door, informing her not to come inside, but two paparazzi photographers, hoping for a scoop, remove the note. Katherine arrives and introduces herself as "Mrs. Goldman". Kevin demands to know why there are two Mrs. Colemans; Val realizes that he cannot keep lying and pulls off Albert's wig, explaining to the Keeleys that while Katherine is his biological mother, Albert is his primary mother figure. Kevin and Louise are taken aback upon learning that Albert and Armand are gay Jewish nightclub owners. Louise breaks down and Kevin announces that they are leaving and demands that Barbara come with them, but the Keeleys have been followed by paparazzi and are trapped as news crews arrive.

The Goldmans, Keeleys, Katherine and Agador consider the best plan of action. Val and Barbara explain why they deceived Kevin and Louise and are forgiven, but the Keeleys fear being tangled up in a scandal if spotted in a gay nightclub. Albert choreographs the Keeleys' escape by dressing them up in drag and having them leave the club as the night's show ends. The plan works and none of the media crews recognize Kevin, Louise or Barbara. The group leaves South Beach with Katherine. Val and Barbara are married in an interfaith ceremony attended by their families.

Cast

- Robin Williams as Armand Goldman - A gay nightclub owner who tries to play it straight when his son's fiancee brings her unsuspecting parents to meet him in South Beach.
- Nathan Lane as Albert - Armand's partner who pretends to be Val's mother by dressing up as, and pretending to be, a woman when the Keeley's arrive. He stars in the nightclub's shows as the drag queen "Starina." Although a man he is Val's mother figure.
- Gene Hackman as Senator Kevin Keeley - Husband of Louise, father of Barbara, and future father-in-law to Val. He is a staunch Republican Senator with conservative social views who is running for re-election and staunchly opposes homosexuality and same-sex marriage. He co-founded the activist group. "Coalition for Moral Order," and struggles to preserve his political career after a close colleague dies while sleeping with a black underage prostitute.
- Dianne Wiest as Louise Keeley - Wife of Kevin, mother of Barbara, and future mother-in-law to Val. She is depicted as passively agreeing with her husband's extreme positions on public morality and social issues.
- Dan Futterman as Val Goldman - Son of Armand Goldman and Katie Archer. He wants to marry Barbara and has his father pretend to be straight when Barbara's parents come to meet them.
- Calista Flockhart as Barbara Keeley - Daughter of Senator Kevin and Louise Keeley, future wife of Val, and future daughter-in-law of Armand. She wants to marry Val, but when she learns that Val's father has a homosexual partner, she lies to her parents by telling them that Val's dad is an artist and his mom is a housewife.
- Hank Azaria as Agador - The Goldman's Guatemalan housekeeper. He too is flamboyantly gay, speaks with a Latin accent and a lisp, and serves as the butler for when the Keeleys come to visit. He detests wearing shoes and longs to work as a drag queen at The Birdcage.
- Christine Baranski as Katherine Archer - Val's biological mother (after having had a one night stand with Armand) and serial divorcee.
- Tom McGowan as Harry Radman.
- Grant Heslov as National Enquirer photographer.
- Kirby Mitchell as Keeley's opportunistic chauffeur.
- Jay Leno (*uncredited*) as Himself.
- Mike Starr (*deleted scenes*) as Harry.

Songs

A number of songs written by Stephen Sondheim were used in the film. The song that Albert rehearses during the sequence with the gum-chewing dancer is entitled "*Little Dream*", and was written specifically for use in the film.[1] Albert's first song as "Starina" is "Can That Boy Foxtrot," cut from Sondheim's Follies. The song that Armand and Katherine sing and dance to in her office, "Love Is in the Air," was originally intended as the opening number for the musical *A Funny Thing Happened on the Way to the Forum* in 1962. The song was cut from the show and replaced with *Comedy Tonight.*[2]

Reception

The Birdcage met with mixed reviews ranging from praise to condemnation in both the mainstream press and the gay press for the portrayals of its gay characters.

The Gay & Lesbian Alliance Against Defamation (GLAAD) praised the film for "going beyond the stereotypes to see the character's depth and humanity. The film celebrates differences and points out the outrageousness of hiding those differences."[3]

Review aggregator *Metacritic* reported that the film received "generally favorable" reviews, with a score of 72% based on 18 reviews.[4] The film currently holds a 77% 'Fresh' rating on Rotten Tomatoes.[5]

Box office

The Birdcage opened on March 8, 1996 and grossed $18,275,828 in its opening weekend, topping the box office.[6] It remained at #1 for the next three weeks before being derailed by the openings of *Primal Fear* and *A Thin Line Between Love and Hate*. By the end of its 14-week run, the film had grossed $124,060,553 domestically and $61,200,000 internationally, coming down to a $185,260,553 worldwide total.[7]

References

[1] Sondheim.com - Putting it together since 1994, http://www.sondheim.com/shows/the_birdcage/
[2] Sondheim.com - Putting it together since 1994, http://www.sondheim.com/shows/a_funny_thing_happened/#cut_songs
[3] GLAAD's press release on *The Birdcage* (http://www.glaad.org/media/archive_detail.php?id=217), retrieved January 20, 2007 from www.glaad.org
[4] "*The Birdcage* reviews" (http://www.metacritic.com/movie/the-birdcage). Metacritic. .
[5] *The Birdcage* (http://www.rottentomatoes.com/m/birdcage/) at Rotten Tomatoes
[6] http://www.boxofficemojo.com/weekend/chart/?yr=1996&wknd=10&p=.htm
[7] *The Birdcage* (http://www.boxofficemojo.com/movies/?id=birdcage.htm) at Box Office Mojo

External links

- *The Birdcage* (http://www.imdb.com/title/tt0115685/) at the Internet Movie Database
- *The Birdcage* (http://www.allrovi.com/movies/movie/vthe-birdcage-v136091) at AllRovi
- *The Birdcage* (http://www.boxofficemojo.com/movies/?id=birdcage.htm) at Box Office Mojo
- *The Birdcage* (http://www.rottentomatoes.com/m/birdcage/) at Rotten Tomatoes
- *The Birdcage* (http://www.metacritic.com/movie/the-birdcage) at Metacritic

Good Will Hunting

Good Will Hunting	
Theatrical release poster	
Directed by	Gus Van Sant
Produced by	Lawrence Bender Scott Mosier Kevin Smith Bob Weinstein Harvey Weinstein
Written by	Ben Affleck Matt Damon
Starring	Matt Damon Robin Williams Ben Affleck Minnie Driver Stellan Skarsgård
Music by	Danny Elfman (score)Elliott Smith (song)
Cinematography	Jean-Yves Escoffier
Editing by	Pietro Scalia
Studio	A Band Apart Lawrence Bender Productions

Distributed by	Miramax Films
Release date(s)	December 5, 1997
Running time	126 minutes
Country	United States
Language	English
Budget	$10 million
Box office	$225,933,435

Good Will Hunting is a 1997 drama film directed by Gus Van Sant and starring Matt Damon, Robin Williams, Ben Affleck, Minnie Driver, and Stellan Skarsgård. Written by Affleck and Damon, and with Damon in the title role, the film follows 20-year-old South Boston laborer Will Hunting, a genius who is forced to see a therapist (Williams) and study advanced mathematics with a renowned professor (Skarsgård) in order to avoid jail time. Through his therapy sessions, Will re-evaluates his relationships with his best friend (Affleck) and his girlfriend (Driver) while confronting his emotional issues and making decisions about his future.

Good Will Hunting was both a critical and financial success. It grossed over US$225 million during its theatrical run, more than twenty-two times its $10 million budget. It was nominated for nine Academy Awards, winning two: Best Supporting Actor for Williams and Best Original Screenplay for Affleck and Damon.

Plot

20-year-old Will Hunting (Matt Damon) of South Boston has a genius-level intellect but chooses to work as a janitor at the Massachusetts Institute of Technology and spend his free time with his friends Chuckie Sullivan (Ben Affleck), Billy McBride (Cole Hauser) and Morgan O'Mally (Casey Affleck). When Fields Medal-winning combinatorialist Professor Gerald Lambeau (Stellan Skarsgård) posts a difficult problem taken from algebraic graph theory as a challenge for his graduate students to solve, Will solves the problem quickly but anonymously. Lambeau posts a much more difficult problem and chances upon Will solving it, but Will runs off. Will meets Skylar (Minnie Driver), a British student about to graduate from Harvard University and pursue a graduate degree at Stanford University School of Medicine in California.

Will is faced with incarceration after assaulting a man who had bullied him as a child. Lambeau arranges for Will to forgo jail time if he agrees to study mathematics under Lambeau's supervision and to see a therapist. Will agrees, but treats his first few therapists with contempt and they refuse to work with him. In desperation, Lambeau calls on Sean Maguire (Robin Williams), his estranged college roommate who also grew up in South Boston and now teaches psychology at Bunker Hill Community College. Unlike the other therapists, Sean pushes back at Will and overcomes his defense mechanisms, and after a few unproductive sessions Will begins to open up.

Will is particularly struck by Sean's story of how he met his wife by giving up his ticket to the historic sixth game of the 1975 World Series after falling in love at first sight. Sean doesn't regret his decision, nor does he regret the final years of his marriage when his wife was dying of cancer. This encourages Will to build a relationship with Skylar, though he lies to her about his past and is reluctant to introduce her to his friends or show her his run-down neighborhood. Will also challenges Sean to take an objective look at his own life, since Sean has been unable to move on from his wife's death.

Will begins to chafe under Lambeau's high expectations and makes a mockery of job interviews that Lambeau arranges for him. Sean cautions Lambeau against pushing the boy too hard. Will walks in on a heated argument between the two over his future and it greatly upsets him. When Skylar asks Will to move to California with her, he panics and pushes her away, revealing that he is an orphan and that his foster father physically abused him. Skylar tells Will that she loves him, but he denies loving her and then leaves her. He next storms out on Lambeau, dismissing the mathematical research he has been doing. Sean points out that Will is so adept at anticipating future failure in his interpersonal relationships that he deliberately sabotages them in order to avoid the risk of emotional pain. When Will refuses to give an honest reply about what he wants to do with his life, Sean shows him the door. Will tells Chuckie he wants to be a laborer for the rest of his life; Chuckie responds that it would be an insult to his friends for Will to waste his potential, and that his fondest wish is that Will leaves to pursue something greater. Will decides to accept one of the job offers arranged by Lambeau.

At another therapy session, Sean and Will share that they were both victims of child abuse, and Sean helps Will to accept that the abuse he suffered wasn't his fault. Having helped Will overcome his problems, Sean reconciles with Lambeau and decides to take a sabbatical to travel the world. When Will's friends present him with a rebuilt Chevrolet Nova for his 21st birthday, he decides to pass on his lucrative job offers and drive to California to reunite with Skylar.

Cast

- Matt Damon as Will Hunting
- Robin Williams as Sean Maguire
- Ben Affleck as Chuckie Sullivan
- Stellan Skarsgård as Professor Gerald Lambeau
- Minnie Driver as Skylar
- Casey Affleck as Morgan O'Mally
- Cole Hauser as Billy McBride
- John Mighton as Tom
- George Plimpton as Dr. Henry Lipkin, Psychologist

Production

Development

Ben Affleck and Matt Damon originally wrote the screenplay as a thriller: Young man in the rough-and-tumble streets of South Boston who possesses a superior intelligence is targeted by the FBI to become a G-Man. Castle Rock Entertainment president Rob Reiner later urged them to drop the thriller aspect of the story and to focus the relationship between Will Hunting (Damon) and his psychologist (Williams). At Reiner's request, noted screenwriter William Goldman read the script and further suggested that the film's climax ought to be Will's decision to follow his girlfriend Skylar to California. Goldman has consistently denied the persistent rumor that he wrote *Good Will Hunting* or acted as a script doctor.[1] In his book, *Which Lie Did I Tell?*, Goldman writes that after reading the script and spending a day with the writers, his only contribution was agreeing with comments that Rob Reiner had already made. He writes, "I think the reason the world was so anxious to believe Matt Damon and Ben Affleck didn't write their script was simple jealousy. They were young and cute and famous; kill the fuckers."[2]

Castle Rock bought the script for $675,000 against $775,000, meaning that Affleck and Damon would stand to earn an additional $100,000 if the film was produced and they retained sole writing credit. However, studios balked at the idea of Affleck and Damon in the lead roles, with many studio executives citing that they wanted Brad Pitt and Leonardo DiCaprio. At the time Damon and Affleck were meeting at Castle Rock, director Kevin Smith was working with Affleck on *Mallrats* and with both Affleck and Damon on *Chasing Amy*.[3] Seeing that Affleck and Damon were having trouble with Castle Rock, Smith and his producer partner Scott Mosier brought the script to Miramax, which eventually caused the two to receive co-executive producer credits for *Hunting*. The script was put into turnaround and Miramax bought the rights from Castle Rock.

After buying the rights from Castle Rock, Miramax gave the green light to put the film into production. Several well-known filmmakers were originally considered to direct, including Mel Gibson, Michael Mann and Steven Soderbergh. Originally Affleck asked Kevin Smith if he was interested in directing. Smith declined, saying they needed a "good director" and that he only directs things he writes and is not much of a visual director. Affleck and Damon later chose Gus Van Sant for the job, whose work in previous films like *Drugstore Cowboy* (1989) had left a favorable impression on the fledgling screenwriters. Miramax was persuaded and hired Van Sant to direct the film.

Filming

Good Will Hunting was filmed on location in the Greater Boston area and Toronto over five months in 1996. Although the story is set in Boston, much of the film was shot at locations in Toronto, with the University of Toronto standing in for MIT and Harvard University and the classroom scenes being filmed at McLennan Physical Laboratories[4] (of the University of Toronto) and Central Technical School. The interior bar scenes set in South Boston ("Southie") were shot on location at Woody's L St. Tavern. The footage during the closing credits is along the Massachusetts Turnpike in Stockbridge, heading west toward the New York border.

The cast engaged in considerable improvisation in rehearsals. Robin Williams, Ben Affleck and Minnie Driver each made significant contributions to their characters. Robin Williams' last line in the film, as well as the therapy scene in which he talks about his character's wife's little idiosyncrasies, were both ad-libbed. The therapy scene took everyone by surprise. According to Damon's commentary in the DVD version of the film, this caused Johnny (the cameraman) to laugh so hard that the camera's POV can actually be seen moving up and down slightly as it shows Damon breaking character by also laughing so hard.

Director Gus Van Sant says in the DVD commentary that, had he known just how successful the film was going to be, he would have left at least a couple of edited scenes intact that were cut purely for considerations of length. One of these involves Skylar's visit to Chuckie in hopes of shedding light on some of Will's eccentricities that Will himself is unwilling to discuss.

The film is dedicated to the memory of poet Allen Ginsberg and writer William S. Burroughs, both of whom died in 1997.

Critical reception

Good Will Hunting received nearly universal acclaim from film critics: It has a 97% "Fresh" rating according to film review compilation website Rotten Tomatoes,[5] and was nominated for many awards (see below).

Matt Damon, Robin Williams and Minnie Driver were all nominated for Academy Awards for the film, with Williams winning. Damon and Affleck won an Oscar for Best Original Screenplay.

Box office

In the film's opening weekend in limited release, it earned $272,912. In its January 1998 wide-release opening weekend, it earned $10,261,471. It went on to gross $138,433,435 in North America for a total worldwide gross of $225,900,000.

Awards

70th Academy Awards

- **Won**: Academy Award for Best Supporting Actor - Robin Williams
- **Won**: Academy Award for Best Writing (Original Screenplay) - Ben Affleck & Matt Damon
- Nominated: Academy Award for Best Picture
- Nominated: Academy Award for Best Actor - Matt Damon
- Nominated: Academy Award for Best Supporting Actress - Minnie Driver
- Nominated: Academy Award for Best Director - Gus Van Sant
- Nominated: Academy Award for Best Song - Elliott Smith (song "Miss Misery")
- Nominated: Academy Award for Original Music Score - Danny Elfman

- Nominated: Academy Award for Film Editing - Pietro Scalia

55th Golden Globe Awards

- **Won**: Golden Globe Award for Best Screenplay - Motion Picture - Ben Affleck & Matt Damon
- Nominated: Golden Globe Award for Best Motion Picture - Drama
- Nominated: Golden Globe Award for Best Actor – Motion Picture Drama - Matt Damon
- Nominated: Golden Globe Award for Best Supporting Actor - Motion Picture - Robin Williams

Other Major Awards/Nominations

- Nominated: Directors Guild of America Award for Outstanding Directorial Achievement in Motion Pictures - Gus Van Sant
- Nominated: Writers Guild of America Award for Best Screenplay Written Directly for the Screen - Ben Affleck & Matt Damon

American Film Institute

- AFI's 100 Years... 100 Songs:
  - Miss Misery - Nominated
- AFI's 100 Years... 100 Cheers - Nominated
- AFI's 100 Years... 100 Movies (10th Anniversary Edition) - Nominated

Soundtrack

Good Will Hunting: Music from the Miramax Motion Picture[6]	
Soundtrack album by Various artists	
Released	December 2, 1997
Genre	Soundtrack, Indie rock, Acoustic rock, Indie folk
Label	Capitol

"Miss Misery," written and recorded for the film by late singer-songwriter Elliott Smith, was nominated for the Academy Award for Best Original Song, but lost to "My Heart Will Go On" from *Titanic*. Starland Vocal Band's "Afternoon Delight" is also featured in the closing credits after "Miss Misery," but does not appear on the soundtrack.

While Danny Elfman's score was nominated for an Oscar, only two cues appear on the film's soundtrack release. Elfman's "Weepy Donuts" was used on NBC's *The Today Show* on September 11, 2006, while Matt Lauer spoke during the opening credits.

1. Elliott Smith - "Between the Bars" (Orchestral)
2. Jeb Loy Nichols - "As the Rain"
3. Elliott Smith - "Angeles"
4. Elliott Smith - "No Name #3"
5. The Waterboys - "Fisherman's Blues"
6. Luscious Jackson - "Why Do I Lie?"
7. Danny Elfman - "Will Hunting" (Main Titles)
8. Elliott Smith - "Between the Bars"
9. Elliott Smith - "Say Yes"
10. Gerry Rafferty - "Baker Street"

11. Andru Donalds - "Somebody's Baby"
12. The Dandy Warhols - "Boys Better"
13. Al Green - "How Can You Mend a Broken Heart?"
14. Elliott Smith - "Miss Misery"
15. Danny Elfman - "Weepy Donuts"

References

[1] see Goldman's memoir *Which Lie Did I Tell?*
[2] Goldman, William (2001). Which Lie Did I Tell?: More Adventures in the Screen Trade. Vintage. pg. 333. ISBN 0375703195
[3] Smith's comments on the *Mallrats* DVD audio commentary
[4] "Trivia for *Good Will Hunting*" (http://www.imdb.com/title/tt0119217/trivia). Internet Movie Database. . Retrieved 17 October 2010.
[5] Good Will Hunting Movie Reviews, Pictures - Rotten Tomatoes (http://www.rottentomatoes.com/m/good_will_hunting/)
[6] Amazon.com: Good Will Hunting: Music from the Miramax Motion (http://www.amazon.com/dp/B000002TM0)

External links

- *Good Will Hunting* (http://www.imdb.com/title/tt0119217/) at the Internet Movie Database
- *Good Will Hunting* (http://tcmdb.com/title/title.jsp?stid=324221) at the TCM Movie Database
- *Good Will Hunting* (http://www.allrovi.com/movies/movie/v1:160083) at AllRovi
- *Good Will Hunting* (http://www.boxofficemojo.com/movies/?id=goodwillhunting.htm) at Box Office Mojo
- *Good Will Hunting* (http://www.rottentomatoes.com/m/good_will_hunting/) at Rotten Tomatoes
- Screenplay on IMSDb (http://www.imsdb.com/scripts/Good-Will-Hunting.html)

Flubber (film)

Flubber	
Theatrical release poster	
Directed by	Les Mayfield
Screenplay by	Bill Walsh (*previous screenplay*) John Hughes
Based on	"A Situation of Gravity" by Samuel W. Taylor
Starring	Robin Williams
Music by	Danny Elfman
Cinematography	Dean Cundey
Editing by	Harvey Rosenstock Michael A. Stevenson
Studio	Great Oaks
Distributed by	Walt Disney Pictures
Release date(s)	November 16, 1997
Running time	93 minutes
Country	United States
Language	English
Budget	$80 million
Box office	$177,977,226

Flubber is a 1997 comedy film and is a remake of *The Absent-Minded Professor* (1961). The film was produced by Walt Disney Pictures starring Robin Williams. Although the film was poorly reviewed, it did well at the box office.

Plot

Professor Philip Brainard (Robin Williams), a professor at Medfield College, is developing a new energy source in an attempt to raise enough money to save the college from closure. His preoccupancy with his research distracts him from his fiancée and the president of Medfield College Doctor Sara Jean Reynolds (Marcia Gay Harden); he has missed two weddings in the past as a result of this, much to the anger of Sara. On the day of the third attempted wedding, Philip is approached by his former partner Wilson Croft (Christopher McDonald), who has profited from ideas he has stolen from Brainard and now desires to steal Sara from Philip and make her his wife, which he declares directly to Philip. Before he can make it to the wedding, his latest experiment shows fast development, forcing him to miss another wedding. The resulting substance created from the experiment is a green slime that proves to be difficult to control and wreaks havoc on the neighborhood before Brainard finally manages to capture him. Weebo (voiced by Jodi Benson), Philip's robot assistant, classifies the substance as "flying rubber", leading Philip to christen him as "Flubber".

Philip discovers that as he bounces, Flubber increases in speed rather than decreasing. After he relays this information to Weebo, she informs him that he has missed the third wedding. Philip goes to Sara's office and attempts to explain the situation to her, but she refuses to listen. Meanwhile, Medfield College sponsor Chester

Hoenicker (Raymond J. Barry) is unhappy that Philip flunked his son Bennett (Wil Wheaton) in chemistry class. That night, Chester sends his two security guards Smith (Clancy Brown) and Wesson (Ted Levine) in an attempt to persuade Philip into giving Bennett a better grade. Philip is oblivious to discovering the two and unwittingly chases off the two goons with a Flubber-coated golf ball and bowling ball. He uses Flubber to give his car the ability of flight. During a test run, he discovers Wilson making the moves on Sara. Afterwards, Weebo attempts to confess her love of Philip, only to be shrugged off as a computer. In response, she secretly creates a holographic human version of herself in hopes of winning him over. Before Weebo can make out with Philip in this form as he sleeps, Philip awakens with another idea for Flubber. He enters an empty basketball court and tests the effects of Flubber on a basketball. Later, he gives Flubber-padded shoes to the unskilled Medfield basketball team to increase their abilities.

Back in Philip's home, a spiteful Weebo unleashes Flubber from his case, allowing him to dance around the house and cause general mayhem. After the close but successful basketball game, Philip's attempt to win Sara back into his favor fails. Philip dumps all of his emotional baggage onto Weebo, saying his absent-mindedness is due to his love of Sara. Weebo records Philip's ramblings and shows the footage to Sara, who then reconciles with Philip. Philip demonstrates Flubber's abilities to Sara and they discuss how he can be used for profit. However, Chester discovers Flubber's existence and sends Smith and Wesson to break into Philip's house and steal Flubber. Weebo attempts to fend off the goons, only to be struck down with a baseball bat. Philip and Sara return home and find that Flubber is gone and Weebo is destroyed. Philip discovers that Weebo created back-up data of herself onto Philip's computer in the event of her demise.

Philip and Sara confront Chester and try to retrieve Flubber, only to find that Wilson was behind the whole scheme. After a battle, Philip and Sara get Flubber back, raise enough money to save the college and finally have a successful marriage, along with Flubber and the daughter of Weebo, called Weebette.

Cast

- Robin Williams as Professor Philip Brainard
- Marcia Gay Harden as Doctor Sara Jean Reynolds
- Christopher McDonald as Wilson Croft
- Raymond J. Barry as Chester Hoenicker
- Clancy Brown as Smith
- Ted Levine as Wesson
- Wil Wheaton as Bennett Hoenicker
- Edie McClurg as Martha George
- Shane Vicker as a pedestrian.
- Jodi Benson as the voice of Weebo
- Leslie Stefanson as Sylvia
- Malcolm Brownson as Father
- Benjamin Brock as Window Boy
- Dakin Matthews as Minister
- Zack Zeigler as Teenage Boy
- Sam Lloyd as Coach Willy Barker
- Scott Michael Campbell as Dale Jepner
- Bob Sarlatte as Rutland Coach
- Bob Greene as Referee
- Tom Barlow as Medfield Basketball Player
- Scott Martin Gershin provided the voice of Flubber
- Julie Morrison as the voice of Weebette

Gag homages

Many gags are embellishments from the 1961 film, with John Hughes (Home Alone) rewriting the original Bill Walsh screenplay (based on Samuel W. Taylor's short story, *A Situation of Gravity*). Even though Walsh died in 1975, he received posthumous credit for this script. Filming began October 8, 1996 in San Francisco.

In the video game The Simpsons: Road Rage, if a character drops Professor Frink off at his destination quickly enough, one of the things he says is, "You must have had Flubber in the gas tank!"

Reception

Box office

Flubber performed well at the box office. It made $92,977,226 in the United States and a total of $85 million in other countries for a grand total of $178 million internationally.[1]

Critical response

It received largely negative reviews. The film holds a 23% approval rating at Rotten Tomatoes based on 31 reviews.[2] Metacritic gives the film a score of 37. The film was submitted for an Academy Award nomination for Best Visual Effects, but didn't get nominated. [3]

References

[1] *Flubber* (http://www.boxofficemojo.com/movies/?id=flubber.htm) at Box Office Mojo Amazon.com
[2] *Flubber* (http://www.rottentomatoes.com/m/flubber/) at Rotten Tomatoes Flixster
[3] *Flubber* (http://www.metacritic.com/movie/flubber) at Metacritic CBS

External links

- *Flubber* (http://www.imdb.com/title/tt0119137/) at the Internet Movie Database
- *Flubber* (http://www.allrovi.com/movies/movie/v158831) at AllRovi
- Official website (http://disney.go.com/vault/archives/movies/flubber/flubber.html)

Deconstructing Harry

Deconstructing Harry	
Theatrical release poster	
Directed by	Woody Allen
Produced by	Letty Aronson Jean Doumanian
Written by	Woody Allen
Starring	Caroline Aaron Woody Allen Kirstie Alley Bob Balaban Richard Benjamin Eric Bogosian Billy Crystal Judy Davis Hazelle Goodman Mariel Hemingway Amy Irving Julie Kavner Eric Lloyd Julia Louis-Dreyfus Tobey Maguire Demi Moore Elisabeth Shue Stanley Tucci Robin Williams
Cinematography	Carlo Di Palma
Editing by	Susan E. Morse
Distributed by	Fine Line Features (USA) Buena Vista International (UK)
Release date(s)	December 12, 1997 (US) April 17, 1998 (UK)
Running time	96 minutes
Country	USA
Language	English
Budget	$20,000,000
Box office	$10,569,071 (USA)

Deconstructing Harry is a black comedy film by Woody Allen released in 1997. This film tells the story of a successful writer called Harry Block, played by Allen himself, who draws inspiration from people he knows in real-life, and from events that happened to him, sometimes causing these people to become alienated from him as a result.

The central plot features Block driving to a university from which he was once thrown out, in order to receive an honorary degree. Three passengers accompany him on the journey: a prostitute, a friend, and his son, whom he has kidnapped from his divorced wife. However, there are many flashbacks, segments taken from Block's writing, and interactions with his own fictional characters.

Plot

One night, Lucy (Judy Davis) gets a taxi to the home of author Harry Block (Woody Allen). She has just read Harry's latest novel. In the novel, fictional Leslie (Julia Louis-Dreyfus) is having an affair with her sister's husband Ken (Richard Benjamin). Lucy is angry because the novel is patently based on her and Harry's own affair. As a result, everyone knows about it. Lucy pulls a gun out of her purse, saying she will kill herself. She then turns the gun on Harry and begins firing. She chases him out onto the roof. Harry insists that he has already been punished: his latest girlfriend Fay (Elisabeth Shue) has left him for his best friend Larry (Billy Crystal). To distract Lucy, Harry tells her a story he is currently writing: a semi-autobiographical story of a sex-obsessed young man named Harvey (Tobey Maguire) who is mistakenly claimed by Death.

In therapy, Harry realizes he has not changed since he was a sex-obsessed youth. Harry discusses the honoring ceremony at his old university, taking place the next day. Harry is miserable that he has nobody to share the occasion with. After the session, Harry asks his ex-wife Joan (Kirstie Alley) if he can take their son Hilliard (Eric Lloyd) to the ceremony. She refuses, stating that Harry is a bad influence on Hilliard. She is also furious at Harry for the novel he wrote. In it, the character Epstein (Stanley Tucci) marries Helen (Demi Moore), but the marriage begins to crumble after the birth of their son.

Harry runs into an acquaintance, Richard (Bob Balaban), who is worried about his health. After accompanying Richard to the hospital, Harry asks him to come to the university ceremony. Richard appears uninterested. Harry then goes to meet his ex-girlfriend Fay, who reveals that she is now engaged. Harry begs Fay to get back together with him. He asks Fay to accompany him to his ceremony, but it clashes with Fay's wedding, scheduled the following day.

That night, Harry sleeps with a prostitute, Cookie (Hazelle Goodman). Harry then asks Cookie to accompany him to his ceremony.

In the morning, Richard unexpectedly arrives to join Harry and Cookie on the journey. On a whim, Harry decides to "kidnap" his son Hilliard. Along the way, they stop at a carnival, then at Harry's half-sister Doris's (Caroline Aaron). Doris, a devoted Jew, is upset by Harry's portrayals of Judaism in his stories, as is her husband (Eric Bogosian). During the journey, Harry also encounters his fictional creations Ken and Helen, who force him to confront some painful truths about his life. Just before arriving at the university, Richard dies peacefully in the car.

Distressed, Harry literally slides out of focus, becoming blurred like one of his own fictional characters. Cookie helps him restore focus. The university's staffers gush over Harry, asking what he plans to write next. He describes a story about a man (based on himself) who journeys down to Hell to reclaim his true love (based on Fay) from the Devil (based on Larry - both being played by Billy Crystal). Harry and the Devil engage in a verbal duel as to who is truly the most evil of the two. Harry gets as far as arguing that he is a kidnapper before the story is interrupted by the arrival of the police. Harry is arrested for kidnapping Hilliard, for possessing a gun (it was Lucy's), and for having drugs in the car (belonging to Cookie).

Larry and Fay come from their wedding to bail Harry out of jail. Harry reluctantly gives them his blessings. Back at his apartment, a miserable Harry fantasizes that the university's ceremony is taking place. Harry realizes that he cannot function in life. He can only function in art. The film ends with Harry returning to his writing.

Cast

Actor	Role
Woody Allen	Harry Block
Richard Benjamin	Ken - Harry's Character
Kirstie Alley	Joan - Harry's former wife
Billy Crystal	Larry/devil - Harry's friend
Judy Davis	Lucy
Bob Balaban	Richard, friend that dies of a heart attack
Elisabeth Shue	Fay, Harry's last girlfriend
Tobey Maguire	Harvey Stern - Harry's character
Jennifer Garner	woman in the elevator - Harry's character
Paul Giamatti	Prof. Abbott
Stanley Tucci	Paul Epstein - Harry's Character
Julia Louis-Dreyfus	Leslie - Harry's Character
Mariel Hemingway	Beth Kramer
Robin Williams	Mel - Harry's Character
Hazelle Goodman	Cookie
Eric Bogosian	Burt - Harry's brother in law
Demi Moore	Helen - Harry's Character
Caroline Aaron	Doris, Harry's sister
Amy Irving	Jane
Shifra Lerer	Dolly - Harry's Character

Awards and nominations

Woody Allen was nominated for an Academy Award for Best Writing, Screenplay Written Directly for the Screen for *Deconstructing Harry*. The film was also nominated for a Golden Satellite Award for Best Motion Picture - Comedy or Musical.

Influences

The film is a general reworking of his earlier 1980 film *Stardust Memories*, which also had an artist go to a ceremony in his honor, while reminiscing over past relationships and trying to fix and stabilize current ones.[1]

Allen is well-known as an admirer of many European directors whose primary body of work was completed sometimes decades before his first script, and his films in particular often draw upon the works of Ingmar Bergman and Federico Fellini. The rough outline of the plot of *Deconstructing Harry*, that of an academic on a long drive to receive an honorary award from his old university while reflecting upon his life's experiences, essentially mirrors that of Bergman's *Wild Strawberries*.[2]

It is also widely acknowledged that Allen based the name of Harry Block on Antonius Block (Max von Sydow), the protagonist from Bergman's *The Seventh Seal*.[1] Some critics, including Roger Ebert, have suggested that the character of Harry Block is based on real-life author Philip Roth and not on Allen himself.[2]

External links

- *Deconstructing Harry* [3] at the Internet Movie Database
- *Deconstructing Harry* [4] at Rotten Tomatoes
- *Deconstructing Harry* [5] at AllRovi

Notes

[1] David Desser, Lester D. Friedman: *American Jewish Filmmakers* . University of Illinois Press 2003, 2nd edition, ISBN 9780252071539, pp. 105

[2] http://rogerebert.suntimes.com/apps/pbcs.dll/article?AID=/19971224/REVIEWS/712240301/1023

[3] http://www.imdb.com/title/tt0118954/

[4] http://www.rottentomatoes.com/m/deconstructing_harry/

[5] http://www.allrovi.com/movies/movie/v158645

Fathers' Day (film)

Fathers' Day	
Theatrical release poster	
Directed by	Ivan Reitman
Produced by	Ivan Reitman Joel Silver
Written by	Francis Veber (film *Les Compères*) Lowell Ganz & Babaloo Mandel (screenplay)
Starring	Robin Williams Billy Crystal Julia Louis-Dreyfus Nastassja Kinski Bruce Greenwood Charles Rocket Patti D'Arbanville
Music by	James Newton Howard
Cinematography	Stephen H. Burum
Editing by	Wendy Greene Bricmont Sheldon Kahn
Studio	Silver Pictures Northern Lights Entertainment
Distributed by	Warner Bros.
Release date(s)	May 9, 1997
Running time	98 minutes
Country	United States
Language	English
Budget	$85,000,000 (estimated)
Box office	$35,681,080 [1]

Fathers' Day is a 1997 comedy film directed by Ivan Reitman and starring Robin Williams, Billy Crystal, Julia Louis-Dreyfus, and Nastassja Kinski. It is a remake of the 1983 French film *Les Compères*.

In the film, Collette Andrews (Kinski) gets two former lovers, cynical lawyer Jack Lawrence (Crystal) and lonely, ex-hippie, suicidal writer Dale Putley (Williams) to help her search for her runaway teenage son Scott by telling each man that he is the father. When Jack and Dale run into each other and find out what's happening, they work together to find Scott and determine the identity of the actual father, who turns out to be Collette's husband, Bob.

The film features an appearance by the musical group Sugar Ray, and Mel Gibson makes a brief uncredited cameo appearance. IMDb credits Gibson as "Scott the Body Piercer". Catherine Reitman and Jason Reitman also have cameos.

Cast

- Robin Williams as Dale Putley
- Billy Crystal as Jack Lawrence
- Julia Louis-Dreyfus as Carrie Lawrence
- Nastassja Kinski as Collette Andrews
- Charlie Hofheimer as Scott Andrews
- Bruce Greenwood as Bob Andrews
- Charles Rocket as Russ Trainor
- Patti D'Arbanville as Shirley Trainor
- Jared Harris as Lee
- Louis Lombardi as Matt

Foreign Adaptations

In South Africa, *Fathers' Day* was released as ***What's Up Pop's?***, a title the distributor decided would be more appropriate for the local market. The name was subsequently changed to ***What's Up Pops?*** for DVD release, when they realized the apostrophe had been used incorrectly.

Reception

The movie was not a success with either critics or audiences. Julia Louis-Dreyfus was nominated for a Razzie Award for Worst Supporting Actress for her work in the film. *Fathers' Day* currently holds a 19% rating on Rotten Tomatoes based on 32 reviews.

References

[1] "Father's Day - Box Office Data" (http://www.the-numbers.com/movies/1997/FATHR.php). The Numbers. . Retrieved 7 August 2011.

External links

- *Fathers' Day* (http://www.imdb.com/title/tt0119109/) at the Internet Movie Database
- *Fathers' Day* (http://www.rottentomatoes.com/m/fathers_day/) at Rotten Tomatoes

Patch Adams (film)

Patch Adams	
Theatrical release poster	
Directed by	Tom Shadyac
Produced by	Mike Farrell Barry Kemp Marvin Minoff Charles Newirth Marsha Garces Williams
Screenplay by	Steve Oedekerk
Story by	Patch Adams Maureen Mylander
Starring	Robin Williams Daniel London Philip Seymour Hoffman Monica Potter
Music by	Marc Shaiman
Cinematography	Phedon Papamichael Jr.
Editing by	Don Zimmerman
Studio	Shady Acres
Distributed by	Universal Studios
Release date(s)	December 25, 1998
Running time	115 minutes
Country	United States
Language	English
Budget	$90 million
Box office	$202,292,902

Patch Adams is a 1998 comedy-drama film starring Robin Williams. Directed by Tom Shadyac, it is based on the life story of Dr. Hunter "Patch" Adams and the book *Gesundheit: Good Health is a Laughing Matter* by Adams and Maureen Mylander. The film is generally considered a box-office success, grossing over twice its budget in the United States alone. However, it was poorly received by most critics.[1]

Plot

In 1969, Hunter Adams (Robin Williams) is a troubled man who voluntarily commits himself into a mental institution. Once there, he finds that helping his fellow inmates gives him a purpose in life and earns the nickname "Patch". Because of this he aspires to become a medical doctor and two years later enrolls at Virginia Medical University, being the oldest first year student. He questions the school's approach to medical care, and clashes with the school's Dean Walcott (Bob Gunton), who believes that doctors must treat patients and not bond with them as people. Because of this and other incidents, including a prank during a medical conference, he is expelled from the school, although he is later reinstated due to his methods actually improving the health of patients. Adams encourages medical students to cultivate relationships with nurses and learn their interviewing skills early, and argues that death should be treated with dignity and even humor.

Adams begins a friendship with fellow student, Carin Fisher (Monica Potter), and develops his idea for a medical clinic built around his philosophy of treating patients through humor and compassion. With the help of Arthur Mendelson (Harold Gould), a wealthy man who was a patient whom Patch met while in the mental hospital, he purchases 105 acres (425,000 m^2) in West Virginia to construct the future Gesundheit! Institute. Together with Carin, medical student Truman Schiff (Daniel London), and some old friends, he renovates an old cottage. When they get the clinic running, they treat walk-in patients without medical insurance, and perform comedy sketches for them.

Carin and Patch's friendship soon turns into romance. She reveals to him that she had been molested as a child, distancing herself from men and dreaming of becoming a butterfly to escape her torment, but Patch reassures her that she can overcome her pain to help others. Encouraged, Carin wants to help a disturbed patient, Lawrence "Larry" Silver (Douglas Roberts), by visiting him at home. Larry turns out to be far more disturbed than anybody expected, and murders Carin, turning the shotgun on himself soon after. Patch is devastated and guilt-ridden by Carin's death. He reconsiders his outlook, and questions the goodness of humanity. He contemplates suicide and questions God for what happened. He then turns to see a butterfly which reminds him of Carin and hope, and so decides to continue his work in her honor. However he is dismissed from the school for a second time because he ran a clinic and practiced medicine without a license. He files a grievance with the state medical board at the advice of his former Med school roommate, Mitch Roman (Philip Seymour Hoffman), and must attend a hearing where it is decided whether he can graduate.

Patch is able to convince the board in a final speech that he did his best to help the people that came to him, and as a doctor it is his responsibility to treat the disease of the body as well as a person's spirit regardless of outcome. The jury accepts Patch's medical methods and decides to allow him to graduate. He receives a standing ovation from the packed hearing room. Even at graduation, Patch cannot help but be a non-conformist. After handing Adams a diploma, Walcott approves of Patch's conformity, to which Patch bows to the professors and the audience, revealing his nude bottom under his gown.

Cast

- Robin Williams as Dr. Hunter "Patch" Adams
- Daniel London as Truman
- Philip Seymour Hoffman as Mitch
- Monica Potter as Carin
- Bob Gunton as Dean Walcott
- Frances Lee McCain as Judy
- Irma P. Hall as Joletta
- Josef Sommer as Dr. Eaton
- Harold Gould as Arthur Mendelson
- Harve Presnell as Dean Anderson
- Michael Jeter as Rudy
- Barry Shabaka Henley as Emmet
- Richard Kiley as Dr. Titan
- Ryan Hurst as Neil
- Peter Coyote as Bill Davis
- Alan Tudyk as Everton

Production notes

The film was shot in three locations: Treasure Island, California (near San Francisco), Asheville (North Carolina) and the University of North Carolina at Chapel Hill. A diner in Point Richmond, (a district in Richmond, California) served as the University Diner. Several interior classroom scenes were filmed on the campus of UC Berkeley.

The producers worked very closely with the Make-A-Wish Foundation. For this reason, all but two of the ill children acting in this film actually have cancer.

The film has several major departures from Adam's real history. One is that the character of Carin is fictional, but is analogous to a real life friend of Adams (a man) who was murdered under similar circumstances. Another difference is the then-47 year old Robin Williams portrays Adams as enrolling in medical school very late in his life, his older age even being brought up in dialogue. In reality, Adams started medical school immediately and his educational progress was quite normal for a physician: He graduated high school at 18, college at 22, and medical school at 26.

Reception

Critical reception

The film received mostly negative reviews from critics. It currently has a score of 23% on Rotten Tomatoes, based on 55 reviews. The review aggregator Metacritic reported that the film averaged a rating of 25%.[2]

Box office performance

The film was released on December 25, 1998 in the United States and Canada and grossed $25.2 million in 2,712 theaters its opening weekend, ranking #1 at the box office. After its first weekend, it was the #2 film for four weeks.[3]

The film grossed US$202,292,902 worldwide — $135,026,902 in the United States and Canada and $67,266,000 in other territories.[4]

Awards

Despite such negative reviews, the film was nominated for an Academy Award for Best Music, Original Musical or Comedy Score by Marc Shaiman.

The film was nominated for Best Picture and Best Actor (Robin Williams) Golden Globe awards in the Musical or Comedy categories.

Reaction of the real Patch Adams

Adams criticized the film, saying it sacrificed a lot of his message in order to make a movie that would sell. He said that out of all aspects of his life and activism, the film portrayed him merely as a funny doctor.[5] Patch Adams also said of Robin Williams, "He made $21 million for four months of pretending to be me, in a very simplistic version, and did not give $10 to my free hospital. Patch Adams, the person, would have, if I had Robin's money, given *all* $21 million to a free hospital in a country where 80 million cannot get care."[6] When film critic Roger Ebert asked Adams his feelings about the film, Adams' first words to him were reportedly, "I hate that movie."[7]

References

[1] Patch Adams Movie Reviews, Pictures - Rotten Tomatoes (http://www.rottentomatoes.com/m/patch_adams/?critic=creamcrop)
[2] Patch Adams - MetaCritic. (http://www.metacritic.com/movie/patch-adams) Retrieved 2009-06-06.
[3] "Patch Adams (1998) - Weekend Box Office Results" (http://www.boxofficemojo.com/movies/?page=weekend&id=patchadams.htm). Box Office Mojo. . Retrieved 2008-02-08.
[4] "Patch Adams (1998)" (http://www.boxofficemojo.com/movies/?page=main&id=patchadams.htm). Box Office Mojo. . Retrieved 2008-02-09.
[5] http://www.chasingthefrog.com/reelfaces/patchadams.php
[6] Interview with Patch Adams on Repubblica.it (http://www.repubblica.it/persone/2010/05/04/news/patch-adams-3804546/)
[7] http://twitter.com/#!/ebertchicago/status/74603410325909504

External links

- *Patch Adams* (http://www.imdb.com/title/tt0129290/) at the Internet Movie Database
- The Real Patch Adams Official Web Site (http://www.patchadams.org/)
- COPATCH- Brazilian group that organizes Adams' trips to Brazil (http://www.copatch.com/)

What Dreams May Come (film)

What Dreams May Come	
Theatrical release poster	
Directed by	Vincent Ward
Produced by	Stephen Deutsch Barnet Bain
Screenplay by	Ronald Bass
Story by	Richard Matheson
Starring	Robin Williams Cuba Gooding, Jr. Annabella Sciorra
Music by	Michael Kamen
Cinematography	Eduardo Serra
Editing by	David Brenner
Studio	Interscope Communications
Distributed by	Universal Pictures PolyGram Filmed Entertainment
Release date(s)	October 2, 1998
Running time	113 minutes
Country	United States
Language	English
Budget	$85 million
Box office	$71,485,043

What Dreams May Come is a 1998 American supernatural drama film, starring Robin Williams, Cuba Gooding, Jr., and Annabella Sciorra. The film is based on the 1978 novel of the same name by Richard Matheson, and was directed by Vincent Ward. The title is taken from a line in Hamlet's *To be, or not to be* soliloquy.[1]

Plot

While vacationing in Italy, Dr. Christopher "Chris" Nielsen (Robin Williams) accidentally meets artist Annie Collins (Annabella Sciorra), with whom he has an instant connection. They marry and have two children: Ian (Josh Paddock) and Marie (Jessica Brooks Grant). Their idyllic life comes to an end when the children die in a car crash, and while things are at first very difficult with Annie mentally breaking down and the risk of divorce hanging over their heads, they manage to pull through.

However, on the anniversary of the day they decided not to divorce, Chris is involved in a car accident that kills him. Initially confused as to why nobody can interact with him, Chris lingers on Earth, watching Annie cope with the loss and attempting to communicate with her, until he understands how this harms her, and he decides to move on.

Chris awakens in Heaven (where everything is controlled and produced by his mind), where a man (Cuba Gooding Jr.) whom Chris recognizes as Albert, his friend and mentor from his medical residency, is there to guide him. As Albert walks Chris through his new abilities, both are surprised when a Blue Jacaranda tree appears unbidden in Chris's personal section of Heaven, matching a tree in a new painting of Annie's, indicating that the couple are a rare case of soul mates. During his tour he also encounters an Asian woman with a nametag reading "Leona", whom he recognizes as his daughter Marie, living in a section shaped like a diorama she loved. The two share a tearful reunion.

Meanwhile, on Earth, Annie is unable to cope with the loss of her husband and commits suicide. Chris, who is initially relieved that her suffering is over, quickly turns to anger when he learns that those who commit suicide are sent to Hell, as it is their nature to create "anti-fantasy" worlds based on their pain. He is adamant that he will rescue Annie from Hell, despite Albert's insistence that no one has ever succeeded in doing so. Albert agrees to find Chris a "tracker" (who takes the form of Sigmund Freud) to help find Annie's soul.

Journeying to Hell, Chris finds himself recalling memories of his son. Remembering how he'd called him the one man he'd want at his side to brave hell with, Chris realizes Albert is Ian: the boy explains that he chose to appear as Albert because he was the only person Chris would ever listen to. Before they part ways, Ian bids Chris to remember how he saved his marriage during the aftermath of the car crash, when Annie's grief led her to be institutionalized, and to their near divorce.

After traversing a field full of the faces of the damned, they come upon a hellish replica of his and Annie's house. The tracker, who reveals himself as the real Albert, warns Chris that if he stays with Annie for more than a few minutes, he may become permanently trapped too, and that all that may be done is allow them a proper goodbye. He also explains to Chris that his loved ones have appeared as other people so that he would allow them to guide him.

Chris enters the house to find Annie unable to remember anything, even that she committed suicide. After he is unable to make her remember, he chooses to join Annie forever in Hell. However, remembering the words he says as he accepts the sacrifice as the same ones he'd given her when she'd been institutionalized, Annie comes to, and Chris awakes with Annie in Heaven once more.

Chris and Annie are reunited with their children (who take on their own appearances once again), and while the four are happy to see each other again, Chris suggests being reborn, so that he and Annie can experience the only thing they won't be able to replicate in Heaven: life. The film ends with Chris and Annie meeting again as young children.

Cast

- Robin Williams as Chris Nielsen
- Cuba Gooding, Jr. as Albert Lewis
- Annabella Sciorra as Annie Collins-Nielsen
- Max von Sydow as The Tracker
- Jessica Brooks Grant as Marie Nielsen
- Josh Paddock as Ian Nielsen
- Rosalind Chao as Leona
- Lucinda Jenney as Mrs. Jacobs
- Maggie McCarthy as Stacey Jacobs

Production

What Dreams May Come was shot largely on Fuji Velvia film and is one of the few films to be done so. The Fuji Velvia film is known among landscape photographers for its vivid color reproduction.[2] Filming locations include various places in Marin County, Alameda County, and Glacier National Park.[3] Part of the "Hell" sequence was filmed on the decrepit and rusted hull of the *Essex* class aircraft carrier USS *Oriskany* (CV-34) while berthed at Mare Island in Vallejo, California. The ship was later sunk to make an artificial reef on May 17, 2006.[4]

Annette Bening was originally cast to play Annie, but extricated herself in advance of production.[5]

The original prints of the film were lost to a fire at Universal Studios' backlot on June 1, 2008. A worldwide search was launched for a copy, which was found in Europe.[6]

The special edition DVD shows an alternate ending — which is the ending from the novel — in which the reincarnation is not a choice, but part of the natural order. Chris and Annie will meet again in their new lives, but Annie must atone for killing herself — her new incarnation will die young, and Chris will spend the remainder of his new life as a widower before the two are once again reunited in Heaven. The film then goes to Sri Lanka where a woman is giving birth to a little girl, presumed to be Annie. In Philadelphia, a little boy is born, presumably Chris. This ending was left roughly edited and unfinished.

Differences from the novel

The novel has significant differences from the film, in both its plot and its vision of the afterlife. Its approach to the love story is considerably less sentimental, its tone more scientific than fantastic.

There are far more references to Theosophical, New Age and paranormal beliefs.[7] Indeed, the author Richard Matheson claims in an introductory note that only the characters are fictional, and that almost everything else is based on research (the book contains an extensive bibliography). Story elements that do not show up in the film include astral projection, telepathy, a séance, and the term "Summerland" (the name for a simplified Heaven in Theosophy, and for Heaven in general in earth-based religions such as Wicca).

The details of Chris's life on Earth also differ strongly in the novel. Only Chris and his wife (called Ann) die. Their children, who are grownups rather than youngsters, remain alive, as minor characters. Albert and Leona are exactly the people they appear to be, and the character played by Max Von Sydow does not appear in the book at all. Albert is Chris's cousin and not African American as in the film, while Leona's ethnicity is not divulged. Chris and Ann are rural, country types rather than the urbanites portrayed in the film, and he is not a pediatrician, nor is she a painter. He's a Hollywood screenwriter, and she has a variety of jobs.

The afterlife imagery is based on natural scenery rather than paintings. The Heavenly environment doesn't automatically mold itself to people's thoughts, as it does in the film; some practice and expertise is required to build things. The novel's depiction of Hell is considerably more violent than in the film. Chris finds it difficult to move, breathe, or even see, and he suffers physical torture at the hands of some of the inhabitants. He does not encounter ships, thunderstorms, fire, or the sea of human faces that he must walk upon in the film. Instead, he and Albert climb across craggy cliffs and encounter such sights as a swarm of insects that attack people's bodies.

Ann is consigned to Hell for only 24 years, not eternity. At the end, which resembles an alternate version of the film but not the standard version, she escapes from Hell by being reincarnated, because she is not ready for Heaven.

Soundtrack

The soundtrack for *What Dreams May Come* was composed and conducted by Michael Kamen and produced by James Seymour Brett. Ennio Morricone completed and recorded a full score for the film. After editorial changes were made, his score was rejected, and Kamen was hired to do the film score.[8] Dawn Soler, the musical supervisor for the film, has said in an interview that Axl Rose intended to have the then-unreleased Guns N' Roses song "This I Love" in the film, but Ward did not use the song. It was later added to the band's album *Chinese Democracy*.

The main theme song ("Chris and Annie's Theme") for this movie was based on The New York Rock Ensemble's song "Beside You," from their 1971 album "Roll Over [9]."

In 2011, the rock band Midas Fate released a single called What Dreams May Come, with the homonymous track and graphic arts being based on the film.

Reception

The film won an Academy Award for its visual effects awarded to Kevin Mack, Joel Hynek, Nickolas Brooks, and Stuart Robertson. It was nominated for the Academy Award for Best Art Direction. It won the Art Directors Guild Award for Excellence in Production Design.

Roger Ebert of the *Chicago Sun-Times* gave a highly positive review, awarding the film three and a half stars out of four, remarking:

> I have my disappointments with it. But I would not want them to discourage you from seeing it, because this is a film that even in its imperfect form shows how movies can imagine the unknown, can lead our imaginations into wonderful places. And it contains heartbreakingly effective performances by Robin Williams and Annabella Sciorra."[10]

James Berardinelli of *ReelViews* gave *What Dreams May Come* three stars out of four, saying:

> Many movies have offered representations of heaven and hell, but few with as much conviction and creativity as *What Dreams May Come*. The plot, which focuses on the sacrifices one man will make for true love, is neither complicated nor original, but, bolstered by the director's incredible visual sense, it becomes an affecting piece of drama.[11]

Stephen Hunter of the *Washington Post* disliked the film, which he felt was "overproduced and underpopulated, with either characters or ideas" and "lacks ... drama."[12] Owen Gleiberman of *Entertainment Weekly* gave the film a C+ rating, saying that

> if the film's morose sentimentality sidesteps ludicrousness, it's also not very dramatic. We feel as if we're stuck inside a two-hour dream sequence. There's a central contradiction in a fairy tale like this one: the film may preach to the audience about matters of the spirit, but its bejeweled special-effects vision of the afterlife can't help but come off as aggressively literal-minded."[13]

When asked his thoughts on the film adaptation of his story, Richard Matheson said, "I will not comment on *What Dreams May Come* except to say that a major producer in Hollywood said to me, 'They should have shot your book.' Amen."[14]

In other media

The film's DVD was referenced in *Family Guy* in the episode "Brian's Got a Brand New Bag" where Peter wouldn't take the DVD for free in a $1 clear out sale.

References

[1] No Sweat Shakespeare (http://www.nosweatshakespeare.com/quotes/soliloquies/hamlet-to-be-or-not-to-be.htm), *To Be Or Not To Be*: Hamlet Soliloquy. Line 11.

[2] Cinema Blend (http://www.cinemablend.com/reviews/What-Dreams-May-Come-461.html), *What Dreams May Come* Movie Review

[3] Film In America (http://www.filminamerica.com/Movies/WhatDreamsMayCome/), *What Dreams May Come*.

[4] Williams, Carol J. (May 10, 2006). "Carrier Will Sink to Serve" (http://articles.latimes.com/2006/may/10/nation/na-oriskany10). *Los Angeles Times* (Tribune Company). . Retrieved August 22, 2010.

[5] http://www.aintitcool.com/node/1961

[6] http://thestudiotour.com/ush/backlot/fire_2008.shtml

[7] Julien R. Fielding, *Discovering World Religions At 24 Frames Per Second*, published in *Journal of Media and Religion* Volume 8, Issue 4, Oct. 2009.

[8] http://users.telenet.be/soundtrack-fm/Reviews/Ennio_Morricone/what_dreams/what_dreams.htm

[9] http://www.allmusic.com/album/roll-over-r45570

[10] Ebert, Roger. *What Dreams May Come* review (http://rogerebert.suntimes.com/apps/pbcs.dll/article?AID=/19981002/REVIEWS/810020306/1023), *Chicago Sun-Times*, October 2, 1998.

[11] Berardinelli, James. *What Dreams May Come* review (http://www.reelviews.net/movies/w/what_dreams.html), ReelViews.net, 1998.

[12] Hunter, Stephen. *What Dreams May Come* review (http://www.washingtonpost.com/wp-srv/style/longterm/movies/videos/whatdreamsmaycomehunter.htm) *Washington Post*, October 2, 1998.

[13] Gleiberman, Owen. *What Dreams May Come* review (http://www.ew.com/ew/article/0,,285180,00.html) *Entertainment Weekly*, October 9, 1998
[14] Richard Matheson interview (http://www.iamlegendarchive.com/matheson.html) at The *I Am Legend* Archive

External links

- *What Dreams May Come* (http://www.imdb.com/title/tt0120889/) at the Internet Movie Database
- *What Dreams May Come* (http://www.allrovi.com/movies/movie/v172903) at AllRovi
- *What Dreams May Come* (http://www.rottentomatoes.com/m/what_dreams_may_come/) at Rotten Tomatoes
- *What Dreams May Come at Vincent Ward Films* (http://vincentwardfilms.com/films/what-dreams-may-come/synopsis/)

Bicentennial Man (film)

Bicentennial Man	
Promotional poster	
Directed by	Chris Columbus
Produced by	Michael Barnathan Chris Columbus Gail Katz
Written by	Isaac Asimov Robert Silverberg Nicholas Kazan
Narrated by	Robin Williams
Starring	Robin Williams Sam Neill Embeth Davidtz Oliver Platt Wendy Crewson Hallie Kate Eisenberg Stephen Root Lynne Thigpen
Music by	James Horner
Cinematography	Phil Meheux
Editing by	Neil Travis
Studio	1492 Pictures
Distributed by	**United States:** Touchstone Pictures **International:** Columbia Pictures
Release date(s)	December 17, 1999
Running time	132 minutes
Country	United States
Language	English
Budget	$100 million
Box office	$93,700,000

Bicentennial Man is a 1999 American drama and science fiction film starring Robin Williams and Sam Neill. Based on the novel *The Positronic Man*, co-written by Isaac Asimov and Robert Silverberg which is itself based on Asimov's original novella titled *The Bicentennial Man*, the plot explores issues of humanity, slavery, prejudice, maturity, intellectual freedom, conformity, sex, love, and mortality. It was directed by Chris Columbus.

Plot

The NDR series robot "Andrew" (Robin Williams) is introduced in 2205 into the Martin family home to perform housekeeping and maintenance duties. The family's reactions range from acceptance and curiosity to outright rejection and deliberate vandalism by their surly older daughter, Grace (Lindze Letherman), which leads to the discovery that Andrew can both identify emotions and reciprocate in kind. When Andrew accidentally breaks a figurine belonging to "Little Miss" Amanda (Hallie Kate Eisenberg), he carves a replacement out of wood. The family is astonished by this creativity and "Sir" Richard Martin (Sam Neill) takes Andrew to his manufacturer, to inquire if all the robots are like him. The CEO of the company sees this development as a problem and wishes to scrap Andrew. Angered, Martin takes Andrew home and allows him to pursue his own development, encouraging Andrew to educate himself in the humanities.

Years later, following an accident in which Andrew's thumb is accidentally cut off, Martin again takes him to NorthAm Robotics for repairs, ensuring first that Andrew's personality will remain unharmed. Andrew requests that while he is being repaired his face be altered to convey the emotions he feels but cannot fully express.

After the wedding of Little Miss he realizes there are no more orders for him to run. Andrew eventually asks for his freedom, much to Martin's dismay. He grants the request, but banishes Andrew so he can be "completely" free. As Andrew leaves, Martin comments that he has stopped referring to himself as "one". Andrew builds himself a home and lives alone. In 2248, Andrew sees Martin one last time on his deathbed. Martin apologizes for banishing him as he silently says his goodbye to Andrew who states it was an honor serving him.

Andrew goes on a quest to locate more NDR series robots to discover if others have also developed sentience. After years of failure he finds Galatea (Kiersten Warren), an NDR robot that has been given feminine attributes and personality. These however are simply aspects of her programming and not something which she developed as with Andrew. Galatea is owned by Rupert Burns (Oliver Platt), son of the original NDR robot designer. Burns works to create a more human look for robots, but is unable to attract funding. Andrew agrees to finance the research and the two join forces to give Andrew artificial human face and hair. He maintains contact with Little Miss. Andrew eventually comes back to greet Little Miss but instead meets Portia, Little Miss's granddaughter, who looks exactly like a younger Little Miss. The now aged Little Miss explains to Andrew that it's a genetic likeness that skipped a generation.

When Andrew comes to the hospital to see Little Miss one last time, he notices the horse he carved for her when she was young. She silently passes away, and Andrew feels the pain of not being able to cry and realizes that every human being he cares for will eventually die.

Andrew begins to study medicine and designs mechanical equivalents of human organs, including a central nervous system, which eventually allows him to acquire tactile sensations. Meanwhile, his friendship with Portia evolves into romance. At first Portia is uncertain about "investing her emotions in a machine" and almost marries someone else, but Andrew confronts her about her emotions and they eventually engage in a romantic and sexual relationship. Upon realizing that his relationship with Portia would never be socially accepted, Andrew petitions the World Congress to recognize him as human, which would allow him and Portia to be legally married, but is rejected; the Speaker of the Congress explains that society can tolerate an everlasting machine, but argues that an immortal human would create too much jealousy and anger for him to be with another human being and he is declared a machine from that day on.

When eventually Portia decides that she doesn't want to have her life forever prolonged by Andrew's medical inventions, Andrew realizes that when she dies, he wouldn't want to live on without her. He works with Rupert (now an old man) to introduce blood into his system and to cause his brain to decay, thereby allowing him to age; Rupert officially welcomes him to the human condition, as it then becomes unknown when exactly Andrew would die. Some time later, Andrew attends the World Congress again, now appearing old and frail, and again petitions to be declared a human being.

On his death bed, with Portia beside him, Andrew watches as the Speaker of the World Congress announces on television the court's decision: that Andrew Martin is officially recognized as human, and that aside from "Methuselah and other Biblical figures," is the oldest human being in history at the age of two hundred years. The Speaker also validates the marriage between Portia and Andrew. Andrew dies while listening to the broadcast, and Portia orders their nurse, a now human-looking Galatea (who also apparently developed self sentience due to the changes that Andrew made on her), to unplug her life support machine. The film ends with Portia about to die hand-in-hand with Andrew, as she whispers to him "*See you soon.*"

Cast

- Robin Williams as Andrew Martin
- Embeth Davidtz as 'Little Miss' Amanda Martin/Portia Charney
- Sam Neill as 'Sir' Richard Martin
- Oliver Platt as Rupert Burns
- Kiersten Warren as Galatea
- Wendy Crewson as 'Ma´am' Rachel Martin
- Hallie Kate Eisenberg as 'Little Miss' Amanda Martin age 7
- Lindze Letherman as 'Miss' Grace Martin age 9
- Angela Landis as 'Miss' Grace Martin
- John Michael Higgins as Bill Feingold, Martin's Lawyer
- Bradley Whitford as Lloyd Charney
- Igor Hiller as Lloyd Charney age 10
- Joe Bellan as Robot Delivery Man
- Brett Wagner as Robot Delivery Man
- Stephen Root as Dennis Mansky, Head of Northam Robotics
- Lynne Thigpen as the second President/Speaker of the World Congress

Accolades

- Academy Awards — Best Makeup
- Blockbuster Entertainment Award — Favorite Actor — Comedy (Robin Williams)
- Blockbuster Entertainment Award — Favorite Actress — Comedy (Embeth Davidtz)
- Hollywood Makeup Artist and Hair Stylist Guild Award — Best Character Makeup — Feature
- Blimp Award — Favorite Movie Actor (Robin Williams)
- Razzie Award — Worst Actor (Robin Williams)
- YoungStar Award — Best Young Actress/Performance in a Motion Picture Comedy (Hallie Kate Eisenberg)

Awards received

- Hollywood Makeup Artist and Hair Stylist Guild Award — Best Special Effects Makeup — Feature

Reception

Bicentennial Man received mixed reviews. The film holds a 38% approval rating on Rotten Tomatoes with 35 out of 93 critics giving it a positive review with an average rating of 4.8 out of 10,[1] with a consensus saying 'Bicentennial Man is ruined by a bad script and ends up being dull and mawkish, while the review aggregator Metacritic gives it a score of 42.[2]

Roger Ebert gave it two out of four stars saying, "*Bicentennial Man* begins with promise, proceeds in fits and starts, and finally sinks into a cornball drone of greeting-card sentiment. Robin Williams spends the first half of the film encased in a metallic robot suit, and when he emerges, the script turns robotic instead. What a letdown."[3] William Arnold of Seattle Post-Intelligencer said the film "Becomes a somber, sentimental and rather profound romantic fantasy that is more true to the spirit of the Golden Age of science-fiction writing than possibly any other movie of the '90s." Todd McCarthy of *Variety* summed it up as "An ambitious tale handled in a dawdling, sentimental way".

References

[1] Bicentennial Man Movie Reviews, Pictures - Rotten Tomatoes (http://www.rottentomatoes.com/m/bicentennial_man)

[2] Search Reviews, Articles, People, Trailers and more at Metacritic (http://www.metacritic.com/video/titles/bincentennialman)

[3] Bicentennial Man :: rogerebert.com :: Reviews (http://rogerebert.suntimes.com/apps/pbcs.dll/article?AID=/19991217/REVIEWS/912170302/1023)

External links

- *Bicentennial Man* (http://www.imdb.com/title/tt0182789/) at the Internet Movie Database
- *Bicentennial Man* (http://tcmdb.com/title/title.jsp?stid=442769) at the TCM Movie Database
- *Bicentennial Man* (http://www.allrovi.com/movies/movie/v1:181283) at AllRovi
- *Bicentennial Man* (http://www.rottentomatoes.com/m/bicentennial_man/) at Rotten Tomatoes
- *Bicentennial Man* (http://www.metacritic.com/movie/bicentennialman) at Metacritic
- *Bicentennial Man* (http://www.boxofficemojo.com/movies/?id=bicentennialman.htm) at Box Office Mojo

Jakob the Liar

Jakob the Liar	
Theatrical release poster	
Directed by	Peter Kassovitz
Produced by	Steven Haft Marsha Garces Williams
Written by	Jurek Becker (novel) Peter Kassovitz & Didier Decoin (screenplay)
Starring	Robin Williams Alan Arkin Liev Schreiber Hannah Taylor-Gordon Bob Balaban
Music by	Edward Shearmur
Cinematography	Elemér Ragályi
Editing by	Claire Simpson
Distributed by	Columbia Pictures
Release date(s)	September 24, 1999
Running time	120 min.
Country	United States
Language	English
Budget	$45 million
Box office	$4,956,401 (domestic) [1]

Jakob the Liar is a 1999 American tragicomedy film directed by Peter Kassovitz and starring Robin Williams, Alan Arkin, Liev Schreiber, Hannah Taylor-Gordon, and Bob Balaban. The movie is set in 1944 in a ghetto in German-occupied Poland in the times of the Holocaust and is based on the book by Jurek Becker about World War II Jewish ghetto life. It is also a remake of the East German DEFA film *Jakob der Lügner* from 1975.

Plot

In the early 1944 Poland, a Polish-Jewish shopkeeper named Jakob is summoned to the German headquarters after being falsely accused of being out after curfew. While waiting for the commander, Jakob overhears a German radio broadcast speaking about Soviet offensives. Returned to the ghetto, Jakob shares his information with a friend, sparking rumors that there is a secret radio within the ghetto. After hestitating, Jakob decides to use the chance to spread hope throughout the ghetto by continuing to tell the optimistic, fantastic tales that he allegedly heard from "his secret radio" and his lies keep hope and humor alive among the isolated ghetto inhabitants. He, however, has a real secret in that he is hiding a young Jewish girl who escaped from an extermination camp deportation train.

The Gestapo learn of the mythical radio, however, and begin a search for the resistance hero who dares operate it. Jakob surrenders himself to the Germans as they demand the person with the radio give himself up or risk hostages being killed. During interrogation, Jakob tells the police commander that he had only listened to the radio inside his office. He is ordered to announce publicly that this was all a lie, so the ghetto's liquidation would then proceed in an orderly fashion. When presented to the public, Jakob refuses to tell the truth, but is shot before he can make his own speech.

In the film's ending, Jakob says, post-mortem, that all the ghetto's residents were then deported and were never seen again. As in the novel, there is an "alternate" fairy tale-style ending where the Soviet forces arrive following Jakob's death, just in time to save the Jews.

Book-film differences

The plot is slightly different in a few places from the book. Notable discrepancies include:

- Lina is not living with Jakob from the beginning, but instead he meets her on his way home from the Gestapo station in the movie's beginning;
- The news of the radio is first told to Mischa, a friend of Jakob, to prevent him from attempting to steal potatoes off of a German military train;
- Jakob is never caught and interrogated; instead he is deported, along with the rest of the Jews, and presumably dies in a death camp;
- The movie's alternate ending has Jakob killed in front of the ghetto, instead of being shot during an escape attempt in the book's alternate ending.

Reception

Produced on a budget of $45 million, *Jakob the Liar* was released on September 24, 1999. According to boxofficemojo.com, it opened in 1,200 theaters and made $2,056,647 in its opening weekend, placing 8th at the box office. The film's total domestic gross was just $4,956,401.

The movie presently holds a rating of "rotten" on Rotten Tomatoes with only 30% positive reviews and an average rating of 4.7/10. Roger Ebert gave the film two stars (out of four), comparing it to the similarly themed *Life is Beautiful* by saying, "I prefer "Life Is Beautiful," which is clearly a fantasy, to "Jakob the Liar," which is just as contrived and manipulative but pretends it is not." He went on to say about the acting in the film: "Williams is a talented performer who moves me in the right roles but has a weakness for the wrong ones. The screenplay and direction are lugubrious, as the characters march in their overwritten and often overacted roles toward a foregone conclusion."[2]

The film earned a Razzie Award nomination: Worst Actor for Robin Williams (also for *Bicentennial Man*).

References

[1] "Jakob the Liar (1999)" (http://www.boxofficemojo.com/movies/?id=jakobtheliar.htm). Box Office Mojo. . Retrieved 2010-01-18.

[2] Roger Ebert's review of "Jakob the Liar (http://rogerebert.suntimes.com/apps/pbcs.dll/article?AID=/19990924/REVIEWS/909240305/)

External links

- *Jakob the Liar* (http://www.imdb.com/title/tt0120716/) at the Internet Movie Database
- *Jakob the Liar* (http://www.allrovi.com/movies/movie/v180793) at AllRovi
- *Jakob the Liar* (http://www.rottentomatoes.com/m/jakob_the_liar/) at Rotten Tomatoes

A.I. Artificial Intelligence

A.I. Artificial Intelligence	
Theatrical release poster	
Directed by	Steven Spielberg
Produced by	Steven Spielberg Stanley Kubrick Jan Harlan Kathleen Kennedy Walter F. Parkes Bonnie Curtis
Screenplay by	Steven Spielberg Ian Watson
Story by	Ian Watson
Based on	"Super-Toys Last All Summer Long" by Brian Aldiss (first act only), Stanley Kubrick's original script
Narrated by	Ben Kingsley
Starring	Haley Joel Osment Jude Law Frances O'Connor Sam Robards Jake Thomas William Hurt
Music by	John Williams
Cinematography	Janusz Kamiński
Editing by	Michael Kahn
Studio	DreamWorks Amblin Entertainment The Kennedy/Marshall Company Stanley Kubrick Productions
Distributed by	Warner Bros. Pictures
Release date(s)	June 29, 2001
Running time	146 minutes
Country	United States
Language	English
Budget	$100 million
Box office	$235,926,552

A.I. Artificial Intelligence, also known as ***A.I.***, is a 2001 science fiction drama film directed, produced and co-written by Steven Spielberg. Based on Brian Aldiss' short story "Super-Toys Last All Summer Long", the film stars Haley Joel Osment, Jude Law, Frances O'Connor, Sam Robards, Jake Thomas and William Hurt. Set sometime in the future, *A.I.* tells the story of David, a child-like android uniquely programmed with the ability to love.

Development of *A.I.* originally began with director Stanley Kubrick in the early 1970s. Kubrick hired a series of writers up until the mid-1990s, including Brian Aldiss, Bob Shaw, Ian Watson and Sara Maitland. The film languished in development hell for years, partly because Kubrick felt computer-generated imagery was not advanced enough to create the David character, whom he believed no child actor would believably portray. In 1995, Kubrick handed *A.I.* to Steven Spielberg, but the film did not gain momentum until Kubrick's death in 1999. Spielberg remained close to Watson's film treatment for the screenplay. *A.I.* was greeted with mixed positive reviews from critics. This film was dedicated to Kubrick's memory after the end credits, saying "For Stanley Kubrick".

Plot

Global warming has led to melting polar ice caps, flooded coastlines and a drastic reduction of the human population. There is a new class of robots called mechas, advanced humanoids capable of emulating thoughts and emotions. David (Haley Joel Osment), a prototype model created by Cybertronics, is designed to resemble a human child and to display love for its human owners. They test their creation with one of their employees, Henry Swinton (Sam Robards), and his wife Monica (Frances O'Connor). The Swintons' son, Martin (Jake Thomas), was placed in suspended animation until a cure can be found for his rare disease. Although Monica is initially frightened of David, she eventually warms to him after activating his imprinting protocol, which irreversibly causes David to project love for her, the same as any child would love a parent. He is also befriended by Teddy (Jack Angel), a robotic teddy bear, who takes it upon himself to care for David's well being.

A cure is found for Martin and he is brought home; a sibling rivalry ensues between Martin and David. Martin convinces David to go to Monica in the middle of the night and cut off a lock of her hair, but the parents wake up and are very upset. At a pool party, one of Martin's friends activates David's self-protection programming by poking him with a knife. David clings to Martin and they both fall into the pool, where heavy David sinks to the bottom while still clinging to Martin. Martin is saved from drowning, but Henry in particular is shocked by David's actions, becoming concerned that David's capacity for love has also given him the ability to hate. Henry persuades Monica to return David to Cybertronics, where David will be destroyed. However, on the way Monica decides to abandon David in the forest (alongside Teddy) to hide as an unregistered mecha instead of being destroyed. David is captured for an anti-mecha Flesh Fair, an event where obsolete mechas are destroyed in front of cheering crowds. David is nearly killed, but the crowd is swayed by his realistic nature (David, unlike other mechas, pleads for his life) and he escapes, along with Gigolo Joe (Jude Law), a male prostitute mecha on the run after being framed for murder.

The two set out to find the Blue Fairy, whom David remembers from the story *The Adventures of Pinocchio*. He is convinced that the Blue Fairy will transform him into a human boy, allowing Monica to love him and take him home. Joe and David make their way to Rouge City. Information from a holographic answer engine called "Dr. Know" (Robin Williams) eventually leads them to the top of Rockefeller Center in partially-underwater Manhattan. They fly to New York a flying submersible vehicle called an amphibicopter they stole from police, who are still chasing Joe. David meets his human creator, Professor Hobby (William Hurt), who excitedly tells David that finding him was a test, which has demonstrated the reality of his love and desire. It also becomes clear that many copies of David are already being manufactured, along with female versions. David sadly realizes he is not unique. A disheartened David attempts to commit suicide by falling from a ledge into the ocean, but Joe rescues him with the amphibicopter. David tells Joe he saw the Blue Fairy underwater, and wants to go down to her. At that moment, Joe is captured by the authorities with the use of an electromagnet. David and Teddy take the amphibicopter to the fairy, which turns out to be a statue from a submerged attraction at Coney Island. Teddy and David become trapped when the Wonder Wheel falls on their vehicle. Believing the Blue Fairy to be real, David asks to be turned into a real boy, repeating his wish without end, until the ocean freezes and his internal power source drains away.

2,000 years later, humans are extinct and Manhattan is buried under several hundred feet of sea ice.[1] Mechas have evolved into a highly advanced alien-looking humanoid form.[2] They find David and Teddy and discover they are functional mechas who knew living humans, making them special and unique. David is revived and walks to the frozen Blue Fairy statue, which cracks and collapses as he touches it. Having received and comprehended his memories, the advanced mechas use them to reconstruct the Swinton home and explain to David via an interactive image of the Blue Fairy (Meryl Streep) that it is not possible to make him human. However, at David's insistence, they recreate Monica from DNA in the lock of her hair which had been saved by Teddy. Unfortunately, she can only live for a single day and the process cannot be repeated. David spends the happiest day of his life with Monica and Teddy, and Monica tells David that she loves him and has always loved him as she drifts to sleep for the final time. David lies down next to her, closes his eyes and goes "to that place where dreams are born".

Cast

- Haley Joel Osment as David, an innovative mecha created by Cybertronics and programmed with the ability to love. He is adopted by Henry and Monica Swinton, but a sibling rivalry ensues once their son Martin comes out of suspended animation. Osment was Spielberg's first and only choice for the role. Osment avoided blinking his eyes to perfectly portray the character, and "programmed" himself with good posture for realism.[3]
- Jude Law as Gigolo Joe, a male prostitute mecha programmed with the ability to mimic love, like David, but in a different sense. To prepare for the role, Law studied the acting of Fred Astaire and Gene Kelly.[4]
- Frances O'Connor as Monica Swinton, David's adopted mother who reads him *The Adventures of Pinocchio*. She is first displeased to have David in her home but soon falls in love with him.
- Sam Robards as Henry Swinton, an employee at Cybertronics and husband of Monica. Henry is reluctant to take David home, and soon sees David as dangerous to his family.
- Jake Thomas as Martin Swinton, Henry and Monica's first son, who was placed in suspended animation. When Martin comes back, he convinces David to cut off a lock of Monica's hair.
- William Hurt as Professor Allen Hobby, responsible for shepherding the creation of David. He resides in New York City, which is crippled by the effects of global warming but still functioning as Cybertronics' headquarters. David is modeled after Hobby's own son, also named David, who died at a young age.
- Brendan Gleeson as Lord Johnson-Johnson, the owner and master of ceremonies of the Flesh Fair.

Voices

- Jack Angel as Teddy, David's robotic teddy bear.
- Ben Kingsley as narrator and the leader of the futuristic mechas. He also appears briefly as one of the technicians who repairs David after he eats spinach.
- Robin Williams as Dr. Know, a holographic answer engine. (Cameo)
- Meryl Streep as Blue Fairy. (Cameo)
- Chris Rock as a mecha killed at the Flesh Fair. (Cameo)

Production

Kubrick began development on an adaptation of "Super-Toys Last All Summer Long" in the early 1970s, hiring the short story's author, Brian Aldiss to write a film treatment. In 1985, Kubrick brought longtime friend Steven Spielberg on board to produce the film,[5] along with Jan Harlan. Warner Bros. agreed to co-finance *A.I.* and cover distribution duties.[6] The film labored in development hell, and Aldiss was fired by Kubrick over creative differences in 1989.[7] Bob Shaw served as writer very briefly, leaving after six weeks because of Kubrick's demanding work schedule, and Ian Watson was hired as the new writer in March 1990. Aldiss later remarked, "Not only did the bastard fire me, he hired my enemy [Watson] instead." Kubrick handed Watson *The Adventures of Pinocchio* for inspiration, calling *A.I.* "a picaresque robot version of *Pinocchio*".[6] [8]

Three weeks later Watson gave Kubrick his first story treatment, and concluded his work on *A.I.* in May 1991 with another treatment, at 90 pages. Gigolo Joe was originally conceived as a GI mecha, but Watson suggested changing him to a male prostitute. Kubrick joked, "I guess we lost the kiddie market."[6] In the meantime, Kubrick dropped *A.I.* to work on a film adaptation of *Wartime Lies*, feeling computer animation was not advanced enough to create the David character. However, after the release of Spielberg's *Jurassic Park* (with its innovative use of computer-generated imagery), it was announced in November 1993 that production would begin in 1994.[9] Dennis Muren and Ned Gorman, who worked on *Jurassic Park*, became visual effects supervisors,[7] but Kubrick was displeased with their previsualization, and at the expense of hiring Industrial Light & Magic.[2]

Stanley [Kubrick] showed Steven [Spielberg] 650 drawings which he had, and the script and the story, everything. Stanley said, "Look, why don't you direct it and I'll produce it." Steven was almost in shock.

Producer Jan Harlan, on Spielberg's first meeting with Kubrick about *A.I.*[10]

In early 1994, the film was in pre-production with Christopher "Fangorn" Baker as concept artist, and Sara Maitland assisting on the story, which gave it "a feminist fairy-tale focus".[6] Maitland said that Kubrick never referred to the film as *A.I.*, but as *Pinocchio*.[2] Chris Cunningham became the new visual effects supervisor. Some of his unproduced work for *A.I.* can be seen on the DVD, *The Work of Director Chris Cunningham*.[11] Aside from considering computer animation, Kubrick also had Joseph Mazzello do a screen test for the lead role.[2] Cunningham helped assemble a series of "little robot-type humans" for the David character. "We tried to construct a little boy with a movable rubber face to see whether we could make it look appealing," producer Jan Harlan reflected. "But it was a total failure, it looked awful." Hans Moravec was brought in as a technical consultant.[2]

Meanwhile, Kubrick and Harlan thought *A.I.* would be closer to Steven Spielberg's sensibilities as director.[12] [13] Kubrick handed the position to Spielberg in 1995, but Spielberg chose to direct other projects, and convinced Kubrick to remain as director.[10] [14] The film was put on hold due to Kubrick's commitment to *Eyes Wide Shut* (1999).[15] After the filmmaker's death in March 1999, Harlan and Christiane Kubrick approached Spielberg to take over the director's position.[16] [17] By November 1999, Spielberg was writing the screenplay based on Watson's 90-page story treatment. It was his first solo screenplay credit since *Close Encounters of the Third Kind* (1977).[18] Spielberg remained close to Watson's treatment, but removed various sex scenes with Gigolo Joe, which Kubrick had in mind.[13] Pre-production was briefly halted during February 2000, because Spielberg pondered directing other projects, which were *Harry Potter and the Philosopher's Stone*, *Minority Report* and *Memoirs of a Geisha*.[15] [19] When he decided to fast track *A.I.*, Spielberg brought Chris Baker back as concept artist.[14]

Teddy used in the movie (Science Fiction Museum and Hall of Fame, Seattle)

The original start date was July 10, 2000,[13] but filming was delayed until August.[20] Aside from a couple weeks shooting on location in Oregon, *A.I.* was shot entirely using sound stages at Warner Bros. Studios. The Swinton house was constructed on Stage 16, while Stage 20 was used for Rouge City and other sets.[21] [22] Spielberg copied Kubrick's obsessively secretive approach to filmmaking by refusing to give the complete script to cast and crew, banning press from the set, and making actors sign confidentiality agreements. Social robotics expert Cynthia Breazeal served as technical consultant during production.[13] [23] Haley Joel Osment and Jude Law applied prosthetic makeup daily in an attempt to look shinier and robotic-like.[3] Costume designer Bob Ringwood (*Batman*, *Troy*) studied pedestrians on the Las Vegas Strip for his influence on the Rouge City extras.[24] Spielberg found post production on *A.I.* difficult because he was simultaneously preparing to shoot *Minority Report*.[25]

Soundtrack

The film's soundtrack was released by Warner Bros. Records in 2001. The original score was composed by John Williams and featured singers Lara Fabian on two songs and Josh Groban on one. The film's score also had a limited release as an official "For your consideration Academy Promo" -- this three CD set commands top dollar prices on e-bay and is the holy grail among fans of the composer, John Williams. Academy Promos have now been discontinued, but they were generally sent out by the studios to other composers and members of the music branch of the Academy of Motion Picture Arts and Sciences for consideration as Best Original Score at the Oscars. The three CD set features many tracks that are unreleased, and not available on the original single CD edition which makes it a must-have collectible.

Release

Marketing

Warner Bros. used an alternate reality game titled *The Beast* to promote the film. Over forty websites were created by Atomic Pictures in New York City (kept online at Cloudmakers.org) including the website for Cybertronics Corp. The Cybertronics CEO is voiced by Topie Nguyen. There were to be a series of video games for the Xbox video game console that followed the storyline of *The Beast*, but they went undeveloped. To avoid audiences mistaking *A.I.* for a family film, no action figures were created, although Hasbro released a talking Teddy following the film's release in June 2001.[13]

A.I. had its premiere at the Venice Film Festival in 2001.[26]

Box office

The film opened in 3,242 theaters in the United States on June 29, 2001, earning $29,352,630 during its opening weekend. *A.I* went on to gross $78.62 million in US totals as well as $157.31 million in foreign countries, coming to a worldwide total of $235.93 million.[27] *A.I.* earned twice as much money overseas as it did in North America, which was fairly unusual for 2001, when foreign grosses had not yet begun to regularly amount to the heavy majority of the receipts for Hollywood films. The film was not clearly a financial success, since the producers collected only a fraction of the listed gross revenue (in particular, studios typically redeem less than half of foreign receipts) against a production and marketing budget of over $100 million.

Critical response

The film received generally positive reviews. Based on 181 reviews collected by Rotten Tomatoes, 73% of the critics gave the film positive notices with a score of 6.6 out of 10. The website described the critical consensus perceiving the film as "a curious, not always seamless, amalgamation of Kubrick's chilly bleakness and Spielberg's warm-hearted optimism. [The film] is, in a word, fascinating."[28] By comparison *Metacritic* collected an average score of 65, based on 32 reviews, which is considered favorable.[29]

Producer Jan Harlan stated that Kubrick "would have applauded" the final film, while Kubrick's widow Christiane also enjoyed *A.I.*[30] However, Brian Aldiss was vocally displeased with the film, stating, "It's crap. Science fiction has to be logical, and it's full of lapses in logic."[31] Richard Corliss heavily praised Spielberg's direction, as well as the cast and visual effects.[32] Roger Ebert wrote that it was "Audacious, technically masterful, challenging, sometimes moving [and] ceaselessly watchable. [But] the movie's conclusion is too facile and sentimental, given what has gone before. It has mastered the artificial, but not the intelligence."[33] On July 8, 2011, Ebert reviewed *A.I.* again when he added it to his "Great Movies" pantheon. Leonard Maltin gives the film a not-so-positive review in his *Movie Guide*, giving it two stars out of four, writing: "[The] intriguing story draws us in, thanks in part to Osment's exceptional performance, but takes several wrong turns; ultimately, it just doesn't work. Spielberg rewrote the adaptation Stanley Kubrick commissioned of the Brian Aldiss short story "Super Toys Last All Summer Long"; [the] result is a curious and uncomfortable hybrid of Kubrick and Spielberg sensibilities." However, he calls John Williams' music score "striking". Jonathan Rosenbaum compared *A.I.* to *Solaris* (1972), and praised both "Kubrick for proposing that Spielberg direct the project and Spielberg for doing his utmost to respect Kubrick's intentions while making it a profoundly personal work."[34] Film critic Armond White, of the *New York Press*, praised the film noting that "each part of David's journey through carnal and sexual universes into the final eschatological devastation becomes as profoundly philosophical and contemplative as anything by cinema's most thoughtful, speculative artists–Borzage, Ozu, Demy, Tarkovsky."[35]

James Berardinelli found the film "consistently involving, with moments of near-brilliance, but far from a masterpiece. In fact, as the long-awaited 'collaboration' of Kubrick and Spielberg, it ranks as something of a disappointment." He particularly criticized the ending: "The film's final half-hour is a curiosity, and not a successful one — a prolonged, needless epilogue which force-feeds us a catharsis that feels as false as it is extraneous to an otherwise fine story."[36] Mick LaSalle gave a largely negative review. "*A.I.* exhibits all its creators' bad traits and none of the good. So we end up with the structureless, meandering, slow-motion endlessness of Kubrick combined with the fuzzy, cuddly mindlessness of Spielberg." Dubbing it Spielberg's "first boring movie", LaSalle also believed the robots at the end of the film were aliens, and compared Gigolo Joe to the "useless" Jar Jar Binks, yet praised Robin Williams for his portrayal of a futuristic Albert Einstein.[37] Peter Travers gave a mixed review, concluding "Spielberg cannot live up to Kubrick's darker side of the future." But he still put the film on his top ten list that year for best movies.[38] Spielberg responded to some of the criticisms of the film, stating that many of the "so called sentimental" elements of *A.I.*, including the ending, were in fact Kubrick's and vice-versa the darker elements were his own.[39] However, Sara Maitland, who worked on the project with Kubrick in the 1990s, claimed that one of the reasons Kubrick never started production on *A.I.* was because he had a hard time making the ending work.[40]

Screenwriter Ian Watson has speculated, "Worldwide, *A.I.* was very successful (and the 4th highest earner of the year) but it didn't do quite so well in America, because the film, so I'm told, was too poetical and intellectual in general for American tastes. Plus, quite a few critics in America misunderstood the film, thinking for instance that the Giacometti-style beings in the final 20 minutes were aliens (whereas they were robots of the future who had evolved themselves from the robots in the earlier part of the film) and also thinking that the final 20 minutes were a sentimental addition by Spielberg, whereas those scenes were exactly what I wrote for Stanley and exactly what he wanted, filmed faithfully by Spielberg."[41]

"People pretend to think they know Stanley Kubrick, and think they know me, when most of them don't know either of us," Spielberg told film critic Joe Leydon in 2002. "And what's really funny about that is, all the parts of *A.I.* that people assume were Stanley's were mine. And all the parts of *A.I.* that people accuse me of sweetening and softening and sentimentalizing were all Stanley's. The teddy bear was Stanley's. The whole last 20 minutes of the movie was completely Stanley's. The whole first 35, 40 minutes of the film – all the stuff in the house – was word for word, from Stanley's screenplay. This was Stanley's vision."

"Eighty percent of the critics got it all mixed up. But I could see why. Because, obviously, I've done a lot of movies where people have cried and have been sentimental. And I've been accused of sentimentalizing hard-core material. But in fact it was Stanley who did the sweetest parts of *A.I.*, not me. I'm the guy who did the dark center of the movie, with the Flesh Fair and everything else. That's why he wanted me to make the movie in the first place. He said, 'This is much closer to your sensibilities than my own.'"[42]

Accolades

Visual effects supervisors Dennis Muren, Stan Winston, Michael Lantieri and Scott Farrar were nominated for the Academy Award for Visual Effects, while John Williams was nominated for Original Music Score.[43] Steven Spielberg, Jude Law and Williams received nominations at the 59th Golden Globe Awards.[44] The visual effects department was once again nominated at the 55th British Academy Film Awards.[45] *A.I.* was successful at the Saturn Awards. Spielberg (for his screenplay), the visual effects department, Williams and Haley Joel Osment (Performance by a Younger Actor) won in their respective categories. The film also won Best Science Fiction Film and for its DVD release. Frances O'Connor and Spielberg (as director) were also nominated.[46]

American Film Institute Lists

- AFI's 100 Years of Film Scores – Nominated[47]
- AFI's 10 Top 10 – Nominated Science Fiction Film[48]

References

[1] Jim Windolf (2007-12-02). "Q&A: Steven Spielberg" (http://www.vanityfair.com/culture/features/2008/02/spielberg_qanda200802?currentPage=4). *Vanity Fair*. . Retrieved 2007-12-02.
[2] "The Kubrick FAQ Part 2: *A.I.*" (http://www.visual-memory.co.uk/faq/index2.html#slot14). *The Kubrick Site*. . Retrieved 2008-08-05.
[3] Haley Joel Osment, A Portrait of David, 2001, Warner Home Video; DreamWorks
[4] Jude Law, A Portrait of Gigolo Joe, 2001, Warner Home Video; DreamWorks
[5] Scott Brake (2001-05-10). "Spielberg Talks About the Genesis of *A.I.*" (http://movies.ign.com/articles/200/200038p1.html). *IGN*. . Retrieved 2008-08-04.
[6] "Plumbing Stanley Kubrick" (http://www.ianwatson.info/kubrick.htm). Ian Watson. . Retrieved 2008-07-07.
[7] Steven Gaydos (2000-03-15). "The Kubrick Connection" (http://www.variety.com/article/VR1117779484). *Variety*. . Retrieved 2008-07-19.
[8] Dana Haris (2000-03-15). "Spielberg lines up *A.I.*, *Report*" (http://www.variety.com/article/VR1117779498). *Variety*. . Retrieved 2008-07-16.
[9] Christian Moerk (1993-11-02). "*A.I.* next for Kubrick at Warners" (http://www.variety.com/article/VR115550). *Variety*. . Retrieved 2008-07-07.
[10] Kenneth Plume (2001-06-28). "Interview with Producer Jan Harlan" (http://movies.ign.com/articles/300/300920p1.html). *IGN*. . Retrieved 2008-08-05.
[11] "The Work of Director Chris Cunningham" (http://www.notcoming.com/features/cunningham/). NotComing.com. . Retrieved 2008-07-19.
[12] "A.I. Artificial Intelligence" (http://www.variety.com/article/VR1117799373). *Variety*. 2001-05-15. . Retrieved 2008-07-19.
[13] Liane Bonin (2001-06-28). "Boy Wonder" (http://www.ew.com/ew/article/0,,165660,00.html). *Entertainment Weekly*. . Retrieved 2008-07-15.
[14] Steven Spielberg, Jan Harlan, Kathleen Kennedy, Bonnie Curtis, Creating *A.I.*, 2001, Warner Home Video; DreamWorks
[15] Christian Moerk (1999-12-23). "Spielberg encounters close choices to direct" (http://www.variety.com/article/VR1117760260). *Variety*. . Retrieved 2008-07-15.
[16] Scott Brake (2001-06-29). "Producing *A.I.*" (http://movies.ign.com/articles/300/300984p1.html). *IGN*. . Retrieved 2008-08-04.
[17] Army Archerd (1999-07-15). "*Annie* Tv'er nab tops talent" (http://www.variety.com/article/VR1117742990). *Variety*. . Retrieved 2008-07-14.
[18] Michael Fleming (1999-11-16). "West pursues *Prisoner*; Spielberg scribbles" (http://www.variety.com/article/VR1117758075). *Variety*. . Retrieved 2008-07-16.
[19] Peter Bart (2000-01-24). "It's scary up there" (http://www.variety.com/article/VR1117761198). *Variety*. . Retrieved 2008-07-15.
[20] Brian Zoromski (2000-06-30). "*A.I.* Moves Full Speed Ahead" (http://movies.ign.com/articles/034/034162p1.html). *IGN*. . Retrieved 2008-08-04.
[21] Scott Brake (2000-08-03). "*A.I.* Set Reports!" (http://movies.ign.com/articles/034/034165p1.html). *IGN*. . Retrieved 2008-08-04.
[22] Christopher "Fangorn" Baker, Rick Carter, *A.I.* From Drawings to Sets, 2001, Warner Home Video; DreamWorks
[23] Bill Higgins (2000-11-06). "BAFTA hails Spielberg" (http://www.variety.com/article/VR1117788785). *Variety*. . Retrieved 2008-08-06.
[24] Bob Ringwood, Dressing *A.I.*, 2001, Warner Home Video; DreamWorks
[25] Charles Lyons (2001-01-18). "Inside Move: Cruise staying busy" (http://www.variety.com/article/VR1117792198). *Variety*. . Retrieved 2008-07-18.
[26] David Rooney (2001-04-16). "'Dust' in the wind for Venice fest" (http://www.variety.com/index.asp?layout=festivals&jump=story&id=1061&articleid=VR1117797100&cs=1). *Variety*. . Retrieved 2008-07-19.
[27] "A.I. Artificial Intelligence" (http://www.boxofficemojo.com/movies/?id=ai.htm). Box Office Mojo. . Retrieved 2008-07-08.
[28] "A.I. Artificial Intelligence" (http://www.rottentomatoes.com/m/ai_artificial_intelligence/). Rotten Tomatoes. . Retrieved 2008-07-08.
[29] "A.I. Artificial Intelligence (2001): Reviews" (http://www.metacritic.com/video/titles/ai?q=A.I.). Metacritic. . Retrieved 2008-07-08.
[30] Army Archerd (2000-06-20). "*A.I.* A Spielberg/Kubrick prod'n" (http://www.variety.com/article/VR1117801772). *Variety*. . Retrieved 2008-08-06.
[31] Bryan Appleyard (2007-12-012). "Why don't we love science fiction?" (http://entertainment.timesonline.co.uk/tol/arts_and_entertainment/books/article2961480.ece). *Times Online*. . Retrieved 2009-09-05.
[32] Richard Corliss (2001-06-17). "*A.I.* – Spielberg's Strange Love" (http://www.time.com/time/sampler/article/0,8599,130942,00.html). *Time*. . Retrieved 2008-08-06.
[33] "A.I. Artificial Intelligence" (http://rogerebert.suntimes.com/apps/pbcs.dll/article?AID=/20010629/REVIEWS/106290301/1023). Roger Ebert. . Retrieved 2008-08-06.
[34] Jonathan Rosenbaum (2001-06-29). "The Best of Both Worlds" (http://www.chicagoreader.com/movies/archives/2001/0107/010713.html). *Chicago Reader*. . Retrieved 2008-08-06.
[35] White, Armond (2001-07-04). "Spielberg's A.I. Dares Viewers to Remember and Accept the Part of Themselves that Is Capable of Feeling" (http://www.nypress.com/article-4331-spielbergs-ai-dares-viewers-to-remember-and-accept-the-part-of-themselves-that-is-capable-of-feeling.html). *The New York Press*. Retrieved 2010-04-26.

[36] James Berardinelli (2001-06-29). "A.I." (http://www.reelviews.net/movies/a/ai.html). ReelViews (http://www.reelviews.net).. Retrieved 2008-08-06.
[37] Mick LaSalle (2001-06-29). "Artificial foolishness" (http://www.sfgate.com/cgi-bin/article.cgi?f=/c/a/2001/06/29/DD239232.DTL). *San Francisco Chronicle*.. Retrieved 2008-08-06.
[38] Peter Travers (2001-06-21). "A.I. Artificial Intelligence" (http://www.rollingstone.com/reviews/movie/5949345/review/5949346/ai_artificial_intelligence). *Rolling Stone*.. Retrieved 2008-08-06.
[39] "Steven Spielberg". Mark Kermode. *The Culture Show*. 2006-11-04.
[40] http://www.visual-memory.co.uk/faq/index2.html#slot14 The Kubrick FAQ Part 2.
[41] http://www.moonmilkreview.com/2010/author-talk-ian-watson-2/
[42] Joe Leydon (2002-06-20). "'Minority Report' looks at the day after tomorrow -- and is relevant to today" (http://www.movingpictureshow.com/dialogues/mpsSpielbergCruise.html). *Moving Picture Show*.. Retrieved 2009-04-29.
[43] "Academy Awards: 2002" (http://www.imdb.com/Sections/Awards/Academy_Awards_USA/2002). Internet Movie Database.. Retrieved 2008-07-14.
[44] "59th Golden Globe Awards" (http://www.imdb.com/Sections/Awards/Golden_Globes_USA/2002). Internet Movie Database.. Retrieved 2008-07-14.
[45] "55th British Academy Film Awards" (http://www.imdb.com/Sections/Awards/BAFTA_Awards/2002). Internet Movie Database.. Retrieved 2008-07-14.
[46] "Saturn Awards: 2002" (http://www.imdb.com/Sections/Awards/Academy_of_Science_Fiction_Fantasy_And_Horror_Films_USA/200). Internet Movie Database.. Retrieved 2008-07-14.
[47] AFI's 100 Years of Film Scores Nominees (http://www.afi.com/Docs/100Years/scores250.pdf)
[48] AFI's 10 Top 10 Ballot (http://www.afi.com/drop/ballot.pdf)

Further reading

- Jane M. Struthers, ed (2009). *A.I. Artificial Intelligence: From Stanley Kubrick to Steven Spielberg: The Vision Behind the Film*. Thames & Hudson. ISBN 978-0-500-51489-4.

External links

- Official website (http://aimovie.warnerbros.com/)
- *A.I. Artificial Intelligence* (http://www.imdb.com/title/tt0212720/) at the Internet Movie Database
- *A.I. Artificial Intelligence* (http://www.allrovi.com/movies/movie/v246161) at AllRovi
- *A.I. Artificial Intelligence* (http://www.rottentomatoes.com/m/ai_artificial_intelligence/) at Rotten Tomatoes
- *A.I. Artificial Intelligence* (http://www.boxofficemojo.com/movies/?id=ai.htm) at Box Office Mojo
- Jude Law Interview (http://video.google.com/videoplay?docid=-7897356503742745317&q=jude+law&pl=true) by Charlie Rose
- Spielberg's AI: Another Cuddly No-Brainer (http://eprints.ecs.soton.ac.uk/6469/1/ai.html) by Stevan Harnad
- A.I./The Kubrick edit - Criticism and comparison (http://www.djfilms.com/AI.html)

The Rutles 2: Can't Buy Me Lunch

The Rutles 2: Can't Buy Me Lunch	
Written by	Eric Idle
Directed by	Eric Idle
Starring	Eric Idle Neil Innes Ricky Fataar John Halsey
Country of origin	UK
Language(s)	English
Production	
Producer(s)	Eric Idle Lorne Michaels
Running time	56 minutes
Chronology	
Preceded by	*All You Need Is Cash*

The Rutles 2: Can't Buy Me Lunch is a 2002 re-telling of the 1978 mockumentary *All You Need Is Cash*, in a modern setting.

Plot

Twenty three years after the original, documentarist Melvin Hall (Eric Idle) interviews mainstream artists, actors, and musicians about the days of the popular band The Rutles, though mostly ending up in the wrong country. The film ends with Melvin and the interviewees laughing.

In the interviews with David Bowie, he is seen holding a copy of the vinyl album *The Rutles 1*, calling it a "piece of marketing extravagance". The interview in the film shows the cover of the album with a black circle that has the words "27 No. 1 Songs On One LP". In the DVD extras, the circle on the album cover says "27 No. 1 Songs On 1 CD", even though this is a vinyl record album. Either way, this was the only time that a Rutles album was practically identical to a Beatles album in both album cover and title.

The plot remains the same to its 1978 counterpart, with a new introduction and conclusion with Idle's character, Melvin Hall.

Cast

- Eric Idle as Narrator / Dirk McQuickly / Lady Beth Mouse-Peddler
- Neil Innes as Ron Nasty
- Ricky Fataar as Stig O'Hara
- John Halsey as Barry Wom
- David Bowie as Himself - Interviewee
- Billy Connolly as Interviewee
- Carrie Fisher as Interviewee
- Jewel Kilcher as Interviewee (as Jewel)
- Steve Martin as Interviewee

- Mike Nichols as Interviewee
- Conan O'Brien as Interviewee
- Salman Rushdie as Interviewee
- Garry Shandling as Interviewee
- Robin Williams as Hans Hänkie
- April Adams as Groupie Interviewee (scenes deleted)
- Clint Black as Interviewee
- Jimmy Fallon as Reporter
- Tom Hanks as Interviewee
- Bill Murray as Bill Murray "The K" (archive footage)
- Graham Nash as Interviewee
- Kevin Nealon as Kevin Wongle
- Catherine O'Hara as Astro Glide
- Jim Piddock as Troy Nixon
- Bonnie Raitt as Interviewee
- David A. Stewart as Interviewee
- James Taylor as Interviewee
- Jann Wenner as Interviewee

Release

The film was made by Eric Idle in 2002, but was shelved and released later.

Reception

The Rutles 2: Can't Buy Me Lunch received mainly negative reviews. Most critics argue it was simply a retelling installment to modern audiences. Idle did not ask for the participation of Fataar, Halsey or Innes for the making of the film, viewing it as more a solo project.[1] It contained no new interviews with the Rutles; Rutle footage consisted of outtakes and unused film produced for the original 1978 documentary. Though Idle had opposed the 1996 release of *The Rutles Archaeology*, he used songs from the album in the film.

References

[1] Mark Caro (2005-05-10). *Art imitates strife: Rutles launch feud* (http://articles.chicagotribune.com/2005-05-10/features/0505100196_1_rutles-neil-innes-holy-grail). Chicago Tribune. .

External links

- *The Rutles 2: Can't Buy Me Lunch* (http://www.imdb.com/title/tt0318641/) at the Internet Movie Database

Insomnia (2002 film)

Insomnia	
Theatrical release poster	
Directed by	Christopher Nolan
Produced by	George Clooney Steven Soderbergh Emma Thomas Broderick Johnson Paul Junger Witt Andrew A. Kosove Edward L. McDonnell
Written by	Erik Skjoldbjærg Nikolaj Frobenius (1997 screenplay) Hillary Seitz
Starring	Al Pacino Robin Williams Hilary Swank Maura Tierney Martin Donovan Nicky Katt Crystal Lowe Paul Dooley
Music by	David Julyan
Cinematography	Wally Pfister
Editing by	Dody Dorn
Studio	Alcon Entertainment Section Eight
Distributed by	Warner Bros. (USA) Buena Vista International (UK and AU)
Release date(s)	May 24, 2002
Running time	118 minutes
Country	United States
Language	English
Budget	$46 million
Box office	$113,714,830[1]

Insomnia is an American psychological thriller film directed by Christopher Nolan and starring Al Pacino, Robin Williams, and Hilary Swank. The film, released on 24 May 2002, is a remake of the 1997 Norwegian film of the same name.

Plot

In the small fishing town of Nightmute, Alaska, 17-year-old Kay Connell (Crystal Lowe) is found murdered. LAPD detectives Will Dormer (Al Pacino) and Hap Eckhart (Martin Donovan) are sent to assist the local police with their investigation.

Concurrently, an intense Internal Affairs investigation in Los Angeles is about to put Dormer under the microscope; Eckhart reveals that Internal Affairs has offered him an immunity deal in exchange for his testimony regarding one of Dormer's past cases. Dormer tries to talk Eckhart out of it, but Eckhart, apparently complicit to some degree in Dormer's misdeeds, says that he has no choice but to accept the deal.

Focusing on the Nightmute case, Dormer comes up with a plan to lure the murderer back to the scene of the crime; however, the stakeout attempt is blown, and the murder suspect flees into the fog, forcing the police to spread out and search for him on foot. During the pursuit, Dormer sees a figure through the fog, which he believes is the armed murder suspect. He fires, and the figure collapses. When Dormer approaches, he discovers that he has mistakenly shot Eckhart. Dormer then runs to help his partner, who believes Dormer shot him intentionally and recoils from him before dying of his wounds. Given the nature of Eckhart's impending testimony, Dormer knows that Internal Affairs will never believe that the shooting was accidental; panicked, he alters the crime scene before crying for help. Ellie Burr (Hilary Swank), a young police officer and Dormer's biggest fan, is put in charge of the investigation of Eckhart's shooting. Dormer uses his influence and reputation to try and mislead her into believing the suspect killed Eckhart.

Over the next few days, Dormer begins losing his grip on reality, plagued with guilt over killing Eckhart and tormented by the resultant insomnia (which is further exacerbated by the perpetual daylight). Dormer then starts receiving anonymous phone calls from the suspect, who claims to have witnessed Dormer kill his partner, and knows of his attempts to cover it up. Dormer is aware that Kay was a fan of a crime writer named Walter Finch (Robin Williams), and books autographed by him were found among her possessions; this then leads Dormer to believe that Finch is somehow involved. Dormer breaks into Finch's apartment to gather evidence, only to be discovered by Finch himself, who gets away. Finch contacts Dormer, who agrees to meet him in public; Finch then offers Dormer a deal, where Dormer is to frame Kay's abusive boyfriend Randy Stetz (Jonathan Jackson) for the murder in exchange for Finch's silence about the Eckhart shooting, forcing Dormer to choose between destroying his own reputation and allowing an innocent man to be sent to prison.

Meanwhile, Burr finds some inconsistencies in Dormer's testimony; she finds a 9mm shell casing at the scene, which conflicts with the bullet type believed to be found in the body, and believes that the direction the suspect fled is improbable. Meanwhile, Finch calls Dormer and tells him that Kay's death was "an accident" — he beat her to death in a blind rage after she rejected his advances. Dormer is appalled, but still feels he has no choice but to keep his end of the deal. The next day, Finch, under Dormer's instruction, gives false testimony at the station, which, along with a weapon planted by Finch, effectively places blame on Randy. Back at the station, Finch offers to give Burr letters indicating that Randy abused Kay, and asks her to come and collect evidence from his second, isolated home the next day.

Dormer returns to his hotel for one last night, where he confides in the hotel owner, Rachel Clement (Maura Tierney), that he fabricated evidence to help convict a pedophile he was certain was guilty of murdering a child, and who would have been set free if Eckhart had testified. She refuses to pass judgment on Dormer, saying that she moved to Alaska because she was trying to "escape something".

Upon returning to Finch's apartment, Dormer discovers that Finch has gone to meet Burr without his evidence, and realizes that Finch intends to kill her. Meanwhile, Burr discovers Kay's dress at Finch's house, and Finch knocks her unconscious. Dormer, fatigued from his insomnia, eventually reaches the cabin and struggles to fight Finch. Burr eventually saves Dormer from Finch, who flees outside to cover; she then holds Dormer at gunpoint, revealing that she knows he shot Eckhart and demanding to know whether he did it on purpose. Dormer admits that he shot his partner, but claims he is no longer certain if it was an accident. From the protection of his shed, Finch fires at them with a shotgun and Dormer devises a plan; while Burr distracts him with gunfire, Dormer sneaks around to Finch's location. A struggle ensues which ends with them shooting each other, killing Finch and mortally wounding Dormer. Burr rushes to the detective's aid, and then comforts him by affirming that Eckhart's shooting was accidental, and tries to toss the shell casing evidence. Dormer stops Burr, telling her not to lose her way, before saying "just let me sleep" as he dies. After a brief moment of contemplation, Burr decides to slip the shell casing back into its plastic evidence bag.

Cast

- Al Pacino as Detective Will Dormer
- Robin Williams as Walter Finch
- Hilary Swank as Ellie Burr
- Maura Tierney as Rachel Clement
- Martin Donovan as Detective Hap Eckhart
- Nicky Katt as Fred Duggar
- Paul Dooley as Chief Nyback
- Crystal Lowe as Kay Connell
- Jay Brazeau as Francis
- Larry Holden as Farrell
- Kerry Sandomirsky as Trish Eckhart
- Lorne Cardinal as Rich
- Katharine Isabelle as Tanya Francke
- Jonathan Jackson as Randy Stetz

Reception

Critics' reviews were very positive, with a "Certified Fresh" rating of 92% on review aggregator Rotten Tomatoes, with an average rating of 7.7/10 from a total of 167 reviews. The website reported the critical consensus, "Driven by Pacino's performance, *Insomnia* is a smart and riveting psychological drama."[2] The film also holds a Metacritic score of 78, based on 36 reviews.[3]

Novelization

Robert Westbrook adapted the screenplay to novel form, which was published by Onyx in May 2002.[4]

References

[1] "Insomnia" (http://www.boxofficemojo.com/movies/?id=insomnia.htm). *Box Office Mojo*. . Retrieved 2009-08-05.
[2] "Insomnia (2002)" (http://www.rottentomatoes.com/m/1114154-insomnia/). *Rotten Tomatoes*. . Retrieved 2011-02-09.
[3] "Insomnia (2002)" (http://www.metacritic.com/movie/insomnia). *Metacritic*. . Retrieved 2011-02-09.
[4] Westbrook, Robert. *Insomnia*. *Onyx*. ISBN 9780451410498.

External links

- Official website (http://dontcloseyoureyes.warnerbros.com/)
- *Insomnia* (http://www.imdb.com/title/tt0278504/) at the Internet Movie Database
- *Insomnia* (http://www.allrovi.com/movies/movie/v260290) at AllRovi
- *Insomnia* (http://www.boxofficemojo.com/movies/?id=insomnia.htm) at Box Office Mojo
- *Insomnia* (http://www.rottentomatoes.com/m/1114154-insomnia/) at Rotten Tomatoes

- Peter Cowie essay on the original at Criterion.com (http://www.criterion.com/asp/release.asp?id=47&eid=4&section=essay)
- Insomnia Screenshot Gallery at NolanFans (http://www.nolanfans.com/insomniagallery.php)

Death to Smoochy

Death to Smoochy	
Theatrical release poster	
Directed by	Danny DeVito
Produced by	Andrew Lazar Peter Macgregor-Scott
Written by	Adam Resnick
Starring	Robin Williams Edward Norton Danny DeVito Catherine Keener Jon Stewart
Music by	David Newman
Cinematography	Anastas N. Michos
Editing by	Jon Poll
Distributed by	Warner Bros.
Release date(s)	March 29, 2002
Running time	107 minutes
Country	United States
Language	English
Budget	$50 million
Box office	$8,382,938

Death to Smoochy is a 2002 American dark comedy film directed by and starring Danny DeVito and starring Robin Williams, Edward Norton, Catherine Keener, and Jon Stewart.

Plot

"Rainbow Randolph" Smiley (Robin Williams), a happily corrupt children's television host, is disgraced by an FBI sting for ripping off parents who want their kids on the show. He is replaced by the "squeaky clean" Sheldon Mopes (Edward Norton) and his character, Smoochy the Rhino. Randolph finds himself unemployed, homeless, and outcast from the television industry by his two-faced associate Marion Stokes (Jon Stewart). In an effort to return to the spotlight, Randolph hatches several schemes to bring down Mopes in hopes of reclaiming his time slot.

Mopes quickly finds himself losing creative control over his show to his hardened producer Nora Wells (Catherine Keener). With the help of his new agent Burke Bennett (Danny DeVito), Mopes renegotiates his contract and is named executive producer. He is approached by Irish mob boss Tommy Cotter (Pam Ferris), who wants Mopes to create a spot on his show for her cousin Spinner (Michael Rispoli), a former boxer whose numerous head injuries have left him with severe brain damage. Sheldon reluctantly adds Spinner to the show, first as a cowbell-wielding game warden, and later on as Smoochy's cousin Moochy.

Rainbow Randolph sets a scheme to destroy Mopes's career and regain his show too all fail. Mopes becomes enraged to learn that Burke signed him up to star in a Smoochy ice show; he feels that the event will exploit children. Burke and Merv Green (Harvey Fierstein), the heads of the corrupt charity running the ice show, unsuccessfully warn Mopes from backing out of the event. Soon afterward, a disguised Randolph dupes Mopes into doing a Smoochy act at a neo-Nazi rally that is raided by the police. Smoochy is labeled a racist and fired. However, when Randolph accidentally lets it slip to Nora that he framed Smoochy, he is arrested. Smoochy's reputation and show are restored. After telling him that his show is back on the air, Nora kisses Mopes and has sex with him, starting a relationship.

Smoochy commits to the ice show. He decides that all proceeds will go to the drug rehab clinic he used to work at, which was closed due to lack of funding; the kids will be given free souvenirs and healthful snacks. Burke and Green retaliate by plotting to kill Mopes and hire a new host who will cooperate with their profit skimming. However, Green and his men accidentally kill Spinner in his Moochy costume; they are discovered and killed by Cotter. Meanwhile, Randolph corners Mopes and Nora in their penthouse and threatens to kill them. They talk him down and discover that he's depressed and genuinely misses entertaining children. An empathetic Mopes offers to let Randolph stay in the penthouse until he recovers.

Burke and Stokes hire heroin addict Buggy Ding Dong (Vincent Schiavelli), another former host, to assassinate Mopes during his ice show. Buggy steals a backstage pass to get inside. However, Randolph, who has been summoned to the ice show, tackles Buggy just as he tries to shoot Mopes from the rafters. Randolph and Buggy struggle for the sniper rifle, until Buggy falls to his death. After Mopes realizes that Burke and Stokes set him up, he chases after Burke into an alley. He pulls a gun and threatens to kill Burke, but Cotter and her men arrive and persuade him to stop. The movie ends with Smoochy and Rainbow Randolph launching a new show together.

Cast

- Robin Williams as "Rainbow" Randolph Smiley
- Edward Norton as Sheldon Mopes/Smoochy the Rhino
- Danny DeVito as Burke Bennett
- Catherine Keener as Nora Wells
- Jon Stewart as Marion Frank Stokes
- Pam Ferris as Tommy Cotter
- Michael Rispoli as Spinner Dunn
- Harvey Fierstein as Merv Green
- Vincent Schiavelli as Buggy Ding Dong
- Danny Woodburn as Angelo Pike
- Tracey Walter as Ben Franks
- Todd Graff as Skip Kleinman
- Robert Prosky (*uncredited*) as Network chairman

Production

The movie was filmed in Toronto and Hamilton, Ontario,[1] along with New York City. Including Union Station, all of the TV studio scenes were shot at the Toronto Film Studios. The scenes involving ice-skating were filmed at Maple Leaf Gardens in Toronto and were choreographed and performed by Canadian figure skaters, including Elvis Stojko.[2]

Reception

The film received mixed reviews from critics. The film currently holds a rating of 42% on review aggregate Rotten Tomatoes.[3] J. Hoberman of *The Village Voice* praised the film, stating that "*Death to Smoochy* is often very funny, but what's even more remarkable is the integrity of DeVito's misanthropic vision."[4]

Though it received a wide release, playing in some 2,164 theaters its opening weekend in the United States, the film was a box office disaster, grossing $4,266,463 its opening weekend, and a mere $8,382,691 overall, with negligible foreign box office receipts.[5] Considering it had a production budget of some $50 million, *Death to Smoochy* was a financial flop. Danny DeVito begins the DVD audio commentary with the lines "Hello. It's Danny. It's been, um... I guess now a few months since the release of *Death to Smoochy*, so the mourning period is over."

Williams's performance earned him a Razzie Award nomination for Worst Supporting Actor.

References

[1] "Internet Movie Database - List of Films shot in Hamilton, Ontario" (http://www.imdb.com/List?endings=on&&locations=Hamilton,+Ontario,+Canada). . Retrieved 2008-01-29.

[2] Death to Smoochy film credits

[3] http://www.rottentomatoes.com/m/death_to_smoochy/

[4] Hoberman, Jim (2002-04-02). "Houses of Mirth" (http://www.webcitation.org/5gq6d0ygW). *The Village Voice*. Archived from the original (http://www.villagevoice.com/2002-04-02/film/houses-of-mirth/1) on 2009-05-17. . Retrieved 2009-05-17.

[5] Death to Smoochy (2002) (http://www.boxofficemojo.com/movies/?id=deathtosmoochy.htm)

External links

- Official website (http://www.deathtosmoochymovie.com/)
- *Death to Smoochy* (http://www.imdb.com/title/tt0266452/) at the Internet Movie Database
- *Death to Smoochy* (http://www.allrovi.com/movies/movie/v259834) at AllRovi
- *Death to Smoochy* (http://www.boxofficemojo.com/movies/?id=deathtosmoochy.htm) at Box Office Mojo
- *Death to Smoochy* (http://www.rottentomatoes.com/m/death_to_smoochy/) at Rotten Tomatoes

One Hour Photo

One Hour Photo	
Directed by	Mark Romanek
Produced by	Christine Vachon
Written by	Mark Romanek
Starring	Robin Williams Michael Vartan Connie Nielsen Dylan Smith Gary Cole Eriq La Salle
Music by	Reinhold Heil Johnny Klimek
Cinematography	Jeff Cronenweth
Editing by	Jeffrey Ford
Distributed by	Fox Searchlight Pictures
Release date(s)	September 13, 2002
Running time	96 minutes
Country	United States
Language	English
Budget	$12 million
Box office	$52,223,306[1]

One Hour Photo is a 2002 American psychological thriller written and directed by Mark Romanek and starring Robin Williams. Fox Searchlight Pictures distributed the film in the United States. *One Hour Photo* also starred Connie Nielsen, Michael Vartan, Gary Cole, and Eriq La Salle. Williams won a Saturn Award for Best Actor (2003) for his work in the film.[2] The film was critically acclaimed and earned an 81% rating at *Rotten Tomatoes*.

Plot

Seymour "Sy" Parrish, a mini-lab photo technician at SavMart's one-hour photo developing clinic in suburban Los Angeles, leads a depressing, solitary life outside of the "heaven-like", hyperreality atmosphere of the department store. Every day he labors to ensure his customers get the best quality photos possible; his work is his life, as he has no one and nothing to go home to at the end of each day. As each workday comes to an end, Sy falls into the inescapable routine of spending his evenings sitting alone in his barren living room, watching television. The only thing in Sy's immaculate apartment he has for companionship is a hamster, caged in his bedroom.

His favorite customers are the Yorkin family: husband Will (Michael Vartan), wife Nina (Connie Nielsen), and their son, Jake (Dylan Smith). He has done their photos for years and, over time, has developed an obsession with the family; he idolizes their happiness and affluence, memorizes every personal detail about them that he can learn, and finally begins to stalk them. Sy secretly makes his own copies of the Yorkins' photos from the film negatives and then puts them on a wall in his apartment in a massive collage. Most of all, he fantasizes about being a member of their family and sharing in the love he assumes they must feel. He is painfully shy and socially inept, however, and his awkward attempts to become closer to the family are gently rebuffed.

Sy eventually manages to spark a connection to Nina when he pretends to have interest in a book he noticed she had purchased on a particular day in the store. For the first time, Nina asks Sy personal questions about his life, realizing that he is indeed a lonely man, something only Jake had noticed earlier. The next day, his boss Bill (Gary Cole) fires him for stealing prints. While inspecting his photos for the last time, Sy discovers that Will is having an affair, and his idyllic conception of the Yorkins as the 'perfect' family is shattered. He comes to hate and envy Will, who has everything Sy longs for, yet doesn't seem to appreciate it.

After losing his job, Sy stalks and takes pictures of Bill's young daughter as revenge for firing him, leading to a police investigation against him. While detectives Van Der Zee and Outerbridge (Eriq La Salle and Clark Gregg) are discovering Sy's obsession, Sy confronts Will and his mistress, Maya (Erin Daniels), during a rendezvous in their hotel room. Armed with a knife and a camera, Sy forces the lovers to pose naked while he takes pictures. After the confrontation, as Sy just sits on the bed in his hotel room, he discovers that the police have arrived in the hotel and tries to escape. The alarm sounds and Van Der Zee pursues him while Outerbridge discovers Will and Maya, physically unharmed but deeply traumatized. After a chase, the police finally apprehend Sy in the parking garage as he attempts to make a break for his car. Upon being arrested, Sy claims, "I just took pictures".

The final scene is set in a police interrogation room where Van Der Zee asks Sy why he terrorized the Yorkins, to which Sy indirectly reveals that his father had made him do "sick, degrading things that children shouldn't do". (The implication, confirmed by Romanek, is that Sy's father exploited him for child pornography.) As the detective prepares to take his confession, Sy asks for the pictures he took at the hotel, which the detective has described as "evidence". They appear to be only shots of household objects and interior furnishings he took after the incident in the hotel. The film closes with a picture of the Yorkin family with Sy. Romanek claims in the DVD commentary that the picture is intended to symbolize an open ending; it is left up to the viewer to decide whether the picture only exists in Sy's mind or if he ever sees the Yorkin family again.

Cast

- Robin Williams as Seymour "Sy" Parrish
- Michael Vartan as Will Yorkin
- Connie Nielsen as Nina Yorkin
- Dylan Smith as Jake Yorkin
- Gary Cole as Bill Owens, Manager
- Erin Daniels as Maya Burson
- Eriq La Salle as Det. James Van Der Zee
- Clark Gregg as Det. Paul Outerbridge
- Paul H. Kim as Yoshi Araki

Release and reaction

One Hour Photo opened to generally positive reviews, earning raves from Roger Ebert,[3] Leonard Maltin, and other noted critics. Ebert called the film "profoundly creepy" and compared it to *Amercian Beauty*.

The film's limited release began on August 21, 2002 in seven theaters, opening to a $321,515 weekend, with an average of $45,930 per theater. Its wide release began on September 13, with a 1,212 theater count. Still, the film made just over $8 million that weekend, and went on to gross $31,597,131 in the US, with an additional $20,626,175 in overseas territories, for an international total of $52,223,306[4] ; this was a moderate box office success, as the budget was around $12 million.

Robin Williams won a Saturn Award for his portrayal of Sy.[5]

The film has an 81% positive rating on the review aggregator site Rotten Tomatoes.[6] The film's aggregate score at Metacritic is 64 out of 100.[7]

Production

Romanek intended the film to be much longer, but the studio ordered it to be cut shorter, and elements rearranged out of concerns about commerciality. The beginning, for example, was moved to the end. Also, several of Sy's narrative monologues were removed, and several scenes were re-shot with fewer lines. The original version also has older musical scores that were not used in the final product. A director's cut is not available to buy, but was shown at the Sundance Film Festival.[8]

Trent Reznor, of the band Nine Inch Nails, composed the original film score, but Romanek opted not to use it. The music can be heard on the Nine Inch Nails EP *Still*.[9]

In accordance with photography being the theme of the movie, many of the characters in the movie take their names from photographers. Examples include: Sy's assistant at the Savmart, Yoshi Araki (named for Nobuyoshi Araki); Det. Van Der Zee (James Van Der Zee); Det. Outerbridge (Paul Outerbridge); Maya Burson (Nancy Burson); and Savmart customers Mrs. von Unwerth (Ellen von Unwerth) and Mr. Siskind (Aaron Siskind). In addition, the hotel at the end of the movie, the Edgerton, is also named for a noted photographer — Harold Eugene Edgerton.

In one of the voice-over pieces Sy can be heard to say "They actually believe that any idiot that attends a two-day seminar can master the art of making beautiful prints in less than an hour. But of course, like most things, there's far more to it than meets the eye." In reality Robin Williams prepared for the role by training for two and-a-half days in a Southern California photo development lab.

In commentary, Romanek has gone on to state that he was partially inspired by the films of 'lonely men' from the 1970s, notably *Taxi Driver*.

In the DVD commentary, Romanek says that Jack Nicholson was first approached to play the lead character. Nicholson turned the role down.

In one scene, Sy watches the film *The Day the Earth Stood Still* while standing in front of his wall laminated with photos of the Yorkin family. In another, he watches the *Simpsons* episode "Cape Feare".

References

[1] http://www.boxofficemojo.com/movies/?id=onehourphoto.htm

[2] Saturn Awards. "Past Saturn Awards" (http://www.saturnawards.org/past.html). www.saturnawards.org. . Retrieved 2002-08-23.

[3] Roger Ebert (2004-05-07). "*One Hour Photo*" (http://rogerebert.suntimes.com/apps/pbcs.dll/article?AID=/20020823/REVIEWS/208230303/1023). ::rogerebert.com::. . Retrieved 2002-08-23.

[4] Box Office Mojo. "One Hour Photo (2002)" (http://www.boxofficemojo.com/movies/?id=onehourphoto.htm). Box Office Mojo. . Retrieved 2002-08-23.

[5] Saturn Awards. "Past Saturn Awards" (http://www.saturnawards.org/past.html). www.saturnawards.org. . Retrieved 2002-08-23.

[6] Rotten Tomatoes. "One Hour Photo Movie Reviews, Pictures - Rotten Tomatoes" (http://uk.rottentomatoes.com/m/one_hour_photo/). Rotten Tomatoes. . Retrieved 2002-08-23.

[7] Metacritic. "One Hour Photo (2002): Reviews" (http://www.metacritic.com/film/titles/onehourphoto). Metacritic. . Retrieved 2002-08-23.

[8] David Geffner. "MAGAZINE" (http://www.dga.org/news/v26_6/indie_Sundance2002.php3). DGA. . Retrieved 2002-08-23.

[9] Trent Reznor (2004-05-07). "Access" (http://web.archive.org/web/20060106205140/http://www.nin.com/access/5_07_04/index.php). nin.com. Archived from the original (http://www.nin.com/access/5_07_04/index.php) on 2006-01-06. . Retrieved 2008-02-19.

External links

- Official website (http://www.foxsearchlight.com/onehourphoto/)
- *One Hour Photo* (http://www.imdb.com/title/tt0265459/) at the Internet Movie Database
- *One Hour Photo* (http://www.rottentomatoes.com/m/one_hour_photo/) at Rotten Tomatoes
- *One Hour Photo* (http://www.metacritic.com/movie/onehourphoto) at Metacritic
- *One Hour Photo* (http://www.boxofficemojo.com/movies/?id=onehourphoto.htm) at Box Office Mojo

Noel (film)

Noel	
Noel film poster	
Directed by	Chazz Palminteri
Produced by	Al Corley Howard Rosenman
Written by	David Hubbard
Starring	Susan Sarandon Paul Walker Penélope Cruz Alan Arkin Marcus Thomas with Robin Williams
Distributed by	Convex Group
Release date(s)	September 12, 2004
Running time	96 minutes
Language	English

Noel is a 2004 Christmas-themed drama film written by David Hubbard and directed by Chazz Palminteri. It stars Susan Sarandon, Penélope Cruz, Paul Walker, Alan Arkin, Daniel Sunjata and an uncredited Robin Williams.

Plot summary

The film centers around five strangers who are linked together — and who meet each other at separate times — by a series of events that take place on Christmas Eve.

The main character is Rose (Susan Sarandon), a woman who is struggling to cope with caring for her mother, an Alzheimer's patient. Meanwhile, Nina (Penélope Cruz) and Mike (Paul Walker) are a young couple on the verge of breaking up due to Mike's increasingly jealous behavior. Elsewhere, Artie (Alan Arkin) is an old waiter who searches for his deceased wife every Christmas Eve. Finally, Jules (Marcus Thomas) is a young man who deliberately damages his hand so he can attend a Christmas party in the emergency room, as that was the only happy memory of his childhood. In addition to the five main characters, the mysterious Charlie (Robin Williams) is introduced as the person who may be able to help Rose finally realize that she must look after herself more, rather than worrying about everyone else.

Main cast

- Susan Sarandon — Rose Harrison
- Penélope Cruz — Nina Vasquez
- Paul Walker — Michael (Mike) Riley
- Alan Arkin — Artie Venizelos
- Marcus Thomas — Jules
- Chazz Palminteri — Arizona
- Robin Williams — Charles (Charlie) Boyd

External links

- *Noel (film)* [1] at the Internet Movie Database
- *Noel (film)* [2] at AllRovi

References

[1] http://www.imdb.com/title/tt0383534/
[2] http://www.allrovi.com/movies/movie/v314070

House of D

House of D	
Theatrical release poster	
Directed by	David Duchovny
Produced by	Jane Rosenthal Bob Yari Richard B. Lewis
Written by	David Duchovny
Starring	David Duchovny Anton Yelchin Robin Williams
Music by	Geoff Zanelli
Cinematography	Michael Chapman
Editing by	Suzy Elmiger
Studio	Tribeca Ovation Entertainment Bob Yari Productions Southpaw Entertainment
Distributed by	Lionsgate
Release date(s)	April 15, 2005
Running time	97 minutes
Country	United States
Language	English French
Box office	$388,532

House of D is 2005 drama film directed by David Duchovny as his directorial debut in film, having previously directed an episode of *The X-Files* for television. The film stars Erykah Badu, Frank Langella, Téa Leoni, Zelda Williams, Anton Yelchin, and Robin Williams. It was screened at the 2004 Tribeca Film Festival.

Plot

An American artist living a bohemian existence in Paris, Tom Warshaw (David Duchovny) is trying to make sense of his troubled adult life by reflecting upon his extraordinary childhood. There is a flashback to Greenwich Village in 1973, as 13-year-old Tommy (Anton Yelchin) is on the brink of becoming a man. While his bereaved single mother (Téa Leoni) mourns the death of his father, Tommy escapes grief by causing trouble at school and making afternoon deliveries with his best friend Pappas (Robin Williams), a mentally challenged janitor. Following the romantic advice offered by Lady (Erykah Badu) – incarcerated in the infamous New York Women's House of Detention for shadowy reasons – Tommy experiences his first taste of love. Yet when an unexpected tragedy radically alters his world, Tommy must take a life-defining choice – one that will compel the adult Tom Warshaw, thirty years later, to confront his unfinished past.

Cast

- David Duchovny as Tom Warshaw
- Anton Yelchin as Tommy Warshaw
- Robin Williams as Pappas
- Téa Leoni as Mrs. Warshaw
- Erykah Badu as Lady / Bernadette
- Frank Langella as Rev. Duncan
- Zelda Williams as Melissa
- Orlando Jones as Superfly
- Willie Garson as Ticket Agent

Critical reception

House of D was given a score of 10% on Rotten Tomatoes with a consensus calling it "A sincere but inept coming of age story." It has received a composite 6.8/10 score by voters on the Internet Movie Database. Box Office Mojo gives the reviews a C+. Many critics attribute the poor reception to the fact that Duchovny wrote, directed and edited the movie, which gave it a lack of creative direction and caused it to meander and to lose focus.

Box office

The film was released in theaters on April 15, 2005. It grossed $36,371 during its opening week. The next week it grossed $7,441. In the film's third week, it grossed $210,826, the most during its run. In the film's fourth and final week, it grossed $30,386, a total of $371,081 worldwide.

DVD release

The DVD was released on October 4, 2005. The DVD contains special features, such as commentary with David Duchovny and the cast and a behind-the-scenes featurette called *The Making of House of D*.

Versions in other languages

The title of the Spanish version distributed in:

- Latin America: *El incomprendido*
- Spain: *Delitos Menores*

References

External links

- Official site (http://www.houseofdthemovie.com/)
- *House of D* (http://www.imdb.com/title/tt0372334/) at the Internet Movie Database
- *House of D* (http://www.boxofficemojo.com/movies/?id=houseofd.htm) at Box Office Mojo
- *House of D* (http://www.rottentomatoes.com/m/house_of_d/) at Rotten Tomatoes

The Final Cut (2004 film)

The Final Cut	
Theatrical poster	
Directed by	Omar Naim
Produced by	Nick Wechsler
Written by	Omar Naim
Starring	Robin Williams Mira Sorvino James Caviezel Mimi Kuzyk Stephanie Romanov Genevieve Buechner Brendan Fletcher
Music by	Brian Tyler
Cinematography	Tak Fujimoto
Editing by	Dede Allen Robert Brakey
Distributed by	Lions Gate Entertainment
Release date(s)	November 11, 2004
Running time	95 minutes
Country	United States Canada Germany
Language	English

The Final Cut is a 2004 film written and directed by Omar Naim. It stars Robin Williams, James Caviezel, Mira Sorvino, Mimi Kuzyk, Stephanie Romanov, Genevieve Buechner and Brendan Fletcher. It was produced by Lions Gate Entertainment and filmed in Vancouver, British Columbia, Canada, and in Berlin, Germany. The film featured original music by Brian Tyler. The story takes place in a near future in which people can pay to have their babies implanted with memory chips. These "Zoe Implants", developed by EYE Tech company, record every moment of their lives, so that they may be viewed by loved ones after one's death. The plot centers on Alan Hakman, a "cutter", whose job it is to edit the Zoe footage into a feature-film length piece, called a "Rememory".

The Final Cut is about subjectivity, memory and history; posing the question, "If history is what is written and remembered, then what happens when memories are edited and rewritten?"

The film won the award for best screenplay at the Deauville Film Festival and was nominated for best film at the Catalonian International Film Festival and Berlin International Film Festival.

Plot

The film opens with Alan Hakman (Williams) as a child, and another child named Louis Hunt, as they enter an abandoned factory. They come to a long wooden plank suspended very high above the floor, and Louis falls after Hakman goads him into crossing the plank. Hakman flees and is not caught. The film advances to Hakman's adult life, portraying him creating two rememories from Zoe implants. It turns out that Hakman is a very skillful cutter whose edits can make "saints out of criminals", and his services are highly valued by rich, immoral people; Hakman sees himself doing a good deed, as a sin-eater who removes past crimes from the dead so they can rest in peace. At the screening of a rememory, a former cutter, Fletcher (Caviezel), offers Hakman $500,000 for the footage he recently acquired of Charles Bannister, a former EYE Tech manager; the footage, which reveals that Bannister was sexually abusing his young daughter, would discredit the entire "cutting" industry. Hakman refuses to surrender it after locating in the footage a person he believes to be Hunt, whom he'd presumed dead from the fall as a child; he sets the "Guillotine", which in the film is the computer used to sort and edit ("cut") the Zoe footage, to search for more images of the man.

Hakman and his colleagues break into the EYE Tech headquarters to locate Hunt's Zoe footage as a second source, and although he does not find Hunt's footage, because his surname also begins with the letter 'H' he discovers a file under his own name. He realizes that he himself has a Zoe implant, violating the cutter's code that no cutter may have one. He did not know he had an implant because both of his parents had passed away suddenly before telling him.

In his distress after the discovery that he is implanted, Hakman brings his lover Delila (Sorvino) into his apartment, and leaves her alone with his Guillotine. He immediately undergoes the first stage of a specialized tattooing procedure to end the implant's ability to record audio, he has to wait a week later to get a second tattoo that will remove video. When he returns he puts bullets in his firearm under the belief that Fletcher and his associate have broken into his apartment to steal the Bannister footage. Instead, he finds Delila poring over the full Zoe footage of her late boyfriend. Hakman apparently has kept the footage and has vicariously used it to fill in what's lacking in his life, experiencing their relationship in all its passion and perhaps turning it into the basis for all the feelings he has for her. Delila becomes angry that her private memory with her boyfriend is used in such a manner, and shoots the Guillotine. The bullet hits the Bannister card, destroying its footage.

When Fletcher and his associate finally break in to steal the Bannister footage, they find out it has been destroyed. Hakman lies to Bannister's wife, telling her that a technical fault destroyed it. Hakman then "cuts" into his own memories, and sees that Hunt did not in fact die when he fell, absolving him of decades of guilt. Hakman visits Hunt's grave, and is joined by Fletcher, who has discovered through the tattoo parlour that Hakman has an implant and that it recorded the critical images from the Bannister footage. Foregoing the biopsy procedure, Fletcher chases Hakman through the graveyard filled with video tombstones, eventually catching up to Hakman but hesitant to shoot him. Fletcher's associate, having concealed his presence during the chase between Hakman and Fletcher, then shoots Hakman, killing him.

In the last shot of the movie, Alan Hakman looks at himself in a mirror through his own eyes. But when he looks away and walks off, the camera keeps watching the empty mirror instead of watching what he sees.

Cast

- Robin Williams as Alan Hakman
- Mira Sorvino as Delila
- James Caviezel as Fletcher
- Mimi Kuzyk as Thelma
- Stephanie Romanov as Jennifer Bannister
- Thom Bishops as Hasan[1]
- Genevieve Buechner as Isabel Bannister
- Brendan Fletcher as Michael
- Joely Collins as Legz the Tattoo Artist
- Michael St. John Smith as Charles Bannister
- Christopher Britton as Jason Monroe

References

[1] (http://www.imdb.com/title/tt0364343/)

External links

- *The Final Cut* (http://www.imdb.com/title/tt0364343/) at the Internet Movie Database
- *The Final Cut* (http://www.allrovi.com/movies/movie/v290206) at AllRovi

The Big White

The Big White	
Promotional poster for *The Big White*	
Directed by	Mark Mylod
Produced by	Michael Birnbaum, Kia Jam, John Schimmel, Andreas Schmid, Andreas Grosch
Written by	Collin Friesen
Starring	Robin Williams, Holly Hunter, Giovanni Ribisi, Alison Lohman, Tim Nelson, Woody Harrelson
Editing by	Julie Monroe
Studio	Capitol Films, VIP Medienfonds 2, Ascendant[1]
Distributed by	Momentum Pictures (UK theatrical)
Release date(s)	December 3, 2005
Running time	105 min.
Country	Canada-New Zealand[1]
Language	English
Budget	$15,000,000[2]

The Big White is a 2005 black comedy picture directed by Mark Mylod starring Robin Williams, Holly Hunter, Giovanni Ribisi, Woody Harrelson, Tim Blake Nelson, W. Earl Brown and Alison Lohman.

Plot

A body left in a dumpster by Mafia hitmen is discovered by financially troubled travel agent Paul Barnell (Robin Williams). Heavily in debt and attempting to find a cure for his wife's apparent Tourette Syndrome, he stages a disfiguring animal attack with the body in order to cash in his missing brother's life-insurance policy, for which a corpse is required.

Local police are convinced, but a promotion-hungry insurance agent (Giovanni Ribisi) is not. The Mafia hitmen are also in search of the corpse for proof to collect their payment. They take Paul's wife (Holly Hunter) hostage to ensure that they will get the body. Paul stays in his brother's cottage.

Paul's missing brother Raymond (Woody Harrelson) returns home, beats him, and demands a portion of the insurance money. By suggesting the insurance agent has assaulted him, Paul speeds up the delivery of the million dollar insurance payment. He has the body exhumed and agrees to exchange it and a portion of the money for his wife. In fear that Raymond will attempt to kill his wife to keep her quiet, Paul considers killing his brother in his sleep, but cannot bring himself to do so.

The next morning Paul leaves his brother asleep and meets the hit-men for the exchange. Raymond is angered at his brother's deception and arrives as well, and is told by the insurance agent, who has finally pieced together what has happened about his million dollar policy.

Raymond then pulls out a pistol and shoots Paul's fleeing wife in the back. He is in turn shot in the stomach by one of the hit-men (Tim Nelson). Paul finds his wife alive, the insurance money he had hidden in his jacket his wife was wearing stopped the bullet. The brothers reflect on childhood memories as Raymond dies.

Using the money, Paul takes his wife on a flight to a tropical location, his love for his wife being the sole motivation for the whole situation.

Production

According to one insider, it was Collin Friesen's script that "drew the talent needed to get the production off the ground."[2] Production was based in Winnipeg, though it was filmed in the Yukon Territory;[2] the film had a $1 million impact on the territory's economy, including the employment of 200 Yukoners.[3] Most of the outdoor scenes and cinematography were shot at summit of the White Pass along the border of Alaska and British Columbia. The bulk of the film was shot in April, 2004.[4] [5]

Reception

In November 2005, *Variety*, after seeing the film at the AFI Fest in Los Angeles, called it "snowed under by misjudgment on every level", with "frigid" commercial prospects.[1] In March 2006, David Mattin of the BBC gave it three stars out of five, saying the film "wants to be a cross between small-screen hits *Northern Exposure* and *Frasier*" but "can't resist the lure of cheap and obvious one-liners"; Mattin calls William's performance is "typically slushy and ultimately likeable" and "Ribisi's a performance that "really shines", but notes that the viewer is mostly subjected to "limp gags based on [Hunter]'s compulsive swearing, and Harrelson's cliché-ridden small-town hick stupidity/"[6]

References

[1] Koehler, Robert (November 16, 2005). "The Big White (Canada-New Zealand)" (http://www.variety.com/review/VE1117928877.html). Variety. . Retrieved 2010-07-22.

[2] "Canadians want movies that taste good" (http://www.cbc.ca/news/viewpoint/vp_bakken/20040624.html). CBC. June 24, 2004. . Retrieved 2010-07-22.

[3] "*Big White* To Be Featured At Yukon International Film Festival" (http://www.gov.yk.ca/news/2006/06-024.html). *Press release*. Yukon official government website. February 1, 2006. . Retrieved 2010-07-22.

[4] 'Action' Skagway! On the set of *The Big White* (http://www.skagwaynews.com/042304thebigwhite.html) an April 23, 2004 article from *The Skagway News*

[5] http://www.strangethingsdone.com/Discourse/BIG_WHITE.pdf

[6] "The Big White (2006)" (http://www.bbc.co.uk/films/2006/03/14/the_big_white_2006_review.shtml). BBC. 20 March 2006. . Retrieved 2010-07-22.

External links

- *The Big White* (http://www.imdb.com/title/tt0402850/) at the Internet Movie Database

Robots (film)

Robots	
Theatrical release poster	
Directed by	Chris Wedge Carlos Saldanha
Produced by	William Joyce John C Donkin Jerry Davis
Written by	Ron Mita Jim McClain David Lindsay-Abaire Lowell Ganz Babaloo Mandel
Starring	Ewan McGregor Robin Williams Greg Kinnear Halle Berry Harland Williams Mel Brooks Amanda Bynes Drew Carey
Music by	John Powell
Editing by	John Carnochan
Studio	Blue Sky Studios
Distributed by	20th Century Fox
Release date(s)	March 11, 2005
Running time	91 minutes
Country	United States
Language	English
Budget	$75 million
Box office	$260,718,330

Robots is a 2005 American computer-animated comedy film produced by Blue Sky Studios for 20th Century Fox, and was released theatrically on March 11, 2005. The story was created by Chris Wedge and William Joyce, a children's book author/illustrator. The two were trying to create a film version of Joyce's book *Santa Calls* but instead they came up with a movie about robots. Joyce served as producer and production designer for the film.[1]

The DVD and VHS of *Robots* were released on September 27, 2005. *Robots* is also the last 20th Century Fox animated film to ever receive a VHS release.

Plot

The film opens with Herb Copperbottom (Stanley Tucci), a dishwasher at Gunk's Greasy Spoon diner, racing through the streets of Rivet Town, elated that he is going to be a father. He and his wife, Lydia (Dianne Wiest), after 12 hours of "labor," finally manage to construct the baby. He is named Rodney (Ewan McGregor), and he becomes a young inventor who dreams of making the world a better place for everyone. Rodney idolizes Bigweld (Mel Brooks), a master inventor and owner of Bigweld Industries. During Rodney's adolescence, he invents a gadget, "Wonderbot", intended to help his father clean the dishes at the restaurant. When Herb's boss, Mr. Gunk (Dan Hedaya), unexpectedly confronts them, Wonderbot breaks dishes, causing Herb to go into debt and Rodney to be fired. Rodney decides to take his invention to Robot City to see Bigweld and get a job as an inventor so that he can help his family. He is encouraged by his father, who confides that he has always regretted not becoming a musician. Rodney arrives in Robot City and meets Fender (Robin Williams), a ramshackle robot scraping by through taking souvenir photos and selling maps to the stars' homes. After a harrowing ride on the crosstown express, Rodney arrives at the gate of Bigweld Industries.

There he learns that Phineas T. Ratchet (Greg Kinnear) has taken over Bigweld Industries and is about to discontinue the manufacture of spare parts. Ratchet believes the company can make more profit if it stops making spare parts for older robots and focuses on selling more expensive upgrades. If any older robots protest they are sent to the underground Chop Shop, where they are shredded and melted down by Ratchet's imposing mother, Madame Gasket (Jim Broadbent). Rodney is thrown out and finds a place to stay, with Fender, at Aunt Fanny's (Jennifer Coolidge) boarding house, along with an assortment of other "Rusties", older robots threatened with the Chop Shop. When the news gets out that spare parts have been discontinued by Bigweld industries, Rodney remembers Bigweld's slogan, "See a need, fill a need", and begins fixing old robots on his own. Upon learning of this financial threat, Gasket orders Ratchet to stop Rodney's work and kill Bigweld.

Rodney finds that Herb has fallen ill, and can not find replacement parts. Rodney decides to try to contact Bigweld directly, so he can beg him to make spare parts again. Wonderbot reminds him that the annual Bigweld Ball takes place that night. Rodney and Fender go to the ball in disguise, only to hear Ratchet announce that Bigweld was unable to attend. Rodney tries to confront Ratchet, but is stopped by security robots. He is saved by Cappy (Halle Berry), a beautiful robot-executive of the company who does not like Ratchet's scheme, and together with Fender and his new girlfriend, Loretta Geargrinder (Natasha Lyonne), they escape from the ball.

Fender walks Loretta home, but he is kidnapped and taken to the Chop Shop. He struggles to escape, losing his lower half in the process. Fender eventually escapes by reluctantly attaching a new pair of female legs. Meanwhile, Rodney and Cappy fly to Bigweld's home. When Rodney inadvertently knocks over a domino, Bigweld appears. Rodney tries to convince Bigweld to return to the helm of his company and once again make spare parts available, but Bigweld refuses. Rodney calls his parents, intending to give up his ambition of becoming an inventor and return to Rivet Town, but his father once again encourages Rodney to pursue his dreams. Rodney rallies the Rusties into fighting back against Ratchet. Fender reveals that Gasket has built a fleet of super-sweepers with the intention of rounding up and destroying all older robots. Bigweld eventually decides to come with the group, having realized what he meant to Rodney.

The group heads for Bigweld Industries, where Bigweld fires Ratchet. Ratchet manages to beat Bigweld senseless, but Rodney and Bigweld flee. Bigweld is repaired just as they enter the Chop Shop, but is captured. A desperate battle ensues between Ratchet's employees and Rodney's repaired robots. During the chaos, Bigweld is rescued by Rodney, the choppers and sweepers are destroyed, and Wonderbot kills Gasket by tossing her into the melter, while Ratchet loses his upgrades and gets stuck on the ceiling with his father. Bigweld goes to Rivet Town to tell Rodney's parents that their son is now his right-hand inventor and eventual successor. Rodney makes his father's dream come true by giving him a three-bell trumpet, playing by sheer improvision that prompts the others to help add other musical tunes; Fender finds the new music to be a mix of Jazz and Funk - "Junk". The audience dances to James Brown's "Get Up Offa That Thing" as a victory celebration.

Voice cast

- Ewan McGregor as Rodney Copperbottom, a young blue robot and aspiring inventor.
- Halle Berry as Cappy, Rodney's love interest.
- Robin Williams as Fender, an old red robot that's always falling apart.
- Amanda Bynes as Piper Pinwheeler, Fender's younger sister.
- Mel Brooks as Bigweld, the jolly inventor and owner of Bigweld Industries; until Rodney met him, Bigweld had slipped into depression at Ratchet's actions.
- Greg Kinnear as Phineas T. Ratchet, the main antagonist.
- Drew Carey as Crank Casey
- Jennifer Coolidge as Aunt Fanny, a kind motherly robot, who takes in "broke" robots; she has the unintentional effect of bumping people with he large rear.
- Harland Williams as Lug
- Jim Broadbent as Madame Gasket, Ratchet's mother.
- Dianne Wiest as Lydia Copperbottom, Rodney's mother.
- Stanley Tucci as Herb Copperbottom, Rodney's father.
- Natasha Lyonne as Loretta Geargrinder, Fender's love interest.

Cameos

- Paul Giamatti as Tim
- Dan Hedaya as Mr. Gunk
- Jay Leno as a Fire Hydrant
- Lucille Bliss as a Pigeon Lady
- Paula Abdul as Wristwatch #1
- Randy Jackson as Wristwatch #2
- Ryan Seacrest as Wristwatch #3
- Al Roker as Mailbox
- John Mahoney as Ratchet's robots.
- James Earl Jones as Darth Vader, voice chip.
- Randall Montgomery as Zinc

Locations

Movie director Chris Wedge says New York City, Toronto, London, and a little future-like city inspired him to make the city.

There are three parts of the city:

- *High End District*: The part of the city where the rich and famous robots live. Buildings and robots are all shiny and nearly everything is futuristic. Everyone here has a metal covering that hides all their inner workings. Bigweld Industries is here.
- *Combustion District*: Middle-class place. It has a few rust spots, and robots have the internal workings similar to a 1950s car. Aunt Fanny's house is here, and the majority of the movie takes place here.
- *Steam District*: The lowest part of the city, and therefore the rustiest. Parts of the district resemble the inventions of the Industrial Revolution, and everywhere is filled with broken machines. Sweepers grab old robots and bring them to Madame Gasket's Chop Shop, where mutant robots then break and melt robots, turning them into upgrades.

Another major location of the film is Rivet Town, home to the Copperbottom family. Two of the buildings there are Gunk's Greasy Spoon and Flathead Floyd's. Rivet Town is based on Watertown, New York, where movie director

Chris Wedge lived during his teens.

Release

The film was the first to feature the new trailer for *Star Wars Episode III: Revenge of the Sith*. The film also featured the exclusive trailer for *Ice Age: The Meltdown*, then called *Ice Age 2*.

Critical response

The film received generally favorable reviews from critics. The review aggregator Rotten Tomatoes reported that 64% of critics gave the film positive reviews, based on 172 reviews.[2] Metacritic gives the a score of 64%, based on 33 reviews.[3]

Most critics liked the visual style and gags but panned the predictable story. The film was nominated for many awards in the category of best animated film, as well as awards for character design, best animated character, voice casting, and sound editing. However, it only won one, the MTV (Mexico) Movie Award for best song, "Un Héroe Real".[4]

The American Film Institute nominated *Robots* for its Top 10 Animated Films list.[5]

Box office

The film was released March 11, 2005 in the United States and Canada and grossed $36 million in 3,776 theaters its opening weekend, ranking #1 at the box office.[6] It grossed a total of $260.7 million worldwide – $128.2 million in the United States and Canada and $132.5 million in other territories.[7]

Music

Soundtrack

Robots: Original Motion Picture Soundtrack	
Soundtrack album by Various Artists	
Released	March 1, 2005
Genre	Alternative rock Pop
Length	41:09
Label	Virgin Records

Robots: Original Motion Picture Soundtrack was released on March 1, 2005 by Virgin Records.[8]

No.	Title	Performer	Length
1.	"Shine"	Ricky Fanté	4:08
2.	"Right Thurr"	Chingy	4:12
3.	"Tell Me What You Already Did"	Fountains of Wayne	1:59
4.	"Wonderful Night"	Fatboy Slim	2:46
5.	"Get Up Offa That Thing" (All Dee Remix)"	James Brown	3:40
6.	"(There's Gotta Be) More to Life"	Stacie Orrico	3:23
7.	"Love's Dance"	Earth, Wind & Fire	4:29
8.	"Low Rider"	War	3:15
9.	"I Like That"	Houston, Featuring Chingy, Nate Dogg and I-20	3:58
10.	"Silence"	Gomez	2:55
11.	"Walkie Talkie Man"	Steriogram	2:15
12.	"Robot City"	John Powell, Featuring Blue Man Group	4:09
Total length:			**41:09**

Other songs in the film include

- "Underground" - Tom Waits
- "Can't Get Enough of Your Love, Babe" - Barry White
- "...Baby One More Time" - Britney Spears

Score

Robots: Original Motion Picture Score	
Film score by John Powell	
Released	March 15, 2005
Genre	Score
Length	43:41
Label	Varèse Sarabande

Robots: Original Motion Picture Score was composed by John Powell and was released on March 15, 2005 by Varèse Sarabande Records.[9]

No.	Title	Length
1.	"Overture"	4:02
2.	"Rivet Town Parade"	0:54
3.	"Bigweld TV / Creating Wonderbot"	2:45
4.	"Wonderbot Wash"	2:08
5.	"Train Station"	3:50
6.	"Crosstown Express"	1:19
7.	"Wild Ride"	1:36
8.	"Madam Gasket"	1:00

9.	"Chop Shop"	1:50
10.	"Meet The Rusties"	2:06
11.	"Bigweld Workshop"	3:13
12.	"Phone Booth"	1:29
13.	"Gathering Forces"	3:28
14.	"Escape"	4:42
15.	"Deciding to Fight Back"	1:13
16.	"Attack of the Sweepers"	1:26
17.	"Butt Whoopin'"	3:42
18.	"Homecoming"	1:33
19.	"Dad's Dream"	1:25
Total length:		**43:41**

References

[1] Jones, Malcolm (March 13, 2005). "Heavenly Metal" (http://www.thedailybeast.com/newsweek/2005/03/13/heavenly-metal.html). *The Daily Beast*. . Retrieved September 1, 2011.

[2] "Robots Movie Reviews, Pictures" (http://www.rottentomatoes.com/m/robots). *Rotten Tomatoes*. Retrieved 2008-02-21.

[3] "Robots Reviews, Ratings, Credits, and More at Metacritic" (http://www.metacritic.com/film/titles/robots). *Metacritic*. Retrieved 2008-02-21.

[4] "Awards for 'Robots' (2005)" (http://www.imdb.com/title/tt0358082/awards). *IMDb*. Retrieved 2010-10-21.

[5] AFI's 10 Top 10 Ballot (http://www.afi.com/drop/ballot.pdf)

[6] "Robots (2005) - Weekend Box Office Results" (http://www.boxofficemojo.com/movies/?page=weekend&id=robots.htm). *Box Office Mojo*. Retrieved 2008-02-21.

[7] "Robots (2005)" (http://www.boxofficemojo.com/movies/?id=robots.htm). *Box Office Mojo*. Retrieved 2008-02-21.

[8] Robots: Original Motion Picture Soundtrack (http://www.allmusic.com/album/r729055) at Allmusic. Retrieved September 17, 2011.

[9] Robots: Original Motion Picture Score (http://www.allmusic.com/album/r731709) at Allmusic. Retrieved September 17, 2011.

External links

- *Robots* (http://www.imdb.com/title/tt0358082/) at the Internet Movie Database
- *Robots* (http://www.bcdb.com/bcdb/cartoon.cgi?film=47509) at the Big Cartoon DataBase
- *Robots* (http://www.allrovi.com/movies/movie/v289664) at AllRovi
- *Robots* (http://www.rottentomatoes.com/m/robots/) at Rotten Tomatoes
- *Robots* (http://www.metacritic.com/movie/robots) at Metacritic
- *Robots* (http://www.boxofficemojo.com/movies/?id=robots.htm) at Box Office Mojo

The Aristocrats (film)

The Aristocrats	
Directed by	Penn Jillette Paul Provenza
Produced by	Paul Provenza Peter Adam Golden[1]
Starring	Various
Music by	Gary Stockdale
Cinematography	Paul Provenza
Editing by	Emery Emery Paul Provenza
Studio	THINKFilm
Distributed by	Lions Gate Pictures
Release date(s)	August 12, 2005
Running time	89 minutes
Country	United States
Language	English
Box office	US$6,377,277

The Aristocrats is a 2005 documentary film about the famous dirty joke of the same name. It was conceived and produced by comedians Penn Jillette and Paul Provenza, edited by Emery Emery, and released to theaters by TH!NKFilm. The film is dedicated to Johnny Carson, as "The Aristocrats" was said to be his favorite joke.[2]

The joke

"The Aristocrats" is a longstanding transgressive joke amongst comedians, in which the setup and punchline are almost always the same (or similar). It is the joke's midsection – which may be as long as the one telling it prefers and is often completely improvised – that makes or breaks a particular rendition.

The joke involves a person pitching an act to a talent agent. Typically the first line is, "A man walks into a talent agent's office." The man then describes the act. From this point, up to (but not including) the punchline, the teller of the joke is expected to ad-lib the most shocking act they can possibly imagine. This often involves elements of incest, group sex, graphic violence, defecation, coprophilia, necrophilia, bestiality, child sexual abuse and various other taboo behaviors.

The joke ends with the agent, shocked and often impressed, asking "And what do you call the act?" The punchline of the joke is then given: "The Aristocrats".

The joke, as first delivered in the film, contains the set-up line "What the heck do you call an act like that?" followed by the punchline "I call it 'The Aristocrats'." The added set-up value of this version of the joke, wherein the pitchman misunderstands the meaning of the phrase "What the heck do you call [that]?" as a request for information, when it is in fact meant to be an expression of incredulity or bewilderment, is lost in subsequent tellings of the joke, with the simpler and less sensible question asked by the agent, "What do you call your act?"

The film itself consists of interviews with various comedians and actors, usually in candid settings. The interviewees engage both in telling their own versions of the joke, and in reminiscing about their experiences with it, the joke's place in comedy history, and even dissecting the logic behind the joke's appeal.

While most of the filmed versions of the joke follow the standard format of a raunchy description followed by the punchline of "the Aristocrats", some versions do vary the joke. Two tellings of it, including that of comedienne Wendy Liebman invert the joke by describing an elegant and beautiful performance act which has been given a lewd and transgressive name. Actor Taylor Negron tells his joke as a mixture of salacious sex acts and calmly delivered observations on life.

Featured celebrities

The following celebrities are featured in the film, telling the joke themselves and/or providing substantial commentary on its history:

- Chris Albrecht
- Jason Alexander
- Hank Azaria
- Shelley Berman
- Billy the Mime
- Lewis Black
- David Brenner
- Mario Cantone
- Drew Carey
- George Carlin
- Mark Cohen
- Carrot Top
- Billy Connolly
- Tim Conway
- Pat Cooper
- Wayne Cotter
- Andy Dick
- Frank DiGiacomo
- Phyllis Diller
- Susie Essman
- Carrie Fisher
- Joe Franklin
- Todd Glass
- Judy Gold
- Whoopi Goldberg
- Eddie Gorodetsky
- Gilbert Gottfried
- Dana Gould
- Allan Havey
- Eric Idle
- Dom Irrera
- Eddie Izzard
- Richard Jeni
- Jake Johannsen
- The Amazing Johnathan
- Alan Kirschenbaum
- Jay Kogen
- Sue Kolinsky
- Paul Krassner
- Cathy Ladman
- Lisa Lampanelli
- Richard Lewis
- Wendy Liebman
- Bill Maher
- Howie Mandel
- Merrill Markoe
- Jay Marshall
- Jackie Martling
- Chuck McCann
- Michael McKean
- Eric Mead
- Larry Miller
- Martin Mull
- Kevin Nealon
- Taylor Negron
- *The Onion* editorial staff
- Otto and George
- Rick Overton
- Gary Owens
- Trey Parker, Matt Stone (as the *South Park* kids)
- The Passing Zone
- Penn & Teller
- Emo Philips
- Peter Pitofsky
- Kevin Pollak
- Paul Reiser
- Andy Richter
- Don Rickles
- Chris Rock
- Gregg Rogell
- Jeffrey Ross
- Jonathan Ross
- Rita Rudner
- Bob Saget
- T. Sean Shannon
- Harry Shearer
- Sarah Silverman
- Bobby Slayton
- The Smothers Brothers
- Carrie Snow
- Doug Stanhope
- David Steinberg
- Jon Stewart
- Larry Storch
- Rip Taylor
- Dave Thomas
- Johnny Thompson
- Peter Tilden
- Bruce Vilanch
- Fred Willard
- Robin Williams
- Steven Wright

Many other comedians were filmed but not included due to time constraints. According to a letter from Penn Jillette to critic Roger Ebert, Buddy Hackett, Troy Henley and Rodney Dangerfield were intended to be included, but died before they could be filmed. Jillette also indicated that, this being Johnny Carson's favorite joke, Carson was also invited to appear, but declined.[3]

Joe Franklin controversy

In the film, Sarah Silverman tells a version of the joke as if it were autobiographical and she had been one of the "Aristocrats" performers as a child. Silverman builds the story to include her family being booked on *The Joe Franklin Show*, and ends with her punch line: a deadpan allegation that Franklin had raped her during a phony rehearsal for the show. *The New Yorker* reported that Sarah Silverman's telling of the joke led veteran talk show host Joe Franklin, who is also featured in the film, to consider filing a defamation lawsuit against the comedian.[4]

On the DVD commentary track, Paul Provenza indicated that he had explained to Franklin that it was only meant to be a joke, and defended Silverman by calling her straight-faced performance Academy Award caliber. Additionally, Silverman told Jillette that it would have been a great publicity stunt if he had filed the suit.

On the April 20, 2011 episode of the WFMU show *Seven Second Delay*, Joe Franklin jokes that he had been so successful lately because he sued Sarah Silverman.[5]

AMC banning

The theater chain AMC refused to show the movie on any of its 3,500+ screens. The theater company tried to avoid an overt ban, by claiming the film had a very limited appeal, causing comedian and co-producer Penn Jillette to comment to MSNBC, "It's the kind of thing that makes you go 'Come on, play fair.' It's not like we're trying to slide this by anybody by calling it *Love Bug 2: Herbie Takes It Up the Ass*."[6]

Friars Club roast footage

The film includes footage of Gilbert Gottfried's telling of the joke at a Comedy Central/Friars' Club roast of Hugh Hefner which had been almost entirely censored when aired on television. Taped not long after the September 11 attacks, the incident occurred at a time when, according to one of the commentators in the *Aristocrats* film, entertainers were uncertain how much comedy was allowed in the aftermath of the attacks. Gottfried followed Rob Schneider, who had received mixed results with his stand-up comedy performance in Hefner's honor. Gottfried began his performance with a joke in which he claimed to have to catch a late flight out of town but was worried because his flight "had a connection at the Empire State Building." The joke, a reference to 9/11, was poorly received by the audience, who showered Gottfried with boos and cries of "too soon." In response, Gottfried told an obscenity-filled rendition of the Aristocrats joke. According to the film, the telling was as much a cathartic experience for the audience as it was a shocking one, regardless of whether viewers were familiar with the joke or not. During his performance, Gottfried told the audience "They might have to clean this up for TV."

References

[1] "Aristocrats (2005)" (http://www.inbaseline.com/project.aspx?project_id=4759578). Inbaseline. . Retrieved 29 October 2011.

[2] HBO The Aristocrats Synopsis (http://www.hbo.com/docs/programs/aristocrats/synopsis.html)

[3] Penn Jillette (21 August 2005). "Letter to Roger Ebert" (http://rogerebert.suntimes.com/apps/pbcs.dll/article?AID=/20050821/ANSWERMAN/508210304/1023). *Movie Answer Man*. RogerEbert.com. . Retrieved 29 October 2011.

[4] Dana Goodyear (24 October 2005). "Quiet Depravity" (http://www.newyorker.com/archive/2005/10/24/051024fa_fact). *The New Yorker*. . Retrieved 29 October 2011.

[5] Andy co-hosts with Joe Franklin at the UCB Theater (20 April 2011) (audio/transcript). Interview. *Seven Second Delay with Ken and Andy*. WFMU. http://www.wfmu.org/playlists/shows/40025. Retrieved 29 October 2011.

[6] TMZ Staff (30 December 2005). "Censored in 2005" (http://www.tmz.com/2005/12/30/censored-in-2005/). *TMZ*. . Retrieved 29 October 2011.

External links

- Official movie site (http://thearistocrats.com/)
- Review / cast listing at nndb.com (http://www.nndb.com/films/138/000099838/)
- *The Aristocrats* (http://www.imdb.com/title/tt0436078/) at the Internet Movie Database
- New York Times Article about the 2005 movie, The Aristocrats (http://www.nytimes.com/2005/06/23/movies/23aris.html)
- Interview with the editor of the film (http://www.sheckymagazine.com/emeryem.htm)
- Critical analysis of the film by Critical-Film.com reviewer Jason Pitt (http://www.critical-film.com/reviews/A/Aristocrats/Aristocrats.html)

Man of the Year (2006 film)

Man of the Year	
Theatrical release poster	
Directed by	Barry Levinson
Produced by	James G. Robinson
Written by	Barry Levinson
Starring	Robin Williams Christopher Walken Laura Linney Lewis Black Jeff Goldblum
Music by	Graeme Revell
Cinematography	Dick Pope
Editing by	Blair Daily Steven Weisberg
Studio	Morgan Creek Productions
Distributed by	Universal Studios
Release date(s)	October 13, 2006
Running time	115 minutes
Country	United States
Language	English
Budget	$20 million
Box office	$41,237,658

Man of the Year is a 2006 Comedy film directed and written by Barry Levinson and starring Robin Williams in the lead role. In addition to Williams, the film features Christopher Walken, Laura Linney, Lewis Black and Jeff Goldblum.

In the film, Williams portrays Tom Dobbs, the host of a comedy/political talk show, based loosely on the real-life persona of Jon Stewart. With an offhand remark, he prompts 4 million people to e-mail their support, then he decides to campaign for President.

The film was released October 13, 2006 and was filmed in Toronto and Hamilton, Canada and parts of Washington, D.C..[1]

Plot

The story opens with Tom Dobbs (Robin Williams), a comedian and host of a satirical talk show who is able to tap into people's frustrations with the sharply divided, special-interest driven political climate. In specific, he makes fun of the American Two-party system. During his warm-up act, an audience member suggests that he run for President. At first, Dobbs laughs off the idea, but following a popular groundswell of support, later announces on the air that he will stand as a candidate. Through his efforts, he gets on the ballot in 13 states and participates in one of the national debates with the Democratic incumbent President Kellogg and Republican U.S. Senator Mills.

A parallel plot follows Eleanor Green (Laura Linney), who works at a voting machine company called Delacroy. According to a television commercial in the movie, the entire United States will be using Delacroy voting machines for the Presidential election. Shortly before the elections, Eleanor notices an error in the voting system, but the head of the company, James Hemmings purposefully ignores her warnings. Initially, Dobbs approaches the campaign seriously - perhaps too seriously, to the chagrin of his staff, especially his manager Jack Menken (Christopher Walken). That turns around the night of the Presidential debates, where, fed up with the posturing of the other candidates, he shifts back into comedian mode, managing to keep the audience laughing and make serious points simultaneously. From then on, he resumes his showman persona, thoroughly shaking up the political landscape. Dobbs surges in polls after the debates, but remains in a distant third to Kellogg and Mills.

Election Day arrives and polls show Dobbs at 17% with Kellogg and Mills tied in the 40s. Dobbs performs better than expected, although not well enough to be close to either of the two major candidates. Early returns show Kellogg beating Mills everywhere. Eleanor says that this is part of the error in the voting systems. Then all of a sudden, Dobbs starts winning states. He first wins Virginia, then North Carolina and then big states such as California, New York and Texas. He now stands at 146 electoral votes and the news states if he wins the remaining states he is on the ballot in, he will become President. Soon afterwards, results show that Tom Dobbs has indeed won the race for President, beating out Kellogg and Mills. Dobbs is extremely shocked - like the rest of the world. While Dobbs and his crew move from shock to celebration, Eleanor remains unconvinced. She considers revealing the computer error to the public, but is attacked in her home by Delacroy Agents and injected with a cocktail of drugs. Upon going to work, her behavior is erratic in the extreme and she is hospitalized for drug abuse. The company uses this as a pretext to fire her. Upon recovering in the hospital, she realizes that very few people would believe her story, but decides that if nothing else, she must tell Dobbs.

Though still suffering from the aftereffects of the drugs in her system, Eleanor eventually makes her way to Jack Menken's birthday party. There, she unconvincingly impersonates an FBI Agent but manages to catch Dobbs' eye, the two dance through the evening and Dobbs gives her his telephone number. Eleanor cannot bring herself to tell Dobbs that he is not really the President-Elect. Later, Dobbs tries to get back in contact with Eleanor by calling Delacroy. This immediately raises the suspicions of the Delacroy leaders and they redouble their efforts to silence Eleanor. Eleanor calls Dobbs and he whisks her off to a paintball fight, followed by Thanksgiving dinner. At dinner, she finally gets him alone to tell him that the elections were a fraud, then leaves. Dobbs wrestles with the idea that he should not have been elected as President and finally decides to break Eleanor's news to the public in a major speech. However, Delacroy pre-empts his announcement with one of their own, stating that Eleanor was caught attempting to throw the election for Dobbs, but that her efforts had no impact on the polls. Eleanor becomes increasingly fearful for her safety, a feeling that is soon justified as Agents break into the hotel room where she is staying to confiscate her computer, the only evidence she had.

Desperate, Eleanor first flees to a mall, where she is found by a Delacroy Agent but escapes. She then drives to find a pay phone so that she can call Dobbs for help. She manages to reach him but is not able to communicate anything before the Delacroy Agent's truck crashes into the phone booth on purpose; she escapes just before the collision but is still injured and is hospitalized a second time. Dobbs goes to the scene and though he cannot understand what she is trying to say, he is convinced that she was telling the truth about the election. During the Weekend Update section of the sketch comedy TV show Saturday Night Live, he finally announces to the public that the elections were flawed and that he should not be President. Dobbs declines to accept victory in a phony election and another election is held in which Dobbs chooses not to participate. President Kellogg wins another term, though, perhaps chastened by the Dobbs phenomenon, is much more sensitive to the populace as a whole rather than the special interests and Dobbs returns to his career as a talk-show host, with Eleanor at his side as his producer and wife. The executives of Delacroy were convicted of fraud. The last seconds of the film shows a mock Time magazine Person of the Year cover with Dobbs chosen as Person of the Year.

Cast

- Robin Williams as Tom Dobbs
- Christopher Walken as Jack Menken
- Laura Linney as Eleanor Green
- Lewis Black as Eddie Langston
- Jeff Goldblum as Stewart
- David Alpay as Danny
- Faith Daniels as Moderator
- Rick Roberts as James Hemmings
- Karen Hines as Alison McAndrews
- Linda Kash as Jenny Adams
- Jacqueline Pillon as Security Tech

Appearing as themselves

- Tina Fey
- Amy Poehler
- Chris Matthews
- James Carville

Casting

Director Barry Levinson originally considered Howard Stern for the role of Tom Dobbs. However, scheduling conflicts prevented Stern from taking on the part.[2]

Reception

Man of the Year received mostly negative reviews, with the critics' aggregate site Rotten Tomatoes giving a rating of 20%.[3] It debuted at #3 at the box office its opening weekend, with a theatrical gross of $12,550,000.[4] Most of the critics noted the abrupt change in tone from comedy to conspiracy film. Many critics rated the entire movie negatively, calling the early humor of the film uninspired and less biting than that of the real-life television comedians Dobbs was modeled after (such as Jon Stewart and Stephen Colbert); others argued that the early political humor of the film was both funny and on-target, but argued that the change in tone to a conspiracy film damaged its effectiveness, and many criticized the love story aspect between Williams and Linney. Stephanie Zacharek of *Salon.com* wrote, "It's a comedy, a political thriller, a love story: Barry Levinson's *Man of the Year* tries to be all things to all people and fails on every count — a little like the generic, ineffectual politicians it's pretending to excoriate".[5]

James Berardinelli of Reelviews.net felt it "makes telling points and has a lot to say, but it loses its voice along with its consistency around the mid-way point".[6] Josh Larsen of the Sun Publications line of newspapers asked straight out, "What is it about Robin Williams that he often appears in these wild misfires, pictures that are so full of promise yet so disastrous in execution?"[7] Frank Lovece of *Film Journal International* placed the well-regarded Levinson's challenge and failure within a larger context: "If satire is what dies on a Saturday night, then political-satire movies are what die on Fridays. Maybe we're used to the TV topicality of *The Daily Show with Jon Stewart* or *Real Time with Bill Maher*, whereas movies are months in the making, turning their current events into history. Yet successful satire needn't be topical - witness *Network*, *Election*, *Dr. Strangelove* - because some verities are timeless. Since when, after all, hasn't there been a populist saying, 'Throw the rascals out'?"[8]

References

[1] "Internet Movie Database - List of Films shot in Hamilton, Ontario" (http://www.imdb.com/List?endings=on&&locations=Hamilton,+Ontario,+Canada). . Retrieved 2008-01-29.

[2] Rabin, Nathan (2008-10-17). "Barry Levinson" (http://www.avclub.com/content/interview/barry_levinson/2). *The A. V. Club*. Onion. . Retrieved 2008-10-17.

[3] RottenTomatoes.com: *Man of the Year* (http://www.rottentomatoes.com/m/man_of_the_year/)

[4] RottenTomatoes.com: *Man of the Year* Numbers (http://www.rottentomatoes.com/m/man_of_the_year/numbers.php)

[5] Salon.com review, by Stephanie Zacharek (http://www.salon.com/ent/movies/review/2006/10/13/man/index_np.html)

[6] Reelviews.net review, by James Berardinelli (http://www.reelviews.net/movies/m/man_year.html)

[7] *The Bolingbrook* [Illinois] *Sun* review, by Josh Larsen (http://www.suburbanchicagonews.com/bolingbrooksun/entertainment/movies/91052,6_5_NA13_MAN_S1.article)

[8] *Film Journal* review, by Frank Lovece (http://filmjournal.com/filmjournal/search/article_display.jsp?vnu_content_id=1003252422)

External links

- Official website (http://www.manoftheyearmovie.net/)
- *Man of the Year* (http://www.imdb.com/title/tt0483726/) at the Internet Movie Database
- *Man of the Year* (http://www.boxofficemojo.com/movies/?id=manoftheyear.htm) at Box Office Mojo
- *Man of the Year* (http://www.rottentomatoes.com/m/man_of_the_year/) at Rotten Tomatoes

Night at the Museum

Night at the Museum	
Promotional poster	
Directed by	Shawn Levy
Produced by	• Shawn Levy • Chris Columbus • Michael Barnathan
Screenplay by	Thomas Lennon Robert Ben Garant
Based on	*The Night at the Museum* by Milan Trenc
Starring	• Ben Stiller • Carla Gugino • Dick Van Dyke • Mickey Rooney • Bill Cobbs • Jake Cherry • Robin Williams • Mizuo Peck • Owen Wilson • Steve Coogan • Patrick Gallagher • Ricky Gervais • Brad Garret • Rami Malek • Kim Raver • Pierfrancesco Favino
Music by	Alan Silvestri
Cinematography	Guillermo Navarro
Editing by	Don Zimmerman
Studio	• 1492 Pictures • Ingenious Film Partners
Distributed by	20th Century Fox
Release date(s)	December 22, 2006
Running time	108 minutes
Country	US
Language	English
Budget	$110 million
Box office	$574,480,841[1]

Night at the Museum is a 2006 fantasy adventure-comedy film based on the 1993 children's book *The Night at the Museum* by Milan Trenc. It follows a divorced father trying to settle down, impress his son, and find his destiny. He applies for a job as a night watchman at New York City's American Museum of Natural History and subsequently discovers that the exhibits, animated by a magical Egyptian artifact, come to life at night.

Released on December 22, 2006 by 20th Century Fox, which presented the 1492 Pictures/21 Laps Entertainment Production in association with Ingenious Film Partners, the film was written by Robert Ben Garant and Thomas Lennon of Comedy Central's *Reno 911!* and MTV's *The State* and produced and directed by Shawn Levy. Also producing for 1492 Pictures were Chris Columbus and Michael Barnathan. The cast includes Ben Stiller, Carla Gugino, Dick Van Dyke, Mickey Rooney, Bill Cobbs, Jake Cherry, Ricky Gervais, and Robin Williams. A new novelization of the screenplay by Leslie Goldman was published as a film tie-in.

A sequel titled *Night at the Museum: Battle of the Smithsonian* was released on May 22, 2009.

Plot

Larry Daley (Ben Stiller) is divorced, unable to keep a stable job, and has failed at many business ventures. His ex-wife (Kim Raver) believes that he is a bad example to their ten years-old son Nick (Jake Cherry), and Larry fears that Nick respects his future stepfather, bond trader Don (Paul Rudd), more than him.

Cecil (Dick Van Dyke), an elderly night security guard about to retire from the American Museum of Natural History, hires Larry despite his unpromising résumé. The museum plans to replace Cecil and two colleagues Gus (Mickey Rooney) and Reginald (Bill Cobbs) with one guard. They advise Larry to leave some of the lights on and warn him not to let anything "in...or out".

Once night comes, Larry discovers that the exhibits come to life, including a living *Tyrannosaurus* skeleton nicknamed "Rexy" who behaves like a dog; a mischievous capuchin monkey named Dexter (Crystal), which always steals Larry's keys; rival miniature civilizations led by Old West cowboy Jedediah (Owen Wilson) and Roman general Octavius (Steve Coogan); an Easter Island Moai (Brad Garrett) obsessed with "gum-gum"; and a wax model of Theodore Roosevelt (Robin Williams).

Roosevelt explains that since an Egyptian artifact—the Golden Tablet of Pharaoh Akhmenrah—came to the museum in 1952, all of the exhibits come to life each night. If the exhibits are outside of the museum during sunrise, however, they turn to dust. Roosevelt helps Larry by restoring order, and he decides to remain as a guard.

On Cecil's advice, Larry studies history to prepare himself better. He also learns from a museum docent, Rebecca Hutman (Carla Gugino), who is writing a dissertation on Sacagawea (Mizuo Peck) but does not feel she knows enough about her subject.

The next night, Larry uses what he has learned to better control the exhibits. Four Neanderthals set fire to a display, however, and one turns to dust when he leaves the museum at dawn, so museum director Dr. McPhee (Ricky Gervais) almost fires Larry. He offers Rebecca a meeting with Sacagawea, but she believes that he is mocking her and the museum.

Larry brings Nick to the museum to show him the exhibits, but none is alive. They find Cecil, Gus, and Reginald stealing the tablet and other valuable objects. Like the exhibits, the guards receive enhanced vitality from the artifact; wishing to retain their health and fund their retirements, the three plan to frame Larry for the thefts, and disabled the tablet to stop the exhibits from interfering. Nick reactivates the artifact, but Cecil locks him and his father in the Egyptian room and flees with the tablet.

Larry releases the Akhmenrah's (Rami Malek) mummy from his sarcophagus. The pharaoh speaks English from many years as an exhibit at Cambridge, and helps Larry and Nick escape. The three find the other exhibits fighting, and Larry convinces them to work together. Although some of the exhibits capture Gus and Reginald without difficulty, Cecil escapes by stagecoach with Larry, Nick, Akmenrah, and Atilla the Hun in pursuit in Central Park, where they stop him and regain the tablet. Rebecca sees the exhibits return to the museum before sunrise and realizes that Larry was telling the truth; he introduces her to Sacagawea.

Dr. McPhee fires Larry due to the chaos during the night, but rehires him when news reports of the strange events around the museum—such as cave paintings in the museum's subway station, dinosaur footprints in Central Park, and cavemen sightings—raise attendance. Larry, Nick, and the exhibits celebrate, while Cecil, Gus, and Reginald are forced to become museum janitors as punishment.

Production

The building featured in the film, which was constructed on a sound stage in Burnaby, is based on the American Museum of Natural History in New York City, external shots of which were used in the movie.[2]

Trainers spent several weeks training Crystal, who plays the troublemaking monkey Dexter, to slap and bite Stiller in the film.

Director Shawn Levy credited Ben Stiller for the ensemble cast: "When actors hear that Ben Stiller is in a movie they want to work with him. It['s] a high-water mark and it absolutely draws actors in and I'm convinced that's a big part of why we got this cast."[3]

Cast

- Ben Stiller as Larry Daley
- Robin Williams as Theodore Roosevelt
- Jake Cherry as Nicky Daley, Larry's son.
- Dick Van Dyke as Cecil Fredericks
- Carla Gugino as Rebecca Hutman
- Mickey Rooney as Gus
- Bill Cobbs as Reginald
- Owen Wilson as Jedediah (Uncredited)
- Steve Coogan as Octavius
- Patrick Gallagher as Attila the Hun
- Rami Malek as Ahkmenrah
- Mizuo Peck as Sacagawea
- Ricky Gervais as Dr. McPhee, Larry's boss.
- Crystal the Monkey as Dexter
- Kim Raver as Erica Daley
- Frank Welker as Rexy
- Dee Bradley Baker as Tutankamun
- Pierfrancesco Favino as Christopher Columbus
- Brad Garrett as The Easter Island Head (Voice)
- Paul Rudd as Don
- Anne Meara-Stiller (Ben Stiller's real-life mother) as Debbie
- Martin Christopher as Meriwether Lewis
- Martin Sims as William Clark
- Ian Campbell as Painter

Music

Songs

- "Friday Night" - performed by McFly; not featured in American version of the film, but heard in some international cuts, used during the end credits. It can be heard on the American DVD on the Spanish dub.
- "September" - performed by Earth, Wind and Fire; used before the end credits where everyone in the museum is partying.
- "Weapon of Choice" - performed by Fatboy Slim; used in the scene where Larry returns to the museum for his second night and is preparing for the chaos.
- "Tonight" - performed by Keke Palmer and Cham; used for the end credits (U.S. theatrical version only).
- "Eye of the Tiger" - performed by Ben Stiller; used in the scene where Larry is bored and messes around with the telephone at the front desk beatboxing the music.
- A Muzak version of "Mandy" by Barry Manilow is used when Larry is standing in the elevator, while escaping from Attila the Hun.
- "Ezekiel Saw Them Dry Bones" is the tune Larry whistles as he passes the empty T. Rex exhibit on his first night.
- "Camptown Races" by Stephen Foster is sung by the townspeople of the American West miniature diorama. This is a period-correct song.
- Alan Silvestri replaced John Ottman as score composer. Silvestri's score was used for the teaser trailer of *Horton Hears A Who!*

Reception

Critical reception

The film received mixed reviews from movie critics, receiving a 44% rating from noted critics and a 39% "Top Critics" rating, both meaning "rotten" at Rotten Tomatoes and a 58/100 rating on Metacritic indicating mixed or average reviews.[4] James Berardinelli of Reelviews gave it 2 stars out of 4, and commented on Stiller's performance by stating "It might be fair to give Ben Stiller an 'A' for effort, but to call what he does in this movie "acting" is a misnomer. He does a lot of running around, occasionally falling down or bumping into things."[5] One positive review by William Arnold of the *Seattle Post-Intelligencer*, gave it a B-, and stated that the film was "Out to impress and delight a family audience with the pageantry of human and natural history, and that's a surprisingly worthy ambition for a Hollywood comedy."[6] However, it received a "fresh" 65% from the RT community.[7] In a case of life imitating art, museum officials at the American Museum of Natural History have credited the film for increasing the number of visitors during the holiday season by almost 20%. According to a museum official, between December 22, 2006, and January 2, 2007, there were 50,000 more visitors than during the same period the prior year.[8]

Box office

Night at the Museum was the highest grossing film in its opening weekend, grossing $30.8 million in 3,685 theaters. For the four-day Christmas holiday weekend, it took in $42.2 million.[1] The movie was also released in IMAX large screen format, often on site at museums of science or natural history such as the Pacific Science Center in Seattle.

In its second weekend, *Night at the Museum* expanded into eighty-three more theaters and took in approximately $37.8 million at the box-office, out-grossing its opening weekend. It maintained its #1 position in its third week, with an additional $24 million. In total, as of Monday, April 30, 2007, the film had grossed $571,069,550: $250,224,440 in the U.S. and Canada, and $320,845,110 in the rest of the world.[9]

DVD release

The film was released on a 2-Disc DVD edition in the United Kingdom on April 2, 2007. It was released on 1-Disc and 2-Disc DVD editions and Blu-ray Disc format on April 24, 2007 elsewhere.

The film became the first non-Disney film to be reviewed by Ultimate Disney, due to the website dealing with other studios besides Disney.[10] [11]

References

[1] "Night at the Museum (2006)" (http://www.boxofficemojo.com/movies/?id=nightatthemuseum.htm). Box Office Mojo. . Retrieved 2009-11-05.

[2] "MovieLocationsGuide.com" (http://www.movielocationsguide.com/Night_at_the_Museum/filming_locations). *Night at the Museum Filming Locations.* . Retrieved January 8, 2007.

[3] "Sun2Surf.com" (http://www.sun2surf.com/article.cfm?id=16582). *Stiller shifts to the Museum.* . Retrieved January 8, 2007.

[4] "RottenTomatoes.com" (http://www.rottentomatoes.com/m/night_at_the_museum/). *Night at the Museum (2006).* . Retrieved January 7, 2007.

[5] "Reelviews.com" (http://www.reelviews.net/movies/n/night_museum.html). *Night at the Museum.* . Retrieved January 7, 2007.

[6] "SeattlePI.com" (http://www.seattlepi.com/movies/296769_museum22q.html). *Shallow 'Museum' exhibits some appealing qualities.* . Retrieved January 7, 2007.

[7] "Night at the Museum - Movie Reviews, Pictures" (http://www.rottentomatoes.com/m/night_at_the_museum/reviews_users.php?page=1&critic=approved&sortby=date&name_order=asc&view=#mo). Rotten Tomatoes. . Retrieved 2011-10-29.

[8] "msnbc.com" (http://www.msnbc.msn.com/id/16549060/). *Movie boosts Natural History Museum visits.* . Retrieved September 11, 2007.

[9] Box Office Mojo - Movie Index, A-Z (http://www.boxofficemojo.com/movie?id=nightatthemuseum.ht)

[10] "UltimateDisney.com" (http://www.ultimatedisney.com/archives-0407b.html). *Non-Disney films to be reviewed by Ultimate Disney..* . Retrieved April 20, 2007.

[11] "UltimateDisney.com" (http://www.ultimatedisney.com/nightatthemuseum-560.html). *"Night at the Museum" at UltimateDisney.com.* . Retrieved April 24, 2007.

External links

- *Night at the Museum* (http://www.imdb.com/title/tt0477347/) at the Internet Movie Database
- *Night at the Museum* (http://www.allrovi.com/movies/movie/v340663) at AllRovi
- *Night at the Museum* (http://www.boxofficemojo.com/movies/?id=nightatthemuseum.htm) at Box Office Mojo
- *Night at the Museum* (http://www.metacritic.com/movie/nightatthemuseum) at Metacritic
- *Night at the Museum* (http://www.rottentomatoes.com/m/night_at_the_museum/) at Rotten Tomatoes
- Night At The Museum Review (http://www.variety.com/review/VE1117932351.html?categoryID=31&cs=1) on *Variety.com*
- Independentfilm.com video interview with Mizuo Peck who played Sacagawea (http://www.independentfilm.com/films/videogalleryfilms/night-at-the-museum-mizuo-peck.shtml)

Happy Feet

Happy Feet	
Promotional poster	
Directed by	George Miller Warren Coleman Judy Morris
Produced by	Bill Miller George Miller Doug Mitchell
Written by	Warren Coleman John Collee George Miller Judy Morris
Starring	Elijah Wood Robin Williams Brittany Murphy Hugh Jackman Nicole Kidman Hugo Weaving
Music by	John Powell Gia Farrell
Cinematography	David Peers
Editing by	Christian Gazal Margaret Sixel
Studio	Kennedy-Miller Productions Animal Logic Films
Distributed by	Warner Bros. Pictures Village Roadshow Pictures
Release date(s)	November 17, 2006 (North America) December 26, 2006 (Australia)
Running time	108 minutes
Country	United States Australia
Language	English
Budget	$100 million
Box office	$384,335,608[1]

Happy Feet is a 2006 American-Australian computer-animated family film with music, directed and co-written by George Miller. It was produced at Sydney-based visual effects and animation studio *Animal Logic* for Warner Bros., Village Roadshow Pictures and Kingdom Feature Productions and was released in North America on November 17, 2006. It is the first animated feature film produced by Kennedy Miller in association with visual effects/design company Animal Logic.

Though primarily an animated film, Happy Feet does incorporate motion capture of live action humans in certain scenes. The film was simultaneously released in both conventional theatres and in IMAX 2D format.[2] The studio had hinted that a future IMAX 3D release was a possibility. However, Warner Bros., the film's production company, was on too tight a budget to release Happy Feet in IMAX digital 3D.[3]

Happy Feet won the Academy Award for Best Animated Feature and was nominated for the Annie Award for Best Animated Feature.

The film was dedicated in memory of Nick Enright, Michael Jonson, Robby McNeilly Green, and Steve Irwin.

Plot

Every penguin sings a unique song called a "heartsong" to attract a mate. If the male penguin's heartsong matches the female's song, the two penguins mate. A penguin named Norma Jean (Nicole Kidman) sings the song "Kiss", whereupon a male penguin named Memphis (Hugh Jackman) sings "Heartbreak Hotel". Norma Jean chooses him as her mate. Norma Jean lays an egg, which is left with Memphis while Norma Jean leaves with the other females to fish. While the males struggle through the harsh winter, Memphis accidentally drops the egg, briefly exposing it to the freezing Antarctic temperatures. The resulting chick - the film's protagonist, Mumble (Elizabeth Daily) - has blue eyes, ever-lasting down feathers, and a terrible singing voice. However, Mumble has a talent that no other penguin has ever seen before: tap dancing. One day Mumble wanders into a secluded area, where he is free to dance without any complaints. Mumble is interrupted when Boss Skua and his posse Dino, Frankie, and Vinnie attempt to eat him. Mumble stalls by asking the leader of the pack about a yellow band that is attached to his right ankle. The Boss Skua tells Mumble that he had been abducted by "aliens". Mumble narrowly escapes the hungry birds by falling into a crevice.

Mumble grows into an adult (Elijah Wood), still half-covered in fluffy down. Mumble joins his class graduates on their first trip into the ocean, where they find a large iceberg to rest on. After interrupting the graduates' song, Mumble is forced to leave, and finds a smaller iceberg. A leopard seal chases him off the iceberg. After escaping the leopard seal, he befriends a small group of bachelors which are Adele Penguins who form a club called "the Amigos": the leader Ramon, the brothers Raul and Nestor, and twin brothers Rinaldo and Lombardo. The Amigos quickly embrace Mumble's dance moves and assimilate him into their misfit group. Mumble's joy is cut short when he accidentally starts an avalanche and causes a hidden human excavator to tumble out from a glacier. Driven by curiosity, he sets out to find the "aliens" responsible for the machine. Mumble has a lot of questions, and the group suggests that he ask Lovelace (a Rockhopper or Macaroni Crested Penguin) who answers questions in exchange for stones and is known as the guru. Lovelace has the plastic rings of a six pack entangled around his neck, which he uses to project his guru image. When asked if the rings were from the aliens, Lovelace denies that aliens exists and claims that the plastic rings were bestowed upon him by mystic beings.

In Mumble's old home, it is mating season, and Gloria (Brittany Murphy) is the center of attention. Although she is surrounded by a large horde of suitors, none of their heartsongs interest her. Ramon tries to help Mumble by singing a Spanish version of "My Way". Gloria is not fooled, however, for she knows Mumble cannot sing. She then notices Ramon behind Mumble's back. Gloria becomes angry and turns her back on Mumble. Gloria continues towards the other males visibly distraught. As a last resort, Mumble tries to persuade her to sing along to his tapping rhythm. Because of her affection for him, she complies. As Mumble's beat speeds up, Gloria finds the chorus to her heartsong, and realizes it is "Boogie Wonderland". Overcome with happiness that they can now be mates, the pair begin dancing, along with the other penguins.

Noah the elder sees their lack of fish as punishment from the Great 'Guin for Mumble's dancing. Mumble tries to explain about the mysterious "aliens", and that they are the cause of the scarceness of fish, but only his mother and Gloria believe him. Noah exiles Mumble from the colony. Mumble vows that he will find the real cause of the famine. He and the Amigos return to Lovelace only to find him being choked by the plastic rings. Lovelace confesses that he got stuck in the rings while swimming near the forbidden shores. He reveals that the forbidden shores are located past the land of elephant seals and beyond the blizzard country. Mumble, the Amigos and Lovelace start their journey. Gloria tries to come, but Mumble, fearing for her safety, drives her off by insulting her singing talents. They travel across vast territories till they reach the shore.

Mumble sees a boat and swims after it. He swims far, and is washed up exhausted onshore. He is rescued and kept at Marine World. He tries to communicate with the "aliens", but when his pleas fail, Mumble nearly succumbs to madness after long confinement. When a girl attempts to interact with Mumble by tapping the glass, he starts dancing, and soon a large crowd gathers. He is released back into the wild, with a Tracking system on his back. He leads the humans to his colony. The other penguins are skeptical, but when Gloria notices the device, they realize that the "aliens" exist. Convinced, the penguins, along with the elders, dance with Mumble to get the humans' attention.

A research team arrives and film the penguins dancing. They bring the footage back and a worldwide debate ensues. The governments realize they are overfishing. Antarctic fishing is banned, and the fish population recovers. At this, the Emperor Penguins and the Amigos celebrate. A dancing baby penguin seen at the end is implied to be the child of Mumble and Gloria.

In the end credits, the characters reunite to dance for the final number, "The Song of the Heart."

Cast

- Elijah Wood as Mumble
- Brittany Murphy as Gloria
- Hugh Jackman as Memphis
- Nicole Kidman as Norma Jean
- Hugo Weaving as Noah the Elder
- Robin Williams as Ramón and Lovelace
- Carlos Alazraqui as Nestor
- Steve Irwin as Trev
- Lombardo Boyar as Raul
- Jeffrey Garcia as Rinaldo
- Johnny Sanchez as Lombardo
- Miriam Margoyles as Mrs. Astrakhan
- Fat Joe as Seymour
- Elizabeth Daily as baby Mumble
- Alyssa Shafer as baby Gloria

Production

Miller cites as an initial inspiration for the film an encounter with a grizzled old camera-man, whose father was Frank Hurley of the Shackleton expeditions, during the shooting of Mad Max 2: "We were sitting in this bar, having a milkshake, and he looked across at me and said, 'Antarctica.' He'd shot a documentary there. He said, 'You've got to make a film in Antarctica. It's just like out here, in the wasteland. It's spectacular.' And that always stuck in my head."[4] *Happy Feet* was also partially inspired by earlier documentaries such as the BBC's *Life in the Freezer*.[5] In 2001, during an otherwise non-sequiter meeting, Doug Mitchell impulsively presented Warner Bros., studio president Alan Horn with an early rough draft of the film's screenplay, and asked them to read it while he and Miller flew back to Australia. By the time they'd landed, Warner Bros. had decided to provide funding on the film. Production was slated to begin sometime after the completion of the fourth Mad Max film, Fury Road, but geo-political complications pushed *Happy Feet* to the forefront in early 2003.

An earlier cut of the film seems to have included a large subplot regarding aliens in the extraterrestrial sense, whose presence was made gradually more and more known throughout, and who were planning to siphon off the planet's resources gradually, placing the humans in the same light as the penguins. At the end, through the plight of the main character, their hand is stayed and, instead, first contact is made. This was chopped out during the last year of production, and has yet to see the light of day in a finished form, although concept art from these sequences were showcased at the Siggraph 2007 demonstration,[6] and are available online, as well.

The animation in *Happy Feet* invested heavily in motion capture technology, with the dance scenes acted out by human dancers. The tap-dancing for Mumble in particular was provided by Savion Glover who was also co-choreographer for the dance sequences.[7] The dancers went through "Penguin School" to learn how to move like a penguin, and also wore head apparatus to mimic a penguin's beak.[8]

Happy Feet needed an enormous group of computers, and Animal Logic worked with IBM to build a server farm with sufficient processing potential. The film took four years to make. Ben Gunsberger, Lighting Supervisor and VFX Department Supervisor, says this was partly because they needed to build new infrastructure and tools. The server farm used IBM BladeCenter framework and BladeCenter HS20 blade servers, which are extremely dense separate computer units each with two Intel Xeon processors. Rendering took up 17 million CPU hours over a nine month period.[9]

Music

Happy Feet is a jukebox musical, taking previously recorded songs and working them into the film's soundtrack to fit with the mood of the scene or character. Two soundtrack albums were released for the film; one containing songs from and inspired by the film, and another featuring John Powell's instrumental score. They were released on October 31, 2006 and December 19, 2006, respectively.

Accolades

Won

Academy Awards

- Best Animated Feature

60th British Academy Film Awards

- Best Animated Feature Film

Golden Globes

- Best Original Song - "Song of the Heart" by Prince

American Film Institute Awards 2006

- Honored as one of the Top Ten Best Films of the Year

Los Angeles Film Critics Association Awards

- Best Animation

New York Film Critics Circle Awards

- Best Animated Film

Golden Trailer Awards[10]

- Best Music

Heartland Awards

- The Truly Moving Picture Award

Kids' Choice Awards

- Favorite Animated Movie

British Academy of Film and Television Arts - Children's Awards

- Best Feature Film

Nominations

Golden Globe Award

- Best Animated Feature

Annie Awards

- Best Animated Feature
- Best Writing in an Animated Feature Production

Satellite Awards

- Best Motion Picture, Animated or Mixed Media

Grammy Awards

- Best Score Soundtrack Album for Motion Picture, Television or Other Visual Media, John Powell, nominee
- Best Song Written for Motion Picture, Television or Other Visual Media: "The Song of the Heart", Prince, nominee

American Film Institute

- AFI's 10 Top 10 - Nominated Animated Film

Top ten lists

The film appeared on numerous critics' top ten lists of the best films of 2006, including AFI's Annual list, which is listed above.[11] [12] AFI's jury said:

"*HAPPY FEET* is a one-of-a-kind motion picture experience. George Miller continues to paint outside the lines of traditional filmmaking, and his genius expands upon the animated art form to illuminate a world where penguins embrace dance and differences to survive and thrive. But that is just the tip of the iceberg, as the environment, religion and the chasm between generations enrich this sweet and subtle tale - one that is fun and funny, brilliant and beautiful, groundbreaking and global in its message."

- 1st - Jack Matthews, *The New York Daily News*
- 1st - Stan Urankar, *Sun News*
- 2nd - William Arnold, *Seattle Post-Intelligencer*
- 2nd - Mark Palermo, *The Coast*
- 3rd - Kirk Honeycutt, *Hollywood Reporter*
- 4th - Edward Douglas, *ComingSoon.net*
- 5th - Scott Foundas, *Village Voice*
- 5th - Peter Rainer, *Christian Science Monitor*
- 5th - Matthieu Santelli, *Critikat (Film review, in French)* [13]
- 5th - Kurt Loder, *MTV*
- 5th - Missy Thompson, *Tooele Transcript Bulletin*
- 6th - Constance Garfinkle, *The Patriot Ledger*
- 6th - Carole Wrona, *Critikat (Top 10 lists for 2006 films, in French)* [14]
- 6th - Lou Lumenick, *New York Post*
- 6th - Kyle Smith, *New York Post*
- 6th - Michael Wilmington, *Chicago Tribune*
- 6th - Keith Cohen, *Sun Newspapers*
- 8th - Rene Rodriguez, *Miami Herald*
- 9th - Schlomo Schwartzberg, *Box Office Magazine*

Home media release

Happy Feet was released on March 27, 2007[15] in the United States in three formats; DVD (in separate widescreen and pan and scan editions), Blu-ray Disc, and an HD DVD/DVD combo disc.[16]

Among the DVD's special features is a scene that was cut from the film where Mumble meets a blue whale and an albatross. The albatross was Steve Irwin's first voice role in the film before he voiced the elephant seal in the final cut. The scene was finished and included on the DVD in memory of Steve Irwin. This scene is done in Steve's classic documentary style, with the albatross telling the viewer all about the other characters in the scene, and the impact people are having on their environment.

Video games

A video game based on the film was developed by A2M and published by Midway Games. It has the same main cast as the film. It was released for the PC, PlayStation 2, GameCube, GBA, NDS, and Wii.[17]

Artificial Life, Inc. has also developed a Happy Feet mobile game for the Japan market.[18]

Reception

Box office

The film opened at #1 in the United States on its first weekend of release (November 17–19) grossing $41.6 million and beating *Casino Royale* for the top spot.[19] It remained #1 for the Thanksgiving weekend, making $51.6 million over the five-day period. In total, the film was the top grosser for three weeks, a 2006 box office feat matched only by *Pirates of the Caribbean: Dead Man's Chest*. As of June 8, 2008, *Happy Feet* has grossed $198.0 million in the U.S. and $186.3 million overseas, making about $384.3 million dollars worldwide. *Happy Feet* was the third highest grossing animated film in the U.S., behind *Cars* and *Ice Age: The Meltdown*. The film has been released in about 35 international territories at the close of 2006.[20] [21] [22]

The production budget was $100 million.[1]

Critical reviews

Happy Feet has received positive reviews from film critics, and received a 74% "Fresh" approval in the Rotten Tomatoes movie review aggregate site, with an 82% percent from the Top Critics.[23]

Analysis

The film has also garnered, since its release, quite a bit of analysis and dissection from various places. Film critic Yar Habnegnal has written an essay, published in *Forum on Contemporary Art and Society*, that examines the themes of encroachment presented throughout the film, as well as various other subtexts and themes, such as religious hierarchy and interracial tensions.[24] And, Vadim Rizov of the Independent Film Channel sees Mumble as just the latest in a long line of cinematic religious mavericks.

On a technical or formal level, the film has also been lauded in some corners for its innovative introduction of Miller's roving style of subjective cinematography into contemporary animation, among other things.

Sequel

Happy Feet Two was produced at Dr. D Studios[25] and released on November 18, 2011. Wood and Williams reprised their roles for the sequel. Brittany Murphy was not be able to reprise her role, due to her death. Matt Damon and Brad Pitt signed on as 'Bill the Krill' and 'Will the Krill', respectively.[26] [27]

Environmental message

As things progress there is increasing emphasis on environmental problems in the Antarctic.

The film's denouement shows a group of researchers taking video of the colony of dancing emperor penguins, and the footage is broadcast globally. After many heated arguments this publicity generates considerable pressure to stop commercial overfishing of the Antarctic.

According to the director, George Miller, the environmental message was not a major part of the original script, but "In Australia, we're very, very aware of the ozone hole," he said, "and Antarctica is literally the canary in the coal mine for this stuff. So it sort of had to go in that direction." This influence led to a film with a more environmental tone. Miller said, "You can't tell a story about Antarctica and the penguins without giving that dimension."[28]

References

[1] Happy Feet (2006) (http://boxofficemojo.com/movies/?id=happyfeet.htm). *Box Office Mojo*. Retrieved 2011-01-02.

[2] "Happy Feet: The IMAX Experience" (http://www.imax.com/ImaxWeb/filmDetail.do?type=comingSoon&movieID=code__.__30). *IMAX*. . Retrieved 2007-03-15.

[3] "Happy Feet Won't Debut in IMAX 3-D" (http://www.vfxworld.com/?sa=adv&code=3631a5a1&atype=news&id=17882). *VFXWorld*. . Retrieved 2007-03-15.

[4] "The filmmaker behind the 'Mad Max' and 'Babe' franchises turns his attention to musical fowl" (http://www.natoonline.org/infocus/06November/happyfeet.htm). *In Focus*. Retrieved 2010-11-13.

[5] "Penguin suits up for a cinema hit" (http://www.theaustralian.news.com.au/story/0,20867,20753501-2702,00.html). *The Australian*. . Retrieved 2008-03-28.

[6] (August 6, 2007). Live from the Happy Feet discussion at Siggraph 2007 (http://brooks.boyd.name/wordpress/2007/08/live-from-the-happy-feet-discussion-at-siggraph-2007). Retrieved 2010-11-13.

[7] Savion Glover (2007). *Happy Feet* (DVD). *Warner Brothers*.

[8] Kelley Abbey (2007). *Happy Feet* (DVD). *Warner Brothers*.

[9] "Animal Logic builds rendering farm with IBM eServer BladeCenter" (http://www-01.ibm.com/software/success/cssdb.nsf/cs/mcag-6h2sr2?opendocument&site=corp). *IBM Australia*. . Retrieved 2010-02-01.

[10] Golden Trailer Awards (http://www.goldentrailer.com/gta7.html). Retrieved 2011-01-02.

[11] "Film Critic Top Ten List, 2006 Critics' Picks" (http://www.metacritic.com/film/awards/2006/toptens.shtml). . Retrieved 2011-01-02.

[12] "The Critics" (http://www.moviecitynews.com/awards/2007/top_tens/critics_01.html). . Retrieved 2011-01-02.

[13] http://www.critikat.com/Happy-Feet.html

[14] http://www.critikat.com/Editorial-8.html

[15] "Happy Feet (2006) - Elijah Wood, Nicole Kidman, Hugh Jackman" (http://videoeta.com/movie.html?via=form&id=78865). Retrieved 2011-01-02.

[16] "Happy Feet to Dance on Blu-ray, HD DVD This March | High-Def Digest" (http://www.highdefdigest.com/news/show/432). Retrieved 2011-01-02.

[17] Happy Feet (http://www.midway.com/rxpage/Game_HappyFeet.html). *Midway.com*. Retrieved 2011-01-02.

[18] (2007-04-24). Parthajit; "Happy Feet Goes Mobile" (http://news.softpedia.com/news/Happy-Feet-Goes-Mobile-52871.shtml). *Softpedia*. Retrieved 2011-01-02.

[19] Weekend Box Office Results for November 17–19, 2006 (http://www.boxofficemojo.com/weekend/chart/?yr=2006&wknd=46&p=.htm). *Box Office Mojo*. Retrieved 2010-11-13.

[20] Happy Feet (2006) - Weekend Box Office Results (http://www.boxofficemojo.com/movies/?page=weekend&id=happyfeet.htm). *Box Office Mojo*. Retrieved 2010-11-13.

[21] IMDb Charts (http://www.imdb.com/chart). *IMDb*. Retrieved 2010-11-13.

[22] Weekend Box Office Results for February 1–3, 2008 (http://www.boxofficemojo.com/weekend/chart). *Box Office Mojo*. Retrieved 2010-11-13.

[23] Happy Feet Movie Reviews, Pictures (http://www.rottentomatoes.com/m/happy_feet). *Rotten Tomatoes*. Retrieved 2010-11-13.

[24] Yar Habnegnal on Happy Feet (http://www.scribd.com/doc/2555518/Yar-Habnegnal-on-Happy-Feet). *Scribd.com*. Retrieved 2010-11-13.

[25] "About Dr. D Studios" (http://www.drdstudios.com). Retrieved 2010-11-13.

[26] (January 19, 2010). "Matt Damon, Brad Pitt to Voice Characters in Happy Feet Sequel" (http://www.showbizspy.com/article/198088/matt-damon-brad-pitt-to-voice-characters-in-happy-feet-sequel.html). *ShowbizSpy.com*. Retrieved 2010-11-13.

[27] "Happy Feet 2's first look at Pitt, Damon" (http://www.rte.ie/ten/2011/0930/happyfeet2poster.html). RTE Ten. 2011-09-30. . Retrieved 2011-10-13.

[28] Kelly, Kate (2006-11-17). "The New Animated Film Happy Feet Doesn't Dance Around Serious Issues" (http://online.wsj.com/public/article/SB116373257478225933-QS7Oc7yiEQI503rfJ2N42OUiVH8_20071119.html?mod=tff_main_tff_top). *The Wall Street Journal*. . Retrieved 2007-03-15.

External links

- Official website (http://www.happyfeetmovie.com)
- *Happy Feet* (http://www.imdb.com/title/tt0366548/) at the Internet Movie Database
- *Happy Feet* (http://www.allrovi.com/movies/movie/v322645) at AllRovi
- *Happy Feet* (http://www.rottentomatoes.com/m/happy_feet/) at Rotten Tomatoes
- *Happy Feet* (http://www.metacritic.com/movie/happyfeet) at Metacritic
- *Happy Feet* (http://www.boxofficemojo.com/movies/?id=happyfeet.htm) at Box Office Mojo
- *Happy Feet* - Review (http://review-online.blogspot.com/2007/03/happy-feet.html)

Everyone's Hero

Everyone's Hero	
Theatrical release poster	
Directed by	Colin Brady Christopher Reeve Daniel St. Pierre
Produced by	Kyle Clark Igor Khait Ron Tippe Christopher Reeve Dana Reeve
Screenplay by	Robert Kurtz Jeff Hand
Story by	Howard Jonas
Starring	Jake T. Austin William H. Macy Rob Reiner Raven-Symoné Whoopi Goldberg
Music by	John Debney Selena Gomez
Cinematography	Jan Carlee Andy Wang
Editing by	John Bryant
Studio	IDT Entertainment
Distributed by	20th Century Fox
Release date(s)	September 15, 2006

Running time	88 minutes
Country	Canada United States
Language	English
Box office	$16,627,188 (Worldwide)[1]

Everyone's Hero is a 2006 computer animated comedy film, directed by Colin Brady, Christopher Reeve (who was working on this film at the time of his death[2]), and Daniel St. Pierre, with music by John Debney. The majority of this film was produced by IDT Entertainment in Toronto with portions outsourced to Reel FX Creative Studios. It was distributed by 20th Century Fox, and released theatrically on September 15, 2006. *Everyone's Hero* had a moderate performance at the box office, earning only $16 million worldwide during its theatrical run, but the film was not released in several major countries.

Plot

The protagonist is young baseball fan Yankee Irving (Jake T. Austin), whose father Stanley (Mandy Patinkin) works as a janitor for New York City's Yankee Stadium. Yankee dreams of playing for the Yankees but can't even play sandlot baseball well enough to avoid being picked last. One day beside the sandlot, he finds a talking baseball he names Screwie (Rob Reiner).

While father and son are in the stadium, a thief steals Babe Ruth's famous bat Darlin' (Whoopi Goldberg), with the result that Yankee's father is blamed and fired; the father blamed Yankee for stealing it and framing his own father. The true thief is Lefty Maginnis (William H. Macy), a pitcher for the Chicago Cubs. Lefty works for Cubs owner Napoleon Cross (Robin Williams), who desires to see the Cubs defeat the Yankees during the 1932 World Series.

Stealing the bat back, Yankee decides to return it to Ruth—and thereby exonerate his father—by journeying across the country to Chicago, where the next World Series' games will be played. Darlin' is able to speak, as does her counterpart Screwie, who she constantly argues and bickers with (though near the end, they finally become friends). Much of the plot is driven by Lefty's comic attempts to retrieve the bat from Yankee, with slapstick results. Other scenes involve Yankee meeting others who will help him in his quest: several hobos (Ed Helms); Marti (Raven-Symone), an African American girl; her baseball player father Lonnie Brewster (Forest Whitaker); and in Chicago, Babe Ruth himself (Brian Dennehy).

A series of improbable coincidences allows Yankee himself to bat for the Yankees, resulting in the archetypal home run (technically, a series of errors after an infield pop-up that allow him to round the bases). This restores the morale of the Yankees, who score 7 more runs to take the lead and win the World Series. Cross tries to talk Babe Ruth out of accepting the victory, saying that Yankee is too young to be a counting player. This leads to the arrest of Cross, who simply says that he was a fan that cheated. When his part in the plan is revealed, Lefty is banished from the team, although he is able to stay out of jail. Yankee also successfully exonerates his father. Yankee returns home, now knowing what is truly important in baseball.

Cast

- Jake T. Austin as Yankee Irving
- Mandy Patinkin as Stanley Irving
- William H. Macy as Lefty Maginnis
- Rob Reiner as Screwie
- Raven-Symoné as Marti Brewster
- Whoopi Goldberg as Darlin'
- Brian Dennehy as Babe Ruth
- Forest Whitaker as Lonnie Brewster
- Robert Wagner as Mr. Robinson
- Dana Reeve as Emily Irving
- Richard Kind as Hobo Andy / Maitre'D
- Joe Torre as New York Yankees manager
- Ed Helms as Hobo Louis
- Conor J. White as Hobo Arnold
- Robin Williams as Napoleon Cross (*uncredited*)
- Richtie Allen as Officer Bryant / Additional Voices
- Patrick Warburton as Coach Larry Benson
- Greta Nilssen as Ella Buntong
- Selena Gomez as emily oscar

Production

With the exception of Ruth, none of the film's characters are based on real people.

The film takes a largely nostalgic tone in its presentation of 1930s American life, though the Great Depression is alluded to, as is the existence of separate Negro Leagues. (Marti's father is a member of the Cincinnati Tigers, though the team was actually founded two years later, in 1934.) The announced morals of the movie are to "keep swinging" (that is, never give up), and the importance of family.

The actual events of the 1932 series, though dramatic, were not followed in the film (perhaps because of rights issues over depictions of the game). For example, the Yankees swept the Cubs in the series, but in the film, they lost three games to set up the classic game 7 scenario.

In one point of the film, Screwy refers to Superman, which is anachronistic due to the fact that Superman did not appear until 1938, and the film is set in 1932, though the reference is clearly intended as a nod to late co-director Reeve, who played Superman in several films.

Reception

Box office

In its opening weekend, the film grossed $6,061,762 million in 2,896 theaters in the United States and Canada, ranking #3 at the box office, behind *Gridiron Gang* and *The Black Dahlia*, was the best debut for an animated film that week. By the end of its run, *Everyone's Hero* grossed $14,522,427 domestically and $2,104,087 internationally, totaling $16,627,188 worldwide.[3]

Critical reception

The film received mixed reviews from most critics. At Metacritic,[4] which assigns a normalized rating out of 100 to reviews from mainstream critics, the film received an average score of 51%, based on 20 reviews, which indicates "mixed reviews" reviews, the film received two negative reviews, twelve mixed reviews and six positive reviews.[5]

New York Daily News, positive review, "Whoever wanders into the theater should leave a winner".

L.A. Weekly, positive review, "The movie's antique Rockwellian look is its greatest pleasure".

Entertainment Weekly, positive review, "*Everyone's Hero* re-creates Depression-era America with surprisingly agreeable anachronistic panache, but a sassy ball and bat don't cut it as compelling cartoon characters, and the not-so-human humans never quite do either (Babe Ruth looks like *Shrek*)".

New York Post, mixed review, "*Everyone's Hero*, a tame CGI cartoon for the simple-minded: the very young, the very old and Yankee fans".

TV Guide, negative review, "An anemic adventure that epitomizes generic feature animation".

Syndication

In the US, Cartoon Network aired *Everyone's Hero* on April 12, 2008 In the Latin America, Cartoon Network Latinoamerica on November 23, 2011.

Soundtrack

Everyone's Hero : Music From The Motion Picture	
Soundtrack album by Various Artists	
Released	June 8, 2011[6]
Genre	Film soundtrack
Label	Columbia Records/Sony Music Soundtrax

The soundtrack, released on the Columbia Records/Sony Music Soundtrax labels, features tracks by the star of the film Raven-Symoné, Grammy-winners Wyclef Jean, Brooks & Dunn, Mary Chapin Carpenter, and various other artists.

1. The Best – John Ondrasik – 3:49
2. Keep on Swinging – Brooks & Dunn – 4:12
3. Dream Like New York – Tyrone Wells – 3:44
4. Chicago (That Toddling Town) – Chris Botti featuring Lyle Lovett – 2:16
5. The Best Day of My Life – John Randall featuring Jessi Alexander – 3:13
6. Keep Your Eye on the Ball – Raven-Symoné – 2:27
7. What You Do – Wyclef Jean featuring Kontrast – 3:12

8. Swing It – Brooks & Dunn – 3:34
9. Take Me Out to the Ballgame – Lonestar – 2:43
10. The Bug – Mary Chapin Carpenter – 3:48
11. The Tigers – John Debney featuring Paris Bennett – 1:46
12. At Bat – John Debney – 3:44

References

[1] *Everyone's Hero* (http://www.boxofficemojo.com/movies/?id=everyoneshero.htm) at Box Office Mojo

[2] *Everyone's Hero* (http://www.imdb.com/title/tt0430779/) at the Internet Movie Database

[3] "*Everyone's Hero* (2006)" (http://www.boxofficemojo.com/movies/?page=main&id=everyoneshero.htm). *Box Office Mojo*. . Retrieved 2011-07-26.

[4] http://www.metacritic.com/movie/everyones-hero

[5] http://www.metacritic.com/movie/everyones-hero/critic-reviews

[6] http://www.amazon.com/Everyones-Hero-Music-Motion-Picture/dp/B000H5TUG8

External links

- Official website (http://www.everyoneshero.com/)
- *Everyone's Hero* (http://www.imdb.com/title/tt0430779/) at the Internet Movie Database
- *Everyone's Hero* (http://www.boxofficemojo.com/movies/?id=everyoneshero.htm) at Box Office Mojo
- *Everyone's Hero* (http://www.rottentomatoes.com/m/everyones_hero/) at Rotten Tomatoes

RV (film)

RV	
Theatrical release poster	
Directed by	Barry Sonnenfeld
Produced by	Douglas Wick Lucy Fisher
Written by	Geoff Rodkey
Starring	Joanna Levesque Robin Williams Cheryl Hines Josh Hutcherson Jeff Daniels Kristin Chenoweth Will Arnett
Music by	James Newton Howard
Cinematography	Fred Murphy
Editing by	Kevin Tent
Studio	Red Wagon Productions Intermedia
Distributed by	Columbia Pictures
Release date(s)	April 28, 2006
Running time	99 minutes
Country	United States
Language	English
Budget	$65 million
Box office	$87,528,173 (worldwide)

RV (released as ***Runaway Vacation*** in some territories) is a 2006 comedy film directed by Barry Sonnenfeld, written by Geoff Rodkey, and starring Robin Williams, Joanna "JoJo" Levesque, Cheryl Hines, Josh Hutcherson, Jeff Daniels, Kristin Chenoweth and Will Arnett. It was released on April 28, 2006 in North America. The film was released on DVD and Blu-ray Disc on August 15, 2006.

Plot

Bob Munro (Robin Williams), a California beverage company executive, is struggling with a dysfunctional family, with Cassie (JoJo) now 15, surly and sarcastic, son Carl (Josh Hutcherson) an adolescent weightlifter who likes Hip hop. At a company picnic, Bob is embarrassed in front of his boss Todd (Will Arnett) by his daughter's militant friend Gretchen (Lauren Ambrose). Looking forward to a big family vacation in Hawaii, Bob is punished by Todd by having to present a merger proposal to the grassroots Alpine Soda company in Boulder, Colorado instead. Concealing the real reason for going to Boulder, Bob rents an RV from the dodgy dealer Irv (Barry Sonnenfeld) and tells his family they are traveling to the Rockies.

On their trip, Bob and his family encounter many mishaps. These include Bob damaging the parking brake, crashing into and running over objects such as shopping carts, flushing out a trio of raccoons with a stink bomb, and fixing a clogged sewage system. Along the way, the Munros meet another traveling family, the Gornickes, consisting of Travis (Jeff Daniels), Mary Jo (Kristin Chenoweth), and their sons and daughter, Earl (Hunter Parrish), Billy "Not Earl" (Alex Ferris), and Moon (Chloe Sonnenfeld). Earl develops a romantic interest in Cassie and Carl starts to like Moon, but thinking that the Gornickes are too strange for them, the adult Munros decide to ditch them; when the Gornickes reappear at another stop, the Munros believe they are stalking them.

Meanwhile, to disguise his business trip, Bob tries to e-mail a proposal outline from his laptop, working in restrooms; eventually, a hitchhiker steals Bob's laptop, leaving him with only a BlackBerry PDA, which he does manage to use to compose and wirelessly send his proposal to his company. The Gornickes then recover the stolen laptop after picking up the same hitchhiker, and pursue the Munros to return it.

Eventually the entire family begins to enjoy their vacation. In order to attend the merger meeting, though, Bob distracts his family by feigning illness and sends them on a hike. The meeting with Alpine Soda is a success, but Bob is invited to talk to the whole company again the next day. Rushing back to his family, Bob takes a treacherous 4 wheel drive trail (it's on this bumpy rutted trail that the film's signature "RV high-centered on a boulder" scene takes place, although unlike the huge lofty granite pinnacle shown in the movie poster, the offending boulder in the ATV trail is actually only a number of inches too tall; Bob manages to dislodge the RV from the boulder by "rocking" ---- forcefully throwing himself forward and backwards in the driver's seat --- until the vehicle eventually wobbles and tips forward enough to slide down from atop the stone), succeeding in fooling them, but while he is attempting a similar ruse the next day, the RV brakes fail again and it rolls into a lake. Bob lets it slip about the real intentions of the Colorado vacation, and his family is upset. Still needing to get to the meeting, a desperate Bob retrieves one of his family's bicycles from the lake and pedals off. Jamie, Carl, and Cassie are then picked up by the Gornickes, and soon realize how well they get along, when Bob appears again, climbing atop the moving bus. After apologizing to his family, Bob is just about to blow off the meeting when it turns out he's right outside the headquarters.

At the second meeting, Bob starts his speech and it goes well, but then -- Bob has an epiphany, and so he recommends against the merger, realizing that Todd would destroy a great independent company. Carl gets angry at Todd and flips him over his shoulder, onto the ground. Moon exclaims "My Hero!" Bob is then fired but he quits anyway, and soon retrieves the sodden-but-still-operable RV from the lake. At the end, Bob is offered a job by the owners of Alpine Soda, who want to go national independently. As the credits roll, the two families are shown dancing and singing the song, "Route 66" (RV Style).

Cast

- Robin Williams as Bob Munro
- Cheryl Hines as Jamie Munro
- Joanna Levesque as Cassie Munro
- Josh Hutcherson as Carl Munro
- Jeff Daniels as Travis Gornicke
- Kristin Chenoweth as Mary Jo Gornicke
- Chloe Sonnenfeld as Moon Gornicke
- Hunter Parrish as Earl Gornicke
- Alex Ferris as Billy "Not Earl" Gornicke
- Will Arnett as Todd Mallory
- Brendan Fletcher as Howie
- Matthew Gray Gubler as Joe Joe
- Barry Sonnenfeld as Irv
- Richard Ian Cox as Laird (as Richard Cox)
- Rob LaBelle as Larry Moiphine
- Brian Markinson as Garry Moiphine

- Ty Olsson as Diablo Pass Officer
- Diane Michelle as Martha the RV (voice) (*uncredited*)

Production

The film began principal photography in the Vancouver area and southern Alberta on May 25, 2005 and finished filming in December 2005.

Soundtrack

The score was written by James Newton Howard and featured several members of the Lyle Lovett Band: Matt Rollings (keyboards), Russ Kunkel (drums), Ray Herndon (guitar), Viktor Krauss (bass), and Buck Reed (pedal steel). Alvin Chea, vocalist from Take 6, provided solo vocals. Additional music was provided by Stuart Michael Thomas and Blake Neely.

Several songs were featured prominently in the film including: "GTO", "Route 66", "Cherry Bomb", and "Stand By Your Man".

Reception

RV grossed $87,528,173 worldwide.[1]

The film received mostly negative reviews from critics. Based on 204 reviews from critics collected by the film review aggregator Rotten Tomatoes, 24% gave *RV* a positive review.[2] Justin Chang of *Variety* said "*RV* works up an ingratiating sweetness that partially compensates for its blunt predictability and meager laughs."[3] Roger Ebert, writing for the *Chicago Sun-Times*, said "There is nothing I much disliked but little to really recommend."[4]

RV won a Golden Raspberry Award for a special category called "Worst Excuse for Family Entertainment", while Kristin Chenoweth was nominated for Worst Supporting Actress.[5]

References

[1] "RV (2006)" (http://www.boxofficemojo.com/movies/?id=rv.htm). *Box Office Mojo*. . Retrieved July 11, 2010.

[2] "RV (2006)" (http://www.rottentomatoes.com/m/1156340-rv/). *Rotten Tomatoes*. . Retrieved July 11, 2010.

[3] Chang, Justin (May 1, 2006). "Family vehicle runs on gentle humor". *Variety* (Reed Business Information) (402.11): 30.

[4] Ebert, Roger (April 28, 2006). "RV review" (http://www.webcitation.org/5r8yY362e). *Chicago Sun-Times*. Archived from the original (http://rogerebert.suntimes.com/apps/pbcs.dll/article?AID=/20060427/REVIEWS/60419007) on July 11, 2010. . Retrieved July 11, 2010.

[5] "27th Annual Golden Raspberry (Razzie) Award "Winners"" (http://www.webcitation.org/5r8ywgyAW). *Golden Raspberry Award Foundation*. 2007. Archived from the original (http://www.razzies.com/history/06winners.asp) on July 11, 2010. . Retrieved July 11, 2010.

External links

- Official website (http://www.sonypictures.com/homevideo/rv/index.html)
- *RV* (http://www.imdb.com/title/tt0449089/) at the Internet Movie Database
- *RV* (http://www.allrovi.com/movies/movie/v323790) at AllRovi

The Night Listener (film)

The Night Listener	
Theatrical release poster	
Directed by	Patrick Stettner
Produced by	Robert Kessel Jill Footlick Jeffrey Sharp John N. Hart, Jr. Armistead Maupin
Screenplay by	Armistead Maupin Terry Anderson Patrick Stettner
Based on	*The Night Listener* by Armistead Maupin
Starring	Robin Williams Toni Collette Rory Culkin Bobby Cannavale Sandra Oh
Music by	Peter Nashel
Cinematography	Lisa Rinzler
Editing by	Andy Keir
Studio	IFC Films Fortissimo Films
Distributed by	Miramax Films
Release date(s)	August 4, 2006
Running time	91 minutes 81 minutes (Edited cut)
Country	United States
Language	English
Budget	$3 million
Box office	$10,639,686

The Night Listener is a 2006 psychological horror film directed by Patrick Stettner. The screenplay by Armistead Maupin, Terry Anderson, and Stettner is based on Maupin's 2000 bestselling novel of the same name, which was inspired by actual events in the author's life.

Plot

Gabriel Noone (Robin Williams), a popular gay New York City radio show host, is dealing with a separation from his partner, Jess (Bobby Cannavale). Noone is given a memoir written by teenager Pete Logand (Rory Culkin), who chronicles the many years of sexual abuse he suffered at the hands of his parents and their friends. Diagnosed with AIDS, the youth has been adopted by Donna Logand (Toni Collette), the social worker who handled his case.

Noone begins a telephone relationship with the boy and Donna. He and Pete become increasingly close and form a father-son relationship, much to the dismay of Jess, especially after he speaks to Donna and suspects she and the boy are the same person. Noone's personal secretary Anna adds fuel to the fire by discussing her research into people who fabricate stories for attention or love. Determined to prove the boy exists and his story is true, Noone decides to pay a surprise visit to him in his hometown in rural Wisconsin. Noone discovers the return address on Peter's correspondence is actually a mail drop. Soon after, while eating in a local diner, he overhears another patron and recognizes her voice as that of Donna. He's stunned to learn she's blind and uses a guide dog. Noone follows her home and Donna senses he has followed her. She invites him into her home and talks openly about Peter, who she says is currently in the hospital undergoing tests. She assures him he can visit the boy the following day, then suddenly becomes angry and tells him she will not allow him to meet her son. Increasingly suspicious, Noone contacts all the hospitals in Madison, the site of the nearest facilities, but none have the boy registered as a patient.

Gabriel's paranoia about the boy's existence grows and, hoping to find proof of his existence, he breaks into Donna's home. A police officer arrests him for breaking and entering and then, mistakenly believing him to be one of the boy's abusers, attacks him with a stun baton before taking him to the station. Noone convinces the police he meant no harm and is released, only to find Donna waiting for him with the news that Pete has died and was staying in a Milwaukee hospital, not one in Madison. Distressed that Noone doesn't believe her, Donna collapses in the middle of a road and tries to hold him with her in the path of an oncoming truck. She then moves everything out of her home and disappears before the police can question her. Noone is now convinced that the boy is a figment of the deranged woman's imagination.

In response to a phone call from Donna, Gabriel goes to a motel where she was staying, and finds Pete's stuffed rabbit and a videotape under a blanket. He plays the video of a child, who seems to be Pete, but who could have been anyone. The phone rings and the caller claims to be the boy, waiting for his mother at the airport. Gabriel asks some questions after finding out that his mother lied about his death, but the caller ends the conversation after Gabriel asks what happened in Donna's past and how she became blind.

Gabriel returns to Manhattan and uses his experience to create *The Night Listener*, a new radio story. In the final scene, Donna is searching for a new home in a coastal town, telling the realtor she needs it for herself and her sick child, who has just lost his leg but will be released the next day. She has drastically changed her appearance and no longer has a guide dog or dark glasses, revealing her blindness was also an act.

Cast

- Robin Williams as Gabriel Noone
- Toni Collette as Donna Logand
- Rory Culkin as Pete D. Logand
- Bobby Cannavale as Jess
- Sandra Oh as Anna
- Joe Morton as Ashe
- John Cullum as Pap Noone
- Lisa Emery as Darlie Noone
- Becky Ann Baker as Waitress

Production

In *The Night Listener Revealed*, an extra on the film's DVD release, Armistead Maupin discusses the inspiration for his novel. In 1992, the author was sent the manuscript of a memoir allegedly written by fourteen-year-old Anthony Godby Johnson, who had been sexually and physically abused by his parents since childhood. Since the galleys included a foreword by novelist Paul Monette, a close friend of Maupin, and an afterward by Fred Rogers of *Mister Rogers' Neighborhood* fame, he had no reason to doubt the story's veracity.

Maupin was impressed with the maturity of the boy's writing and called him. The two quickly developed a close telephone relationship, and Maupin frequently discussed the boy's various physical ailments (he had been diagnosed with AIDS) with his adopted mother. Several months later, Maupin's then-lover Terry Anderson (who co-wrote the screenplay), who had spoken to the boy on occasion, had a conversation with his mother and was struck by how much she and the boy sounded alike. As he became increasingly suspicious about the situation, Maupin became more and more determined to believe the boy really existed. Only after his many attempts to visit him were aborted by his mother did Maupin begin to think Anderson's belief that he was caught up in a scam was correct.

Following the publication of the novel, a friend of Maupin who wrote for *The New Yorker* instigated an investigation, and the story was reported by *20/20*. During filming, stars Robin Williams and Toni Collette both received fan letters written in the same distinctive handwriting as that of the boy, whose existence has never been proven or disproved.

Release

Box office

The film premiered at the Sundance Film Festival and was shown at the Berlin International Film Festival before opening on 1,367 screens in the US, earning $3,554,134 in its opening weekend. The film went on to gross $7,836,393 domestically and $2,785,502 in foreign markets for a total box office of $10,621,895.[1]

Critical reception

A.O. Scott of the *New York Times* called the film a "well-meaning, flat-footed screen adaptation [that] has its creepy, suspenseful moments ... but it shrinks a rich, strange story to the dimensions of an anecdote ... the psychological and intellectual implications that hover over the story are lost in the spooky atmospherics and overshadowed by Ms. Collette's off-kilter showboating."[2]

Mick LaSalle of the *San Francisco Chronicle* described it as "a movie with lots of heart but no heartbeat ... it feels infected by a malaise ... yet the film has intelligence and integrity and cannot be dismissed."[3]

Michael Phillips of the *Los Angeles Times* said, "It's a small but crafty and well-acted picture ... The pacing and staging of the later scenes could use a little more electricity and momentum and a little less restraint. Yet *The Night Listener* keeps you watching. And listening."[4]

David Rooney of *Variety* thought it was "tediously solemn" and a "dawdling mystery thriller [that] manages to flatten two protagonists that had far more depth in the novel ... Lenser Lisa Rinzler gives the film a somber, elegant look, and Peter Nashel's score adds a layer of intensity. But it takes more than a few brooding strings to make a film taut and tense. The pace drags increasingly, trudging through the protracted final reels to a clumsy wrap-up with too many concluding scenes, none of them effective."[5]

References

[1] "BoxOfficeMojo.com" (http://www.boxofficemojo.com/movies/?id=nightlistener.htm). .

[2] Scott, A. O. (February 7, 2005). "*New York Times*, August 4, 2006" (http://movies2.nytimes.com/2006/08/04/movies/04list.html). *The New York Times*. . Retrieved May 25, 2010.

[3] LaSalle, Mick (August 25, 2010). "*San Francisco Chronicle*, August 4, 2006" (http://www.sfgate.com/cgi-bin/article.cgi?f=/c/a/2006/08/04/DDGH3KA1BI1.DTL). *The San Francisco Chronicle*. .

[4] "*Los Angeles Times*, August 4, 2006" (http://www.calendarlive.com/movies/reviews/cl-et-listener4aug04,0,592323.story). .

[5] Rooney, David (January 22, 2006). "*Variety*, January 22, 2006" (http://www.variety.com/index.asp?layout=features2006&content=jump&jump=review&head=sundance&nav=RSundance&articleid=VE1117929305&cs=1&p=0). .

External links

- Official website (http://www.thenightlistener-movie.com/)
- *The Night Listener* (http://www.imdb.com/title/tt0448075/) at the Internet Movie Database
- *The Night Listener* (http://www.boxofficemojo.com/movies/?id=nightlistener.htm) at Box Office Mojo
- *The Night Listener* (http://www.rottentomatoes.com/m/the_night_listener/) at Rotten Tomatoes
- Film trailer (http://www.apple.com/trailers/miramax/thenightlistener/)
- Robin Williams interview (http://www.moviehole.net/interviews/20060805_interview_robin_williams.html)
- Armistead Maupin interview (http://www.flipsidemovies.com/armisteadmaupin.html)

License to Wed

Licence to Wed	
Promotional poster	
Directed by	Ken Kwapis
Produced by	Mike Medavoy Robert Simonds
Written by	Kim Barker Tim Rasmussen Vince Di Meglio Wayne Lloyd
Starring	Robin Williams Mandy Moore John Krasinski Eric Christian Olsen
Music by	Christophe Beck
Cinematography	John Bailey
Editing by	Kathryn Himoff
Studio	Village Roadshow Pictures Phoenix Pictures
Distributed by	Warner Bros. Pictures
Release date(s)	July 3, 2007
Running time	101 minutes
Country	United States
Language	English
Budget	$35 million
Box office	$69,307,224

License to Wed (spelled ***Licence to Wed*** outside the United States) is a 2007 romantic comedy film starring Robin Williams, Mandy Moore, and John Krasinski and directed by Ken Kwapis. The film was released in theaters on July 3, 2007.

Plot

Sadie Jones (Mandy Moore) has always longed to marry the man of her dreams in her family church. Though she has found her lifetime companion in Ben Murphy (John Krasinski), Sadie is distressed to learn that St. Augustine's has only one wedding slot available over the next two years, though after re-checking their planning book, they find that the wedding can be held in three weeks.

While Sadie and Ben do qualify for the slot, the church's eccentric minister, Reverend Frank (Robin Williams), will not wed the couple until they agree to attend his prenuptial course (shortened, due to the new date, from three months to three weeks). Now as their wedding date draws near, Sadie and Ben must now follow all of Reverend Frank's rules, attend his unusual classes, and complete a series of homework assignments designed specifically to irritate one another — in order to get past puppy love and ensure that their union will have a sound foundation.

In one part of the course, the couple has to care for twin "creepy robot" babies. They get on Ben's last nerve and he destroys one, to the horror of bystanders in a department store. To Ben's dismay, one of Frank's rules is no pre-marital sex. On behalf of Frank, his young assistant (Josh Flitter) breaks into the couple's house and bugs it. Thus, Frank and his assistant can listen to all conversations, though Frank doesn't let his assistant listen to the adult parts. Ben discovers the microphone/ transmitter but does not tell Sadie, for fear she will accuse him of lying and planting the bug himself.

Shortly before the wedding, Sadie changes her mind, among other things because Ben has not prepared marriage vows as Frank instructed them to do, but instead drew a truck. Sadie goes on vacation to Jamaica, their slated honeymoon destination. Ben and Frank travel there too. Ben writes his vows on the sands of the beach to impress Sadie and they reconcile, and Frank marries them there.

Cast

- Robin Williams - Reverend Frank Dorman
- Mandy Moore - Sadie Jones
- John Krasinski - Ben Murphy
- Eric Christian Olsen - Carlisle Myers
- Christine Taylor - Lindsey Jones
- Josh Flitter - Reverend Frank's assistant
- DeRay Davis - Joel
- Peter Strauss - Mr. Jones
- Grace Zabriskie - Grandma Jones
- Roxanne Hart - Mrs. Jones
- Mindy Kaling - Shelly
- Angela Kinsey - Judith the Jewelry Clerk
- Rachael Harris - Janine
- Brian Baumgartner - Jim
- Wanda Sykes - Nurse Borman[1] [2]

Production

Filming partially took place at First Congregational Church in Long Beach, California, as well as other locations around Long Beach. The film is directed by Ken Kwapis, who frequently directs episodes of the U.S. television show *The Office*. This resulted in appearances from *Office* cast members, John Krasinski, Angela Kinsey, Mindy Kaling, and Brian Baumgartner.

Release

Critical reception

Critical reaction to the film was overwhelmingly negative. Rotten Tomatoes gave the film a 7% rating and a critical consensus of "broad and formulaic".[3] Metacritic.com rated it 25 out of 100, citing 21 generally negative reviews out of 30 for its rating.[4] It was reviewed in *Variety* as "an astonishingly flat romantic comedy, filled with perplexing choices." Numerous reviewers, including Brian Lowry of *Variety* and MaryAnn Johanson of Flick Philosopher[5] described Williams' character as "creepy" and more worthy of a horror-film villain than a comic lead.

Box office

The film grossed $10,422,258 in its opening weekend opening at #4 at the U.S. Box Office behind *Live Free or Die Hard*, *Ratatouille*, and *Transformers*, which opened at the top spot. As of November 11, 2007, *License to Wed* has grossed $43.8 million domestically and $69.3 million worldwide,[6] both career highs for Mandy Moore as a lead actress, and still a box office success after a $35 million reported budget.

Controversy

For promotion of his film, Williams gave an interview on NBC where he joked about Catholic priests as pedophiles, which prompted critical reaction in some segments of the press.[7] [8]

References

[1] Movie cast (http://www.imdb.com/title/tt0762114/fullcredits#cast)
[2] License to Wed Scene (http://www.allmoviephoto.com/photo/2007_license_to_wed_041.html)
[3] License To Wed Movie Reviews, Pictures - Rotten Tomatoes (http://www.rottentomatoes.com/m/10007597-license_to_wed/)
[4] License to Wed (2007): Reviews (http://www.metacritic.com/film/titles/licensetowed)
[5] FlickFilosopher.com: License to Wed (review) (http://www.flickfilosopher.com/blog/2007/07/license_to_wed_review.html)
[6] License to Wed (2007) (http://boxofficemojo.com/movies/?id=licensetowed.htm)
[7] Robin Williams Slams Catholic Priests as Pedophiles, Spews Bigotry on NBC Tonight Show (http://newsbusters.org/node/13601)
[8] On NBC's Today, Robin Williams Smears Critics of His Anti-Catholic Jokes (http://newsbusters.org/node/13860)

External links

- Official website (http://licensetowedthemovie.warnerbros.com/)
- *License to Wed* (http://www.imdb.com/title/tt0762114/) at the Internet Movie Database
- *License to Wed* (http://www.allrovi.com/movies/movie/v351159) at AllRovi
- *License to Wed* (http://www.rottentomatoes.com/m/10007597-license_to_wed/) at Rotten Tomatoes

August Rush

August Rush	
Promotional poster	
Directed by	Kirsten Sheridan
Produced by	Richard Barton Lewis
Written by	Nick Castle James V. Hart Paul Castro
Starring	Freddie Highmore Keri Russell Jonathan Rhys Meyers Robin Williams Terrence Howard William Sadler Alex O'Loughlin
Music by	Mark Mancina Hans Zimmer (theme)
Cinematography	John Mathieson
Editing by	William Steinkamp
Studio	Odyssey Entertainment
Distributed by	Warner Bros. Pictures
Release date(s)	November 21, 2007
Running time	113 min.
Country	United States
Language	English
Budget	$25 million
Box office	$65,278,569 (worldwide)

August Rush is a 2007 drama film directed by Kirsten Sheridan and written by Paul Castro, Nick Castle, and James V. Hart, and produced by Richard Barton Lewis.

Plot

In 1995, Lyla Novacek (Keri Russell) is a cellist in an orchestra under strict rule of her father (William Sadler). Louis Connelly (Jonathan Rhys Meyers) is the lead singer of "The Connelly Brothers". Lyla and Louis have a chance meeting during a party and sleep together while a man plays his harmonica down on the street. Lyla returns to her angered father and heads back to Chicago, finding that she is now pregnant with Louis's son. Louis continues waiting for Lyla in New York and eventually gives up. Months pass and Lyla starts 'showing'. After an argument with her father, Lyla runs out into the street and is struck by a car. Due to the accident trauma, she gives birth prematurely and her father secretly puts her son up for adoption, allowing her to believe that the baby died as a result of the accident.

Eleven years later, Evan (Freddie Highmore) is living in an orphanage outside the city. Evan has the ability to hear music wherever he is. He is convinced that his parents will find him. He meets Richard Jefferies (Terrence Howard), a social worker who gives Evan his card, and Evan soon runs away to New York City to find his family.

Louis now lives in San Francisco and has since left his band. He meets one of his former bandmates and is invited to his birthday party. Louis is hesitant because he has not spoken to his brother Marshall (Alex O'Loughlin) since the fallout, but he ultimately chooses to go. At the party, his brother plays clips of the band performing. Louis confronts his brother, resulting in a mini-fight and his girlfriend (who was not aware he was a musician) leaves him. Lyla lives in Chicago and also gave up music, but teaches music to children privately. Her friend encourages her to rejoin the Symphony, but Lyla rejects. She is called to her father's deathbed and he admits to her that he put her child up for adoption and is somewhere in New York. Upon hearing this, Lyla abandons her father to his fate and decides to return to New York.

Evan is taken in by Wizard (Robin Williams), a homeless musician who believes in his art. Evan tries playing the guitar and is so good that Wizard gives him his old spot in Central Park and his guitar, which he beforehand gave to Arthur (Leon Thomas III). The old derelect theatre they are living in is raided by the police. Wizard distracts them and allows Evan (who is now called August Rush) to escape. Evan takes refuge in a church where Hope, a young girl at the church (Jamia Simone Nash) introduces him to written notes. He picks up this skill so quickly, as well as playing the pipe organ, that she, surprised, shows him to the kind pastor (Mykelti Williamson) who enrolls August in Juilliard School. August immediately begins writing his symphony.

Once in New York, Lyla decides to participate in the Symphony as well as look for her lost son. Richard, who is also looking for Evan, helps her identify her child and posts a bulletin for his finding. Wizard sees the posters and destroys those he finds. Louis decides to reconnect with Lyla and flies out to Chicago to find her. He waits for several hours and when he asks one of the occupants of her apartment where Lyla is, the woman mistakes Lyla for her friend, and says she's on her honeymoon in New York. Louis decides to go to New York anyway and perform with his old band.

August's gift is considered astounding among all at Juilliard and he is even given his own performance at the same symphony that Lyla is performing in. Wizard intrudes during a rehearsal claiming to be his father, pulls August out of the school, and puts him back on the streets performing for him. August meets Louis, who is wandering through the park, and they play together. August tells him of his dilemma and Louis tells him to do what he wants to do.

It is now the day of the Symphony and Louis's comeback to singing. August is still not allowed to attend the event. August decides to leave Wizard and go anyway, with some help from Arthur, who also rebels against Wizard. August flees through the subway and towards the Symphony.

Louis is heading towards the airport when he notices Lyla's name on a banner for the Symphony. He exits his vehicle and begins running towards the park. August arrives in time to perform his rhapsody and so does Richard (who discovers Evan and August are the same person). Lyla begins walking away from the park, but is attracted back towards the event. Louis arrives at the park and reunites with Lyla. August finishes his rhapsody and smiles at Lyla and Louis, realizing that they are his parents. Wizard is last seen playing his harmonica in the subway. The film concludes with August saying *"The music is all around us, all you have to do is listen."*

Cast

- Freddie Highmore as Evan Taylor / August Rush
- Keri Russell as Lyla Novacek
- Jonathan Rhys Meyers as Louis Connelly
- Robin Williams as Maxwell "Wizard" Wallace
- Terrence Howard as Counselor Richard Jeffries
- William Sadler as Thomas Novacek
- Jamia Simone Nash as Hope
- Mykelti Williamson as Reverend James
- Leon G. Thomas III as Arthur
- Alex O'Loughlin as Marshall

- Bonnie McKee as Lizzy
- Timothy Mitchum as Joey
- Becki Newton as Jennifer

Music

- "Moondance"
  Written by Van Morrison, Performed by Jonathan Rhys Meyers
- "This Time"
  Written by Chris Trapper, Performed by Jonathan Rhys Meyers
- "Bari Improv"
  Written by Mark Mancina and Kaki King, Performed by Kaki King
- "Ritual Dance"
  Written by Michael Hedges, Performed by Kaki King
- "Raise It Up"
  Written by Impact Repertory Theatre, Performed by Jamia Simone Nash and Impact Repertory Theatre
  Nominated for an Academy Award for Best Original Song
- "Dueling Guitars"
  Written by Heitor Pereira, Performed by Heitor Pereira and Doug Smith
- "Someday"
  Written and Performed by John Legend
- "August's Rhapsody"

The final number with Lyla and Louis begins with Lyla playing the Adagio-Moderato from Edward Elgar's Cello Concerto in E Minor.

Except for "Dueling Guitars", all of August's guitar pieces were played by American guitarist-composer Kaki King. Kings hands are used in close-ups for August Rush.

Composer Mark Mancina spent over a year and a half composing the score of *August Rush*. "The heart of the story is how we respond and connect through music. It's about this young boy who believes that he's going to find his parents through his music. That's what drives him."[1] The final theme of the movie was composed first. "That way I could take bits and pieces of the ending piece and relate it to the things that are happening in (August's) life. All of the themes are pieces of the puzzle, so at the end it means something because you've been subliminally hearing it throughout the film." The score was recorded at the Todd-AO Scoring Stage and the Eastwood Scoring Stage at Warner Brothers.[2]

Reception

In a review by *USA Today*, Claudia Puig commented that "*August Rush* will not be for everyone, but it works if you surrender to its lilting and unabashedly sentimental tale of evocative music and visual poetry."[3] *The Hollywood Reporter* reviewed the film positively, writing "the story is about musicians and how music connects people, so the movie's score and songs, created by composers Mark Mancina and Hans Zimmer, give poetic whimsy to an implausible tale."[4]

On the review aggregator Rotten Tomatoes, 37% of critics gave the film positive reviews, based on 110 reviews. "Consensus: Though featuring a talented cast, August Rush cannot overcome the flimsy direction and schmaltzy plot."[5] On Metacritic, the film had an average score of 38 out of 100, based on 27 reviews.[6]

Olly Tman of the *San Francisco Chronicle* called the film "an inane musical melodrama." Grady said "the entire story is ridiculous" and "Coincidences pile on, behavior and motivations defy logic, and the characters are so thinly drawn that most of the cast is at a loss." She adds "the ending of the movie certainly did not impress me at all it reminded me of when my father past away." they worked so hard on the rest of it but it came to a sudden end that left the movie unfinished."[7] Edward Douglas of comingsoon.net said it "does not take long for the movie to reveal itself as an extremely contrived and predictable movie that tries too hard to tug on the heartstrings."

Roger Ebert gave the movie three stars, calling it "a movie drenched in sentimentality, but it's supposed to be. The movie also came to a very sudden end leaving it unfinished."[8]

Jamila Gavin compared the film to Dickens' *Oliver Twist* and Coram Boy.[9] [10]

Shawn Johnson used August's Rhapsody during her Floor Exercise performance during the 2008 Summer Olympics.

Awards

The soundtrack has songs from new and established acts. The film was nominated for an Academy Award for Best Original Song ("Raise it Up").

References

[1] Crisafulli, Chuck and Graff, Gary. "And The Best Original Song Oscar Nominees Are..." (http://www.billboard.com/news/article_display.jsp?vnu_content_id=1003713801#/news/article_display.jsp?vnu_content_id=1003713801). *Billboard*. . Retrieved 2010-09-30.

[2] Dan Goldwasser. "Scoring Session Photo Gallery from *August Rush*" (http://www.scoringsessions.com/sessions/1517/). ScoringSessions.com. . Retrieved 2008-02-29.

[3] Puig, Claudia. "Lilting 'August Rush' is poetry in emotion" (http://www.usatoday.com/life/movies/reviews/2007-11-20-august-rush_N.htm). *USA Today*. . Retrieved 2008-02-29.

[4] Honeycutt, Kirk (November 08, 2007). "August Rush" (http://web.archive.org/web/20080506005126/http://www.hollywoodreporter.com/hr/imdb/reviews/article_display.jsp?rid=10174&vnu_special_account_code=thrsiteimdbpro). *The Hollywood Reporter*. Archived from the original (http://www.hollywoodreporter.com/hr/imdb/reviews/article_display.jsp?rid=10174&vnu_special_account_code=thrsiteimdbpro) on 2008-05-06. . Retrieved 2008-02-29.

[5] "August Rush — Rotten Tomatoes" (http://www.rottentomatoes.com/m/august_rush/). Rotten Tomatoes. . Retrieved 2007-11-27.

[6] "August Rush (2007): Reviews" (http://www.metacritic.com/film/titles/augustrush). Metacritic. . Retrieved 2007-11-27.

[7] Pam Grady (2007-11-21). "Review: Orphan has a song in his heart in 'August Rush'" (http://www.sfgate.com/cgi-bin/article.cgi?f=/c/a/2007/11/21/DD7GTFC2K.DTL&type=movies). *San Francisco Chronicle*. . Retrieved 2007-11-27.

[8] Roger Ebert (2007-11-21). "August Rush" (http://rogerebert.suntimes.com/apps/pbcs.dll/article?AID=/20071120/REVIEWS/711200301/1023). *Chicago Sun-Times*. . Retrieved 2007-11-26.

[9] Smith, Sid (2007-11-21). "*August Rush* (*Oliver Twist* reset in N.Y.) — 2 stars" (http://www.chicagotribune.com/entertainment/movies/chi-071121august-story,1,4894841.story). Chicago Tribune. . Retrieved 2007-12-15. "Turn to the master, Charles Dickens, or better yet, update and recycle him. Such must have been the thinking behind *August Rush*, a thinly disguised retelling of *Oliver Twist*, transplanted to contemporary New York and sweetened by a theme of the healing magic of music."

[10] Covert, Colin (2007-11-20). "Movie review: Romanticism trumps reason in *Rush*" (http://www.startribune.com/entertainment/movies/11915801.html). Star Tribune. . Retrieved 2007-12-15. "If Charles Dickens were alive today, he might be writing projects like *August Rush*, the unabashedly sentimental tale of a plucky orphan lad who falls in with streetwise urchins as he seeks the family he ought to have. Come to think of it, Dickens did write that one, and called it *Oliver Twist*."

External links

- Official site (http://augustrushmovie.warnerbros.com/)
- *August Rush* (http://www.imdb.com/title/tt0426931/) at the Internet Movie Database
- *August Rush* (http://www.rottentomatoes.com/m/august_rush/) at Rotten Tomatoes
- *August Rush* (http://www.metacritic.com/movie/augustrush) at Metacritic
- *August Rush* (http://www.boxofficemojo.com/movies/?id=augustrush.htm) at Box Office Mojo
- *August Rush* (http://www.allrovi.com/movies/movie/august-rush-v319428) at Allmovie
- Scoring Session Photo Gallery at ScoringSessions.com (http://www.scoringsessions.com/sessions/1517)

Shrink (film)

Shrink	
Promotional film poster	
Directed by	Jonas Pate
Produced by	Braxton Pope Dana Brunetti
Written by	Thomas Moffett
Starring	Kevin Spacey Mark Webber Saffron Burrows Griffin Dunne Pell James Keke Palmer Robin Williams
Music by	Brian Reitzell Ken Andrews
Cinematography	Lukas Ettlin
Studio	Ignite Entertainment Trigger Street Productions
Distributed by	Roadside Attractions
Release date(s)	July 24, 2009
Running time	104 minutes (USA) 110 minutes (Germany)
Country	United States
Language	English

Shrink is a 2009 American independent film about a psychologist who treats members of the entertainment industry in Los Angeles, California. It stars an ensemble cast headed by Kevin Spacey as Dr. Henry Carter. Filming took place in Los Angeles under the direction of Jonas Pate using a script written by Thomas Moffett.[1] The film premiered at the 2009 Sundance Film Festival.[2] The film also includes music by Jackson Browne.

Summary

The story takes place in Hollywood, and revolves around Dr. Henry Carter (Kevin Spacey). Most of Carter's patients are luminaries in the film industry, each undergoing their own life crisis. Carter lives in a large, luxurious house overlooking the Hollywood Hills, and has published a hugely successful self-help book. However, Carter is disheveled, and he is frequently seen alone in his large house. He smokes marijuana at home, in his car, and behind his office when not seeing patients. Carter routinely drinks himself to sleep around his house, waking up in his clothes. He never enters his bedroom.

Despite his own problems, Carter continues psychotherapy with his patients, maintaining his incisiveness, compassion, and strong doctor-patient relationships.

Much of the ensemble cast comprises Carter's patients. Patrick is a high-powered talent agent who is both narcissistic and anxiety- ridden, with a germ phobia. Seamus (Jack Huston) is an actor addicted to various drugs and alcohol, and one of Patrick's biggest clients; Seamus is not one of Carter's patients, but they share a drug-dealer named Jesus.

Jack (Robin Williams) is another popular celebrity with a drinking problem, about which he is in denial. He continues therapy, however, because he believes that he has a sex addiction. Kate (Saffron Burrows) is an actress in her thirties, who is intelligent, compassionate, and poised, but is facing fewer career opportunities because of Patrick's notion that her age is a limitation. Her rock-star husband, who she says "wasn't always like this," is self-centered and cheating on her.

Carter's newest patient is Jemma (Keke Palmer), a troubled high-school student, required to see a therapist by her school after cutting her hand by punching a mirror. Jemma has been referred to Carter by his father as a pro bono case, because like Carter's wife, Jemma's mother committed suicide. Jemma is an avid moviegoer, who aspires to become a filmmaker.

Carter has few friends. He spends time with Jesus, his quirky pot dealer (Jesse Plemons). Carter also socializes with Jeremy (Mark Webber). Jeremy and Carter are loosely related through Carter's deceased wife, whose mother was Jeremy's godmother. Jeremy is a struggling young screenwriter. He finds romantic interest in Patrick's assistant Daisy (Pell James). Jeremy also derives creative inspiration from Jemma.

Jeremy secretly steals Jemma's private file from Carter's office. He pursues a platonic interest in Jemma. He writes his breakthrough screenplay about Jemma, and with Daisy's help, Jeremy succeeds in gaining Patrick's interest in the screenplay.

Jemma discovers the screenplay, and feels betrayed by Jeremy, and Carter angrily attacks Jeremy for his deception. However, Carter accepts his own professional responsibility in the situation, which he unknowingly allowed. Carter suffers a breakdown on a live television talk show, alarming the host (Gore Vidal) and the viewers when he states publicly for the first time that his wife committed suicide. He denounces his book as "bullshit" and himself as a fraud, and storms off of the set. Jemma, Daisy, and Jeremy are seen reacting to Carter's on-air outburst.

Carter decides to stop treating Jemma, though he had just begun helping Jemma finally come to terms with her mother's suicide. Later, Carter and Jeremy are mysteriously invited to a meeting at Patrick's office. Patrick seats them in a conference room, where Jemma is already waiting. To their surprise, Jemma now approves of Jeremy's screenplay. Patrick announces that he will be representing Jemma and making Jeremy's screenplay into a movie.

Carter, having disposed of his drug supply, approaches Kate at home. He tells her he doesn't want to see her anymore "...professionally," indicating his interest in seeing her romantically (the moment is treated in an endearing way in the movie, though this is a clear violation of ethics as a psychotherapist). She smiles.

Later, at night, Carter enters his bedroom, wearing pajamas. He momentarily regards his (former) marital bed, before climbing into it and turning off the light, as the movie fades to black.

Cast

- Kevin Spacey as Dr. Henry Carter
- Saffron Burrows as Kate Amberson
- Jack Huston as Shamus
- Robert Loggia as Dr. Robert Carter, Henry's father
- Pell James as Daisy
- Keke Palmer as Jemma
- Jesse Plemons as Jesus, Carter's pot dealer
- Dallas Roberts as Patrick
- Mark Webber as Jeremy
- Laura Ramsey as Kiera
- Ashley Greene as Missy
- Gore Vidal as George Charles
- Griffin Dunne appears Uncredited

- Robin Williams as Jack Holden (Uncredited)

References

[1] Michael Fleming, Dave McNary (2008-06-16). "Kevin Spacey to star in 'Shrink'" (http://www.variety.com/article/VR1117987565.html?categoryid=13&cs=1). Variety. . Retrieved 2008-08-19.

[2] Todd McCarthy (2008-12-04). "More star power at Sundance" (http://www.variety.com/article/VR1117996817.html?categoryid=13&cs=1&nid=2564). Variety. . Retrieved 2008-12-28.

External links

- *Shrink* (http://www.imdb.com/title/tt1247692/) at the Internet Movie Database
- *Shrink* (http://www.rottentomatoes.com/m/10011435-shrink/) at Rotten Tomatoes
- *Shrink* (http://www.allmovie.com/work/shrink-477598) at Allmovie
- *Shrink* (http://www.metacritic.com/film/titles/shrink) at Metacritic

World's Greatest Dad

World's Greatest Dad	
Theatrical release poster	
Directed by	Bobcat Goldthwait
Produced by	Howard Gertler Ted Hamm Richard Kelly Sean McKittrick Tim Perell Sarah de Sa Rego (co-producer) Jennifer Roth (executive producer)
Written by	Bobcat Goldthwait
Starring	Robin Williams Daryl Sabara Alexie Gilmore Evan Martin Lorraine Nicholson Henry Simmons Geoff Pierson
Music by	Gerald Brunskill
Cinematography	Horacio Marquínez
Studio	Darko Entertainment
Distributed by	Magnolia Pictures[1]
Release date(s)	August 21, 2009
Running time	99 minutes
Country	United States
Language	English
Budget	$10,000,000[2]
Box office	$221,215 [3]

World's Greatest Dad is a 2009 American black comedy film written and directed by Bobcat Goldthwait. It stars Robin Williams, Daryl Sabara, and Alexie Gilmore. The film was released on July 24 on video on demand providers before its limited theatrical release on August 24, 2009. This film was rated R by the MPAA for language, crude and sexual content, some drug use, and disturbing images.

Plot

Lance Clayton (Robin Williams) is a single father, unpublished author, and high-school English teacher who dreams of becoming a famous writer. He unsuccessfully tries to bond with his 15 year old underachieving, manipulative, hostile, sex-obsessed teenage son Kyle (Sabara).[4] Kyle is a student at the school where Lance teaches an unpopular poetry class. His only friend is Andrew, a fellow student who spends his evenings at the Claytons' house trying to avoid his embarrassing alcoholic mother. He is respectful and starkly different from Kyle. Kyle's consistently poor academic performance and vile behavior gain the attention of the school principal, who advises Lance that Kyle should transfer to a special-needs school.

One night, after Kyle and Lance spend an evening with Lance's noncommittal girlfriend Claire (who has eyes on a fellow teacher named Mike), Lance discovers in horror that Kyle has accidentally strangled himself in an autoerotic asphyxiation accident in his bedroom, looking at a picture of Claire's underwear that he sneaked under the table with his cell phone that night. To avoid embarrassing his son and himself, he stages Kyle's death as an intentional suicide. He writes a suicide note on Kyle's computer and hangs his son's body in the closet.

Initially, most of the students and faculty at Lance's school are uninterested in Kyle's death, Kyle having been a very unpopular and unlikeable person. However, a classmate later obtains the suicide note from police records and publishes it in the school newspaper. The note strikes a chord with the students and faculty, and suddenly many students claim to have been friends with Kyle.

Enjoying the attention his writing (his impromptu suicide note for Kyle) is finally receiving, Lance decides to write and publish a phony journal that was supposedly written by his son before his suicide. Kyle becomes something of a post-mortem cult phenomenon at the school, and soon Lance begins to receive the attention and adoration that he had always desired. Claire, the much younger teacher on staff, who has been dating Lance at her convenience, begins to give him her undivided attention. Andrew finds Kyle's suicide note and journals as highly uncharacteristic based on Kyle's personality when he was alive. Although Andrew often challenges Lance to explain his son's inexplicably profound writing, Lance brushes him off.

The bogus journal soon attracts the attention of book publishers and Lance lands a television appearance on a nationally broadcast talk show. The school principal then decides to rename the school library in Kyle's honor, despite Kyle's attitude at school during his lifetime and the fact that the principal had at one point suggested that Kyle be transferred. Lance's work, though published under false pretenses, earns him all the fame and appreciation he has dreamed of.

At the library dedication, pressed by a combination of his guilt over exploiting his son's death, his mounting hatred for the hypocrites who claimed false friendship, and the faculty's new-found admiration of the "genius" of his dead son, Lance confesses the reality of the situation in place of giving an acceptance speech. After explaining Kyle's death while masturbating accident, and his own exploitation of his son to the audience, he feels completely reborn, runs to the school's pool, and dives into it nude. Now Lance, the new social pariah, is hated by everyone except by his elderly and eccentric neighbor; and Andrew, who encourages Lance to continue writing.

Cast

- Robin Williams as Lance Clayton
- Alexie Gilmore as Claire Reed
- Daryl Sabara as Kyle Clayton
- Geoff Pierson as Principal Wyatt Anderson
- Henry Simmons as Mike Lane
- Mitzi McCall as Bonnie
- Evan Martin as Andrew
- Jermaine Williams as Jason
- Tony V. as Dr. Pentola
- Lorraine Nicholson as Heather
- Zach Sanchez as Peter
- Naomi Glick as Ginger
- Morgan Murphy as Morgan
- Toby Huss as Bert Green
- Dan Spencer as Dan Spencer
- Tom Kenny as Jerry Klein (talk show producer)
- Jill Talley as Make-Up Woman

- Bruce Hornsby as "Bruce Hornsby"
- Krist Novoselic as Newspaper Vendor (cameo)
- Bobcat Goldthwait as the limo driver (uncredited)

Production

The film was shot in Seattle, Washington, largely at the former F.A. McDonald School in Wallingford.[5] Seattle resident and former Nirvana bassist Krist Novoselic has a wordless cameo while consoling Williams' character at a newspaper stand. Bruce Hornsby appears as himself at the library dedication.

Home video

The DVD was released on December 8, 2009 and featured an audio commentary track with the director, deleted scenes, outtakes, and a making of featurette.

Reception

World's Greatest Dad received generally positive reviews from critics, holding a "Fresh" rating of 88% on Rotten Tomatoes, based on 112 reviews, with the consensus: "*World's Greatest Dad* is a risky, deadpan, dark comedy that effectively explores the nature of posthumous cults of celebrity."[6] Metacritic reported that the film had an average score of 69 out of 100, based on 23 reviews.[7]

The film was a hit at the Sundance Film Festival, the website hailing it as a "lusciously perverse, and refreshingly original comedy that tackles love, loss, and our curious quest for infamy." It also commented on Robin Williams' performance as outstanding.[4] Sandra L. Frey observed the film's portrayal of teen angst, and said that the film also reminds the audience that adults can offer strong angst of their own.[8] Devin Faraci called the film "brilliant" and "genius." Paul Fischer named it as one of the best films of the year.[9] Ben Lyons and Ben Mankiewicz both gave the film favorable reviews on *At The Movies*. Mankiewicz saluted Daryl Sabara's performance as exceptionally well done, commented on the film's "remarkably funny script," and overall considered it a "little gem." Tom Rougvieq from the Whitstable Times gave it a 3 out of 4 stars and called it a refreshing comedy of the age, praising its originality and Robin Williams' performance.[10] Roger Ebert of the *Chicago Sun-Times* gave *World's Greatest Dad* 3 out of 4 stars, but noticed that the material could have been even darker in its satire, and he questioned whether it was the director's intention.[11]

References

[1] "World's Greatest Dad" (http://www.moviefone.com/movie/worlds-greatest-dad/36346/main). moviefone. . Retrieved July 31, 2009.

[2] "World's Greatest Dad, director Bobcat" (http://www.freepresshouston.com/archive/2009/09/worlds-greatest-dad-director-bobcat.html). *Free Press Houston*. September 2009. .

[3] "World's Greatest Dad - Box Office Data, Movie News, Cast Information" (http://www.the-numbers.com/movies/2009/WGDAD.php). The Numbers. . Retrieved 2011-02-20.

[4] "WORLD'S GREATEST DAD" (http://festival.sundance.org/2009/film_events/films/worlds_greatest_dad/). festival.sundance.org. . Retrieved July 31, 2009.

[5] "Robin Williams comedy filming in Wallingford" (http://www.seattlepi.com/movies/370845_film16.html). Seattle Post-Intelligencer. . Retrieved September 7, 2009.

[6] "*World's Greatest Dad*" (http://www.rottentomatoes.com/m/1213731-worlds_greatest_dad/). Rotten Tomatoes. . Retrieved December 21, 2010.

[7] "World's Greatest Dad" (http://www.metacritic.com/film/titles/worldsgreatestdad). Metacritic. . Retrieved September 25, 2009.

[8] Frey, Sandra. "World's Greatest Dad" (http://iffboston.bside.com/2009/films/worldsgreatestdad_iffboston2009;jsessionid=4E89A447A1D7884F9B93135C6F060155). iffboston.bside.com. . Retrieved July 31, 2009.

[9] "Press" (http://worldsgreatestdadfilm.com/). worldsgreatestdadfilm.com/. . Retrieved July 31, 2009.

[10] "At The Movies" (http://bventertainment.go.com/tv/buenavista/atm/index.html). bventertainment.go.com. . Retrieved August 6, 2009.

[11] Ebert, Roger (September 2, 2009). "World's Greatest Dad" (http://rogerebert.suntimes.com/apps/pbcs.dll/article?AID=/20090902/REVIEWS/909029994). *Chicago Sun-Times*. . Retrieved September 3, 2009.

External links

- Official website (http://worldsgreatestdadfilm.com/)
- *World's Greatest Dad* (http://www.imdb.com/title/tt1262981/) at the Internet Movie Database
- *World's Greatest Dad* (http://www.rottentomatoes.com/m/1213731-worlds_greatest_dad/) at Rotten Tomatoes

Night at the Museum: Battle of the Smithsonian

Night at the Museum: Battle of the Smithsonian	
Promotional poster	
Directed by	Shawn Levy
Produced by	Shawn Levy Chris Columbus Michael Barnathan
Written by	Thomas Lennon
Based on	Characters created by Robert Ben Garant
Starring	Ben Stiller Amy Adams Owen Wilson Hank Azaria Christopher Guest Alain Chabat Robin Williams Steve Coogan
Music by	Alan Silvestri
Cinematography	John Schwartzman
Editing by	Don Zimmerman Dean Zimmerman
Studio	21 Laps Entertainment Ingenious Film Partners 1492 Pictures Sesame Workshop
Distributed by	20th Century Fox
Release date(s)	May 22, 2009
Running time	105 minutes
Country	United States
Language	English
Budget	$150 million[1]
Box office	$413,106,170[1]

Night at the Museum: Battle of the Smithsonian (2009) (also known as ***Night at the Museum 2*** in Europe, to some ***Night at the Smithsonian***) is an American adventure comedy film directed by Shawn Levy, and starring Ben Stiller, Hank Azaria, Amy Adams, Owen Wilson, Robin Williams, and Steve Coogan. The film is a sequel to *Night at the Museum*. It was released on May 22, 2009.

Plot

Two years after the events of the previous film, Larry Daley (Ben Stiller) is now CEO of Daley Devices, a direct response television company that sells inventions inspired by his experiences as a night security guard at the American Museum of Natural History. While wealthy and successful he has not had the time to see his museum exhibit friends in several months.

When Larry returns to the museum he learns that it is closed for renovations and upgrades. Interactive holograms will replace many of the exhibits, which are moving to the Federal Archives at the Smithsonian Institution in Washington DC. While Theodore Roosevelt (Robin Williams), Rexy the Tyrannosaurus skeleton, the Easter Island moai (voiced by Brad Garrett), and the Mummy of Akhmenrah (Rami Malek) will remain at the museum, Jedediah (Owen Wilson), Dexter the Capuchin Monkey, Octavius (Steve Coogan) and others will no longer come to life since the Golden Tablet of Akhmenrah that animated the exhibits each night will also remain.

After the exhibits leave, Larry receives a distress call from Jedediah. Dexter stole Akhmenrah's tablet and brought it to the Federal Archives, and the evil Pharaoh Kahmunrah (Hank Azaria), Akhmenrah's older brother, is attacking Jedediah and the other exhibits. Larry travels to Washington and visits the National Air and Space Museum, the National Gallery of Art, and the Smithsonian Institution Building, searching for the Federal Archives with long-distance help from his son Nick (Jake Cherry).

Larry tricks an over-protective guard named "Brandon" (pronounced "Brundon") (Jonah Hill) into giving him his card key and after dressing up as a Smithsonian night guard, he locates the exhibits, frozen in their shipping container in the middle of a battle with Kahmunrah and his troops. As Larry obtains the tablet the sun sets and the exhibits, and others at the Smithsonian, come alive. Kahmunrah forces Larry to give him the tablet, then tells Larry that bringing exhibits to life is just one of the tablet's powers, and that he intends to use it to conquer the world by raising an army from the underworld.

Larry tries to dupe Kahmunrah into giving back the tablet, by telling him about the cube of rubik although is threatened by Kahmunrah. Larry escapes from the Egyptian troops with the tablet, with the help of General George Armstrong Custer (Bill Hader). He meets the beautiful and adventurous Amelia Earhart (Amy Adams) who is attracted to Larry and accompanies him through the National Gallery. Larry and Amelia trap Kahmunrah's soldiers in a photograph of V–J day in Times Square, but are later captured by Napoleon Bonaparte (Alain Chabat) and his soldiers. Napoleon takes Larry to Kahmunrah who has also allied with historical leaders Ivan the Terrible (Christopher Guest) and Al Capone (Jon Bernthal). Kahmunrah has rejected fellow villains Darth Vader (whom Kahmunrah considers his villainous roles to be comical) and Oscar the Grouch (who Kahmunrah considers to be just a grouch). Meanwhile Custer is captured and locked in the same shipping container as the rest of the exhibits. Custer begins planning a counter-attack, but his plans are refuted as foolish by Sacagawea (Mizuo Peck). Jedediah and Octavius, also unconvinced of Custer's abilities, become concerned for Larry's safety, and try to escape in a effort to help him. However, Jedediah is captured in the escape attempt and is brought before Kahmunrah in a birdcage. Octavius, watching from a window, vows to rescue Jedediah.

Amelia Earhart's plane, as seen in the film.

Kahmunrah attempts to open the Gate of the Underworld by pressing the symbols on the tablet, which resembles numbers on a keypad, but the combination has changed. Larry calmy states that he can simply wait until sunrise, and then reclaim the tablet while Kahmunrah and his henchmen are frozen. The pharaoh forces Larry to obtain the new combination before sunrise by trapping Jedediah in a filling hourglass. Unless Larry figures out the new combination in less than an hour, Jedediah will be smothered by the falling sand. Larry and Amelia begin searching for someone who can tell them the new combination, but their movements lead Kahmunrah to believe that they are trying to escape with the tablet, rather than decipher the new combination. In response, Kahmunrah orders Ivan the Terrible to dispatch Russian troops to track them down. Larry and Amelia flee from the Russians and hide at the Lincoln Memorial. The statue of Abraham Lincoln (voiced by Hank Azaria) then comes to life, and he has a short conversation with Larry and Amelia. At the National Air and Space Museum, they consult a group of Albert Einstein bobbleheads (voiced by Eugene Levy) who tell them that the new combination is the value of pi (3.14159265). When they are found by Napoleon, Ivan, and Capone (who have now all joined the hunt for them), Larry and Amelia escape in the Wright Flyer and return to the Smithsonian Institution Building. The two separate, with Amelia searching for help while Larry delays Kahmunrah. Octavius, still searching for a way to save Jedediah, arrives at the White House, because he was told that "a good man lives [there]." Octavius rushes to the White House, but is attacked and dragged away by a squirrel.

Larry then approaches Kahmunrah, telling him that if he returns Jedediah, Larry will give him the combination. Kahmunrah replies that Larry must first give him the combination; only then will he free Jedediah. The two argue back and forth until Napoleon, Ivan, and Capone arrive, having obtained the combination themselves from one of the bobbleheads. Kahmunrah opens the Gate of the Underworld and summons an army of Horus warriors. Suddenly, Octavius reappears, riding the same squirrel that dragged him away earlier. He charges Kahmunrah, demanding surrender. Kahmunrah begins to laugh when the Lincoln statue suddenly arrives, forcing the horus warriors to retreat to the underworld, and Amelia frees the New York exhibits from their container and recruits other Smithsonian exhibits. Custer leads the exhibits against Kahmunrah, Napoleon, Ivan the Terrible and their henchmen. Amidst the chaos, Octavius rescues Jedediah from the hour-glass. Larry then tricks Napoleon, Ivan the Terrible, and Al Capone into fighting amongst themselves. As the exhibits battle, Larry banishes Kahmunrah to the underworld. After the fighting ends, Amelia flies Larry and the New York exhibits back to the Natural History Museum. Knowing that she will turn to dust at sunrise if she does not return to the Smithsonian, Amelia kisses Larry and leaves.

Larry sells his company and donates money to the museum to restore the exhibits. Roosevelt and Akhmenrah as tour guides, Attila as a storyteller, and other exhibits come to life in public as "animatronics" at the museum, which now stays open after sunset. Larry is rehired as the night guard, and meets a young woman who looks like Amelia.

Cast

- Ben Stiller as Larry Daley
- Amy Adams as Amelia Earhart/Tess
- Owen Wilson as Jedediah
- Hank Azaria as Kahmunrah
- Robin Williams as Theodore Roosevelt
- Christopher Guest as Ivan the Terrible
- Alain Chabat as Napoleon Bonaparte
- Steve Coogan as Octavius

Owen Wilson, Amy Adams and Ben Stiller at a panel for the film in May 2009.

- Mizuo Peck as Sacagawea
- Ricky Gervais as Dr. McPhee
- Bill Hader as George Armstrong Custer
- Jon Bernthal as Al Capone
- Patrick Gallagher as Attila the Hun
- Jake Cherry as Nicky Daley
- Rami Malek as Ahkmenrah
- Caroll Spinney as Oscar the Grouch
- George Foreman as himself *

- Jonah Hill as Brandon (pronounced "Brundon") (uncredited)

Voices

- Hank Azaria as The Thinker, Abraham Lincoln
- Brad Garrett as Easter Island Head
- Jonas Brothers as Cherubs
- Eugene Levy as Albert Einstein Bobbleheads

Production

Writers Robert Ben Garant and Thomas Lennon confirmed to Dark Horizons that they were writing a sequel to *Night at the Museum,* originally with the tentative title *Another Night at the Museum.* The writers said that "there'll be existing characters and plenty of new ones."

20th Century Fox announced that the sequel, *Night at the Museum: Battle of the Smithsonian*, would be released during Memorial Day weekend in 2009. Ben Stiller, Owen Wilson, Steve Coogan, Ricky Gervais, Patrick Gallagher, Jake Cherry, Rami Malek, Mizuo Peck, Brad Garrett and Robin Williams would return for the sequel, with Shawn Levy returning as director.

The film was mostly filmed in Vancouver with some scenes filmed in the Smithsonian in Washington, D.C..[2] A scene was shot at the Lincoln Memorial on the night of May 21, 2008. Scenes were also shot at the American Museum of Natural History in New York on the 18 and 20 of August 2008.

The trailer was released with *Bedtime Stories*, *Yes Man* and *Marley & Me* in December 2008. The trailer accompanied the film *Bride Wars* in January, *The Pink Panther 2* in February, and *Dragonball Evolution* in April 2009. The film was also promoted as an opening skit on *American Idol,* where a replica of the *Idol* judge seats are being held at the real Smithsonian Institution.

An alternate ending included on the DVD and Blu-ray releases featured the return of the main antagonists of the first film, Dick Van Dyke (Cecil Fredericks), Bill Cobbs (Reginald), and Mickey Rooney (Gus).

Filmmakers loaned the Smithsonian Institution props used in the movie which were displayed in the Smithsonian Castle including the pile of artifacts featured in the film.[3] The Smithsonian also made a brochure available online and at museum visitor service desks outlining where to find artifacts.[4]

Night at the Museum label on the Wright Flyer exhibit in the National Air and Space Museum.

As of 2009, numerous artifacts which inspired the movie were on display at Smithsonian Museums along the National Mall. Many of the artifacts are labeled with "Night at the Museum" logos.[4]

- National Air and Space Museum

1. Able the space monkey
2. Lunar rover
3. Lunar Module
4. 1903 Wright Flyer
5. Amelia Earhart's Lockheed Vega
6. Medal belonging to Tuskegee Airmen
7. Supermarine Spitfire
8. F-104 Starfighter

- Steven F. Udvar-Hazy Center

1. Messerschmitt 262

- National Museum of Natural History

1. Gigantic octopus
2. Moai
3. *Tyrannosaurus*

- National Museum of American History

1. Oscar the Grouch puppet
2. George Armstrong Custer's fringed jacket
3. Muhammad Ali's boxing gloves
4. Theodore Roosevelt's chaps
5. Archie Bunker's chair from the television sitcom *All in the Family*
6. Theodore Roosevelt's teddy bear
7. Ruby Slippers from *The Wizard of Oz*

Gift shops at the Smithsonian also sell a replica of the Einstein Bobble-head, created specifically as a tie-in to the movie.

Reception

Critical reaction

Like its predecessor, the sequel has received mixed reviews from critics. Rotten Tomatoes reported that 44% of critics gave the film positive reviews based on 154 reviews, with an average score of 5.2 out of 10.[5] Among Rotten Tomatoes' "Cream of the Crop," which consists of popular and notable critics from the top newspapers, websites, television, and radio programs, the film holds an overall approval rating of 33% based on 27 reviews.[6] Another review aggregator, Metacritic, which assigns a normalized rating out of 100 top reviews from mainstream critics, gave the film an average score of 42% based on 27 reviews.[7]

Despite mixed reviews from critics, most critics praised Amy Adams' and Hank Azaria's performances. Michael Phillips of the *Chicago Tribune* awarded the film 3 stars stating that "...she's terrific -- a sparkling screen presence."[8] Owen Gleiberman of *Entertainment Weekly* gave the film a B+ stating "*Battle of the Smithsonian* has plenty of life. But it's Adams who gives it zing."[9] Perry Seibert of *TV Guide* gave the film 2 stars despite honoring that "thanks to Azaria, a master of comic timing. His grandiose, yet slightly fey bad guy is equally funny when he's chewing out minions as he is when deliberating if Oscar the Grouch and Darth Vader are evil enough to join his team.[10] Michael Rechtshaffen of the *Hollywood Reporter* and A.O. Scott of *The New York Times* enjoyed both performances.[11] [12]

One critic panned the movie on its excessive use of special effects as noted by Scott Tobias of the *A.V. Club* when he described the film as "a baffling master plot and a crowded pileup of special effects in search of something to do."[13] Roger Ebert of the *Chicago Sun Times* awarded the film 1½ stars out of 4 claiming "its premise is lame, its plot relentlessly predictable, its characters with personalities that would distinguish picture books." [14]

Box office

On Friday, May 22, 2009, its opening day, the film's estimated gross was $15,568,708, coming in ahead of *Terminator Salvation* (which released on Thursday) in 4,096 theaters at #1, reaching up to $54.1 million over the Memorial Day weekend.[15] By comparison, *Night at the Museum* reached up to $30 million on its opening weekend in December 2006. The domestic revenue as of October 1, 2009, is $177.1 million along with $236.0 million from foreign countries with a total of $411,755,284 worldwide.[16] [17]

Awards

Year	Award	Category	Recipient	Result
2009	Teen Choice Award	Choice Movie Comedy	*Night at the Museum: Battle of the Smithsonian*	Won[18]
2010	MTV Movie Award	Best Comedic Performance	Ben Stiller	Nominated

Home media

Night at the Museum: Battle of the Smithsonian was made available December 1, 2009 on DVD and Blu-ray as a two-disc Special Edition and a three-disc Digital Copy Edition.[19]

Video game

The video game based on the film was released on May 5, 2009. It was fairly well-received in comparison to the majority of film-based video-games, netting a 7.5 out of 10 from IGN.com.

Artworks featured

- *American Gothic*, painting by Grant Wood
- *Balloon Dog*, sculpture by Jeff Koons
- *Crying Girl*, painting by Roy Lichtenstein
- *La Petite Danseuse de Quatorze Ans* (*Little Dancer of Fourteen Years*), sculpture by Edgar Degas
- *Le Penseur* (*The Thinker*), sculpture by Auguste Rodin
- *Venus Italica*, sculpture by Antonio Canova
- *Nighthawks*, painted by Edward Hopper
- *V-J day in Times Square*, picture taken by Alfred Eisenstaedt
- *Sierra Nevada*, painting by Albert Bierstadt
- *Shad Fishing at Gloucester, Delaware River*, painting by Thomas Eakins
- Works by Alexander Calder and Jackson Pollock
- "LOVE", sculpture by Robert Indiana

Sequel

Ben Stiller admitted that a sequel is "a possibility" and on January 22, 2010, co-writer Thomas Lennon said to *Access Hollywood*, "That after the success of two *Night at the Museum* films, its no surprise that 20th Century Fox is looking to develop a third and that those suspicions are indeed true and how could you not? I think it's a really outstanding idea to do 'Night at the Museum 3,' in fact," he said. "I wonder if someone's not even already working on a script for that," he added with a raised eyebrow. "I cannot confirm that for a fact, but I cannot deny it for a fact either... It might be in the works."[20] In an interview, Stiller confirmed the sequel, however, he said that it was only in the "ideas stage". [21]

References

[1] "Night at the Museum: Battle of the Smithsonian (2009)" (http://www.boxofficemojo.com/movies/?id=nightatthemuseum2.htm). Box Office Mojo. . Retrieved 2011-10-29.

[2] "The Smithsonian In the Movies" (http://siarchives.si.edu/exhibits/SIintheMovies/index.htm). Siarchives.si.edu. . Retrieved 2011-10-29.

[3] Puente, Maria (2009-05-25). "Smithsonian gets top billing in the new 'Night at the Museum'" (http://www.usatoday.com/travel/destinations/2009-05-18-smithsonian-museum_N.htm). *USA Today*. . Retrieved 2009-10-13.

[4] "See the Artifacts That Inspired the Movie" (http://www.gosmithsonian.com/nightatthemuseummovie/). Smithsonian Institution. . Retrieved 2009-10-13.

[5] "Night at the Museum: Battle of the Smithsonian Movie Reviews, Pictures" (http://www.rottentomatoes.com/m/night_at_the_museum_2_escape_from_the_smithsonian/). *Rotten Tomatoes*. IGN Entertainment. . Retrieved 2009-08-10.

[6] "Night at the Museum: Battle of the Smithsonian Movie Reviews, Pictures - Cream of the Crop" (http://www.rottentomatoes.com/m/night_at_the_museum_2_escape_from_the_smithsonian/?critic=creamcrop). *Rotten Tomatoes*. IGN Entertainment. . Retrieved 2009-05-22.

[7] "Night at the Museum: Battle of the Smithsonian (2009): Reviews" (http://www.metacritic.com/film/titles/nightatthemuseum2?q=Night at the Museum: Battle of the Smithsonian). Metacritic. . Retrieved 2009-05-22.

[8] "Toys in the nation's attic - Amy Adams a treasure in the 'Museum' sequel" (http://www.chicagotribune.com/entertainment/movies/chi-tc-mov-night-museum-0520-052may20,0,6390332.story). *Chicago Tribune*. 2009-05-20. . Retrieved 2009-05-22.

[9] "Night at the Museum: Battle of the Smithsonian" (http://www.ew.com/ew/article/0,,20279927,00.html). *Entertainment Weekly*. 2009-05-19. . Retrieved 2009-05-22.

[10] "Night At The Museum: Battle Of The Smithsonian: Review" (http://movies.tvguide.com/night-museum-battle-smithsonian/review/297477). *TV Guide*. . Retrieved 2009-05-22.

[11] "Film Review: Night at the Museum: Battle of the Smithsonian" (http://www.hollywoodreporter.com/hr/film-reviews/film-review-night-at-the-museum-battle-of-1003974548.story). *Hollywood Reporter*. 2009-05-20. . Retrieved 2009-05-22.

[12] Scott, A. O. (2009-05-22). "Movie Review: Night at the Museum: Battle of the Smithsonian (2009) - Dad's at Another Museum. Does That Make Him an Exhibitionist?" (http://movies.nytimes.com/2009/05/22/movies/22nigh.html?ref=movies). *The New York Times*. . Retrieved 2009-05-22.

[13] "Night at the Museum: Battle of the Smithsonian Review - A.V. Club" (http://www.avclub.com/articles/night-at-the-museum-battle-of-the-smithsonian,28233/?utm_source=channel_film). A.V. Club. 2009-05-21. . Retrieved 2009-05-22.

[14] Ebert, Roger (2009-05-20). "Night at the Museum: Battle of the Smithsonian Review" (http://rogerebert.suntimes.com/apps/pbcs.dll/article?AID=/20090520/REVIEWS/905209993). *Chicago Sun-Times*. . Retrieved 2009-05-22.

[15] "Daily Box Office" (http://boxofficemojo.com/daily/chart/?sortdate=2009-05-22&p=.htm). *Box Office Mojo*. May 22, 2009. . Retrieved May 26, 2009.

[16] "Night at the Museum: Battle of the Smithsonian" (http://www.boxofficemojo.com/movies/?id=nightatthemuseum2.htm). *Box Office Mojo*. June 5, 2009. . Retrieved June 5, 2009.

[17] Frank Segers (2009-06-21). "New 'Transformers' bows No. 1 overseas" (http://www.hollywoodreporter.com/hr/content_display/news/e3i34e2ede5adb7e1e8e8cbf7a6dbae2373). *Hollywood Reporter*. . Retrieved 2009-06-22.

[18] Teen Choice Awards winners (http://www.google.com/hostednews/ap/article/ALeqM5gzwwpelzmXR7OGixpNf7x4tyyiVgD99VR9CO0)

[19] Amazon.com: DVD Release for Night at the Museum: Battle of the Smithsonian (http://www.amazon.com/dp/B001PR0Y4E)

[20] "'Night At The Museum 3' In The Works | Access Hollywood - Celebrity News, Photos & Videos" (http://www.accesshollywood.com/night-at-the-museum-3-in-the-works_article_28049). Access Hollywood. 2010-01-21. . Retrieved 2011-10-29.

[21] http://www.moviehole.net/201147786-ben-stiller-confirms-night-at-the-museum-3-talks-zoolander-2-script

External links

- *Night at the Museum: Battle of the Smithsonian* (http://www.imdb.com/title/tt1078912/) at the Internet Movie Database
- Guide to Smithsonian museums displaying artifacts featured in the movie (http://www.gosmithsonian.com/nightatthemuseummovie/)
- *Night at the Museum: Battle of the Smithsonian* (http://www.allrovi.com/movies/movie/v426891) at AllRovi
- *Night at the Museum: Battle of the Smithsonian* (http://www.rottentomatoes.com/m/night_at_the_museum_2_escape_from_the_smithsonian/) at Rotten Tomatoes
- *Night at the Museum: Battle of the Smithsonian* (http://www.boxofficemojo.com/movies/?id=nightatthemuseum2.htm) at Box Office Mojo

Old Dogs (film)

Old Dogs	
Theatrical release poster	
Directed by	Walt Becker
Produced by	Andrew Panay Peter Abrams Robert Levy
Written by	David Diamond David Weissman
Starring	Robin Williams John Travolta Kelly Preston Seth Green Lori Loughlin Bernie Mac Matt Dillon
Music by	John Debney
Cinematography	Jeffrey L. Kimball
Editing by	Ryan Folsey Tom Lewis
Studio	Walt Disney Pictures Stoopid Monkey Tapestry Films
Distributed by	Walt Disney Studios Motion Pictures
Release date(s)	November 25, 2009
Running time	88 minutes
Country	United States
Language	English
Budget	$35 million
Box office	$96,753,696[1]

Old Dogs is a 2009 American ensemble comedy film directed by *Wild Hogs*'s Walt Becker and starring Robin Williams and John Travolta with an ensemble supporting cast played by Kelly Preston, Matt Dillon, Justin Long, Seth Green, Rita Wilson, Dax Shepard, and Bernie Mac. It was released in theaters on November 25, 2009 and was released on DVD March 9, 2010.

The movie is dedicated to both Bernie Mac (who died in August 2008 and had his final acting role in the film) and Jett Travolta (John Travolta's son who died in January 2009).

Old Dogs received poor reception from film critics. *The Orlando Sentinel* called the film "badly written and broadly acted."[2] The *Chicago Daily Herald* said the film "should be put out of our misery."[3] The *San Jose Mercury News* and *The Boston Globe* both described the film as a "turkey."[4] [5] Reviews in the *Milwaukee Journal Sentinel* and *AV Club* said the movie was not recommended for adults or children.[6] [7]

Despite the negative criticism, it was a minor box office success, beating its budget.[1]

At the 30th Golden Raspberry Awards ceremony, *Old Dogs* was nominated in four categories: Worst Picture, Worst Actor for John Travolta, Worst Supporting Actress for Kelly Preston and Worst Director for Walt Becker, but "lost" in all categories.

Canadian rocker Bryan Adams wrote the theme song for the film, "You've Been a Friend to Me".

Plot

Dan Rayburn (Robin Williams) and Charlie Reed (John Travolta) are best friends and co-owners of a successful sports marketing firm. Seven years prior, Dan, recently divorced, married Vicki (Kelly Preston) after being whisked away by Charlie for a tropical vacation. The wedding, however, is short lived. Seven years later, Vicki resurfaces to tell Dan that their short marriage resulted in something he never suspected: twins Zach (Conner Rayburn) and Emily (Ella Bleu Travolta).

Vicki, facing jail time for her work as an environmental activist, asks Dan to take care of the kids while she does her time. Thinking this might be his chance to get back with Vicki, Dan agrees, but only if Charlie will help him since neither have any experience taking care of kids. At the same time, the two must finalize a huge marketing deal with a Japanese company; something they've always dreamed of, but will take all of their talents to clinch.

Because Dan's condo does not allow children, he has to board with Charlie. Whilst this is happening, Charlie and Dan are close to securing the biggest account in the history of their careers with a Japanese corporation. Charlie and Dan's attempts to take care of the kids are well-intentioned, but very misguided. On a trip with the kids to an overnight camp, a hard-nosed camp instructor (Matt Dillon) becomes convinced that Dan and Charlie are homosexual partners. The trip ends with a bang after Dan accidentally sets a beloved statue of the camp's founder on fire.

The kids then proceed to spill and replace Charlie and Dan's prescriptions, mixing them up in the process. Dan then must play a game of golf with the Japanese executives while experiencing extreme side effects and Charlie tries to woo Amanda (Lori Loughlin) with a face frozen by the pills.

Desperate to help Dan communicate with the children despite his inexperience with children, Charlie recruits his friend Jimmy Lunchbox (Bernie Mac), a flamboyant children's entertainer, who is famous around the world. Jimmy comes by and straps Dan and Charlie in motion control puppet suits so Charlie can help Dan make all the right moves with his daughter while having a tea party. The suits malfunction, but Dan speaks from the heart, winning over Emily but his speech makes Jimmy emotional. Everything is great with Vicki as she returns home. However, the guys have sealed their Japanese deal, sending junior associate Craig (Seth Green) to Tokyo. When Craig goes missing after arriving there, Charlie and Dan must fly to Tokyo themselves to work. Dan must leave the kids and Vicki despite his (and their) desire to be a family.

Once in Tokyo, Dan realizes that what he really wants is to be a good father. He leaves the meeting without sealing the deal, rushing with Charlie to Vermont for the kids' birthday party. They aren't able to get into the Burlington Zoo in time and are forced to break in with the help of Craig. However, they mistakenly wind up in the gorilla enclosure. Though Dan and Charlie escape, Craig is captured by the gorilla (which takes a strong liking to him).

Dan then pays a birthday party performer hired by Vicki to use his jet pack and suit, flies into the ceremony and wins his kids back over. When the jet pack stops working in mid-air, he is taken to an ambulance on a stretcher. One year later, Dan and Vicki are together, Charlie has married Amanda, and Craig has become like a new "uncle" to the kids.

Cast

- Robin Williams as Dan Rayburn
- John Travolta as Charlie Reed
- Kelly Preston as Vicki Greer
- Seth Green as Craig White
- Lori Loughlin as Amanda
- Ella Bleu Travolta as Emily Greer
- Conner Rayburn as Zach Greer

Minor

- Sab Shimono as Yoshiro Nishamura (as Saburo Shimono)
- Dax Shepard as Child Proofer Gary (**uncredited**)
- Luis Guzmán as Child Proofer Nick (**uncredited**)
- Bernie Mac as Jimmy Lunchbox
- Matt Dillon as Troop Leader Barry
- Rita Wilson as Jenna
- Justin Long as Troop Leader Adam (**uncredited**)
- Ann-Margaret as Martha
- Laura Allen as Kelly
- Amy Sedaris as Condo Woman
- Kevin W. Yamada as Riku
- Bradley Steven Perry as Soccer Kid
- Dylan Sprayberry as Soccer Kid
- Paulo Costanzo as Zoo Maintenance (**uncredited**)
- DeRay Davis as Zoo Security Guard (**uncredited**)
- Paul Thornton as Restaurant Patron (**uncredited**)
- Residente as Tattoo Artist

Muppet Performers

The following have performed the puppets in Jimmy Lunchbox's show:

- Bruce Connelly -
- Josh Cohen -
- Joe Kovacs -
- John Kennedy -
- Edward Noel MacNeal -
- Matt Vogel -

NOTE: Two of the puppets identified in Jimmy Lunchbox's show are Bozark the Elephant from *Animal Jam* and Scales the Dragon from *Little Mermaid's Island.*

Reception

Critical response

The film received extremely negative reviews, and Rotten Tomatoes gave the film a 5% rating based on 77 aggregated reviews, making it certified "rotten"[8] and based on a selection of 19 of their top "Top Critics" the film achieved a rating of only 5%.[9] The film was ranked number three on their list of the ten most moldy films of 2009.[10] At Metacritic, *Old Dogs* received an aggregated rating of 19 based on 22 reviews, indicating "overwhelming dislike."[11] Film critic Roger Ebert gave *Old Dogs* a rating of one star out of a possible four.[12] Ebert opened his review commenting, "'Old Dogs' is stupefying dimwitted. What were John Travolta and Robin Williams *thinking* of? Apparently their agents weren't perceptive enough to smell the screenplay in its advanced state of decomposition".[12]

The Salt Lake Tribune gave *Old Dogs* a rating of zero stars out of a possible four, and criticized the film for "hammy acting and sledgehammer editing".[13] Film critic Roger Moore of *The Orlando Sentinel* gave *Old Dogs* a rating of one and a half stars out of a possible four.[14] "Trashing Old Dogs is a bit like kicking a puppy. But here goes. The new comedy from some of the folks who brought us Wild Hogs is badly written and broadly acted, shamelessly manipulative and not above stopping by the toilet for a laugh or two," wrote Moore.[14]

Bill Goodykoontz of *The Star Press* gave the film a critical review, and commented, "'Old Dogs,' which stars Robin Williams and John Travolta as a couple of aging bachelors who suddenly have twins thrust upon them, delivers everything you'd expect. Which is: not much."[15] He concluded his review with, "Let's hope Williams, Travolta and the rest got a fabulous payday for "Old Dogs." Because otherwise, you know, woof."[15] In a review for *The Arizona Republic*, Goodykoontz gave the film a rating of one and a half stars out of a possible five.[16]

Writing for the *San Jose Mercury News* in an analysis of movies that were released around Thanksgiving, Randy Myers placed *Old Dogs* below "The Scraps: Leftovers that should be immediately placed in Fido's bowl."[4] Myers commented, "We have a winner in the Thanksgiving movie turkey contest."[4] Dennis Harvey of *Variety* wrote, "Too bad this shrilly tuned comedy doesn't demand more than clock-punching effort from everyone involved."[17] Tim Robey of *The Telegraph* savaged the film, saying, "*Old Dogs* is so singularly dreadful it halts time, folds space and plays havoc with the very notion of the self."[18] He added to the review, "Being a film critic is a wonderful job, but there are weeks when the bad film delirium strikes and we'd all be better off in straitjackets. A colleague opined to me the other day that this might be the deadliest run of releases in his 20-year history on the job, and I can completely see that." He also said, "You'd have to hate your family to take them to this!" He gave the film zero stars.

Writing for *The Philadelphia Inquirer*, Carrie Rickey gave the film a rating of two and a half stars out of four.[19] Rickey commented of the multiple cameos in the film, "A child of 5 can see that these brief appearances serve to pad a gauze-thin script."[19] The review concluded, "*Old Dogs* may not be good. But the sight of pesky penguins pecking Travolta and Green in the embrace of an unlikely partner makes it just good enough."[19] Pete Hammond of *Boxoffice* gave the film 3/5 stars, and concluded, "*Old Dogs* may not reach the box office heights of *Wild Hogs* but its fun family friendly attitude should guarantee a healthy holiday haul."[20]

Box office

In its first day, *Old Dogs* opened in fifth place, with a take of $3.1 million.[21] [22] It was beat out in first-day box office results by *New Moon*, *The Blind Side*, *2012*, and *Ninja Assassin*.[21] [22] The film came in fourth in its second day with $4.1 million, for a two-day pickup of $7.2 million.[23] The film remained in fourth place for its third day, with a box office take of $6.8 million.[24] Overall, the film grossed $96,753,696 worldwide on a budget of $35,000,000.[25]

The movie was also a moderate success on DVD, gaining more than twenty millions of dollar domestically during its first two mounths of release.[26]

References

[1] "Old Dogs (2009) Box Office Mojo" (http://boxofficemojo.com/movies/?id=olddogs.htm). Box Office Mojo. . Retrieved 2010-08-09.

[2] http://blogs.orlandosentinel.com/entertainment_movies_blog/2009/11/movie-review-old-dogs-no-new-tricks.html

[3] http://www.dailyherald.com/story/?id=339223

[4] Myers, Randy (November 24, 2009). "Thanksgiving Movie Guide: From the main courses to the doggie scraps" (http://www.mercurynews.com/entertainment/ci_13850907?nclick_check=1). *San Jose Mercury News*. . Retrieved 2009-11-24.

[5] Burr, Ty (2009-11-25). "Old Dogs" (http://www.boston.com/ae/movies/articles/2009/11/25/old_dogs_lacks_a_plot_purpose/). *The Boston Globe*. .

[6] http://www.jsonline.com/entertainment/movies/71974927.html

[7] http://www.avclub.com/articles/old-dogs,35742/

[8] "Old Dogs (2009)" (http://www.rottentomatoes.com/m/10009596-old_dogs/). *Rotten Tomatoes*. Flixster. . Retrieved 2010-01-17.

[9] "Old Dogs (2009) - Top Critics" (http://www.rottentomatoes.com/m/10009596-old_dogs/?critic=creamcrop). *Rotten Tomatoes*. Flixster. . Retrieved 2010-01-17.

[10] "ROTTEN TOMATOES: 11th Annual Golden Tomato Awards: Moldy" (http://www.rottentomatoes.com/guides/rtawards/moldy/). *Rotten Tomatoes*. Flixster. . Retrieved 2010-01-17.

[11] "Old Dogs" (http://www.metacritic.com/film/titles/olddogs). *CBS Interactive Inc.*. Metacritic. 2009. . Retrieved 2009-11-25.

[12] Ebert, Roger (November 24, 2009). "Old Dogs" (http://rogerebert.suntimes.com/apps/pbcs.dll/article?AID=/20091124/REVIEWS/911249994/1023). *RogerEbert.com* (Chicago Sun-Times). . Retrieved 2009-11-25. 1/4 stars

[13] The Salt Lake Tribune staff (November 24, 2009). "5-minute movie reviews: 'Old Dogs,' 'Ninja Assassin'" (http://www.sltrib.com/themix/ci_13857602). *The Salt Lake Tribune*. . Retrieved 2009-11-24.

[14] Moore, Roger (November 23, 2009). "Movie Review: Old Dogs, no new tricks" (http://blogs.orlandosentinel.com/entertainment_movies_blog/2009/11/movie-review-old-dogs-no-new-tricks.html). *Movies with Roger Moore* (Orlando Sentinel). . Retrieved 2009-11-24.

[15] Goodykoontz, Bill (November 23, 2009). "REVIEW" 'Old Dogs' could use new tricks" (http://www.thestarpress.com/article/20091123/ENTERTAINMENT04/91123024). *The Star Press*. . Retrieved 2009-11-24.

[16] Goodykoontz, Bill (November 24, 2009). "'Old Dogs'" (http://www.azcentral.com/thingstodo/movies/articles/2009/11/24/20091124olddogs1226.html). *The Arizona Republic*. . Retrieved 2009-11-24.

[17] Harvey, Dennis (November 24, 2009). "Old Dogs" (http://www.variety.com/review/VE1117941669.html). *Variety*. . Retrieved 2009-11-24.

[18] "Old Dogs, review" (http://www.telegraph.co.uk/culture/culturecritics/timrobey/7471621/Old-Dogs-review.html). *The Daily Telegraph* (London). 2010-03-18. .

[19] Rickey, Carrie (November 24, 2009). "Old Dogs" (http://www.philly.com/philly/entertainment/movies/20091124_Old_Dogs.html). *The Philadelphia Inquirer*. . Retrieved 2009-11-24.

[20] Hammond, Pete (2009-11-25). "Old Dogs Movie Review" (http://boxoffice.com/reviews/2009/11/old-dogs.php). *Boxoffice*. www.boxoffice.com. . Retrieved 2009-11-28.

[21] DiOrio, Carl (November 26, 2009). ""Moon" begins long weekend atop box office" (http://www.reuters.com/article/filmNews/idUSTRE5AK14C20091127). *The Hollywood Reporter* (Reuters). . Retrieved 2009-11-27.

[22] Ellwood, Gregory (November 26, 2009). "Box Office: 'New Moon's' $14.3 million dominates 'Ninja' and 'Old Dogs'" (http://www.hitfix.com/articles/2009-11-26-box-office-new-moon-s-14-3-million-dominates-ninja-and-old-dogs). *HitFlix* (HitFix Inc). . Retrieved 2009-11-27.

[23] D'Alessandro, Anthony (November 27, 2009). "Football player elbows vampires on Turkey day" (http://www.variety.com/article/VR1118011882.html). *Variety* (Reed). . Retrieved 2009-11-28.

[24] Briody, Tim (November 28, 2009). "Black Friday Box Office Analysis" (http://www.boxofficeprophets.com/column/index.cfm?columnID=12271). *Box Office Prophets* (Box Office Prophets, a division of One Of Us, Inc.). . Retrieved 2009-11-28.

[25] "Old Dogs (2009) Box Office" (http://www.the-numbers.com/movies/2009/OLDOG.php). The-Numbers. . Retrieved 2010-01-23.

[26] "Old Dogs - DVD Sales" (http://www.the-numbers.com/movies/2009/OLDOG-DVD.php). The-Numbers. . Retrieved 19 November 2011.

External links

- Official website (http://disney.go.com/disneypictures/olddogs/)
- *Old Dogs* (http://www.imdb.com/title/tt0976238/) at the Internet Movie Database
- *Old Dogs* (http://www.allrovi.com/movies/movie/vold-dogs-395873) at AllRovi
- *Old Dogs* (http://www.boxofficemojo.com/movies/?id=olddogs.htm) at Box Office Mojo
- *Old Dogs* (http://www.metacritic.com/movie/olddogs) at Metacritic
- *Old Dogs* (http://www.rottentomatoes.com/m/10009596-old_dogs/) at Rotten Tomatoes

The Richard Pryor Show

The Richard Pryor Show	
The Richard Pryor Show title card	
Format	Sketch comedy, variety
Created by	Richard Pryor
Starring	Richard Pryor
Country of origin	United States
No. of seasons	1
No. of episodes	4
Production	
Running time	45–48 minutes
Broadcast	
Original channel	NBC
Audio format	Monaural
Original run	September 13, 1977 – October 4, 1977

The Richard Pryor Show is an American comedy variety series starring Richard Pryor. It premiered on NBC on Tuesday, September 13, 1977 at 8 p.m. opposite ABC's popular television shows *Laverne & Shirley* and *Happy Days*.

The show was produced by Rocco Urbisci for Burt Sugarman Productions. It was conceived out of a special that Pryor did for NBC in May 1977. Because the special was a major hit, both critically and commercially, Pryor was given a chance to host and star in his own television show.

Series run

The Richard Pryor Show lasted four episodes during the 1977 season. It was a far cry from the goofy, cookie cutter "bad comedy skits with songs" type of variety show that dominated the airwaves of the day. Pryor's program was a true variety show, featuring an unpredictable mix of satire, social commentary, conceptual comedy, improvisation, slapstick, and the occasional dramatic bit. From the start, the show faced controversy about its time slot and subject matter.

Pryor's contract stated that the show was to air at 9 p.m., but it was aired at 8 p.m. Many people wondered why NBC would put one of America's most controversial and profanity-laced artists in the middle of "family hour" on Tuesdays. Many more wondered why the network slotted the show opposite the most popular shows of the day, all but assuring its failure.

Pryor was ready to quit before production even began because of network intervention, indifference, and incompetence during the development stage. He was eventually wooed back, agreeing to do four episodes of the show instead of the ten originally required by his contract. The four episodes were produced, and they aired in consecutive weeks, but the network interference that almost canceled the show before it began returned when the first episode's introductory bit was cut just before air. The bit began with a close-up of Pryor's face as he explained that he was not going to have to give anything up in order to bring his brand of comedy to network television. Then the camera pulled back to show an apparently nude Pryor with his genitals removed (Pryor wore a full-length body stocking, so no nudity was shown).

The Richard Pryor Show did not do well in the ratings while the programs that preceded it and followed it were highly rated. After Pryor fulfilled his contractual obligations, neither he nor the network pursued any further episodes or specials.

Cast

- Richard Pryor
- Robin Williams
- Paul Mooney
- Tim Reid
- John Witherspoon
- Sandra Bernhard
- Edie McClurg
- Marsha Warfield

The main cast consisted of Pryor as various characters. Some of the more popular characters were Pryor playing a money-seeking priest, a wino, and a white-hating rock star. The rest of the cast consisted of comedians, some of who went on to have popular careers in Hollywood.

Episodes and controversy

Pryor only filmed four episodes of the show, and there were controversies beyond the first episode's title-card scene. A skit in which Pryor appeared as a machine gun-toting rocker who kills all of his white fans also caused a stir. The second episode also featured a controversial skit that showed a woman in a park describing what her first lesbian experience was like. Probably one of the shocking and revealing moments of the show came during the last episode of the show. During the final episode, a roast skit was given similar to ones by the Friars Club or hosted by Dean Martin. The show's cast roasted Pryor, who sat with his head down laughing mildly while regulars on the show either had kind remarks or very scornful ones.

DVD release and syndication

Because Pryor's status as a comedic and Hollywood icon continued to grow, a two-volume DVD set was released on March 23, 2004. The DVDs include the special that Pryor did that was the inspiration for the series.

In February 2010, the African-American-themed cable network TV One aired a five-hour marathon of *The Richard Pryor Show*, which consisted of the original special, followed by all four episodes of the series. The broadcast marked one of only two times that the show had been aired on television since its original run on NBC. In the late 1990s,it was re-shown as a summer filler show after most of their other series had either been canceled or fulfilled their regular seasons. In February 2011, TV One re-aired the episodes again in honor of black history month.

On March 11, 2010, *The Top 10 Greatest Sketches from The Richard Pryor Show* was released by **Alright, Dude Productions**, featuring a mini-documentary format on Pryor's history, the conception of the show, and eventually moving into the actual countdown portion.

External links

- *The Richard Pryor Show* [1] at the Internet Movie Database
- *The Richard Pryor Show* [2] at TV.com

References

[1] http://www.imdb.com/title/tt0075567/
[2] http://www.tv.com/show/2536/summary.html

Mork & Mindy

Mork & Mindy	
First season title card	
Genre	Science fiction sitcom
Created by	Garry Marshall Dale McRaven Joe Glauberg
Starring	Robin Williams Pam Dawber Elizabeth Kerr Conrad Janis Jeffrey Jacquet Jay Thomas Gina Hecht Tom Poston Jim Staahl Jonathan Winters
Theme music composer	Perry Botkin, Jr.
Country of origin	United States
Language(s)	English
No. of seasons	4
No. of episodes	95 (List of episodes)
Production	
Executive producer(s)	Anthony W. Marshall Garry Marshall
Producer(s)	Bruce Johnson Brian Levant Dale McRaven Ed Scharlach Tom Tenowich
Camera setup	Multi-camera
Running time	22–24 minutes
Production company(s)	Henderson Production Company Miller-Milkis Productions Paramount Television
Distributor	CBS Television Distribution
Broadcast	
Original channel	ABC
Audio format	Monaural
Original run	September 14, 1978 – May 27, 1982
Chronology	
Preceded by	*Love, American Style* *Happy Days*

Related shows	*Laverne & Shirley* *Blansky's Beauties* *Out of the Blue* *Joanie Loves Chachi* *The New Love, American Style*

Mork & Mindy is an American science fiction sitcom broadcast from 1978 until 1982 on ABC. The series starred Robin Williams as Mork, an alien who comes to Earth from the planet Ork in a small, one-man egg-shaped spaceship. Pam Dawber co-starred as Mindy McConnell, his human friend and roommate. Mork and Mindy married in the show's final season.

In 1997, the episode, *Mork's Mixed Emotions*, was ranked #94 on TV Guide's "100 Greatest Episodes of All Time" list.[1]

Premise and initial success

The series was a spin-off from the sitcom *Happy Days*. The character of Mork, played by a then-unknown Robin Williams, first appeared in the Happy Days Season 5 episode, "My Favorite Orkan," which was a take on the 1960s sitcom, *My Favorite Martian*. Williams' character Mork attempts to take Richie Cunningham back to his planet of Ork as a human specimen, but his plan is foiled by Fonzie (though all this turned out to be simply a dream Richie had). The character proved to be popular enough with the audience to go forward with the planned series of his own. In *Mork & Mindy*, Mork resides in the present-day city of Boulder, Colorado, of the late-1970s and early-1980s as opposed to the late-1950s setting of *Happy Days*.

Mork's egg-shaped spacecraft lands on Earth with a mission to observe human behavior. Mork is assigned his mission by Orson, his mostly-unseen and long-suffering superior (voiced by Ralph James), who has sent Mork to Earth to get him off Ork, due to the fact humor is not permitted on Ork. To fit in, Mork dresses in Earth clothing (a suit, which he wears backwards). He befriends 21-year old Mindy (Pam Dawber) after she is stranded one evening after an argument with her boyfriend. Mork offers assistance, and Mindy, not seeing his back or the on-backwards suit, assumes he is a priest, mistaking his wardrobe gaffe for a priest's collar. Mindy is taken by Mork's willingness to listen (unknown to her, he is simply observing her behavior as part of his mission), and the two become friends. They walk back to her apartment, when Mindy sees his backwards suit and Mork's rather unconventional behavior for a priest. She asks him who he really is, and the innocent Mork, having not learned how to lie, tells her the truth.

After discovering Mork is an alien, Mindy promises to keep his true identity a secret and allows him to move into her attic. However, Mindy's father, Fred (Conrad Janis), expresses outrage that his daughter is living with a man (particularly one as bizarre as Mork). Fred's mother-in-law, Cora (Elizabeth Kerr), presents a much less conservative view, and approves of Mork and the living arrangement. Mindy and Cora also work at Fred's music store where Cora gives music lessons to a young child named Eugene (Jeffrey Jacquet), who becomes Mork's friend. Also seen occasionally were Mindy's snooty old friend from high school, Susan (played by Morgan Fairchild) and the possibly-insane Exidor (played by Robert Donner).

Storylines usually centered on Mork's attempts to understand human behavior and American culture as Mindy helps him to adjust to life on Earth. At the end of each episode, Mork reports back to Orson on what he has learned about Earth. These end-of-show summaries allow Mork to comment humorously on social norms.

It usually ends up frustrating Mindy as Mork can only do things according to Ork customs. For example, lying to someone, or not informing them it will rain is considered a practical joke (called "splinking") on Ork.

Mork's greeting was "Na-Nu Na-Nu" (pronounced "nah-noo nah-noo") along with a hand gesture similar to Mr. Spock's Vulcan salute from *Star Trek* combined with a handshake. It became a popular catchphrase at the time, as did "Shazbot" (Shozz-bot), an Orkan profanity that Mork used. Mork also said "kay-o" in place of okay.

This series was Robin Williams' first major acting break and became famous for Williams' use of his manic improvisational comedic talent. Williams would make up so many jokes during filming that eventually, the scripts had specific gaps where Williams was allowed to perform freely. In many scenes, Dawber apparently had to bite her lip to avoid laughing and ruining the take.

The series was hugely popular in its first season. The Nielsen ratings were very high, ranking at #3 behind *Laverne & Shirley* (#1) and *Three's Company* (#2), both on ABC, which was the highest rated network in the US in 1978. The show even garnered slightly higher ratings than the show that spawned it, *Happy Days* (#4).[2] [3] However, the network management sought to improve the show in several ways. This was done in conjunction with what is known in the industry as counterprogramming, a technique in which a successful show is moved opposite a ratings hit on another network. The show was moved from Thursdays, where it outrated CBS' *The Waltons*, to Sundays where it replaced the cancelled sci-fi series *Battlestar Galactica*. The show now aired against two highly-rated shows: NBC's anthology series entitled *The Sunday Big Event* and CBS' revamped continuation of *All in the Family* entitled *Archie Bunker's Place*.[2]

Second season

The second season saw an attempt to seek younger viewers and premiered a new, disco arrangement of the gentle theme tune.

The characters of Fred and Cora were dropped from the regular cast. It was explained that Fred went on tour as a conductor with an orchestra, taking Cora with him. Fred and Cora made return appearances in later episodes. Recurring characters Susan and Eugene made no further appearances after season one and were never mentioned again.

New cast members were added. Among the new supporting characters were Remo and Jean DaVinci (Jay Thomas and Gina Hecht), a brother and sister from New York City who owned a new neighborhood deli where Mork and Mindy now spent a lot of time. Also added as regulars were their grumpy neighbor Mr. Bickley (who was seen occasionally in the first season and ironically worked as a verse writer for a greeting-card company) portrayed by Tom Poston, and Nelson Flavor (Jim Staahl), Mindy's snooty cousin who ran for city council.

The show's main focus was no longer on Mork's slapstick attempts to adjust to the new world he was in, but on the relationship between Mork and Mindy on a romantic level.

In a two-part, second-season episode, Raquel Welch appeared as Captain Nirvana of the Necrotons, an alien species of beautiful women that were enemies of the Orkans.

Due to the abrupt changes to the show and time slot, ratings slipped dramatically (from #3 to #27). The show was quickly moved back to its previous timeslot and efforts were made to return to the core of the series; unfortunately ratings did not recover.

Decline

Third season

For the third season, Jean and Remo were retained as regulars.

Mindy's father and grandmother returned to the series. The show acknowledged this attempt to restore its original premise, with the third season's hour-long opener titled *Putting The Ork Back in Mork*.

Several new supporting characters were added to the lineup. Joining were two children from the day-care center where Mork worked. They were the intellectual Lola and the gluttonous Stephanie. Also added was Mindy's close friend Glenda Faye Comstock (Crissy Wilzak). Crissy lasted one season as a regular.

When these ideas failed to improve ratings, many wilder ideas were tried to attempt to capitalize on Williams' comedic talents. The season ended at #49 in the ratings.

Fourth season

Despite the show's steady decline, ABC agreed to a fourth season of *Mork*, but executives wanted changes.

In the fourth season, Mork and Mindy were married. Jonathan Winters, one of Williams' idols, was brought in as their child, Mearth. Due to the different Orkan physiology, Mork laid an egg, which grew and hatched into the much older Winters.[4] It had been previously explained that Orkans aged "backwards", thus explaining Mearth's appearance and that of his teacher, Miss Geezba (portrayed by then 11-year-old actress Louanne Sirota). Other attempts included the use of special guest stars. Unfortunately, those changes failed to increase ratings, and the show ended at a dismal No. 60. After four seasons, and 95 episodes, *Mork & Mindy* was canceled.

Happy Days connection

Actor-director Jerry Paris was inspired to create the character of Mork after directing an unusual and memorable episode of *The Dick Van Dyke Show* in which van Dyke's Rob Petrie believed the Earth had been surreptitiously invaded by walnut-eating aliens who stole humans' thumbs and imaginations.[5] When he moved on to direct *Happy Days*, he introduced Mork in a similarly atypical season-five episode entitled *My Favorite Orkan*.[5] [6] In it, Richie tells everyone he has seen a flying saucer, but no one else believes him. Fonzie tells him that people make up stories about UFOs because their lives are "humdrum". Then while Richie's at home, Mork walks in. He freezes everyone with his finger except Richie and says he was sent to Earth to find a "humdrum" human to take back to Ork. Richie runs to Fonzie for help. When Mork catches up to him, he freezes everyone, but finds himself unable to freeze Fonzie due to The Fonz's famous and powerful thumbs. Mork challenges Fonzie to a duel: finger vs. thumb. After their duel, The Fonz admits defeat, and Mork decides to take Fonzie back to Ork instead of Richie. Then, Richie wakes up and realizes he was dreaming. There is a knock on the door and much to Richie's dismay, it is a man who looks exactly like Mork except in regular clothes asking for directions. When production on *Mork & Mindy* began, an extra scene was filmed and added to this episode for subsequent reruns. In the scene, Mork contacts Orson and explains that he decided to let Fonzie go, and was going to travel to the year 1978 to continue his mission. In the pilot episode of Mork and Mindy, Orson tells Mork that he is assigning him to study the planet Earth. Mork remembers that he's been to Earth before to collect a specimen (Fonzie) but he "had to throw it back, though. Too small."

Fonzie and Laverne of *Laverne & Shirley* appeared in the first episode of the show. In this segment, Mork relays to Mindy his trip to 1950s Milwaukee where Fonzie sets Mork up on a date with Laverne.

Mork returned to *Happy Days* in a 1979 episode in which Mork tells Richie that he enjoys coming to the 1950s because life is simpler and more "humdrum" than in the 1970s. Fonzie sees Mork and immediately tries to run away, but Mork freezes him and makes him stay. He eventually lets him go, but not before Fonzie asks Mork to reveal two things about the future: "cars and girls". Mork's response is "In 1979... both are faster." to which the Fonz replies "Whoa!" The episode is mostly a retrospective in which clips are shown as Richie and Fonzie try to explain the concepts of love and friendship to Mork.

DVD releases

Paramount Home Entertainment and CBS DVD have released the first three seasons of *Mork & Mindy* on DVD in Regions 1, 2 and 4.

DVD name	Ep#	Release dates		
		Region 1	**Region 2**	**Region 4**
The Complete First Season	25	September 7, 2004	October 29, 2007	September 19, 2007
The Second Season	26	April 17, 2007	April 7, 2008	March 6, 2008
The Third Season	22	November 27, 2007	September 1, 2008	September 4, 2008
The Fourth Season	22	TBA	TBA	TBA

Syndication

Mork & Mindy was syndicated off network by Paramount beginning in the Fall of 1982. Many stations (nearly all independent stations) bought the program to use as a transition from cartoons to sitcoms in the 5 p.m. hour. Still, the show's ratings in syndication were disastrous. By 1983 most stations that owned the show rested it much of the time running it in the summer, during which time weaker programming tended to air back then. Very few stations renewed the show a few years later. By 1987, the show only aired in a handful of TV markets. With the expansion of cable channels available, the show began airing on cable. Nick at Nite reran the show from March 4, 1991 to November 27, 1995.[7] The show has also aired on FOX Family Channel in the late 1990s. It has aired in recent years on Me TV.

Ratings

- 1978-1979: #3
- 1979-1980: #27
- 1980-1981: #49
- 1981-1982: #60

Cast

- Mork: Robin Williams
- Mindy McConnell: Pam Dawber
- Fred McConnell: Conrad Janis
- Grandmother Cora: Elizabeth Kerr
- Mr. Bickley: Tom Poston
- Mearth: Jonathan Winters
- Remo Davinci: Jay Thomas
- Jean Davinci: Gina Hecht
- Nelson Flavor: Jim Staahl

Recurring characters

- Susan Taylor (Morgan Fairchild), Mindy's snooty ex-friend from high school. In the episode, *Mork's First Christmas*, a glimpse into why Susan is such a shallow person was shown. As she and Mindy are turning out the lights to the apartment, Susan comments that it seems like Mork's first Christmas, wherein Mindy says that his family never celebrated Christmas. As Mindy enters her bedroom, Susan turns out the light saying (out of Mindy's earshot), "Mork and I have a lot in common." (This part of the scene is usually cut during reruns.)
- Exidor (Robert Donner), an eccentric man (with possible mental illness) who regards himself as a prophet. He is often seen wearing a flowing white robe with a blue sash. He knows that Mork is an alien but nobody believes him. He was the leader of a cult called The Friends of Venus, of which he was the only member; he regularly

engaged in conversations with imaginary members of his cult (such as "Pepe" and "Rocco"), but he was the only person who could see them. Most times he is found yelling at his imaginary cult. He makes the comment "Entourages can be the pits!". Later, since the Venusians had abandoned him, he began to worship O.J. Simpson. He also had a plan to become "Emperor of the Universe" by becoming a rock star—but his musical instrument of choice was the accordion. Exidor appears to be something of a squatter, as on at least two separate occasions he turned up in homes not his own. Once, Mork visited Exidor at a very nice apartment where he supposedly lived with his imaginary girlfriend and her twin sister. Another time, he turned up "on vacation" in Mindy's family home, where he apparently believed there was a beach in the living room closet. ("Everybody out of the water! Can't you see that fin?") He eventually got married, in a "forest" which was Mindy's attic. Mindy thought his wife would be imaginary, but turned out to be a real woman named "Ambrosia". The insane Exidor became highly popular with audiences and prompted wild applause from the studio audience when entering a scene.

- Mr. Sternhagen (Foster Brooks), Mindy's boss when she got a job at a local TV station. He is overbearing and demanding of Mindy when sober, but occasionally turns up drunk and cheerful. (Brooks was a comedian noted for his "drunk" act.)
- Glenda Faye Comstock, Mindy's friend played by show producer Crissy Wilzak.
- Todd Norman Taylor a.k.a. TNT (Bill Kirchenbauer), an obnoxious and arrogant womanizer. He later teaches Mork to drive at the "FastLane Driving School."
- Cathy McConnell (Shelley Fabares), Fred's new younger wife and Mindy's stepmother.
- Lola (Amy Tenowich), the young philosopher, and Stephanie (Stephanie Kayano), the chubby girl who loves to eat. Two children from the daycare center Mork works at later in the series.
- Billy (Corey Feldman), also a daycare center child, wants to be like his namesake Billy the Kid. Mork introduces him to the Orkan hero Squellman the Yellow.
- Arnold Wanker (Logan Ramsey), The landlord of Mindy's music store.[8] [9] He dies in the Fred's music store, but Mork, misinterpreting the comments made to his wife, brings him back to life (a "one-in-a-billion" chance.)

Filming locations

In an interview with Garry Marshall on June 30, 2006, Pat O'Brien mentioned that *Mork & Mindy* was filmed on Paramount stage 27, the former studio for his infotainment program *The Insider*.

The house from the show is located at 1619 Pine Street, just a few blocks away from the Pearl Street Mall in Boulder. This was also used in the show as Mindy's actual address in Boulder, as shown in the episode, *Mork Goes Public*.

The same house was later used for exterior shots on the series *Perfect Strangers* in Episode 21 of Season 5, *This Old House*, where the cousins, Larry and Balki, remodel a home for a fix and flip in hopes of huge profits. Often mistaken, it was not the house the cousins moved into with their wives during the final two seasons. In addition, it was used in three episodes of Family Matters as Myra's house.[10]

1619 Pine Street, Boulder, Colorado was used for the external shots of Mindy's house on *Mork & Mindy*

Spin-offs and adaptations

- In the United Kingdom, a long-running comic strip version was written by Angus P. Allan, illustrated by Bill Titcombe, and printed in children's television magazine, *Look-In*. Several British-produced annuals were also released that tied in with the series.

- A subsequent Saturday morning cartoon entitled *The Mork & Mindy / Laverne & Shirley / Fonz Hour* ran on ABC from 1982 to 1983. The *Mork & Mindy* segments were a prequel with Mindy as a student in high school. The character of Eugene returned in this spin-off voiced by Shavar Ross.
- In 2005, a made-for-television movie entitled *Behind the Camera: The Unauthorized Story of Mork & Mindy* aired on NBC.
- In 1979, a short-lived Brazilian version of the series appeared as *Superbronco*. It was produced by Rede Globo and starred comedian Ronald Golias and actress Liza Vieira.

References

[1] "Special Collectors' Issue: 100 Greatest Episodes of All Time". *TV Guide* (June 28-July 4). 1997.

[2] Brooks, Tim; Earl Marsh (2003). *The Complete Directory to Prime Time Network and Cable TV Shows*. Ballantine Books. ISBN 0-345-45542-8.

[3] Screen Source: Top TV Shows, 1970's (http://www.amug.org/~scrnsrc/top_tv_shows_70s.html)

[4] "TV Playbook: *Let's Add a Kid!*" (http://uk.tv.ign.com/articles/935/935812p1.html). *IGN*. . Retrieved 2010-08-15.

[5] Weissman, Ginny; Coyne Steven Sanders (1993). *The Dick Van Dyke Show* (http://books.google.com/books?id=yw4clpRWbg4C&pg=PA60&dq="danny+thomas"+walnuts+thumbs&ei=iLwdS4qSOpi0MIXZ8PEI&cd=3#v=onepage&q="danny thomas" walnuts thumbs&f=false). Macmillan. p. 60. ISBN 0312087667. .

[6] "*Happy Days*: My Favorite Orkan (1978)" (http://www.imdb.com/title/tt0596274/). *Internet Movie Database*. . Retrieved 2009-12-09.

[7] Nick at Nite Log - 1985-present

[8] *Mork & Mindy* (http://www.youtube.com/watch?v=aVQbgaHBojw) (TV). USA: Henderson Production Company. .

[9] "Mork & Mindy - To Tell the Truth" (http://www.imdb.com/title/tt0651264/). IMDb. . Retrieved 26 April 2011.

[10] *We're Going to Disney World (Part 2)*, *Crazy For You (Part 1)*, and *Crazier for You (Part 2)*

External links

- *Mork and Mindy* (http://www.imdb.com/title/tt0077053/) at the Internet Movie Database

America 2-Night

America 2-Night	
Format	Situation comedy
Created by	Norman Lear
Starring	Martin Mull Fred Willard Frank De Vol Tommy Tedesco
Country of origin	United States
No. of episodes	65
Production	
Running time	22–24 minutes
Broadcast	
Original channel	Syndication
Audio format	Monaural
Original run	April 10, 1978 – July 7, 1978
Chronology	
Preceded by	*Fernwood 2 Night*

America 2-Night is the continuation of the talk-show parody series *Fernwood 2 Night*. It ran from April to July 1978. As in *Fernwood*, Barth Gimble (Martin Mull) was the host and Jerry Hubbard (Fred Willard) was his co-host. Happy Kyne (Frank De Vol) and the Mirth-Makers was the band.

Synopsis

The setting of the show was moved from the fictional Fernwood, Ohio, to the fictional "Tri-City" area of Alta Coma, Petaluma, and the City of Merchandise in California. According to Hubbard's announcement at the beginning of every show, Alta Coma was "the unfinished furniture capital of the world". This new setting made it easier for celebrities to come on the show as themselves. Among the celebrities who guested are Charlton Heston, Carol Burnett, Burt Lancaster, Steve Allen, Milton Berle, Rita Moreno, Rob Reiner, Mark Hamill, and Gary Coleman. In the final episode, Mull and Willard guested as themselves.

The show was broadcast on the fictional UBS network (presumably a reference to the film *Network*), whose logo featured an ear (a takeoff on CBS's "Eye" logo) and whose slogan was "We put U before the BS".

In 2001, Martin Mull and Fred Willard reprised their roles in a stage appearance and retrospective at the US Comedy Arts Festival in Aspen, Colorado.

Recurring characters

- William W.D. 'Bud' Prize (Kenneth Mars)
- Tony Rolletti (Bill Kirchenbauer)
- Virgil Simms (Jim Varney)
- Jason Shine (Robin Williams)
- Chuck Emmitt Saugis (Paul Willson)

Syndication

Reruns of *America 2-Night* aired on Nick at Nite from 1990 to 1993.

External links

- *America 2-Night* [1] at the Internet Movie Database

References

[1] http://www.imdb.com/title/tt0076976/

Faerie Tale Theatre

Faerie Tale Theatre	
The 6-DVD box set cover by Starmaker II.	
Also known as	***Shelley Duvall's Faerie Tale Theatre***
Genre	Fairytale fantasy
Format	Children's anthology series
Created by	Shelley Duvall
Presented by	Shelley Duvall
Starring	Various
Country of origin	United States
Language(s)	English
No. of seasons	6
No. of episodes	27 (List of episodes)
Production	
Executive producer(s)	Shelley Duvall
Running time	50 min.
Broadcast	
Original channel	Showtime
Original run	September 11, 1982 – November 14, 1987
Chronology	
Followed by	*Tall Tales & Legends*
Related shows	*Shirley Temple Theatre*

Faerie Tale Theatre (also known as ***Shelley Duvall's Faerie Tale Theatre***) is a live-action children's television anthology series retelling popular fairy tales. Shelley Duvall serves as narrator, host and executive producer of the program, and occasionally stars in episodes. The series was followed by another, shorter series called *Tall Tales & Legends* which followed the same format as *Faerie Tale Theatre* and focused on classic American folk tales. Both series feature well known actors and directors, and were inspired by the children's television series *Shirley Temple Theatre* (also known as *The Shirley Temple Show* and *Shirley Temple's Storybook*).

Faerie Tale Theatre originally aired on Showtime from 1982 to 1987. It later aired as edited re-runs on the Disney Channel[1] as well as in syndication on various television stations,[2] including PBS[3] [4] and BookTelevision.[5]

Background

Shelley Duvall began conception of *Faerie Tale Theatre* while filming *Popeye*. She reportedly asked her co-star, Robin Williams, his opinion on "The Frog Prince," a fairy tale she was reading during production.[6] Williams would later star in the pilot episode of the series, "The Tale of the Frog Prince".

Episodes

Every episode opens with Shelley Duvall introducing herself and welcoming the viewer to the show, after which she would provide a brief synopsis of the story that would follow. All the episodes feature live-action twist adaptations of fairy tales in costume by many well-known actors and are directed by such diverse directors as Tim Burton and Francis Ford Coppola. Though Duvall introduced each show, she has starring roles in only two of the episodes: "Rumpelstiltskin" (airing in 1982) and "Rapunzel" (airing in 1983). Many episodes feature backdrops and settings inspired by specific artists and children's book illustrators,[7] including Maxfield Parrish ("The Frog Prince"), Norman Rockwell ("Goldilocks and the Three Bears"), Arthur Rackham ("Hansel and Gretel"), Edmund Dulac ("The Nightingale"), Gustav Klimt ("Rapunzel"), N.C. Wyeth ("Rumpelstiltskin", "Snow White"), Kay Nielsen ("Sleeping Beauty"), and George Cruikshank ("Thumbelina"), as well as filmmakers, such as Jean Cocteau ("Beauty and the Beast").

Home video and DVD releases

Faerie Tale Theatre was released on VHS, Betamax, CED and Laserdisc in the 1980s through mid 1990s, by Playhouse Video, CBS/Fox, and later Razz Ma Tazz Entertainment/Cabin Fever Entertainment.

Starmaker II held the rights to the series from 2004 to 2006, and at first released 26 episodes as individual DVDs.[8] This was followed by a double-sided 4-disc box set and then a 6-disc box set, each version containing the same 26 episodes. The "Greatest Moments" episode was not included in this release.

After 2006, Koch Vision held the series' distribution rights, and in November 2006 licensed the rights worldwide (excluding DVDs in North America) to the British company 3DD Entertainment.[9] [10] A new remastered 7-disc box set, including the lost "Greatest Moments" episode, was released by Koch Vision on September 2, 2008.[11] In 2009, Koch Vision released the episodes by theme on six DVD compilations: *Tales from the Brothers Grimm*, *Funny Tales*, *Tales from Hans Christian Andersen*, *Princess Tales*, *Magical Tales*, and *Bedtime Tales*.[12]

When released on DVD by Starmaker II and Koch Vision, the following scenes were cut from the series:

- "Goldilocks and the Three Bears": Papa Bear and Mama Bear trying to fix Cubby Bear's chair; the Charades scene is shortened.
- "The Pied Piper of Hamelin": Julius Caesar Rat's monologue.
- "Rumpelstiltskin": the Miller's daughter singing with the animals in the forest (this scene was also unavailable on the VHS releases).

References

[1] Bianculli, David (September 26, 1995). "Cable Viewers Suffer Unkindest Cuts Of All" (http://www.nydailynews.com/archives/entertainment/1995/09/26/1995-09-26_cable_viewers_suffer_unkinde.html). *New York Daily News*. .

[2] Nanwalt, Sasha (August 6, 1989). "TELEVISION; Shelley Duvall Tries Scaring Up A New Audience" (http://www.nytimes.com/1989/08/06/arts/television-shelley-duvall-tries-scaring-up-a-new-audience.html?sec=&spon=&pagewanted=all). *The New York Times*. .

[3] Lomartire, Paul (April 21, 1992). "'BEDTIME STORIES' A FINE SHOW FOR KIDS" (http://nl.newsbank.com/nl-search/we/Archives?p_product=PBPB&p_theme=pbpb&p). *Palm Beach Post*. .

[4] KLRU TV Schedule - Search By Title: List of KLRU programs (http://www.klru.org/schedule/SearchByTitles.php?Letter=F) klru.org

[5] "Program Schedule" (http://web.archive.org/web/20070329062045/http://www.booktelevision.com/Schedule.aspx). BookTelevision. March 29, 2007. Archived from the original (http://www.booktelevision.com/Schedule.aspx) on March 29, 2007. .

[6] Suskin, Steven (2008-09-07). "THE DVD SHELF: "Mad Men" Season One, and Duvall's "Faerie Tale Theatre"" (http://www.playbill.com/news/article/120999.html/pg2). Playbill.com. . Retrieved 2008-09-08.

[7] Stengel, Richard and Denise Worrell (July 25, 1983). "Video: Cinderella Puts On a Show" (http://www.time.com/time/magazine/article/0,9171,954020,00.html). *Time*. .

[8] Bianculli, David (October 28, 2004). "Old Family Treasures Unearthed On DVD" (http://www.nydailynews.com/archives/entertainment/2004/10/28/2004-10-28_old_family_treasures_unearth.html). *New York Daily News*. .

[9] "3DD Takes On New Properties from U.S. Companies" (http://web.archive.org/web/20071219182009/http://www.worldscreen.com/newscurrent.php?filename=3dd110306.htm). *World Screen*. November 3, 2006. Archived from the original (http://www.worldscreen.com/newscurrent.php?filename=3dd110306.htm) on December 19, 2007. .

[10] "International Market: 3DD Entertainment" (http://web.archive.org/web/20080601131451/http://www.cynopsis.com/content/view/927/53/). *Cynopsis: Multi-Cultural & International Edition*. November 6, 2006. Archived from the original (http://www.cynopsis.com/content/view/927/53/) on June 1, 2008. .

[11] "Shelley Duvall's Faerie Tale Theatre: The Complete Collection (2008)" (http://www.amazon.com/Shelley-Duvalls-Faerie-Tale-Theatre/dp/B001AZIRV8/). Amazon.com. . ASIN: B001AZIRV8

[12] Catalog (http://kochvision.com/) kochvision.com

External links

- *Faerie Tale Theatre* (http://www.imdb.com/title/tt0199214/) at the Internet Movie Database
- *Faerie Tale Theatre* (http://www.tv.com/show/3196/summary.html) at TV.com
- *Faerie Tale Theatre* (http://epguides.com/FaerieTaleTheatre) at epguides.com

Second City Television

SCTV ***Second City Television***	
Also known as	***Second City TV*** (1976–1981) ***SCTV Network 90*** (1981–1983) ***SCTV Channel*** (1983–1984)
Genre	Sketch comedy
Created by	No specific creator credit given Developed by Bernard Sahlins, Andrew Alexander (See "creation" section in article)
Starring	John Candy Robin Duke Joe Flaherty Eugene Levy Andrea Martin Rick Moranis Catherine O'Hara Harold Ramis Tony Rosato Martin Short Dave Thomas
Country of origin	Canada
Language(s)	English
No. of seasons	6 (over an 8-year period)
No. of episodes	135
Production	
Running time	30 minutes (1976-1981) 90 minutes (1981-1983) 45 minutes (1983-1984)
Broadcast	
Original channel	Global (1976-1979) CBC (1980-1983) NBC (1981-1983) Superchannel (1983-1984)
Picture format	NTSC (480i)
Original run	September 21, 1976 – July 17, 1984

Second City Television (SCTV) is a Canadian television sketch comedy show offshoot from Toronto's The Second City troupe that ran between 1976 and 1984.

Premise

The basic premise of the show is that "SCTV" is an independent television station in the city of Melonville. Melonville is a nickname for Chatham, Ontario, as Chatham is a major melon producer. Rather than broadcasting the usual TV rerun fare, the station produces a bizarre and humorously incompetent range of cheap local programming. This can range from a soap opera called "The Days of the Week" ("Monday... Tuesday... Wednesday... these are... the days of the week"), to game shows like "Shoot At The Stars" in which celebrities are literally shot at like targets in a shooting gallery, to full blown movie spoofs like "Play it Again, Bob" in which Woody Allen (Rick Moranis) tries to get Bob Hope (Dave Thomas) to star in his next film.

A typical episode of SCTV would present a compendium of programming seen on the station throughout their programming day. This would mean a given episode could contain everything from SCTV news broadcasts to sitcoms, dramas, talk shows, kids shows, and/or game shows. Episodes would also feature a range of SCTV-produced promos and commercials, such as spots for "Al Peck's Used Fruit" or "Shower In A Briefcase", or a PSA which helpfully describes "Seven Signs You May Already Be Dead".

Also seen fairly frequently (particularly in the later episodes) were behind-the-scenes plots focusing on life at the station. These plots often featured Guy Caballero (Joe Flaherty), the cheap, tyrannical owner and president of SCTV, who was in a wheelchair only so that people would "respect" him; weaselly, sweating station manager Maurice "Moe" Green (Harold Ramis), who was succeeded by flamboyant, leopard-skin clad station manager Mrs. Edith Prickley (Andrea Martin); vain variety star Johnny La Rue (John Candy); washed-up entertainers like singer Lola Heatherton (Catherine O'Hara) and "funnyman" Bobby Bittman (Eugene Levy); news anchors Floyd Robertson (Flaherty) and Earl Camembert (Levy), talk-show host Sammy Maudlin (Flaherty), beer-addled brothers Bob and Doug McKenzie (Moranis and Thomas), plus many other characters, all played by the SCTV cast.

The small cast (usually six to eight people at any given time) played a wide variety of other roles on the show, ranging from program hosts to commercial spokespersons for the fictional station. They also mimicked numerous popular celebrities who would appear on SCTV programming; a list of SCTV impersonations appears later in this article.

History

Show creation

There is much dispute as to who created the SCTV series. The show itself bears no "created by" credit, although it gives "developed by" credits to Bernard Sahlins and Andrew Alexander.

What is clear is that in 1976, Andrew Alexander, then the producer of Toronto's Second City stage show, was looking to expand his company into the realm of TV production. He called together the current cast of the stage show (including Candy, Flaherty, Thomas and Levy) to discuss a format for a Second City TV series. Also in attendance at the meeting were Second City vets Del Close, Sheldon Patinkin, and Harold Ramis and business partner Bernard Sahlins.

According to Dave Thomas' account in *SCTV: Behind The Scenes*, various ideas were batted around, then—and here's where meeting attendees remember things differently—either Close or Patinkin came up with the idea of presenting programming from the world's smallest TV station. The cast immediately jumped on the idea as a workable model for presenting virtually unlimited range of characters, sketches, and ideas while still having a central premise that tied everything together. From there, the actual content of the show (the characters, the situations, the Melonville setting, etc.) was all the work of the cast, with contributions from producers Alexander and Sahlins.

Alexander remained as producer/executive producer throughout SCTV's run. Sahlins stayed for the first two seasons as a producer. Patinkin was a first-season writer and *de facto* editor and post-production supervisor. Close had no further involvement with the series.

Seasons 1 & 2: 1976-79

SCTV was initially produced in 1976 at the Toronto studios of the Global Television Network, then a small regional network of stations in Southern Ontario. For the first six episodes, new episodes were seen once a month. For the next seven episodes (beginning in February 1977, and continuing through the spring of 1977) new episodes were seen every second week. Then, in September 1977, Global ordered 13 additional episodes, which were seen once a week from September through December.

These irregularly scheduled 26 episodes (produced over a period of 15 months) were considered one "season" for syndication purposes. All of the original cast (except Harold Ramis) were from the Toronto branch of The Second City theatre improv troupe, and many had previously worked together on *The David Steinberg Show*. Ramis was a Second City vet, but with the Chicago troupe.

The original SCTV cast consisted of John Candy, Joe Flaherty, Eugene Levy, Andrea Martin, Catherine O'Hara, Harold Ramis, and Dave Thomas. All also served as writers on the show, although Martin and O'Hara did not receive writing credits on the earliest episodes. Ramis served as SCTV's original head writer, but only appeared on-screen as a regular during the first season (spread out over two years).

For the second season (1978–79), SCTV became a weekly series on Global, and was seen in syndication throughout Canada and parts of the United States. After episode 3 of the second season, Ramis was no longer in the cast but continued to receive credit as the show's head writer until towards the end of the season.

Season 3: 1980-81

The show was off the air for the 1979-80 season, but returned to production after producer Andrew Alexander and Allarcom-ITV Edmonton owner Charles Allard struck a deal to produce SCTV in ITV Studios in Edmonton, Alberta.

Candy, O'Hara, and Ramis dropped out at this juncture. Added to the cast (and writing room) were Tony Rosato, Robin Duke, and Rick Moranis. Moranis, a friend of Dave Thomas, would be the only cast member not to have come from the ranks of Second City.

This season of the show was seen in Canada on the CBC, and in scattered markets in the US in syndication.

Seasons 4 & 5: 1981-83

In 1981, *SCTV* was picked up as a 90-minute show by NBC as a mid-season replacement (for *The Midnight Special*). Less than two months after Season 3 ended, SCTV was back on the air for Season 4, airing first as *SCTV Network 90*, then as *SCTV Network,* late Friday nights. For this iteration, Rosato and Duke dropped out (ending up as cast members of *Saturday Night Live*), and Candy and O'Hara returned. Because of the rush to generate material for this new 90-minute show, several early season 4 episodes were partially or even entirely made up of repeats of previously taped sketches from Seasons 1 to 3. Rosato, Duke and Ramis are often featured in these repeat sketches, uncredited.

Season 4 (25 episodes) ran on an irregular basis from May 1981 to July 1982. Beginning in January 1982, production of the show moved back to Toronto, where it would stay for the remainder of its run.

Writer/performer Martin Short was added to the cast at the end of Season 4, filming three episodes before O'Hara, Thomas, and Moranis all left. One of those episodes was aired as the Season 4 finale in July 1982; the other two were held for the start of Season 5 (14 episodes), which began in October 1982. For the remaining 12 episodes of Season 5, the cast of Candy, Flaherty, Levy, Martin, and Short were augmented by supporting players John Hemphill and Mary-Charlotte Wilcox, neither of whom were official cast members. Also in Season 5, Ramis and O'Hara each returned for one episode apiece as guest stars.

The last new *SCTV* episode for NBC was seen in March 1983. During its network run, the show garnered 15 Emmy nominations, winning two (both for outstanding writing in a variety or music program). For both Seasons 4 & 5, the show continued to air on the CBC in Canada as a full hour, edited down from the NBC shows.

Season 6: 1983-84

In the fall of 1983, NBC wanted the late Friday night timeslot for the new *Friday Night Videos*. SCTV was offered a slot on early Sunday evenings by NBC, but because they would have had to alter the show's content to appeal to "family" audiences (per a 1975 amendment to the Prime Time Access Rule) as well as face CBS' dominant *60 Minutes,* the producers declined.

Instead, for its final season, the show moved to pay-TV channels Superchannel in Canada and Cinemax in the United States, changing the name slightly to *SCTV Channel*. The running time was now 45 minutes, and new episodes (18 in total) were seen every second week from November 1983 to July 1984. For this final season, the cast consisted solely of Flaherty, Levy, Martin, and Short, although Candy, Thomas, and O'Hara all made guest appearances. Writer/performers Hemphill and Wilcox once again appeared semi-regularly.

Significance

SCTV initially adapted its comedy from existing sketches and improvisation from the Second City stage show. However, especially after expanding to a ninety minute format, *SCTV* quickly pushed the envelope on television sketch comedy. While showing some influence from *Monty Python's Flying Circus* and *Saturday Night Live*, *SCTV* eschewed both the live television format and even filming before a live studio audience. This was mostly to save money, but it also allowed more attention and care to be taken in building a premise and supporting it.

Having a moderately low budget and limited resources, *SCTV* got a reputation for making the most out of what it had, reusing sets and particularly taking advantage of expert makeup and hairstyling. With the luxury of being able to take long periods of time in the makeup chair, elaborate characters could be built. Not being bound by expensive and elaborate prosthetics, cast members and makeup artists worked together to create their characters, referring to the process in interviews as "Improvisation in the chair."

To add to the feel of the show — that of a low-budget local television station that went national — the *SCTV* crew recruited their dance troupe from the writers on the show, led by costumer Juul Haalmeyer. The "Juul Haalmeyer Dancers" were spectacularly maladroit, parodying dance teams on variety shows through their sheer ineptness, and ultimately attracting a cult fandom of their own. (Juul Haalmeyer himself reports still being asked for autographs years later.)

The core premise of the show allowed for tremendous variety in presentation, but unlike *Monty Python*, which often would cut from one sketch to another without any resolution, the *SCTV* format required television style bridges. One technique they used was to build premises into "promos" for shows that would never run (such as "Melvin and Howards", a parody of the movie *Melvin and Howard* which featured Melvin Dummar, Howard Hughes, Howard Cosell, Curly Howard, and Senator Howard Baker on a road trip singing old tunes). Another was to take longer pieces that failed and cut them into promos or trailers. These short elements wound up being the equivalent of "blackout" pieces on the Second City stage. However, the internal logic of the series — that this actually **was** a television station producing low-budget programming — was never lost. SCTV's techniques helped inform and influence later shows, with clear influence on *The State*, the *Upright Citizen's Brigade*, and *The Kids in the Hall*.

Later shows built a tight theme, sometimes acting as a metaparody — such as the Emmy-winning "Moral Majority" episode where advertisers and special interest groups forced significant changes to SCTV's programming; "Zontar", a parody of the Larry Buchanan film *Zontar, The Thing from Venus* which featured an alien race seeking to kidnap SCTV's on-air talent for "a nine-show cycle plus three best-ofs" (which was the actual deal NBC worked out with *SCTV* that season); and an ambitious parody of *The Godfather* featuring an all-out network war over pay television between SCTV, CBS, NBC, ABC, and PBS - the last featured mafia-style hits on the sets of *The Today Show*, *Three's Company*, and *The NFL Today* as well as an extended sequence with guest star John Marley as an off-beat

Leonard Bernstein, spoofing his *Godfather* role of Hollywood mogul Jack Woltz.

In another such episode, a janitorial union went on strike, forcing the station to broadcast the network feed from CBC Television. Parodies of Canadian television ensued, such as *Hinterland Who's Who*, *Front Page Challenge*, and *It's a Fact*, as well as promos for *Monday Night Curling*, hosted by two orange-jacketed sportscasters who were both named Gord, and *Magnum, P.E.I.*, with John Candy as a private detective chasing his quarry through the scenic potato patches of Prince Edward Island. Meanwhile, in behind-the-scenes labour negotiations, Eugene Levy's **Sid Dithers** played the union president, barely able to see over the conference table as he detailed the progress of the strike-talks ("Fifteen minutes for lunsch? Ye can't even blow on your shoop!")

While these shows continued to incorporate the broad range of television parodies the show was known for, they also had a strong narrative thread which set the show apart from other sketch comedy shows of the time.

The show would also have a huge influence on *The Simpsons*. In the DVD commentary for "Homer vs. The Eighteenth Amendment" (in which Dave Thomas guest stars), everyone says how much they loved the show and how influential it was because "it was so funny". Matt Groening goes on to say that he was specifically inspired by the town of Melonville, its own little universe with many recurring characters, and that that was the type of universe he wanted for *The Simpsons*. Both Dave Thomas and Andrea Martin have guest starred on *The Simpsons*.

Mystery Science Theater 3000 (another program that also enjoyed a "cult" following like that of SCTV) at times featured references to the show and its characters; for example, during the film *Space Mutiny*, a character with an outrageous hairdo is said to resemble Martin Short's Ed Grimley and prompted numerous impersonations of said character. In another example, near the end of the film *Danger! Death Ray* a character throws a watch out of a window, prompting Crow T. Robot to cry "SCTV is on the air!"

The entire troupe was given a star on Canada's Walk of Fame in 2002. John Candy, Martin Short, Eugene Levy, and Catherine O'Hara also have individual stars.

Features

SCTV parody shows included *Natalie Wingneck*, a *Tarzan*-style spoof in which Martin played a girl raised by geese after her family died in a plane crash. A parody of the popular western drama *The Life and Times of Grizzly Adams* — retitled *Grizzly Abrams* — depicted the burly wilderness hero as the owner of a wild tortoise which took weeks to lead police to the skeletal remains of its master, trapped beneath a fallen log.

Battle of the PBS Stars was a parody of ABC television's *Battle of the Network Stars* athletic competitions that pit performers against each other in running and swimming events. SCTV's version featured a team of public television stars captained by William F. Buckley (played by Flaherty) vs. a team led by Carl Sagan (played by Thomas), with confrontations that included Fred Rogers of *Mister Rogers's Neighborhood* fame (played by Short) in a boxing match with chef Julia Child (played by Candy).

The People's Global Golden Choice Awards sent up the countless show-biz shows in which the industry honors itself. Presenters include stars ranging from Elizabeth Taylor (played by O'Hara) to Jack Klugman (Flaherty) reading off the nominees in each category, with SCTV's chief Guy Caballero secretly having conspired to guarantee that every award goes to his own network's stars.

The TV station concept provided *SCTV* the ability to lampoon virtually any television genre, as well as commercials, promos, network IDs, and more. Some of the most memorable sketches involved parodies of low-budget late-night ads, like *Al Peck's Used Fruit* (they enticed viewers to visit by offering free tickets to *Circus Lupus*, the Circus of the Wolves; mocked-up photos depicted wolves forming a pyramid and jumping through flaming hoops). Equally memorable were the faux-inept ads for local businesses like *Phil's Nails*, *Chet Vet the Dead Pet Remover*, and *Tex and Edna Boil's Organ Emporium*.

Impersonations

Impersonations were also an integral part of the comedy, with almost every cast member playing multiple roles as well-known personalities. Some impressions included:

Star	Impersonations
John Candy	Orson Welles Julia Child Luciano Pavarotti Divine Curly Howard Richard Burton Tip O'Neill Jimmy the Greek Hervé Villechaize Alfred Hitchcock
Robin Duke	Shelley Winters Imogene Coca Linda Ronstadt
Joe Flaherty	Gregory Peck Gavin MacLeod Donald Sutherland Peter O'Toole Kirk Douglas Charlton Heston Henry Fonda Bing Crosby William F. Buckley, Jr. Geraldo Rivera Charles Bronson Alan Alda Gene Siskel Richard Nixon Jack Klugman Slim Whitman Larry Fine Salvador Dali
Eugene Levy	Ricardo Montalban Henry Kissinger Judd Hirsch Bud Abbott John Charles Daly Floyd Lawson Milton Berle Neil Sedaka Howard Cosell Ralph Young Perry Como Gene Shalit

Andrea Martin	Barbra Streisand Liza Minnelli Linda Lavin Joni Mitchell Joyce DeWitt Indira Gandhi Connie Francis Bernadette Peters Ethel Merman Karen Black Patti Duke Marsha Mason Brenda Vaccaro Charo Mother Teresa Sophia Loren
Rick Moranis	Merv Griffin Woody Allen Gordon Lightfoot Ringo Starr Dick Cavett Phil Silvers George Carlin Brent Musburger Michael McDonald Al Waxman David Brinkley James Stewart Elton John Richard Dreyfuss Neil Young
Catherine O'Hara	Katharine Hepburn Morgan Fairchild Jane Fonda Dorothy Killgallen Mary Tyler Moore Elizabeth Taylor Maggie Smith Lucille Ball Tammy Faye Bakker Brooke Shields
Tony Rosato	Lou Costello Ella Fitzgerald Lou Ferrigno Edward Asner Tony Orlando

Martin Short	Jerry Lewis Pierre Elliott Trudeau Dustin Hoffman David Steinberg Robin Williams Fred Rogers Kenneth D. Taylor Paul Anka Hoyt Pollard Jamie Farr Scott Baio Deney Terrio Howie Mandel Howie Meeker Tony Sandler Tom Hayden Gore Vidal Brian Linehan
Dave Thomas	Bob Hope Richard Harris DeForest Kelly Liberace Bennett Cerf Michael Caine G. Gordon Liddy Roger Ebert Neil Simon Lee Iacocca Carl Sagan John Ritter Walter Cronkite Fred Travalena

Sketches and characters

Popular sketches and recurring characters include:

- *Mailbag*, *SCTV*'s take on a vox populi segment where near-apoplectic host **Bill Needle** (Thomas) would answer viewer mail. The show's length was continually cut, however, until Needle was down to mere seconds of airtime.
- *Farm Film Report* aka *Farm Film Celebrity Blow-Up*: Two hicks named **Big Jim McBob** (Flaherty) and **Billy Sol Hurok** (Candy) (a spoof of Billie Sol Estes and Sol Hurok) interview celebrities and ultimately encourage them to blow up (creating the catch-phrase "blow'd up good, blow'd up *real* good!"). Exploding guests included Dustin Hoffman, David Steinberg (both played by Short), Bernadette Peters (Martin), Meryl Streep (O'Hara), and a lispy Neil Sedaka (Levy).
- *Polynesiantown*: a parody of modern-day film noir. In its attempt to emulate the movie *Chinatown*, this extended one-shot sketch ended with a crane shot that pushed the show so over budget that the sketch's producers got in trouble with the network. The show's writers incorporated this behind-the-scenes drama into the show's long-term continuity, sending the career of John Candy's fictional actor/producer/superstar **Johnny LaRue** into a tailspin as a result of this budget mishap.
- *The Sammy Maudlin Show*: Flaherty is the afro-coiffed, knee-slapping, overly-effusive host welcoming a panel of "stars" who did nothing but heap lavish praise on each other and applaud their pointless profundities. Originally a parody of Sammy Davis, Jr.'s short-lived gab-fest, *Maudlin* (the word means overly sentimental, treacly) evolved into a late-night universe all its own. Levy is "a comic in all seriousness" as egomaniacal funnyman **Bobby Bittman**, with his repeated catch-phrase "how are ya?" Bittman's younger brother **Skip Bittman**, played by

Moranis, eventually appeared on *Maudlin* as well, with disastrous results. Martin skewered Liza Minnelli and Lorna Luft with "real terrific" combo-character **Lorna Minnelli** (in one wickedly funny skit, she accepts an award telling the audience "If my mother were here tonight" and is then interrupted by a drunken Johnny LaRue who finishes, "you wouldn't be"); O'Hara inhabited pill-popping boozer **Lola Heatherton**, a Joey Heatherton-Lola Falana amalgam who greeted fans with her trademark shriek, *"I love you! I wanna bear your children!"*; John Candy portrayed constantly-chuckling Ed McMahon-style sidekick/sycophant **William B. Williams**, who often wound up kneeling on the floor as guests came out and the couch filled up. The *Maudlin* regulars would later appear together in the Rat Pack movie parody *Maudlin's Eleven*.

- *The Days of the Week* was a soap-opera spoof, with the continuing saga of terminally ill rock star Clay Collins (Moranis) trying to marry slutty fiancee Sue Ellen (O'Hara) in the few days left to him by his tactless doctor Sabian (Levy). A second plot hatched by corrupt doctor Wainwright (Candy) has small-time criminal Rocco (Flaherty) con the wealthy Violet McKay (O'Hara) into accepting him as her long-lost son Billy, even though Rocco is so inept that he mistakes Mojo the maid (Martin) for his mother. A third story has the suave swindler Harrington (Thomas) try to seduce the suicidally depressed May Madlock (Martin) out of the land she owns.
- *Mel's Rock Pile* was a knockoff of the Citytv dance show *Boogie* and closely resembled *American Bandstand.* Hosted by **"Rockin' Mel" Slirrup** (Levy), a nervous, bespectacled nerd who played lame pop songs for surly in-studio teen guests. One memorable episode of *Mel's Rock Pile* featured an appearance by Sex Pistols-type band *The Queen Haters*, featuring the entire Short-era cast in perfect '80s punk-band mode. Another featured Thomas as Richard Harris, performing *MacArthur Park* live in the studio—complete with lengthy instrumental breaks. This caused an uncomfortable Mel to try and fill the otherwise "dead" air. Harris dances endlessly in total agony during the elongated orchestral stretches, while the show moves on to other skits. The song finally ends when an audience member hurls a brick at his chest.
- Martin Short's **Jackie Rogers, Jr.** was an earnestly smarmy albino Las Vegas headliner with a grating, lisping laugh in a manner similar to Sammy Davis, Jr. Rogers was partial to sequined jumpsuits, Jack Jones-style song standards, and "eligible ladies". Later, Rogers would run for political office but drop out of the race when he realizes it's cramping his show-biz lifestyle.
- Short's somewhat-unclassifiable uber-nerd **Ed Grimley** (later featured on *Saturday Night Live* when Short became a regular) was an SCTV fixture, appearing on numerous assorted shows, commercials, promos, and "behind-the-scenes" dramas. Grimley had an obsession for the game show Wheel of Fortune and host Pat Sajak, both of which "made him quite mental, I must say," as he frequently insisted.
- *Half-Wits* and *High-Q* were parodies of quiz shows *College Bowl* and *Reach For The Top* hosted by a highly-irritable Alex Trebek approximation named **Alex Trebel** (Levy), a thinly-veiled riff on the real-life *Jeopardy!* host.
- *The 5 Neat Guys*, an absurdly clean-cut, '50s style vocal group (á la The Four Freshmen), were portrayed by Candy, Flaherty (as the drunk one), Levy, Moranis, and Thomas. The "5" sang songs like "I've Got a Hickey on My Shoulder", "Pimples and Pockmarks" and other memorable tunes. Several of their songs contrasted with their squeaky-clean image, however, such as "She Does It", "Patsy Has the Largest Breasts In Town", and "Who Brought the Egg Salad Sandwiches".
- **Connie Franklin**, a caricature of Connie Francis portrayed by Andrea Martin. Franklin appeared on the Sammy Maudlin Show but also appeared in a parody of mail-order record commercials. Franklin's songs are universally depressing; one contains the lyrics, "I'm losing my hearing, I've lost sight in one eye. I'm sorry, I didn't hear you, did you really say goodbye?"
- Another Martin Short character, talk-show host **Brock Linehan** was a parody of real-life Canadian interviewer, the late **Brian Linehan**. Linehan was famous for his overpreparation, which Short satirized by going in the opposite direction: on SCTV's version of the Linehan show, called *Stars in One*, all the research compiled about any particular episode's guest was totally and completely wrong, making for some unhappy guests and one frustrated, uneasy host.

- **Harry, the Guy with the Snake on his Face** (Candy). Harry ran Melonville's adult book and X-rated video stores.
- "Video deejay" **Gerry Todd** (Moranis) hosted an all-night "televised-radio" type of video show. Moranis' turtleneck-sporting, smooth-talking radio-personality parody was perfectly pitched—complete with casually-pronounced "vuddeeo"--and eerily presaged the first group of MTV VJs.
- **Mayor Tommy Shanks** (Candy) is Melonville's "easygoing" (corrupt) mayor who is prone to sudden fits of rage and physical violence, yet gives regular fireside chats on SCTV while feeding treats to a stuffed dog that sits motionless by his side. Throwing out one non-sequitur after another, Shanks manages to convey absolutely nothing of relevance during his broadcasts. Eventually, Shanks succumbs to mental illness and is institutionalized. While still in the institution, he runs for re-election with the campaign slogan "Get me outta here!" and wins by a landslide. Some sources erroneously claim the character was named after Edmonton jazz musician (and future Senator) Tommy Banks. However the character pre-dates SCTV's move to Edmonton by two years (first being referenced in the Toronto-shot episode 2.8 "The Mirthmakers/Happy Endings", aired 4 November 1978) and furthermore does not resemble Banks in any way.
- *SCTV News* (later *Nightline Melonville*), anchored by Flaherty as mostly professional (but alcoholic) newscaster **Floyd Robertson** and Levy as geeky, clueless **Earl Camembert**, a model of oblivious self-importance. The members of the SCTV news-team were named after Canadian news anchors Lloyd Robertson and Earl Cameron respectively, but otherwise bore no resemblance to their real-life counterparts (Camembert was in fact based on American newsman Irv Weinstein). Unlike Saturday Night Live's similar news parody *Weekend Update*, which typically uses actual news headlines as set-ups for more satirical humour, *SCTV News* used more absurdist humor, with its news stories often focusing on events happening within the Melonville continuity. Another source of humour for this segment was the contrast between the hapless Camembert (whose name is inexpicably pronounced "Canenbare") and the more respected Robertson, who usually ended up playing straight man to Camembert's antics. A running gag involved the news team's tendency to give the hard news items to Robertson (such as the latest earthquake to hit the tiny nation of Togoland) and the trivial or poorly-prepared stories to his co-anchor (such as a fire at a doily factory).
- *Monster Chiller Horror Theatre*: This fright-film showcase featured laughably non-frightening z-movies like *Dr. Tongue's 3-D House of Stewardesses* and *Tip O'Neill's 3-D House of Representatives*. Dr. Tongue was played by Candy and *Monster Chiller Horror Theatre* was hosted by Flaherty's character **Count Floyd** -- a vampire who mysteriously howled like a wolf. Count Floyd was revealed in a later episode to be *SCTV News* anchorman Floyd Robertson working a second job. This was a comic homage to the early days of television, where the kiddie show hosts at smaller TV stations were often actually members of the local news staff in costume.
- **The Shmenge Brothers** (Candy and Levy) and their polka band, **The Happy Wanderers**, based upon Czechoslovakian-born Edmonton-based polka cable show host *Gaby Haas*. Like Bob and Doug McKenzie, the Shmenges were breakout characters and their popularity resulted in the HBO special *The Last Polka* (a parody of Martin Scorsese's *The Last Waltz*). (Candy would go on to play another polka clarinetist in *Home Alone*, which also starred O'Hara). In one episode, the Shmenges performed a memorable tribute to composer John Williams. The band's name is based on the Friedrich-Wilhelm Möller song "The Happy Wanderer," which was frequently performed by polka artists.
- **Harvey K-Tel**, portrayed by Thomas. K-Tel, a parody of rapid-fire mail-order commercial announcers, spoke in a rapid patter both on and off the air. The character's name is derived both from the Canadian mail-order commercial company K-tel and the actor Harvey Keitel.
- The famous CCCP1-Russian television episode in which SCTV is taken over by Soviet programming. At first, nothing seems out of the ordinary at the station: on the air, Levy plays Perry Como in a promo for *Still Alive*, a TV-special in which Como's trademark relaxed style is taken to ludicrous extremes. The nearly-comatose Como sings one song while propped up against a dancer, another swaddled in bed with the covers pulled up to his chin, and performs a third number sprawled face-down and almost-motionless on the floor, mic lying next to his mouth,

one finger moving to the beat. But SCTV is suddenly knocked off the air, replaced by an illegal signal from the Soviet television network. Throughout, the old Union of Soviet Socialist Republics, which is abbreviated USSR in English but CCCP in Russian (the Cyrillic for "SSSR"), is referred to as "three-C-P-one". From there, all the "shows" are Russian-themed spoofs: *Tibor's Tractor*, a situation comedy about a talking tractor similar to *My Mother the Car*--only with the voice of Nikita Khrushchev; a game-show, *What Fits into Mother Russia?*, which celebrates the USSR's massive size; *Upo-Scrabblenyk*; and *Hey, Giorgy*--"everybody's favourite Cossack"--with the memorable line "Uzbeks drank my battery fluid!", uttered when Moranis's Lada won't start outside an alehouse. (Popping the hood reveals the old-style battery's six cells sporting bendy straws.) The CCCP1 episode was shot with "new Russian mini-cam," a massive electronic device the size of a small car that had to be dragged around by three technicians.

- A *Jazz Singer* parody which reversed the story by having musical guest Al Jarreau play a popular jazz singer who wants to become a cantor (hazzan). His father is a disapproving pop-music impresario played by Levy's befuddled **Sid Dithers**. Hasidic Dithers, four feet tall and cross-eyed behind Coke-bottle glasses, spoke with a thick early vaudeville-style Yiddish accent ("San Fransishky? So how did you came: did you drove, or did you flew?"). The payoff of this parody made for a classic SCTV moment: Jarreau has become a synagogue cantor, fulfilling his dream against his father's wishes, and he wonders if his father will ever speak to him again – until, during the service, he is interrupted by a disco-clad Dithers standing in the doorway in dancing shoes, spangled jacket, and corn-rowed hair.
- *Tex & Edna's Organ Emporium* a series of parodies of local car dealer TV ads with Tex and Edna (Thomas and Martin) imploring viewers to "Come on down!" to buy their organs.
- *Thursday Night Live*, an atrociously low-budget ripoff of *Fridays* and *Saturday Night Live* created by Guy Caballero who wanted to go hip by making this show, however, it is nothing more than a long collage of uncontrollable laughter and hooting from the rowdy audience and many uncovincing samplings of profanity and corny drug jokes. The guest host was Earl Camembert, who during the monologue, does a bad impression of Steve Martin by going "Well, I beg your pardon!".
- *Towering Inferno*, a satire of the 1974 Irwin Allen film, with each cast member playing multiple roles, trying to escape "the world's thinnest, tallest building" that catches on fire. Martin was at this point the only female cast member, so they were forced to use doubles when two women appeared in the same shot. Candy actually says, "you take the Edith Prickley double and I'll take the other girl and get out of here," deliberately acknowledging the fake as a wink to the audience. There is also a nuclear reactor on the top of the building, with a spinning restaurant above it.

Bob & Doug McKenzie

Ironically, the most popular sketch was intended as throwaway filler. Bob & Doug McKenzie, the dim-witted, beer-chugging brothers in a recurring Canadian-themed sketch called *Great White North*, were initially developed by Rick Moranis and Dave Thomas (**Bob & Doug**, respectively) as a sardonic response to the CBC network's request that the show feature two minutes of "identifiably Canadian content" in every episode.

The characters ultimately became icons of the very Canadian culture they parodied, spinning off albums, a feature film (*Strange Brew*), commercials, and numerous TV and film cameos. Bob and Doug helped to popularize the stereotypical Canadian trait of adding "eh" to the end of sentences, a facet of Canadian life that is often gently ridiculed in American shows featuring Canadian characters. Lines from the sketch, such as "take off, you hoser!", became part of North American popular culture. Thomas later revealed in his 1996 book *SCTV: Behind the Scenes* that the other members of the cast grew bitter at the immense financial and popular success he and Moranis received from their Bob & Doug McKenzie albums, ultimately leading to their departing the show.[1] Joe Flaherty and John Candy accused Thomas of using his position as head writer to increase the visibility of Bob & Doug, even though the original segments were largely unscripted.[2] An *SCTV* episode even poked fun at the duo's popularity. Station manager Guy Caballero declared that they had become SCTV's top celebrities, supplanting Johnny LaRue. This led to the pair being given a Bob & Doug "special" with Tony Bennett as their guest, which wound up being a disaster.[3]

Recently, Moranis and Thomas recreated Bob and Doug in the form of a pair of moose in the animated feature *Brother Bear* from Disney. During Canadian rock band Rush's 2007 *Snakes And Arrows* tour, Moranis and Thomas reprised their Bob and Doug Mackenzie roles in an introductory clip projected on the rear screen for the song "The Larger Bowl".[4] Previously, Rush used Joe Flaherty in his Count Floyd persona to introduce their song "The Weapon" during their 1984 *Grace Under Pressure Tour*. Rush vocalist Geddy Lee sang the chorus on the hit single "Take Off" from the 1982 Mercury Records album *Great White North* by Bob and Doug McKenzie. That chorus was aired in a 2002 episode of *The Simpsons* which depicted the Simpson family visiting Toronto.

Special guests and musical guests

The show's NBC years brought with them a network edict to include musical guests (in part because of their use on *Saturday Night Live*, which NBC executives considered the model for *SCTV*, despite their being very different shows). At first, the *SCTV* cast, writers, and producers resisted special guests, on the theory that famous people wouldn't just "drop into" the Melonville studios. However, they soon discovered that by actually working these guests into different shows-within-shows, they could keep the premise going while also giving guest stars something more to do than show up and sing a song.

As a result, Dr. John became a featured player in the movie "Polynesiantown", John Mellencamp (no longer known as Johnny Cougar) was Mister Hyde to Ed Grimley's Doctor Jekyll in "The Nutty Lab Assistant", Natalie Cole was made into a zombie by a cabbage in "Zontar", and the Boomtown Rats were both blown up on "Farm Film Celebrity Blow Up" and starred in the *To Sir, with Love* parody "Teacher's Pet". It reached a point where Hall & Oates appeared on a "Sammy Maudlin Show" segment, promoting a new film called "Chariots of Eggs", which was a parody of both *Chariots of Fire* and *Personal Best*, only to show scenes from the faux movie as clips. Canadian singer-songwriter Ian Thomas (the real-life brother of cast member Dave Thomas) was the "topic" on a "Great White North" sketch. Carl Perkins, Jimmy Buffett, Joe Walsh, The Tubes, and Plasmatics also appeared on the "Fishin' Musician".

This, along with *SCTV*'s cult status, led to the show's celebrity fans clamoring to appear. Later on, Tony Bennett credited his appearance on Bob and Doug McKenzie's variety-show debacle "The Great White North Palace" as triggering a significant career comeback. Sketch comedy giant Carol Burnett did an ad for the show in which an alarm clock goes off next to her bed, she rises up suddenly and advises those who couldn't stay up late enough (the NBC version aired from 12:30 to 2 a.m.) to go to bed, get some sleep, then wake up to watch the show. Burnett later briefly appeared in a climactic "courtroom" episode of "The Days of the Week".

Former Chicago *Second City* player, *Saturday Night Live* cast member and film actor Bill Murray also guest-starred on a "Days of the Week" installment, as a photography buff scrambling to make it to the wedding of singer-songwriter Clay Collins (Rick Moranis) and town slut Sue-Ellen Allison (Catherine O'Hara) in time to take pictures of the event. In that same episode, he also played two other roles: Johnny LaRue's biggest fan who is subsequently hired to be LaRue's bodyguard (and who pushes his homemade LaRue t-shirts when possible); and he also appeared as Joe DiMaggio in a commercial for DiMaggio's restaurant, where he promised anyone who could strike him out a free meal (the strikeout challenges then took place in the middle of the dining room, with many patrons injured by speeding baseballs).

Robin Williams guest-starred in a sketch called *Bowery Boys in the Band*, in which his Leo Gorcey-like character tries to hide a gay lifestyle from his Huntz Hall-inspired pal (played by Short). Williams also mimicked actor John Houseman eloquently reading the Melonville telephone book.

Canadian actors including Jayne Eastwood, Monica Parker, and Peter Wildman appeared on the show occasionally as guests. Catherine O'Hara's sister, singer-songwriter Mary Margaret O'Hara, also appeared in a bit part in the episode "Broads Behind Bars". William B. Davis, still a decade away from his signature role as The X-Files'

"Smoking Man" also has a bit role in one 1983 episode.

Laugh track

One other point of contention between *SCTV* and several different networks they were on was the use of laugh tracks. As *SCTV* wasn't a live show, it paced its comedy accordingly, and several pieces were more outré than standard network fare. The use of a laugh track often stepped clumsily on the punchlines as a result, and there are some reports that the laugh track editor admitted to not getting *SCTV*'s humour and just threw laughs in wherever they would fit.

The laugh track used in early episodes was actually recorded using audience reactions during live performances in the Second City theatre.

Syndication and music rights

In 1984, after production on the series finally ended, the *Second City Television* syndicated half-hour episodes and *SCTV Network* 90-minute episodes were re-edited into half-hour shows for a revised syndicated package, which consisted of 156 re-edited half-hours. In 1990, a separate package of 26 half-hours (edited from the pay-TV *SCTV Channel* episodes) aired on The Comedy Channel (and later Comedy Central) in the United States. Like the original syndicated series, the US and Canadian versions of the 1984 package differed, with the Canadian half-hours a couple of minutes longer; the running order of episodes also differed between the two countries. By the late 1990s, the re-edited *SCTV Channel* episodes were added to the regular SCTV syndicated package; three additional half-hours (all from the 1980-1981 season) were restored to the package, knocking the episode count up to 185 half-hours.

The syndicated series re-aired on NBC in from 1999 through early 2001, in the 185 half-hour format. This shows were presented under the banner of *Later presents SCTV* -- "Later" was a recently cancelled Cynthia Garrett-hosted talk show, which SCTV essentially replaced. For some reason, NBC still wanted to keep the "Later" brand alive, so the shows opened with a unique introduction featuring the *Later* logo below the *SCTV* logo, and a brief voice-over by host Rita Sever. The repeats ended in 2001 with the launch of *Last Call with Carson Daly*.

For years, *SCTV* was unavailable on video tape (apart from one compilation, *The Best of John Candy on SCTV*), or in any form except these re-edited half hour programs. Originally, the producers and editors putting the original shows together never bothered to get clearance to use copyrighted music — for example, the "Fishin' Musician" show ended with Bing Crosby singing "Gone Fishin'", even though *SCTV* never obtained the clearance rights to use copyrighted music recordings.

It has been sometimes believed that the sole reason for SCTV not appearing on DVD before, is that the series did not originally get clearance for the numerous music cues used throughout the six seasons that SCTV was produced. Although the producers did neglect to clear the music for SCTV during production, this has no legal bearing on the use of the music for the DVD releases. However, this could indeed have had a detrimental effect on how smoothly those rights were granted for the use of music on the DVD releases. The ease of obtaining music clearance rights for a given music cue may depend upon the context in which that music cue is used, as well as the willingness of the copyright holder to allow the use of their music in any shape or form.

The shows couldn't be reproduced on DVD or video tape until after the laborious rights issues were resolved and clearances were received. In some cases (as with the aforementioned Crosby song) clearances couldn't be secured after the fact and new music had to be edited in its place for the 2005 DVD releases of the 90-minute shows. In a few cases where the music is intrinsic to the premise of the sketch (such as the sketches "Stairways to Heaven", "The Canadian National Anthem" and "Gordon Lightfoot Sings Every Song Ever Written") and rights could not be obtained, sketches have been dropped from the DVDs.

DVD releases

Shout! Factory has released SCTV on DVD in Region 1. To date, all episodes from Season 4 & 5 (which aired on NBC) have been released in 4 Volumes and a Best-of DVD has been released which features episodes from Seasons 2 & 3. It is not known if the remaining episodes (Seasons 1-3,6) will be released at some point.

DVD Name	# of Ep	Release Date	Additional Information
SCTV- Vol 1: Network 90	9	June 8, 2004	
SCTV- Vol 2	9	October 19, 2004	
SCTV- Vol 3	9	March 1, 2005	
SCTV- Vol 4	12	September 13, 2005	

Other Releases

- *Christmas With SCTV*: **Released October 4, 2005**
- *SCTV- Best of The Early Years*: **Released October 24, 2006**

2008 on-stage reunion

On May 5 & 6, 2008 most of the cast reunited for a charity event 'The Benefit of Laughter' at the Second City Theatre in Toronto.[5] Eugene Levy, Martin Short, Andrea Martin, Catherine O'Hara, and Joe Flaherty took part. The event was a fundraiser for The Alumni Fund, which helps support former Second City cast and crew members facing health or financial difficulties. There is no word yet if the performances will be released.

The initial press release for this event also included Dave Thomas, but he reportedly bowed out due to illness.

SCTV Golden Classics 2010

To honor the 50th anniversary of The Second City, ***SCTV Golden Classics*** aired nationwide on public television stations beginning March 2010.[6] It will feature some memorable skits from the comedy television series.

References

[1] Thomas, Dave. *SCTV: Behind the Scenes*. New York: McClelland & Stewart, 1996.

[2] "Take off, eh?" Review of *Two-Four Anniversary* special at www.macleans.ca (http://www.macleans.ca/culture/entertainment/article.jsp?content=20070507_105097_105097)

[3] Plume, Kenneth. "Interview with Dave Thomas (Part 1 of 5)" at movies.img.com, February 10, 2000.

[4] "Rush out for latest Rush Concert DVD Snakes & Arrows." Review at www.epinions.com on December 5, 2008.

[5] Ouzounian, Richard (May 6, 2008). "All the hits, as good as we remember" (http://www.thestar.com/entertainment/article/421833). *The Star* (Toronto). . Retrieved May 23, 2010.

[6] "SCTV Golden Classics | WLIW21 Productions" (http://www.wliw.org/productions/comedy/sctv-golden-classics/558). Wliw.org. 1959-12-16. . Retrieved 2011-03-02.

Further reading

- Thomas, Mike (2009), *The Second City unscripted : revolution and revelation at the world-famous comedy theater* (http://books.google.ca/books?id=TyGOO2JjU1sC&lpg=PA100&dq=Second City Television&pg=PR1#v=onepage&q&f=true), Villard, ISBN 9780345514226
- Robbins, Jeff (2007), *Second city television: a history and episode guide* (http://books.google.ca/books?id=FPFX6daYP0MC&lpg=PP1&dq=Second City Television&pg=PP1#v=onepage&q&f=true), McFarland & Co, ISBN 9780786431915

External links

- The Second City (http://www.secondcity.com/tvfilm/)
- SCTV.ORG (http://sctv.org/)
- SCTV Guide (http://www.sctvguide.ca/)

A Wish for Wings That Work

A Wish for Wings That Work	
Book front	
Author(s)	Berkeley Breathed
Illustrator	Berkeley Breathed
Cover artist	Berkeley Breathed
Country	United States
Language	English
Genre(s)	Children's
Publisher	Little Brown & Co
Publication date	1991
Pages	32
ISBN	0316106917

A Wish for Wings That Work: An Opus Christmas Story was a children's book by Berkeley Breathed that was published in 1991. It was made into an animated television special that same year. The story is 30 pages long, and contains large color pictures every other page, and small black and white ones over the writing.

Plot

The story centers on Opus the Penguin (who was at the time one of the main characters in Breathed's comic strip *Outland*). Opus is downhearted because as a penguin, he cannot fly. He orders a machine and assembles it; when it comes time to test the machine by jumping off a three mile high cliff, Opus decides to do something less dangerous, and goes home to make anchovy Christmas cookies. He does not give up on his dream though, and makes a Christmas wish to Santa Claus for "wings that will go!". On Christmas Eve, Santa is making his usual delivery when he loses his reindeer and crashes into the lake. Opus jumps in and uses his natural swimming skills to pull Santa out. To thank Opus for his daring rescue, a group of ducks pick him up and take him flying through the air.

TV special

A Wish for Wings that Work	
DVD cover	
Directed by	Skip Jones
Produced by	Peggy Regan
Written by	Berkeley Breathed
Starring	Michael Bell Joe Alaskey John Byner Tress MacNeille Alexaundria Simmons Andrew Hill Newman Frank Welker Robin Williams Dustin Hoffman
Music by	Thomas Chase Steve Rucker
Editing by	Larry C. Cowan
Distributed by	Amblin Television Universal Television
Release date(s)	December 13, 1991
Country	United States
Language	English

On December 13, 1991, an animated special was released. It was directed by Skip Jones and was produced by Steven Spielberg's Amblimation animation studio for Universal Cartoon Studios. It was then given a DVD release for the first time on November 6, 2007.

Critical reception

Lisa Horowitz of *Variety* gave the special a positive review, saying that it "crams a lot of action and intelligence into its half-hour". She also praised the animation and vocal performances.[1]

Breathed, who was credited as the writer and executive producer of the special, was disappointed with the overall results. His displeasure with the special was shown in a 2003 Washington Post interview where someone asked where a copy of the special can be found on VHS or DVD. Breathed's response was:

Hopefully in the rubbish pail. We can do better than that and we will with an eventual Opus film.. but I'm glad you enjoyed it. I presume your family was on speed when they watched it. I would imagine it helps.

In a later 2007 interview, Breathed claims that the reason he dislikes the special was simply "unspectacular ratings" and his humour "wasn't meant for television, even if it was done right." Another reason was his "lack of writing experience" and the director was way over his head. He stated that he wanted Sterling Holloway to provide the voice for Opus.

References

[1] *Variety Television Reviews 1991-1992* (http://books.google.com/books?id=RxHbPxbBM1AC&pg=PP261&dq="a+wish+for+wings+that+work"&hl=en&ei=_QT_TKKpHMr9ngeo3qzwCQ&sa=X&oi=book_result&ct=result&resnum=2&ved=0CDUQ6AEwAQ#v=onepage&q="a wish for wings that work"&f=false). Taylor & Francis. ISBN 0-8240-3796-0. .

External links

- Berkeley Breathed's website (http://www.berkeleybreathed.com)
- *A Wish for Wings That Work* (http://www.imdb.com/title/tt0103272/) at the Internet Movie Database
- Washington Post interview, mentions the TV Special (http://www.washingtonpost.com/ac2/wp-dyn?pagename=article&contentId=A47999-2003Nov16&notFound=true)

The Larry Sanders Show

The Larry Sanders Show	
title card	
Format	Comedy[1]
Created by	Dennis Klein Garry Shandling[1]
Starring	Garry Shandling Jeffrey Tambor Rip Torn Penny Johnson Janeane Garofalo Jeremy Piven Wallace Langham[2]
Composer(s)	Frank Fitzpatrick[2]
Country of origin	United States[1]
No. of seasons	6[1]
No. of episodes	89[1] (List of episodes)
Production	
Executive producer(s)	Brad Grey Garry Shandling Paul Simms Peter Tolan Fred Barron[2]
Location(s)	Los Angeles[1]
Cinematography	Peter Smokler Christian Santiago[2]
Camera setup	Multi-camera [3]
Running time	approx. 21-26 minutes[1]
Production company(s)	Brillstein-Grey Entertainment Columbia Pictures Television HBO Partners with Boundaries[1]
Distributor	Sony Pictures Television HBO
Broadcast	
Original channel	HBO[1] BBC2
Original run	August 15, 1992[1] – May 31, 1998[1]
External links	
Website [4]	

The Larry Sanders Show is a satirical television sitcom that aired from August 1992 to May 1998 on the HBO cable television network in the United States.[1] It starred stand-up comedian Garry Shandling as vain, neurotic talk show host Larry Sanders, and centered on the running of his TV show, and the many people behind the scenes. It is notable for featuring celebrities playing exaggerated, self-parodying versions of themselves, and for its character-based humor. Other series which subsequently aired on HBO, such as *Curb Your Enthusiasm*, *Extras*, and *Entourage*, shared these traits.

The series, in which Shandling used his experience as a guest host on *The Tonight Show*, is ranked by various critics and fans as one of the best TV comedies of the 1990s.[5] The series ranked #38 on TV Guide's 50 Greatest TV Shows of All Time, the only HBO comedy to make the list.[6] It was also included in *Time* magazine's list of the "100 Best TV Shows of All Time."[7]

The show won 24 major awards, including three Primetime Emmy Awards, five CableACE Awards, four American Comedy Awards, two British Comedy Awards, a BAFTA Award and a Satellite Award. It also received 86 nominations, including 56 Primetime Emmy Awards nominations, five Directors' Guild of America nominations, six Writers' Guild of America nominations, six American Comedy Awards nominations, three Golden Globe nominations, three Satellite Awards nominations and a GLAAD Award nomination.[3]

Premise

Plot

The show revolves around Larry Sanders (Garry Shandling), host of the fictional late night talk show *The Larry Sanders Show*. It chronicles the daily life of Larry; the show's producer, Arthur "Artie" (Rip Torn); Larry's sidekick, Hank Kingsley (Jeffrey Tambor); and the production staff, as they attempt to produce a successful talk show each night while dealing with celebrities, the network and everything in between. Episodes focus on both the professional and personal lives of the characters, with most shows focusing on Larry Sanders. However, ancillary characters are also prominently featured, among them Jerry, the show's head writer for the first and second seasons; Phil, the head writer beginning in season two; Beverly, Larry's assistant; Darlene, Hank's assistant until the fourth season; Brian, Hank's assistant beginning in the fourth season; Paula, the show's booker until the fifth season; and Mary Lou, the assistant booker and then booker starting in the fifth season.

Different kind of sitcom

The Larry Sanders Show mixed video-taped footage of the fictional broadcast show (which was recorded in front of an actual live studio audience) with "behind the scenes" footage shot on film (for example, Larry talking to his guests during the commercial break or the everyday workings of the office between shows). As such, it featured real-life celebrity guests as they appear on the talk show, but also as they appeared behind the scenes. This gave writers and the celebrity guest the opportunity to send up their media image while making the show more realistic.

Much like Shandling's other work, *The Larry Sanders Show* presented its main character as rather selfish and neurotic (but also likable and charming), and it contained some "meta" touches, such as in the final episode, in which it is established that Garry Shandling exists in the Larry Sanders universe, and is the subject of a complaint by Sean Penn, involving Garry's narcissism and his behavior toward Penn's wife on the set of Hurlyburly.

Catchphrases

The show had two catchphrases used throughout its entire run, the most notable being "Hey now", a phrase Hank repeats in the opening credits of the fictional talk show, and whenever he greets someone. In one episode, Hank says he invented the phrase when he accidentally said it to someone and liked it. In 2007, TV Land ranked "Hey Now" as the 87th Best Television catch phrase. "No flipping" is a phrase Larry uses to go to commercial breaks, encouraging the at-home audience not to use their remotes to flip to another channel. In the series finale, the last thing Larry says on the show is, "You may now flip."

Episodes

Further information: List of The Larry Sanders Show episodes

<table>
<tr><th>Season</th><th>Episodes</th><th>Premiere Date</th><th>End Date</th><th>Timeslot</th></tr>
<tr><td>1</td><td>13</td><td>August 15, 1992</td><td>November 7, 1992</td><td>Saturdays at 10:00 PM</td></tr>
<tr><td>2</td><td>18</td><td>June 2, 1993</td><td>September 29, 1993</td><td rowspan="4">Wednesdays at 10:00 PM</td></tr>
<tr><td>3</td><td>17</td><td>June 22, 1994</td><td>October 12, 1994</td></tr>
<tr><td>4</td><td>17</td><td>July 19, 1995</td><td>November 22, 1995</td></tr>
<tr><td>5</td><td>13</td><td>November 13, 1996</td><td>February 26, 1997</td></tr>
<tr><td>6</td><td>11</td><td>March 15, 1998</td><td>May 31, 1998</td><td>Sundays at 10:00 PM</td></tr>
</table>

Series overview

Season 1

The first season premiered on August 15, 1992 and ended on November 7, 1992, and was an immediate success. For the first season, the show always began with Hank's introduction, and some early episodes of the show began with the opening credits of the fictional talk show, The Larry Sanders Show. In later seasons, the episodes often began without the fictional opening credits.

Some popular episodes of the season are: "The Garden Weasel", in which the network wants Larry to do live commercials during the show; "The Spider Episode", in which Larry is afraid to do a sketch which involves spiders; "The New Producer", in which the network wants to replace Artie; "Out of the Loop", in which Artie doesn't want Larry to know that Jerry and Sally have been having sex on his desk; "The Flirt Episode" in which Larry tries not to flirt with Mimi Rogers; and the season finale "The Hey Now Episode", in which Larry and Artie try to make Hank appreciate the show more.

The season was nominated for eight Emmy Awards, including Outstanding Comedy Series, but lost to *Seinfeld.* However, *The Larry Sanders Show* became the first cable TV series to be nominated for an Emmy Award for Outstanding Comedy Series. Garry Shandling was nominated for Outstanding Lead Actor in a Comedy Series. Rip Torn and Jeffrey Tambor were nominated for Outstanding Supporting Actor in a Comedy Series. Dana Carvey and Carol Burnett were nominated for Outstanding Guest Actor and Guest Actress in a Comedy Series. Dennis Klein and Garry Shandling was nominated for Outstanding Writing in a Comedy Series for the Pilot episode. Garry Shandling, Paul Simms, Peter Tolan and Rosie Shuster were nominated in for the same category for "The Spider Episode".

Season 2

The second season premiered on June 2, 1993 and ended on September 29, 1993.

Jeremy Piven grew tired of playing the character Jerry, head writer of the fictional Larry Sanders Show talk show; because his character was not given much of a background. He left during season two on the episode "Larry's Birthday", where Artie fired him because of his behavior on the show. Jerry later came back on the series finale to say good luck to Larry on his final show. Eventually, Phil replaced Jerry as the show's head writer. The story arc in this season involved Larry beginning a new relationship with his first wife, after he had divorced his second wife.

Some popular episodes of the season were: "Larry's Agent", in which Larry tries to fire his agent; "Broadcast Nudes", in which Hank wants Darlene to pose naked in *Playboy* magazine (Linda Doucett, the actress who played Darlene and also Garry Shandling's girlfriend at the time, would later actually appear in the magazine); "Larry's Birthday" in which Larry doesn't want anyone throwing a party for his birthday; this is also the episode where Jerry (the head writer of the show) is fired; "The Grand Opening", in which Hank tries to promote his new restaurant; "Off Camera", in which Artie has to deal with all the stress that Larry suffers every show; and the season finale "L.A or N.Y?", in which Larry leaves the show and moves to Montana, to protest the network's desire to shift the show's base from L.A. to New York.

The show was nominated for four Emmy Awards, including Outstanding Comedy Series, but lost to *Frasier* and would continue losing to the same series for the rest of its run. Rip Torn was nominated for Outstanding Supporting Actor in a Comedy. Todd Holland was nominated for Outstanding Directing in a Comedy Series for the episode "Life Behind Larry". Garry Shandling, Paul Simms, Drake Sathers, Victor Levin and Maya Forbes where nominated for Outstanding Writing in a Comedy Series for the episode "Larry's Agent".

Season 3

The season premiered on July 22, 1994 and ended on October 12, 1994. The original title credits of the show appear less frequently this season.

Some of the most popular episodes of the season were: "Montana", in which the show gets back on the air after Larry discovers that life in Montana is not to his liking; "You're Having My Baby", in which a woman claims that she is having Larry's baby; "Hank's Night in the Sun", in which Hank fulfills his dreams of becoming guest host for the show; "The Mr. Sharon Stone Show", which Larry dates Sharon Stone and finds out what it means to be the less famous member of a show biz couple; and the season finale "End of the Season" in which Larry gets engaged to Roseanne Barr.

The season was nominated for six Emmy awards, including, for the third year in a row, for Outstanding Comedy Series, but lost to *Frasier* again. Garry Shandling was nominated as Outstanding Lead Actor in a Comedy Series. Rip Torn was nominated for Outstanding Supporting Actor in a Comedy Series. Todd Holland was nominated for Outstanding Directing in a Comedy Series for "Hank's Night in the Sun". Peter Tolan was nominated for Outstanding Writing in a Comedy Series for Hank's Night in the Sun. It received another nomination in that same category, Garry Shandling and Peter Tolan for "The Mr. Sharon Stone Show". This season also received a Golden Globe nomination for Garry Shandling for Best Lead Actor in Musical or Comedy. It received one nomination for the Directors Guild of America Award for Todd Holland for "The Mr. Sharon Stone Show".

Season 4

The season premiered on July 19, 1995 and ended on November 22, 1995.

Darlene, Hank's loyal assistant left the show at the end of season three (the actress who portrayed her was previously in a relationship with Shandling, but the couple had become estranged between seasons). Supposedly Darlene was on vacation, but on the second episode of the fourth season, a letter arrived from Darlene telling Hank she decided to quit as his assistant to follow someone she describes as "a holy man" living in India. Later that same episode, Hank hires Brian, has reservations about him when he learns he is gay, but decides to keep him on when Brian is indirectly instrumental in Larry inviting Hank to join him for a game of poker. Darlene returned along with Jerry on the show's finale to congratulate Larry on his final show.

Some of the most popular episodes of the show included: "Rosanne's Return", in which Larry has to face Roseanne Barr after their engagement broke off; "Arthur After Hours", in which it is revealed what Artie does after the show had an unsuccessful broadcast; "Jeanne's Visit", in which Larry's ex-wife, Jeannie, visits the show, "Hank's Sex Tape", in which Hank becomes incensed when Phil circulates a tape of him having sex; and the season finale "Larry's On Vacation", in which Sandra Bernhard tries to take over the show .

The season was nominated for 12 Emmy awards, including for Outstanding Comedy Series, but lost for the third time in a row to *Frasier*. But this year *The Larry Sanders Show* received its first Emmy award: Rip Torn won Outstanding Supporting Actor in a Comedy Series. Jeffrey Tambor was also nominated in the same category. Garry Shandling was nominated for Outstanding Lead Actor in a Comedy Series, and the show received two nominations for Outstanding Directing in a Comedy Series: One for Todd Holland for "Arthur After Hours", another for Michael Leachmann for "I was a Teenage Lesbian". The show: one for Garry Shandling, Steve Levitan and Maya Forbes for the episode "Roseanne's Return", another for Peter Tolan for the episode "Arthur After Hours", and another for Jon Vitti for "Hank's Sex Tape". Janeane Garofalo was nominated for Outstanding Supporting Actress in Comedy Series. Rosie O'Donnell and Mandy Patinkin were nominated for Outstanding Guest Actress and Guest Actor in Comedy Series. Garry Shandling was nominated for the second time in a row for Best Actor in a Musical or Comedy Series at the Golden Globe Award. This season received four Writers' Guild of America Awards, one for Garry Shandling, Steve Levitan and Maya Forbes for "Roseanne's Return", another for John Riggi for "Hank's New Assistant", another for Peter Tolan for "Arthur After Hours" and finally one for Peter Tolan for "Eight". It received one Director's Guild of America Award nomination for Todd Holland for the episode "Arthur After Hours".

Season 5

The season premiered November 13, 1996 and ended on February 26, 1997. There is only one episode that began with the original credit sequence of the series.

Janeane Garofalo decided to leave due to decreasing screen time for her character Paula, the show's booker. Mary Lou, her assistant, replaced her as booker. In this season the show got a writer named Wendy. Also in this season, Jon Stewart became a frequent guest who threatened to replace Larry on the show.

Some of the most famous episodes of the series were made in this season: "Everybody Loves Larry", in which Larry starts suspecting that David Duchovny has sexual feelings for him;[8] "My Name is Asher Kingsley", in which Hank explores his Jewish roots, much to the crew's dismay; "Ellen, or Isn't She?", in which Larry and Artie try to find if Ellen DeGeneres is really a lesbian; "The New Writer", in which Wendy begins working as a writer for the show, much to Phil's dismay; "The Book", in which Larry is convinced to write an autobiography; "Pain Equals Funny", in which Paula leaves the show; and the season finale, "Larry's New Love", in which Hank is afraid the network is trying to replace him.

The show was nominated for 16 Emmy awards, breaking the record for most nominations for a Comedy Series for an individual Emmy year. The record was maintained for ten years, until 30 Rock received 17 nominations. The show was nominated for the fifth time for Outstanding Comedy Series, and was considered a front-runner for

Primetime Emmy Award, but was defeated again by *Frasier*. Garry Shandling was nominated for Outstanding Lead Actor in a Comedy Series. Rip Torn and Jeffrey Tambor were nominated for Outstanding Supporting Actor in Comedy Series. Janeane Garofalo was nominated for Outstanding Supporting Actress in a Comedy Series. It received two nominations for Outstanding Directing in a Comedy Series; one for Todd Holland for Everybody Loves Larry, another for Alan Myerson for "Ellen, Or Isn't She?". It received three nominations for Outstanding Writing in a Comedy Series; one for Garry Shandling, John Markus and Judd Apatow for the episode "Ellen, Or Isn't She?", another for Peter Tolan for "My Name is Asher Kingsley", another for Jon Vitti for Everybody Loves Larry. David Duchovny and Ellen DeGeneres received nominations for Outstanding Guest Actor and Guest Actress in a Comedy Series. The show was nominated for the Golden Globe Award for Best Series-Musical or Comedy. It received two Directors' Guild of America Award nominations; one for Todd Holland for Everybody Loves Larry, another for Alan Myerson for Ellen, Or Isn't She?. It was also nominated for two Writers' Guild of America Awards; one for Maya Forbes for The Book and another for Garry Shandling, John Markus and Judd Apatow for Ellen, Or Isn't She?.

Season 6

This was the final season of The Larry Sanders Show. It premiered on March 15, 1998 and ended on May 31, 1998. There is only one episode which began with the original show's opening.

Most of the changes of the show occurred offscreen this season. Many of the show's writers left the show (all except Garry Shandling, Peter Tolan, and Judd Apatow), and a new writing staff was hired. Todd Holland, who directed more than 48 episodes of the show, only directed two episodes the sixth season. This season was also markedly less comedic than earlier ones. Sid, the cue card guy at the show, commits suicide on the 8th episode of the season, but this was not considered a huge change, because there were only three episodes left in the series at that point.

Some of the most popular episodes of the season were: "Another List", in which the network threatens to replace Larry with Jon Stewart unless he makes some changes; "The Beginning of the End", in which the show gets a new creative consultant who wants to make big changes in the show; "Adolf Hankler", in which Hank has to play Adolf Hitler, while Larry is on vacation and Jon Stewart guest hosts; "Beverly's Secret", in which Beverly tries to tell the father of her baby she's pregnant; "Putting the 'Gay' Back in Litigation", in which Brian (Hank's assistant) sues Phil and the show for sexual harassment due to Phil's gay jokes; and the series finale: "Flip", in which the cast gets ready for their final broadcast and Larry and Artie deal with Hank and the emotions of the crew.

For its final Emmy year, it received 10 nominations, receiving its final nomination for Outstanding Comedy Series, but it lost once again to *Frasier*, for the fifth year in a row. Nevertheless, it won two Emmys: one for Todd Holland for Outstanding Directing in a Comedy Series for his direction of the final episode of the show, another for Garry Shandling and Peter Tolan for Outstanding Writing in a Comedy Series also for the final episode of the show. Garry Shandling was nominated Outstanding Lead Actor in Comedy Series. Rip Torn and Jeffrey Tambor were nominated for Outstanding Supporting Actor in Comedy Series. It received one nomination for Outstanding Writing for a Comedy Series: Richard Day, Alex Gregory and Peter Huyck for "Putting the 'Gay' Back in Litigation." It received only one nomination for Directors' Guild of America Award: Todd Holland for the episode "Flip."

Series finale

After six years on the air, HBO and Garry Shandling announced that the show would not continue for a seventh season. The series finale aired in May 1998.

Garry Shandling says he was very proud of the show's popularity and was sad it couldn't continue. Members of the cast and crew expressed disappointment and even depression with the end of the show. The finale was written by Garry Shandling and Peter Tolan, and was directed with Todd Holland. They both won Emmy Awards for directing and writing the final episode. The episode was filmed in March 1998, the same month the season premiered, with a running time of 53 minutes (90 with commercials), unlike all the other episodes with a running time of 22 to 28 minutes.

The episode aired 16 days after the finale of *Seinfeld* aired on May 31 and was watched by 2.5 million viewers, which was a significant number for HBO. The finale got very positive reviews from critics, especially in comparison to *Seinfeld*'s season finale. Coincidentally, Jerry Seinfeld appears as himself in the *Larry Sanders* finale.

The episode was nominated for five Emmy Awards and won two: Outstanding Directing in a Comedy Series for Todd Holland and Outstanding Writing in a Comedy Series for Shandling and Tolan.

Cast and characters

Main Characters

The following is a list of cast and characters who have appeared in all or some seasons of the show.[2]

- Garry Shandling as Larry Sanders, the show's primary character.
- Rip Torn as Arthur ("Artie"), the show's producer
- Jeffrey Tambor as Larry's sidekick, Hank Kingsley
- Penny Johnson as Larry's personal assistant, Beverly
- Janeane Garofalo as the show's booker Paula (until the 5th season)
- Mary Lynn Rajskub as the show's booking assistant/booker Mary Lou (from episode 69)
- Jeremy Piven as head writer Jerry (until episode 25)
- Wallace Langham as writer/head writer Phil
- Linda Doucett as Hank's personal assistant Darlene (until episode 48; Doucett was Garry Shandling's live-in girlfriend at the time of production[9])
- Scott Thompson as Hank's personal assistant Brian (from episode 50)
- Megan Gallagher as Larry's second ex-wife Jeannie (episodes 1-13, 53)
- Kathryn Harrold as Larry's first ex-wife Francine (episodes 14-31)
- Deborah May as network executive Melanie Parrish
- Bob Odenkirk as Larry's agent Stevie Grant
- Sarah Silverman as writer Wendy (episodes 70, 74, 75, 87, 88)
- Sid Newman as Sid the cue-card guy (various episodes)

Guests

Most episodes featured celebrity guests who usually played themselves appearing on the fictional *Larry Sanders Show*, and who were often the primary source of conflict between Sanders and his co-workers. The following is a list of some of the celebrity guests who appeared at one time or another on the show.[2]

- Kip Addotta
- Jason Alexander
- Tim Allen
- Jennifer Aniston
- Tom Arnold
- Alec Baldwin
- Roseanne Barr
- T-Bone Burnett
- Brett Butler
- Drew Carey
- Jim Carrey
- Carrot Top
- Dana Carvey
- Dave Chappelle
- Angie Dickinson
- Illeana Douglas
- David Duchovny
- Peter Falk
- Chris Farley
- Farrah Fawcett
- Sally Field
- Phil Hartman
- Colin Hay
- Hugh Hefner
- Chris Isaak
- Jake Johannsen
- Kristen Johnston
- Jonathan Katz
- Barry Levinson
- Richard Lewis
- Warren Littlefield
- Jon Lovitz
- Rob Lowe
- Julianna Margulies
- Norm Macdonald
- Bernadette Peters
- Tom Petty
- Regis Philbin
- Tom Poston
- Victoria Principal
- Charles Nelson Reilly
- Carl Reiner
- Doc Severinsen
- Tom Shales
- Nicollette Sheridan
- Brooke Shields
- Pauly Shore
- Richard Simmons
- Gene Siskel
- Lea Thompson
- Alex Trebek
- Vince Vaughn
- Jimmie Walker
- George Wendt
- Paul Westerberg
- Andy Williams

- Drew Barrymore
- Warren Beatty
- Beck
- Ed Begley, Jr.
- James Belushi
- Richard Belzer
- Sandra Bernhard
- Corbin Bernsen
- Clint Black
- Eric Bogosian
- Michael Bolton
- Terry Bradshaw
- Carol Burnett
- Chevy Chase
- Shawn Colvin
- Tim Conway
- Bob Costas
- Elvis Costello
- Courteney Cox
- Norm Crosby
- Billy Crystal
- Fred De Cordova
- Ellen DeGeneres
- Dana Delany
- Danny DeVito
- Laura Dern
- Harvey Fierstein
- Bridget Fonda
- George Foreman
- Jeff Foxworthy
- Al Franken
- Daisy Fuentes
- Jennie Garth
- Gina Gershon
- Jeff Goldblum
- Bobcat Goldthwait
- Jim Gray
- Rosey Grier
- Mary Gross
- Andy Kindler
- Greg Kinnear
- Larry King
- Bruno Kirby
- Heidi Klum
- Kris Kristofferson
- k.d. lang
- Eriq La Salle
- Wendy Leibman
- Laura Leighton
- Jay Leno
- Sugar Ray Leonard
- David Letterman
- Bill Maher
- Marlee Matlin
- Ed McMahon
- Larry Miller
- Rita Moreno
- Martin Mull
- Kevin Nealon
- Maureen O'Boyle
- Rosie O'Donnell
- Catherine O'Hara
- Ryan O'Neal
- Sarah Jessica Parker
- Sean Penn
- Rob Reiner
- Burt Reynolds
- Michael Richards
- Don Rickles
- John Ritter
- Mimi Rogers
- Wayne Rogers
- Winona Ryder
- Bob Saget
- Pat Sajak
- Adam Sandler
- George Segal
- Jerry Seinfeld
- Tom Snyder
- Suzanne Somers
- David Spade
- John Stamos
- Gloria Steinem
- Howard Stern
- Shadoe Stevens
- Jon Stewart
- Ben Stiller
- Jerry Stiller
- Sting
- Sharon Stone
- Dave Thomas
- Robin Williams
- Henry Winkler
- Steven Wright
- Warren Zevon

Jeff Cesario was the butt of a long running joke, being frequently "bumped" when booked to appear.

In a commentary on the season 1 DVD, Shandling says the guests were invariably happy to parody their media images and generally shared the same sense of humor as himself and the other writers.[10]

Crew

Directors

The show had many directors for its run.[2] The most frequent director was Todd Holland, who directed 52 episodes.[2] Holland is also the only director to have directed episodes in all six seasons.[2] Holland was the head director for season two, three, four and five.[2] Garry Shandling was the primary director for the sixth season, having directed three episodes of the season, while Holland directed only two.[2] Another major director was Ken Kwapis; although he only directed episodes of the first and second season, overall he directed 13 episodes.[2] Kwapis was the head director in the first season.[2] Some directors who directed only one episode in show's run are: Dennis Erdman, Paul Flaherty, John Riggi, Michael Lange, David Mirkin, Melonie Mayron and Judd Apatow.[2] Directors who directed two or more episodes are: Michael Lehmann and Alan Myerson.[2] The show received one Emmy Award for directing. It went to Todd Holland for directing the series finale "Flip".[3]

Writers

More than 40 writers wrote episodes of the show.[2] Garry Shandling and Peter Tolan were the head writers for the entire six-season run.[2] Garry Shandling and Dennis Klein wrote the pilot episode of the show.[2] Shandling wrote 38, while Tolan wrote 23 episodes.[2] Shandling and Tolan received an Emmy Award for writing the series finale "Flip".[3] Other writers on the show were Maya Forbes, Paul Simms, Judd Apatow, John Riggi, Jon Vitti, Chris Thompson, Dennis Klein, Drake Sather, Molly Newman, Lester Lewis, Becky Hartman Edwards and Jeff Cesario.[2]

Reception

Critical reaction

After the show ended, the *New York Post* called it "One of the Greatest Achievements in Television". *LA Weekly* called it "Very Funny". *Time* said it was "The Closest Sitcom Ever Came to Perfect Pitch". *The Washington Post* called the show "Brutally and Blatantly Hilarious" and *USA Today* gave it four stars.

Many critics alike called it one of the greatest television shows of all time. Metacritic gives the show a metascore of 96%, based on 8 reviews. Ken Tucker from *Entertainment Weekly* said "Revisiting former colleagues and friends to find out how they felt about both Larry Sanders and Garry Shandling amounts to a monumental display of ...fearless revelation and humor."[11] Doug Elfman from the *Chicago Sun-Times* said "It is simply the one of the best sitcoms ever". Ivan Morales calls it "the greatest HBO sitcom of all time".

Awards and honors

Award	Category	Recipient
American Comedy Awards 1994	Funniest Supporting Male in a TV Series	Rip Torn
American Comedy Awards 1998	Funniest Male Performance in a TV Series	Garry Shandling
American Comedy Awards 1999	Funniest Male Guest Appearance on a TV Series	David Duchovny
American Comedy Awards 1999	Funniest Female Guest Appearance on a TV Series	Ellen DeGeneres
British Comedy Awards 1997	Best International Comedy Show	
British Comedy Awards 1999	Best International Comedy Show	
BAFTA Awards 1999	Outstanding International Program	Garry Shandling
CableACE Awards 1993	Outstanding Comedy Series	
CableACE Awards 1994	Outstanding Comedy Series	
CableACE Awards 1995	Outstanding Comedy Series	
CableACE Awards 1996	Outstanding Comedy Series	
Emmy Awards 1998	Outstanding Individual Achievement in Writing in a Comedy Series	Peter Tolan & Garry Shandling (for "Flip")
Emmy Awards 1998	Outstanding Individual Achievement in Directing in a Comedy Series	Todd Holland (for "Flip")
Emmy Awards 1996	Outstanding Supporting Actor in a Comedy Series	Rip Torn
Peabody Awards 1998		"Flip"
Peabody Awards 1993		
Rose d'Or 1997	Sitcom	
Satellite Awards 1997	Best Television Series — Comedy or Musical	
Television Critics Association Awards 1997	Outstanding Achievement in Comedy	
Television Critics Association Awards 1998	Outstanding Achievement in Comedy	

BAFTA Television Awards

- 1998: Best International Programme or Series (**won**)

Directors Guild of America (DGA)

- 1994: Outstanding Directing — Comedy Series (Todd Holland for "The Mr. Sharon Stone Show", nominated)
- 1995: Outstanding Directing — Comedy Series (Holland for "Arthur After Hours", nominated)
- 1996: Outstanding Directing — Comedy Series (Holland for "Everybody Loves Larry", nominated)
- 1996: Outstanding Directing — Comedy Series (Alan Myerson for "Ellen, Or Isn't She", nominated)
- 1998: Outstanding Directing — Comedy Series (Holland for "Flip", nominated)

GLAAD Media Awards

- 1996: Outstanding Series — Comedy (nominated)

Golden Globe Awards

- 1994: Best Actor - Musical or Comedy Series (Garry Shandling for playing "Larry Sanders", nominated)
- 1995: Best Actor — Musical or Comedy Series (Shandling, nominated)
- 1996: Best Series - Musical or Comedy (nominated)

Image Awards

- 1997: Outstanding Supporting Actress — Comedy Series (Penny Johnson for playing "Beverly Barnes", nominated)

Satellite Awards

- 1996: Best Actor - Musical or Comedy Series (Garry Shandling for playing "Larry Sanders", nominated)
- 1996: Best Actor — Musical or Comedy Series (Rip Torn for playing "Arthur", nominated)
- 1996: Best Series - Musical or Comedy (**won**)
- 1997: Best Actor — Musical or Comedy Series (Shandling, nominated)
- 1997: Best Series — Musical or Comedy (nominated)

Writers Guild of America (WGA)

- 1995: Best Writing — Episodic Comedy (Garry Shandling for "Roseanne's Return", nominated)
- 1995: Best Writing — Episodic Comedy (John Riggi for "Hank's New Assistant", nominated)
- 1995: Best Writing — Episodic Comedy (Peter Tolan for "Arthur After Hours", nominated)
- 1996: Best Writing — Episodic Comedy (Tolan for "Eight", nominated)
- 1997: Best Writing — Episodic Comedy (Shandling for "Ellen, Or Isn't She?", nominated)
- 1997: Best Writing — Episodic Comedy (Maya Forbes for "The Book", nominated)

Other honors

After the show ended, it came to be considered one of the finest TV shows of all time. The biggest honor it received was a spot on Time magazine's 100 Greatest Shows of All Time. In 2008, Entertainment Weekly ranked *The Larry Sanders Show* the 28th Greatest Show of the past 25 years. Also, TV Guide named it the 38th Greatest Show of All Time, the only HBO comedy to make it to the list.[6] During its six year run, The Larry Sanders Show won 24 awards including three Emmy awards. In 1997, the episode "Everybody Loves Larry" was ranked #39 on TV Guide's 100 Greatest Episodes of All Time.[12]

After the show

After the show ended, many members of the cast and crew enjoyed other success in television or movies. Garry Shandling returned to his roots of stand-up comedy. He also worked as a voice actor in the children's film *Over the Hedge*. Rip Torn guest-starred on *30 Rock*, and was nominated for an Emmy for Outstanding Guest Actor in a Comedy Series for his performance.

Jeremy Piven portrayed Ari Gold in the HBO series *Entourage* and Spence Kovak on the ABC sitcom *Ellen*. He has won three Emmy awards, a Golden Globe Award and several other awards for his performance in the show. Jeffrey Tambor played George Bluth Sr. in the critically acclaimed FOX sitcom, *Arrested Development*. He was nominated for two Emmy awards for Outstanding Supporting Actor in a Comedy Series. He also appeared in the first two Hellboy films. Janeane Garofalo, Penny Johnson and Mary Lynn Rajskub all appeared on the television show *24*. Wallace Langham appeared on *CSI: Crime Scene Investigation*.

Judd Apatow, one of the producers of the show and writers, had a successful career after the show, making many adult comedy films such as *Knocked Up*, *Pineapple Express*, *The 40-Year-Old Virgin*, and *Funny People*. Brad Grey, the show's executive producer, produced the Martin Scorsese film *The Departed* and was the executive producer on *The Sopranos*. Writer Peter Tolan would find success as a Hollywood screenwriter with *Analyze This* and create his own hit TV show with *Rescue Me*.

DVD releases

In 2000, *The Larry Sanders Show: The Best Episodes* was released by Sony Pictures UK in Region 2. The compilation contains the episodes: #302, "Montana" (Robin Williams); #403, "Hank's Sex Tape" (Henry Winkler, Norm Macdonald); #408, "Larry's Big Idea" (Courteney Cox, David Letterman); #411, "I Was a Teenage Lesbian" (Brett Butler). Also included are two first season episodes (#109, "The Guest Host;"#113, "The Talk Show"), as well as the second season episode, "The List" (#203) which was left out of the US cable syndication package offered to Bravo. However, it is available to local affiliates.

On February 26, 2002 Sony Pictures Home Entertainment released the complete first season on DVD in Region 1.

On April 17, 2007, Sony Pictures Home Entertainment released a best-of compilation featuring episodes from all six seasons entitled *Not Just the Best of the Larry Sanders Show*.[13] The 4-disc DVD set features 23 episodes and features 8 hours of bonus material.

On November 2, 2010, Shout! Factory released **The Larry Sanders Show: The Complete Series** on DVD in Region 1 (USA). The 17-disc set features extensive bonus features including featurettes, commentaries & outtakes. Shout! Factory has also released the seasons as stand-alones one by one.

Books

- *Confessions of a Late-night Talk-show Host: The Autobiography of Larry Sanders* (ISBN 067102910X) was written by Garry Shandling in-character as Larry Sanders. It was released October 4, 1999. The book was the topic of season five's episode ten, which was also under the same title.

References

Notes

[1] *The Larry Sanders Show* (http://www.imdb.com/title/tt0103466/) at the Internet Movie Database

[2] "Full cast and crew for "The Larry Sanders Show"" (http://www.imdb.com/title/tt0103466/fullcredits#cast). *IMDb*. . Retrieved December 4, 2010.

[3] "Awards for "The Larry Sanders Show"" (http://www.imdb.com/title/tt0103466/awards). *IMDb*. . Retrieved December 4, 2010.

[4] http://www.sonypictures.com/homevideo/thelarrysanderscollection

[5] Weinraub, Bernard (December 10, 1992). "AT WORK WITH Garry Shandling; Late-Night TV, Ever More Unreal" (http://www.nytimes.com/1992/12/10/garden/at-work-with-garry-shandling-late-night-tv-ever-more-unreal.html?scp=10&sq=larry sanders show&st=Search). *The New York Times*. . Retrieved December 4, 2010. "The reaction to "Larry Sanders", perhaps the most widely acclaimed new comedy on television, has stunned him."

[6] Cosgrove-Mather, Bootie (April 26, 2002). "TV Guide Names Top 50 Shows" (http://www.cbsnews.com/stories/2002/04/26/entertainment/main507388.shtml). *CBS News*. . Retrieved December 4, 2010. "38. The Larry Sanders Show (HBO)"

[7] Poniewozik, James. "The 100 Best TV Shows of All-TIME" (http://www.time.com/time/specials/2007/completelist/0,,1651341,00.html). *Time Magazine*. . Retrieved December 4, 2010.

[8] Mink, Eric. 'SANDERS' AND THE ART OF THE REAL (http://www.nydailynews.com/archives/entertainment/1996/11/12/1996-11-12__sanders__and_the_art_of_the.html), *The New York Daily News*, April 12, 1996, October 4, 2010.

[9] "Bio" (http://www.imdb.com/name/nm0234720/bio) on IMDB

[10] Todd Holland (1992) [DVD 1992] (in English) (Audio commentary). *The Larry Sanders Show - The Entire First Season* (Liner notes). Sony Pictures. 0767847563.

[11] Tucker, Ken. Not Just the Best of The Larry Sanders Show (2007) (review) (http://www.ew.com/ew/article/0,,20033916,00.html), *Entertainment Weekly*, April 12, 2007, accessed October 4, 2010.

[12] "Special Collector's Issue: 100 Greatest Episodes of All Time". *TV Guide* (June 28-July 4). 1997.

[13] Sony Pictures - The Best of Larry Sanders Collection (http://www.sonypictures.com/homevideo/larrysanderscollection/because.html)

External links

- HBO official site (archived from 2001) (http://web.archive.org/web/20010123211 7/http://www.hbo.com/larry/)
- Epguides - episodes and air dates guide (http://epguides.com/LarrySandersShow/)
- *The Larry Sanders Show* (http://www.imdb.com/title/tt0103466/) at the Internet Movie Database
- *The Larry Sanders Show* (http://www.tv.com/show/213/summary.html) at TV.com

Homicide: Life on the Street

Homicide: Life on the Street	
Homicide: Life on the Street title card (Seasons 1–4)	
Format	Police procedural Drama
Created by	Paul Attanasio
Starring	(see below)
Country of origin	United States
No. of seasons	7
No. of episodes	122 (plus TV movie) (List of episodes)
Production	
Running time	approx. 1 hour (per episode)
Broadcast	
Original channel	NBC
Original run	January 31, 1993 – May 21, 1999
Chronology	
Related shows	*Law & Order* *Law & Order: Special Victims Unit*

Homicide: Life on the Street is an American police procedural television series chronicling the work of a fictional version of the Baltimore Homicide Unit. It ran for seven seasons (122 episodes) on NBC from 1993 to 1999, and was succeeded by a TV movie, which also acted as the de-facto series finale. The series was originally based on David Simon's book *Homicide: A Year on the Killing Streets*. Many of the characters and stories used throughout the show were based on events depicted in the book, which was also used for Simon's own series, *The Wire* on HBO.

Although *Homicide* featured an ensemble cast, Andre Braugher emerged as the series' breakout star through his portrayal of Frank Pembleton.[1] The show won Television Critics Association Awards for Outstanding Achievement in Drama in 1996, 1997, and 1998. It also became the first drama ever to win three Peabody Awards for best drama in 1993, 1995, and 1997. In 1997, the episode "Prison Riot" was ranked No. 32 on TV Guide's 100 Greatest Episodes of All Time.[2] In 2007, it was listed as one of *Time* magazine's "Best TV Shows of All-*TIME*."[3] In 1996 *TV Guide* named the series 'The Best Show You're Not Watching'.[4]

The show inspired the spin-off *Homicide: Second Shift*, which was shown exclusively online.

The regular cast

Character	Duration (Regular)	Duration (Guest)	Portrayed by	Rank
John Munch	1–7	N/A	Richard Belzer	Detective
Meldrick Lewis	1–7	N/A	Clark Johnson	Detective
Al Giardello	1–7	N/A	Yaphet Kotto	Lieutenant
Tim Bayliss	1–7	N/A	Kyle Secor	Detective
Frank Pembleton	1–6	N/A	Andre Braugher	Detective
Kay Howard	1–5	N/A	Melissa Leo	Detective / Sergeant
Beau Felton	1–3	N/A	Daniel Baldwin	Detective
Stanley Bolander	1–3	N/A	Ned Beatty	Detective
Steve Crosetti	1–2	N/A	Jon Polito	Detective
Julianna Cox	5–6	N/A	Michelle Forbes	Chief Medical Examiner
Laura Ballard	6–7	N/A	Callie Thorne	Detective
Stuart Gharty	6–7	4–5	Peter Gerety	Detective
Mike Kellerman	4–6	7	Reed Diamond	Detective / P.I.
Megan Russert	3–4	5	Isabella Hofmann	Capt. / Lt. / Detective
Paul Falsone	6–7	5	Jon Seda	Detective
Terri Stivers	6–7	5	Toni Lewis	Detective
J. H. Brodie	5	4	Max Perlich	Crime Scene Videographer
Rene Sheppard	7	N/A	Michael Michele	Detective
Michael Giardello	7	N/A	Giancarlo Esposito	F.B.I. Agent

Overview

Homicide: Life on the Street was adapted from *Homicide: A Year on the Killing Streets*, a non-fiction book by *Baltimore Sun* reporter David Simon, based on his experience following a Baltimore Police Department homicide unit. Simon, who became a consultant and producer with the series, said he was particularly interested in the demythification of the American detective. While detectives are typically portrayed as noble characters who care deeply about their victims, Simon believed real detectives regarded violence as a normal aspect of their jobs.[5] Simon sent the book to film director and Baltimore native Barry Levinson with the hopes that it would be adapted into a film, but Levinson thought it would be more appropriate material for television because the stories and characters could be developed over a longer period of time. Levinson believed a television adaptation would bring a fresh and original edge to the police drama genre because the book exploded many of the myths of the police drama genre by highlighting that cops did not always get along with each other, and that criminals occasionally got away with their crimes.[6] Levinson approached screenwriter Paul Attanasio with the material, and *Homicide* became Attanasio's first foray into television writing. Subsequently, all episodes of *Homicide* display the credit, "Created by Paul Attanasio" at the end of their opening sequence, a credit which both Eric Overmyer and James Yoshimura dispute on the DVD audio commentary to the season 5 episode, "The Documentary", claiming instead the show was created by Tom Fontana and Yoshimura. The series title was originally *Homicide: A Year on the Killing Streets*, but NBC changed it so that viewers would not believe it was limited to a single year; the network also believed the use of the term "life" would be more reaffirming than the term "killing streets".[7] The opening theme music was composed by Baltimore native, Lynn F. Kowal, a graduate of the Peabody Institute of the Johns Hopkins University in Baltimore.[8]

"The greatest lie, I think, in dramatic TV is the cop who stands over a body and pulls up the sheet and mutters, 'Damn' and looks down sadly. To a real homicide detective, it's just a day's work."

David Simon[5]

Homicide's purpose was to provide its viewers with a no-nonsense, police procedural-type glimpse into the lives of a squad of inner-city detectives. As opposed to many television shows and movies involving cops, *Homicide* initially opted for a bleak sort of realism in its depiction of "The Job", portraying it as repetitive, spiritually draining, an existential threat to one's psyche, often glamor- and glory-free—but, nonetheless, a social necessity. In its attempt to do so, *Homicide* developed a trademark feel and look that distinguished itself from its contemporaries. For example, the series was filmed with hand-held 16 mm cameras almost entirely on-location in Baltimore (making the idiosyncratic city something of a character itself). It also regularly used music montages, jump cut editing, and the three-times-in-a-row repetition of the same camera shot during particularly crucial moments in the story. The episodes were also noted for interweaving as many as three or four storylines in a single episode. NBC executives often asked the writers to focus on a single homicide case rather than multiple ones, but the show producers tended to resist this advice.[7]

Despite premiering in the coveted post-Super Bowl time slot, the show opened to lackluster ratings, and cancellation was an immediate threat. However, the show's winning of two Emmy Awards (for Levinson's direction and Fontana's writing of the pilot episode) and the success of another police drama—the more sensational *NYPD Blue*—helped convince NBC to give it another chance beyond the truncated, nine-episode-long first season. (Incidentally, *Homicide*'s four-episode second-season renewal ties it with *Seinfeld* as the lowest number of episodes ordered in network history.) *Homicide* consistently ranked behind ABC's *20/20* and CBS's *Nash Bridges* in the Nielsen ratings. Despite the poor ratings, reviews were consistently strong from the beginning of the series. Commentators were especially impressed with the high number of strong, complex, well-developed and non-stereotypical African American characters like Pembleton, Lewis and Giardello.[9]

The police department scenes were shot at the historic City Recreation Pier in the Fells Point neighborhood in Baltimore. Although NBC occasionally pressured the show's producers to write happy endings to the homicide cases, the network gave an unusual amount of freedom for the writers to create darker stories and non-traditional detective story elements, like unsolved cases where criminals escape.[10] Nevertheless, in its attempt to improve *Homicide*'s ratings, NBC often insisted on changes, both cosmetic and thematic. For example, by the beginning of the third season, talented but unphotogenic veteran actor Jon Polito had been ordered dropped from the cast. At around this same time, the network also began clamoring for more on-screen romance and violence. In order to have episodes NBC considered more eye-catching air during "sweeps" periods, it sometimes aired them out of order, often to the detriment of story arcs that had developed over several episodes or even entire seasons. Probably the most infamous of such gaffes was NBC's decision to broadcast an episode featuring the program's first sex scene ("A Model Citizen") prior to the airing of the much acclaimed episode, "Crosetti". (The detective, Polito's character, had been in Atlantic City on vacation since the end of the second season's four episodes; for reasons never fully explained—but perhaps not difficult to surmise—he returns to Baltimore and drowns himself rather than return to his job.) As a result of this deviation from the producers' intended order, viewers of "A Model Citizen" found out from a comment made by his ex-partner, Detective Meldrick Lewis, merely that Crosetti had died but not how or when.

Considered by critics to be one of television's most authentic police dramas, as well as an excellent dramatic series propelled by a talented ensemble cast, *Homicide* garnered three straight TCA (Television Critics Association) Awards for Outstanding Achievement in Drama from 1996 to 1998 and was the first drama ever to win three of the prestigious Peabody Awards for best drama (1993, 1995, 1997).

The reality of *Homicide*'s low Nielsen ratings hovered over all things, however, and always left the show in a precarious position; it also had a harder time gaining a large audience because fewer viewers are at home watching TV on Friday nights. To NBC's credit, though, the network managed to keep what *TV Guide* referred to as "The Best Show You're Not Watching" on the air for five full seasons and seven seasons in all. In July 1997, NBC gave the series producers an ultimatum to make *Homicide* more popular than *Nash Bridges* or face cancellation. When this goal was not reached, the studio gave serious consideration to canceling the show, but a number of unexpected shocks at NBC increased *Homicide*'s value. Among those factors were the loss of the popular series *Seinfeld* and the $850 million deal needed to keep *ER* from leaving the network.[10]

Homicide was at one time syndicated on Lifetime and Court TV as well as the all-crime television cable station Sleuth, and airs occasionally on WGN America. Episodes of *Homicide* have aired on TNT as part of several crossovers the series had with *Law & Order*, which TNT owns broadcast rights for; in these cases both crossover episodes aired back to back. It was recently televised on the Centric channel.

All seven seasons are available on DVD. One DVD set combines the first two seasons. Additional sets contain the complete third, fourth, fifth, sixth, and seventh seasons. A boxed set shaped like a filing cabinet features an additional disc containing the *Homicide* TV movie and the relevant *Law & Order* crossover episodes – those without this disc had to rely on *Law & Order* recap clips on the season DVDs. Significantly, the DVDs contain the episodes in the producers' intended order, not the order in which NBC aired them.

The show has spawned changes in the real life Baltimore homicide unit. As seen in the show, the unit originally used a dry erase board in order to visually track detectives' progress at solving crimes. After the show began to air, the Baltimore Police Department discontinued the practice, believing the board, which concentrated on "clearance rates" for crimes, had a negative impact on publicity. It was brought back later at the insistence of the detectives.[11]

Broadcast History

Season	Time Slot
1 (1993)	Wednesday at 9:00 pm
2 (1994)	Thursday at 10:00 pm
3 (1994-1995)	Friday at 10:00 pm
4 (1995-1996)	
5 (1996-1997)	
6 (1997-1998)	
7 (1998-1999)	

Plot

Seasons 1 and 2

The first season saw the introductions of Detectives Frank Pembleton (Andre Braugher), Stan Bolander (Ned Beatty), Kay Howard (Melissa Leo), Meldrick Lewis (Clark Johnson), John Munch (Richard Belzer), Tim Bayliss (Kyle Secor), Beau Felton (Daniel Baldwin) and Steve Crosetti (Jon Polito), as well as Commander, Lieutenant Al Giardello (Yaphet Kotto).

The first departure came in the second season, when Jon Polito was cut from the show, marking the end of Steve Crosetti, a departure that would be explained in the third season.

Season 3

The third season dealt with the death of Crosetti, who made his last appearance in the season 2 finale. Isabella Hofmann joined the cast as Lieutenant Megan Russert, the commander of the other Homicide shift, it also dealt with her promotion to Captain, and saw the last appearances of Felton and Bolander (Daniel Baldwin, Ned Beatty).

Seasons 4 and 5

The fourth season saw the departure of Daniel Baldwin and Ned Beatty, who play Felton and Bolander, who had both been given a suspension. Bolander went on to retirement, and Felton, recruited for deep undercover work, was killed in the line of duty. They would not return until the movie. This season also sees Mike Kellerman (Reed Diamond) join the cast. Isabella Hofmann (newly demoted, Detective Meg Russert) left at the end of Season 4, but returned in the Season 5 finale, in which she, Kay Howard (Melissa Leo) and J.H. Brodie (Max Perlich) would make their last appearances.

Season 6

The sixth season was the first not to feature Leo as Sergeant Kay Howard, and the last to feature Braugher as Detective Frank Pembleton. Jon Seda, Callie Thorne and Peter Gerety joined the cast as Detective's Paul Falsone, Laura Ballard and Stuart Gharty. Max Perlich is no longer present, nor is Detective Meg Russert (Isabella Hofmann).

Season 7

Following the events of the season 6 finale, Detective Frank Pembleton (Braugher) and Detective Mike Kellerman (Diamond) are no longer regulars, Braugher would not return until the movie, while Diamond made a 2-episode guest appearance. Michael Michele stars in this season as Det. Rene Sheppard and Giancarlo Esposito is cast as Giardello's son Mike, who is assigned to Homicide as an FBI Liaison.

Homicide: The Movie

In 2000, following the conclusion of the show, a TV film titled *Homicide: The Movie* was shown on NBC. The squad's former Lieutenant, Al Giardello, was running for mayor on a controversial pro-drug-legalization platform, and is close to victory when he is gunned down. The assassination attempt inspires the return of the entire unit, past and present, in an effort to apprehend the gunman.

Crossovers

Homicide had three two-part crossovers with *Law & Order*.

- Season 4, Episode 12: "For God and Country"
  - Guest Characters - Rey Curtis, Lennie Briscoe & Claire Kincaid
- Season 6, Episode 5: "Baby, It's You"
  - Guest Characters - Rey Curtis, Lennie Briscoe, Jack McCoy & Jamie Ross
- Season 7, Episode 15: "Sideshow"
  - Guest Characters - Rey Curtis, Lennie Briscoe & Jack McCoy

Cameo crossovers

Homicide episode	Crossover with	Nature of crossover
4x04: A Dolls Eyes	Chicago Hope	The organs of the murder victim, a young boy, are shipped to various hospitals across the country. The heart is placed in a cooler with the destination label "Chicago Hope Hospital", and during a montage is received in Chicago by a heart surgeon played by Mandy Patinkin, who also plays surgeon Jeffrey Geiger in *Chicago Hope* (the character is unnamed in the *Homicide* episode, the implication being that he is the same character).
N/A	Multiple	The character John Munch, played by Richard Belzer, has appeared in several other shows, such as *The Beat*, *The X-Files*, *Arrested Development*, *The Wire* and *Law & Order: Trial by Jury* and *Law & Order: SVU*.

Other cast members

Recurring cast members

In addition to the regular cast, *Homicide* featured a number of recurring characters, who starred alongside the ensemble. Wendy Hughes (Carol Blythe), Ami Brabson (Mary Pembleton) and Željko Ivanek (Ed Danvers) are possibly the most notable, with the former appearing in Season 1, and the other 2 appearing in Seasons 1–6 and Seasons 1–7, respectively. Clayton LeBouef played Colonel George Barnfather throughout the run. Ralph Tabakin also played Dr. Scheiner in all 7 seasons. In addition to them, the recurring cast also included: Gerald F. Gough as Col. Burt Granger (seasons 1–3); Lee Tergesen as Officer Chris Thormann (seasons 1, 5); Sean Whitesell as Dr. Eli Devilbiss (seasons 1, 3–4, 6–7); Michael Willis as Darin Russom (seasons 1–7); Sharon Ziman as Naomi (seasons 1–7); Judy Thornton as Judy (seasons 2–7); Herb Levinson as Dr. Lausanne (seasons 2–7); Gary D'Addario as Lt. Jasper (seasons 3–7); Walt MacPherson as Capt. Roger Gaffney (seasons 3–7); Harlee McBride as Alyssa Dyer (seasons 3–7); Rhonda Overby as Reporter Dawn Daniels (seasons 3–7); Kristin Rohde as Officer Sally Rogers (seasons 3–7); Mary B. Ward as Beth Felton (season 3); Christopher Meloni as Bounty Hunter Dennis Knoll (season 7); Erik Dellums as Luther Mahoney (seasons 4–5); Mekhi Phifer as Junior Bunk (seasons 5–6); Hazelle Goodman as Georgia Rae Mahoney (season 6); Ellen McElduff as Billie Lou Hatfield (seasons 5–7); Austin Pendleton as Dr. George Griscom (season 7), and Jason Stanford as Joe Ryblack (season 6–7).

Notable guest appearances

A number of well-known actors and celebrities appeared on the show, including Steve Allen, Lewis Black, Wilford Brimley, Steve Burns, Steve Buscemi, Bruce Campbell, Joan Chen, Vincent D'Onofrio, Jeffrey Donovan, Tate Donovan, Charles Durning, Charles S. Dutton, Richard Edson, Kathryn Erbe, Edie Falco, Peter Gallagher, Paul Giamatti, John Glover, Moses Gunn, Luis Guzmán, Jake Gyllenhaal, Marcia Gay Harden, Neil Patrick Harris, Pat Hingle, James Earl Jones, Terry Kinney, Bruno Kirby, Julianna Margulies, Jena Malone, Christopher Meloni, David Morse, Terry O'Quinn, Joe Perry, Chris Rock, J.K. Simmons, Fisher Stevens, Jerry Stiller, Eric Stoltz, Tony Todd, Lily Tomlin, Kate Walsh, Isaiah Washington, Robin Williams, Elijah Wood, and Alfre Woodard, among many others. Jason Priestley joined the cast in the climactic television movie, during which his character referred to Pembleton and Bayliss as "legends". Typically, well-known actors making guest appearances on *Homicide* were cast in fully developed roles central to the episode in which they appeared. Robin Williams' sensitive portrayal of a grieving widower and father in the early episode, "Bop Gun", is a notable example, as is Steve Buscemi's role as a suspected gunman in the third-season "End Game."

Recurring characters of particular note include the Mahoney crime family. Luther Mahoney, a recurring villain throughout seasons four and five, is a crime and drug kingpin who uses others to do his dirty work and masterfully manipulates the law to repeatedly escape conviction and hide his connection to the crimes committed by his underlings. At first, he is depicted as an almost friendly rival, with both Mahoney and the police mutually amused by Mahoney's antics. Gradually, however, the police—particularly Kellerman and Lewis—grow frustrated with

Mahoney, until Lewis viciously beats him during an arrest, and Kellerman fatally shoots Mahoney under questionable circumstances.

In the following season, the Mahoney organization is taken over by Luther's sister Georgia Rae, who seeks both legal and illegal forms of revenge against the Baltimore Police Department.

Mekhi Phifer makes several appearances as Junior Bunk, a dim-witted street thug who is initially depicted as someone with the potential to go straight. His crimes grow increasingly violent, however, and in his final appearance he is revealed to be Georgia Rae's son, with the real name "Nathaniel Lee Mahoney". Junior's final appearance takes place after the character has been hardened by jail time, and the once minor criminal deals the homicide department a major blow with a multiple shooting in the police station, killing three uniformed cops (extras) and injuring two of the main characters. In retaliation, the police declare all-out war on the Mahoney crime organization. Several cops, including Bayliss, are injured, and several criminals, including Georgia Rae, are killed as a result; in addition, both Pembleton and Kellerman turn in their badges.

However, some celebrities made essentially cameo appearances which were more lighthearted in nature. Director (and Baltimore native) John Waters appeared twice, once as a nameless bartender listening to a disconsolate Detective Bolander, and another time as a talkative prisoner awaiting transfer from New York to Baltimore (escorted by Det. Mike Logan, played by Chris Noth). Out traveling on his motorcycle, Jay Leno stopped in at the Waterfront to have a soft drink, quickly departing after finding his bartenders strangely silent. In one particularly self-referential episode, journalist Tim Russert appeared as himself, bickering about Christmas presents with his "cousin", Lieutenant Megan Russert. Film director Barry Levinson, who also executive produced *Homicide*, acted as himself directing an episode for a show-within-a-show called *Homicide* in the episode, "The Documentary".

Both the mayor of Baltimore (Kurt Schmoke) and the governor of Maryland (Parris Glendening) made brief appearances in the episode about the death of Beau Felton, appearing at the memorial press conference for Felton's death in the line of duty.

Episodes

For a list of the episodes, see List of Homicide: Life on the Street episodes

All episodes have been released on DVD, A&E Home Video has released all 7 Seasons of *Homicide: Life on the Street* on DVD in Region 1. In addition to this the TV movie ***Homicide: The Movie*** made after the regular series ended was released on DVD in Region 1 by Trimark Pictures on May 22, 2001.

DVD Name	Episodes	Release dates		
		Region 1	Region 2	Region 4
The Complete 1st and 2nd Seasons	13	May 27, 2003	February 26, 2007 (Series 1)	June 30, 2009
The Complete 3rd Season	20	October 28, 2003	July 16, 2007 (Series 2)	September 30, 2009
The Complete 4th Season	22	March 30, 2004	September 24, 2007 (Series 3)	December 2, 2009
The Complete 5th Season	22	September 28, 2004	February 4, 2008 (Series 4)	February 2, 2010
The Complete 6th Season	23	January 25, 2005	May 5, 2007 (Series 5)	May 5, 2011[12]
The Complete 7th Season	22	June 28, 2005	June 2, 2007 (Series 6)	TBA
Homicide: The Movie	1	May 22, 2001	N/A	N/A
The Complete Series	122	November 14, 2006	March 29, 2010	N/A

Nielsen ratings

- Season 1: #24—12,717,000[13]
- Season 2: N/A
- Season 3: #89—7,822,800[14]
- Season 4: #66—8,535,100[14]
- Season 5: #68—7,760,000[14]
- Season 6: #77—7,546,000[15]
- Season 7: #66—10,238,200[16]

Impact on African American cinema

Homicide was noteworthy amongst network TV shows in its multi-dimensional depictions of various African Americans throughout the show. While not specifically an African-American-themed show, it was set in majority African-American Baltimore, Maryland and would naturally display various issues and characteristics of the city's African-American community. *Homicide* managed to cross several racial barriers that were not crossed on previous television series, and portrayed by and large a more progressive depiction of African-American characters than other previous television series.[17] The show was commended at several award ceremonies themed to African-American cinema, such as the NAACP-sponsored Image Awards which would nominate both the show itself and its major cast members such as Andre Braugher, Giancarlo Esposito, Clark Johnson, Yaphet Kotto, Toni Lewis, and Michael Michele and for various awards.[18]

References

[1] Fretts, Bruce (1998-05-01). "The show that wouldn't die" (http://www.ew.com/ew/article/0,,282863,00.html). *Entertainment Weekly*. . Retrieved 2008-12-18.

[2] "Special Collectors' Issue: 100 Greatest Episodes of All Time". *TV Guide* (June 28 – July 4). 1997.

[3] Poniewozik, James (September 6, 2007). "The 100 Best TV Shows of All-*TIME*" (http://www.time.com/time/specials/2007/article/0,28804,1651341_1659188_1652056,00.html). *Time* (Time.com). . Retrieved March 4, 2010.

[4] *TV Guide Book of Lists*. Running Press. 2007. pp. 212. ISBN 0-7624-3007-1.

[5] Simon, David (1998-11-04). *Anatomy of "Homicide: Life on the Street"* (http://www.imdb.com/title/tt0324999/) (Documentary). Baltimore, Maryland: Public Broadcasting Service. .

[6] Kalat, David P. (1998). *Homicide: Life on the Street: The Unofficial Companion*. Los Angeles, California: Renaissance Books. p. 102. ISBN 1580630219.

[7] Levinson, Barry (2003) (Audio commentary). *Homicide Life on the Street – The Seasons 1 & 2* (DVD). A&E Home Video.

[8] "Lynn F. Kowal" (http://www.imdb.com/name/nm1862139/). . Retrieved 2009-09-28.

[9] Leonard, John (1998-11-04). *Anatomy of "Homicide: Life on the Street"* (http://www.imdb.com/title/tt0324999/) (Documentary). Baltimore, Maryland: Public Broadcasting Service. .

[10] Bogosian, Theodore (1998-11-04). *Anatomy of "Homicide: Life on the Street"* (http://www.imdb.com/title/tt0324999/) (Documentary). Baltimore, Maryland: Public Broadcasting Service. .

[11] "Homicide: Life on the Street, The Board" (http://www.borderline-productions.com/jimking). . Retrieved 2008-12-19.

[12] http://www.ezydvd.com.au/item.zml/819008

[13] http://www.classictvhits.com/tvratings/1993.htm

[14] http://fbibler.chez.com/tvstats/recent_data/1994-95.html

[15] "Final Ratings for '97–'98 TV Season" (http://www.sfgate.com/cgi-bin/article.cgi?f=/c/a/1998/05/25/DD61876.DTL&type=chart). *The San Francisco Chronicle*. September 16, 2010. .

[16] http://web.archive.org/web/20091029011819/http://geocities.com/Hollywood/4616/ew0604.html

[17] Mascaro, Thomas A. (2004-03-22). "Homicide: Life on the Street: progress in portrayals of African American men" (http://www.encyclopedia.com/doc/1G1-115399891.html). *Journal of Popular Film and Television*. ISSN 0195-6051. OCLC 4652347. . Retrieved 2007-09-23.

[18] "Awards for "Homicide: Life on the Street"" (http://www.imdb.com/title/tt0106028/awards). .

- Bobby, J. (c. 2000). "The Homicide: Life on the Street Glossary" (http://novemberrain.free.fr/GlossaireHLOTS.htm). Retrieved 2007-09-24.

External links

- *Homicide: Life on the Street* (http://www.tv.com/show/110/summary.html) at TV.com
- *Homicide: Life on the Street* (http://www.imdb.com/title/tt0106028/) at the Internet Movie Database
- *Homicide: The Movie* (http://www.imdb.com/title/tt0226771/) at the Internet Movie Database
- Homicide: Links on the Sites (http://www.borderline-productions.com/hlotslinks/) – News links, web sites, merchandise

Life with Bonnie

Life with Bonnie	
The cast of *Life with Bonnie* in a season two advertisement.	
Format	Sitcom
Created by	Bonnie Hunt Don Lake
Written by	Bonnie Hunt Sam Denoff Doug Ellin Don Lake Norma Safford Vela
Directed by	John Bowab Bonnie Hunt
Starring	Bonnie Hunt Mark Derwin Charlie Stewart Marianne Muellerleile David Alan Grier Anthony Russell Holly Wortell Chris Barnes Frankie Ryan Manriquez Samantha Browne-Walters (Season 1)
Country of origin	United States
No. of seasons	2
No. of episodes	44
Production	
Running time	22 minutes
Broadcast	
Original channel	ABC
Original run	September 17, 2002 – April 9, 2004

Life with Bonnie is an ABC television sitcom that originally aired from 2002 to 2004. The show outlined the life of character Bonnie Malloy, who juggled her personal life and a TV talk show position. The series was created by Bonnie Hunt and Don Lake, and produced by Miss Hunt's company, Bob & Alice Productions, in association with Touchstone Television, Inc. The show had fair ratings in the first season but struggled in the second, causing ABC to cancel it. *Life With Bonnie* was also shown on Living TV during ABC's airings.

Cast

- Bonnie Hunt as **Bonnie Malloy** - Bonnie is the mother of 2 children (3 in season 1), loving wife, and host of a local TC talk show. Bonnie tries to maintain a public image of the perfect wife and mother, but in reality her life is chaotic.
- Mark Derwin as **Mark Malloy** – Mark, a doctor, is Bonnie's husband and the father of her children. He looks on as she tries to balance her hectic life. Mark is much less concerned about what other people think than Bonnie is, which causes problems on occasion. He has a generally more professional demeanour, and sometimes doesn't understand why Bonnie continues to put up with annoying people in her life.
- Charlie Stewart as **Charlie Malloy** – Charlie is Bonnie's son. Charlie shares most of his scenes with his friend Frankie. His role is small and usually unscripted although he adds priceless comedy to the show.
- Samantha Browne-Walters as **Samantha Malloy** (Season 1) - Samantha played Bonnie's eldest child, yet another ingredient in Bonnie's hectic life. She was removed from the cast when season 2 started, without one mention of her whereabouts or fate.
- Marianne Muellerleile as **Gloria** – Gloria is Bonnie's live-in housekeeper/nanny. It was stated in the show that she was only intended to stay there until Charlie started school, but despite the fact that she actually provided little help, they couldn't let her leave because they had grown attached to her.
- David Alan Grier as **David Bellows** – David is the producer of the "Morning Chicago" show. David is most often seen yelling and frantically rushing to get things for the show in order while pushing his lectern around the studio.
- Anthony Russell as **Tony Russo** – Tony plays Bonnie's affable piano player on the "Morning Chicago" show. Bonnie's housekeeper Gloria has a crush on Tony.
- Holly Wortell as **Holly** – Holly is Bonnie's make-up artist on the "Morning Chicago" show. She often gives advice on Bonnie's marriage issues and seems to date many men.
- Chris Barnes as **Marv** – Marv is the cue-card guy on the "Morning Chicago" show. Marv is very protective of Holly, who does not return his interest.
- Frankie Ryan Manriquez as **Frankie** – Frankie is Charlie's best friend and spends most of his time at the Malloy home. He contributes many funny anecdotes about his screwed-up family.

Guest stars

- Rip Taylor (as "Rappin' Rip" in four episodes)
- Tom Hanks (as himself in the episode "What If?")
- Robin Williams (as Kevin Powalski in the episode "Psychic")
- David Duchovny (as Johnny Volcano in 2 episodes)
- Carl Reiner (as "Mr. Portinbody" in 3 episodes)
- Teri Garr (as "Mrs. Portinbody" in the episode "Buy the Book")
- Martin Mull (as "Le Nord" in 2 episodes (and yes, his name is pronounced "Le Nord"))
- The Smothers Brothers (as contractors in the episode "Everything Old is New Again")
- Jonathan Winters (as a writer with multiple personalities)
- Jack LaLanne (as himself)
- Morgan York (as Christine Harris in the episode "Dare To Be Different")

Episodes

Season 1: 2002-2003

Episode #	Episode title	Original airdate
1-1	"Pilot"	September 17, 2002
1-2	"Weather or Not"	September 24, 2002
1-3	"Dream"	October 1, 2002
1-4	"Don't Act Your Age, Just Act"	October 8, 2002
1-5	"Duets"	October 15, 2002
1-6	"Is It Just Us?"	October 22, 2002
1-7	"A Day in the Life"	October 29, 2002
1-8	"Happy Day"	November 5, 2002
1-9	"Money Plus Marlens Makes Four"	November 12, 2002
1-10	"Partly Sunny"	November 19, 2003
1-11	"What If?"	November 26, 2003
1-12	"Christmastime in the City"	December 12, 2003
1-13	"Okay, Thanks"	December 17, 2003
1-14	"Deuce is Wild"	January 8, 2003
1-15	"Assaulted Nuts"	January 14, 2003
1-16	"Psychic"	February 4, 2003
1-17	"The Graduate"	February 11, 2003
1-18	"Buy This Book"	February 18, 2003
1-19	"In Need of Assistants"	March 11, 2003
1-20	"Stealing Home"	March 18, 2003
1-21	"Ding, Ding, Ding Went the Truth"	March 25, 2003
1-22	"Till Next Time"	March 25, 2003

Season 2: 2003-2004

Episode #	Episode title	Original airdate
2-1	"Ironing Out Your Differences"	September 26, 2003
2-2	"Pontiac Bonnie-Ville"	October 3, 2003
2-3	"Everything Old Is New Again"	October 10, 2003
2-4	"No Matter Where You Go, There You Are"	October 17, 2003
2-5	"Boyhood to Womanhood"	October 24, 2003
2-6	"The Merry Ole Land of Oz"	October 31, 2003
2-7	"Places, Stat!"	November 4, 2003
2-8	"Queer Eye for the Straight Lie"	November 14, 2003
2-9	"Boomerang"	November 21, 2003

2-10	"Food for Thought"	December 5, 2003
2-11	"It's a Wonderful Job"	December 12, 2003
2-12	"Trifecta, Try Friendship"	January 9, 2004
2-13	"Live and Let Live"	January 23, 2004
2-14	"Space Heaters"	January 30, 2004
2-15	"Dare to Be Different"	February 13, 2004
2-16	"Nightshift"	February 20, 2004
2-17	"Act Natural"	February 27, 2004
2-18	"Therabeautic"	March 5, 2004
2-19	"Striking a Match"	March 19, 2004
2-20	"Don't Stress, Express"	March 26, 2004
2-21	" Nip, Tuck and Roll"	April 2, 2004
2-22	"Father and Son: A Table for Two"	April 9, 2004

External links

- *Life with Bonnie* [1] at the Internet Movie Database
- *Life with Bonnie* [2] at TV.com

References

[1] http://www.imdb.com/title/tt0320053/
[2] http://www.tv.com/show/9461/summary.html

Mind of Mencia

Mind of Mencia with Carlos Mencia	
Format	Stand-up comedy and Sketch comedy
Created by	Carlos Mencia
Starring	Carlos Mencia Joseph Mencia
Country of origin	United States
No. of seasons	4
No. of episodes	55
Broadcast	
Original channel	Comedy Central
Original run	July 6, 2005 – July 23, 2008

Mind of Mencia is an American television comedy series on the cable channel Comedy Central. Hosted by Carlos Mencia, it aired from 2005 to 2008.

History

The first season of *Mind of Mencia* ran from July 6, 2005 to September 28, 2005, premiering on Comedy Central with an initial order of ten episodes. Soon after that the series was renewed for a second season, set to air in winter of 2006.[1] Season 2 premiered on March 22, 2006. The first season was released on DVD on March 21, 2006 to coincide with the premiere. The second season became Comedy Central's ninth highest rated program.[2]

In a May 2006 *Wall Street Journal* article, Mencia said he initially resisted requests by his network to take a deal to do a stand-up comedy album on the Comedy Central label, but will now likely appear on one.[3]

After the fourth season, Comedy Central canceled the show due to suffering ratings.

Cast members

- Carlos Mencia
- Joseph Mencia
- Brad Williams
- Ray Payton

Guest appearances

- James Adomian
- Dave Attell
- Robin Bain
- Josh Blue
- Peter Boyle
- Frank Caliendo
- Edge
- Pablo Francisco
- Joey Greco
- Chris Hansen
- Estelle Harris
- Tony Hawk
- Gabriel Iglesias
- Courtney Jackson
- Ken Jeong
- Jamie Kennedy
- Angela Kinsey
- Phil LaMarr
- Bobby Lee
- Mario Lopez
- Method Man
- Cheech Marin
- Tracy Morgan
- Amaury Nolasco
- Lupe Ontiveros
- P.O.D.
- Smush Parker
- Jeff Richards
- Gene Simmons
- Aries Spears
- Three 6 Mafia
- Daniel Tosh
- Billy Dee Williams
- Robin Williams
- Debra Wilson
- John Witherspoon
- Tom Virtue

Recurring characters/sketches

Stereotype Olympics

In season two they put stereotypes to the test. Few of the stereotypes stood up to the test.

Punji

Punji is a Hindu storekeeper who insults customers with obvious physical and/or social problems, before telling them to "get the park out of my store". He often expresses the wish to be reincarnated as something the person is not likely to ever see/use (for example, he says "I hope I am reincarnated as your feet, so you will never see me again" to an obese woman). Before going on his tirades, he begs for forgiveness from various Hindu gods such as Shiva and Vishnu. Punji has been a storekeeper at "Heaven-11", a store that sells wives, and an electrical store.

Carlosaurus Rex

Carlosaurus Rex is a call-in kid's show that deals with serious/mature matters. The show is a parody of *Barney & Friends* and was originally hijacked from a Barney-like character, Larry the Lizard. Examples of the mature matters the show deals with include:

- A kid telephones the show, saying that his parents sent their dog "to live on a farm" (a euphemism parents use to explain the death of a family pet). Carlosaurus sings him a song explaining that the kid's dad shot the dog and dumped the body into a river.
- A boy calls, saying that "all my other friends like girls, but I think I like boys!". Carlosaurus sings him a song, "If you think you might be gay then you're gay!" (to the tune of "If You're Happy and You Know It"), whereupon the boy is then heard saying, 'Hey, Mom, I'm gay!".
- A kid asks if touching himself when he wakes up is wrong. Carlosaurus sings him a song to the tune of "Rock-a-bye Baby":

  Rock-a-bye, Billy,

  Time for sleep!

  You've washed your face,

  You've brushed your teeth.

  Now grab some lotion and that crunchy sock.

  Think of Jessica Alba while stroking your-- "...Listen kids I'm trying to tell you!"

Judge Carlos

Carlos plays a judge, and with the help of The Ghost of Johnny Cochran looks at real life recent court cases.

The Adventures of Carlitos

An animated cartoon based on Carlos' life as a kid.

DVD releases

Each DVD set includes uncensored versions of each season's episodes with bonus features including commentary, a behind the scenes featurette, and deleted scenes.

Season	DVD release date	Episodes
1	March 21, 2006	13
2	April 3, 2007	16
3	October 23, 2007	16
4	November 11, 2008	10

References

[1] "Carlos Mencia Can Sit Back And Count The Beans" (http://www.thefutoncritic.com/news.aspx?id=20051031comedycentral01), TheFutonCritic.com, 31 October 2005.

[2] "Comedy Central delves deeper into the 'Mind of Mencia' and orders third season" (http://www.comedycentral.com/press/press_releases/2006/071206_mencia_thirdseason_pickup.jhtml). Comedy Central. . Retrieved 2006-10-21.

[3] Joe Flint. "Comedy Central Corners The Laughs Business," (http://online.wsj.com/public/article/SB114704678745746219-Ba_TbhjP4t0Vm2i___hvEuVCSMA_20060606.html?mod=tff_main_tff_top) *The Wall Street Journal*, May 8, 2006.

External links

- Official website (http://www.comedycentral.com/shows/mind_of_mencia/index.jhtml)
- *Mind of Mencia* (http://www.imdb.com/title/tt0468999/) at the Internet Movie Database
- *Mind of Mencia* (http://www.tv.com/show/38890/summary.html) at TV.com
- *Comedy Central Corners The Laughs Business* by Joe Flint, Wall Street Journal, May 8, 2006. p.B1 (http://online.wsj.com/public/article/SB114704678745746219-Ba_TbhjP4t0Vm2i___hvEuVCSMA_20060606.html?mod=tff_main_tff_top)

Law & Order: Special Victims Unit (season 9)

Law & Order: Special Victims Unit *Season 9*	
DVD cover art	
Country of origin	United States
No. of episodes	19
Broadcast	
Original channel	NBC
Original run	September 25, 2007 – May 13, 2008
Home video release	
DVD release	
Region 1	May 26, 2009
Region 2	August 31, 2009
Region 4	September 30, 2009

This page contains a list of episodes for **season 9** of the television series, *Law & Order: Special Victims Unit*.

Cast

- Christopher Meloni as Det. Elliot Stabler
- Mariska Hargitay as Det. Olivia Benson
- Richard Belzer as Sgt. John Munch
- Diane Neal as ADA Casey Novak
- Ice-T as Det. Fin Tutuola
- Adam Beach as Det. Chester Lake
- B. D. Wong as Dr. George Huang
- Tamara Tunie as Dr. Melinda Warner
- Dann Florek as Capt. Don Cragen

Recurring

- Vincent Spano as FBI Agent Dean Porter

Guest stars

This season *Law & Order: Special Victims Unit's* guest stars consisted of; Cynthia Nixon, Laura Allen, Bronson Pinchot, Annie Potts, Melissa Joan Hart, Anwan Glover, Kyle Gallner, Aidan Quinn, Julie White, Elizabeth McGovern, Steven Weber, Jared Harris, Beverly D'Angelo, Forrest Griffin, Nicole "Coco" Austin, Mark Valley, Method Man, Gloria Reuben, Fiona Hutchison, Mae Whitman, Erika Christensen, Rhea Perlman, Alexander Gould, John Schuck, James Waterston, Janine Turner, Mark Moses, Bill Pullman, Bailey Chase, Robin Williams, Mo Rocca, Stephen Collins, Matthew Davis, and Sam Waterston as District Attorney Jack McCoy.

Episodes

- In the following table, "U.S. viewers (millions)" refers to the number of Americans who viewed the episode on the day of original broadcast.

<table>
<tr><th>Season no.</th><th>Series no.</th><th>Title</th><th>Directed by</th><th>Written by</th><th>Original air date</th><th>Prod. code</th><th>U.S. Viewers (millions)</th></tr>
<tr><td>1</td><td>184</td><td>"Alternate"</td><td>David Platt</td><td>Neal Baer & Dawn DeNoon</td><td>September 25, 2007</td><td>09003</td><td>12.10[1]</td></tr>
<tr><td colspan="8">Detectives Benson and Stabler suspect that Janis Donovan (Cynthia Nixon), a woman with Dissociative Identity Disorder, may have harmed her own daughter. Their investigation is met with initial resistance from her psychiatrist, Dr. Henry Carlisle (Bronson Pinchot). Captain Cragen is temporarily re-assigned due to problems with his detectives last season, and newly promoted Sgt. John Munch is assigned as Acting Squad Commander.

The detectives discover that Janis has four other alternate personalities. As the episode progresses, the detectives witness these personalities, culminating when one of Janis's personalities throws a chair across the room. Later in the episode, Janis and her sister are reunited after serving time in jail. The day after Janis and her sister go home together, their parents are found murdered in their beds. Janis's fingerprints are found on the gun. When Janis goes to trial, she displays one of her alternate personalities, choking Novak. Janis is found not guilty by reason of mental defect. Afterwards, it is revealed that everything was an act she and her sister cooked up to create a fake motive to kill their parents. When Stabler and Benson go to visit Janis in the psychiatric hospital, Janis confesses to everything and her sister, who was visiting with Janis, is arrested for being a co-conspirator.</td></tr>
<tr><td>2</td><td>185</td><td>"Avatar"</td><td>Peter Leto</td><td>Paul Grellong & Chris Emposimato</td><td>October 2, 2007</td><td>09004</td><td>11.66[2]</td></tr>
<tr><td colspan="8">Rachel McGarrett (played by Christina Brucato), a participant in virtual reality video games, goes missing. Her boyfriend, Dan Friedich (Ryan Lynn), is a suspect in the case and is discovered to suffer from sexsomnia which caused him to attempt to rape her sister, Kristi McGarrett (played by Liza Joyce). In an effort to locate Rachel, Detectives Olivia Benson and Elliot Stabler use her avatar to track her kidnapper down.</td></tr>
<tr><td>3</td><td>186</td><td>"Impulsive"</td><td>David Platt</td><td>Jonathan Greene</td><td>October 9, 2007</td><td>09001</td><td>12.19[3]</td></tr>
<tr><td colspan="8">Sarah Trent (Melissa Joan Hart) is a high school teacher, suspected of statutorily raping her student, Shane Mills (played by Kyle Gallner), after he is diagnosed with gonorrhea. Sarah claims that Shane actually raped her. The team finds that Shane has a brain disorder making him obsessed with sex (he hires prostitutes, photoshops scantily-clad women and masturbates with high frequency) and he confesses to raping his teacher. Shane is given another chance and is sent to a rehabilitation clinic, but the situation quickly changes gears when Shane himself is raped in the clinic.</td></tr>
<tr><td>4</td><td>187</td><td>"Savant"</td><td>Kate Woods</td><td>Judith McCreary</td><td>October 16, 2007</td><td>09005</td><td>12.54[4]</td></tr>
<tr><td colspan="8">Ben Nicholson (Aidan Quinn) discovers that his mentally challenged daughter, Katie (played by Paulina Gerzon), who has Williams syndrome, is the only witness to the savage beating of his wife (Judy Kuhn), which placed her in a coma. Detectives Benson and Stabler and ADA Novak work with Katie to reconstruct the night the beating took place.</td></tr>
<tr><td>5</td><td>188</td><td>"Harm"</td><td>Peter Leto</td><td>Josh Singer</td><td>October 23, 2007</td><td>09002</td><td>12.17[5]</td></tr>
<tr><td colspan="8">The detectives investigate the fatal stabbing of a private school teacher (Elizabeth Morton), who had volunteered at a victim's rehabilitation center. The teacher had been working with an Iraqi man whose story helped uncover some military secrets, which may have led to her murder.
• Elizabeth McGovern, Patrick Page, and Steven Weber guest star.</td></tr>
<tr><td>6</td><td>189</td><td>"Svengali"</td><td>David Platt</td><td>Kam Miller</td><td>November 6, 2007</td><td>09006</td><td>11.75[6]</td></tr>
<tr><td colspan="8">A college student is found murdered in an attack that bears the hallmarks of infamous serial killer Robert Morton (Jared Harris). Detectives Benson and Stabler investigate Morton and discover his loyal following, which includes a man whose comic books glorify Morton's murders. When Cecilia (played by Shannon Woodward), the last person to have seen the victim alive, goes missing, the detectives are pressed to save her life. Benson also finds herself in danger when the investigation angers Morton's followers.</td></tr>
<tr><td>7</td><td>190</td><td>"Blinded"</td><td>David Platt</td><td>Jonathan Greene</td><td>November 13, 2007</td><td>09009</td><td>12.49[7]</td></tr>
</table>

<table>
<tr><td colspan="8">The discovery of a kidnapped girl leads Detectives Benson and Stabler to her abductor, Saul Picard (played by Arye Gross), who is a violent, schizophrenic artist. As Detective Stabler prepares to take Saul into custody, he head butts Stabler, slamming his head into a car window which shatters on impact. As Stabler wakes up in the hospital room he is unable to see anybody around him. Novak must face her own dark past while attempting to convict Picard, whose reaction post-psychiatric treatment to his crimes complicates the case.
• Note: First appearance in the *Law & Order* series of Jack McCoy (Sam Waterston) as the District Attorney.</td></tr>
<tr><td>8</td><td>191</td><td>**"Fight"**</td><td>Juan J. Campanella</td><td>Mick Betancourt</td><td>November 20, 2007</td><td>09007</td><td>11.66[8]</td></tr>
<tr><td colspan="8">A brutal murder leads the detectives into the dangerous world of MMA (mixed martial arts). The investigation leads to two brothers who confessed that they had to rape the victim to enter a gang. The case gets harder when the leader of the gang and prime suspect is accidentally crushed to death in a trash compactor and one of the brothers lies to protect the other.
• Gaius Charles, Arlen Escarpeta, Forrest Griffin, Adina Porter, Coco Austin, Stephanie Andujar, Anwan Glover, and Lenny Venito guest star.</td></tr>
<tr><td>9</td><td>192</td><td>**"Paternity"**</td><td>Kate Woods</td><td>Amanda Green</td><td>November 27, 2007</td><td>09010</td><td>12.29[9]</td></tr>
<tr><td colspan="8">The murder of a young boy's nanny leads Detectives Benson and Stabler to suspect her Internet love interest, "Casanova" (Steven Bauer). However, the nanny's employers (played by Mark Valley and Anastasia Griffith) soon get troubles of their own when the father finds out that his son is not his biological son. Stabler's family suffers a tragedy leaving his unborn child in serious danger after Benson and Kathy are hurt in a car accident.</td></tr>
<tr><td>10</td><td>193</td><td>**"Snitch"**</td><td>Jonathan Kaplan</td><td>Mark Goffman</td><td>December 4, 2007</td><td>09008</td><td>11.72[10]</td></tr>
<tr><td colspan="8">Detectives Benson and Stabler investigate when a Nigerian polygamist's wife is killed, and the husband fears that his testifying in a crime may have led to his wife's demise. Benson and Stabler suspect that the man's cultural tradition may have been the cause of his wife's murder when they find a website that exposes potential witnesses to the crime that he was testifying for.
• Method Man, Gloria Reuben, Steven Weber, Hakeem Kae-Kazim, and Tracy Middendorf guest star.</td></tr>
<tr><td>11</td><td>194</td><td>**"Streetwise"**</td><td>Helen Shaver</td><td>Paul Grellong</td><td>January 1, 2008</td><td>09011</td><td>12.35[11]</td></tr>
<tr><td colspan="8">The SVU squad are called in when a wealthy teenager (Natalie Hall) is found murdered in Central Park. The case soon develops into an investigation of a community of homeless children.
• Mae Whitman and Madeline Taylor guest star.</td></tr>
<tr><td>12</td><td>195</td><td>**"Signature"**</td><td>Arthur Forney</td><td>Judith McCreary</td><td>January 8, 2008</td><td>09012</td><td>15.17[12]</td></tr>
<tr><td colspan="8">Detectives Benson and Lake investigate the murder of a female alongside a man with a bullet inside his head; they soon team up with Special Agent Cooper (Erika Christensen), who's tracking a serial killer by the name of "The Woodsman", but things turn weird when the male victim is identified as the serial killer and Special Agent Cooper seems to be hiding something of her own.</td></tr>
<tr><td>13</td><td>196</td><td>**"Unorthodox"**</td><td>David Platt</td><td>Josh Singer</td><td>January 15, 2008</td><td>09013</td><td>12.14[13]</td></tr>
<tr><td colspan="8">The sexual assault of a Jewish boy (Braeden Lemasters) prompts the attention of Benson and Stabler. Initially an orthodox Jewish rabbi (Bob Dishy) is suspected to be the one responsible for the raping the kid, but the case turns into a media circus as a flood of young victims are revealed, with all the clues pointing to one of their classmates. It's discovered that a 14-year-old boy (Alexander Gould) is the rapist, but he doesn't go to prison because (thanks to a psychological evaluation) he is declared mentally ill, as a result of daily exposure to pornography.
• Cara Buono, Rhea Perlman, Novella Nelson, Linda Emond, and Zoe Lister-Jones guest star.</td></tr>
<tr><td>14</td><td>197</td><td>**"Inconceivable"**</td><td>Chris Zalla</td><td>Dawn DeNoon</td><td>January 22, 2008</td><td>09014</td><td>12.97[14]</td></tr>
<tr><td colspan="8">When fertilized embryos disappear from a sperm bank, examination of a security tape points the detectives to two publicity-hungry extremists. Meanwhile, Benson ponders her own decisions about fertility and motherhood.
• Mark Moses, Janine Turner, Gabrielle Anwar, Meredith Eaton, James Waterston, Richard Masur, Meredith Zinner, and Emilio Delgado guest star.</td></tr>
<tr><td>15</td><td>198</td><td>**"Undercover"**</td><td>David Platt</td><td>Mark Goffman</td><td>April 15, 2008</td><td>09015</td><td>13.27[15]</td></tr>
<tr><td colspan="8">After a young girl (Shareeka Epps) is found raped in a community garden, Benson and Stabler realize the girl has a mother who is in a female correction facility. After the rape kit on the girl goes missing, the detectives realize one of the corrections officers at the facility is raping and brutalizing women. Without the rape kit, however, Benson and Stabler have no proof, so Benson goes in undercover at the same facility to catch the officer, but is almost raped herself in the basement of the facility.
• Johnny Messner, Todd Stashwick, LaChanze, Hassan Johnson, Tawny Cypress, Matthew Cowles, and Dinah Lenney guest star.</td></tr>
</table>

<table>
<tr><td>16</td><td>199</td><td>"Closet"</td><td>Peter Leto</td><td>Ken Storer</td><td>April 22, 2008</td><td>09016</td><td>11.50[16]</td></tr>
<tr><td colspan="8">When investment banker Jeremy Haynes is found murdered, suspicion turns to his boyfriend Lincoln Haver (Bailey Chase), a professional football player who could lose everything if the truth about his sexuality came to light. When information about Haver's sexual orientation is leaked to the media, Benson comes under fire for her relationship with a reporter (Bill Pullman).
• Robert John Burke, Rick Hoffman, Beverly D'Angelo, Richard Lewis, and David Del Rio also guest star.</td></tr>
<tr><td>17</td><td>200</td><td>"Authority"</td><td>David Platt</td><td>Neal Baer & Amanda Green</td><td>April 29, 2008</td><td>09017</td><td>12.06[17]</td></tr>
<tr><td colspan="8">The 200th episode of the show features an engineer, Merritt Rook (Robin Williams) who has been posing as a cop to make people do abnormal things all in the act of trying to convince people to oppose authority. He turns his trial into a media circus and the case gets more complicated when Rook abducts Benson. He tries to make Elliot inflict pain on her by way of a Milgram experiment, but he refuses.
• When Rook's "No Sheep" crew freeze in their tracks at Grand Central Station, it is based on Improv Everywheres' 2006 performance [18].</td></tr>
<tr><td>18</td><td>201</td><td>"Trade"</td><td>Peter Leto</td><td>Jonathan Greene</td><td>May 6, 2008</td><td>09018</td><td>10.44[19]</td></tr>
<tr><td colspan="8">When a pregnant woman's body is found raped and murdered inside her burnt loft the team investigates a family of coffee importers. The suspects are numerous ranging from the woman's fiance (Matthew Davis) to his father (Stephen Collins). Further investigation reveals a twisted love rectangle between the woman, her fiance, the father and even the son's lawyer Michelle Borth.</td></tr>
<tr><td>19</td><td>202</td><td>"Cold"</td><td>David Platt</td><td>Judith McCreary</td><td>May 13, 2008</td><td>09019</td><td>10.83[20]</td></tr>
<tr><td colspan="8">The SVU squad is left at ends when they have a dead cop on their hands and Det. Chester Lake is their prime suspect. They discover Lake was investigating a ten-year-old cold case and the cop may have been involved in the rape of one girl and the rape-murder of another girl. Lake tracks down the surviving victim and convinces her to testify against the partner of the dead cop who also raped and helped murder the other girl. However, as the case quickly goes downhill in the courtroom, Novak withholds evidence in desperate hopes of winning a conviction, but her efforts fail to win her a conviction. In the end, Novak is censured for her misconduct and Lake hunts down and kills the cop, while Fin, upset at Elliot for gaining his cellphone records in hopes of finding out if he had informed Lake of the detective's progress, announces his intent to transfer out of SVU.
• Adam Beach and Diane Neal leave the cast.</td></tr>
</table>

References

[1] "With Break-Out Performances from New and Returning Series, NBC Ties for Premiere Week's Top Spot in 18-49" (http://www.thefutoncritic.com/ratings/2007/10/02/with-break-out-performances-from-new-and-returning-series-nbc-ties-for-premiere-weeks-top-spot-in-18-49-25605/20071002nbc01/). *The Futon Critic/NBC* (The Futon Critic/NBC). October 2, 2007. . Retrieved September 11, 2011.

[2] Seidman, Robert (October 3, 2007). "Nielsen Overnight TV Ratings, Tuesday Oct 2" (http://tvbythenumbers.com/2007/10/03/nielsen-overnight-tv-ratings-tuesday-oct-2/1040). *The Nielsen Company* (TV by the Numbers). . Retrieved August 7, 2010.

[3] Seidman, Robert (October 10, 2007). "Overnight Results for Tuesday Oct 9" (http://tvbythenumbers.com/2007/10/10/fox-wins-the-night-cuban-dances-on/1188). *The Nielsen Company* (TV by the Numbers). . Retrieved August 7, 2010.

[4] Seidman, Robert (October 17, 2007). "Overnight Results Tuesday 10/16: Red Sox on the Brink" (http://tvbythenumbers.com/2007/10/17/overnight-results-tuesday-1016-red-sox-on-the-brink/1308). *The Nielsen Company* (TV by the Numbers). . Retrieved August 7, 2010.

[5] Seidman, Robert (October 24, 2007). "Overnight Results 10/23: Fox Wins" (http://tvbythenumbers.com/2007/10/24/overnight-results-1023-fox-wins/1433). *The Nielsen Company* (TV by the Numbers). . Retrieved August 7, 2010.

[6] Seidman, Robert (November 7, 2007). "Overnight Results 11/6: Fox Leads with House" (http://tvbythenumbers.com/2007/11/07/overnight-results-116-fox-leads-with-house/1656). *The Nielsen Company* (TV by the Numbers). . Retrieved August 7, 2010.

[7] Seidman, Robert (November 14, 2007). "Overnight Results 11/13: FOX is in the House" (http://tvbythenumbers.com/2007/11/14/overnight-results-1113-fox-is-in-the-house/1772). *The Nielsen Company* (TV by the Numbers). . Retrieved August 7, 2010.

[8] Seidman, Robert (November 21, 2007). "Overnight Results 11/19: House is a Demo Hit" (http://tvbythenumbers.com/2007/11/21/overnight-results-1119-house-is-a-demo-hit/1872). *The Nielsen Company* (TV by the Numbers). . Retrieved August 7, 2010.

[9] Seidman, Robert (November 28, 2007). "Overnight Results 11/27: Huge Dancing Finale" (http://tvbythenumbers.com/2007/11/28/overnight-results-1127-huge-dancing-finale/1932). *The Nielsen Company* (TV by the Numbers). . Retrieved August 7, 2010.

[10] Gorman, Bill (December 12, 2007). "Top NBC Primetime Shows, December 3–9" (http://tvbythenumbers.com/2007/12/12/top-nbc-primetime-shows-december-3-9/2107). *The Nielsen Company* (TV by the Numbers). . Retrieved August 7, 2010.

[11] Gorman, Bill (January 8, 2008). "Top NBC Primetime Shows, Dec 31 – Jan 6" (http://tvbythenumbers.com/2008/01/08/top-nbc-primetime-shows-dec-31-jan-6/2336). *The Nielsen Company* (TV by the Numbers). . Retrieved August 7, 2010.

[12] Seidman, Robert (January 9, 2008). "Overnight Results for Tuesday, January 8" (http://tvbythenumbers.com/2008/01/09/overnight-results-for-tuesday-january-8/2344). *The Nielsen Company* (TV by the Numbers). . Retrieved August 7, 2010.

[13] Seidman, Robert (January 16, 2008). "Overnight Results for Tuesday, January 15" (http://tvbythenumbers.com/2008/01/16/overnight-results-for-tuesday-january-15/2409). *The Nielsen Company* (TV by the Numbers). . Retrieved August 7, 2010.

[14] Seidman, Robert (January 23, 2008). "Overnight Results for Tuesday, January 22" (http://tvbythenumbers.com/2008/01/23/overnight-results-for-tuesday-january-22/2445). *The Nielsen Company* (TV by the Numbers). . Retrieved August 7, 2010.

[15] Seidman, Robert (April 16, 2008). "Nielsen Ratings Tue, April 15: American Idol Wins / Kristy Lee Cook Must Lose!" (http://tvbythenumbers.com/2008/04/16/nielsen-ratings-tue-april-8-american-idol-wins-kristy-lee-cook-must-lose/3364). *The Nielsen Company* (TV by the Numbers). . Retrieved August 7, 2010.

[16] Seidman, Robert (April 23, 2008). "Nielsen Ratings Tue, April 22: American Idol and Hell's Kitchen Cook for FOX" (http://tvbythenumbers.com/2008/04/23/nielsen-ratings-tue-april-22-american-idol-and-hells-kitchen-cook-for-fox/3485). *The Nielsen Company* (TV by the Numbers). . Retrieved August 7, 2010.

[17] Seidman, Robert (April 30, 2008). "Nielsen Ratings Apr 29: Is A Drunken Paula Abdul Good for Ratings?" (http://tvbythenumbers.com/2008/04/30/nielsen-ratings-apr-29-is-a-drunken-paula-abdul-good-for-ratings/3559). *The Nielsen Company* (TV by the Numbers). . Retrieved August 7, 2010.

[18] http://improveverywhere.com/2008/01/31/frozen-grand-central/

[19] Seidman, Robert (May 7, 2008). "Nielsen Ratings May 6: FOX and Idol Take a Hit, But Still Win" (http://tvbythenumbers.com/2008/05/07/nielsen-ratings-may-6-fox-and-idol-take-a-hit-but-still-win/3665). *The Nielsen Company* (TV by the Numbers). . Retrieved August 07, 2010.

[20] Seidman, Robert (May 14, 2008). "Nielsen Ratings May 13, 2008: American Idol Still Crushes Field" (http://tvbythenumbers.com/2008/05/14/nielsen-ratings-may-13-2008-american-idol-still-crushes-field/3772). *The Nielsen Company* (TV by the Numbers). . Retrieved August 07, 2010.

External links

- Official episode guide (http://www.nbc.com/law-and-order-special-victims-unit/about/recaps/#cat=9)
- Season 9 episodes (http://www.tvguide.com/tvshows/law-order-special-victims-unit/episodes-season-9/100257) at TVGuide.com
- Season 9 episodes (http://tv.msn.com/tv/series-episodes/law-and-order-special-victims-unit.1/) at MSN.com
- Season 9 episodes (http://www.tv.com/law-and-order-special-victims-unit/show/334/episode.html?season=9&tag=list_header;paginator;9) at TV.com
- Season 9 episodes (http://www.imdb.com/title/tt0203259/episodes#season-9) at IMDb.com
- *Law & Order: Special Victims Unit* Season 9 (http://lawandorder.wikia.com/wiki/SVU_Season_9) on the Law & Order wiki (http://lawandorder.wikia.com/wiki/Law_&_Order_wiki)

SpongeBob SquarePants

SpongeBob SquarePants	
The current "off-screen" logo, enacted in 2009.	
Genre	Comedy
Created by	Stephen Hillenburg
Developed by	Derek Drymon Tim Hill Nick Jennings
Creative director(s)	Derek Drymon (Season 1-3) Vincent Waller (Season 4-present)
Voices of	Tom Kenny Bill Fagerbakke Rodger Bumpass Carolyn Lawrence Clancy Brown Mr. Lawrence
Theme music composer	Hank Smith Music
Opening theme	"SpongeBob SquarePants" performed by Pat Pinney
Ending theme	"Cierre Bob Esponja"
Composer(s)	Nicolas Carr
Country of origin	United States
No. of seasons	8
No. of episodes	167 320 (Segments) (List of episodes)
Production	
Executive producer(s)	Stephen Hillenburg Paul Tibbitt (Season 5-present)
Producer(s)	Dina Buteyn **(Supervising Producers)** Derek Drymon (Season 1-3) Paul Tibbitt (Season 4-present)
Running time	22–23 minutes
Production company(s)	United Plankton Pictures Nickelodeon Animation Studios
Distributor	MTV Networks International
Broadcast	
Original channel	Nickelodeon
Picture format	480i: SDTV (1999–present) 1080i: HDTV (2009–present)

Audio format	Advantage Audio Services (1999–2009) (NTSC) Advantage Audio Services 8.0 (2009–present) Dolby Surround 5.1 (2009–present) (NTSC)
Original run	May 1, 1999 – present
External links	
Website [1]	

SpongeBob SquarePants (often referred to simply as ***SpongeBob***) is an American animated television series, created by marine biologist and animator Stephen Hillenburg. Much of the series centers on the exploits and adventures of the title character and his various friends in the underwater city of Bikini Bottom. The series' popularity has prompted the release of a media franchise, contributing to its position as Nickelodeon's highest rated show, the most distributed property of MTV Networks, and among Nicktoons' most watched shows.[2] As of 2011, *SpongeBob SquarePants* is the only Nicktoon from the 1990s that has not ended yet. The show is listed 15th in IGN's top 100 animated series list. It is also known for being one of Nickelodeon's longest running TV shows.

The basis for *SpongeBob SquarePants* was formed by Hillenburg in 1984 while teaching and studying marine biology at the Ocean Institute in Dana Point, California, where he wrote the comic strip *The Intertidal Zone*, which starred various anthropomorphic forms of sea life, many of which would evolve into *SpongeBob SquarePants* characters. He left the institute to become an animator in 1987, and later attended the California Institute of Arts in 1992. In the institute, he made his thesis film *Wormholes* (1992), which led to his hiring as a director, writer, producer, storyboard artist, and executive producer of the series *Rocko's Modern Life* by creator Joe Murray. He started to develop the series in 1996 following *Rocko's Modern Life*'s, and pitched the series to Nickelodeon in 1998 and was later greenlit for a first season.

The pilot episode of *SpongeBob SquarePants* first aired episodes in the United States on Nickelodeon on May 1, 1999, following the *Nickelodeon Kids' Choice Awards*. The first episodes were called "Help Wanted", "Reef Blower", and "Tea at the Treedome". The "official" series premiere followed on July 17, 1999, with the second episode, "Bubblestand/Ripped Pants." The show reached enormous popularity by 2000 during the second season, and has remained popular since. A feature film of the series was released in theaters on November 19, 2004. The series celebrated its tenth anniversary on July 17, 2009. *SpongeBob* was renewed for a ninth season on January 3, 2011.[3] So far the series has aired 320 individual episodes.

Characters

SpongeBob SquarePants is an energetic and optimistic sea sponge (although his appearance more closely resembles a kitchen sponge) who lives in a pineapple under the sea with his pet snail, **Gary**, who meows like a cat. Although Gary only actually speaks in a few episodes, (mainly in "Sleepy Time" in SpongeBob's dream world, where Gary is portrayed as a librarian with an English accent) the characters have shown an ability to understand him. Living two houses down from SpongeBob is his best friend, **Patrick Star**, a dim-witted yet friendly pink seastar who lives under a rock. Even despite his "Mental Setbacks", Patrick still sees himself as intelligent. SpongeBob's next-door neighbor and co-worker is **Squidward Tentacles**, an arrogant and ill-tempered squid who lives in an Easter Island moai and dislikes his neighbors (especially SpongeBob) for their child-like behavior. He enjoys playing the clarinet and painting self-portraits, but hates his job working at the Krusty Krab.

Another close friend of SpongeBob's is **Sandy Cheeks**, a squirrel from Texas. Sandy is an expert at karate and lives in an underwater tree dome. When not inside her tree dome, she wears an astronaut-like suit because she cannot breathe underwater. SpongeBob and Squidward's employer is former officer cadet for the Bikini Bottom Navy force and war veteran **Eugene Krabs**, a miserly crab obsessed with money, who is the owner of the Krusty Krab restaurant. Mr. Krabs has a whale daughter, Pearl, who is a teenage cheerleader. The reason why Mr. Krabs' daughter is a whale is unknown. Mr. Krabs' archenemy is **Sheldon Plankton**, a small green copepod who owns a low-rank fast-food restaurant called the Chum Bucket across the street from the Krusty Krab. Plankton spends most of his time planning to steal the recipe for Mr. Krabs's popular Krabby Patty burgers to obtain success (occasionally with the assistance of his computer wife, Karen), though his schemes always end in failure.

Voice cast

Main cast

- Tom Kenny as SpongeBob SquarePants, Gary the Snail
- Bill Fagerbakke as Patrick Star
- Carolyn Lawrence as Sandy Cheeks
- Rodger Bumpass as Squidward Tentacles
- Clancy Brown as Mr. Krabs
- Mr. Lawrence as Plankton

Recurring cast

- Mary Jo Catlett as Mrs. Puff
- Lori Alan as Pearl
- Jill Talley as Karen and various characters
- Dee Bradley Baker as Bubble Bass, Squilliam Fancyson, Perch Perkins, various characters
- Tom Kenny as French Narrator, Harold SquarePants, Patchy the Pirate, Dirty Bubble (2010–present), various characters
- Bill Fagerbakke as Mayor of Bikini Bottom and various characters
- Rodger Bumpass as Dr. Gill Gilliam and various characters
- Mr. Lawrence as Larry the Lobster, Johnny-Elaine and various characters
- Sirena Irwin as Claire Bubblebottom-SquarePants, Mrs. Krabs (2005–present) and various characters
- Stephen Hillenburg - Potty the Parrot (2000–2004)
- Paul Tibbitt as Mrs. Krabs (2001–2002) and Potty the Parrot (2005–present)
- Ernest Borgnine as Mermaid Man
- Tim Conway as Barnacle Boy
- Marion Ross as Grandma SquarePants
- Brian Doyle-Murray as The Flying Dutchman
- John Rhys-Davies as Man Ray (2001–2002)
- Bob Joles as Man Ray (2005–present)
- Charles Nelson Reilly as Dirty Bubble (1999–2002)
- John O'Hurley as King Neptune
- Mark Fite as various characters
- Thomas F. Wilson as various characters
- Carlos Alazraqui as various characters

Setting

Much of the series' events take place in Bikini Bottom, an underwater city located in the Pacific Ocean beneath the real life tropical isle of Bikini Atoll.[4] Stephen Hillenburg has stated that much of Bikini Bottom was based on the real life city of Seattle.[5] Much of this is supported within the context of the episodes themselves; however, despite implications of the city's location as well as analogies to real life, Hillenburg has stated that he wishes to leave the city isolated from the real world, explaining the *Baywatch* parody scene from *The SpongeBob SquarePants Movie* as simply a reference to his favorite show of all time.[5] [6] The citizens of Bikini Bottom live in mostly aquatic-themed buildings, and use "boatmobiles", an amalgamation of cars and boats, as a mode of transportation.

Each episode of *SpongeBob SquarePants* is self-contained, with references to previous episodes being rare. Episodes have ended with the entire town being destroyed, the entire cast being irreparably harmed, or other catastrophic events, only for everything to return to normal the next episode without any mention of what happened before.

History

Origins

Creator Stephen Hillenburg initially conceived *SpongeBob SquarePants* in 1984, while he was teaching and studying marine biology at what is now the Orange County Ocean Institute.[7] During this period, Hillenburg became fascinated with animation, and wrote a comic book entitled *The Intertidal Zone* starring various anthropomorphic forms of sea life, many of which would evolve into *SpongeBob SquarePants* characters,[8] including "Bob the Sponge", who was the co-host of the comic and resembled an actual sea sponge, as opposed to SpongeBob who resembles a kitchen sponge.[9] In 1987, Hillenburg left the institute to pursue his dream of becoming an animator,[8] [9] and began to envision the possible concept of a project involving anthropomorphic sea life, drawing several rough sketches.[9] In 1992, Hillenburg began to attend the California Institute of the Arts to study animation, having been accepted into the institute by Jules Engel, who was impressed with Hillenburg's previous work.[8] [10] [11]

Creator Stephen Hillenburg became an animator during his period of study at the California Institute of Arts.

While attending animation school, Hillenburg received a job on the children's TV series *Mother Goose & Grimm*, and worked on the series from 1991 to 1993. When attending the California Institute of the Arts, he made his thesis film entitled *Wormholes*,[9] which was funded by the Princess Grace Foundation and was later displayed at various animation festivals.[9] In 1993, Hillenburg graduated from the institute, earning a Master of Fine Arts in experimental animation.[8] In 1995, Joe Murray, creator of *Rocko's Modern Life*, met Hillenburg at an animation festival, and offered him a job as a director of the series.[9] [12] [13] [14] Hillenburg then joined the Nickelodeon animated series as a writer, producer, and storyboard artist during the series' third season, continuing his position for much of the fourth season.[9] [14] [15] The third season episode "Fish-N-Chumps" (November 12, 1995) was directed by Hillenburg, and involved Rocko, Heffer, and Filburt going on a fishing trip, oblivious to the fact that a pair anthropomorphic fish are attempting to catch them from underwater.[12] [16] While working on *Rocko's Modern Life*, Hillenburg became friends with Tom Kenny, who was later approached by Hillenburg to become the voice of SpongeBob SquarePants,[17] and future *SpongeBob SquarePants* collaborators Mr. Lawrence, Paul Tibbitt and others.

Rocko's Modern Life ended in 1996.[18] Shortly following this, Hillenburg began working on *SpongeBob SquarePants*, teaming up with several Nickelodeon veterans and *Rocko* crew members.[9] [16] To voice the character of SpongeBob, Hillenburg approached Tom Kenny, who had worked with him on *Rocko's Modern Life*.[17]

Originally, SpongeBob was to be named *SpongeBoy*, but this name was already in use.[19] This was discovered after voice acting for the original seven minute pilot was recorded in 1997. The Nickelodeon legal department discovered that the name was already in use for a mop product.[20] Upon finding this out, Hillenburg decided that the character's given name still had to contain "Sponge" so viewers would not mistake the character for a "Cheese Man." Hillenburg decided to use the name "SpongeBob." He chose "SquarePants" as a family name as it referred to the character's square shape and "had a nice ring to it".[21]

While pitching the cartoon to Nickelodeon executives, Hillenburg donned a Hawaiian shirt, brought along an "underwater terrarium with models of the characters", and Hawaiian music to set the theme. The setup was described by Nick executive Eric Coleman as "pretty amazing".[22] When given money and two weeks to write the pilot episode ("Help Wanted"),[10] Derek Drymon, Stephen Hillenberg, and Nick Jennings returned with, described by Nickelodeon official Albie Hecht, "a performance he wished he had on tape".[23] Although described as stressful by executive producer Derek Drymon,[10] the pitch went "very well"; Kevin Kay and Hecht had to step outside because they were "exhausted from laughing", making the cartoonists worried.[23]

Hillenburg era (1999–2004)

SpongeBob's first season was only a modest success during its initial run after the series' debut in 1999, but the show still garnered enough popularity that Nickelodeon quietly renewed it for a second season. Beginning with this season, production of the series switched from traditional cel animation to digital ink and paint. During the second season's run, the show quickly achieved enormous and world wide popularity, leading to an immediate third season pick-up. The show's continued success eventually led to the creation of a feature film called *The SpongeBob SquarePants Movie*, which was intended to be the end of the series. However, shortly after the film's release, Nickelodeon renewed the series for a fourth season. Also following the film's release, Stephen Hillenburg resigned as show runner, causing a shift in the series' production crew, as well as several of the series' writers. Following the end of the Hillenburg era, the animation style changed to 3D computer animation (although it would still use digital ink and paint).

Post-movie era (2005–present)

The series' fourth season began in May 2005, and was ordered a fifth season in December 2005, bringing the show's total episode count to 100.[24] In December 2006, *SpongeBob* was approved for a sixth season. The fifth season began in February 2007.[25] On July 23, 2007, Nickelodeon began airing a special event, called the "SpongeBob New–New–New–New–New–Week" in which from Monday to Friday, a new episode would air.[26] This continued until the end of the second week. Later on November 12, 2007, a TV movie aired titled *Atlantis SquarePantis*, guest starring David Bowie as the voice of Lord Royal Highness. In March 2008, it was announced that *SpongeBob* would have an additional thirty-nine episodes, which includes the remaining episodes of the sixth season, and a seventh season.[27] [28] [29]

On July 14, 2009, a primetime *SpongeBob* tenth anniversary documentary titled *Square Roots: The Story of SpongeBob SquarePants*, aired on VH1, discussing the history of the show, and its impact on popular culture.[30] Starting on July 17, 2009 at 8:00 PM EST, Nickelodeon aired a 50½-hour marathon titled "The Ultimate SpongeBob Sponge Bash." The marathon included the premiere of 11 new episodes, countdowns of celebrities' and viewer-chosen top 10 episodes, and more.[31] On November 6, 2009, a second TV movie debuted on Nickelodeon, titled *Truth or Square*, in which SpongeBob, Patrick, Squidward, and Mr. Krabs are accidentally locked inside the Krusty Krab freezer on the night of the restaurant's eleventy-seventh anniversary celebration. While trapped inside, the friends look back on their shared memories with "shocking" reveals.[32] Several celebrities made live-action cameo appearances on *Truth or Square*, including Rosario Dawson, LeBron James, Tina Fey, Will Ferrell, Craig Ferguson, Robin Williams and Pink, while Ricky Gervais provided opening and closing naration for the special.[33] Also Victoria Beckham lent her voice as Queen Amphitrite, a Brit-accented goddess of the sea in an episode titled

"The Clash of Triton," a half-hour special that aired on July 5, 2010.[34] [35]

SpongeBob SquarePants is currently slated to surpass *Rugrats* as the longest running Nicktoon in number of episodes sometime during its eighth season. *Rugrats* aired 172 episodes in its run; *SpongeBob*, when the eighth season completes, will have 178.[36] The series was further extended to a ninth season in January 2011, bringing its total to 204 episodes. It will become the first Nicktoon to reach 200 episodes.[37] It will also be the second Nicktoon to have made it to its ninth season.

The eighth season started on March 26, 2011, when "Oral Report" and "A Friendly Game" aired. "Sentimental Sponge" aired the next weekend, on April 2, 2011. The next episode did not air until June 4, 2011, when a SpongeBob SquarePants new episode marathon started, that aired 1 new episode every Saturday, for the month of June.

Music

The theme music was composed by Derek Drymon, Mark Harrison, Stephen Hillenburg and Blaise Smith as part of Hank Smith Music, and is primarily based on the sea shanty, "Blow the Man Down". The song is sung by Painty the Pirate, voiced by Patrick Pinney, and can be found on the soundtrack *SpongeBob SquarePants: Original Theme Highlights*. A cover of the song by Avril Lavigne can be found on the *SpongeBob SquarePants Movie* soundtrack. Another cover by the Violent Femmes, which aired as a commercial on Nickelodeon to promote season two, can be viewed in the special features of the Nautical Nonsense/Sponge Buddies DVD. A choral version was recorded for the SpongeBob Christmas special where the last repetition of "SpongeBob SquarePants" was replaced by, "It's the SpongeBob Christmas special." The theme song is occasionally used as marching cadence. An instrumental version of the opening theme is used in Italy. The series' music editor and main composer is Nicolas Carr. Most of the background music used in the series comes from the Associated Production Music (APM) Library, some of which have also been used in shows such as *The Simpsons*, *The Ren & Stimpy Show*, *The Mighty B!*, *Rocko's Modern Life*, *The X Factor*, *Camp Lazlo*, *My Gym Partner's a Monkey*, *Bill Nye the Science Guy*, and *The Adventures of Pete & Pete*. For competition-based episodes, some of Sam Spence's NFL Films music is used (such as "A Golden Boy Again" used in episodes such as The Fry Cook Games and "Ramblin' Man from Gramblin" is used in Mermaid Man and Barnacle Boy V. "The Lineman" is also used extensively in Mermaid Man and Barnacle Boy episodes). Ironically, one of Spence's more famous songs for the NFL Films library of music is an orchestral version of "Drunken Sailor" called "Up She Rises", first suggested by Steven Sabol to his father Ed because he liked the song at summer camp.

Hawaiian steel guitar music is used for comedic and dramatic effect in the show. Various compositions featuring the Hawaiian steel convey happy, sad, or goofy emotions and situations. Many are traditional Hawaiian melodies such as "Aloha 'Oe" and are usually sampled from the above-mentioned APM music library, and are from time to time performed by classic steel guitar artists, including The Woodies, The Langhorns, and The MelTones. Creator Hillenburg states that much of the music in the series was inspired by 1950s Hawaiian steel guitar tunes.[6] Another aspect of the series' musical score is traditional sea shanties, which are used for the musical themes in the show. The most commonly used song in the series is "Drunken Sailor," though a ukulele version of the "Twelfth Street Rag" is often heard in the background as well. Unlike other Nickelodeon shows, SpongeBob features well-known independent musicians who contribute to its soundtrack. Alternative rock bands such as Wilco, The Shins, The Flaming Lips and Ween, as well as metal bands Pantera, Motörhead and Twisted Sister have made appearances on the show and movies soundtracks.

Reception

Popularity and appeal

SpongeBob SquarePants was the first "low budget" Nickelodeon cartoon, according to the network, to become extremely popular. Low-budget cartoons had not garnered as much esteem as higher-rated, higher-budgeted shows, although when *SpongeBob SquarePants* aired in 1999, it had gained a significant enough number of viewers in the ratings to be considered popular, eventually reaching worldwide popularity by 2000. *SpongeBob* follows other Nickelodeon shows that have attracted "older" followers: Other shows have followed in this trend as well: *The Fairly OddParents* won a similar fan base when it premiered in 2001, and is now second only to *SpongeBob* in popularity. Though the show debuted in 1999, *SpongeBob* did not become hugely popular until around 2000, and it has remained popular since then. Since 2004, IGN made *SpongeBob SquarePants* 15th in its top 100 animated series of all time list.

Heavy metal group Metallica even released a T-shirt featuring cartoon versions of themselves playing live with the characters SpongeBob and Patrick. British rock singer David Bowie was a special guest on the SpongeBob SquarePants episode Atlantis SquarePantis, which aired on November 12, 2007.[38] The episode drew total 8.8 million viewers, the biggest audience in the show's eight-year history.[38]

The show became so popular with adolescents and adults that the series was broadcast on MTV and featured on Spike TV. A quote by Patrick, "It's gonna rock!" from the episode Mid-Life Crustacean, has been used as a promotional tag-line for rock stations. Ren and Stimpy, among others, had followed a similar path. *The SpongeBob SquarePants Movie* features a cameo appearance by actor David Hasselhoff, in a parody of his role from the *Baywatch* TV series. In April 2009, as a tie-in to the special "SpongeBob vs. The Big One", Burger King distributed two different commercials geared toward children and adult audiences. In ads broadcast on major networks, the commercial shows rapper Sir Mix-a-Lot recording a music video for his new song, “SpongeBob Got Back”.

Awards and nominations

Year	Association	Category	Nominee	Result
2000	Golden Reel Award	Best Sound Editing in Television Animation — Music	Episodes: "Mermaid Man and Barnacle Boy" and "Pickles"	Won
2000	Golden Reel Award	Best Sound Editing in Television Animation — Sound	Episode: "Karate Choppers"	Won
2001	Annie Awards	Outstanding Individual Achievement for Voice Acting by a Female Performer in an Animated Television Production	Mary Jo Catlett as Mrs. Puff in "No Free Rides"	Nominated
2001	Annie Awards	Outstanding Individual Achievement for Voice Acting by a Male Performer in an Animated Television Production	Tom Kenny as SpongeBob in "Wormy"	Nominated
2001	Annie Awards	Outstanding Individual Achievement for a Song in an Animated Production	Peter Straus and Paul Tibbitt for the song "The Very First Christmas"	Nominated
2001	Golden Reel Award	Best Sound Editing in Television Animation — Sound	Episodes: "Rock Bottom" and "Arrgh"	Won
2001	Golden Reel Award	Best Sound Editing in Television Animation — Music	Episodes: "Fools In April" and "Neptune's Spatula"	Nominated
2002	Emmy Awards	Outstanding Animated Program (For Programming Less Than One Hour)		Nominated
2002	Golden Reel Award	Best Sound Editing in Television – Animation	Episodes: "Secret Box" and "Band Geeks"	Won
2002	Golden Reel Award	Best Sound Editing in Television Animation — Music	Episodes: "Jellyfish Hunter" and "The Fry Cook Games"	Nominated

2002	Television Critics Association Awards	Outstanding Achievement in Children's Programming		Won
2003	Emmy Awards	Outstanding Animated Program (For Programming Less Than One Hour)	Episodes: "New Student Starfish" and "Clams"	Nominated
2003	Golden Reel Award	Best Sound Editing in Television Animation — Music	Episodes: "Wet Painters" and "Krusty Krab Training Video"	Won
2003	Golden Reel Award	Best Sound Editing in Television Animation	Episodes: "Nasty Patty" and "Idiot Box"	Won
2003	Kids' Choice Awards	Favorite Cartoon		Won
2004	Emmy Awards	Outstanding Animated Program (For Programming Less Than One Hour)	Episode: "SpongeBob B.C. (Before Comedy)"	Nominated
2004	Golden Reel Award	Best Sound Editing in Television Animation — Music	Episodes: "The Great Snail Race" and "Mid-Life Crustacean".	Won
2004	Golden Reel Award	Best Sound Editing in Television Animation — Music	Episode: "Mid-Life Crustacean".	Nominated
2004	Kids' Choice Awards	Favorite Cartoon		Won
2005	Annie Awards	Best Animated Television Production		Won
2005	Emmy Awards	Outstanding Animated Program (For Programming Less Than One Hour)	Episodes: "Fear of a Krabby Patty" and "Shell of a Man"	Nominated
2005	Golden Reel Award	Best Sound Editing in Television: Animated	Episodes: "Pranks A Lot" and "SpongeBob Meets the Strangler"	Nominated
2005	Kids' Choice Awards	Favorite Cartoon		Won
2005	Satellite Awards	Best Youth DVD	Complete Second Season DVD	Nominated
2005	Television Critics Association Awards	Outstanding Achievement in Children's Programming		Nominated
2006	Annie Awards	Best Writing in an Animated Television Production	C.H. Greenblatt, Paul Tibbitt, Mike Bell, and Tim Hill in "Fear of a Krabby Patty"	Won
2006	Golden Reel Award	Best Sound Editing in Television: Animated	Episode: "Have You Seen This Snail?"	Nominated
2006	Kids' Choice Awards	Favorite Cartoon		Won
2007	Emmy Awards	Outstanding Animated Program (For Programming Less Than One Hour)	Episodes: "Bummer Vacation" and "Wigstruck"	Nominated
2007	Kids' Choice Awards	Favorite Cartoon		Won
2007	Television Critics Association Awards	Outstanding Achievement in Children's Programming		Nominated[39]
2008	Annie Awards	Best Voice Acting in an Animated Television Production	Tom Kenny in "Spy Buddies"	Nominated
2008	Golden Reel Award	Best Sound Editing in Television: Animated	Episode: "SpongeHenge"	Nominated
2008	Kids' Choice Awards	Favorite Cartoon		Nominated
2008	Emmy Awards	Outstanding Animated Program (For Programming Less Than One Hour)	Episodes: "The Inmates of Summer" and "The Two Faces of Squidward"	Nominated
2008	Philippines Kids' Choice Awards	Favorite Cartoon		Won
2009	Kids' Choice Awards	Favorite Cartoon		Won
2009	Indonesia Kids Choice Awards	Favorite Cartoon		Won
2009	Annie Awards	Direction in an Animated Television Production	Episode: "Penny Foolish"	Nominated

2009	Golden Reel Awards	Best Sound Editing: Television Animation	Episode: "Suction Cup Symphony"	Nominated
2009	Teen Choice Awards	Choice TV Animated Show		Won
2009	Emmy Awards	Special Class Animated Program	Episode: "Dear Vikings"	Nominated
2010	Golden Reel Awards	Best Sound Editing: Television Animation	Episode: "SpongeBob vs. The Big One"	Nominated
2010	Annie Awards	Best Home Entertainment Production	"SpongeBob vs. The Big One" DVD	Nominated
2010	Annie Awards	Best Animated Television Production for Children		Nominated
2010	Annie Awards	Best Voice Acting in a Television Production	Tom Kenny in "SpongeBob's Truth or Square"	Won
2010	Kids' Choice Awards	Favorite Cartoon		Won
2010	Indonesia Kids Choice Awards	Favorite Cartoon		Won
2010	Emmy Awards	Outstanding Special Class Animated Program		Won
2011	Annie Awards	Best Animated Television Production for Children		Won
2011	Annie Awards	Music in a Television Production	Jeremy Wakefield, Sage Guyton, Nick Carr, Tuck Tucker	Won
2011	Kids' Choice Awards	Favorite Cartoon		Won
2011	Emmy Awards	Outstanding Short-format Animated Program	Episode: "That Sinking Feeling"	Nominated

Criticism and controversy

In 2005, a promotional video which showed SpongeBob along with other characters from children's shows singing together to promote diversity and tolerance,[40] was attacked by an evangelical group in the United States because they saw the character SpongeBob being used as an advocate for homosexuality.[41] James Dobson of Focus on the Family accused the makers of the video of promoting homosexuality due to a pro-tolerance group sponsoring the video.[41]

The incident led to questions to whether or not SpongeBob is homosexual. In 2002, SpongeBob creator Stephen Hillenburg denied this, despite the fact that SpongeBob's popularity with gay men grew. He clarified that he considers the character to be "almost asexual".[42] [43] After Dobson made the comments, Hillenburg repeated this assertion that sexual preference was never considered during the creation of the show.[44] Tom Kenny and other production members were shocked and surprised that such an issue had arisen.[20]

Dobson later asserted that his comments were taken out of context and that his original complaints were not with SpongeBob, the video, or any of the characters in the video but with the organization that sponsored the video, *We Are Family Foundation*. Dobson indicated that the *We Are Family Foundation* posted pro-homosexual material on their website, but later removed it.[45] After the controversy, John H. Thomas, the United Church of Christ's general minister and president, said they would welcome SpongeBob into their ministry. He said *"Jesus didn't turn people away. Neither do we".*[46]

Jeffrey P. Dennis, author of the journal article "The Same Thing We Do Every Night: Signifying Same-Sex Desire in Television Cartoons," argued that SpongeBob and Sandy are not romantically in love, while adding that he believed that SpongeBob and Patrick "are paired with arguably erotic intensity." Dennis noted the two are "not consistently coded as romantic partners," since they live in separate residences, and have distinct groups of friends, but claimed that in the series, "the possibility of same-sex desire is never excluded."[47] Martin Goodman of *Animation World Magazine* described Dennis's comments regarding SpongeBob and Patrick as "interesting."[48]

A 2011 study conducted at the University of Virginia, published in the journal *Pediatrics*, suggested that allowing preschool audiences to watch the series caused short term disruptions in mental function and attention span. The study had three groups of four-year-olds each engage in activities; one group watched *SpongeBob*, another watched

Caillou, and the third group drew pictures. After nine minutes, the children were tested on mental functions; the group watching *SpongeBob* scored significantly lower than the other two groups, whose results were roughly equal to each other.[49] A Nickelodeon executive responded that the show was not intended for an audience of that age and that the study used "questionable methodology and could not possibly provide the basis for any valid findings that parents could trust."[50]

Other media

Amusement rides

SpongeBob SquarePants 4-D is located in Six Flags Over Texas, Noah's Ark Dive-In Theater in Noah's Ark Waterpark and Flamingo Land and opened in Six Flags Over Texas and Noah's Ark Dive-In Theater in 2007. The ride features water squirts, real bubbles, and other sensory enhancements. The SpongeBob SquarePants 4-D ride opened at the Wisconsin Dells, Wisconsin in the summer of 2007. SpongeBob appears at the Mall of America's new Nickelodeon theme park re-branded from the Mall of America's Park at MOA, formerly Camp Snoopy, to Nickelodeon Universe in the Minneapolis-St. Paul suburb of Bloomington, Minnesota. The new theme park features a SpongeBob-themed Gerstlauer Euro-Fighter custom roller coaster, the SpongeBob SquarePants Rock Bottom Plunge, which has replaced the Mystery Mine Ride and Olde Time Photo store on the west end of the theme park. The theme park opened March 15, 2008.

The Chicago Shedd Aquarium hosts a 15 minute feature of SpongeBob in 4-D with vibrating "special FX" movie seats accompanied by bubbles, wind, a distinct pickle smell, and tickles throughout the film. The feature ran through 2009 being temporarily replaced on November 27.[51]

Film

Paramount Pictures and Nickelodeon Movies produced *The SpongeBob SquarePants Movie*, a film adaption of the *SpongeBob SquarePants* animated series released on November 19, 2004. The film was directed by series creator Stephen Hillenburg, and was written by long-time series writers Hillenburg, Derek Drymon, Tim Hill, Kent Osborne, Aaron Springer, and Paul Tibbitt. Nickelodeon official Albie Hecht, Drymon, Hillenburg, Julia Pistor, and Gina Shay produced the film, while much of the film's music was composed by Gregor Narholz. this movie was originally going to be the series finale, but because of the film's popularity and universal critical acclaim, Stephen Hillenburg decided to make more episodes. The film follows SpongeBob, who expects to be bestowed the title of manager for Mr. Krabs' new restaurant, *The Krusty Krab 2* (although this restaurant is never seen or mentioned for the rest of the series). However, the position is given to Squidward instead, causing SpongeBob to go into a state of depression. Jealous of Mr. Krabs' success, Plankton initiates his final plan, *Plan Z*, which involves framing Mr. Krabs for the theft of King Neptune's crown. SpongeBob and Patrick then go on a quest to retrieve Neptune's crown and save the lives of both Mr. Krabs and the rest of Bikini Bottom from Plankton's scheme. The film also guest stars Jeffrey Tambor as King Neptune, Scarlett Johansson as the king's daughter Mindy, Alec Baldwin as Dennis the Hitman, and David Hasselhoff as himself.[52] It received a largely positive critical reception and grossed over $140 million worldwide.

Merchandise

Merchandise based on the show ranges from Kraft Macaroni & Cheese, Go-Gurt, Kellogg's cereal, and video games to boxer shorts, flip-flops, pajamas, t-shirts, slippers, Pez dispensers, and radios. The show also spawned a large and popular merchandise line at Hot Topic, Claire's, Waldenbooks, Borders Books, Barnes & Noble, Best Buy, RadioShack, Target, Big Lots, Walmart, Shopko, Pamida, Meijer, Kmart, Sears, JCPenney, Kohl's, Lowe's, T.J. Maxx, Toys "R" Us and the defunct stores Ames, KB Toys in the United States as well as the Zellers, Wal-Mart Canada, and Toys "R" Us stores in Canada, and a limited selection of merchandise in Australia at Kmart Australia,

Target Australia, Big W, and The Warehouse.

Kids' meal tie-ins have been released in fast-food restaurants in many different parts of the world, including Burger King in Europe and North America, as well as Wendy's in North America, and Hungry Jack's in Australia. A McDonald's Happy Meal tie-in with SpongeBob-themed Happy Meal boxes and toys has not been released in North America yet, but was released in Europe and other international markets in the summer of 2007.[53] In Australia, the advertisement for the McDonald's SpongeBob Happy Meal won the Pester Power Award for the fact that the ads are enticing young children to want its food because of the free toy. In Japan, they had a kids meal tie-in with KFC which featured different toys based on the TV series.[54] As a tie-in beverage for the *SpongeBob SquarePants Movie*, 7-Eleven convenience stores created a pineapple-flavored Slurpee in 2004, which was discontinued in 2005.

In 2007, some new high-end SpongeBob-themed electronics have been introduced by Imation Electronics Products under the Npower brand, such as MP3 players, digital cameras, a DVD player, and a flatscreen television.[55] Other items featuring SpongeBob include a special edition Monopoly board game, Life and Operation board game as well as a SpongeBob SquarePants edition of Ants in the Pants and Yahtzee. There are also rarer items such as SpongeBob Surfboards and electric guitars.

Pictures of SpongeBob SquarePants also started to appear on the labels of 8 oz. cans of Green Giant cut green beans and frozen packages of Green Giant green beans and butter sauce which featured free stickers in 2007 as part of an initiative to get kids to eat their vegetables.[56] In the United Kingdom, a SpongeBob SquarePants magazine is currently being published by Titan Magazines every four weeks. It was first published on February 3, 2005. The issue published on February 1, 2007 was the second anniversary of the magazine. The magazine contains comic strips, fan letters, competitions and several features including games.

A *SpongeBob SquarePants* 2009 calendar has been released featuring the caption on the bottom right corner of the front cover, "Celebrating his 10th Anniversary!", which was on May 1 and July 17, 2009 respectively.[57] On March 31, 2009 three songs from the show were released as downloadable content for the music video game series *Rock Band*. Nickelodeon has also created a Facebook page and Twitter account for SpongeBob. His best friend, Patrick Star, has been given a page on Facebook as well.

The popularity of SpongeBob translated well into sales figures. In 2002, SpongeBob SquarePants dolls sold at a rate of 75,000 per week, which was faster than Tickle Me Elmo dolls were selling at the time.[58] SpongeBob has gained popularity in Japan, specifically with Japanese women. Nickelodeon's parent company Viacom purposefully targeted marketing at women in the country as a method of the *SpongeBob SquarePants* brand. Skeptics initially doubted that SpongeBob could be popular in Japan as the character's design is very different to already popular designs for Hello Kitty and Pikachu.[59]

Episodes

Including the pilot, there are 304 total individual *SpongeBob SquarePants* episodes that have aired. There are still some episodes that have been announced but have still not yet aired. So far, *SpongeBob SquarePants* is in its eighth season. Season 8 has been announced and will have 26 new episodes bringing the number of episodes up to 178. Season 8 started on March 26, 2011 and will air episodes 153-178.

Season	Episodes	Season premiere	Season finale	DVD releases		
				Region 1	Region 2	Region 4
1	20 (41)	May 1, 1999	April 8, 2000	October 28, 2003	November 7, 2005	November 30, 2006
2	20 (39)	October 26, 2000	July 26, 2003	October 19, 2004	October 23, 2006	November 30, 2006
3	20 (37)	October 5, 2001	October 11, 2004	September 27, 2005	December 3, 2007	November 8, 2007
4	20 (38)	May 6, 2005	July 24, 2007	September 12, 2006 January 9, 2007	November 3, 2008	November 7, 2008
5	20 (41)	February 19, 2007	July 19, 2009	September 4, 2007 November 18, 2008	November 16, 2009	December 2, 2009
6	26 (47)	March 3, 2008	July 5, 2010	December 8, 2009 December 7, 2010	November 29, 2010	December 2, 2010
7	26 (50)	July 19, 2009	June 11, 2011	December 6, 2011[60]	N/A	N/A
8	26	March 26, 2011	TBA	N/A	N/A	N/A
9	26	TBA	N/A	N/A	N/A	N/A

Special episodes

Year	Episode
2000	"Christmas Who?"
2002	"Party Pooper Pants"
2003	"The Sponge Who Could Fly"
2004	"Ugh"
2005	"Have You Seen This Snail?"
2006	"Dunces and Dragons"
2007	"Friend or Foe?"
2008	"Pest of the West"
2008	"WhoBob WhatPants?"
2009	"SpongeBob vs. The Big One"
2010	"SpongeBob's Last Stand"
2010	"The Clash of Triton"
2010	"The Great Patty Caper"
2011	"Frozen Face-Off"
2011	"Ghoul Fools"
2011	"A SquarePants Family Vacation"

TV movies

Year	TV Movie
2007	*Atlantis SquarePantis*
2009	*Square Roots: The Story of SpongeBob SquarePants*
2009	*SpongeBob's Truth or Square*

Theatrical films

Year	Movie
2004	"The SpongeBob SquarePants Movie"

Notes

[1] http://spongebob.nick.com/

[2] Stock, Rosina (June 24, 2009). "Nickelodeon Celebrates Pop Culture Icon SpongeBob SquarePants decade" (http://mnilive.com/2009/06/nickelodeon-celebrates-pop-culture-icon-spongebob-squarepants-decade/). *Media News International*. . Retrieved July 14, 2009.

[3] Andreeva, Nellie (2011-01-03). "Nickelodeon Renews 'SpongeBob SquarePants' For Ninth Season" (http://www.deadline.com/2011/01/nickelodeon-renews-spongebob-squarepants-for-ninth-season/). Deadline.com. . Retrieved 2011-08-20.

[4] QSR Staff (June 7, 2001). "Burger King SpongeBob SquarePants" (http://www.qsrmagazine.com/articles/news/story.phtml?id=3354). *QSR Magazine* (QSRmagazine.com). . Retrieved August 19, 2010.

[5] "SpongeBob SquarePants" (http://members.outpost10f.com/~lindax/spongebob/spongebob-information.html). *SpongeBob SquarePants information*. . Retrieved February 10, 2009.

[6] Banks, Steven (September 24, 2004). *SpongeBob Exposed! The Insider's Guide to SpongeBob SquarePants*. Schigiel, Gregg (Illustrator). Simon Spotlight/Nickelodeon. ISBN 978-0689868702.

[7] Banks, pp. 8-9

[8] Banks, p. 9

[9] Hillenburg, Stephen (2003). *The Origin of SpongeBob SquarePants. SpongeBob SquarePants: The Complete First Season* (DVD). Paramount Home Entertainment.

[10] Drymon, Derek (2003). *The Origin of SpongeBob SquarePants. SpongeBob SquarePants: The Complete First Season* (DVD). Paramount Home Entertainment.

[11] "Nickelodeon Taps Patrick Creadon and Christine O'Malley to Produce First-Ever SpongeBob SquarePants Documentary" (http://sev.prnewswire.com/film-motion-picture/20090119/NY6023619012009-1.html). *Press Release* (Viacom). January 19, 2009. . Retrieved February 1, 2009.

[12] Murray, Joe (2003). *The Origin of SpongeBob SquarePants. SpongeBob SquarePants: The Complete First Season* (DVD). Paramount Home Entertainment.

[13] Neuwirth, p. 50

[14] " Lisa (Kiczuk) Trainor interviews Joe Murray, creator of Rocko's Modern Life (http://www.title14.com/rocko/contributors/murray.html)," *The Rocko's Modern Life FAQ*

[15] Banks, pp. 9-10

[16] Banks, p. 10

[17] Orlando, Dana (March 17, 2003). "SpongeBob: the excitable, absorbent star of Bikini Bottom" (http://www.sptimes.com/2003/03/17/Xpress/SpongeBob__the_excita.shtml). St Petersburg Times. . Retrieved November 8, 2008.

[18] " Rocko's Modern Life (http://www.joemurraystudio.com/tv/rocko.shtml)". *Joe Murray Studio*.

[19] Banks, p. 31

[20] Farhat, Basima (Interviewer) (December 5, 2006) (mp3). *Tom Kenny: Voice of SpongeBob SquarePants – Interview* (http://www.thepeoplespeakradio.net/archives/mp3/tps-2006-12-05-kenny.mp3) (Radio production). The People Speak Radio. . Retrieved November 8, 2008.

[21] Neuwirth, p. 51

[22] Coleman, Eric (2003). *The Origin of SpongeBob SquarePants. SpongeBob SquarePants: The Complete First Season* (DVD). Paramount Home Entertainment.

[23] Hecht, Albie (2003). *The Origin of SpongeBob SquarePants. SpongeBob SquarePants: The Complete First Season* (DVD). Paramount Home Entertainment.

[24] "More SpongeBob on Nickelodeon" (http://www.star-ecentral.com/news/story.asp?file=/2005/12/27/tvnradio/12578379&sec=tvnradio). *Star Online eCentral*. December 27, 2005. . Retrieved April 24, 2008.

[25] "SpongeBob SquarePants Season 5 Episode Guide on" (http://www.tv.com/spongebob-squarepants/show/3428/episode.html?season=5&tag=list_header;paginator;5). Tv.com. . Retrieved September 14, 2010.

[26] "Nickelodeon July Highlights" (http://www.animationinsider.net/article.php?articleID=1402). *Animation Insider*. June 25, 2007. . Retrieved November 8, 2009.

[27] "Nickelodeon Picks-Up Returning Animated Hits" (http://www.viacom.com/news/Pages/newstext.aspx?RID=1118469). *Viacom.com*. March 13, 2008. . Retrieved March 15, 2008.

[28] "Nickelodeon Upfront 2008" (http://www.animationinsider.net/article.php?articleID=1656). *Animation Insider*. March 13, 2008. . Retrieved March 16, 2008.

[29] "Nick Orders New Eps of "SpongeBob," "OddParents" and Other Series" (http://www.news.toonzone.net/article.php?ID=22274). *ToonZone*. March 13, 2008. . Retrieved March 19, 2008.

[30] Goldman, Eric (January 9, 2009). "SpongeBob SquarePants Meets Johnny Depp - TV News at IGN" (http://tv.ign.com/articles/943/943426p1.html). Tv.ign.com. . Retrieved September 14, 2010.

[31] "Ultimate SpongeBob SpongeBash Weekend - Raving Toy Maniac - The Latest News and Pictures from the World of Toys" (http://www.toymania.com/news/messages/11311.shtml). Toymania.com. . Retrieved September 14, 2010.

[32] "2009 Is The Year To Get 'Happy Squared' As Nickelodeon Celebrates 10 Years Of SpongeBob SquarePants" (http://news.prnewswire.com/DisplayReleaseContent.aspx?ACCT=104&STORY=/www/story/01-09-2009/0004952081&EDATE=). News.prnewswire.com. . Retrieved September 14, 2010.

[33] "News Headlines" (http://www.cnbc.com/id/31524589/site/14081545). Cnbc.com. . Retrieved September 14, 2010.

[34] "Victoria Beckham : Posh Spice lands princess role in Spongebob Squarepants | Entertainment Biz!" (http://www.entertainmentandshowbiz.com/victoria-beckham-posh-spice-lands-princess-role-in-spongebob-squarepants-2009041214227). Entertainmentandshowbiz.com. April 12, 2009. . Retrieved September 14, 2010.

[35] "Victoria Beckham to Square Off with SpongeBob" (http://www.people.com/people/article/0,,20270930,00.html). *Us Magazine*. April 8, 2009. . Retrieved October 12, 2009.

[36] "'SpongeBob' Renewed for 26 Episodes" (http://www.thewrap.com/article/spongebob-renewed-26-episodes-11810). *The Wrap*. December 15, 2009. . Retrieved December 16, 2009.

[37] "SpongeBob SquarePants renewed for season nine" (http://tvseriesfinale.com/tv-show/spongebob-squarepants-season-nine-18999/). TV Series Finale. 2011-01-03. . Retrieved 2011-08-20.

[38] Starr, Michael (November 15, 2007). "Bowie "sponge" makes splash" (http://www.nypost.com/seven/11152007/tv/bowie_sponge_makes_splash_402981.htm). *New York Post*. . Retrieved December 7, 2007.

[39] "NBC 'Lights' Up Critics' Nominations" (http://www.zap2it.com/tv/news/zap-2007tcaawardnominations,0,935063.story). *Zap 2 It*. June 5, 2007. . Retrieved July 8, 2008.

[40] BBC Staff (January 20, 2005). "US right attacks SpongeBob video" (http://news.bbc.co.uk/1/hi/world/americas/4190699.stm). BBC News. . Retrieved June 11, 2007.

[41] "Spongebob, Muppets and the Sister Sledge writer suffer criticism" (http://www.usatoday.com/life/television/2005-01-22-kids-video_x.htm). *USA Today*. Associated Press. January 22, 2005. . Retrieved June 11, 2007.

[42] BBC Staff (October 9, 2002). "Camp cartoon star 'is not gay'" (http://news.bbc.co.uk/1/hi/entertainment/tv_and_radio/2313221.stm). BBC News. . Retrieved June 11, 2007.

[43] Silverman, Stephen M. (January 28, 2005). "SpongeBob Asexual, Not Gay: Creator" (http://www.people.com/people/article/0,,1021976,00.html). *People*. . Retrieved August 26, 2009.

[44] "SpongeBob isn't gay or straight, creator says" (http://www.iol.co.za/index.php?set_id=1&click_id=22&art_id=vn20050129114540161C803463). Reuters. January 29, 2005. . Retrieved November 9, 2008.

[45] Chang, Pauline J. (January 28, 2005). "Dobson clarifies Pro-Gay SpongeBob Video Controversy" (http://www.christianpost.com/article/20050128/20875.htm). The Christian Post. . Retrieved June 11, 2007.

[46] Till, Francis (February 4, 2005). "Ministry celebrates SpongeBob: Gay, happy, yellow, orange, whatever, he's welcome" (http://www.nbr.co.nz/home/column_article.asp?id=11260&cid=1&cname=Media). *National Business Review*. . Retrieved June 11, 2007.

[47] Dennis, Jeffrey P. " The Same Thing We Do Every Night: Signifying Same-Sex Desire in Television Cartoons (http://www.encyclopedia.com/doc/1G1-110113188.html)." *Journal of Popular Film & Television*. Fall 2003. Volume 31, Issue 3. 132-140. 9p, 3bw. Within the PDF document the source info is on p. 137 (6/10)

[48] Goodman, Martin. "Deconstruction Zone — Part 2." *Animation World Network*. Wednesday March 10, 2004. 4 (http://www.awn.com/articles/drtoon/deconstruction-zone-part-2/page/4,1). Retrieved on October 28, 2009.

[49] Lillard, Angeline and Jennifer Peterson. The Immediate Impact of Different Types of Television on Young Children's Executive Function (http://pediatrics.aappublications.org/content/early/2011/09/08/peds.2010-1919). Pediatrics 2011; peds.2010-1919; published ahead of print September 12, 2011, doi:10.1542/peds.2010-1919.

[50] Tanner, Lindsey (September 12, 2011). SpongeBob in hot water from study of 4-year-olds (http://hosted.ap.org/dynamic/stories/U/US_MED_SPONGEBOB_STUDY?SITE=AP&SECTION=HOME&TEMPLATE=DEFAULT). *Associated Press*. Retrieved September 12, 2011.

[51] "Chicago | Plan a Visit | Now Playing in 4-D" (http://www.sheddaquarium.org/4dtheater.html). Shedd Aquarium. . Retrieved September 14, 2010.

[52] Johansson, Scarlett (2005). *The Absorbing Tale Behind The SpongeBob SquarePants Movie. The SpongeBob SquarePants Movie* (DVD). Paramount Home Entertainment.

[53] "SponbgeBob SquarePants Happy Meal" (http://translate.google.com/translate?hl=en&sl=it&u=http://www.megamodo.com/2007111368-spongebob-con-lhappy-meal-mcdonalds/&ei=RtliSsjdCceBtgf15oD6Dw&sa=X&oi=translate&resnum=1&ct=result&prev=/search?q=Spongebob+con+l%E2%80%99Happy+Meal+McDonald%E2%80%99s&hl=en&rlz=1B2GGFB_enUS223US224). *Megamodo*.
.

[54] "SpongeBob SquarePants KFC toys in Japan" (http://www.viacom.com/view_release.jhtml;jsessionid=OQP0BQE5ORHWSCQBAFLQ4CY?inID=10000007&inReleaseID=227116). .

[55] "SpongeBob SquarePants" (http://npower2.memorexelectronics.com/html/product_family.php?FID=8&SID=2&opento=2). *Npower Electrionics*. . Retrieved April 24, 2008.

[56] "Nickelodeon Expands Healthy Food Initiative with Green Giant" (http://promomagazine.com/entertainmentmarketing/news/nickelodeon_healthy_food_initiative_green_giant_053107/). Promomagazine.com. May 31, 2007. . Retrieved September 14, 2010.

[57] SpongeBob 2009 Calendar (http://images.calendars.com/images/124/12420/200900000533_fc.jpg)

[58] Strauss, Gary (May 17, 2002). "Life's good for SpongeBob" (http://www.usatoday.com/money/covers/2002-05-17-spongebob.htm). *USA Today*. . Retrieved November 8, 2008.

[59] Kageyama, Yuri (January 24, 2007). "SpongeBob Goes Trendy to Win Japan Fans" (http://www.sfgate.com/cgi-bin/article.cgi?f=/n/a/2007/01/24/entertainment/e091755S47.DTL). *The San Francisco Chronicle*. . Retrieved November 8, 2008.

[60] http://www.tvshowsondvd.com/news/SpongeBob-SquarePants-Season-7/15919

References

- Banks, Steven (September 24, 2004). *SpongeBob Exposed! The Insider's Guide to SpongeBob SquarePants*. Schigiel, Gregg (Illustrator). Simon Spotlight/Nickelodeon. ISBN 978-0689868702.
- Neuwirth, Allan (2003). *Makin' Toons: Inside the Most Popular Animated TV Shows and Movies*. Allworth Communications, Inc. pp. 50, 252–253. ISBN 1581152698.

External links

- Official site (US) (http://spongebob.nick.com)
- Official site (Asia) (http://spongebob.nick-asia.com)
- Official site (Australia) (http://www.nickelodeon.com.au/fullynick/tvshows/shows/index.php?show_id=31)
- Official site (UK) (http://www.nick.co.uk/#/spongebob_squarepants/)
- *SpongeBob SquarePants* (http://www.imdb.com/title/tt0206512/) at the Internet Movie Database
- *SpongeBob SquarePants* (http://www.tv.com/show/3428/summary.html) at TV.com
- *SpongeBob SquarePants* (http://www.bcdb.com/cartoons/Other_Studios/N/Nickelodeon/Nicktoons_Productions/SpongeBob_SquarePants/index.html) at the Big Cartoon DataBase
- *SpongeBob SquarePants* (http://www.ytv.com/programming/shows/SpongeBob_SquarePants/) at YTV.com
- *SpongeBob SquarePants* (http://epguides.com/SpongeBobSquarePants/) at Epguides

Wikis

- SpongeBob SquarePants Wikia (http://SpongeBob.wikia.com/wiki/Main_Page)
- SpongePedia (http://en.spongepedia.org)
- SpongeBob SquarePants NeoSeeker Wiki (http://spongebob.neoseeker.com/wiki/Main_Page)

Alan Carr: Chatty Man

Alan Carr: Chatty Man	
The second title card from 2010-present	
Format	Chat show
Presented by	Alan Carr
Country of origin	United Kingdom
No. of series	7
No. of episodes	57 (to 6 November 2011)
Production	
Producer(s)	Open Mike Productions
Location(s)	The London Studios
Running time	50-70 minutes
Broadcast	
Original channel	Channel 4
Original run	14 June 2009 – Present
Chronology	
Related shows	Sunday Night Project The Justin Lee Collins Show
External links	
Website [1]	

Alan Carr: Chatty Man (also simply known as ***Chatty Man***) is a British comedy chat show presented by comedian Alan Carr. The award-winning show[2] is on Channel 4. The show features interviews with celebrity guests, sketches, topical chat and music.

The show was first on as a pilot in late May 2009, the show proved popular with the public and was commissioned for a series. The first episode drew in a total of 2.15 million viewers. To date, the show has rebroadcast 7 series and 55 episodes. Carr has signed a new deal worth £4 million, which will keep the show on air to 2014, spanning another four more series.[3]

Filming

A structural difference from other British chat shows is that while the guests for each episode of *Chatty Man* all tape on the same day, there is no on screen interaction between the guests. A guest will be introduced and be interviewed, and then they are gone when the next guest comes out. An advantage to this taping process is the fact that Carr is able to pretape interviews with certain guests. If a particular guest is unavailable to be interviewed on the chosen week, an interview can be pre-taped and slotted in during the next week's editing. Often, at the end of a series, the final episode can be made up of three pretaped interviews (as well as a musical performance) taped earlier in that particular series' run, thus eliminating one tape date.

Issues

An interview with Marilyn Manson was recorded in mid 2009, however, due to Manson's drunkenness, plans to air the interview were scrapped.[4]

Lily Allen was slated to appear on the show for an interview and to perform with Professor Green, but she ended up pulling out at the last minute for medical reasons, along with Green. Due to this being her second time pulling out of *Chatty Man*, Alan Carr publicly berated her on the Web.[5]

Episodes

Series 1

Date	Episode number	Guests	Performance	Ratings
Filmed in May	Pilot 1	Jerry Springer, Denise Van Outen and Robert Webb[6] [7]	Pet Shop Boys performed "Did You See Me Coming?"	
Filmed in May	Pilot 2	Ronnie Corbett, Joanna Page, Gok Wan and The Noisettes[6] [8]	The Noisettes performed "Don't Upset the Rhythm"	
14 June 2009	1	Bruce Forsyth, Ross Kemp, Heather Graham and Pet Shop Boys	Pet Shop Boys performed "Did You See Me Coming?"	2.15 million viewers
21 June 2009	2	Samuel L. Jackson, Katy Perry and Ivana Trump	Katy Perry performed "Waking Up in Vegas"	1.80 million viewers
28 June 2009	3	Jerry Springer, Martina Navratilova and The Black Eyed Peas	The Black Eyed Peas performed "I Gotta Feeling"	
5 July 2009	4	David Walliams, Dawn French, Kirstie Allsopp, Phil Spencer and La Roux	La Roux performed "Bulletproof"	1.64 million viewers
12 July 2009	5	Fern Britton, Sarah Harding, Kanye West and Mr. Hudson	Mr. Hudson and Kanye West performed "Supernova"	1.86 million viewers
19 July 2009	6	Jonathan Ross, Denise Van Outen, Mickey Rourke and JLS	JLS performed "Beat Again"	1.52 million viewers
26 July 2009	7	Rupert Everett, Barbara Windsor, Kevin Bishop and The Enemy	The Enemy performed "Be Somebody"	
2 August 2009	8	Shane Warne, Patsy Kensit, Gok Wan and Calvin Harris	Calvin Harris performed "Ready for the Weekend"	
9 August 2009	9	Peter Andre, Natalie Imbruglia, Frank Skinner and The Noisettes	The Noisettes performed "Wild Young Hearts"	1.82 million viewers
16 August 2009	10	Jack Dee, Amanda Holden, Alan Dale and Pixie Lott	Pixie Lott performed "Boys and Girls"	1.26 million viewers

Series 2

A second series began airing on 19 November 2009.[9] A Christmas and New Year's special were been confirmed and aired in December.

Date	Episode number	Guests	Performance	Ratings
19 November 2009	1	Mariah Carey, Noel Fielding and Simon Pegg	Mariah Carey performed "I Want to Know What Love Is"	
26 November 2009	2	Ruth Jones and James Corden, Chris Moyles, Westlife and Alesha Dixon	Alesha Dixon performed "The Light"	1.21 million viewers
3 December 2009	3	Kate Hudson, David Mitchell, Sharon Osbourne and Chipmunk and Talay Riley	Chipmunk and Talay Riley performed "Look For Me"	
10 December 2009	4	Michael McIntyre, Chris Evans and Miley Cyrus	Miley Cyrus performed "Party in the U.S.A."	1.49 million viewers
17 December 2009	5	Bette Midler, Johnny Vegas and JLS	JLS performed "One Shot" feat. The Back Blue Boys	
22 December 2009	6 (Christmas Special)	Cilla Black, Justin Lee Collins, Eoghan Quigg, David Walliams, Christopher Biggins, Abigail Clancy and The Saturdays	The Saturdays performed "Ego" and "All I Want for Christmas Is You"	1.60 million viewers
29 December 2009	7 (New Year's/Hogmanay Special)	Davina McCall, Catherine Tate, David Tennant and Spandau Ballet	Spandau Ballet performed "Gold"	1.70 million viewers

Series 3

A new series began on 4 February 2010 for 8 episodes. The first episode was taped on 27 January, according to Sro Audiences.[10]

Date	Episode number	Guests	Performance	Ratings
4 February 2010	1	Ricky Gervais, Katie Price, Vinnie Jones and Corinne Bailey Rae	Corinne Bailey Rae performed "Paris Nights/New York Mornings"	2.07 million viewers
11 February 2010	2	Daryl Hannah, Nicholas Hoult, Sid Owen and Patsy Palmer and Mika	Mika performed "Blame it on the Girls"	
18 February 2010	3	Alex Reid, Jimmy Carr, Janice Dickinson and Kesha	Kesha performed "Blah Blah Blah"	1.98 million viewers
25 February 2010	4	Courtney Love, Steve Jones and Rihanna	Rihanna performed "Rude Boy"	
4 March 2010	5	Ant & Dec, John Barrowman, Jo Frost and Ellie Goulding	Ellie Goulding performed "Starry Eyed"	
11 March 2010	6	Lindsay Lohan, Torvill and Dean, Frankie Boyle and Mary J. Blige	Mary J. Blige performed "I Am"	
18 March 2010	7	Miranda Hart, Russell Howard, Justin Bieber, David Haye and Florence and the Machine	Florence and The Machine performed "Dog Days Are Over"	
25 March 2010	8	Kim Cattrall, Boy George and N-Dubz	N-Dubz performed "Say It's Over"	

Series 4

Series 4 premiered on 20 June for a 12-episode run.

Date	Episode number	Guests	Performance	Ratings
20 June 2010	1	Russell Brand, Pamela Anderson, Matthew Morrison, Kevin McHale, Jenna Ushkowitz, and Plan B	Plan B performed "Prayin"	1.79 million viewers
27 June 2010	2	Katie Price and Alex Reid, James Corden and Enrique Iglesias	Enrique Iglesias performed "I Like It"	1.87 million viewers
4 July 2010	3	Shakira, Louie Spence, Nikki Reed, Kellan Lutz, Ashley Greene, Xavier Samuel and Kelis	Kelis performed "4th of July (Fireworks)"	1.50 million viewers
11 July 2010	4	Grace Jones, Gok Wan and JLS	JLS performed "The Club Is Alive"	
18 July 2010	5	Kylie Minogue, John Bishop and Jared Leto	Kylie Minogue performed "All The Lovers" and "Get Outta My Way"	1.73 million viewers
25 July 2010	6	Vic Reeves, Bob Mortimer, Ulrika Jonsson, Joanna Page and Scissor Sisters	Scissor Sisters performed "Running Out"	1.64 million viewers
1 August 2010	7	Alice Cooper, David Walliams and The Saturdays	The Saturdays performed ""Missing You""	1.37 million viewers
8 August 2010	8	Robin Williams, Bobcat Goldthwait, Olly Murs, Jason Manford, Alex Jones and Tinchy Stryder	Tinchy Stryder performed "In My System"	1.36 million viewers
15 August 2010	9	Ricky Gervais, Stephen Merchant, Minnie Driver and Alexandra Burke	Alexandra Burke performed "Start Without You"	1.41 million viewers
22 August 2010	10	Drew Barrymore, Gary and Danielle Lineker, Phill Jupitus and Goldfrapp	Goldfrapp performed "Believer"	1.59 million viewers
29 August 2010	11	Whoopi Goldberg, Jedward, Kim Cattrall and McFly	McFly performed "Party Girl"	
5 September 2010	12	Paul O'Grady, Katy Perry, Davina McCall and Brandon Flowers	Brandon Flowers performed "Crossfire", Katy Perry performed "Teenage Dream"	1.54 million viewers

Series 5

Series 5 began on 13 December 2010 and includes 3 Christmas/New Year's specials.[11]

Date	Episode number	Guests	Performance	Ratings
13 December 2010	1	David Hasselhoff, Simon Bird, Joe Thomas, James Buckley, Blake Harrison, Colin Farrell, Jim Sturgess and Cee Lo Green	Cee Lo Green performed "It's OK"	1.75 million viewers
20 December 2010	2	Michael McIntyre, Stacey Solomon, Shaun Ryder and Cheryl Cole	Cheryl Cole performed "Promise This" and "The Flood"	2.25 million viewers
26 December 2010	3 (Christmas Special)	Chris Evans, Mickey Rourke, Catherine Tate and The Wanted	The Wanted performed "Lose My Mind"	1.41 million viewers
2 January 2011	4 (New Years Special)	Matt Lucas, Dame Edna Everage and McFly	McFly performed "Nowhere Left To Run"	1.52 million viewers
17 January 2011	5	Jonathan Ross, Kevin Bridges, Jack Whitehall and Adele	Adele performed "Rolling in the Deep"	
24 January 2011	6	James Corden, Benedict Cumberbatch, Kerry Katona and Jamiroquai	Jamiroquai performed "Lifeline"	

31 January 2011	7	Billie Piper, Usher, Russell Tovey, Lenora Crichlow, Sinead Keenan and Duran Duran	Duran Duran performed "All You Need is Now"	
7 February 2011	8	Juliette Lewis, Dermot O'Leary, Miranda Hart and The Streets	The Streets performed "Going Through Hell"	
14 February 2011	9	Samuel L. Jackson, Lee Mack and JLS	JLS performed "Eyes Wide Shut"	
21 February 2011	10	Jo Brand, Tom Hardy, Amy Childs, Mark Wright, Sam Faiers, James Argent, Nanny Pat, and Ellie Goulding	Ellie Goulding performed "Lights"	

Series 6

Series 6 will move to Friday nights beginning on 17 June.

Date	Episode number	Guests	Performance	Ratings
17 June 2011	1	Jonathan Ross, David Haye and Jennifer Lopez	Jennifer Lopez performed "I'm Into You"	1.78 million viewers
24 June 2011	2	Elle Macpherson, Bruce Forsyth, Louis Walsh, Wonderland and Kaiser Chiefs	Kaiser Chiefs performed "Little Shocks"	1.40 million viewers
1 July 2011	3	Thandie Newton, Ben Miller, Jo Frost, Liam Gallagher and Beady Eye	Beady Eye performed "The Beat Goes On"	1.53 million viewers
8 July 2011	4	Eddie Izzard, Chris Moyles, Prof. Brian Cox and Hard-Fi	Hard-Fi performed	1.81 million viewers
15 July 2011	5	Matt Smith, David, Taylor Ann and Hayley Hasselhoff, JLS and Miles Kane	Miles Kane performed "Inhaler"	1.63 million viewers
22 July 2011	6	Mathew Horne, Denise Welch, Sherrie Hewson, Carol McGiffin, Charlie Day, Jason Bateman, Jason Sudeikis and The Kooks	The Kooks performed "Is It Me?"	1.58 million viewers
29 July 2011	7	Bradley Cooper, Stephen Merchant, One Direction and Will Young	Will Young performed "Jealousy"	1.67 million viewers
5 August 2011	8	Justin Timberlake, Mila Kunis, Simon Bird, Joe Thomas, James Buckley, Blake Harrison and Jessie J	Jessie J performed "Who's Laughing Now"	1.85 million viewers

Series 7

Series 7 will move back to Sunday nights beginning on 30 October.

Date	Episode number	Guests	Performance	Ratings
30 October 2011	1	Nicole Scherzinger, Simon Pegg, Nick Frost and Matt Cardle	Matt Cardle performed "Letters"	1.80 million
6 November 2011	2	Dermot O'Leary, David Walliams, Westlife, Mary J. Blige and The Saturdays	The Saturdays performed "My Heart Takes Over"	1.14 million
13 November 2011	3	Louis Walsh, Gary Barlow, Tulisa Contostavlos, Kelly Rowland, Terry Wogan, Tinie Tempah and Kasabian	Kasabian performed "Re-Wired"	1.28 million
20 November 2011	4	Dannii Minogue, Peter Kay and Lady Gaga	Lady Gaga performed "Marry The Night"	1.39 million
27 November 2011	5	Lee Evans, Bear Grylls and One Direction	One Direction performed "What Makes You Beautiful"	1.1 million
4 December 2011	6	Ricky Gervais, Warwick Davis, Vernon Kay, Alesha Dixon, Craig Revel Horwood, Bruno Tonioli and Ed Sheeran	Ed Sheeran performed "Lego House"	1.24 million

25 December 2011	7 (Christmas Special)	David Walliams, Ruth Jones, Jedward and Steps	Steps performed	
31 December 2011	8 (New Year's Specstacular)	Jonathan Ross, Micky Flanagan, Melanie Sykes, Gok Wan, Kirstie Allsopp, Alesha Dixon, Bruno Tonioli, Heston Blumenthal, JLS and The Ting Tings	JLS performed and The Ting Tings performed	

References

[1] http://www.channel4.com/chattyman

[2] "TV Choice Best Entertainment Award" (http://www.tvchoicemagazine.co.uk/awards/2010/winners/best-entertainment-show). tvchoicemagazine.co.uk. 2010-09-07. . Retrieved 2010-10-10.

[3] http://tellymix.co.uk/general-telly/36031-alan-carr-and-graham-norton-both-sign-new-4-million-deals-for-their-chatshows.html

[4] "Information on Alan and Marilyn Manson" (http://www.alancarr.net/diary/2009/07/angelheart.html). Alancarr.net. 2009-07-13. . Retrieved 2010-03-05.

[5] "Alan Carr hits out at Lily Allen after she pulls out of his chat show over illness" (http://www.dailymail.co.uk/tvshowbiz/article-1293138/Alan-Carr-blasts-Lily-Allen-pulls-chat-illness.html). *Daily Mail* (London). 8 July 2010. .

[6] "Alan Carr talks about his new Channel 4 chat show as well as Susan Boyle, Madonna and why he'd never have surgery! | Dean Piper's World" (http://www.deanpiper.com/index.php/2009/06/13/alan-carr-talks-about-his-new-channel-4-chat-show-as-well-as-susan-boyle-madonna-and-why-hed-never-have-surgery/). Deanpiper.com. 2009-06-13. . Retrieved 2010-03-05.

[7] (http://www.joeholgate.co.uk/b2/blogs/blog2.php/2009/06/05/alan-carr-s-new-show-chatty-man)

[8] 04:46 PM. "Alan Carr's Chat Show - Coming Soon! - ThisisBigBrother.com - UK TV Forums" (http://www.thisisbigbrother.com/forum/viewthread.php?tid=112035). ThisisBigBrother.com. . Retrieved 2010-03-05.

[9] Syeda Irtizaali. "Blog - Chatty Man!" (http://blogs.channel4.com/thetvshow/2009/08/27/chatty-man/). Blogs.channel4.com. . Retrieved 2010-03-05.

[10] "sro audiences" (http://www.sroaudiences.com/). sro audiences. . Retrieved 2010-03-05.

[11] http://www.channel4.com/programmes/alan-carr-chatty-man/episode-guide/series-5/episode-1

External links

- *Alan Carr: Chatty Man* (http://www.channel4.com/chattyman) at channel4.com
- *Alan Carr: Chatty Man* (http://www.tv.com/show/77404/summary.html) at TV.com
- *Alan Carr: Chatty Man* (http://www.comedy.co.uk/guide/tv/alan_carr_chatty_man/) at the British Comedy Guide
- The Official Alan Carr website (http://www.alancarr.net)

Happy Feet Two

Happy Feet Two	
Theatrical poster	
Directed by	George Miller
Produced by	George Miller Bill Miller Doug Mitchell
Written by	George Miller Gary Eck Warren Coleman Paul Livingston
Starring	Elijah Wood P!nk Ava Acres Sofía Vergara Brad Pitt Matt Damon Hugo Weaving Anthony LaPaglia Hank Azaria Johnny A. Sanchez Lombardo Boyar Carlos Alazraqui Michael Cornacchia Danny Mann Meibh Campbell Lil P-Nut Mark Klastorin
Music by	John Powell Pink
Studio	Village Roadshow Pictures Kennedy-Miller Mitchell Films Dr. D Studios
Distributed by	Warner Bros. Pictures
Release date(s)	November 18, 2011 (United States) December 26, 2011 (Australia)
Running time	117 minutes
Country	Australia United States
Language	English
Budget	$135 million[1]
Box office	$106,050,000 [2]

Happy Feet Two is a 3D computer-animated family film film directed by George Miller, who co-directed the original film *Happy Feet*. The film is a sequel to *Happy Feet* and stars Elijah Wood, Pink, E.G. Daily, Sofía Vergara and Common. *Dr. D Studios*[3] in Sydney, Australia produced the film, which premiered in North American theaters on November 18, 2011 in Digital 3D and IMAX 3D. The film was released with a *Looney Tunes* short called *I Tawt I Taw a Puddy Tat*.[4]

Plot

After Moments of Happy Feet, Mumble (Elijah Wood) and Gloria's (Pink) son Erik (Ava Acres) is reluctant to try dancing as most of the penguins in Emperor-land do. Erik's first attempt at dancing embarrasses and outcasts him from the rest of the penguins. After Ramon's misguided advice that Emperor-Land isn't fit for outcast penguins like themselves, Erik and his two friends Boadicia (Meibh Campbell) and Atticus (Lil P-Nut) follow Ramon back to Adélie-Land. Upon returning, Ramon learns that Adélie-Land has been ruled by a God-like penguin named The Mighty Sven (Hank Azaria). Sven is the last of his kind who survived death by his ability to fly. Erik instantly becomes enamored with Sven, who takes a liking to him as well as there are "many brave warriors named Erik" back in Svenland. Sven and Lovelace tell the story of The Mighty Sven, who was rescued by a Russian vessel and rehabilitated alongside Lovelace. One night Sven discovers the "aliens" that saved them cooking and eating chicken meat. He flees the boat with Lovelace in tow. The two wind up on the shore of Antartica, where Sven performs his first miracle by revealing moss to the local penguins. Ramon accuses Sven of being a fraud and a false idol, until Sven uses his power of "Sven Think" to help Ramon find a mate. Ramon instantly falls in love with Carmen (Sofía Vergara), another Adélie penguin who shows no interest in him. Mumble follows the chicks' footprints to Adélie land and orders them to return to Emperor-Land. The chicks refuse, especially Erik, who has adopted Sven as a hero. Sven encourages Erik to believe in himself, because "Sven believes in you", before sending Erik back to Emperor-land with Mumble.

Meanwhile, the story shifts to two krill in the midst of a swarm. Will (Brad Pitt) is an adventurous and existentialist krill determined to discover what lies beyond the krill swarm. His friend, Bill, (Matt Damon) reluctantly follows him to ensure his safety. Once separated from the swarm, Will and Bill realize that krill are at the bottom of the food chain, created to be eaten. Inspired, Will ventures out to evolve and "move up the food chain", eating a real creature instead of being eaten.

On the way back from Adélie-Land, Mumble tells Erik that he is unique to the world and that he will someday find his calling. Erik, still inspired by Sven's words of wisdom, quickly dismisses Mumble's advice. While trying to cross a perilous ice bridge, the penguins encounter Bryan the Beach Master (Richard Carter) and his two young sons, who refuse to let the penguins pass. Suddenly the ice gives away and Bryan is trapped in a deep crevice below the ice. Mumble sets out to free Bryan by antagonizing a sleeping leopard seal until it chases him down. In actuality, it is the work of Bill and Will "moving up the food chain" and trying to eat a creature with a face that awakens the seal. During the fight, Mumble manages to use the leopard seal to shatter the wall of ice between Bryan and the sea, saving his life. Seeking acceptance from Erik, Mumble is disheartened to learn Erik attributed the feat of courage to Sven Think, Sven's motivational process of achieving what one wants by willing it to happen. Bryan returns to the Elephant Seal beach, but not before thanking Mumble and promising to return the favor to him at any time.

When the penguins returns to Emperor-Land they are shocked to discover a large iceberg has struck their home, trapping the entire Emperor Penguin population below large walls of ice. Boadicia ventures out to Adélie Land to recruit the help of Ramon, the Amigos and all the Adélie penguins to bring fish to the doomed Emperor penguins. In the meantime Mumble, Erik and Atticus deliver meager supplies of fish to the trapped penguins. Erik, still convinced penguins can fly through Sven Think, attempts to deliver a fish to Gloria by flying and nearly tossing himself over the edge of the iceberg. Mumble scolds Erik for his beliefs, claiming that no penguin can fly and that none of the Emperor Penguins will be able to escape. Once Erik realizes Emperor-Land is destined to die, he begins to break down. Gloria sends Mumble off to hunt for fish, calming Erik and the rest of the hysterical Emperor-Land through song (Bridge of Light). In the process, Bill becomes inspired to create another swarm of krill but Will refuses, preferring to adhere to his new predator lifestyle.

The next morning, a large flock of Skua attack the trapped Emperor-Land. Noah the Elder (Hugo Weaving) encourages the penguins to stand up to the birds (Anthony LaPaglia, Michael Cornacchia) through perseverance and unity. When all hope seems lost, Boadica returns with the entire Adélie-Land, led by Sven, to aid the trapped Emperor Penguins. Sven orchestrates a cooperative effort to feed the trapped Emperor Penguins through hunting and bringing back a flow of fish from the sea.

During this period Will becomes increasingly agitated with Bill's behavior and ventures out alone, into the Adélie feeding swarm, to join "fellow predators". In the process he is whisked away attached to a fish carried by Sven and down into the trapped Emperor-Land.

Suddenly the Adélie penguins recognize the same Russian vessel that saved Sven and Lovelace. Sven, terrified for his life, flees and hides from the humans. Lovelace, meanwhile, swims to the top of an iceberg and dances to attract the ship's attention. He successfully leads the humans back to Emperor-Land, where they begin carving a path up the side of the iceberg to freedom. Halfway through the effort, a large storm rolls in, forcing the penguins to huddle up and the humans to flee. The next morning Sven returns, reporting that the ocean has frozen over significantly and there is no chance of the humans returning or the Adélie Penguins transporting food over such a distance. Tensions arise as the Emperor Penguins become frantic at the lack of food and attempt to launch themselves into the air and "fly" out of the crevice. Erik urges Sven to teach the penguins how to fly, but he reveals his true nature. Sven is a not a penguin at all, but a Puffin-- and puffins can fly. He admits that after the loss of Svenland, he was lonely and grew to love the penguins who accepted him as a family. Dejected, Sven flies off. Mumble, after watching snow fall into a crevice between chunks of iceberg, begins to tap-dance on the ice and lead the Adélie penguins in a dance to force snow between the ice and weaken it. The plan works well until several chunks break loose, sending a large portion of the Adélies into the doomed crevice. In attempting to save Erik from plummeting over the edge, Mumble injures his foot and is unable to dance and lead the Adélies. Ramon realizes Carmen is trapped below and, risking his own life, jumps off the iceberg to be with her. As he professes his love to her, she immediately falls in love with him.

Sven becomes aware of the dancing and proves himself to be a worthy dancer despite public outcry against him. He leads the remaining Adélies in dance (Dragostea din tei) while Erik and Mumble venture off to the Elephant Seal beach.

Meanwhile Will, weary from the dangers he experienced as a predator on the surface, ventures back into the sea to find Bill, but not before experiencing the penguin's dancing. He is suddenly forced down a crack in the ice and into the sea beneath Emperor-Land. He reunites with Bill and his swarm, who tell him he has the purpose of changing the world and evolving the swarm. Once Bill told the swarm of their position on the food chain and their lives as pure herbivores, they followed him to the safety of the inaccessible ice below Emperor-Land.

Mumble and Erik arrive at Elephant Seal Beach where Bryan is in the middle of a fight of dominance between another large male. Mumble pleads with the elephant seals to help free the Emperor Penguins. Bryan, initially hesitant to return a favor at such a pivotal time of the year, becomes aggressive and threatens Mumble off the beach. Erik, unnerved by the lack of honor and respect from Bryan, discovers his true ability- a strong operatic voice. He sings an impromptu opera, commemorating Mumble as his hero for his acts of bravery and chides Bryan for his lack of compassion and gratitude towards him. At the Wrap up he runs up and hugs Mumble, accepting him as his inspiration. Touched by Erik's song, the elephant seals travel to Emperor-Land to free the penguins (Rawhide). The penguins and the seals begin slamming the ice on beat, joined by the krill below the ice, to the tune of "Under Pressure". Finally, the iceberg crumbles enough for the Emperor Penguins to climb out of the crevice and reunite with their families.

Cast

- Elijah Wood as Mumble
- Robin Williams as Ramon/Lovelace
- Pink as Gloria
- Hank Azaria[5] as The Mighty Sven[6]
- Brad Pitt as Will the Krill[7]
- Matt Damon as Bill the Krill[7]
- Ava Acres as Erik
- Meibh Campbell as Boadica
- Lil P-Nut as Atticus
- Carlos Alazraqui as Nestor
- Johnny A. Sanchez as Lombardo
- Lombardo Boyar as Raul
- Jeffrey Garcia as Rinaldo
- Magda Szubanski as Miss Viola
- Sofía Vergara as Carmen[8]
- Anthony LaPaglia as (Boss Skua) (Yellaleg) (Alpha Skua)[9] (cameo just Happy Feet)
- Michael Cornacchia as Frankie
- Danny Mann as (Dino) (Brokebeak)
- Gabe Newell as Archie the Killer Whale
- Hugo Weaving as Noah the Elder[10]
- Richard Carter as Bryan The Beach Master, an Elephant Seal
- Common as Seymour
- Elizabeth Daily provides the singing voices for Erik and Boadica

Development

Elijah Wood, Robin Williams and Hugo Weaving reprised their previous performances as Mumble, Ramón, Lovelace, and Noah. Also returning for the film were Carlos Alazraqui, Johnny A. Sanchez, Lombardo Boyar and Jeffrey Garcia as Nestor, Lombardo, Raul, and Rinaldo.[11] No other actors repeated their earlier performances.

Brittany Murphy, who originally voiced Mumble's love interest Gloria, was set to reprise her role and begin recording sometime in 2010,[12] but died from pneumonia on December 20, 2009. Steve Irwin, who played Trev the elephant seal, died in a stingray attack on September 4, 2006, before *Happy Feet* was released. Pink and Richard Carter both replaced Murphy and Irwin, and Pink contributed a song ("Tell Me Something Good", also by Pink, was contributed to the soundtrack of the first film), and Brad Pitt and Matt Damon voiced the tiny krill, Will and Bill.[13][14] Hank Azaria also signed on to voice The Mighty Sven.[15] E.G. Daily, who played young Mumble in the previous film, played the vocals for Mumble's choreophobic son Erik and the daughter of Miss Viola Boadicea, as well as additional voices. Sofía Vergara appears in the film as a new character.[16] There is to be a live action scene in the movie as in the first *Happy Feet*.[17] Mitchell Hicks has signed up as the movie's choreographer.[18]

Reception

Critical response

Happy Feet Two received mixed reviews from film critics. Review aggregator Rotten Tomatoes reported that 42% of critics gave positive reviews, based on 72 reviews.[19] *Happy Feet Two* currently holds a Metascore of 50 out of 100 on Metacritic. Richard Corliss of *Time* gave the film a positive review and said that Miller is "not content to duplicate the pleasures of his first penguin film; he dares to go bigger, deeper, higher — happier." [20]

Box-office performance

On its opening weekend, *Happy Feet Two* earned $21,237,068 while playing on 3,606 screens.[21] This is barely half of the $41,533,432 that the first *Happy Feet* made on its opening weekend in November 2006. Approximately 50% of *Happy Feet Two*'s box-office take came from the 2,825 screens that showed it in 3D.[22] Thus, when adjusted for ticket price inflation, *Happy Feet Two* achieved less than 45% of the attendance figures of its predecessor. Major box-office prediction websites were almost unanimously predicting an opening weekend of $35 million - $45 million, so *Happy Feet Two's* box-office performance has thus far been underwhelming. Among 2011's animated films, *Happy Feet Two's* opening weekend ranks 8th. Kurt Orzeck of the *Vancouver Sun* has reported that "due to the poor performance of Happy Feet Two, 600 of the 700 employees at the Sydney-based Dr. D. Studios, the digital production studio behind the animated movie, have reportedly received their walking papers."[23]

Merchandise

Video game

Happy Feet Two: The Video Game was developed by KMM Games for PlayStation 3, Xbox 360 and Wii. WayForward Technologies developed the Nintendo 3DS and Nintendo DS versions.[24]

Soundtrack

The soundtrack album for the film was released by WaterTower Music on CD on November 21, 2011 and on iTunes on November 15, 2011. Unlike the previous film's two album releases—one for its songs and one for its score—both the songs and John Powell's score are included on this album. The film's theme song, "Bridge of Light", is performed by P!nk, who also lends her vocals to the character Gloria.

Tracklist

1. "Happy Feet Two Opening Medley" (featuring the Happy Feet Two Chorus) – Common as Seywer, P!nk as Gloria & Lil' P-Nut
2. "The Mighty Sven" (featuring Robin Williams as Ramon) – Hank Azaria as Sven and the Happy Feet Two Chorus
3. "Bridge of Light" – P!nk as Gloria & the Happy Feet Two Chorus
4. "Papa Oom Mow Mow" – Happy Feet Two Chorus
5. "Dragostea Din Tei" – Hank Azaria as Sven & the Happy Feet Two Chorus
6. "Erik's Opera" – E. G. Daily as Erik and Omar Crook
7. "Rawhide" – Elephant Seal Chorus
8. "Under Pressure/Rhythm Nation" – P!nk as Gloria & the Happy Feet Two Chorus
9. "Tightrope" (Ice Cold Mix) [featuring P-Nut & the Happy Feet Two Chorus] – Janelle Monáe

The deluxe edition of the album contains an addition of 5 songs performed by Ozomatli; these songs and more can also be found on the soundtrack for the video game, released on iTunes on November 8, 2011.

References

[1] Kaufman, Amy (2011-11-17). "Movie Projector: 'Breaking Dawn' to suck life out of 'Happy Feet'" (http://latimesblogs.latimes.com/entertainmentnewsbuzz/2011/11/box-office-breaking-dawn-happy-feet.html). *Los Angeles Times*. Tribune Company. . Retrieved 2011-11-17.

[2] "Happy Feet Two" (http://boxofficemojo.com/movies/?id=happyfeet2.htm). *Box Office Mojo*. Retrieved November 26, 2011.

[3] Pip Bulbeck (2011), *From 'Great Gatsby' to 'Happy Feet Two': 7 Hot Movies, Series Coming Out of Australia* (http://www.hollywoodreporter.com/news/great-gatsby-happy-feet-two-251547),

[4] Adam B. Vary (2011), *Tweety Bird and Sylvester the Cat do battle in new Looney Tunes short -- EXCLUSIVE CLIP* (http://insidemovies.ew.com/2011/11/14/tweety-bird-sylvester-looney-tunes-clip-exclusive/),

[5] "Hank Azaria confirmation" (http://www.mediamarketjournal.com/2011/05/happy-feet-2-teaser-trailer). *MediaMarketJournal.com*. 2011-05-27. . Retrieved 2011-06-17.

[6] "Another New Character" (http://trailers.apple.com/trailers/wb/happyfeettwo). *Trailers.Apple.com*. . Retrieved 2011-6-1 4.

[7] "Happy Feet 2's first look at Pitt, Damon" (http://www.rte.ie/ten/2011/0930/happyfeet2poster.html). RTE Ten. 2011-09-30. . Retrieved 2011-10-13.

[8] "Sofia Vegara's role in Happy Feet Two revealed" (http://www.news.com.au/entertainment/celebrity/sofia-vegaras-tattoo-tribute-to-sad-heath/story-e6frfmqr-1226034442207). *News.com.au*. 2011-06-04. . Retrieved 2011-06-14.

[9] "More Cast" (http://happyfeettwo.warnerbros.com/index.html). *HappyFeetTwo.WarnerBros.com*. . Retrieved 2011-06-15.

[10] "Hugo Weaving's confirmed" (http://cinemovie.tv/cinemovie_new/component/content/article/51-trailers/1497-movie-trailer-happy-feet-2-). *CineMovie.tv*. . Retrieved 2011-06-17.

[11] "Record Brilliance, Feb 4, 2010" (http://malamar.blogspot.com/2010/02/record-brilliance.html). *Malamar.BlogSpot.com*. Retrieved 2010-11-19.

[12] Byrnes, Holly; Crawford, Carly (2009-12-21). "Brittany Murphy planned to have New Year in Australia" (http://www.news.com.au/entertainment/movies/brittany-murphy-plotted-new-year-escape-to-australia/story-e6frfmvr-1225812575550). *News.com.au*. .

[13] "Enticing glimpse of projected triumphs" (http://www.theaustralian.com.au/news/arts/enticing-glimpse-of-projected-triumphs/story-e6frg8n6-1225906549211). *TheAustralian.com*. Retrieved 2010-11-19.

[14] "George Miller Casting: Teresa Palmer in Mad Max 4: Fury Road, Matt Damon and Brad Pitt in Happy Feet 2" (http://www.slashfilm.com/2010/01/15/george-miller-casting-teresa-palmer-in-mad-max-4-fury-road-matt-damon-and-brad-pitt-in-happy-feet-2). */Film*. Retrieved 2011-05-27.

[15] Antonette Collins (2010-02-04). "Sydney welcomes patter of Happy Feet 2" (http://www.abc.net.au/news/stories/2010/02/04/2810411.htm). *ABC News*. . Retrieved 2010-02-14.

[16] "Sofia Vergara Joins The Smurfs & Happy Feet 2" (http://www.comingsoon.net/news/movienews.php?id=64636). *ComingSoon.net*. Retrieved 2010-11-19.

[17] Garth Franklin (2011-06-05). "Live action in Happy Feet Two?" (http://www.darkhorizons.com/news/20770/miller-s-happy-feet-2-uses-fury-cameras). *DarkHorizons.com*. . Retrieved 2011-06-13.

[18] "A New Dancing Expert" (http://www.thesauce.info/2009/08/28/mitchell-hicks-putting-his-boots-into-happy-feet-2). *TheSauce.info*. . Retrieved 2011-06-14.

[19] "Happy Feet Two Movie Reviews" (http://www.rottentomatoes.com/m/happy_feet_two/). *Rotten Tomatoes*. Flixster. . Retrieved Nuvember 24, 2011.

[20] Movie Review: Happy Feet Two: Mr. Miller's Poppy Penguins Save Their Own Planet | Entertainment | TIME.com (http://entertainment.time.com/2011/11/17/happy-feet-two-mr-millers-poppy-penguins-save-their-own-planet/)

[21] Happy Feet Two (2011) - Box Office Mojo (http://boxofficemojo.com/movies/?id=happyfeet2.htm)

[22] Weekend Report: 'Breaking Dawn's Huge Debut Just Shy of 'Twilight' Record - Box Office Mojo (http://boxofficemojo.com/news/?id=3312&p=.htm)

[23] Orzeck, Kurt (November 25, 2011). "'Happy Feet Two' flop leads to 600 layoffs: Report" (http://www.vancouversun.com/story_print.html?id=5768216&sponsor=). *Vancouver Sun*, accessed November 25, 2011.

[24] "Official Video Game of Happy Feet 2" (http://www.prnewswire.com/news-releases/warner-bros-interactive-entertainment-announces-happy-feet-two---the-videogame-122935898.html). *PRNewsWire.com*. 2011-05-01. . Retrieved 2011-06-13.

External links

- Official website (http://happyfeettwo.warnerbros.com/index.html)
- *Happy Feet Two* (http://www.boxofficemojo.com/movies/?id=happyfeet2.htm) at Box Office Mojo
- *Happy Feet Two* (http://www.imdb.com/title/tt1402488/) at the Internet Movie Database
- *Happy Feet Two* (http://www.rottentomatoes.com/m/happy-feet-2-in-3d/) at Rotten Tomatoes

Article Sources and Contributors

Robin Williams *Source*: http://en.wikipedia.org/w/index.php?oldid=465367766 *Contributors*: *drew, -ginkgobiloba-, 09nick, 12.49, 2goth, 6afraidof7, 78.26, 8.132, ADM, AKR619, AMittelman, AQuandary, Abby 96, Acceber123, Access Denied, Ace Class Shadow, Ace Fool, Acroterion, Addshore, Adultnature1989, Afabbro, Afri, Ageekgal, Ahkond, Ahoerstemeier, Ajm81, Akcarver, Al.locke, Alakey2010, Alamandrax, Alansohn, Alanviv, Alex20850, Alexf, Alias Flood, Alkivar, All Hallow's Wraith, Allstarecho, Allthenamesarealreadytaken, Alphachimp, Alphax, Alvaro, Amalthea, Amariyah, Amazins490, Amchow78, Ameliorate!, Andrei S, Andrewlp1991, Andreworkney, AndyRoberts7, Anomaly1, AnoreX, Antandrus, Apparition11, Aquamammal, ArcAngel, Arda Xi, Aresef, ArmadilloFromHell, Armbrust, Arniep, Arthur Rubin, Artichoke-Boy, Aspects, Astorknlam, Astuishin, Atif.t2, Atlan, Atlant, AuburnPilot, Aude, Auntof6, Aust0220df, Austinrh, AvYoshi, Avb, AvicAWB, Avillia, Awesomeomar, Azn.inv4zn, B4hand, Bab alemzadeh, Bacteria, Badgernet, Baird, Bamgermany2000, Bamjd3d, Bardnet, Barticus88, BashBrannigan, Basilbrushybrush, Batchtaster, Bazj, Bballduke511, Bbatsell, Bdwilliamscraig, Bearcat, Beatlesfan12, Begoon, Bejinhan, Belasted, Bellylamp216, Ben-Zin, Bencherlite, Bento00, BeringStrait, BernieKearny333, Bevo, Bhall37, Bialytock&Bloom, Bill Hicks Jr., Bill37212, Billbrasky168, Bite, Blakebs, Blanchardb, Blegendman, Blm07, Blue954, Bmillersus1992, Bobo192, Bongwarrior, Boojum, Bookgrrl, Boris995, BostonRed, Braves fan10, Brian Kendig, Brianjd, Bridgecross, Bruce1ee, Bubba73, Buchanan-Hermit, Buckboard, Bucketsofg, Bullytr, Bushcarrot, Buttonpincher, CIreland, CStyle, CWii, Cabrosa, Cactusrob, Caesura, Caliga10, Callcentermonkey, Calsicol, Caltas, Calton, Cameron D. Carver, Can't sleep, clown will eat me, Canihaveacookie, CanisRufus, Captain Disdain, Carlosrealm, Carmichael95, Cartoon Boy, CaseInPoint, Casliber, Cat's Tuxedo, Cath reen, Cbrett42, Cburnett, Ccacsmss, Celebritywiki, Chabba77, Chamal N, Chanlyn, Chantessy, Charlesdrakew, Chench, Chicheley, Chicken man222, Chrisch, Christopher Parham, Christopherpbus1, CieloEstrellado, Cirt, Cj005257, Ckatz, Clarityfiend, ClonedPickle, Closedmouth, Cmichael, Coder Dan, Colingj, Coll7, Colonies Chris, Cometstyles, Commander Keane, CommonsDelinker, Coolmanwc4, Copland64, Correogsk, Countess Nessa, CovenantD, Crash Underride, Crazyagingman, Crazycomputers, Crazynas, Crestville, Crohnie, Cruefest08, Cst17, Cubs Fan, Curps, CurtisJohnson, CycloneGU, CyrilIsBackBaby, D6, DJ Clayworth, DaffyDuck619, Dale Arnett, DanArmiger, Dances with weasels, Daniel sugden, DanielNuyu, Danmoore, DanniBHM, Dansteele, Dantecubed, Darguz Parsilvan, DarkFalls, DarkMissy, Darkcore, Darth Mike, DarylNickerson, DasallmächtigeJ, Dave.Dunford, Davehi1, DavidFarmbrough, DavidJ710, DavidRF, Davidfraser, Davidjed, Dcrasno, Degrassi ST, Demoman87, Deor, DepressedPer, DesmondRavenstone, Dethme0w, Diloretojazz, Dinertime444, Dinkytown, Disavian, Discospinster, Dismas, Distad, Djay70k, Djbj16, DocWatson42, Dockingman, Doczilla, Dogman15, Doilyn1, Domingo Portales, Donaldd23, DonnyD97, Doradus, DoubleAW, DoubleBlue, Doug4422, Doughty74, Downwards, Doylesrader, Dp462090, Dr who1975, DrGaellon, Dra, Dralwik, DreamGuy, Dtemp, Dudesleeper, Dwarfmonster, Dwslassls, E946, EKindig, Ead061, Ed g2s, EdenMaster, Edge o Matic 2005, EdgeNavidad, Edgecution03, Edinburgh Wanderer, Edwy, Eeekster, Eep², Egg Centric, Eh jack you late, Eirik, Ejfetters, El chulito, Elcapitane, Elcocinero, Elinnea, Elipongo, Ellsworth, Elsuperbeanerman, Emerson7, Empiresj1, Ercolino, ErdoSa, Erik, ErikNY, Escape Orbit, Esrogs, EurekaLott, Evanreyes, Eversman, Evilchino, Extra info, FJCKeos, Fabian Hassler, Fallout boy, Fame, Fan-1967, Faradayplank, Feydey, Fi265, Fieldday-sunday, Filip nohe, Firien, FirstPrinciples, Fishhead2100, Flami72, Floydgeo, Flyguy33, Fmmarina, Forteblast, Fourthords, Fram, FranksValli, Fraslet, Freak104, Freakofnurture, Frecklefoot, Freeman6, FrenchIsAwesome, FriscoKnight, Fschoenm, Funstitch, Furrykef, Fvasconcellos, Fæ, G-Man, GADFLY46, GC Buffalo, Gail, Gaius Cornelius, Ganfon, Gargaj, Garion96, Gatotsu911, Gavri, Gbms86, Gdo01, Ged UK, Gilliam, Gilo1969, Gimmetrow, Glennwells, Gmacbrown, Gmosaki, Gnowor, Gnowxilef, Gogo Dodo, GoingBatty, Goldenrowley, Gonei72, Goofy14, Goosefraba99, Gr8lyknow, Grafen, Grazon, Green man in the trees, Greendesk, Gregsabia, Gritironskillet, Grsz11, Grypson, Gsh, Guat6, Gunkyboy, Gurch, Guroadrunner, Gurubrahma, Guy M, Guy15, Gwernol, HANDBONE, HG707, Hadal, HalfShadow, Hall Monitor, Harris7, Hateless, HawkShark, Hayden4258, Hdevil, HeadNog, Hecko X, Heinleinscat, Hektor, Heliomance, Henshin-A-Go-Go, Heyy2345, Hillock65, Hjal, Hmains, Hmrox, Hokeman, Hourick, Howenstein115, Hu, Hubbard rox 2008, Hulkrules22085, Hullaballoo Wolfowitz, Hunter Kahn, Hyliad, I'm No Winner, IAmTheCoinMan, II MusLiM HyBRiD II, Iamwisesun, Ian Pugh, Iantnm, Iced Kola, Igno2, Igoldste, ImperatorExercitus, In fact, Infrogmation, Innercontinental, InspectorSands, Intelati, Invincible Ninja, InvisibleK, Iohannes Animosus, Irishguy, Ironholds, IrrTJMc, Islandboy99, J.delanoy, JCDenton2052, JForget, JHMM13, JNW, JYolkowski, JaGa, Jab843, Jack O'Lantern, JackO'Lantern, Jackfork, JackofOz, Jackslevin, JacksonESP, Jacobgreenbaum, Jagged 85, Jajhill, Jaldridge86, Janke, Jarkeld, Jarraddamiani, Jasenlee, JasonAQuest, Jasonbres, Javawizard, Jay, Jazzilady, Jbl1975, Jeandepaul, Jedi Striker, Jedi94, Jeff79, Jeffman52001, JeffreyAtW, Jenwindy, Jeromealden 85, Jerzy, Jessiejames, Jhendin, Jhsounds, Jiang, Jienum, Jill Tuck, Jim Michael, JimVC3, Jimbo1192, Jimifloydrix, Joanne ong, Joey80, John O'C, John Vandenberg, Johno100, Jojhutton, Jondude11, Joseph A. Spadaro, Jossi, Joyous!, Juansidious, Juliancolton, JustinInAtlanta, Justme89, Jvcdude, Jw21, Jwking, Jwolfe, Jzummak, Kainaw, Kaiwhakahaere, Kakashi-sensei, Kansan, Karen Johnson, Karin127, Karrmann, Kaylynn1998, Kbdank71, Kchishol1970, Kdm85, Kelly, Kenb215, Keno, Keristrasza, Kevin, Kevin J Chase, Kgrad, Kidlittle, Kieff, Kilo-Lima, Kiloalpha, Kingturtle, Kipple, Kirrages, Kitsunegami, Kittybrewster, Kiwibeca, Kman618, KnowledgeOfSelf, Koavf, Kotrt99, Koyaanis Qatsi, Kramertron, Kronnang Dunn, Kuru, Kwake20, Kyesac, Kyle Barbour, Kylegtr3, L Kensington, LOL, LaVidaLoca, Lacon432, Ladida, Ladydayelle, Lamrock, Latics, Lawrence142002, Lee Houston, Junior, Lee S. Svoboda, Leebo, Leon..., Levineps, Lexxus12, LilMane, Lilac Soul, Lima Neto, Little Savage, Little grape, Livitup, Llavigne, Longwalkshortpier, Looper5920, Loopy, Lothar von Richthofen, Lotje, LovelyLillith, Lucas B. de Souza, Lucy-marie, Lugnuts, Luna Santin, Lunar Jesters, Lupo, Lurlock, Lyght, Lynx13371989, Lyverbe, M.S.K., MAWforever27, MBisanz, MER-C, MF14, MaJic, Macromonkey, Mad Hatter, Madchester, MagedMahfouz, Makemi, Makron78, Malke 2010, Mandarax, Mandy for ever, Mannafredo, MarcK, Marcus Brute, Mark E, Markus Matei, Markusanthony, MarnetteD, Maruchan, Mary Read, Mastermanxp, MattTM, Mattie67, Mclover08, Mechanical digger, Megan1967, Mel Etitis, Melicans, Metnik, Michael Calwell, Michael Devore, Michael Drew, Michael Greiner, MightyWarrior, Mike Garcia, Mike Rosoft, MikeWazowski, Mikeman4510, Million Moments, Millsy 35, Minesweeper, Minutiaman, Miquonranger03, Mironfist, Miskwito, Misterrick, Mixino1, Mizazah, Mkhbgpa, Mlcjuggler, Mmernex, Mo7aisen, Morganfreeman12, Moshe Constantine Hassan Al-Silverburg, Mouse is back, Mr Adequate, Mr Beale, Mr Hall of England, Mr Stephen, Mr. Brain, Mr. Jibbers, Mr.jack, MrDarcy, MrDolomite, MrMoustacheMM, Mra, Mrblondnyc, Mrsanitazier, Mrtthefoo, Mrwojo, MsDivagin, Mushroom, Music2611, Myself0101, NAHID, NBbeauty, NWill, Najoj, Namcos, Nauraran, NawlinWiki, Nbick, Nborders1972, Neddyseagoon, Neilc, Neschek, New Order, Nintendofan88, Ninteneo1379, Nirinsanity, Niteowlneils, Nlu, No Guru, Nofadofa, Nrbelex, NuclearWarfare, Nues20, Number87, O, Oanabay04, Ohconfucius, Ohnoitsjamie, OlofE, Olorin28, Omicronpersei8, Omizzle77, Onasphere, OnePt618, Oobopshark, Orca1 9904, Otto4711, Overstrain, OwenX, Oxymoron83, PHDrillSergeant, PTR, PTSE, Pac123456, Pacreca, Passportguy, Paste, Pastordavid, Paul A, Paul Benjamin Austin, Pax:Vobiscum, Pedro thy master, Pegship, Pelotas, Peppycup12, Perardi, PericlesofAthens, Persian Poet Gal, Peter G Werner, PhantomS, Phbasketball6, Phil Sandifer, Phthoggos, Piano non troppo, Pic82101, PierceG, Pimlottc, Pinkkeith, Pipelinejohnson, Piuka, Plasma east, Plastic editor, Poindexter Propellerhead, Polisher of Cobwebs, Portia327, Portillo, Primarypenguin, PrimeHunter, ProjectTux, Pseudomonas, Psyche825, Pumpkingrrl, Punktarist684, Purgatory Fubar, QuasyBoy, Quebec99, QueenHenry, QuizzicalBee, R. fiend, RCX, RWFanMS, Rabidanimals, Rachelcgen, Radiopathy, RaiderTarheel, Rajah, Rasmus Faber, RattleandHum, RattyPussFACE, Rbb l181, Rcarey1979, Realar, Realm of Shadows, Reaper Eternal, Red Specter, Rei, Reisio, Retired username, Reyk, Reywas92, Rich Farmbrough, Richardcavell, Rilr, Rjwilmsi, Rms125a@hotmail.com, RobJ1981, RobbieFal, RobbieNomi, Robert Moore, RobertG, RobertGustafson, Rocio44, Rock55, Rocketjames2, Rockhopper10r, Rocking.kaustav, Rodhullandemu, Rofthorax, Rossami, Rossrs, Rossumcapek, Rracecarr, Rshiflet, Rtkat3, Ruebush, Runewiki777, Rusted AutoParts, Rwlinda, RypER, Ryulong, S2333, SAMbo, SD6-Agent, SGGH, SJP, SPQRobin, Sadchild, Saforrest, Sakurambo, Salamurai, Samosa Poderosa, SandyGeorgia, Sarah, Saucybetty, SavageEdit, Savant1984, Scarian, SchfiftyThree, Schmendrick, ScorpSt, Seaphoto, Secant1, Secfan, Selmo, Serasuna, Sevenstones, Severa, Sfmammamia, Sgeureka, Shadowjams, Shamrox, Sheara33, ShelfSkewed, Sheva7anto, Shirulashem, Shoeofdeath, Shojego, Shouriki, Sicilarch, SidP, Signalhead, Silent Tom, Silvanu, Simharrison, SimonMayer, Sintonak.X, Sionus, Sk8terdud333, Skippermytim, SkyWalker, Skysmith, Slavik81, Slp1, Smartiger, Solatha, Solipsist, Solitaryxchild, SomeAvailableName, Sonia1986, Sophie means wisdom, Sophitus, Sorenlarrington, SpadeAxis, Spagett, SpeedyGonsales, Spellcast, Spider669, Spirifil, Spockthecow, Sport woman, Sroc, Sry85, Starswept, Stephenb, Steve Farrell, SteveRamone, Stevertigo, Stewggrifin, Stuthehistoryguy, SupaDane, Superfreaky56, Supertigerman, Surcer, Susfele, Swat360, Symphony Girl, Syvanen, THATSBETTER, TJRC, TJUser, TMC1982, TNA RAGE 5150, TOO, TOR, TRBP, Tachitsuteto, Taestell, Tai kit, Tarquin, Tassedethe, Tbhotch, Tdowling, Tell-Tale Ghost, TenPoundHammer, TerraHikaru, The Amazing Dancing Bear, The Anome, The Dark Lord of Wiki, The Filmaker, The Giant Puffin, The Haunted Angel, The King of Australia, The Man in Question, The lorax, The mitten man, The wub, TheCustomOfLife, TheFatJamoc, TheFreeloader, TheHairyan05, Thedarkestclear, Thedjatclubrock, Theroachman, Thewayforward, ThuranX, TigerShark, Tijuana Brass, Tim Thomason (usurped), Timberframe, Tinton5, Tjmayerinsf, Todd unt, Toddst1, Tohd8BohaithuGh1, Tomgyrl31, Tomheyd, Tony1, Torqueing, Tpbradbury, Tpg1989, Trainik, Tranio24, TrapStilton, Tregoweth, Treybien, Tumadoireacht, Twh66, Twix1875, Tyler, Tylisasweet, Tyup, U2clay, Ukexpat, Ulric1313, Ultraviolet scissor flame, Uncle Milty, UninvitedCompany, Uromax, Ursatz, Vaoverland, Vbd, Vendettax, Vergency, Vermooten, VeryVerily, Voltron, Vtguy4242, Vzbs34, WCFrancis, WLU, WP addict 0, Wabby, Wafulz, Waggers, Waliy sherpa, WarioLoaf, Washburnmav, Wayman975, Wayne Slam, Wedineinheck, Who, Whywhenwhohow, Wik, Wiki alf, WikiPikiUser, Wikicali00, Wikipedical, Wikipete, WildCowboy, WildMIKE123, WildWildBil, Wildhartlivie, William Avery, Williamspuckett, Wimt, Windsor Help Desk, Wittylama, Wmahan, Wnick99, Wolfmankurd, Wolfpeaceful, Wolfy9005, Woohookitty, WpZurp, Wrathchild, Xanxz, Xeno, Xenophon777, Xezbeth, Xoke, Xp54321, Xzamuel, Yamanbaiia, Yamla, Yancyfry jr, Yekdorb, Yekrats, Yellowdesk, Yinzland, Yonskii, Yossarian, Yottamol, Yurivict, ZStoler, Zarabelda, Zeno McDohl, ZeroJanvier, Zoe, Zutopiaa, Zzyzx11, Александър, 1832 anonymous edits

Popeye (film) *Source*: http://en.wikipedia.org/w/index.php?oldid=464246390 *Contributors*: AN(Ger), Acjelen, ActivExpression, AdamDeanHall, Alientraveller, Aliuken, Andres, Anárion, Arcadian, Auntof6, B Touch, Baseball Bugs, Bluejay Young, Bobblewik, Bokan, Brammen, Brighterorange, Brittany Ka, Bryan H Bell, CBeilby, CLW, Clydewr, CoolKatt number 99999, Count Ringworm, Cypherpunk, Czolgolz, DVassallo, David Gerard, Davidhorman, Deriobamba, Doniago, Donmike10, Erik9, Esanchez7587, Ewulp, FMAFan1990, Flowan, Gamaliel, Garion96, Goustien, Grey Shadow, Howcheng, InnocuousPseudonym, Irishguy, ItsTheClimb17, JamesBWatson, Jayunderscorezero, Jbl1975, Jedi94, JesseMeza, Jfarajr, John Prattley, JohnnyChicago, JonathanDP81, Jperrylsu, Junafani, Kchishol1970, Khaosjr, Klaatuprime, Lamato, Lawrence142002, Le Gibbon, Leithp, LeoBunny, Lightmouse, Lupine Proletariat, MARQUIS111, Macduff, Matt Deres, MegX, MonkeeJuice, Newseditor, Nikofeelan, Oakshade, Oanabay04, Oblic, Paul A, Pegship, Pennyforth, Pepso2, Peyre, Quilly, Rebecca, Rebochan, ReverendG, Rich Farmbrough, Rock4arolla, Rodhullandemu, Rwlinda, Schroeder74, Ser Amantio di Nicolao, Shadowjams, SidP, Siebrand, Slgrandson, Son of adam, Sottolacqua, Spaceman42, SteinbDJ, Student7, Suchalady, SummerPhD, TMC1982, Testerman Westminster, The 80s chick, ThomasAnime, Tom Tresser, Tregoweth, Treybien, Tsange, TutterMouse, Tuttt, VideoRanger2525, Wahkeenah, Websurfer246, Westham4eva0204, Wiggin Tree, Wikisilki, Willy91, Wolvesnthemist, Woohookitty, Wykebjs, Yashveer r, Zachlast, Zundark, 210 anonymous edits

The World According to Garp (film) *Source*: http://en.wikipedia.org/w/index.php?oldid=464013679 *Contributors*: Alientraveller, Arno Matthias, Beware the Unknown, Big Bird, Bovineboy2008, Cat Parade, Debresser, Djflem, Dnn71, GrahamHardy, Guest9999, Hejsa, Jg2904, Katalaveno, Kollision, Kubek15, Kvdh, Mathew5000, Philbertgray, Radosław10, Rglenn, Rjfost, RoyBatty42, SFTVLGUY2, ShelfSkewed, Shining.Star, SidP, Sp33dyphil, Sugar Bear, Tjsocr1, TracyLinkEdnaVelmaPenny, Зейнал, 42 anonymous edits

The World According to Garp *Source*: http://en.wikipedia.org/w/index.php?oldid=462665969 *Contributors*: ***Ria777, Americanunderworld, Andycjp, AshcroftIleum, AugieWest, Bearcat, Benjiboi, Beware the Unknown, Cburnett, Cobaltcigs, Creationlaw, Cruxcriticorum, CutOffTies, Cutler, Czolgolz, Darguz Parsilvan, Darwinek, David Gerard, Demonslave, Dewey000, DocWatson42, Donmike10, Ed Poor, EdQuine, Edgamart, EeepEeep, Ellsworth, Ewlyahoocom, Facts707, Frecklefoot, Ggally, GrahamHardy, Grey Shadow, Guest9999, Gyrofrog, H-girl, Haddison, Hbent, Hejsa, Heron, Highpriority, Ilion2, Ilyaunfois, Indefinitevirtue, JJL, JamesMLane, Jogers, Joyous!, K1Bond007, Katalaveno, Katface, KelleyCook, Kevinalewis, Koyaanis

Qatsi, Kuyabribri, Kvn8907, LGagnon, Lee M, M.C. Brown Shoes, Marc Venot, Mathew5000, Mercurywoodrose, MikeCapone, Modernist, Narfal, Nevilley, NinjaLore, Ophion, Ottershrew, Patrick, Paul Drye, RafaAzevedo, Rai27, Ravichandar84, Redlemur, RevRagnarok, Rich Farmbrough, Riki, Rjwilmsi, S Luke, Sadads, ScottyBoy900Q, Sontag12, Speedoflight, Sugar Bear, Template namespace initialisation script, Tesselene, Tfine80, The Anome, Timothy Titus, TimothyHorrigan, Tony1, Treybien, Valentinejoesmith, VanBremen, Volmix, Vranak, WBoutros, Waacstats, Wackelpudding, Xezbeth, Yllosubmarine, Zoidbergmd, Zoltarpanaflex, Zotdragon, Зейнал, 106 anonymous edits

The Survivors (1983 film) *Source*: http://en.wikipedia.org/w/index.php?oldid=406300106 *Contributors*: A. Carty, After Midnight, Coder Dan, Colonies Chris, DeWaine, Jeffman52001, Jonathan Versen, Kchishol1970, Keraunoscopia, Kollision, LigaDue, Lklundin, Lugnuts, Open Human, Qrsdogg, Sayerslle, Skier Dude, Sknayfan, Sugar Bear, THEN WHO WAS PHONE?, Tassedethe, TheMovieBuff, Tjsocr1, Ulric1313, Wafulz, 42 anonymous edits

Moscow on the Hudson *Source*: http://en.wikipedia.org/w/index.php?oldid=462582556 *Contributors*: AbsoluteGleek92, Altenmann, Autobogg, BD2412, Colonies Chris, David Gerard, Demonslave, Derbent 5000, Donmike10, Dyl, Ed Poor, Ericgoldman, FollowGuard, Frecklefoot, Glennwells, Jedikaiti, Jeff G., Jenrae, Jordgubbe, Jrdioko, Leszek Jańczuk, Lord Cornwallis, Lugnuts, Mazca, Morefun, Pegship, Rekiwi, Ryder555, Salamurai, Sam Hocevar, Saucemaster, Skier Dude, SteinbDJ, Supernumerary, Tapir2001, Template namespace initialisation script, Tonywalton, Tvmode, Vague Rant, 达伟, 42 anonymous edits

Seize the Day (film) *Source*: http://en.wikipedia.org/w/index.php?oldid=464373215 *Contributors*: John of Reading, KurakCrossley, Paulgaita, Tassedethe, TheMovieBuff, Treybien, 1 anonymous edits

Club Paradise *Source*: http://en.wikipedia.org/w/index.php?oldid=463752036 *Contributors*: AGK, Bensin, Blue954, Bovineboy2008, Dalexwats, David Gerard, Donmike10, Erik9, Fernandobouregard, FollowGuard, FrankRizzo2006, Ivancurtisivancurtis, JDspeeder1, Jeffman52001, Minaker, Polisher of Cobwebs, Schroeder74, Shawn in Montreal, Sledgeh101, Slgrandson, Supernumerary, Tassedethe, The JPS, Timesman626, 17 anonymous edits

The Best of Times (film) *Source*: http://en.wikipedia.org/w/index.php?oldid=465423657 *Contributors*: AN(Ger), American Eagle, Appraiser, BostonRed, BudMann9, CardinalDan, David Gerard, GVnayR, Grandpafootsoldier, Jojhutton, Keeper76, Koavf, Looper5920, Madcapsjs, Mallanox, Mwalsh00, Nehrams2020, Noirish, Physicistjedi, Polisher of Cobwebs, Rorschach29, Rxcxxy, Sayerslle, Schroeder74, SilkTork, Sreejithk2000, Supernumerary, Taestell, TheRingess, Thefourdotelipsis, Tholly, Treybien, XSG, 59 anonymous edits

Good Morning, Vietnam *Source*: http://en.wikipedia.org/w/index.php?oldid=465395187 *Contributors*: *drew, Akono, Alexpopo, Ashley Pomeroy, Athaenara, Avij, B jonas, Beyond My Ken, Bobet, Bobo192, Boffob, Bovineboy2008, Brettalan, Bridgecross, Canterbury Tail, CapitalR, Cat's Tuxedo, Cbrown1023, Cburnett, Chester polarbear, Chris the speller, Classicfilms, Classicrockfan42, Comelloyellow, ConervativeTenn, Dakern74, Darev, Darkness2005, Darth Rage, Dave-ros, David Gerard, DeWaine, Der Meister, DevAnubis, Diagraph01, Easchiff, Ed Poor, Ed c 1969, Erik, Espen, Esrob, Evanstim, Evenfiel, Flashjordan, FlieGerFaUstMe262, Flyguy33, Forteblast, Fschoenm, Fuhghettaboutit, Gamaliel, Goofy12, Gyrferret, HappyDog, Heimstern, HeirToPendragon, Hfarmer, Idkeverythingistaken, Insanity Incarnate, Ipridian, J.D., JackalsIII, Jalabi99, Jeffman52001, Jim1138, Jnocook, Josh Parris, Jzummak, Kbdank71, Kchishol1970, Khukri, Kidlittle, Kintetsubuffalo, LGagnon, Lady Aleena, Laraspal00, Levineps, MARQUIS111, Mandsford, Margoon, Mark Sublette, Meeewkung, MegX, Mike Selinker, Mlaffs, NPalmius, Nehrams2020, Ngebendi, Not a dog, NotACow, PBP, Palica, Pearle, Perey, Polisher of Cobwebs, Ptcamn, Puckly, Quentin X, Radiohawk, Radosław10, Rbmoore, RealFerrari, RepublicanJacobite, ReyBrujo, Ribbet32, RicJac, Ricky81682, Rjwilmsi, Rogerd, Romanc19s, RoyBoy, SGGH, Salamurai, Sfaustin3, Shadowjams, ShelfSkewed, Shirt58, Sidewinded, Sietse Snel, Skywatcher68, Sledgeh101, SmartGuy, Snojoe, StanMarsh19, Stefanomione, Szumyk, Tanonero, Tassedethe, Tekmatic38, Tommyt, Tucu Mann, Tumadoireacht, Tyler.szabo, Ulric1313, Undertaker1562, Uxorion, Varlaam, Who, Whywhenwhohow, Wikipeterproject, Y2kcrazyjoker4, Yashveer r, Zoe, אנדר-ויק, 218 anonymous edits

Awakenings *Source*: http://en.wikipedia.org/w/index.php?oldid=462070077 *Contributors*: AN(Ger), Ahoerstemeier, Al042077, Alangdon86, Anders.Warga, Asymptote, BeApower, Bihco, Bovineboy2008, Burglekutt, Bzuk, Cburnett, Cpcheung, DeWaine, Demonslave, Dethomas, Dogah, Don Pasquale, Drmies, Drpickem, Dwanyewest, Dzubint, Easchiff, Ejs-80, Ekabhishek, Erik, Erik Kennedy, Evixir, Fatal exception, Feureau, FrankRizzo2006, From the North, Garion96, Green Cardamom, GregorB, Guestia, Hankwang, Harry, Irishguy, ItsTheClimb17, JamesBWatson, JeffyP, Jienum, Jimp, John K, Jordanceltiesfan, JzG, Kane5187, Kateedgar, Koro Neil, Kusma, LGagnon, Lady Aleena, Lindsay G. King, LtMuldoon, Luokehao, Mahjong705, Marxus, Mileykanerobert, NWill, NYScholar, Nabokov, Notinasnaid, Oanabay04, Okki, OldakQuill, Pegship, Peppage, Quentin X, Quintote, Qwe, Rbb l181, Reaper Eternal, Retiono Virginian, RichMac, Rockvee, Ron whisky, Salopian, Shakirfan, Shawisland, Shawn81, ShelfSkewed, SilkTork, Someguy1221, Somerwind, Stuart.drewer, Sven Erixon, TMC1982, Terrryjones, The Anome, The Sock of Maelgwn, Thraxas, Tollini, Tool2Die4, Toussaint, Treybien, Tvoz, Vfp15, Vl'hurg, Vlad, WadeSimMiser, WatchAndObserve, Websurfer246, West.andrew.g, Wiki Builder93, Wildhartlivie, Woohookitty, Wool Mintons, Zigger, Zoe, 143 anonymous edits

Dead Poets Society *Source*: http://en.wikipedia.org/w/index.php?oldid=465112535 *Contributors*: *drew, 5 albert square, 97198, AboveTheLogic, AbsoluteGleek92, Akageorge, Alansohn, Andrewpmk, Andy@ACS, Anetode, Angel caboodle, Angr, Anna Lincoln, Aquatics, Artist Walser, Artiste-extraordinaire, Artoasis, Ashershow1, Aspects, Atlant, Augustus Rookwood, Avb, Ayrton Prost, BMR4, Badagnani, Bahar101, Ball of pain, Bassmancalum, Bearian, Belovedfreak, Ben76266, Bender235, Benea, Berenise, Best O Fortuna, Betacommand, Biggspowd, Bigninja0433, Bihco, BillFlis, Bindingtheory, Binksternet, Blueaster, Bobmoney711, Bodnotbod, Boss1000, Bovineboy2008, Brianga, Bruceanthro, Btmelt11, Bubba hotep, BudMann9, Bullzeye, C1k3, C628, Caleb Aaron Osment, Calliaume, CapitalSasha, CaseyPenk, Cbrown1023, Cburnett, Chanheigeorge, Chris 42, Chris 73, Christian Storm, ColtM4, Cometstyles, Cop 663, Count Ringworm, Ctifumdope, Curtainhere, Cyberdoc777, D.alexa, D4g0thur, DARTH SIDIOUS 2, DJ Clayworth, DMCer, DMacks, DVD R W, Davehi1, David Gerard, David.Mestel, DavidDouthitt, Defrosted, Demonslave, Denimadept, DerHexer, Derbent 5000, Dirac1933, Dismas, Dissentor, Dodo bird, Doniago, Donmike10, DoxTxob, Dpotter, DurtyWilly, Dylan620, EH74DK, ESkog, Easchiff, Edlitz36, Egmontaz, Ekabhishek, Elli the baker, Emoangeltosha, Epbr123, Esprit15d, Etherhuffer666, EvertoExcel, EvgenyGenkin, Excirial, F W Nietzsche, FJPB, Faigl.ladislav, Feraudyh, Feross, Finn-Zoltan, FisherQueen, Fitzdocs, Foochar, Friendsfreak126, Frob, Frut, Gaius Cornelius, GalliasM, Gargaj, Gillean666, Gimmetoo, GoingBatty, Grafen, Grandpallama, Grungekid262, Gulliveig, Gwernol, HangingCurve, Harpsicalz, Havocrazy, HawkE65, Heatherfire, Heff01, HokieRNB, Hom sepanta, Hypnometal, Ianbob306, Ima boi, Impala2009, Imsxby, InShaneee, Iner22, Irishguy, Isil Helyanwe, IvanP, J04n, JForget, JHunterJ, JKKP, JackofOz, Jaldridge86, James Emtage, JamieJones, Jason Palpatine, Jay Gatsby, Jesse Hamm, Jessfrog43, Jet5343, Jezzabr, Jjc92787, Jnelson09, Johnchiu, Johnleemk, Jonathan.Bruce, Jrhoadley, Juntas, JzG, KF, KJS77, Kakofonous, Kazekko, Kbdank71, Kchishol1970, Kckoch, Khaosjr, Kintetsubuffalo, KirbyMaster14, Kizor, KnightRider, Koavf, Kollision, Kookyunii, Koszmonaut, Kristen Eriksen, Krsont, Kusma, Kwiki, L'aime, LGagnon, Lamrock, Laraspal00, LaszloWalrus, Leftus, Legotech, Levineps, Liesdamnlies, Logan, Longhair, Luigimon, MJBoa, MachoCarioca, Magioladitis, Magnus.de, Majorclanger, Maniska076, Maralia, Marc Venot, Marechal Ney, Marriedtofilm, MathNOTmeth, Matt Deres, Maxis ftw, Mbhunter, Mcbridej1313, Meamvagabond, Mediaman2, Mentifisto, Michael Farris, MickyGrenade, Mike Rosoft, Mo0, MonkeeJuice, Mr. Canadian, MrSomeone, Mrwojo, MustacheRider, N734LQ, NG 4 93, NWill, Nafi1122, Nafkar, Namangwari, Ncamren, Neilstar32, Netkinetic, Netscott, Ngebendi, Nightfreak, Ninaswims927, Nintendofan88, Noobeditor, Not a dog, NuclearWarfare, Oedii, Ohconfucius, Omghgomg, OneWeirdDude, Orange Suede Sofa, PKFlashOmega, PRRfan, Paperlan, Paradiso, Paragon12321, PassionOrPain, Pat1792A, Paxse, Pdubz18, Penbat, Phbasketball6, Philip Trueman, Philippe, Pi72, Pjoef, Player 03, Prashanthns, Purplebackpack89, Q8-falcon, RainbowOfLight, Randrewsman, RattleandHum, Redhaven27, Rednwhite, Renaboss, RepublicanJacobite, Res2216firestar, RicJac, Richardofoakshire, Rillian, Riwibb, Roaring Siren, Rob T Firefly, Robertson-Glasgow, Roricka, RxS, SEWilco, Sajbmz, Sampi, Samwisep86, Scientizzle, ScottyBoy900Q, Scout101, Sdedeo, Seanredshaw, Seascapeza, Sheogorath, Shouriki, Sionus, SixFourThree, Slingerble, SomethingWittyHere, Sottolacqua, Spelledasleep, SpuriousQ, Sry85, Sslop, Stibu, Stilgar135, Sullivan9211, Suriel1981, Susurrus, Szumyk, TMC1982, Taruru, Tbhotch, Tempodivalse, Tewapack, The Thing That Should Not Be, TheFarix, Thecheesykid, Theoldanarchist, Thismightbezach, Tide rolls, Tien.le, TimJing, Tjmayerinsf, Tohd8BohaithuGh1, Tommy2010, Tony Sidaway, Tool2Die4, Tough Little Ship, Treybien, Turkeyphant, TutterMouse, Tyraios, Udelluv, Username650, Valermos, Vampirefiend541, Venerated, Vex Delay, Vipinhari, Vivio Testarossa, Vlad, Voyagerfan5761, Wabliska, Wavelength, Werdna, WhisperToMe, Whitedge1, Whouk, Wikieditor06, Willcrys 84, Windchaser, Wjejskenewr, Wolfdog, Woohookitty, Wtmitchell, Xsxex, Yamamoto Ichiro, Yetanothercheesecakeman, Yiyun, Zeketheo, ZeroJanvier, Zntrip, Zoe, 930 anonymous edits

Cadillac Man *Source*: http://en.wikipedia.org/w/index.php?oldid=430398016 *Contributors*: Aleph-4, Andareed, Bisbis, DeWaine, Dwanyewest, Ed Poor, FMAFan1990, Grandpafootsoldier, Horkana, Jay Firestorm, Jeffman52001, Marc Shepherd, Matt Kurz, Nice poa, Pearle, Pegship, Polisher of Cobwebs, Premeditated Chaos, Prijutme4ty, QuasyBoy, Radosław10, STEV56, Schmendrick, Schmiteye, Shsilver, TexMurphy, TheMovieBuff, Treybien, Varlaam, WikHead, Wikiaf1, Yarbo's Tooth, 11 anonymous edits

Dead Again *Source*: http://en.wikipedia.org/w/index.php?oldid=464514672 *Contributors*: (aeropagitica), AN(Ger), AllySDude, Andrzejbanas, Atticuslai, B00P, Backtable, Bbb23, Beardo, Beast from da East, Bender235, CSOCSOCSO, ColinFine, Colonies Chris, Cromulent Kwyjibo, D6, Darkness2005, Dave B, David Gerard, Demonslave, Easchiff, Ellsworth, Elshewy, Everyking, Frecklefoot, Gabbort, Grandpafootsoldier, J.D., JHunterJ, Jamesbanesmith, Jg2904, Johnlongbond, Jwy, Kencf0618, Kslain, Lugnuts, Martarius, Martin S Taylor, Paul A, Pegship, Pingku, Polisher of Cobwebs, Quentin X, QuizzicalBee, RepublicanJacobite, Rjwilmsi, SCOCSOOCSOSC, Scarian, Schwenkstar, Sfan00 IMG, Shawn in Montreal, ShiftyNinja, Space Rodeo, Sreejithk2000, Stimmj, Talon6, TheMovieBuff, Tim!, Treybien, WickerGuy, Xezbeth, ZimZalaBim, ZodKneelsFirst, Zoz, 55 anonymous edits

The Fisher King (film) *Source*: http://en.wikipedia.org/w/index.php?oldid=457973715 *Contributors*: Acakewouldbenice, Agentsage, Andrzejbanas, Andycjp, Arasaka, Athanasius1, Azucar, Bensin, Berlot7, Blackjanedavey, Bobet, Bovineboy2008, CanisRufus, Cburnett, Charivari, Chris 73, Count Ringworm, Cubs Fan, Cuchullain, D6, Darkness2005, David Gerard, DeWaine, Discospinster, Donny, Doord127, Dpbsmith, Dudeman5685, Dutzi, Dwanyewest, Elendil's Heir, Emurphy42, EurekaLott, FMAFan1990, Fastilysock, Finlay McWalter, Francisco Valverde, Fred Bradstadt, G34j, GTBacchus, Georgef85, Gevorg89, Gleech, Gobonobo, GoldenMeadows, GorgeCustersSabre, Greenrd, GregU, Helion Omega, Imgaril, Inurhead, J.D., Jackel, Joanberenguer, Julia Rossi, Kate, Koavf, Kuralyov, Liftarn, Lord Bob, Lugnuts, Mandarax, Mattstan, MaximumMadnessStixon, MetaManFromTomorrow, Michel BUZE, Micione, Mickea, MikeWazowski, Morgands1, Moshe Constantine Hassan Al-Silverburg, MrPanyGoff, Nasmformyzombie, Notmicro, Oakshade, One Salient Oversight, Paul A, Planders, RattleandHum, Reeperbahn, RepublicanJacobite, Sam Hocevar, Santryl, Schroeder74, Scopetta, Signalhead, Signinstranger, Silent Tom, SpNeo, SpikeJones, Staecker, Stillnotelf, Str1977, TallulahBelle, Template namespace initialisation script, That Guy, From That Show!, The Wrong Man, TheRealFennShysa, Thebanjohype, Tommyt, Trut-h-urts man, Waerloeg, Wildhartlivie, Wool Mintons, Wyatt Riot, Xezbeth, ZeroJanvier, Zodiac0, Zoe, 115 anonymous edits

Hook (film) *Source*: http://en.wikipedia.org/w/index.php?oldid=465282686 *Contributors*: 5 albert square, A Raider Like Indiana, AN(Ger), Ainoskedu, Alientraveller, Alissa98cp, AlistairMcMillan, Alligators1974, Andrzejbanas, Andyjay729, Annericelover, Anticipation of a New Lover's Arrival, The, Antiuser, Arbero, Arman88, Aron1, AskFranz, Australian Matt, Autopilots, Avb, B4hand, BMMEZ, Baldghoti, Batmanand, Bdingg, Bear208, Bejnar, Ben-Bopper, Betty Logan, Bfoaz, Biggspowd, Bignole, Black Kat, Boduke343, Bolman Deal, Bonga, Boonjava, Branddobbe, Brant Jones, BrownHairedGirl, Bubbleoui, Buh6173, C. A. Russell, Caim, Caleson, CelticJobber, CharlotteWebb, Cholmes75, Chowbok, Chrisp510, Ckatz, Closedmouth, Cooksey, Cryabbey, Cueball8384, Cyclone77, Cypherpunk, D6, DRosenbach, DaffyDuck619, Darkness2005, Das cool, Deltalima, Demonslave, Dieschwarzetur, Discospinster, Doctor Hexagon, Double.a.19, Dr. Blofeld, Dupz, Dynesclan, EJBanks, Easchiff, Eclectic hippie, Eeekster, Efilipek, Elfguy, Ellsworth, Emote, Energy Dome, Enviroboy, Epbr123, Erik, FMAFan1990, Falstaft, Finn-Zoltan, Firsfron, Fourthords, Friginator, Furrykef, Garion96, Geopgeop, George A. M., GiantKingz, Goa103, GoingBatty, Goldenmelody722, GrifterWolf, HMFS, Hailey C. Shannon, HalfShadow, Harley Quinn hyenaholic, Harluu, Hedyfrancis, Henhouse808, Hfctorch, High Orbit, Hill of Beans, Hires an editor, Hooked91, IAngelofFuryI, ILovedYouToDeth, IllaZilla, Ink 13, Irishguy, Ischorr, JBK405, JDDJS, JHFTC, JaGa, Jamesbanesmith, JasonAQuest, Jedi Striker, Jhsounds, Jienum, JimVC3, Joelvanatta, Johnlongbond, Jonathan.Bruce, Jonghyunchung, Joseph 098, Jtalledo, Juggernautthunderclap, JuneGloom07, Jusdafax, Kageskull, Karin127, Kelly Martin, Kinneyboy90, Kittentornado, KojieroSaske, Koolo, Krazykenny, Kusma, LGagnon, Laurabennett14, Levineps, LilHelpa, Linda, LiteShell, Loudmouth 2, Ludwigparis, Lugnuts, MARQUIS111, Majorly, MakeRocketGoNow, Mandarax, Mary Read, Meddling, Mentifisto, Moviefan2k4, Mr.Xp, Mr.rbt, Musik of Anarchy, Mutt'sIndy5, Mütze, NICHOLAS LAMINACK, NICHOLAS THE MIGHTY, NWill, Nalvage, NeoBatfreak, NeverLand91, Nikai, Nkm, Nroxz, Number87, Nuttycoconut, Nv8200p, O, Onorem, PS2pcGAMER, Patrick1982, Paul A, Paul panhook, PaulHanson, Pegship, Pictureuploader, Powerofjuju, Psantora, Quentin X, Qxz, R. fiend, Racecarguy360, RattleandHum, Razorflame, Redeagle688, Reywas92, RicJac, Rich Farmbrough, Rich257, Ricky81682, Riverstepstonegirl, Rjanag, Rjwilmsi, Ronhjones, Runefurb, SGreer1113, Sadads, Scarecroe, Scoutersig, Sego57, Seko, ShadowHntr, Shanek1980, Shannara, ShelfSkewed, Shirt58, Sjones23, Sleepyjuly, Sniperz11, Sottolacqua, Sp33dyphil, Splash, Srushe, Stan39520, Stelmaris, Sverdrup, Swhuck, Syrannicus, Szyslak, TAnthony, TMC1982, TaintedMustard, Tamariki, Tertiary7, Test3, Tetrix, The 80s chick, The Famous Movie Director, The JPS, The Thing That Should Not Be, The Ungovernable Force, The soapboxer, TheRedPenOfDoom, Thumperward, TimGillespie, Tin013, Tom H12, Tozoku, TracyLinkEdnaVelmaPenny, Tregoweth, Treybien, Triddle, Tristan Morin, Tupac Apocalypso, UPMan16, Undeniably.insane, Unitednut, WHS, WTRiker, Wackymacs, Ward3001, Wasted Sapience, WesleyDodds, Who, Whysanitynet, Wikiwisesense, Wildroot, Will-B, Williamnilly, Windbear Chime Guy, Woohookitty, Yachtsman1, Yanksox, Yashveer r, Yuri Elite, ZEJ999, Zepp900, Zii XFS, Zombie Jeff, Zz414, 593 anonymous edits

Toys (film) *Source*: http://en.wikipedia.org/w/index.php?oldid=464429521 *Contributors*: Ahmednh, Allixpeeke, Andrzejbanas, Anglius, AnonMoos, Antaeus Feldspar, Anthony Appleyard, Appraiser, Articrono, Az1568, BANZ111, Balmung0731, Barticus88, Ben-Bopper, BigCow, Bigar, Biggspowd, Bondegezou, Bosco13, Branddobbe, Bridgecross, CWSWeb, CallidoraBlack, Canterbury Tail, Cap.Blackard, Cat's Tuxedo, CecilPL, Cigarette, Cliff1911, Corvun, CouplandForever, Cyberry, DGRM13, DOSGuy, DaRocksteady, Dahveed76, Dansham, Demoman87, Demonslave, Dingno, Dryguy, Dwanyewest, Dyaa, Eluchil404, Epbr123, Epistemophiliac, Errand, Exok, FCYTravis, Fnerchei, FollowGuard, Fourthords, FrankRizzo2006, Freshh, Fuhghettaboutit, GVnayR, Gaius Cornelius, Ginkgo100, Glacier109, Gnfnrf, GoingBatty, Golbez, Hailey C. Shannon, Hello32020, Henry W. Schmitt, Holme053, Improv, Jaranda, Jeepday, John Smith M.D., Ph.D, JokerWylde, Justin W Smith, Kitch, Krellion, Kusma, Laurinavicius, Lawrence142002, Lifterus, Linkor, Linkspamremover, LokiClock, Lugnuts, MARQUIS111, MarnetteD, Matthew Fennell, Mhking, Mhrycak25, Mickeyg13, Mistress Selina Kyle, Munci, Myrealana, Mysekurity, N30n-night, Nandesuka, Neg, Nehrams2020, Nick, O1ive, Ohnoitsjamie, Pascalzib, Pearle, Pegship, Pelusa, Pennicilan, Pgk, Planet-man828, Prime 2004, Quentin X, Quicklin, Radosław10, RedWolf, Rjwilmsi, Ron whisky, Rtkat3, Sagaciousuk, Salamurai, Seajayla, ShadowHntr, Shanes, Silent Tom, SimonMayer, Spidermanrox, SpikeJones, TJ Spyke, Tassedethe, Template namespace initialisation script, TexasAndroid, Texture, TheMadBaron, TheObtuseAngleOfDoom, Tjsocr1, Tomsega, Toxicroak, Travelingman99, Ucanlookitup, Voice of Treason, WalterGR, Warreed, Wickethewok, William Graham, Yetikirby, Yonskii, Zzuuzz, 173 anonymous edits

Aladdin (1992 Disney film) *Source*: http://en.wikipedia.org/w/index.php?oldid=465063399 *Contributors*: **mech**, 1088park, 2Pac, 5 octaves, A purple wikiuser, AGW, AKR619, Aaaxlp, AaronY, Abdurahman49, Abu1987, AdamDeanHall, Adraeus, Agent 918, Agustinaldo, Ahoerstemeier, Aidepikiw0000, Aka042, Akshayaj, Al3xil, AlbertSM, Alegoo92, Allissonn, Alumni, AmDrag21, Amplifier123, And1987, Andreaus, Andres, Andrew Maiman, Andrewpmk, Andrewrp, Andromeda, Andrzejbanas, Andycjp, AngChenrui, Angela, Angelofdeath275, Angie Y., Angmering, AnmaFinotera, Annabella2006, Annebb11, Apostrophe, Arainach, Arbero, Arcadia24, Ardavu, Arielbelle1621, Armetrek, Atlant, Autiger, Avant Guard, Avaya1, Axem Titanium, Azure Haights, AzureAzul, B Touch, BD2412, Bad Graphics Ghost, Ballofbluestring, Bambifan101, Batman tas, Battlebeast, Bazzargh, Bburton, Bdesham, Beemer69, Beetstra, Benschar, BesigedB, Bigcheesebebbs, Bigtophat, Biiru, Binx, Blackcat12, Blitz Lutte, Bob Castle, Bobamnertiopsis, Bobo192, Bobyllib, Bovineboy2008, Btornado, BulsaraAndDeacon, Burkemancometh, ByeNow, Cactusjump, Caesura, Cakeofages, Caldorwards4, Calion, CameronPG, CanadianLinuxUser, Cartoonrama, Cat's Tuxedo, Causa sui, Cdeujm, Cetra, Cfolz88, CharlotteWebb, Chepetoño, Chickenmonkey, Chowbok, Chris the speller, Chris1219, Chrislintott, Christianster45, Chzz, Clarkefreak, Clearbu2, Cliffb, ClonedPickle, CodeMonk, Colliric, Colorfulharp233, ContiAWB, Corpx, Crackshoe, Crblchn555, Cromwellt, Cubs Fan, Cutesparkina67, Cybercobra, Cynicalkane, DEX1115, DRosenbach, DTwirler, DabMachine, Dadaist6174, DaffyDuck619, Daibhid C, Dakart, Damien Prystay, Damnreds, Danglada, Darklilac, Darkness2005, DarthSidious, Daveswagon, David Gerard, Dawn Bard, Dcoetzee, DeadEyeArrow, Debresser, Demonslave, DepartedUser4, Derumi, Descendall, Dewelar, Diego Grez, Dieschwarzetur, DisneyAnimeFreak92, Disneyfolly, Disneyfolly2, Disneyluv, Dkkicks, Dkupser, Dlae, Dmn, Dnusair, DoubleBlue, Dougtremblay, Drazzib, Drewcifer3000, DropDeadGorgias, Drunkenpeter99, Dumersk, Dyl, EWS23, Easy4me, EditingManiac, Editor182, Efghij, El Krem, Elonka, Emurphy42, Epbr123, Eratticus, Eric119, Erik, Esn, Estoy Aquí, Estrose, EveryDayJoe45, Everyking, Exert, F1315NJ, Fantasy, Fastzander, Fibonacci, Figureskatingfan, Flair Girls, Flammifer, Fligglegiggle, FlyingPenguins, Fourthords, Fractyl, FriscoKnight, Frollo, Funguy06, FunkMonk, FuriousFreddy, Furrykef, GD 6041, Galactic war, Garion96, Gary King, GeeJo, GentlemanGhost, Georgia guy, Gigamaligabyte, Gilliam, Gimmetrow, GlassCobra, Goth67, Goustien, Granpuff, GreatScottoftheAwesomes, Gtrmp, Gurch, Gwernol, Hadal, Hal7Li7e, Halo, HannahMiley, Harley Quinn hyenaholic, Harryd1007, Heenan73, Heimstern, Heron, Hibana, Hiphats, Histrion, Homesliced174, Hondo77, Hope(N Forever), Horkana, Hyliad, I Enjoy Commenting, IRT1904, IW.HG, Ianblair23, Icemountain2, Igordebraga, Ilike2pizza, InShaneee, Indosauros, Inky, Insanity Incarnate, Irishguy, It Is Me Here, Itxia, Ivirivi00, J.delanoy, JFaddoul, JQF, Jackalt, Jason Palpatine, Jaxer, Jean-Jacques Georges, Jedi Striker, Jedi94, Jeff G., Jienum, Jimnyc62, Joeshoe, John of Reading, John254, JohnDoe0007, JohnRussell, Joseph A. Spadaro, Josh Gentry, Joy, Jpark3909, JuWiki2, Julien faddoul, Junkfly, Just A Lad, JustPhil, JustWong, Jvsett, KJS77, KMF, Karen Johnson, Kassjab, KathrynLybarger, Kbdank71, Kchishol1970, Keith Paynter, Kellywatchthestars, Kevin j, Keyser Söze, Killiondude, King of Hearts, Kitkatface, Kiwiboy1221, Kizor, Kkm010, Klausness, KnowledgeOfSelf, Koavf, Kosunen, Kwamikagami, LGagnon, Lacrimosus, Larry laptop, LaukkuTheGreit, LeaveSleaves, LesIsMore9o9, Levineps, Liftarn, Lightlowemon, Lightmouse, Ling.Nut, Ljones, Lord Opeth, LordBleen, LowSelfEstidle, Lowellian, LtPowers, Lugnuts, Luna Santin, MHarrington, Madforthefiddle, Make, Malcham7, Mamolu, Marcsin, Marcus2, MarjorieCook, MarnetteD, Mary Read, Maserati edict, Master Bigode, Master Deusoma, Master z0b, Matthew Cantrell, Maxim, Maxis ftw, Maxwell Rochette, MearsMan, Mengsk, Mezzy mok, Michael Hardy, Michaelsbll, Mickeymousechen, Mikekearn, Mimihitam, MindlessXD, Mitch1981, Mitsuki152, Mlaurenti, ModerateOne, Mooky 7 sa, Mr Beale, Mr Bound, Mr Sasquatch, MrItty, Mtjaws, Mwalimu59, Mynameisnotpj, N. Harmonik, NDfan007, NHRHS2010, NawlinWiki, Nehrams2020, Nemeses9, NerdMaster15, Niceley, Nick123, Nintendo Maximus, Nintendude, Niteowlneils, No substitute for you, Nqnpipnr, Nrbelex, Nymf, ObsessiveJoBroDisorder, Oda Mari, OjeB, Ollj, One, Oscar22, Oscara, Ost316, Otohime, Overlord11001001, Oxymoron83, PJ Pete, PacificBoy, Palnatoke, Palpatine, Paul A, Pavel Vozenilek, Pennyadodumuss, Peppage, Percy Snoodle, Philip Stevens, Pikawil, Plactus, Plainnym, PlaywrightSt, Prayerfortheworld, Prkr 07, Prof. MagneStormix, Psych2008, PurpleChez, Q11, Qtoktok, QuasyBoy, Quintote, QuirkyAndSuch, Quuxplusone, R13n13, Rcwc, Reagar, Redjedia, Redrose64, Reedy, Revth, RexNL, Reywas92, Rfsilveira, Rhindle The Red, Rich Farmbrough, Richard ruffian, RickK, Ricky81682, Rjwilmsi, Rmhermen, Robsinden, RockMFR, Rogerd, Rory Cox, Rror, Rusted AutoParts, Salamurai, Salavat, Sam, SandDune1, Sango123, Sb1990, Scanlan, Scarlet Lioness, SchfiftyThree, Schnauf, Scot.eaton, Scottryan, Seinfreak37, Selmo, Seresin, Shadow24816, Shakirfan, Shanegamer13, ShelfSkewed, Shii, Shinku Hisaki, Shnout, Siddharth Mehrotra, SilentWind, SilkTork, SimonP, Sirius85, Sjones23, Skier Dude, Skycoh8er, Slakr, Slt10T, Small5th, Smalljim, SmartGuy, Smurdah, Snailwalker, Snowy 1973, Socal gal at heart, Sohailstyle, Someone else, Somsack, Sottolacqua, Soundofmusicals, Sparky the Seventh Chaos, Spidey104, Spirits003, Spitfire19, Sroc, Stan Shebs, StarSpangledKiwi, Stardust6000, StebenXC, Stemonitis, Stephenb, Steve1138, Sugar Bear, SuperDude115, SuperFlash101, Superherongpogi, Supermorff, Supernumerary, Switchercat, Synflame, TAnthony, TKD, TPIRFanSteve, Tabletop, TangentCube, Tanthalas39, Taran Wanderer, Tartan, Tassedethe, Tavilis, Tbhotch, Template namespace initialisation script, Tenchichan, The 80s chick, The Filmaker, The JumpStation, The Prince of Darkness, The Rogue Penguin, The Thing That Should Not Be, The mitten man, TheLeopard, TheListUpdater, Theangryblackwoman, Thedemonhog, Thefourdotelipsis, Themeparkfanatic, Themeparkgc, Tim Auke Kools, TimBentley, TimeCruiserMike, Timwi, Tiswaser, Tony1, TonyTheTiger, Tool2Die4, Touch Of Light, Tregoweth, Tripod86, TuneyLoon, Tustin2121, TwoOneTwo, Txomin, Typhoon966, Ubardak, UltimatePyro, Useight, User27091, Uther Dhoul, Vague Rant, Valdezlopez, Varlaam, VashiDonsk, Vegaswikian, Versus22, Visual planet, Voyagerfan5761, Wafulz, Warpozio, Watamala, Wearend4, Wedineinheck, Wereon, WesleyDodds, Wheelchair Epidemic, Whomp, Whywhenwhohow, Wicherwill, WikHead, WikiKingOfMishawaka, Wikieditor1988, Wikiman999224, Will2k, WilyD, Wiredpup, Witchbaby, Wknight94, Wmahan, Wolfcruiser, Woodylogan, Woohookitty, WpZurp, WullieMan, Ww2censor, Wysprgr2005, Xer, Yashouzoid, Yashveer r, Yelsikneb, Youknowme70, YourEyesOnly, Ysangkok, Zanimum, Zarl11, Zero1328, Zidane4028, Zohab, Zone46, Zotdragon, Δ, 1048 anonymous edits

The Timekeeper *Source*: http://en.wikipedia.org/w/index.php?oldid=463944597 *Contributors*: 23skidoo, ACSE, After Midnight, Allstar86, Arcticdawg, Atomuran, AtticusX, Attilios, Bedford, Bernstein2291, Billdanbury, Blm07, Bobblehead, Bradd Sky, Canterbury Tail, CommonsDelinker, DReifGalaxyM31, Danim, DeFender1031, Debresser, Deror avi, Dlrp87, Doczilla, Favonian, Fethers, FigmentJedi, Gaius Cornelius, Gdgourou, Hailey C. Shannon, Hill of Beans, Hooon, Jordancatalano, Kirkfenton, Knowledge Seeker, Koavf, Kuralyov, Kusma, LordBleen, LordJord, Luckybolt, Lyght, M-le-mot-dit, Mahdisney, ManoaChild, Mdawg89, Michael Hardy, Mitsukai, Mkaycomputer, MrInsla, MrItty, Narnaiexpert, Nehrams2020, Pegship, Phydend, RadioFan, Randomgbear, Rich Farmbrough, Rjwilmsi, RomanXNS, Salavat, Santryl, Sawblade5, Slysplace, Speedway, Stevemcl, Tabletop, Tim!, Timberlax, Tone, Trivialist, Turquoisefish, WOSlinker, WesUGAdawg, Whoville, Zanimum, 186 anonymous edits

FernGully: The Last Rainforest *Source*: http://en.wikipedia.org/w/index.php?oldid=461029951 *Contributors*: A8UDI, AdamDeanHall, Alan Liefting, Alansohn, AndrewHowse, Andrzejbanas, Angel caboodle, Angie Y., AnmaFinotera, Anonymous from the 21st century, Apokryltaros, Arx Fortis, Basawala, Ben-Bopper, Bender235, Bovineboy2008, Brad Rousse, Canley, Carlwev, Cartooner32, Cat's Tuxedo, Chris the speller, Columbia, Cromwelman, Danucciguzman, DarkFalls, David Gerard, Dcflyer, DeWaine, Denkealsobin, DethMetalDrummer, Dl2000, Don P.I.M.P, Dr. Blofeld, ESkog, Eeee, Eekerz, Eratticus, Erik, Evilgidgit, Fizan, Freikorp, Freshh, FuriousFreddy, G716, Gdo01, Gilliam, Glottal Stop, Herbee, Hornean, Hoverfish, Hulleywood, Ichiru, Iknowyourider, Imaginaryoctopus, J.delanoy, JeezBreeze, Jmac3568, John254, Josiah Rowe, Jrobknicks123, KidzOnlyFan, King kong922, Klassykittychick, Kollision, Kuru, Liberty's Library Waiters, Liface, Little.miss.sunshine, Lizakimoto, Longhair, Loqi, Lugnuts, Luke4545, MadManAmeica, Mariofan88, MarnetteD, MonkeeJuice, Montecarlocars, MorrisS, Mr. Power-Mad!, Mr. Worldster, Munci, N5iln, Nate Spidgewood, Nemeses9, Nightscream, NorrYtt, OGoncho, Oblivious, Omgteal, Onomea, Orderinchaos, OverlordQ, PMDrive1061, Pascal.Tesson, Phydend, Piano non troppo, Plasticspork, Pnkrockr, Quijote3000, RainbowWerewolf, Rebochan, Redwood Elf, Remurmur, Rmccowen, Scyker, Sgtdude, Shawn2082, Sjones23, Slgrandson, Slowking Man,

StarLegacy, StebenXC, Swotboy2000, TJUser, Tasermon's Partner, TehDogfather, TenPoundHammer, Terra-chan, The 80s chick, The Watusi, TheBadgerFromYourNightmares, TheValentineBros, Themania, Thumperward, Tregoweth, Tricky Wiki44, Tryforceful, UberMan5000, UsaSatsui, Vameon, Vancouver Outlaw, WhisperToMe, Witchbaby, Wussycat, XuxiRawe22, Zartok-35, 248 anonymous edits

Shakes the Clown *Source*: http://en.wikipedia.org/w/index.php?oldid=462092549 *Contributors*: Andrzejbanas, Attilios, Ben-w, Binksternet, Bmclaughlin9, Boratsagdiyev, Bowlderizer, Cameron.walsh, Cbrown1023, Ceoil, D6, Darrenhusted, ElHornberg, Evb-wiki, Felicity4711, Fuhghettaboutit, GlassCobra, GoingBatty, Jamesbanesmith, Jeffman52001, Jkazoo, Joeystuff, John32404, Kerowyn, KevinWho, Koavf, Kukini, Magioladitis, Malcolm, Mileycyruseminem, Neanderthalprimadonna, Ol Chappy, Pornovision, RW Dutton, Sexbeatle, SlubGlub, Sugar Bear, Surfmaui, Sus scrofa, Tassedethe, TenPoundHammer, TigerK 69, Uucp, Wdflake, АлександрВв, 37 anonymous edits

Mrs. Doubtfire *Source*: http://en.wikipedia.org/w/index.php?oldid=464842990 *Contributors*: 2Pac, AJR, Acb123sisir, AdamSmithee, Adambro, Adamshappy, Airplaneman, Akerans, Alexd17, Alexd18, Alfirin, Alloy, Alro, Americanhero, Andrzejbanas, Angr, Annalise, Annie Lennox, AnthonyA99, Antmusic, Aoecean, ApprenticeFan, Aralvarez, Arctic Night, Argyll Lassie, Arkady Rose, Arthur Holland, Arthur Rubin, Arx Fortis, Astroview120mm, BD2412, Babaloozy, Baccyak4H, Backslash Forwardslash, BarryTheUnicorn, Baseball Bugs, Before My Ken, Ben Ben, Bennybp, Bento00, Beorhtwulf, Beyond My Ken, Bidgee, Biggspowd, Bigsteeve, Black raven2525, BlackTerror, Bob Castle, Bobet, Bongwarrior, Boo1210, BranFlake96, Bravo Plantation, Briandutremble, Brumski, Burto88, COMPFUNK2, CanadianCaesar, Cardsplayer4life, Cat-five, Cavenba, Cbdorsett, Cbrown1023, CeruleanFilms, Cgnabod, Chavando, Chocolateeclaire, ChrisP2K5, ClonedPickle, Cobain, Colonies Chris, ContiAWB, Coolcaesar, Countz3r0, Cst17, Cute 1 4 u, D-rew, D6, DARTH SIDIOUS 2, DBaba, DaisukeVulgar, DanielNuyu, Darkness2005, Darkwolf021, Darth Mike, David Gerard, DavidA, DavidHolden, DavidLevinson, Dell9300, Delldot, Derek Markus, Djbroox, Dlloyd, Dominik92, Donald Albury, Donmike10, Dr. Blofeld, DreamMcQueen, Drunkenpeter99, Dsiphor98, Dutzi, Dwanyewest, EdGl, Edward321, Einsteinbud, Eirik, ElrRigby, EoGuy, Erik, Everyking, Evil saltine, Extransit, Fabricationary, Falcon8765, FeelsLikeHome, FetchcommsAWB, Fieldday-sunday, Filmstalker, Flyguy33, Fourthords, FreewayDan, Freikorp, Frut, Funguy06, Furrykef, Fyyer, G33klvr, Gamaliel, Giant89, Gilliam, Glane23, Gpollock, Grandpafootsoldier, Granpuff, Grenavitar, Guy M, HalfShadow, Harrygorilla, Hi1714, Huon, Interrobang², Invincible Ninja, Iohannes Animosus, Irk, IronGargoyle, Jack Schlederer, Jacobr1020, Jadelucca, JaffaCakeLover, Jaldridge86, Jamacfarlane, Jamesbanesmith, Jeff G., Jeffman52001, Jellzzz, Jienum, Jill Tuck, Jnelson09, Joe3333, Johnlongbond, Johno100, Johnuniq, Jonay81687, Joseph A. Spadaro, JustPhil, Jzummak, Kahlil88, Katiker, Kbdank71, Kchishol1970, Kidlittle, Kilo-Lima, Klam69r, Kollision, Koolaidohyea, LGagnon, Lady Aleena, Levineps, Limetolime, Linklewtt, LorenzoB, Lots42, Lt. Frank Drebin, Luckyherb, MJD86, Magomarl, Mahjong705, Martin451, Mav, Meteorico, Micahbrwn, Millahnna, Min1Phoeb2, Mjrmtg, Moncrief, Mosherdude91, Mr. Billion, Mr. Laser Beam, Mr. Matté, MrDisTrv, Naturalfloridian, Nbettencourt, Ndrly, Nicknackrussian, Nickrj, Noidea26, NotACow, Nymf, Nyttend, Nyxaus, Oarfisher, Obsessmuch, OhioBuckeyeBill, Ojorojo, OneWeirdDude, Only, Orbitalwow, PDH, PM800, Paul-L, Piepants, Pigsonthewing, Pinethicket, Pinkbutterfly91, Planet-man828, Plasticspork, Ppntori, Prodego, Psy guy, Psychoboyjack, Pyfan, QuasyBoy, Quentin X, Radosław10, Rahuloof, Rakshasa7, RaseaC, Rayhill09, Rbb l181, Red dwarf, Retired username, Revolver Ocelot 1994, Ric168, Richardcarroll1981, Ricky81682, Rivecoder, Riverstepstonegirl, Rjwilmsi, Ron whisky, Ronz, Rosstech, Ryanmalik01, SSJ 5, Saebvn, Sam Vimes, Sb2007, Scanbus, SchfiftyThree, Schmiteye, SchuminWeb, Sd31415, Sfaustin3, ShakataGaNai, ShelfSkewed, Shirtwaist, ShortShadow, SidP, Sims2aholic8, Sjones23, Sjyglm, Skippy-9, Skullfission, Slgrandson, Smalljim, Sottolacqua, Sound of white, Sreejithk2000, Statalyzer, Stefan, Stemurph88, Steveo2, Studiedgenius, Sullyboy204, SuperBrickDude, SuperDude115, SyntaxError55, TAnthony, TMC1982, Tamnguyen88, Tarquin, Tassedethe, Tawniz, Tbhotch, Tedius Zanarukando, Teo64x, TexMurphy, The Giant Puffin, The Shadow-Fighter, The dark lord trombonator, The mitten man, The wub, TheCustomOfLife, TheHidingAmaranth, TheRealFennShysa, Think777, Thismightbezach, Tide rolls, Tinton5, Toki, TomGreen, Tool2Die4, Trachtemacht, TrbleClef, Triwbe, TubularWorld, Twisted4000, USN1977, UberMan5000, UltimatePyro, Uniquifiant, Vega84, Violetriga, Viridae, Voyagerfan5761, Walkiped, Walter 1080, Welshleprechaun, WhatGuy, Who, Wikicali00, WikipedianMarlith, Wildhartlivie, Will-B, Willirennen, Wisdom89, Wolfdog, WolframSiever, Woohookitty, Xiaomao, Y2kcrazyjoker4, Yashveer r, Younkinconnor92, Zanoni, 743 anonymous edits

Being Human (film) *Source*: http://en.wikipedia.org/w/index.php?oldid=439747493 *Contributors*: 1dragon, Academic Challenger, AdamDeanHall, Andrwsc, Big Bird, Bovineboy2008, Catamorphism, Deiz, Donald McKinney, Duncancumming, Edwinstearns, Enochlau, Fastily, Freshh, G3rrick, Grandpafootsoldier, Hagerman, Horkana, Killing Vector, Locaracle, Lucky number 49, MPerel, MarnetteD, Neddyseagoon, Razzfan, ReverendG, Ricky81682, Rnb, Rubyuser, SISLEY, SilkTork, Skier Dude, Stevertigo, TheMovieBuff, Treybien, Wool Mintons, 36 anonymous edits

In Search of Dr. Seuss *Source*: http://en.wikipedia.org/w/index.php?oldid=458045282 *Contributors*: Absolon, Alakazam, Andrei G Kustov, Balloonguy, Cholmes75, David Gerard, Drpickem, ExoSynth, Flankk, Jacob valliere, Jevansen, Kitia, MiltonT, Mr. Absurd, Mtjaws, Pjoef, Plrk, Rjwilmsi, Smitty, TMC1982, TenPoundHammer, The Anome, Tim1357, TrapStilton, TubularWorld, Tylisasweet, 44 anonymous edits

Jumanji *Source*: http://en.wikipedia.org/w/index.php?oldid=465302197 *Contributors*: 041744, Abomasnow, Aericanwizard, Ahkond, Alansohn, AmsyyLeSavage, Amtwinkles, Andrzejbanas, Anetode, Animum, Anthony Appleyard, Armbrust, Awesomeomar, BassPlyr23, Belinrahs, Binkyuk, Biruitorul, Blanket hogger, BlueMario1016, Bongwarrior, Bovineboy2008, Breawycker, Brownma17, Caiaffa, Can't sleep, clown will eat me, Cannibal2, Capricorn42, Cbrown1023, Cctoide, CharlotteWebb, Chenzw, Chris G, Closedmouth, Coder Dan, Colonies Chris, Computer97, Comrade Kesha, Conti, ContiAWB, Crablogger, Creesyboo, Crumbsucker, Cyberherbalist, Czolgolz, DCEdwards1966, Daking, Danucciguzman, Darkness2005, David Gerard, David171193, Db099221, DeWaine, Degscult, Dekisugi, Denisarona, DerekDD, Detnchris14, Dickclarkfan1, Dieschwarzetur, Donmike10, Dpeifer, Draconiator, Dwanyewest, EJBanks, EMMAjaneMURPHYflobert, Ebyabe, Ed Poor, Efficacious, Eliavsd, Ellissound, Empty2005, Emurphy42, Eraysor, Erik, Evilgidgit, Excirial, FMAFan1990, Falcon9x5, Fieldday-sunday, Flewis, Flower Priest, FollowGuard, Fourthords, FrankRizzo2006, GM11, Gabe1972, Galactic war, Garion96, Gemini 925, George Ho, Gevorg89, GhostFace1234, GoingBatty, Haon 2.0, Happygogirl, Happypatatoes, Harinara21, Harryboyles, Heather-Grace, Heegoop, HeinzDoofenshmirtz, Hort Graz, Hu12, Hugh Manatee, IGeMiNix, II MusLiM HyBRiD II, Iammilind, Ian Lee, Immblueversion, Inwind, Iridescent, JAF1970, JNighthawk, JQF, Jafeluv, JamesBWatson, Jason Palpatine, Jay Firestorm, Jelly Soup, JesseRafe, Jetligi2, Jhsounds, Jienum, Jjamison, John of Reading, John67832, Kanonkas, Karaoke Prince, Kbdank71, Kdennis86, Keilana, Kid2500, Kidlittle, King of Hearts, Kingfisherswift, Kittysmith123, Klapi, Kmecha7, Konczewski, Kooky World Guy, Kubieziel, KusanagiTsuragi, Lacrimosus, Lady Aleena, LadyJ3000, Lg16spears, LightSpirit06, LilHelpa, Limetolime, ListedRenegade, LittleMenace2K3, Loom91, Maelnuneb, Marktreut, Master Deusoma, Mauriciopenac, Mcanmoocanu, Merotoker, Merotoker1, Merqurial, Michael Devore, Michaelas10, Michaelsbll, Mightily Oats, Misabel, Mjrmtg, Moneasha, Moshe Constantine Hassan Al-Silverburg, Mostly Rainy, MovieMan123, Nagy, Name Theft Victim, Ndboy, Nehrams2020, NeoBatfreak, Neoarchon, Nick45726, Noclevername, OneWeirdDude, Onebrothertoomany, PatrickSauncy, Pcbene, Pegship, Peppergreen, Plasticspork, Portillo, PrinceCharming, Pstraten, Quibik, R.G., Raijinili, Raikoh117, Ranitagoyle, RealityTelevisionFan, Rehevkor, RepublicanJacobite, RobJ1981, Robert Moore, Romanc19s, Rossj81, Rsage, Rtkat3, Ryan101672, Ryanbstevens, Rypcord, SGGH, Scog, Seeleschneider, Shadowjams, Shannonmuir, Silencingthedead, Silent Tom, Sir Vicious, SirSoliloquy, Sjones23, SkrallAgori, Smijes08, Snowolf, Soap, Sohaib Khan, Sololhj, Stardust8212, Steven25615, Strangeconstantblue, Sudachi, Supernumerary, SynergyBlades, T-borg, TMC1982, Tassedethe, Tbhotch, Teddyb, Tekwani, The 80s chick, The Rogue Penguin, The Thing That Should Not Be, The mitten man, TheMovieBuff, TheProf07, TheRealFennShysa, Thirteen squared, Tomia, Tony1, Treybien, Trippyboi91, Trusilver, Tylerhuyser, Typhoon966, Ultraphil, Useight, Vanished user 39948282, Visokor, Voicingmaster, Vssun, Werideatdusk33, Whitepaw, WikiLubber, Will-B, Wolfer68, Woohookitty, Yashman18, Yomiel, Zvar, 838 anonymous edits

Nickelodeon Kids' Choice Awards *Source*: http://en.wikipedia.org/w/index.php?oldid=462137516 *Contributors*: 201Two, 34MERVE96, 3yoda, 5 albert square, 75th Trombone, 9potterfan, A.t.360, ABC1356msep1, ALIENBOY122, AMERICAN MIGHT, AMK152, Ajraddatz, Al.locke, Alextwa, Americanhero, Anarchy 97, Anetode, Angelic-alyssa, Aoi, Archanamiya, Aristotle1990, Art1991, Arthena, Atakid96, AussieLegend, Average Earthman, Azumanga1, B.hygate, Backtable, Barkyboy999, Baseball Bugs, Bband11th, BeanyFans, Beeblebrox, Beshoy h, Bestkid92, Big Bad Baby, BigrTex, Blean, Blehfu, Bluquail, Bmg2282, Bob 2.0, Bob the Rabbid, Bob0012, Bobo192, Bonadea, BoogerD, BornonJune8, Bryant1236, BsaPR1996, Btty2154, CR85747, Caldorwards4, Cammador, Canis Lupus, Captiian, CartoonNothing, Catgut, Causa sui, Chad1m, Chane 815, Chard513, Christopher Tsakonas, Citicat, Cleavon B., Clockwisekid, Closedmouth, Cmdrjameson, Coffee12345, CommonsDelinker, Corvus cornix, Crazysunshine, Crazywrestler, Crumbsucker, Ctjf83, D99figge, DMacks, Daboss94, Dalekusa, Daniel Callegaro, DanielDeibler, Daniphunk7557, Dannycas, Danski14, Daqenue, DarkAdonis255, Davehi1, Dellpcr, Denisarona, Devohawks75, Discospinster, Dmanskater11, DougsTech, Dragonslayer1234, Dycedarg, Dylanlip, E2eamon, Easy4me, Eddiemercado, Editorofthewiki, Eduardo Sellan III, Eli730, Elizium23, Emlin82, Euclynthajunior, Evan1109, EwkRocks, Explicit, Fabricationary, Falcon8765, Fastily, Fifo, Flan456, Flauto Dolce, Forrestdfuller, Forum User, Fratrep, Frehley, GVOLTT, Galliano7, Garkeith, Garlic knots, Geniac, Ghewgill, Ginkgo100, Glane23, Groudon199, Guitarherochristopher, Guy1423, Gwernol, HERMiT cRAB, Hadger, Hans Dunkelberg, HappySquared, Hdt83, IP202.51.194.13, Ia802, Ignotus91987, Ik.pas.aan, Ikiroid, Intelligance, Iridescent, Irishancest, Irishguy, Ishdarian, J.delanoy, J4lambert, JDDJS, JHoltzman, JJonathan, Jack1214, Jackie10000, Jake Wartenberg, Jedi94, Jeffrey Mall, Jeneral28, Jennavecia, Jetblue2, Jhhawesome, Jjrules08, Jnk2008, Jnk2009, Jnk2011rockz, John, John13-69, Jon89, Jonathan89, Jonathannew7, Jonghyun0411, Jorgito0246, Jose Me, Jovenhispana, Jpablo95, JuWiki, Juanacho, Jun Bug.jr, Jusdafax, Justme89, Jzxpertguitarist, KG200, Kevin2008000, Kingpin13, KinseyLOL, Kneale, Kopachris, Krazycev13, Kylebrennan1, L Kensington, LAUGH90, LFaraone, LOL, Laframboise-trixter, Lampbane, Landinrock, Lear's Fool, Lerdthenerd, Leroy573, Lewis odane, Lightmouse, Lithium-Cove, Little Mountain 5, Logan, Lopestitomatheus34, Ltdanp, M2K 2, M3rlyzZ, Majorclanger, Mansib Intisar Khan, MaraNeo127, Martin19, Martin451, Mason1213, Mauler90, MaxW444, McSly, Mcbridelr, Medos2, Meerkatxoxo, MegaKN, Mercurywoodrose, Merseymasala, Metagraph, Mika-ng, Mike3497, MikeyMouse10, Mikiemike092791, Millahnna, Mingardia, MitchelMussoLover, Mr3urious, Mrmoocow, Mro, Mrschimpf, MsDivagin, Mtyr, MuZemike, N5iln, Nanami Kamimura, Nappyrootslistener, Nasnema, Nataly8, Nerdygeek101, Next-Genn-Gamer, Nickyvfall, Nifboy, Nights Not End, Not Accessible, Oblic, Obscurans, Oldcbsfan, Omgilovegod, Oo7565, Oreos, Orphan Wiki, Panser Born, ParamountCartoons93, Patricklikewoah, Patriot174, Peanutmarie 775, Penpaldog, PeterSymonds, Phantom784, PhnomPencil, Pikalax, Pikamander2, Pinkey60, Praefectorian, Pswiney, Quadparty, QuasyBoy, Qwertluis, Qwyrxian, R. S. Shaw, Rafaelsilveira, Red Director, RedX619, ReganAnneee, Remstar, Renanx3, Rezashah12, Rezashah4, Rhedsox27, Rivemont, Rjd0060, RobJ1981, Rockhead1220, Rod14, Rory096, Rox yajox, Rubixmike14, RussellAN, Ryulong, SFOetthekid, Saggymoney2008, Scarian, Sciurinæ, Sedna1365, Sgs101, Shadowx5206, Shannernanner, Sidewinders, Silverthehedgehog9348745, Sirbrickrock, Siwelb, Slyfence, Smiley Miley Disney, Smogilski, Socby19, Soccer5525, SouljaBoy10, SpOnGeFaN818, Sponge1987, SpongeMcFly2015, SpongeSebastian, Spongefrog, Spongeyfan, SpuriousQ, Squirepants101, Stellafranco65, Stepo9, Stitchon, Stix765, Stlsportsfan2316, Stu34art, Stupidgodladyfromthemistmovie, Styrofoam1994, Summersrj, SuperHamster, SuperSonicTH, Sydh, THEN WHO WAS PHONE?, TITROTU, TMC1982, TRBP, Talpik, Tbhotch, Teenchoiceawards, Tempodivalse, Tfkalk, The Eye of Timaeus, The Thing That Should Not Be, TheBlackAvengersGuard1, TheNewMinistry, Thefreakshow, This is Drew, Tinton5, Tomd2712, Tommy2010, Tony Sidaway, Tony414, TrapStilton, Trevor MacInnis, Tvtonightokc, Twispace3000, Ucla90024, Uncle Dick, Ungvichian, UnitedStatesian, VJ13A, Vague Rant, Vanessarks, Versus22, Vian kadal, Victoria93s, Vinta81, VoteyDisciple, WTRiker, Wack'd, Wafulz, Wayne Slam, Welsh, Weng1028, Wenli, West.andrew.g, WhatGuy, Whattimeisituk, WigglesFan1991, WikHead, Wiki Raja, WikiWynn, Wikialexdx, Wikipeedio, Wikipeters, Wilson44691, Wintonian, Wizardman, Wizkid357, Woohookitty, WookieInHeat, Xboxman107, Xx kidschoice xx, Yoshi032192, You2life, Youngamerican, Youngcc7, Zaffar12, Zasswass, Zon1235, Zzyzx11,

厚狭原彰鋼, 1864 anonymous edits

To Wong Foo, Thanks for Everything! Julie Newmar *Source*: http://en.wikipedia.org/w/index.php?oldid=455379201 *Contributors*: Aarchiba, AgnosticPreachersKid, Airjamison23, Alakazam, Allister MacLeod, AngelOfMusic, Angelo De La Paz, Bdve, Bearcat, Bwjs, CJMylentz, CantabrigianAlicia, Chzz, Cleduc, Colonies Chris, Craigy144, Cyberroach, D6, Darkness2005, David Gerard, David Shankbone, Detaler, Dgmjr05, Dingno, Discospinster, Dismas, Djflem, Dlloyd, Donmike10, Downwards, Drew Smith, Easchiff, Elonka, FetchcommsAWB, FrankRizzo2006, Freshh, Gabe1972, Glanhawr, Hirolovesswords, Ianblair23, Ipstenu, ItsTheClimb17, Ivankipling, JGKlein, Jakezing, Jeffq, JesseRafe, Jevansen, JimmB, Joseph A. Spadaro, Kateire, KenelmJames, Kieff, Koavf, LadyNorbert, Lalunadiosa, Lil Flip246, Lugnuts, MarnetteD, Mensurs, Mike Halterman, Mike Payne, Mjrmtg, MrBojanglesNY, Mrblondnyc, Myatt315, NightBear, Niteowlneils, Nostaljack, Nv8200p, Obedience, ObsessiveJoBroDisorder, Oppso, Ost316, Otto4711, OwenBlacker, Pennyforth, Phoenixrod, Plasticspork, Psantosj, RWFanMS, Rabbabodrool, Renebeto, RicJac, Rusted AutoParts, Samwaltz, SatyrTN, SkittlzAnKomboz, SlimVirgin, Speedoflight, Steam5, Supasaru, Swid, TAnthony, Tawniz, TenPoundHammer, The 80s chick, Thumperward, Tim Long, Tjmayerinsf, UtherSRG, Uucp, Vis-a-visconti, Werldwayd, Whomp, XLR8TION, Xprivate eyex, 157 ,אנדר-ויק anonymous edits

Nine Months *Source*: http://en.wikipedia.org/w/index.php?oldid=457471330 *Contributors*: 97198, Anthony Appleyard, ArielGold, Arnaudh, BigCow, Bovineboy2008, Bryan Derksen, Burks821, Canley, Cbrown1023, Condorjoe, D6, Dana boomer, Dewey Finn, DoubleCross, Dwanyewest, E edwards ellis, EcksWILLecks, GhostFace1234, Gonioul, Grandpafootsoldier, Inaxdaze, Jaxl, Jdperkins, Kabjdb10, Kate, Kusma, LGagnon, Levineps, Liftarn, Nehrams2020, Niteowlneils, Noirish, Paulinho28, Radosław10, RicJac, Schmiteye, Searcher 1990, Shining.Star, Shshshsh, Smallman12q, Soumyasch, Sreejithk2000, Team venture, Tomv, Tony Keen2, Treybien, Unregistered.coward, Woohookitty, YUL89YYZ, 44 anonymous edits

Aladdin and the King of Thieves *Source*: http://en.wikipedia.org/w/index.php?oldid=465138108 *Contributors*: Aaaxlp, Acidburn24m, AdamDeanHall, Addict 2006, Angie Y., AnmaFinotera, Aoi, Arcadia24, Ardavu, Aurigas, Avant Guard, Azure Haights, Bencherlite, Benny6000, Bovineboy2008, Brenont, Burori, CXCV, Cactusjump, Cardsharp21, Cclarke, Chasingsol, Chickenmonkey, Chris the speller, Chris1219, ClonedPickle, Crablogger, Czolgolz, Darklilac, Debresser, Dio Only Uses a Knife, DisneyAnimeFreak92, Djsasso, Dnusair, Dysprosia, Erik, Everyoneandeveryone, FKmailliW, Forteblast, FriscoKnight, Gabrielkat, Garion96, Gatotsu911, GeeJo, Geniac, Geopgeop, Gmaspoiledbrat, GoingBatty, Gracenotes, GreenGumby, Grizzwald, GroovySandwich, Gtrmp, Hailey C. Shannon, HoserHead, IllaZilla, Ixfd64, J.delanoy, JaGa, JadeBoco, Jake Wartenberg, Javert, Jienum, Jmac3568, Joe Sewell, JohnDBuell, Jojhutton, Josiah Rowe, JuJube, Kageno, Kbdank71, Koavf, Kusma, LaukkuTheGreit, Lenin and McCarthy, Lighteningluster, Lokai, Lord Opeth, Magnificator, Mandarax, MarnetteD, Master Deusoma, Matthew Cantrell, Mercury McKinnon, Miilousuede, Mr.Nobody, MrDarcy, Nemeses9, Niceley, Nintendo Maximus, Nintendoman01, Ocatecir, OneWeirdDude, PBP, PMDrive1061, Paul A, PeruAlonso, PhantomS, Piano non troppo, Polisher of Cobwebs, Poor Yorick, RadioKirk, Ramminges, Reedy, Refinnejann, Reviewking1, Rich Farmbrough, Robsinden, Rtkat3, Rx4evr, Ryanmalik01, SaliereTheFish, ShelfSkewed, Sjones23, Smetanahue, Sparky the Seventh Chaos, TJUser, TKD, Tabletop, TehDogfather, Tetrahedron93, The 80s chick, The Filmaker, Tigerpawz, Tktktk, To play cool like that, Tomaketu, TracyLinkEdnaVelmaPenny, TravelingCat, Tregoweth, Tyciol, UltimatePyro, Valermos, Vegas949, Wack'd, Wafulz, WikHead, Zanimum, Zhen Lin, АлександрВв, 261 anonymous edits

Hamlet (1996 film) *Source*: http://en.wikipedia.org/w/index.php?oldid=460850816 *Contributors*: Ajplmr, Ajshm, AlbertSM, AndyJones, Ann77, Ausir, Azucar, Bovineboy2008, Brain, CJMylentz, Catamorphism, Chris the speller, Comicist, Cthuljew, Cubs Fan, Deltabeignet, Deposuit, Doc glasgow, Donald McKinney, Downstage right, Ed Poor, Esn, Fmbpwyhd, Gabbort, Generica, Girolamo Savonarola, Goustien, Hal 10000.0, Hmains, JHFTC, Jevon Tompkins, Jg2904, Jogers, Jordancelticsfan, Joseph A. Spadaro, Josh Parris, Judesba, JudgePat, Julle, KarenViceroy, Kitch, Korny O'Near, Kuralyov, Lachatdelarue, Leedsrhino, LinkTiger, Lugnuts, Lupin, M.nelson, MER-C, MarnetteD, Matthew Auger, Mav, Mdiamante, Meta faye, Mike R, Mikeo, Montecarlocars, Nevilley, Oneiros, Patriarch, Paul A, Paul Barlow, Paul441391, Pfistermeister, Phaeton23, Pufferfish101, Qui1che, RedWolf, RicJac, Robertbyrne, Sbpat21, ScottMHoward, SeanEB, Seaphoto, Sesesq, ShelfSkewed, Shining.Star, Stevekeiretsu, Supernumerary, Swordman182, TFNorman, Tassedethe, Tbhotch, The Drama Llama, TheFeds, TheMovieBuff, Thebdj, ThuranX, Tim!, Tintazul, Towzzer, Tregoweth, Trivialist, Ushionna, VolatileChemical, VonV, Websurfer246, Wrad, Wysdom, Xover, YUL89YYZ, Yworo, Zigger, 112 anonymous edits

Jack (1996 film) *Source*: http://en.wikipedia.org/w/index.php?oldid=459973218 *Contributors*: 7Beckham, AN(Ger), ASB16v, Abby 82, Abby 96, Abigailtoby, Adentong, Arasaka, Arjun01, Armyrifle9, Artichoke-Boy, Asbestos, AshTFrankFurter2, Babcockd, Bastiche, Bluemoose, Bluquail, Bobbybobboy999, Cab88, CanadianCaesar, Canley, Cooksey, CountdownCrispy, D-Day, D6, DD2K, DDima, Darkness2005, Darrenhusted, David Gerard, DeWaine, Discospinster, Dkkicks, Dudesleeper, Easchiff, EdChem, Ellissound, Frankenpuppy, Frankg, Freedomlinux, Freshh, Furrykef, Glitch010101, Granpuff, Greaser, GusF, HairyPerry, HexaChord, Icarus3, J.delanoy, JamesLucas, Jason One, Jay*Jay, Jedzz, Jhenderson777, John K, Koavf, Leroyinc, MachoCarioca, Madhero88, Magioladitis, Mahanga, Martpol, Matthew Yeager, Maximillion Pegasus, Maximus Rex, MeltBanana, Metrofilmko, Millahnna, MonkeeJuice, MrRuidavets, N5iln, Nasirakd, Nelliebellie, NerdyScienceDude, OGoncho, Pardy, Peinwod, Persian Poet Gal, Pietaster, PizzaIceCreamCandyCake1, QQQ, Qxz, Rahulmachal, Ratchetcomand, RicJac, Rich Farmbrough, Rtkat3, Schmiteye, Secfan, Sgoldman10, Shaunthered, Shimmera, Shultz, Silverandcold, Snowolfd4, Sreejithk2000, Sroc, StayTunedForDanger134, The JPS, TheTruthiness, Thefourdotelipsis, Thegreat100, Thingg, TracyLinkEdnaVelmaPenny, Treybien, Trut-h-urts man, Tryptofeng, Ville Siliämaa, Will-B, YUL89YYZ, Zenohockey, 187 anonymous edits

The Birdcage *Source*: http://en.wikipedia.org/w/index.php?oldid=457973576 *Contributors*: 6SJ7, A Softer Answer, AGK, AN(Ger), Abidari, AbsoluteGleek92, Achester99, AdamWeeden, Adcro, All Hallow's Wraith, Andrzejbanas, AnmaFinotera, Apollotiger, Apparition11, Arthurian Legend, Artichoke-Boy, Asianchick, Averette, Bearcat, Bobet, Bwjs, Can't sleep, clown will eat me, CanadianLinuxUser, CardinalDan, Cbrown1023, Ccacsmss, CharlotteWebb, ClockworkSoul, Cochese516, Crimson Ghost, Daisee, Darkness2005, David Gerard, Demonslave, Discospinster, Dlloyd, Dml, Donarreiskoffer, Doniago, Dudie101, Dylan620, Easchiff, Edward321, Eirik, Emurphy42, Erik, Films addicted, Fireaxe888, Freshh, FromtheWordsofBR, Fuhghettaboutit, Gaius Cornelius, GeneralBelly, Ghirlandajo, Gilliam, GirasoleDE, Gonioul, GorgeCustersSabre, GrahamHardy, Great Leonopteryx, Ground Zero, Grzegorz Wysocki, Guy M, HappyInGeneral, Heron, Hightower 40, Iceberg3k, Idinic, Irishguy, JB82, Jienum, Johno100, Jzummak, Kbdank71, Kerowyn, Kieranthompson, KnowledgeOfSelf, Koyaanis Qatsi, Kristagoss, Kubigula, LGagnon, Lady Aleena, Lalunadiosa, Levineps, LiberalPhan, Mecv, Millahnna, Moshe Constantine Hassan Al-Silverburg, Msisley, Nehrams2020, Nekohakase, Not a dog, NotACow, ObsessiveJoBroDisorder, OrthodoxeSizilien, OwenBlacker, Parable1991, Pdcook, Pegasus1138, Pnkrockr, PokeHomsar, R'n'B, Ratchetcomand, RattleandHum, Rbb 1181, Rocky stallone, Rodrigogomespaixao, Rrburke, Ryanmalik01, Samir, Scorchfire, ShelfSkewed, Silivrenion, Solid Reign, Someone else, Sottolacqua, Spellmaster, Ssilvers, Stopmenow100, Supernumerary, Tassedethe, Tavilis, Tawniz, Tbsdy lives, Thatcher, The Filmaker, The Rambling Man, The Wrong Man, The mitten man, TheCustomOfLife, Tony Sidaway, Tothebarricades.tk, Treybien, VanPelt101, Venece09, Ward3001, Weetjesman, Wikignome0529, WilliamMelvin, Willking1979, Woohookitty, Wool Mintons, XLR8TION, Xezbeth, ZPM, 221 anonymous edits

Good Will Hunting *Source*: http://en.wikipedia.org/w/index.php?oldid=463668001 *Contributors*: 9258fahsflkh917fas, AThestral, AVtime, AaronY, AbsoluteGleek92, Abu badali, Acalamari, Aecis, Afa86, Akamad, Aklobe10, Alex.petralia, AlphaGreyHound, Altzinn, Ameriwet, Amitch, Andrewc1117, Andrzejbanas, Angel caboodle, Angelic Wraith, Anomie, Arcadian, ArmadilloFromHell, Arthur Holland, Asdflkjqwer, Asuskay, Asyndeton, Axl, Azathar, BD2412, Batman2005, Bazketballr, Beardo, Bender235, Betterworld, Bigtimepeace, Bill shannon, Biot, Blackjanedavey, Blake Burba, Blanchardb, BlueMoonlet, Bobbyo99, Boggie, Bovineboy2008, Brownsc, Busillis, C. A. Russell, C0lmjl, CBM, CDA, CambridgeBayWeather, Catgut, Cbrown1023, Cburnett, Ccady, CelticJobber, Chimeric Glider, Chris the speller, ChrisB, Chubbles, Cinebard, Clarityfiend, Cliff smith, Comelloyellow, Crotchety Old Man, Cuaya, Custardninja, Cyclonenim, Czj, D brace, D4, DANE RAMADAN YOUSSEF, DANE YOUSSEF, DJ Clayworth, DOHC Holiday, Da10g, DancingMan, DanielNuyu, Darrenhusted, Davemcarlson, David Gerard, David Schaich, DeWaine, Deagle AP, Delldot, Deltabeignet, Demian.5, Derbent 5000, Dilcoe, Dingno, Dirac1933, Discospinster, Donmike10, Donpelota, Doradus, Dracconl36, Dramatist, Dranster, Dream of Goats, Drunkenpeter99, Drysarcasm, Dudesleeper, Durin, Ed Poor, Ed g2s, Edward, Ejk81, Ekabhishek, Ekwos, Elistoughton, Elmondo21st, Eric Douglas Statzer, Erik, Esperant, Ethanidor11, Evans1982, Everard Proudfoot, Eyesplice, F.N. Wombat, FF2010, FMAFan1990, Fakeblueeyess, FallenWings47, Fdssdf, Ferdinand Pienaar, Fgf2007, FiachraByrne, Foxmulder, Fred Bradstadt, FromtheWordsofBR, Gabbe, Gamaliel, Gareth E Kegg, Gareth Jones, Garion96, Gczffl, Geetotiger, Glacier109, Godsfire, Granpuff, Hadal, Hanacy, HappyInGeneral, Hede2000, Hexslinger, Hkhenson, Hmsulski, Hydrogen Iodide, Hyperquantization, IJVin, IKNS, Ian13, Ianhurley, IllaZilla, Intractable, Irishguy, ItsTheClimb17, J. Charles Taylor, JDDJS, Janhouse00, Jaseman125, JeffreyN, JesseRafe, Jiffy Clay, Jjohan35, Jkeesh, Jmlk17, Joeyvallone, Jogers, John254, Johnseita, Johnwcowan, Jonay81687, Jonkerz, Jtir, Jujutacular, Jusdafax, KAH, Kar98, Kasparov, Katalaveno, Katxo, Kbdank71, Keo-san, Kesla, Kidlittle, Killdevil, Koavf, Kollision, Krtek2125, Kukini, Kungfuadam, LGagnon, La Pianista, Lareine, Larry V, Lasneyx, Lawikitejana, Laymanas, Lcarsdata, Lentower, Levineps, Livitup, LongLiveMusic, Loodog, LostLikeTearsInRain, Lowellian, Lynch1000s, Lynch9000s, MJBoa, MachoCarioca, Madcoverboy, Mandel, Mang0es, Martarius, MattTM, Mattrodi, Maximus Rex, Michael Dorosh, Michael Hardy, Millahnna, Mjrmtg, Mr. Chicago, Mrand, Mspraveen, MuZemike, MuppetMower, Musicalantonio, Naniwako, Nehrams2020, Neilc, NellieBly, NickW557, Nightscream, Nintendofan88, Niro87, Noirish, Noozgroop, Notheruser, Novacatz, Ny156uk, OTB, Oatmeal batman, ObsessiveJoBroDisorder, Ofsevit, Ohmnamoh, Oko, Oneworld25, Ontopofthewall, Orange Goblin, Osu.mann, Owen, P1415926535, Passportguy, Patrick, Patstuart, Pethan, Phbasketball6, Plasticspork, Polihale, Pomte, Porffiry, Postcard Cathy, Precious3230, Prometheus235, Qjuad, Quaeler, Quentin mcalmott, Qwerty Binary, RDBury, RODERICKMOLASAR, Rajah, Randomjohn, RattleandHum, Recycler1973, Redeagle688, Reywas92, Riana, Rich Farmbrough, Ricky81682, Rlei1130, RobNS, RoddyYoung, Ronhjones, Runtime, SJP, SNIyer12, SQGibbon, Salix alba, Sam, SamBaly, Santryl, Savolya, Schlumpff, Scooby7292, Scrabbleship, Seegoon, Sergay, Shamrox, Shotgunefx, SidP, Silent Tom, Silentjames, SimonP, Sir Paul, Skier Dude, Socialservice, Softlavender, Sottolacqua, Southieinfo, Spellmaster, Spicoli77, Spider-Carnage Earth-X, Spore789, Ssbohio, Steven Walling, Stick Fig, Sugarlover101, Svetlana Miljkovic, TJRC, Tachmann, Tariqabjotu, Tech77jp, Ted Wilkes, TedE, Teiladnam, TenPoundHammer, Tfine80, The Bugs Bunny, The Filmaker, The Invisible Man, TheMovieBuff, Theatheistgerm, Thecheesykid, Thething88, This, that and the other, ThuranX, Tills, Tim1965, TimVickers, Timkmak, Timneu22, Tins128, Tommyt, TonyTheTiger, Tool2Die4, Treybien, Truffles64, Tsujigiri, Turidoth, Ukexpat, UnitedStatesian, VERITASPURE, Vera Cruz, VicShah, Vincent Gray, Virginia Bell, Vjamesv, VolatileChemical, Waldir, Wales, Wandering Man, Ward3001, Wfeidt, WikiKingOfMishawaka, Will2k, Wingman4l7, Wizardman, WoodenTaco, Xbox6, Yaksar, Yintan, Your Lord and Master, ZZninepluralZalpha, ZeroJanvier, Zoe, Zro, 735 anonymous edits

Flubber (film) *Source*: http://en.wikipedia.org/w/index.php?oldid=465222977 *Contributors*: Ace246able, AdamDeanHall, AeneasTulsa, Agustinaldo, Alansohn, Aleenf1, Alexfrance250291, All Hallow's Wraith, Angelofdeath666, Arania, Asterism, Astroview120mm, Before My Ken, Bela Mulder, Ben Ben, BenjyBoy2000, Bluecatcinema, Bodnotbod, Bovineboy2008, CIreland, Can't sleep, clown will eat me, Capricorn42, Cat's Tuxedo, Catamorphism, Christiancox, Christianster45, Christopherlin, Closedmouth, Coasttocoast, DJHerbie53, Darkness2005, DaveTheRed, David Gerard, Deadmallsanita, Dee15gon, Difluoroethene, Discospinster, Dismas, Dj1112, Dlohcierekim, Dotzodiac, Dupz, Dwaipayansinha, Editor2020, Edlin2, Enok Walker, Epbr123, Eplack, Eric119, Error792, Ewlyahoocom, FenristheWolf, Flamingblur, Flowerpotman, Fredrik, Geraldo Perez, Gevorg89, Gman42, GrayFox92, HalJor, Hobbesy3, Hookem329, Horkana, Ianjones1900, Icairns, Icey, Ichthyoid, IrrationalSanity, JDspeeder1, Jamesbanesmith, Jammus, Jienum, Jill Tuck, Jivecat, John Littlewood, Johnlongbond, JonathanDP81, Juan Cruz, Jweiss11, Kaybugg1, Keegan, Klosterdev, Knee427, KrytenKoro, Kukini, Kx1186, Lacon432, Largoplazo, LilHelpa, Lilbill0005, Lord Pistachio, Lugnuts, Magioladitis, MakeRocketGoNow, Matt Deres, Meanwolf21,

Michaelsbll, Mikeblas, Mishae, Moonroe, Myanw, Nakon, Nemesis of Reason, Neoyan, OdinReborn, Ohthelameness, One, Optichan, Otisbdart, Ouzo, PaidInFull1987, Pegship, Penbat, PhilKnight, Phoenixvalley, Pol430, Prolog, Promethean, Puffin, Quentin X, Quinsareth, Ramki66, Reywas92, Riisikuppi, Rrburke, Rtkat3, Rufous-crowned Sparrow, Runewiki777, SGGH, Sfbenton, Shirulashem, Silent Tom, Simon12, Sjones23, Sophus Bie, Spiffyxd, Stickee, Supernumerary, Swimdb, Szyslak, TMC1982, Tassedethe, Tealwisp, Ted87, TheAschMan, TheMovieBuff, TheRealFennShysa, Theditor, ThefirstM, Theseven7, ThylekShran, Tom, Twexler, Unnatural20, Useight, Valermos, Venece09, WJBscribe, WadeSimMiser, Werldwayd, West.andrew.g, WikHead, Wimt, Wysprgr2005, Xanzzibar, Yintan, Zepp95, Ziva 82, 357 anonymous edits

Deconstructing Harry *Source*: http://en.wikipedia.org/w/index.php?oldid=460642944 *Contributors*: All Hallow's Wraith, Andrzejbanas, Arite, Ashmoo, Attilios, Azucar, Bender235, Bruvensky, Catamorphism, Cliff1911, Darrenhusted, Darz Mol, David Gerard, DeWaine, Dibyajyotighosh, Djflem, DoctorWho42, Donald McKinney, Donmike10, ESkog, Gabbe, JustAGal, Kmhkmh, La loi du récit, Levineps, MachoCarioca, Moshe Constantine Hassan Al-Silverburg, Mrblondnyc, Polisher of Cobwebs, Qp10qp, RicJac, Rosalbissima, Rtcnz, Scanlan, ScottyBoy900Q, Sevenarts, Shlomif, Sillstaw, Skier Dude, Squiddy, Stefanomione, Supernumerary, Tenar80, Thebogusman, ZimZalaBim, 45 anonymous edits

Fathers' Day (film) *Source*: http://en.wikipedia.org/w/index.php?oldid=464260150 *Contributors*: AN(Ger), Azucar, Bencey, Bluemoose, Briantw, Condorjoe, Da10g, David Rush, DeWaine, Ermanon, Fernandobouregard, FollowGuard, FrankRizzo2006, George Ho, Gonioul, Gtrmp, Jaxl, Kjlovescats, Lady Aleena, Ljones, Luckyj, Millahnna, Prayudhi, Rosalbissima, Rusted AutoParts, Shawisland, ShelfSkewed, SpNeo, The Giant Puffin, Wool Mintons, 27 anonymous edits

Patch Adams (film) *Source*: http://en.wikipedia.org/w/index.php?oldid=462176350 *Contributors*: 97198, Adamzanzie, Adrory, Aibdescalzo, AimeeRose, Alex43223, Andrzejbanas, Andy Marchbanks, Apostrophe, Bahar101, BarryTheUnicorn, Bencey, Bibbly Bob, Blammo77, Bluecatcinema, Bobblewik, Bobet, Bonadea, Bovineboy2008, Brianga, Cartwarmark, Ccacsmss, CeruleanFilms, Chanlyn, CharlotteWebb, ChrisfromHouston, Cjdkoh, Crieff405, Darev, Darkness2005, David Gerard, Delpino, Dgstangel, Donmike10, Download, Dudesleeper, EJBanks, Fastily, Fitchhollister, Flip619, Fourmeyer4, Freakofnurture, Frecklefoot, Furrykef, GnarlyLikeWhoa, Guoguo12, Harditya123456789, Harel, Havelock, Irishguy, J04n, JP1978, JSweit8573, JTBX, Jahrtag69, JamesAM, Jangleleggs, Jcbarr, Jeandré du Toit, JnB987, Joepiekarski, Jonny2x4, Josh VC, Juanmarodri, Ka Faraq Gatri, Karl 334, Katana Geldar, Kchishol1970, Kilbosh, Kkarma, Knizar, Kontra, Langeluksh, Legitimus, Levineps, Loren.wilton, LtMuldoon, Lugatta, Luigibob, LurkingInChicago, MarnetteD, MartinPoulter, Matpe815, Meshach, Mike.lifeguard, Mm40, Mr. Billion, Nigholith, Nithin.philips, Oliphaunt, Pamelaa16, Parnagerstar, PaulHanson, Pearle, Peter Pan, Physics sam, Picapica, Pixelface, Quentin X, Radiohawk, Radosław10, Red.echelon, Reepnorp, RicJac, Rizla, Rmky87, Ryan1484, Santryl, Sarvagyana guru, SchuminWeb, Sd31415, Sjuturu, Sreejithk2000, Steam5, Sweeperchick8705, Szyslak, TRS de, Tabletop, Tassedethe, Thorpe, Threesom666, Thryduulf, Tinton5, Treybien, USMA, Vannav, Vegaswikian, Versus22, Visionholder, Washburnmav, Wilhelmina Will, Wool Mintons, Wordy1, Wysdom, Yankees10, 229 anonymous edits

What Dreams May Come (film) *Source*: http://en.wikipedia.org/w/index.php?oldid=464669695 *Contributors*: 'Doc' Scurlock, 1013-christi, 2T, 42Strangelove, AN(Ger), Across.The.Synapse, Andrzejbanas, Andycjp, Anoriega, Antandrus, Arguss, Atlan, BenFrantzDale, Beyond My Ken, Bovineboy2008, Boyblackuk, Bwithh, Capnchicken, Chickenmonkey, Ckatz, Clarityfiend, Cpm990, Crimsonmargarine, Czolgolz, D6, David spector, Denny, Dom Kaos, Donteatyellowsnow, Ed Poor, Ekabhishek, ElectricalTill, Ellsworth, Erik, FeanorStar7, Fountain01, FrankRizzo2006, Frecklefoot, Freshh, GrahamHardy, Grandpafootsoldier, Haninay, HawkMcCain, Herbie290, Hipster21, HorsePunchKid, Iceberg3k, Iridescent, Ixfd64, Jfiling, Jrue, JustAGal, Kasper2006, Kasreyn, Kate, Kollision, Konczewski, Kushboy, Kusma, Kwekubo, Lady Aleena, Levineps, Liko81, Lugnuts, Madjaxter, Mandarax, Marbehraglaim, MasterXiam, Mijoco4510, Mike Ege, Mintleaf, Moreschi, MurrayCraven24, MusicMaker5376, NZFilmHistory, Nice poa, Niteowlneils, Notmicro, OrigamiNinja, Pegship, PepeGuitar, Phbasketball6, Philodox-ohki, Pictureuploader, Poco a poco, Polylerus, Prestonmcconkie, Pro bug catcher, Prosfilaes, Rachgia, Reconsider the static, Rsgmmack, ScottyWZ, Shadow Android, ShadowyCaballero, Shanedidona, SidP, Sjones23, Something Wicked 451, Sottolacqua, Sperril, Steam5, Sz1335, TFunk, TJRC, Tamariki, Tearsinraine, The Duke of Waltham, The JPS, TheMovieBuff, Thingg, Thom, Thorpe, Tjsocr1, Treybien, UDScott, UnitedStatesian, Vegas Bleeds Neon, Waerloeg, Welsh-dragoon, WereSpielChequers, Wigsey, Wikicali00, Wilhelm meis, Xezbeth, YUL89YYZ, Yukichigai, 193 anonymous edits

Bicentennial Man (film) *Source*: http://en.wikipedia.org/w/index.php?oldid=464980046 *Contributors*: *drew, 2T, Academic Challenger, Adam.J.W.C., Aitias, Ajcheema, Ajosephantony, Alansohn, Alex2631, Alynna Kasmira, Amcbride, Andrei G Kustov, Andrzejbanas, AnemoneProjectors, Arasaka, Attilios, Azucar, BJB, BSI, Bbx, Bender235, Bovineboy2008, Bramton1, BrickExist57, Brouhaha, Bse3, Btipling, Captain Infinity, Chrishy man, Cralize, Cst17, DCLXVI, Danieljackson, DebbieV76, Dennis Bratland, Der Blaue Wolf, Dewey Finn, Dougofborg, Drwarpmind, Dutchmonkey9000, E. Ripley, Easchiff, Elmorth, Emurphy42, Erainor, Esn, FaithLehaneTheVampireSlayer, Flyingidiot, FollowGuard, Fourthords, Fox816, Frankg, FrenchIsAwesome, Freshh, Gabbe, Garion96, Gil Gamesh, Grandpafootsoldier, Gundato, Halil marx07, Heavy bolter, ISD, ImSpidey2, Inkslinger, J.delanoy, J04n, JAF1970, JForget, Jedd the Jedi, Jeepday, Jeff Muscato, JustPhil, Katalaveno, Katana Geldar, Khalinin2010, Kimdino, Lach Graham, Levineps, Logical Fuzz, Lots42, Lwmte, MPD01605, Macg4cubeboy, Mallanox, Markiel, MikeWazowski, Mikemill, Millahnna, Misza13, Mitch Ames, Mr MaRo, Mysdaao, Natbug123, Ndenison, NeVic1, Ouzo, Parkjunwung, Philippe, Phoenix Hacker, Player35664, ProtoBuster, Radosław10, RicJac, Rmt2m, Ryanbstevens, Ryulong, SMcCandlish, SavageEdit, Savolya, Senator Palpatine, Shakin2012, Shiemy, Shir-El too, Signalhead, Sjm757, Snigbrook, Taipan198, Tedius Zanarukando, Tertiary7, The Clawed One, The grey side, TheNewPhobia, Toyokuni3, Trcunning, Treybien, Ttonyb1, Tyro Kith, Useight, VRH, Verrai, WadeSimMiser, Welsh, WikHead, Wine Guy, Woohookitty, 256 anonymous edits

Jakob the Liar *Source*: http://en.wikipedia.org/w/index.php?oldid=464497426 *Contributors*: Ajaxrools, Andrei Rublev, Cirdan747, Cybercobra, D6, Darev, David Gerard, DeWaine, Dudeman5685, Ejkook, Ennerk, Floquenbeam, FollowGuard, Fothergill Volkensniff IV, Inge-Lyubov, J 1982, JM.Beaubourg, Jackol, Jimmy Knoxville, Laurinavicius, Leandrod, LilHelpa, Lucinor, Ndenison, Observer 144, Olivier, ParaGreen13, Pegship, Phaeton23, Pharos, Prayudhi, RicJac, RobNS, Rrburke, Skittleys, Surrealplaces, Tedius Zanarukando, Thomasionus, Timesman626, Treybien, Trilemma, Twp, Valvs, Xanderall, Yossarian, Zen 38, Zombie433, 44 anonymous edits

A.I. Artificial Intelligence *Source*: http://en.wikipedia.org/w/index.php?oldid=465452414 *Contributors*: *Ria777*, 23skidoo, 2T, 2rusty22, AKR619, AaronW, AaronY, AbsoluteGleek92, AceTracer, Adamzanzie, Ahoerstemeier, Ajm81, Alectrona, Alexbalchen, Alientraveller, AlistairMcMillan, All Hallow's Wraith, Allixpeeke, Ameliorate!, AmethystPhoenix, AndrewHowse, Andrzejbanas, Angel caboodle, Angr, Anthony Appleyard, Arbero, Artihcus022, Asbestos, AskFranz, Asmallwhitecube, Astronaut, Avaloan, Avantgame, AzureCitizen, Balsa10, Batmanand, Blackjanedavey, Blt33, Bobblehead, Bobo192, Bovineboy2008, Boxclocke, Bryan Derksen, Bulgaroctonus, Burpelson AFB, Burschik, CannedLizard, Caspian, CecilWard, Cesarm, Chad44, Chaosdruid, CharlesFosterKane123, ChesterG, Chicagorob1, ChrisiPK, Christian75, Chuq, Closedmouth, Cmelsted, Cocoaguy, Coder Dan, Colds7ream, Collard, ContiAWB, CoolKatt number 99999, Crumbsucker, Curps, Cvindustries, Damiens.rf, Dan4142, Dan8700, DanielCD, Dante Alighieri, Dark hyena, Darkness2005, David Gerard, Deletros, DirkvdM, Discospinster, Djfspence, Dlrohrer2003, DmcReif, Dom Kaos, Doradus, Dr. Blofeld, DrBob, Drake Clawfang, Druff, Drunkenpeter99, Dss1bond, Dumoren, Duncan5qwerty, Earle Martin, Ecthelion83, Editor510, Elfguy, Ellsworth, Emuzesto, Erik Zachte, Erik9, ErinM, Erp Erpington, Evans1982, Ewlyahoocom, FMAFan1990, Fabulous Creature, FaithLehaneTheVampireSlayer, Fallout boy, Fighting for Justice, Films addicted, Fluffernutter, Fourthords, Francisco Valverde, FrankRizzo2006, Frecklefoot, Fred Bradstadt, Freedomlinux, Freshh, Gabbe, Gaheris, Gangster Octopus, Garion96, Gatherton, Gbraad, Getana, Ghirlandajo, Glittery86, Gnuyen, Gogo Dodo, Gorm, Goustien, Grandpafootsoldier, Grant65, Grognard3, Gryffindor, Gtrmp, Happy Evil Dude, Harac, Harnad, Hede2000, Heilemann, Hermitage17, HighEnergyProtons, Hiphats, Home Row Keysplurge, Horkana, Husond, Hyliad, IKato, Iandiver, Imagechaos, Impaciente, InfamousPrince, Islandboy99, Ithinkhelikesit, JB82, JForget, Jafetdexter, James Emtage, Jamesontai, JasonAQuest, Jclemens, Jedi Master Fort, Jeff Muscato, Jetforme, Jguad1, Jiawen, Jmax-, JoeLeydon, JoeLoeb, John-107, Johners, Jolivetti, Judgesurreal777, Judson, JustPhil, Jwk3, Karynannestuckey, Kbdank71, Kea, KeithJonsn, Kernitou, Kieranthompson, Kingoomieiii, Koavf, Kody9100, Kona1611, Konczewski, Korath, Kosmopolis, Kosunen, Ktalon, Kubrick 908, Kylelovesyou, Ladiesman925, Lastorset, LilHelpa, Logical Gentleman, Lord Opeth, MacGyverMagic, MachoCarioca, Magnius, Malickfan86, Mallanox, Manuel Anastácio, Marco.rambaldi, MarnetteD, Martarius, MartinDK, Materialscientist, Matteh, Matty j, Maximus Rex, McNoddy, Mckaysalisbury, Melvalevis, Menchi, Metlin, Michael Devore, Michaelbusch, Mighty Antar, Mika1h, Mikeo, Millahnna, Miranda, Mircead, Mirror Vax, Mista-X, Mitaphane, Mjb, Mjparry716, Mjrmtg, Mjwilso7, Mnealon, Modi mode, Monty845, Mrmewe, Mrwojo, Muchosucko, Mysdaao, N5iln, NAHID, NXK, Nabokov, Navstar, Norm mit, Norminator, Nv8200p, Olivier, Orangemike, Orpheus Machina, Oscarthecat, P0lyglut, PR Hero, Pag293, Pantologywhore, Passive, Patrick, Paul A, Pb30, Pedist, Pedro cunha, Pegship, Pejman47, Peter Greenwell, Phazer1980, Pingveno, Pipedreamergrey, Plasticspork, Poketape, Polisher of Cobwebs, Ppntori, ProhibitOnions, Prtyjedi, Quadraxis, R'n'B, Raabscuttle, RadicalBender, RalfiParpa, Ramo0031, Rapscallion, Reball01, ReyBrujo, Rich Farmbrough, Richiekim, Rjwilmsi, Rlee0001, RobyWayne, Rojomoke, Rsocol, Rsrikanth05, Rtkat3, Rusted AutoParts, RyanGFilm, Rydra Wong, S Luke, SCPM08, SMC, ST47, Salamurai, SamEtches, Sarahmcphee, Saudade7, Sağlamcı, Schewek, ScottyBoy900Q, Shenme, Shimgray, Sin-man, SiobhanHansa, Sirveaux, Siurekrek, Sj, Sm8900, Smartsmith, Soc8675309, Softlavender, SonicNirvana, SpaceFlight89, Splash, Spookfish, Staecker, Stephenchou0722, Stoshmaster, Str1977, Sverdrup, TCorp, THINMAN, Tabletop, TaerkastUA, Template namespace initialisation script, Tethet2Tethet, The JPS, The Singing Badger, The Transhumanist, The Wookieepedian, TheGreenwalker, TheGrza, TheLastAmigo, TheLordGLod, Thedarkestclear, Theoldanarchist, ThomasO1989, Thoreau 222, Tiger Trek, Timotheus Canens, TinyMark, Tobit2, Todd unt, Tomdobb, Tommyt, Tony1, TonyW, Trcunning, Treybien, Tuncrypt, Typhoon966, Tyw7, TøM, UDScott, Ukt-zero, Ulric1313, Unyoyega, VI, Vainqueur, Van helsing, Vikrant42, Viriditas, Vision3001, Voldemore, Vrenator, Vroomfondel, Vzbs34, Waldir, Ward3001, WatchAndObserve, Wayne Slam, Wdfarmer, Wereon, Who, WickerGuy, Wik, Wik4, Wildroot, Will4311, Wlmg, Woohookitty, Xezbeth, Xklsv, Xylke, Year 2144, Yongxinge, Yorkshiresky, Yossarian, Yworo, ZENDELBACH, Zafiroblue05, Zen56749, Zepperdude, ZeroJanvier, Zoe, Zoicon5, Zooterkin, Zzyzx11, Мурад 97, 658 ,דניאל צבי anonymous edits

The Rutles 2: Can't Buy Me Lunch *Source*: http://en.wikipedia.org/w/index.php?oldid=463907903 *Contributors*: Bearcat, Beetstra, Bencey, Blast Ulna, Crablogger, Dawkeye, Dhartung, Discographer, DougHill, Elephant Talk, Erik Henning Edvardsen, Evanh2008, FHSerkland, James Preston, Kuralyov, Liquidmetalrob, MarnetteD, Mclay1, Mr Larrington, Oanabay04, Otto4711, Roger McCoy, Salamurai, ScottMHoward, Sgeureka, Spartaz, Sreejithk2000, Thewhiteswan9, TonyTheTiger, Torchiest, Toughpigs, Treybien, WOSlinker, Whosasking, 23 anonymous edits

Insomnia (2002 film) *Source*: http://en.wikipedia.org/w/index.php?oldid=465095018 *Contributors*: 13 of Diamonds, 8th Ohio Volunteers, AEMoreira042281, AbsoluteGleek92, Alan daniel, Alaric Deschain, All Hallow's Wraith, Andrzejbanas, Arbero, Arcayne, Azucar, BLGM5, Bacteria, Beetstra, Beyond My Ken, Bináris, Bovineboy2008, Brad, Bradley0110, Brock2097, Carc5959, CeruleanFilms, Coltenstokes, ContiAWB, Cop 663, Cosmoline, Cresix, Darrenhusted, David Gerard, Donmike10, Dr. Blofeld, DylanW, Earle Martin, Edlitz36, Erik, Fakeman100, Fosibodu, Francesco 13, FrankRizzo2006, Freshh, GoldDragon, Grandpafootsoldier, Gregcaletta, Gscshoyru, Guizou, HMFS, HappyInGeneral, Henryodell, IlDuce89, IronGargoyle, J04n, JackalsIII, JackofOz, Javabourne, Jayunderscorezero, JimDunning, JoeLoeb, Joebaum, Jon Ascton, Laikatiger, Lakers, Lamro, Ljones, Lontano, LtMuldoon, MONGO, Man of wealth and taste, Mathew5000, Melaena, Mgiganteus1, Modest Genius, Mongreilf, Moshe Constantine Hassan Al-Silverburg, Mwelch, NcSchu, Nehrams2020, Odemars, PadieHere, Parallel33, PokeHomsar,

Reaverdrop, RicJac, Roaring Siren, S.dedalus, Schizodelight, ShelfSkewed, Shirt58, Siddhant, Sspeik, Supernumerary, The Filmaker, The Singing Badger, Tim1357, Treybien, VigneshManickam, Ward3001, Weichei, Wolverine7044, Woohookitty, Yaco, 101 anonymous edits

Death to Smoochy *Source*: http://en.wikipedia.org/w/index.php?oldid=465058296 *Contributors*: *drew, AN(Ger), AbsoluteGleek92, AdamDeanHall, Afa86, Alexander.Keays, Andrzejbanas, Angie Y., Antmusic, ArmadilloFromHell, Aspects, B3t, Bentogoa, Bevita, Brandon.macuser, Briaboru, Bwjs, CSOCSOCSO, Charlieshick, Darkwind, David Gerard, Davidhorman, Demoman87, Dschmidt, FrankRizzo2006, FugStat, Gabbe, GoingBatty, Gurch, HJ Mitchell, Huangdi, ISNorden, Ikebowen, Infrogmation, Insommia, Jabronimus, Jason One, Jc215flip, Jellocube27, Jetfire85, JoeLoeb, Joshua4, Juggernautthunderclap, Kbdank71, Keilana, Kelly Martin, Kgldude, Kieff, Kollision, Loki at6, Lontano, Lots42, Lucashoal, Lugnuts, Majarvis, Man of wealth and taste, Marcus Brute, Marimvibe, Master Deusoma, Master of Puppets, Mattlittlej, Michael Hardy, Mike Searson, Mikesmash, Mild Bill Hiccup, Miss kat, Mrblondnyc, Musik of Anarchy, Nemeses9, Nhl4hamilton, Omicronperseі8, PalindromicAnagram, Phoenix720, RattleandHum, Razzfan, RicJac, Ricky81682, Rjwilmsi, Rusted AutoParts, Seb35, Ser Amantio di Nicolao, SmartyBoots, Smatthewman, SoccrFwd13, Sterry2607, Sugar Bear, Supernumerary, SwitChar, T.cornall, TJ Spyke, TallulahBelle, The Transhumanist, Themepark, TommyBoy, Treybien, Uucp, Varlaam, Wile e2005, William Graham, Wtbe7560, Xezbeth, 157 anonymous edits

One Hour Photo *Source*: http://en.wikipedia.org/w/index.php?oldid=463909598 *Contributors*: *drew, Aaron Brenneman, AbsoluteGleek92, Aiken drum, Algae, All Hallow's Wraith, Americanhero, AndTheCrowdGoesWild, Andrzejbanas, Apoltix, Bento00, Bovineboy2008, Brad Rousse, Browny1213, Bwiki, Captain vlad, Ccacsmss, Codernaut, Commander Shepard, CoolKatt number 99999, CyberGhostface, Darren Jowalsen, David Gerard, Debresser, Delta40, Demonslave, Diluuk, Djrobgordon, Dogah, Druff, Dukinhower, Eekerz, El duderino, Emishi, Empty2005, Erik, Erisie, Everett Akay, Feureau, Fourthords, Frecklefoot, Gabbe, Gargaj, Gazpacho, Greenpopman, Gurko, Holi Teacakes, IKato, Ierifff, Irishguy, J21, Jab843, Jack324, Jared Preston, Jay-W, Jh51681, JoeLoeb, Joshdboz, JustPhil, KJK::Hyperion, Kasreyn, King of Hearts, Kronnang Dunn, LaMenta3, LadyJ3000, Liquidblue8388, Litalex, Longhair, LtMuldoon, M.C. Brown Shoes, Mallanox, Martarius, MatthewGoodfan101, Mattphesto, Message From Xenu, Michael Devore, Mike1971inter, Morpose, Moshe Constantine Hassan Al-Silverburg, Mosherdude91, NeoVampTrunks, Nick San, Noirish, Not a dog, Nv8200p, Ouroboris, Pegship, Pernelldh, Purpose Observatory, Quuxplusone, Radiohawk, Rcrocha, Red Specter, Richardcavell, Roaring Siren, Rosalbissima, RyanGFilm, Scarian, Seoidau, Shannon Tucker, Shinshoryuken, Sirkh1, SoSaysChappy, Something Wicked 451, Sthgtsman, The Filmaker, The JPS, The misha, The-Pope, Themagicalpixieelf, TimidObserver, TomEatsCake, Tonku, Tony Sandel, Totoro-chan, TrbleClef, Treybien, Twas Now, Twendai, Tyger63, Whomp, Wongston, Wtfdavemustaine, Xezbeth, Yukichigai, Zetetic Apparatchik, Zotdragon, 201 anonymous edits

Noel (film) *Source*: http://en.wikipedia.org/w/index.php?oldid=465050057 *Contributors*: *drew, AN(Ger), Ajshm, Andycjp, Antofa, Armbrust, Bartleby79, David Rush, Don Joe, ENDelt260, Ed Poor, Erik, GrayFullbuster, John, JzG, Kberkely65, MikeWazowski, Naniwako, Neurolysis, RattleandHum, Rjwilmsi, Shiftedreality, Signalhead, Skier Dude, Sreejithk2000, Tata1711, Tato.nascimento1979, Tdogg241, Thegreat100, Tide rolls, Tim1357, Tomerico74, Urashimataro, Valermos, Xezbeth, 33 anonymous edits

House of D *Source*: http://en.wikipedia.org/w/index.php?oldid=462367747 *Contributors*: 777sms, Bluezy816, Bruce1ee, Cladeal832, Correogsk, Dan56, DubCrazy, Fungusdookie, Ghirlandajo, GrahamHardy, Grandpafootsoldier, GregorB, ItsTheClimb17, Jenks24, LaffyTaffy24, LinkToddMcLovinMontana, Lugnuts, Markaci, MikeAllen, Mrperson27, Nick, Oda Mari, Okiefromokla, Oodus, Pegship, Pharos, Pjoef, Proof Pudding, ReZips, Schmeller, Semajdraehs, Skier Dude, ThinkBlue, Tractorkingsfan, TracyLinkEdnaVelmaPenny, Varlaam, Wadofglue, 75 anonymous edits

The Final Cut (2004 film) *Source*: http://en.wikipedia.org/w/index.php?oldid=463445104 *Contributors*: *drew, AaronY, Abantha1, Alansohn, Alex2631, Alksub, Andrzejbanas, Animekill, Arbero, Atlantima, Bovineboy2008, Chowbok, Cs302b, DTRY, DavidOaks, E20Ci, ERcheck, Easchiff, Erik, Freshh, Hoverfish, Iwanttofly4, Jason Palpatine, JzG, Kerowyn, Kusma, Levineps, Lew19, Lightmouse, MSJapan, Mallanox, Martarius, Michael Snow, MikeAllen, Milant, Murvey888, Noelledeg, Nopira, Notmicro, Pcap, Postdlf, PubliusFL, Q8-falcon, Robin S, Shadrack-dva, ShelfSkewed, Soetermans, SpNeo, Spider-Carnage Earth-X, Spidlock, Steam5, TJ Spyke, Tassedethe, Thorpe, Tony Sandel, Topdeck, Transfinite, Treybien, Underwater, Vespristiano, WBTtheFROG, Walterk29, ZZninepluralZalpha, 71 anonymous edits

The Big White *Source*: http://en.wikipedia.org/w/index.php?oldid=419264085 *Contributors*: David Gerard, Donmike10, Donteatyellowsnow, Eetvartti, Fariborz29, GoldieRush, Leavemade, LilHelpa, Longhair, Magister Mathematicae, Mordicai, NWill, Nehrams2020, Pigsonthewing, Polisher of Cobwebs, Prcr, SandyGeorgia, SilkTork, Skier Dude, Sreejithk2000, Sugar Bear, Supernumerary, Susurrus, Taestell, Tassedethe, TubularWorld, Woohookitty, Wunderpilot, 27 anonymous edits

Robots (film) *Source*: http://en.wikipedia.org/w/index.php?oldid=465416791 *Contributors*: 28421u2232nfenfcenc, 5 albert square, Active Banana, AdamSmithee, Adnghiem501, Agent008, AirLiner, Airplaneman, Ajshm, Alansohn, Albert109, AlexDBNB, AlwaysUnderTheInfluence, Alyssa kat13, Ambulnick, Andonic, AndrewHowse, Angie Y., Animation815, Animedude360, Apsmanuel, Armistej, Aspects, Avicennasis, BRG, BadCRC, Belovedfreak, Benv-b92, Bibliomaniac15, Big Bad Baby, Bigheaded, Blackbone 5000, Blanchardb, Bold Clone, Boo1210, Bovineboy2008, Cabdude, Carniolus, Cartoon Boy, Cat's Tuxedo, Cbrown1023, Cglassey, Chaosdruid, Cheat2win, Closedmouth, Coltenstokes, CptCutLess, Creidieki, D6, Daedalus969, Dakart, Dancter, Daniel913, Darkwind, DavidCane, Deadlock, DiogenesNY, Doomsdayer520, Dragon76, Drat, Drewdy, Drunkenpeter99, Enigmaticanant, Ephidel, Evilgidgit, Ewlyahoocom, Ezekieloak, Faerun, Fatachebanner, Favonian, Freakofnurture, FrogTape, Gabbe, Gaius Cornelius, George100, Granpuff, Harutake, Hippi ippi, Hondasaregood, Horkana, Hotwiki, IKR1, InfamousPrince, Irishguy, J'onn J'onzz, J.delanoy, J04n, JAY2damncoolchap, JDspeeder1, JM.Beaubourg, JSH-alive, JamesAM, Jc37, Jedi Davideus, JesseMeza, Jojhutton, Joshua-Ed-Guy, Jumbo Juice, JustPhil, Justinhful, Kashakak, Kbh3rd, Keithh, Kglman6, Kidlittle, Kieranthompson, Kismetmagic, Klassykittychick, Knee427, Koavf, Kungfuadam, Lanway, Lavamagnet, Lee M, Leonidas23, LilHelpa, Lilanglwannabe, Logoboy95returns, Lots42, Luckystar41292, Luna Santin, M.corbett, MacsBug, Madscientist102, Malcolmo, Mallanox, Man of wealth and taste, MarjorieCook, MasterA113, Mikokat, Millahnna, Momoricks, MonkeeJuice, NCurse, Nehrams2020, NickelodeonFan95, Niduzzi, Nohat, Nunu1997, Nzd, Od Mishehu AWB, Oren0, Originalsinner, Ouzo, P.h, Pabter, PacificBoy, Pburka, Piano non troppo, Pikawil, Pixelface, Pollinator, Pumpie, QuietApocalypse, RUL3R, Rdsmith4, Reaper Eternal, RedHillian, Reflex Reaction, RelentlessRecusant, RepublicanJacobite, Richfife, RobertG, RobyWayne, Rusted AutoParts, Rwlinda, Safety Cap, Sak31122, Salamurai, SarahMGGG, ScudLee, Secfan, Sega381, Semidriver214, Silent Tom, Sjones23, Skier Dude, SnapSnap, Socby19, Spa-Franks, Spen gottogo, Stevertigo, Stubblyhead, SummerPhD, Supernumerary, THEN WHO WAS PHONE?, TKD, Tbhotch, Tcatron565, Terence, The Big Chunk, The Bread, TheMovieBuff, TheRealFennShysa, TheValentineBros, Theparamountlogofanclub, Therealestoutthere101, Thuresson, Tombomp, Tregoweth, Treybien, Ultraviolet scissor flame, Valermos, Violetriga, Viriditas, VofSteel, Wecantdoanythingaboutit, Wikidude10000, Wikigold96, Wilhelmalexis, Wolfpeaceful, Woohookitty, Wtmitchell, Wwwwolf, Wyatt915, Xezbeth, YOUSUCK37, Yanimich69, Ynhockey, Zak Hammat, Zapacna, ZeroJanvier, 591 anonymous edits

The Aristocrats (film) *Source*: http://en.wikipedia.org/w/index.php?oldid=457934058 *Contributors*: 041744, 09gebejo, 23skidoo, After Midnight, Andrzejbanas, AtticusX, Audiodude, Backslash Forwardslash, Bakilas, Bewildebeast, Boscoboy, Bovineboy2008, Brtkrbzhnv, Classic rocker, Criticalfilm, DMacks, Damian Yerrick, David Gerard, Doctofunk, Dweller, Emerson7, Emeryemery, Ergito, FJPB, Fourthords, Garion96, Gekritzl, Gohst, GrahamHardy, Harmil, Historymike, Hoof Hearted, Iamtheworldsgreatest, Iridescent, JasonAQuest, Jay-W, Jmudge, JnB987, John of Reading, Jolivetti, Jotunar, KConWiki, Kbh3rd, Kirjapan, Kyorosuke, Lightmouse, LindsayH, Meegs, MickO'Bants, Mrfreakyinastar, Mrzaius, Muddtallica, Mütze, NapoliRoma, Naufana, Nick C, NotACow, Obi-Jon, Ohioreader, Otto4711, Parkerfrey, PhilSchabus, Plastic editor, Postdlf, Qalaud, Reepnorp, Rockstar180, Sadads, Savethemooses, Scix, Sethkills, Shamrox, Shawn in Montreal, SmartGuy, Sophruhig Vita@comcast.net, Steve Bob, StradivariusTV, Sugar Bear, Swordblade182, THATSBETTER, TPIRFanSteve, The Famous Movie Director, The Literate Engineer, The velociraptor, ThePatman, Theoneintraining, Thisis0, Tony Sandel, Tregoweth, Trialsanderrors, Trivialist, Trogga, Truthiness Jones, Vanillawaif, Varlaam, Violetriga, WAS, WSUCanuck, Xeno, Zadduel86, 118 anonymous edits

Man of the Year (2006 film) *Source*: http://en.wikipedia.org/w/index.php?oldid=465509274 *Contributors*: AN(Ger), AbsoluteGleek92, Ace Class Shadow, AdelaMae, Alison, Amazingracer, Aml830, Andrei G Kustov, Andrzejbanas, Aoystreck, ArmadilloFromHell, Art LaPella, Auric, Booyabazooka, Bwjs, Calwatch, Cat-five, Chairboy, ColdRush, Commando303, ConradPino, Daverich313, David Gerard, Donald McKinney, Drgorman, Easchiff, Ed Poor, EditingManiac, Egon Eagle, Elcocinero, Electiontechnology, Elliott golding, Emurphy42, Enderknight17, Fourthords, Franklinpierce4, FrozenPurpleCube, Fuhghettaboutit, Gadget850, Guat6, Herunar, Husnock, Ianiceboy, Ibanez RYM, Ike-bana, Iquadri, Irishguy, J04n, JBK405, JQF, Jmlk17, Jusjih, Karrmann, Kbdank71, Kit Foxtrot, Kross, Kuralyov, Leroyinc, Levineps, Lights, Loremipsum, MAINEiac4434, MJBurrage, MK2, MSJapan, Mahjong705, Mouse is back, Neddyseagoon, Nhl4hamilton, Nightscream, Noclevername, Obi-WanKenobi-2005, ObsessiveJoBroDisorder, Oscarthecat, Otto4711, Pairadox, Passive, Patrick, Philodox-ohki, Portillo, Q8-falcon, Radosław10, RattleandHum, Reid1867, Richard Barrett, Rjwilmsi, Robertvan1, Ronen Perry, Rwlinda, Sarware, Sciurinæ, Searcher 1990, Seinfreak37, Sonjay11, Soundslikealotofhooplah, Stefanomione, Subman758, TTE, Tassedethe, Taty2007, Tenebrae, The Giant Puffin, Thebeck, Tony Sidaway, Tonzo, Torritorri, Truthiness Jones, UberMan5000, Uucp, Varlaam, Viewdrix, Zerath13, 136 anonymous edits

Night at the Museum *Source*: http://en.wikipedia.org/w/index.php?oldid=461254848 *Contributors*: 1965Tim, 1994rw, 4444hhhh, 78.26, Abby724, Acelanyth, Adambro, AdjustShift, Aircorn, Airplaneman, Albinochaos, Alientraveller, Alliepally24, Amaraiel, American Eagle, Andrew0501, Andrzejbanas, Andycjp, Angleterre, AnmaFinotera, Anniemariel99, AnonMoos, Arasaka, Art1991, Asams10, Asfarer, Atorero, Auntof6, AwesomeDude8, AzaToth, Azucar, BGyss, Babygator23, Badapro, Bark, Barosaurus Lentus, Batman2005, Bearcat, Bedford, Bender235, Benstiller22222, Betty Logan, Bibliomaniac15, Bigal0427, Biggybilal, Bigmoviezone, Bignole, Billastro, Blahblah32blahblah, Bobet, Bold Clone, Bolman Deal, Booksworm, Boris Barowski, Bovineboy2008, Brad, BrandonAlexanderMills, Braydwilde, Briaboru, Brian Kendig, Bruce Hall, Buchanan-Hermit, Bud0011, CBM, CK10, CM7Y, CWenger, Calgary, Can't sleep, clown will eat me, Carcharoth, CardinalDan, Cat's Tuxedo, Cculber007, Cessator, Cflm001, Chamillitaryboi94, Chaparyan, Chris Mason, ChrisCork, Cigraphix, Clygeric, Cognita, Coolboy223, Copsi, CrazedEwok, CycloneChibi, Czolgolz, DJ Clayworth, DReifGalaxyM31, Damiens.rf, DancingQueenGirl, Danntm, Danreitz, Danwojo812, Darkness2005, Darkwingdave, Darrik2, Das Baz, Davehi1, David Gerard, Davidwhite544, Davie4264, DeadGuy, Debresser, Dekimasu, DennisPNorman, Des1804, Deucalionite, Dewey Finn, Difluoroethene, Digata200, DinoCraze, Dntrwl, Dogman15, Donmike10, Dora Nichov, Dougie K, Downwards, Dp76764, Draknfyre, Dreadstar, DudeBrownie, Dunkenud, Dylan Lake, EVula, Ebyabe, Ed, Egglord, Eggy4, Elcairo, Eloipfeiffer, Empoor, Eqdoktor, Erik, Evanreyes, Evilgidgit, Excirial, F13nd, Falcon8765, Fastzander, Feeeshboy, Firsfron, FisherQueen, Fitzwilliam, Fluffernutter, Fm90, Fourthords, FrankRizzo2006, Freddie R. Aldous, Fusek71, G4ruleo, GM11, GPanesarJatt, GTAGeek123, Gaius Cornelius, Garion96, GeneralYin, Geniac, Get mahim, Gildir, Giraffedata, GoingBatty, GrahamHardy, Granpuff, Grieferhate, Grizzwald, GroovySandwich, Grsz11, Grubber, Gurudata, GusF, Happyme22, Harveyhanson, Historiographer, Homer29, Hoverfish, Hydrargyrum, Ianblair23, Ianthegecko, Idont Havaname, Immblueversion, InfamousPrince, Ipstenu, Irishguy, Irrationalfan, Ishsahai, IvanLanin, J.delanoy, JAltman752, JDDJS, JDspeeder1, JMolo1115, JPG-GR, JQF, JamesAM, JamesBWatson, Jamesbanesmith, Jason Palpatine, Jasonbres, Jdmxrain, Jfmajo, Jleon, Johann Wolfgang, Jojhutton, JonathanDP81, Josephfg, Joutsen-DD, Jpbowen, Jrt989, Jstohler, Junejoyjonny, JustPhil, Justin1276536, KGasso, Kaihoku, Karrade247, Kbdank71, Keithmc2, King Bowser 64, King of Hearts, Kintetsubuffalo, Kinu, Kitch, Kitia, KittyKat 1987, Knightj,

Kollision, Krazycev13, Krellion, Kubigula, Kuralyov, KyleRGiggs, LOL, Larry laptop, Le fantome de l'opera, Legaleagle86, Legitimus, Lemonflash, Lence, Leszek Jańczuk, Levineps, Libatius, Litalex, LiteraryMaven, Locos epraix, Logan, Lotsincommon, Loudmouth 2, Luigi-ish, Luna Santin, Luwilt, M.O.X, MacGyverMobile, Madchester, Maelwys, Magioladitis, Malcolm, Mammamiamania, Mankiller2000, Marco Alfarrobinha, Markeer, MarnetteD, Mat wang, Mattbuck, Mattsmasher0000, Maxim, Menchi, Merotoker1, MetroStar, Micione, Midkay, MightyAtom, Mikelr, Mikemoral, MilitHist, Millahnna, Milton1918, Minglex, Minnesota Jones, Misterkillboy, Mjrmtg, Mlanza, Mmccl2, MoMo19947, ModernDino, Moshe Constantine Hassan Al-Silverburg, Moviefan1, Movieguru2006, Mr. Prez, MrRadioGuy, Msw1002, Murraybill, Myscrnnm, NAHID, NHRHS2010, Nachoman-au, Nae'blis, Nehrams2020, NeilEvans, Neirgb818, NickelodeonFan, Night Gyr, NorthernThunder, Nouse4aname, NrDg, Nricardo, Ntsimp, OOODDD, Orenburg1, Orsoni, Paaa, Pegship, Penwhale, Peteb16, PhnomPencil, PoeIssac62, PoeticVerse, Prem555, Puffy Treat, Quantumobserver, R'n'B, R13n13, Razzkazz, Rbdfan17118, RealityTelevisionFan, Relyna, RetypePassword, Reywas92, Rhino131, Ric36, RicegoneWILD, Richfife, Rick-Levitt, Rickterp, Rjwilmsi, Robertandrade, Romanc19s, Ron Ritzman, Rtkat3, Rukifelth, Rusted AutoParts, Rwlinda, Ryanb006, SFTVLGUY2, SGCommand, SJP, SQGibbon, Samjohn95, Satori Son, Scarecroe, Schmiteye, Sci13960, Shadow1, Shawisland, ShelfSkewed, Shortie43504, Simone15, Simply south, Sixedheart, Sjones23, Sjyglm, Sky Attacker, SkyWalker, Southsloper, Spinerod, Squids and Chips, SteveO, Stryik, Styrofoam1994, Superbowlbound, Supernumerary, Syrthiss, T-borg, TKD, TMC1982, Tachikoma64, Tacofan, TaerkastUA, Tahitia, Tassedethe, Tcatron565, Tea and crumpets, Technobabble1, Teh roflmaoer, Tenorcnj, The Clawed One, The Cool Kat, The Giant Puffin, The Rogue Penguin, The Ronin, The Shadow-Fighter, TheMisunderstoodMisfit, TheMovieBuff, TheQuoteBuff, TheStrayCat, Themeparkfanatic, Themillofkeytone, TheoClarke, Thesis4Eva, Thething95, Thief12, Thincat, Tide rolls, Tigerpoet, Titoxd, Tkynerd, Tone, Tony Sidaway, Treybien, TylerXKJ, Typhoon966, Tyrc, UberMan5000, UberUltimate, Useight, Uucp, Vader200591, Varlaam, Verne Equinox, VigilancePrime, Vlad4, VodkaJazz, VolatileChemical, WBardwin, WIKI-GUY-16, WOSlinker, Wainstead, Ward3001, Wavy G, Websurfer246, WereSpielChequers, WikHead, Wiki Raja, Wikimachine, Will-B, Willking1979, Winter04, Wisekwai, Wyatt Riot, Xezbeth, Yamamoto Ichiro, Yggdriedi, Ylee, Ylem, Ytfc23, Yukichigai, ZaacE., ZeldaQueen, ZimZalaBim, Zinko777, Zomic13, 1067 anonymous edits

Happy Feet *Source*: http://en.wikipedia.org/w/index.php?oldid=464319741 *Contributors*: 041744, 1samwyz3, 99DBSIMLR, A7x, AAA!, ACBest, AEMoreira042281, AKGhetto, ALadinN, AN(Ger), AUG, Aang-kai, Aaron Schulz, Aaronaeb, Abce2, Abdurahman49, AddDeWitt, Ailley, AirLiner, Ajmint, Akcarver, Alandavidson, Alansohn, Albino Bebop, Albrozdude, Ale jrb, Alejo123, Alexforcefive, Alfirin, Alhoon, Alrightypewriter, Alxeedo, Amarkov, Ameliorate!, Ancientanubis, And1987, Andrewpmk, Andrzejbanas, AndySimpson, Andycjp, Angam, Angr, AnmaFinotera, Ann Stouter, Antandrus, Anthony Appleyard, Apple1013, Aralvarez, Archerchef, Archie325, ArchonMagnus, Arrkhal, Art1991, Aseelmunzirbarghouti, Ashmoo, Aspects, Athaenara, AuburnPilot, Aunatrea, Auntof6, Autocratique, Avs5221, BA 744, Bac2futurfan, Baltimorehare, BarrettM82, Bazzargh, Bedford, Bencey, Benjaminlobato, Benzy19, Berserkerz Crit, Bettia, Bgunsberger, Big Bird, Bigmoviezone, Bill, Blue Dingo, BlueMario1016, Bob the Rabbid, Bobdylanfan, Bored461, Bovineboy2008, Brandon, Breno, BrotherFlounder, Bryan H Bell, Bt8257, Bumm13, C.Fred, CBM, CTVampSlayer, Canglesea, Casper2k3, Cat's Tuxedo, Catgut, Cbrown1023, Cbuckley, Ccacsmss, Chanlyn, Chard513, CharlotteWebb, Checkerfly, Chibibibi, Chowbok, Chrislk02, Church of emacs, Cigammagicwizard, Cinephobia, Classicfilms, Closenplay, CloudNine, Cloudbound, Clyde Miller, Cncxbox, Codetiger, ColdFusion650, Colonies Chris, Conmancool17, Conti, ContiAWB, Cooldani95, Countmall, Crystallina, CrystallinetheHedgidna, Ctbolt, Cunard, Cxz111, CyberSkull, Cyrus XIII, Cyster, DH85868993, Dakane, Dale Arnett, Dancey2, Dancter, DanielEng, Darth Panda, David in DC, Deb, Debresser, Declan Clam, Deej30, Delldot, Denisgomes, DennyColt, DerHexer, Design, Destron Commander, DevastatorIIC, Dfrg.msc, Directormtb, Discospinster, Diti, DivineAlpha, Dkp, Dogface, Dominicrusho, Dpenguinman, Dpm12, Dreadstar, Dreslough, Drunkenpeter99, Duschinono, Dwmr, EJBanks, Ebyabe, Edwpat, Elcairo, Elendil's Heir, Elil, Emerson7, Enpitsu, Eqdoktor, Eric82oslo, Erik, Erik9, Esanchez7587, Esn, Esrever, Evancrss, Everyguy, Ex nihil, Exozero, Extraordinary Machine, F, FF2010, FMAFan1990, FMAN, Fagstein, Falconfly, Falconleaf, Famer, Faradayplank, Fastily, Favonian, Fayenatic london, FeldBum, Figure-Headed Guy, Firelordazulon, Firetrap9254, Flair Girls, Flami72, Flubeca, Fluffernutter, Forsteri, Franck Drake, Free-encyclopedia, Freshh, FriscoKnight, FuriousFreddy, Fusek71, Fuzzy510, GDonato, Gadfium, Gail, Gdavidp, Gdo01, GerardKennedy, Gilliam, Glen, Got118115147, Goth67, Gothmog26, GracieLizzie, Gurch, Guybrush, Gwernol, Gyrferret, Happyfeetluvr22, Happyft, Hdt83, HeartofaDog, HenkvD, Henry W. Schmitt, HenryJthefilmist, Hensleyb, Herbm, Hewie7, Hgkamath, Hiddekel, Hinatagal101, Hjfhksdjf, Holdaway, Hooperbloob, Horseagle, IKR1, Iamwisesun, Ian T, Ianjones50, Ianthegecko, Icseaturtles, ImSpidey2, InfamousPrince, Inter16, Irishguy, Irk, IronGargoyle, J Bar, JAF1970, JLaTondre, Jabbathenut, JackSparrow Ninja, JamesAM, Jane-21, Janke, JarakMaldon, Jason.cinema, Jedi94, Jeff3000, Jeltag-the-Ferret, Jemstone66, Jerry, Jimeree, Jinjoo, Jitterro, Jjdebaca, Jmanigold, JoeSmack, JohnI, Johndburger, Jon513, Jonathan.s.kt, Josh Parris, Joshfriel, Jp.bc, Jrhoadley, Jt spratt, Jtryan, Juliaholcomb, Jusdafax, Jwy, KConWiki, Kaneshirojj, Karin127, KathrynLybarger, Kchishol1970, Keilana, Kelisi, Kenicks, Kevin McE, Keyser Söze, Kirill Lokshin, Kjhstuph, Klosk12, Knute, Kollision, Konczewski, Kotsu, Krisster, Kuralyov, Kwah-LeBaire, Las Vegas JD, Leafyplant, Leflyman, Legedevin, LegioXIII-SPQR, Leonard^Bloom, Leslie kawakami, LibLord, Little Mountain 5, Lo2u, Longhair, Lordmuffin, Loren.wilton, Lradrama, Lubrio, Luigi-ish, Luis1972, LukeSurl, Luna Santin, MADMAX1998, MER-C, MPD01605, MackSalmon, Mackeriv, Macunuva, Madman, Maideniron, Malerin, Manderiko, Marcg106, MarkSutton, MartinDK, Maxim, McNoddy, Mecko192, MeegsC, MegX, Melanie Jordan, Meno25, Midnight Comet, Midnightcomm, MikeLondon, Mikecraig, Mikeymoo333, Milerz91, Millahnna, Mimzy1990, MindWraith, Minochige, Miranda, Miskwito, MistaTee, Mj khazali, Monkeys 9711, Monz, Movingimage, Mr Stephen, MrClegg, MrMacMan, Mschel, Mushroom, Myanw, N. Harmonik, Natureguy1980, NavarroJ, Nehrams2020, Neutrality, New Jack Swing, Nhrenton, Nickksnow, Nina phunsta, Nintendofan88, Nitrosuperspeed, No Guru, Nocarsgo, Norsehorse89, Notfound, Nr1moviefan, NrDg, Nssdfdsfds, Nuggetchild, Ocatecir, Octane, Optigan13, Orderinchaos, Oscarthecat, Otingocni, Overcasts, Oxymoron83, Ozone77, Ozzieboy, PHXsuns3434, PJ Pete, PMDrive1061, Paddyslacker, Paradoxian, ParalysedBeaver, Peecee1978, Pejorative.majeure, Penciltapper, Pendo 4, Pengo, PennsylvaniaPatriot, Persnickety, PeruAlonso, Peteb16, Peter Ellis, Peterl, PhattyFatt, Phbasketball6, Philip Trueman, Phone beeps, Pigeonarmy, Pigman, Pineapplex, Pingveno, Pixelface, Pnevares, Pnkrockr, PokeFan2006, Ppk01, PrinceRegentLuitpold, PrisonMan, Procrastinatrix, Prolog, Pronoiac, Ptikobj, Quentin X, Quesar, QuintanaDS, RB972, RFBailey, Radosław10, Raghuvansh r, Rangerkom, Rapomon, RattleMan, Raymond arritt, Raymondwinn, RealityTelevisionFan, Reinoe, Rescue Guy, Revrant, Rhindle The Red, Rholton, Riana, Ric168, Richard Barrett, Richfife, Ring2011, Rje, Rjwilmsi, Rklawton, Rmallins, RobMarvin, Robin Chen, Rockysmile11, Ronhjones, Rougeblossom, Royboy193456, Rtkat3, Ruby (Land Before Time) Lover, Rusted AutoParts, Rwlinda, RyanGerbil10, Ryulong, SISLEY, SKS2K6, SabineLaGrande, Sad mouse, Sander123, Sardanaphalus, Scalytail, Schissel, Scout of truth, Scratte Lover, Sd31415, Seattlenow, Secret Saturdays, Semchin, Sera404, Sergeant.cross, Sesshomaru, Shaolin128, ShawnVW, ShelfSkewed, Shoito, Shortmalay, Shotwell, Shuffdog, SidP, Siddharth Mehrotra, Silent Tom, Simonus, Singster90, SixteenBitJorge, Sjones23, Skudrafan1, Skypurevis, Slatz-123, Smalljim, Smash, Smurffluvr, Snowman Guy, Snowolf, Solumeiras, Sotakeit, Sp3000, Spazure, Spitacular, Squallhart, Staecker, StarSpangledKiwi, Statarius, Sterry2607, Steven Weston, Steven Zhang, Steverapaport, Strom, Superghost987, SyntaxError55, Synthe, Szyslak, TDC99, TKD, TPIRFanSteve, Tad Lincoln, Tamariki, Tarra emerald51394, Tastes like lead, Tayljon, Tbboy13, TeaDrinker, Teak the Kiwi, The 80s chick, The Gilly, The Merciful, The Rogue Penguin, The Thing That Should Not Be, The Wild West guy, The wub, TheAnimal117, TheCoffee, TheST, Theworldstinks, Thirteen squared, Tiago nicastro, Tiddly Tom, Tide rolls, TinFoil, Titoxd, Tmlpalmsurfer, Tntnnbltn, Tomithicus, TonyTheTiger, Tpal3, TrapStilton, Tregoweth, Trivialist, TwilightMan, Underneath-it-All, Uthabiti, UtherSRG, Uzume, VG Cats Tipe 2, Veinor, VernoWhitney, Viroxor, WWGB, Wafulz, Ward3001, Warpozio, Websurfer246, Weiko676, WestKateLobsterMan14, Wheels0132, WhisperToMe, Wikieizor, Wikipe-tan, Williamnilly, WillyofToxteth, Wimt, Xnuala, XxTrillvillexX9, Y2kcrazyjoker4, Yamaguchi先生, Yardserror, Yllosubmarine, Zak Hammat, Zanimum, Zoe, Zzuuzz, Ζεύς, Basil, 1643 anonymous edits

Everyone's Hero *Source*: http://en.wikipedia.org/w/index.php?oldid=463240681 *Contributors*: 2Pac, AbsoluteGleek92, AlbertHerring, Arkadium, Baehr, Barek, Bbb23, Big Fin Guy, Cbrown1023, Christianster45, Cooksey, Coppertop Guy, David Gerard, Derek21, Dictyosiphonaceae, DigitalKaede, Drunkenpeter99, Dylanknows, Empoor, Esn, Forthofer, Freak104, Fredinandus, Freshh, Garion96, HappyUser, High School Musical909, Iheartwiki19, Ilion2, Immblueversion, Irishguy, J 1982, Jack O'Lantern, Johnlongbond, Justinfr, Kasper2006, Kimchi.sg, Kitsunegami, Ladsgroup, Lava100100, Lugnut215, Lugnuts, MER-C, Materialscientist, Mbmbmb123456789, MichaelQSchmidt, Ndboy, Nehrams2020, Nezickson, NrDg, Nymf, Onedanshow, Oneononetvseries, P1cooly, Pearle, Pegship, Qelery, Red1530, Redeagle688, Rje, Rtkat3, Rwlinda, SamEtches, SamtheBravesFan, Sc straker, Secret Saturdays, SidP, Simply Agrestic, Sjones23, Slithymatt, Spiffy sperry, Spoilwork, Starcheerspeaksnewslostwars, Strong Devon, Tabletop, TenPoundHammer, Tommy11111, Tregoweth, Trivialist, Varlaam, Vchimpanzee, WikiLubber, Willgustavo, Wmahan, Woodshed, Wtooher, Yanksguy26, Youngcc7, Zu Ninja, 231 anonymous edits

RV (film) *Source*: http://en.wikipedia.org/w/index.php?oldid=464992402 *Contributors*: 2 of 8, All Hallow's Wraith, Alphachimp, Amchow78, Andrzejbanas, Annatot, Ar-wiki, Ardavu, Arknascar44, Arroww, Aycan, B.Wind, Beardo, Behnam mancini, Ben-Bopper, Bgold4, Bioberg, Bovineboy2008, Branddobbe, Browndog72, Buchanan-Hermit, CO, Can't sleep, clown will eat me, Cassie1230, Ceecookie, Chantessy, Cheddarjack, Cjmarsicano, Claygate, Colonies Chris, Crumbsucker, Dale Arnett, Darthvader1, David Gerard, DeC, DerHexer, Dhartung, Dirkbb, Dl2000, Dppowell, Drake Clawfang, Drewdy, Eduemoni, Edward, ElectricSkrill, Empty2005, FilmFan69, FollowGuard, FrankRizzo2006, Freakofnurture, Freddie R. Aldous, Free Bear, Freshh, Fuhghettaboutit, Galactusz, Gareth Jones, Gdamasceno, Ghosts&empties, Glass of water, Granpuff, GrayFox92, Haakon, Headstrong neiva, Huangm, Iansanderson, Iokerapid, Irishguy, Ixfd64, JHeinonen, Jack O'Lantern, Jumping cheese, Kathylove, Kbdank71, Kidcorona, Klow, Kollision, Kwi, Lahiru k, Longhair, Magg 608, Mat wang, Materialscientist, Max22, McNaughty1987, Mikemor92, Misterkillboy, Monkeys 9711, MrShamrock, MrWhipple, Myscrnnm, Nova Prime, NutsForFacts, OOODDD, Omicronpersei8, PJ Pete, Piano non troppo, Pizzadinosaur, Polylerus, Pulsar822, Q8-falcon, QuasyBoy, Queenmomcat, RattleandHum, Reece 555, Richfife, Robertvan1, Russ kavalunah, Rwlinda, RyanFaley, Seanie16, Sjones23, Sjorford, Sjsitler92, Skier Dude, SkyWalker, Snoogans, Soetermans, Spookeyes, StangStud, Steinninn, Stevo D, Stuthomas4, Supernumerary, TJ Spyke, Tassedethe, Tazz765, Tcatron565, Thatcher, The Shadow-Fighter, Thegreat100, Therealeggplant, Thirteen squared, Tinton5, TracyLinkEdnaVelmaPenny, Treybien, Unregistered.coward, Useight, VG Cats Tipe 2, WOSlinker, Websurfer246, Wikieditboy, Wknight94, Zak Hammat, Ὁ οἶστρος, 278 anonymous edits

The Night Listener (film) *Source*: http://en.wikipedia.org/w/index.php?oldid=458085180 *Contributors*: AbsoluteGleek92, Alyssa hoffel, Andrzejbanas, AndyRoberts7, Bovineboy2008, Chiaange, Clavecin, Cpoupart, Crculver, Cuchullain, DTRHStudios, David Gerard, Deconstructhis, Djflem, Elizabennet, Erik, Exok, Funwisconsinguy2007, Gabbe, Irishguy, JHunterJ, Kc12286, Kevinalewis, Kruse56, Kuda, Leuko, LtMuldoon, Master Deusoma, Matthiashess, Nightscream, Odoital25, Omicronpersei8, Park3r, Pegship, Possum, Prekario, Pricer1980, Puerca, Radosław10, Rwlinda, Ryulong, Sarranduin, Shan246, SiobhanHansa, Sjones23, Somercet, TAnthony, Thismightbezach, Tmohr, Tony Sandel, Tony Sidaway, Toussaint, Treybien, Ustyuzhanin, Werldwayd, Wittylama, Ysangkok, ZETAZEN, Zu Ninja, 67 anonymous edits

License to Wed *Source*: http://en.wikipedia.org/w/index.php?oldid=461722736 *Contributors*: AAA!, ADM, AN(Ger), AbsoluteGleek92, All Hallow's Wraith, Amulet Heart, Andonic, Andrzejbanas, Arcoirris, Bbmm, Beetstra, Bobo92, Bovineboy2008, CRRaysHead90, CambridgeBayWeather, Chaosmical, Chibiheart, Coffee12345, Dahamsta7, Damian Yerrick, Darrenhusted, Dgalmavs07, Doctorfluffy, DoubleCross, Esperant, Fritz Saalfeld, Grandpafootsoldier, Grenavitar, Henryodell, Husond, Irishguy, JDspeeder1, Jabbathenut, Jeremy Butler, Kidlittle, KnowledgeOfSelf, Kogsquinge, Leroyinc, Levineps, Lugnuts, Mahanga, Marcthepirate, Marktoo4, Mensurs, MikeWazowski, Mr. Quertee, Msw1002, Nash17, Nehrams2020, Nemo24, Patrick, Portillo, Rilbiz, Rockysmile11, Rwlinda, SignorSimon, Skier Dude, Spidey104, Suckstobeabum, Tell-Tale Ghost, TheMovieBuff, Thegreat100, Thulasi12345, Tony Sidaway, Treybien, Walkiped, Web-Man, Wingsandsword, 206 anonymous edits

August Rush *Source*: http://en.wikipedia.org/w/index.php?oldid=465227475 *Contributors*: Aaron90omar, Abovetherim440, Adriaan, Agadant, Airproofing, Aitias, Alexf, AlisonLiu, All Hallow's Wraith, Anajana, AskFranz, Axem Titanium, Azumanga1, Bahar101, Bender235, Bentu, Cayla, Cg-realms, Chaucer1387, ChazBeckett, Cheesek1, CheetSpeek, Chris9086, Cinderelly007, Cjfield, Clpo13, Corvus cornix, Courtkittie, CyberSkull, CylonCAG, Dancter, Danieltuan, Darkfrog24, Darrenhusted, Darth Panda, Dbabbitt, DearPrudence, Dgoldwas, Discospinster, Djflem, Doze, Dsdukcy, Easchiff, Enviroboy, EoGuy, Epbr123, Erik, Excirial, Extraordinary Machine, Fairweather01, Farras Octara, FeanorStar7, Fighting for Justice, Fleetflame, Fodient, Fru1tbat, Garion96, Girlxxfade, GoingBatty, Grandpafootsoldier, GusF, Happyharry345, Hcnebono, Hematek, Heroes&hollyoaks, IW.HG, IndulgentReader, InfamousPrince, Irish yank22, Irishguy, ItsTheClimb17, Jades113, James Hade, Jangnathan, Jasheehy, Jfire, Jim1138, Joan.rr, Jomach08, JonHarder, JonnyDomestik, Jonpaulusa, Kelly Denham, Kingdom2, Kintetsubuffalo, Kittykatmc, Kollision, Ladyevol, Lightmouse, Liko81, LittleBigSpoon, Ltrifone, Lucky Mitch, Macduff, Marquis De Carabas, Mateo.ortega, McKnight88, Melty girl, Minimac, Miss kat, Mjrmtg, Monica Guerrero, Munsumee, Musicophiliac, My76Strat, N5iln, NOLA504ever, Ndboy, Neolandes, Nepenthes, Nimajji, Nnivanov, Noclador, Nutana, Padillah, Patar knight, Patrick, Paul Erik, PeaceNT, Pegship, Philip Trueman, Pixelface, Plasticspork, Plau, Polisher of Cobwebs, Possum, PrisonMan, Protonk, Qst, Quentin X, RBBrittain, RasputinAXP, Raymondwinn, Redbarronalpha1, Rfc1394, Rich Farmbrough, Rje, RoadDogXVIII, Robertvan1, Ron whisky, Ronark, Ronhjones, Rossrs, Rror, Rusted AutoParts, Rwlinda, Sadietruth, Sakaniprod, Salamurai, SandSan, Sceptre, SchfiftyThree, Scientizzle, Sciurinæ, Scott Dial, Scribbles02010, Ser Amantio di Nicolao, Shadowjams, Shilo2345, Shruti14, Sigmund Freud, Snigbrook, SpikeJones, Sreejithk2000, Stanlum, Steven J. Anderson, Steven Zhang, Sullyboy204, Svntnth, T-Prime85, THRintern, TJRC, Tassedethe, Tavilis, Tbhotch, Teknolyze, TenPoundHammer, Tetyl, The very last username, TheOtherJesse, Thedarxide, Thegreat100, Thejesster14, Theresa knott, ThinkBlue, TracyLinkEdnaVelmaPenny, WaKo944, Walkiped, Whiteflamez, WikiSea, Wikipediarules2221, Wookiepower2, Xsile, Yeganehaym, Zoz, 505 anonymous edits

Shrink (film) *Source*: http://en.wikipedia.org/w/index.php?oldid=464430459 *Contributors*: AnonymousAnimus, Bencey, Bovineboy2008, Bronks, DeCa MaCh, DeadlyAssassin, Djbj16, Erikire, Esceptic0, Fastilysock, Grandpafootsoldier, IvanStepaniuk, Karl gregory jones, LtMuldoon, MAXYZ1243, ManfrenjenStJohn, McGeddon, Mutinus, Nathan, Pollinosisss, RepublicanJacobite, Responsibilityveritas, Slapnuts909, SpaceFlight89, Sprintabm, Treybien, Typhoon966, Tyrannosword, Woohookitty, 36 anonymous edits

World's Greatest Dad *Source*: http://en.wikipedia.org/w/index.php?oldid=465367918 *Contributors*: Akulo, Alpha Quadrant, Artichoke-Boy, Bandstand1102, Bender235, Burmiester, C.S.Strowbridge, CalumH93, Cheddarjack, Coder Dan, Commander Keane, Dd86, Flarephoenix332, Forteblast, Francis J Schmidt, Gnowxilef, HMFS, HiDrNick, Jackie, Jay-sonluncan, Justin W Smith, Koavf, Kollision, Lugnuts, MER-C, MJBurrage, Marek69, Mikeo, MrSaturn33, NapoliRoma, Nick Number, Oronhey, ParaGreen13, R'n'B, RDBury, Richard Arthur Norton (1958-), Rwalker, Shadowjams, Skinriver, Swinterich, Tassedethe, Thatguyflint, Thurinym, Tjsocr1, Ulric1313, Varlaam, ÀrdRuadh21, 113 anonymous edits

Night at the Museum: Battle of the Smithsonian *Source*: http://en.wikipedia.org/w/index.php?oldid=465329397 *Contributors*: 2009history, ABF, Aaronjhill, Acebloo, Aldamira, Alexandru Stanoi, Alexcas11, AlienDragon, All Hallow's Wraith, Alphius, American Eagle, And1987, AndrewAllen15, Andrzejbanas, AnonMoos, Anonymous Dissident, Art1991, BD2412, Bacchus87, Bachcell, Badapro, BanjoKazooieRulz, Barosaurus Lentus, Bedford, Benatfleshofthestars, Bencey, Bender Roblox, Big Bird, Bill conery, Billyseth, Blurpeace, Bobo192, Bobyllib, Bold Clone, Bovineboy2008, Bubbleoui, Burks821, CR85747, Cameron Scott, Centurion44, Cessator, Chickenlegs501, Chris Hobeck, Chris the speller, Chris.roland, Christianster94, CocaCirca2009, Coder Dan, Commander Shepard, ConstantineChernabog, ContiAWB, Courtens, Crashdog76, Crazy4metallica, Crohnie, Cureden, DaGreenGates, Dale Arnett, Danteorange123, Darkness2005, Darrenhusted, Deanmo19, Dgoldwas, Dhabolt, DiamondDragon, Diego948, Dinokid, Djbj16, Djdannyp, DmcReif, Doc9871, Dog on flea, Donmike10, Drekscot, Dryranm, DudeBrownie, Dutzi, E and b, Eh! Steve, Elliethomson, Emily Windsnap, Enter Movie, EoGuy, Erik, Extralars, Falcon8765, Fastilysock, Ferrariguy90, Fierce Beaver, FineBabcockRosenberg212, Foofbun, FrankRizzo2006, Franpi.s, Freemenhardwick, Frodo1666, FromtheWordsofBR, GOBLUE56, GSK, GUllman, GeoWPC, Geprljn, Giantdevilfish, Goku1st, Granpuff, Gray484, Grieferhate, Gw2005, HandsomeFella, Hannu, Happy5214, Hardy1956, Hiphats, Hithere2008, Hoppybunny, Huwthehair, Hydrogen Iodide, Hyju, I Feel Tired, IJA, Inceptional637, InfamousPrince, IronGargoyle, ItsTheClimb17, Itstimeformileycyrus, Iuio, J.delanoy, JBs1VideoGirl, JDDJS, JQF, Jacksonmerritt, Jacobsnchz, Jal11497, JamesBWatson, Jamesm118, JasonDW, Jasonbres, John, Jojhutton, Jolivio, Jpbowen, Justin1276536, JuventusGamer, Karloffornia, Kbdank71, Kbtpoif, Kimberlayyyyy, Kjghjhg, Knee427, Konczewski, Ktr101, Kumioko, Kuralyov, Kuyabribri, Letmechooseaname, Liquidluck, Locos epraix, Lotsincommon, Lub-Dub-Man, Lucas.tej, Lukefan3, M.O.X, Mabeenot, Maddie1988, Manmat10, Marcos314159, MarnetteD, Martin451, Matty-chan, Melvalevis, Messenger777, Mike 41000000000, MikeWazowski, MilitHist, Mjrmtg, Mononomic, Mph703, Mr. Prez, Mr.Linderman, Mrdirector215, MuZemike, Mysdaao, Nardog, Narnia2514, NawlinWiki, Ndboy, Nechigawara, Nehrams2020, NeilN, Nellynel7619, Nicktroptopolis, Ninelon, NinjaRatchetW, Niteshift36, NorthernThunder, Nricardo, Oncamera, OpenFuture, Ophois, Orenburg1, Oxico, Parsecboy, Paulinho28, Pcuser42, Petergriffin9901, PhilKnight, Phillster578, Piano non troppo, PocketMedia, Pokerdance, Prem555, PrincessofLlyr, RadioFan, Raelle, Redeagle688, Reywas92, Rich Farmbrough, Richard Arthur Norton (1958-), Roaring Siren, Rockin56, RokinRyan, Roxas13066, Rtkat3, Rwalker, Rwe1138, Rx4evr, SHSB09, Sallicio, SassyYoshi, Sdalmonte, Sean 1118, Secret Saturdays, Seeleschneider, Sep10ber, Shaunthered, ShelfSkewed, SigKauffman, Sisko199, Sjones23, SkyWalker, Skyress1, SnakeChess5, Sparky1234567890, SpikeJones, Spongefrog, Staka, Steam5, Stepho-wrs, Stevejarrettnc, T3chl0v3r, TMC1982, TaerkastUA, Tdi7457, Teiladnam, Tennispro45, The Clawed One, The Shadow-Fighter, TheDingbat, TheMovieBuff, TheRealFennShysa, TheStrayCat, Theatrepr, Thegreat100, Themfromspace, Tomtom9041, Tubeyoumania, Typhoon966, Uncle Dick, UrukHaiLoR, Uucp, Vampus, Varlaam, Vermin2, Versus22, WesleyDodds, Whm2, WildMIKE123, Wjejskenewr, Wwoods, Ylee, Zhoos, Zzguitar14, ماني, 1236 anonymous edits

Old Dogs (film) *Source*: http://en.wikipedia.org/w/index.php?oldid=463528637 *Contributors*: A3oertENG, Alexandru Stanoi, AndrewAllen15, Angel caboodle, AnmaFinotera, Anonymous9498, Art1991, AwesomeDude898, Ben-Bopper, Bovineboy2008, Brendaninct, Cavarrone, Ccacsmss, Cheddarjack, Christianster94, Cineplex, Cirt, Cody is Awesome!, Daintiest, Danger, Dansham, Danteorange123, Danteorange2012, Darrenhusted, Dewey Finn, Djbj16, DocWatson42, DoubleBlue, Dragonmaster88, Drpickem, Eeyore7739, ErikvanB, Fieldday-sunday, Fierce Beaver, Flami72, FollowGuard, Foodrockshard, Freshh, FromtheWordsofBR, Gamester76, Garion96, German.Knowitall, Grandpafootsoldier, Horkana, Insanity Incarnate, Iohannes Animosus, ItsTheClimb17, Jabrona, Jackie1171, Jake Wartenberg, Jamesbanesmith, Javert, Jedi94, Jhsounds, Kevinbrogers, Kollision, LilHelpa, LtMuldoon, Maddie!, Mandarax, Marceki111, Mateusz5500, MaxRebo120, MikeAllen, Mikemor92, Millahnna, MiniK287, MisterYuck, MovieMan123, My New Animated Life, NeoBatfreak, Neovu79, Nicholas0, Obi-WanKenobi-2005, Onebadtown, Oxymoron83, PMDrive1061, PSP 321, QuasyBoy, Razzfan, Rjwilmsi, Roaring Siren, Rowedahelicon, Rtkat3, Scoutjd, SeibbuteletLover2009, Seibbuteletwtf(ftw), ShelfSkewed, Shicoco, Simulation90, Sivvmeister, SkyWalker, Sowhat00, Spongefrog, StangStud, Stout1070, Super Steve, Tdi7457, The Movie King!, The Rogue Penguin, The Shadow-Fighter, TheMovieBuff, TheRealFennShysa, Thegreat100, Tigerpawz, Tinton5, To play cool like that, Tomdobb, Treybien, Trivialist, Trust Is All You Need, Ulric1313, Unfinishedportrait, Unimaginable666, Vanthorn, Warreed, Wool Mintons, Zak Hammat, Ziva David, 192 anonymous edits

The Richard Pryor Show *Source*: http://en.wikipedia.org/w/index.php?oldid=460220208 *Contributors*: Bearcat, Bhumiya, BornonJune8, Bubba73, Caroldermoid, Chris814, CobraWiki, Couillaud, DStoykov, DaveK74, Drmies, Fdssdf, Fhb3, Freakofnurture, Jakz34, Kingturtle, Kmweber, Markeer, Neelix, Otto4711, Panta Section, PaulHanson, Pinkadelica, Pryorconvictions, RKJL, RepublicanJacobite, Sochwa, SymmaTree, TAnthony, TMC1982, Tengku syariful, Thiseye, Wrightaway, 41 anonymous edits

Mork & Mindy *Source*: http://en.wikipedia.org/w/index.php?oldid=463989270 *Contributors*: -OOPSIE-, A bit iffy, Aaron charles, Akira625, AnakngAraw, AnonMoos, Ariefwn, Backling, Bearcat, Beland, Belasted, Bitbut, Bjschwar, Bmrbarre, Boing! said Zebedee, Bongwarrior, BornonJune8, BostonRed, Brad, Bratsche, BrettAllen, Brettfern, Brianlane, Brittany Ka, Broquaint, Brykmantra, BuffaloChip97, CX23882-19, CambridgeBayWeather, Captain Infinity, Cath reen, Ccacsmss, CedrictheWelshDragon, Chairboy, Charlycrs, ChrisCork, Cirt, Cmdrjameson, Coastergeekperson04, CobraWiki, Collier626, Colonies Chris, Cyrano6957, DanBri, Dannyking@wikipedia.org, Darguz Parsilvan, David Gerard, DavidA, Dayewalker, Deltabeignet, Dl2000, Doin' it for the shorties, Donaldd23, Doniago, Dr. Submillimeter, Dreadstar, Dwanyewest, Dwp49423, Edititok, Eduarodi, Electricbolt, EmiOfBrie, Emurphy42, Epbr123, Eric Ceaser, Eyreland, Fabartus, Format, Frecklefoot, Freyr35, Furrykef, GRBerry, Gcapp1959, Gdo01, Geniac, Gmaspoiledbrat, Godgundam10, Gogo Dodo, GoingBatty, HelloAnnyong, Iam4Lost, IguanaScales, Iltever, Incognito9810, Irishguy, JAF1970, JHunterJ, JT72, Jaknouse, Jaldridge86, JamesClayton77, JamesReyes, Jay Firestorm, Jbl1975, Jeffq, Jfarajr, Jigen III, Jim1138, Jim856796, JimmyMcJim, Jivecat, Jmac27@aol.com, JoanneB, John wesley, Johnny Pez, Joshua1995, Joyous!, Jurqeti, Jvhertum, KConWiki, Karaveks voice, Karl the Idiot, Kchishol1970, Keeves, Kintetsubuffalo, Kyuko, Kâlî, Lady Aleena, Latka, LeonWhite, Liftarn, Lighthope, Lihaas, LilHelpa, Listener55, Love vigilante, Ludde23, Lukobe, M4gnum0n, MCBastos, Macduff, Magnius, MakeRocketGoNow, Manofradio, Manutius, Marasmusine, Mboverload, McGeddon, Mdumas43073, MegX, Mentifisto, Mike R, Moncrief, Motor, Mrblondnyc, Mrschimpf, Mrwojo, Nborof, NeilEvans, NeilN, NekoDaemon, NickBurns, Niteowlneils, Notbyworks, Oanabay04, Oliver Pereira, Pedant, Phantom2299, Philwelch, Pinkadelica, PioneerGrrrl, ProtoBuster, Radiohawk, Raiku Samiyaza, Rettetast, Reuben, Riluve, Robert Moore, Robinspoiler, Rtkat3, Ruralchest, Ryanmalik01, Sade, Savolya, Schroeder74, Sebastian1794, SidP, Skywalker80100, Slanoue, Spacepotato, Ss112, Stemonitis, Stephenb, Steveskill, TAnthony, TJF74, TMC1982, TPIRFanSteve, Tarc, Techsmith, ThatDamnDave, The GateKeeper07, The JPS, The wub, Timc, Timrollpickering, Tomknibb, Tony Sidaway, Tregoweth, Tvtonightokc, Unknown Unknowns, Val42, Vizjim, Vjamesv, Vvevo, Weregerbil, Wereon, Wheelerclown, Who, Wiki alf, Wikidan829, Wmahan, Woohookitty, Wrightaway, Wyldstaar, Xnatedawgx, Xsonda538, Zomno, 284 anonymous edits

America 2-Night *Source*: http://en.wikipedia.org/w/index.php?oldid=451282850 *Contributors*: Azumanga1, Betacommand, Cloogle12, CobraWiki, Ghosts&empties, Iamcuriousblue, Jim856796, Kingturtle, Mrblondnyc, Pegship, Pinkadelica, Rich Farmbrough, Rjwilmsi, Robert Moore, TMC1982, TPIRFanSteve, The JPS, Therefore, 10 anonymous edits

Faerie Tale Theatre *Source*: http://en.wikipedia.org/w/index.php?oldid=460628186 *Contributors*: 23skidoo, AdamDeanHall, Bearcat, Colonies Chris, Crystal il Cigno, D13399, Date delinker, Defying Gravity, Editit, Fladoodle, Goustien, Hailey C. Shannon, Hektor, Ichbinklugja, Jaconrad, Jedzz, Jeffiejeff, Jeremiah11, Kelly Martin, Killing Vector, Kouban, Lord Opeth, Lunar Jesters, MBareng, Mildew93, NawlinWiki, Penny Dreadful, Pinkadelica, ProjectPlatinum, Rjwilmsi, Sahasrahla, TMC1982, The 80s chick, Toes mctwiddle, TonyTheTiger, Ume, Wickeder90, Wwoods, 87 anonymous edits

Second City Television *Source*: http://en.wikipedia.org/w/index.php?oldid=461287098 *Contributors*: 10metreh, 23skidoo, 68Kustom, AMCKen, AdamDeanHall, Adoorajar, Ae-a, Aitch Eye, Alan smithee, AlanUS, Albiefett, Aleal, Allenk893, Anastrophe, Antmusic, Astrolatry, Azumanga1, BD2412, Bcarlson33, Bdrischbdemented, Bearcat, Beirne, Big palooka, Bjones, Bozhawk, Bratsche, Brendan Moody, Bryan Derksen, CODOR, CSWarren, Cab88, CambridgeBayWeather, CanisRufus, Capnquirky, Captain Infinity, Catapult, Chris814, Christinetaylor, Cliff1911, Co-Incidental Guy, Colonies Chris, Dainichijess, Dale Arnett, Daniel Benfield, Danielhouse, Dante Alighieri, Danthemankhan, Davehi1, Deacon of Pndapetzim, Demon blazer, Denelson83, Dhodges, Dirwuf, Dl2000, Doubter, Dr Erick, DropDeadGorgias, Drunkenpeter99, Ds13, Dtremenak, Dual Freq, Dubkiller, Dunks58, Dysepsion, DéRahier, EAderhold, Emaf, EmiOfBrie, Emurphy42, Epolk, Ergative rlt, Eric Burns, Eric119, Esasus, FMAFan1990, Fernandobouregard, Freefry, Freshacconci, Gaius Cornelius, GrandpaPap, Greg Salter, Ground Zero, Gtrmp, Guffawing Crow, Gyrofrog, HDS, Henry Flower, Hiphats, Hotspur, Howenstein115, Hydroxonium, Iam4Lost, Ianking, Ianthegecko, Infrogmation, Ironass, JB82, JCPClevo, JForget, JLaTondre,

JMyrleFuller, Jakesy34, Jeffreykopp, Jgm, Joegoodfriend, Johnny Pez, Josh Parris, Jpeeling, Julesd, KatefanO, Kchishol1970, Kevlar67, Koavf, L0b0t, LWG, LancasterII, Landroo, Lawyer2b, M1ss1ontomars2k4, MJBurrage, MWielage, Mahatma Randy, Marcmus, Mario500, MattAM4, McCart42, McGeddon, Mike hayes, Minaker, Mlc1958, Mokwella, Morkis, Moxy, Mr. Chicago, Mrblondnyc, Mrschimpf, Mtstroud, Muckapedia, Murphymc, Musimax, Nehrams2020, NekoDaemon, NellieBly, Neschek, NickZ, Ninten, Nuwriter, Oakjoan, Ohnoitsjamie, Open2universe, Ottawahitech, Pjedicke, Planetneutral, Prokopenya Viktor, PsychoJason, Pwgus, QuasyBoy, Rayzuquin, Rdash, RedWolf, Robert Moore, Rogerd, Rolypolyman, Rudyardk, Scani, Scorpion0422, Sctvguide, Sdp, Sewing, Shark96z, Shrodingerskitty, Shsilver, SidP, Spot87, SteinbDJ, Stereorock, SteveHFish, Steven J. Anderson, Stickguy, TGC55, TMC1982, Tabletop, Tassedethe, Telestylo, Threerandot, Timc, Timvasquez, Tobycat, Toddsschneider, Togi55, Troiscoins, Tvtonightokc, Twintone, Two halves, Tzittnan, Unreal7, Vbartilucci, Vegaswikian, WAJWAJ, Wahoo76, Wbwn, WikiDolenz, Woohookitty, YUL89YYZ, Yossarian, Zanimum, Zxcsde, 341 anonymous edits

A Wish for Wings That Work *Source*: http://en.wikipedia.org/w/index.php?oldid=465203116 *Contributors*: Alientraveller, Alison22, Belovedfreak, Chowbok, Czolgolz, Dravecky, Dynamite XI, Good Olfactory, Hammon27, Hiding, JaDangerz, Jenblower, John of Reading, Loggie, MaJic, Majorclanger, MakeRocketGoNow, Miszal3, Murgh, Novalis, Pegship, Rich Farmbrough, Skier Dude, Stefanomione, TenPoundHammer, Trivialist, Ulric1313, VolatileChemical, WhisperToMe, Wool Mintons, 41 anonymous edits

The Larry Sanders Show *Source*: http://en.wikipedia.org/w/index.php?oldid=464102406 *Contributors*: 23skidoo, AaronPaige, AaronY, Adduke, Agnosticraccoon, Andrewlp1991, Annifridfour, AnonMoos, Arkan67, Asc85, Aspects, Barmy Fotheringay-Phipps, Baseball Bugs, Bdegfcunbbfv, Beardo, Before My Ken, Bencey, Benscripps, Beyond My Ken, Bgautrea, Bobtoomey, Bodnotbod, Bogswallop, Bwithh, CAN, CCKyle, CR85747, CanadianCaesar, Ceoil, Ch'marr, Ched Davis, Chris the speller, Chriscooperlondon, Citymovement, Classicswatchtv, Clerks, Cliff1911, CobraWiki, Colonies Chris, ContiAWB, Coullj, DANZIG666, Darrenhusted, Davidcx, DeadDeers, Delldot, Discospinster, Drunkenpeter99, Dubkiller, Duke33, Dunks58, EEMIV, Ed g2s, Erik9, Eugenian, Eye of the Mind, Fernandobouregard, Fosibodu, GMc, Gareth Aus, Gareth E Kegg, Generally Sentient, Gmaspoiledbrat, GoorooV, Grafen, Harley Hudson, Hey Teacher, Hotstreets, ISD, Iam4Lost, Ianblair23, Iohannes Animosus, Ipragér, JForget, JLaTondre, JMyrleFuller, Jack Cox, Jeremy Butler, Jevansen, Jlouise311, JoanneB, JoeCool59, Joemac5367, John Fader, John of Reading, Jordgette, Junglecinema, JustAGal, Jxan3000, Kaihsu, Kaizenyorii, Kbtv123, Koavf, Kronecker, Kâlî, LMorland, Lee M, LeilaniLad, Lew19, LilHelpa, Livefastdieold, MER-C, MakeRocketGoNow, Martarius, Marty2Hotty, Matthew Woodcraft, Mboverload, Mchstream688, Meco, Mickturbo, Mike Rosoft, Mike1971inter, Mikeyj962, Mr. Brain, MrWeeble, Mrblondnyc, NWill, NickBush24, Noaya.v, Nova Prime, Occono, P4k, Pablo X, Pat Berry, Pawnkingthree, Peanutcactus, Phil Bastian, Phoampiper, Pinkville, Plastic editor, PrimeHunter, Quentin X, Qutezuce, R.A Huston, RalfiParpa, ReXorcist, Rebroad, Recognizance, Registered user 92, Retropolis1, Rhino8888, Rich257, Richardcavell, Rjwilmsi, Rogerd, Ronhjones, Royote, Saikokira, Sanfranfan88, Sfpesq, Shamrox, Sheilnaik, Shelly1986, Silent Tom, Skykevah, Skylights76, Skywalker80100, Slanoue, Slowmover, Sonicsean89, Sottolacqua, Squandermania, Stamfordlion08, Stephen Bain, Stephenb, Straussian, Stx423, SubSeven, Suffusion of Yellow, SummerWithMorons, SuperFlash101, Symplectic Map, TMC1982, TPIRFanSteve, Tabletop, Telestylo, The GateKeeper07, The JPS, The Moose, Thebogusman, ThunderPeel2001, TimidObserver, TonyTheTiger, Trusilver, Turkeyphant, Tvtonightokc, UDScott, VarlosZ, VolatileChemical, Vslashg, WCityMike, Wapcaplet, Wayman975, Wikipedical, Wocky, Xezbeth, YUL89YYZ, Yoshi64, Yossarian, 爆笑運合, 460 anonymous edits

Homicide: Life on the Street *Source*: http://en.wikipedia.org/w/index.php?oldid=464852544 *Contributors*: ABCxyz, AOC25, Aillema, Alpha Quadrant, AndrewJKD, AndrewWickliffe, ApathyMonger, Aristophanes68, Assawyer, Aude, AussieLegend, AxelBoldt, BD2412, Bearcat, Before My Ken, Bellhalla, BierHerr, Bjones, Blake-, Bloomy, Bovineboy2008, Brad, Briaboru, Brunton, Buddemeyer, Budman08, Bwithh, CR85747, Chetvorno, Chimino, Chris the speller, Chupaboy2002, Ckatz, Clancy60, Cmdrjameson, CobraWiki, Coffee, Comicist, Conradege, CoolKatt number 99999, Cordrym, Cravergay, D Monack, Dale Arnett, DanDud88, Dauster, DavidLevinson, Daysleeper47, Detective Bayliss, Dhartung, Djln, DocWatson42, Don't Feed the Pie Man, Donny, Dputig07, Drunkenpeter99, Dual Freq, Duoraven, Dwdmang, EMPY, Econrad, EdwinHJ, Eliz81, Ericamick, FMAFan1990, Fbb fan, Fleming60, Fourthords, Freticat, Froid, GMc, GoingBatty, Grammaticus Repairo, Groovemaneuvers, Grutness, Gtown1968, GusF, Hades6483ny, Hammersfan, Harley Hudson, Hattrem, Hlotslinks, Hooluvsya, Hunter Kahn, Iam4Lost, Indrian, IndulgentReader, J Greb, JHCC, JHunterJ, JaGa, James26, Jarry1250, Jeandré du Toit, Jeff Muscato, Jimaking, Joanberenguer, Johnbillups, JordoCo, Joseph Q Publique, Juggler2005, KConWiki, Kbdank71, Khaosworks, Kleb t, Krash, Kusma, Langston Bonasera, Lisasmall, Logan Barek, Lordz, Lvr, MBK004, Magnet For Knowledge, MakeRocketGoNow, Malik Shabazz, MarnetteD, Martial75, Marysunshine, Massofspikes, Matthew, MatthewTStone, Mboverload, MegastarLV, MetatagDeVries, Michael Rawdon, Mika1h, Milch78, Minaker, Mistat94, Mister Six, Movementarian, Mrblondnyc, Mudwater, Munnp001, Natty4bumpo, Necessary Evil, Nehrams2020, Netoholic, Newkirk Plaza David, Nlu, Oatmeal batman, Ohconfucius, Oknazevad, Open2universe, Paralympic, PatBrennan, Pb30, Phydend, Piledhigheranddeeper, Polynova, PrePressChris, ProperlyRaised, RainbowOfLight, Raja99, Realrap, Redfarmer, RepublicanJacobite, Rich Farmbrough, Richard75, RickNomai, Ricky81682, Rizzoli Isles, Rlquall, Roadrunner3000, RockRNC, RoyBatty42, ScreenwriterJeb, Sdornan, ShelfSkewed, Skomorokh, Skywalker80100, Spikeballs, Spotteddogsdotorg, Squalk25, Stangbat, Stephenyoxall29, Stilgar135, Stubblyhead, T. Anthony, T@nn, TAnthony, TMC1982, Tallyho70, Teiladnam, The Earwig, The GateKeeper07, The JPS, The Lake Effect, TheMovieBuff, Thebogusman, Thefourdotelipsis, Theoldanarchist, ThomasK, Tony1, Ttenchantr, UDScott, UltimatePyro, UtherSRG, Vi Veri Veniversum Vivus Vici, Vincelord, WOSlinker, WWB, Wadems, Wellesradio, Wernher, Wildhartlivie, Woohookitty, Wwoods, Yu homicide, ZPM, Zeus, 592 anonymous edits

Life with Bonnie *Source*: http://en.wikipedia.org/w/index.php?oldid=439394941 *Contributors*: 0555, AndrewJKD, Anthony Appleyard, Bovineboy2008, Bunchofgrapes, Canderson7, Ckatz, CraWill, Danigro89, Dina, Enigmaman, Havul Anigav, Hira Virk, IanManka, Ibanez RYM, JYi, Jimmy, Lightdarkness, Loansince, Luna Santin, M Vallee, MOOOOOPS, Matthew, Milton Stanley, OffsBlink, Open2universe, Pinkadelica, QuasyBoy, Ragmen, Robert Moore, Salamurai, SchuminWeb, Senkris, Sgeureka, Sky Captain, SpikeZoft, StuartBrewer, TJ Reyes, The JPS, The wub, TonyTheTiger, Wereon, Wikitoddia, 57 anonymous edits

Mind of Mencia *Source*: http://en.wikipedia.org/w/index.php?oldid=460678141 *Contributors*: 1 wit da force, 293.xx.xxx.xx, 98E, ??lostiNconfusIoN??, A Daffy Duck, ACSE, AKB10, ASDFGHJKL, Abidel, Adam1090, Adn486, Adolphus79, Affluent Rider, AgentPeppermint, Alansohn, Alasdair, Alefu, Alex248, Andrew Parodi, AndrewJKD, Andrewlp1991, Andy120290, Anetode, AnonGuy, Arctic.gnome, Areya, Ariasne, Astronomy Divine, AxiomShell, Bacteria, Barneca, Baseballimillion, Bdve, Betaeleven, BigD79, Bigolfish, Biker Biker, BlueLotusLK, Bob98133, Boccobrock, Bonadea, Bongwarrior, Boomtown Rat, Bovineboy2008, Brat32, Braves fan10, BreadLand, Brittonware, Browngorilla, Btty2154, Bueller 007, CMJMEM, CTZMSC3, CambridgeBayWeather, Can't sleep, clown will eat me, CaptainFalcon23, Careless hx, Chamal N, Chillllls, Chipangalokes, ChristopherM, Chunky Rice, Cirosan, Classic rocker, Closedmouth, Computerjoe, Comrade438, ConCompS, Couch potato365, Covingtons, Craig t moore, Crash Underride, Cubs Fan, CyrilB, DJ BatWave, DJac75, DSRH, DVD R W, Damir H., DanielCD, Danigro89, Danny1234567, Danny13, Dano135, Danski14, Davidboley, DiamondDragon, Donkathankyou, Douglasr007, Download, Dreadpiratetif, DuKot, Dugwiki, EddieVanZant, Enigmaman, Epbr123, Euphrosyne, Eviljake360, Explicit, Extransit, F.Barrera, Falcon8765, Falseikon, Faradayplank, Fastswimguy, Feitclub, Fernandobouregard, Flashpenny, Floyd09, GVOLTT, Gaius Cornelius, Gamer928, Gameworldduelist2, Gdo01, Geneshallet, Gert7, Ghostprincess, GoingBatty, Graham87, Grandpallama, Gurch, Gyrorobo, Hasimweezy, Heimstern, HelloAnnyong, Hellomeanshello, ILovePlankton, Iamgreat66, Ibanez RYM, Illnab1024, Inclusivedisjunction, Inka 888, Interiot, Iokerapid, Isis4563, J.delanoy, JHP, Jackryan, JakeV, Jaman013, Jbarnes2, Jeffrey O. Gustafson, Jenniferlbridges, Jersyko, Jesus107, Jmlk17, Jmw0000, Joeyramoney, Joffeloff, Jorcoga, Josh471776, Jossi, JuJube, Jusdafax, KConWiki, KING Vernon, Kane Freak8, Karasuhebi, Kdhilst, KevboJH, Kevinwells, Kidlittle, KimboSlice, Kirrages, Koavf, Krashkorse, L337p4wn, Lando242, Lawikitejana, LeaveSleaves, Legolasss, LinoPop, LizardJr8, Lord Ed, Lord Oblivion, Luna Santin, MBK004, Madhero88, Magister Mathematicae, MannyShiznit, Marviiin g, Materialscientist, Mattbillows, MattieTK, Maxwell7985, Mbc362, Megalodon99, Michael Greiner, MiguelRL, Mistercow, Moe Epsilon, Mojska, Mr. Gas Mask, Mr. Lefty, Mrgreen520, Mschel, Msh210, MuZemike, Mystikranger, N419BH, N5iln, NY4INFO, NY4Life, Nakon, Nantoz, Ncasci, Ned Holness, Newager, Newsaholic, Nhprman, Nick Bond, NickCT, NickW557, Nikki311, Nneonneo, Nograv, NordicStorm, Nosaints4life, Not1337, Nutster, Omicronpersei8, OneTopJob6, Overthinkingly, OwenX, Oxymoron83, PSROXB, Parcequilfaut, Pearle, Peter Chastain, Peter Karlsen, Phearson, Pinkadelica, Pinoyartist99, Pit-yacker, Precious Roy, Preeeemo, PrestonH, Producercunningham, Propalicious, Protonk, Quintote, Qworty, R. fiend, RA0808, RJASE1, RJFJR, RainbowOfLight, Rayy49, Reach Out to the Truth, Reaper Eternal, Rettetast, RexNL, Reywas92, Ricky81682, Rjwilmsi, Rollinman, Ronhjones, Rosing95, Rsm99833, S.A.B.Z, SPPV, Saget53, Salis60, Salvio giuliano, Satan son666, Schrodinger82, Seaphoto, Sekort Sev Lewt, Senner, Seraphim, Seresin, Sess44, Sesu Prime, Sgt. boxx, ShadowZach, Shanes, Shoeofdeath, SidP, Skyline63, Sleeperhold24, Sliker Hawk, Someoneinmyheadbutit'snotme, SorryGuy, Soundtrackzz, SouthParkAdmirer, Spellmaster, SpyMagician, Stoph, Super bean187, SxeFluff, Sylent, SystemPatch, THEN WHO WAS PHONE?, TITROTU, TMC1982, TakerLives, Tassedethe, TenPoundHammer, Tgunner, Thatguyulove, The undertow, Thebluesharpdude, Thechampishere91, Thecheesykid, Thedjatclubrock, Thedudezor, Thingg, Thumperward, Thunder Wolf, Tide rolls, Tikiwont, TimBrock, Tizona1, Tom-Tom, Travelbird, TreacherousWays, Triscafoole, Tromboneplayer, Tupac13th, Tuspm, Useight, Vanished User 1004, Velella, Versus22, Voyagerfan5761, WadeSimMiser, Wadems, Warzarmz, Wickedsick001, WikHead, Wiki render, WikiDao, Wikibout, Wrestlinglover, Wtmitchell, Wwtfchampnumero1, Wysprgr2005, Yancyfry jr, Z4ngetsu, Zone46, Zscout370, Zsinj, Шизомби, 1056 anonymous edits

Law & Order: Special Victims Unit (season 9) *Source*: http://en.wikipedia.org/w/index.php?oldid=460509071 *Contributors*: Adamfinmo, Akerans, AussieLegend, BLGM5, BLGM7, BabyGirl91, BakerBaker, BattleshipMan, Beardo, Boo1210, Brainscar, Caleiva, Ccacsmss, CharlotteWebb, Chickie4, CobraWiki, Courcelles, DanDud88, Davejohnsan, DavianThule, DocWatson42, Drmargi, Drunkenpeter99, F, Gahks, Garion96, Gravidef, Grsz11, Grundle2600, Highspeed, Jamdonaldson, Jetong, Ladida, Lowellian, Mathew5000, MelbourneStar, Mgfan222, MikeAllen, Mistat94, Moonriddengirl, Mr. Laser Beam, Naraht, Nishkid64, Ohconfucius, Ozzieboy, Pascal666, Plastikspork, QuasyBoy, Redfarmer, Rgmofnyc, Rmd1023, Rocafella, SVU4671, Staffwaterboy, Takeit10, Talix, Tassedethe, Terraskye, TestPilot, TheEnterprise, Ulric1313, WikiJunkie13, Wrightaway, 141 anonymous edits

SpongeBob SquarePants *Source*: http://en.wikipedia.org/w/index.php?oldid=464661605 *Contributors*: -000, .:Alex:., 00Ladyluck00, 01kkk, 041744, 12elleman, 13mullja, 1620050, 1bigj, 1oddbins1, 1q2w3e4r, 32e6bw, 451-r, 744cody, 76df457hjkozdfg, 989soccer, 98E, A, A Softer Answer, A legend, A.t.360, A2-computist, ABC1356msep1, ACV777, AJL1957, AMK152, AOB, ASDFGHJKL, ATC, AThing, Aa35te, Aamirrobinson, Abby724, Abc210, Abce2, Abney317, AbneySBN, Abrightcoldday, Abu Amal Bahraini, Academic Challenger, Ace4135, Acecombatant, Acmilan10italia, Acrazyguy, Adamski24, Addict 2006, AdultSwim, Aesopos, Ag97, Agent-347, Agent4453, AgentCDE, AgentPeppermint, Ahoerstemeier, Aikidockd, Aiman abmajid, Aiman619, AirLiner, Airhogs777, Airmario3, Ais523, Aitias, Ajdawg27, Al1976, Alansohn, Albert wesker, Albion69, Alex Lindell, Alex cartmen, Alfakim, Allmightyduck, Alpha Quadrant (alt), Alphachimp, Alphasqd7, Alstinsono, Aluisios, Alumni, Aminullah, Amy523, AndreniW, Andrew Hampe, Andrewrox, Andvari7, Andy M. Wang, Andycjp, AngelicEnigma, Anger-Cola, Angrydad101, Angusmcr, AniRaptor2001, Anilocra, Animum, Anirvan, Annonymousmaniaciii, Anomenat, Anonymi, Anonymous editor, Anonymous from the 21st century, Answar, AnteaterZot, Antonrojo, Antoshi, Aperiodic, Aphid360, Apofisu, Apostrophe, Apothecia, Apple1013, AppleKid2424, Arcadie, Arctic Night, ArglebargleIV, Armageddon1994, Arniep, Arthurtran, Arubaman14, Ashleshrocks94, Ashleyy osaurus, Ashmurthy, Ashury, Aspensti, Aspirex, AstrOace, Atlantima, Atomicpuffball, AuburnPilot, Aude, AussieLegend, Autobahnsho, Avala, AvatarDude, Aviator1141, Aviturner2, Awesome93, Awesomecakes, Awesomeguyman, Ayrton Prost, AzaToth, Azcollect, Azncommunist198, BD2412, BF153, BNSF1995, BOB358, BREMANTE, Baa, Bac2futurfan, Back to the Past 23, Badboy 365, Bagpipeturtle, Banana7070, Bantosh, Bart133, Barticus88, Bartman1776, Basilisk4u, Batman tas, Bb1, Bbabybear02, Bbatsell, BeanyFans, Bearcat, Bearsfootball516, Beatlesnicole, Beefball, Belfour owns, Belovedfreak, Ben k., Bender235, Betacommand, Betos00, Bevo, Bgnkid, Big Bad Baby, Big Bird, Bill,

Bill Conrad, Billinghurst, Binglebongle2000, Binksternet, BioYu-Gi!, Bippo Ernesti, Birdy541, Bitbit, Black Falcon, Blackbone 5000, Blackjack48, Blackwatch21, BlazeTheMovieFan, Blubbermarble, BlueCaper, BlueMario1016, Bly1993, Bmcnabb, Bob 2.0, Bob2276, Bobber1, Bobblewik, Bobbyboy248, Bobet, Bobfilling, Bobisbob2, Bobo192, Boing! said Zebedee, Bok269, Bolt, Bomac, Bonadea, Bongwarrior, Bonusballs, Boogieshmoo, BookDen, Booksrule9, Boomchakanaka101, BorgQueen, Born2killx, Boss1000, Bovineboy2008, Bowser, King of the Koopas, Bowserkid24, Bowsy, Boxstaa, Boznia, Brad, Bradeos Graphon, Brainulator9, Brandon J. Marcellus, Brandon Marcellus, Brat32, BrawlerJ E 1300, Brawlmantis80, Brenda Jackson, Brian radon1, Brilliand, Brisbane99, Britain97, BritishWatcher, Brittonshayne, Brooktree, Brucelee1224, Bryankreutz 77, Buh6173, Bulldog73, Bun39, Burger32, Burner0718, Burntsauce, Butros, Buttle, Buzhwa2001, Bwanatoto, ByteofKnowledge, C12H22O11, C1k3, CBFan, CFCF, CJ2005B, CJS102793, CQJ, CRWXT, Cactus.man, Caitlizzle, Calaxa, Calc93, Caldorwards4, Caleson, Calicore, Caltas, CalvinRocksMySocks, Cammador, Camw, Can't sleep, clown will eat me, Canderson7, Canihuan300, Canuckguy, Cap777, Capitalistroadster, Cappio, Captain Infinity, Captain Insano shows no mercy, Captain elmo, Captaindisturbo, Captainpancreas, Carly1376, Carmelapple, Carol Bold, CarolGray, Caroline Sanford, CartoonNetworkFan100, CartoonSpot121, Casey906262, Casper182, Casper2k3, Cat's Tuxedo, CatMan, Catgaard, Cats2, CattleMan, Cedders, Celestra, Cellmate27, Cerpintaxt12, Chairboy, Championnumber1, Changer32, Chanlyn, Chantessy, Chapnzaba, CharCharOverOver11, Chaser, Chazzy17773, Cheeseisgood4539, Cheggsrgood, Chemicalrubber, CherryFlavoredAntacid, Chet nc, Chewparka, ChicosBailBonds, Chikinpotato11, Chitala, Chowdit, Chris the speller, Chris83, ChrisP2K5, Chrislk02, Chrismaster1, Christopher Parham, Christopherwils, Cineplex, Citicat, Ckatz, Claimgoal, Clamster5, Clamztheman123, ClapBoy380, Clarkburkhardt, Classicalfan2, Clconway, Cleavon B., Clintville, Clock clock, Clubpenguinclubpenguin, Cmitch, CoJaBo, Coastergeekperson04, Cocoaguy, Coderedck, Codetheshu, Coldguy78, Colinsweet, Comicbook30, Commando303, CommonsDelinker, Computer97, ComradeBilbo, Conman666, Connor mezza, Connorflanagan, Contortrix, Cookie81923, Cool aire of 1998, Cool545, Coolboy11, Coolboy818, Cooldood703, Coolsprings, Corpx, Cortexcrashfluff, Cory pratt, Cousin Yugi, CovenantD, Cpaliga, Crablogger, Craigaswartout, Crazy Fox, CrazyLegsKC, Crazycomputers, Crazygreg55, Crypter24k, Cryptic, Crypticfirefly, Crystallina, Cssiitcic, Curlyro, Curps, Curtmack, CyberTech-100, Cyberface, D-Day, DARTH SIDIOUS 2, DBZGirl, DJ Clayworth, DJ WikiBob, DJ0215997, DJ1AM, DTM, DaProx, Dachannien, Dachshundboy25, DaichiS4815162342, Damicatz, Dan D. Ric, Dan East, DanGer JuLeS, Dangerandrew, Daniel Carrero, Danigro89, Danny8247, Dannycas, Dared111, Dark Tichondrias, DarkAdonis255, DarkMario91, DarkXWeatherX, DarknessLord, Darkrokker224, Darkside 88, Darkvaughn, Darkwhistle, Darth Goku, Darth Jadious, Darth Knight, Darth Mike, Darthdj31, Dascott, Dashana, Dave1722, Davehi1, Daverocks, DavidApi, Davidizer13, Davidmaxwaterman, Davidvs1st, De Boni 2007, DeadEyeArrow, Deathsquad53, Deena237, Degenerate-Y, Dekkanar, Delandoffrance, Delcity, Deli nk, Delldot, Delo666, Dennis Brown, Dennisjiewenliu, DennyColt, Der4, DerHexer, Derek R Bullamore, Deutschgirl, Dharssan123, Dictionarygirl137, Digifiend, Dillmister, Dillonlaw, DisMupp, Disciple of Colbert, Discospinster, Disney avatar, Disneyadventurernicholas, DjRanger37, Djpwnzorz, Dmarex, DobbyD, Doctorindy, Doikhoikin, Dokortd, Dollarsindata, Dolphinbub19, Dolphonia, Doman12, Dominic, Dommico, Donbodo, Doodoobutter, Doodoodoo, Dooly00000, DoomsDay349, Dopar, Dough4872, Douglas12, Dpm12, DrChristmas, Drashleymorris, Dream Focus, Drewdy, Drfsupercenter, Drilnoth, DriveMySol, Drm1026, Drop of Soul, Drunkenpeter99, Dryke, Dskluz, Dtp882, Duckduck96, Duckeboy, Dude78, Dudemanjazz, DuoDeathscyther 02, Dusta619, Dusty Nenman, Dwonderful, Dxtrfn80, Dylan620, Dylan6758, DynamoDegsy, EVIL!, Earteaga97, East718, Easter Monkey, Ebo707, Eci bulldawg1608, EdC, Editfriendly22, Edrainkona, Eelyworm, Effer, Egwoestman, Eh! Steve, ElKevbo, Elassint, ElementalKnight, Elephant whispers, Elil, Elinews, Elkman, Elofan, ElphabaThropp95, Eltigremania, Emir34, Emmysq, EnglishEfternamn, Enigmatic2k3, EntertainU, Enviroboy, EoGuy, Ep347, Epson291, Eqdoktor, Erebus555, Ericeee10, Ericguttormson, Erik9, Erock23432, EronMain, Erwkern3, Esanchez7587, Escape Orbit, EscapingLife, Essjay, Eubulides, EurekaLott, Evan1109, Evanellis2, Everyking, Evilguy, EvocativeIntrigue, Excirial, ExtraordinaryMan, Extremecheese, F1Krazy, Fahrenme, Falconleaf, Fang Aili, Fangusu, Farvin111, Fashnek, Fastily, Fastlane250, FayssalF, Felixboy, FerretBrains, Fikricoban, Firegnome, Firsfron, Fishcake15, FisherQueen, Fixer 20.0, FlaminChar, Flamingspinach, Flapdragon, Flare13, FlareNUKE, Flcelloguy, Fluzwup, Flyguy649, Flyoffacliff, ForestH2, Forum User, Fowen123, Fragglet, Frank Anchor, FrankCostanza, Frantzedward.cha, Fred Bradstadt, FredFredBurger88, Freedomeagle, Freeleet, Freemenhardwick, Frit, FromtheWordsofBR, FrozenPurpleCube, FuelTiger, Funkalucious, Funneegurl4, Funnyboy240, Funnybunny, Furbytubby, Furbytubby2, Furrykef, GMc, GV39, GVOLTT, GVnayR, Gab.popp, Gabriel mark, Gagoy, Gail, Gaius Cornelius, Games97, GangstaEB, Gardevoir11, Gary King, Gatorademan, Gaunter, Gavri, GaylordHopscotch, Gazpacho, Gdo01, Ged UK, Geg, Geneb1955, General456, George2001hi, GeorgeMoney, Georgehoward, Gerdel, Germanbini, Ghujik, Gilgamesh, Gill Giller Gillerger, Gilliam, Gizwidget, Gjd001, Glass Sword, GloriousLeader, Gnangarra, Gnfnrf, Godfart02, Gogo Dodo, GoingBatty, Gojira09, Goldbook, Goofgoobers, Goofygoobers, Goombapatrol, Gopal81, GordyHowell, Got118115147, GraemeL, Grammaticus Repairo, Granpuff, Grayshi, GrdScarabe, Greatmilenko43, Greenwolfzero, Gregorof, GroovySandwich, Groudon199, Grunty14, Gscshoyru, Gtbob12, Gtg204y, Guilty504cmk, Gupper1, Gurch, Gusworld, Gwernol, Gyrferret, HBow3, Hadger, Hahnchen, Hall Monitor, Hammersoft, HanaSolo, HanyouAlchemist, Haon 2.0, Happy5214, Happyme22, Haroldpennywink, Harry Blue5, Hchrishicks, Hearts of clear lake, Heimstern, HeirToPendragon, Heli12, Hellevision123, Hellokity, HenryBurkenstein, Hessamnia, Hey Teacher, Hi123987, Hibernian, Hithere2008, Ho0d, Holiday56, HollyAm, Holothurion, Homewrecker27, Honey Bee Real, Hope(N Forever), Hoppybunny, HorseGirl070605, Hrwiki, Hsnrcool, Hugh Jass, Hugo999, Husond, Huwbwici, Hypershock, I dream of horses, I want a big stereo, IFuZiONI, Iago4096, Ibdania, Icelandic Hurricane, Icep, Idol 2006, Ieph, Iiariah, Ik.pas.aan, Ikiwi99929, Ilikepie2221, Ilmari Karonen, Iluvmesodou, Im A Shark, Immblueversion, Imnotminkus, Impala99, Imroy, In America!, In-Correct, InShaneee, Independents for Truth, Indium, InfallibleRoxi, Info845, Infrogmation, Inkybutton, Insanity Incarnate, Intelati, Inter16, Interchange88, Interrobang², Invader SpongeBob, Invertzoo, Invinciman, Ipso2, Iridescent, IsaacAA, Islander, IstvanWolf, Itsame, Ixfd64, Izaic3, J Di, J.delanoy, J04n, J3wishVulcan, JDoorjam, JHunterJ, JL93, JLaTondre, JMBZ-12, JMcQuire, JMyrleFuller, JNeal, JWSCIS, Jacek Kendysz, Jack 6428, Jack Bz, Jack9293, Jacob1a2b3c, JacobS, Jacobsaunders1993, Jaden2555, Jaimie Henry, Jake34567, Jakeiyounis2, James086, JamesBWatson, JamesBurns, Jan0195, JaneDaw, Janejellyroll, Janke, Jared34, Jaredthomas, JasonXV, Jasonbres, JavierMC, Jaxl, Jay, Jay Firestorm, Jaybenad, Jb007ltkill, Jchally, Jdh94, Jdjd021, Jdlddw, Jdylan, Jeandré du Toit, Jeff G., Jeff3000, Jefffire, Jeffro100, Jefftheman45, Jeremie@theLab, Jeremy.Sanders, Jermerc, Jerry, Jerrysmp, Jess567, Jesuschrist120, Jetblue2, Jf froese, Jharp07, Jhkgf, Jibajabba, Jimmy8593, Jj98, Jjack66, Jkfp2004, Jmbaechle, Jmlk17, JoeDawgJAC, Joedeshon, Joekid, Joekid23334, John, John Reaves, John Smith (test), JohnCD, JohnathanChiotti, Johnnycobra, Jon Doh, Jon186, Jonathanledgard555, Jonghyunchung, Jonnytaylor, Jonohill, Jonthestrummer, Jorgito0246, Joseph Fleisher, Joshua H-Star-R, Joshua36, Joshweiser, Jossi, Jpark3909, Jslynch, Jsmaye, Jspyster1, Ju66l3r, Judgeking, Juhachi, Jujutacular, Juliancolton, June1998, Jusdafax, JustWong, JustaDAH!fan, Justaskme96, Justin Eiler, Justinhful, KATkanga, KEITH567, KFP, KGasso, KH1MOVIE, Kagome 77, Kakaru kl, Kalo150, Kanabekobaton, Kane1047, Kangy, Kaobear, Kaoruchan, Katy,Girl, Kawaiisaffy, Kazvorpal, Kcrooks728, Kechie, Keilana, KeithH, Kelly Martin, Kenneth Hardeman, Kennytheboywonder, Keraunoscopia, Kesac, KevboJH, Kevosaraus Rex, Keyblade, Kglaser, Khaoz 0, Kidlittle, Kildareuser, Kimera Kat, King of Hearts, KingBubbaWii24, KingNeptune2, Kingboyk, Kingpin13, Kinkadjou, Kinneyboy90, KinseyLOL, Kirkad0021, Kirkgaard, Kitty398, KittyKo'sCute, Kjammer, Kjbleu, Kjinho213, Klewung, Kman1320, Kman543210, Kmaster22, Kmccoy, Knockout27, Kontikikev, Konzack, Kornfan71, Krazymonkee72, Krich, Ktn1, Kubigula, Kui97, Kukini, Kuratowski's Ghost, Kuru, Kyle Barbour, Kyle1081, Kyle1278, Kylexy289, L arts hater08, LAPS, LBM, La Pizza11, Lahiru k, Landfish7, LawerenceSmit, Lazlo25, Leader Vladimir, Leaderofearth, Legedevin, Legendarydairy, Leifanator, Lemonflash, Lenin and McCarthy, Leonard^Bloom, Leowan, Lesliepear, Lessthanthree, Leszek Jańczuk, Letter 7, Lewis odane, Lightdarkness, Lima bean of the north, Limetolime, LindsayH, Ling.Nut, Lita5dozen, LittleRoughRhinestone, Live Light, Lizziebabes90, Loadmaster, Lolsponge, LongBay, Longebane, Longhair, Lord Jarrod, Lord Moe, Lordhawkins, Louieais, LovesMacs, Lpfan117, Luckybolt, Ludo716, Luigi128, Luigi30, Luizalves, Luk, Luke Farrelly-Spain, Lumarine, Luminifer, Luna Santin, Lussiersister, LutherBifteck, Luvinchicken45692, Luvtheheaven, Lwalt, Lyle Piratehog IV, M477, MC Goggles, MDPP, MER-C, MJ94, Macellarius, Machchunk, Macintosh User, Mactrac, Madchester, Madhero88, Magegg, Magical StarSign, Magister Mathematicae, Magiwand, Makowsky, Makron1n, Malcolm, Mamajama690, Mandarax, Mangomaster501, Mannschaftskapitän, Mannyyo, Manop, ManwhichGirl2012, Marcellusb, Marcus2, Marek69, Marink, Mariogamer15, Marioluigi98, Marioman22, MarkGallagher, Markebson, Markogarza, Marktwain6991, Markwarnes, MarshallF, Martial75, Masonshowalter, Mastrchf91, Matema, Matt0401, Maxaradius, Maxheritage, Maxim, Maxl, Mazca, McGeddon, Mcrteen13, MeLstaRR, Meaningful Username, Meaty85203, Meatyking, Mecool12, MegX, MegastarLV, Melnorme, Mentality, Merumerume, Mervn, Metropolitan90, Meursault2004, Mewtwowimmer, Mfowler11, Mgangku, Mgfan22, Mgradz, Michael Devore, Michael93555, MichaelMaggs, Micromaster, MightyWarrior, Mike Dillon, Mike Foker, Mike Rosoft, Mike s, Mike45555, MikeVitale, Mikeman4510, Miketyler2010, MilfordBoy991, Milklover44566, MindWraith, Minna Sora no Shita, Minnesota1, Misgnomer, MissingNo11, Mister macphisto, Mmx1, Mnbvcxzmnbvcxzmnbvcxzmnbvcxz, Mobo85, ModerateTy, Moe Epsilon, Mohamed Ishan, Mokoniki, Moncrief, Monkeyboy12310, Monkeys 9711, Montana's Defender, Montchav, Moojgoo, MosheA, MotherFerginPrincess, Mr Kupo, Mr. Krabby Patty, Mr. Lefty, Mr. big144, Mr.Cartoon, Mr.Rachel, Mr.Z-man.sock, MrJoshbumstead, MrLeap, MrMarmite, MrPixar, Mrdinwiddy, Mrfunnyd, Mrsanitazier, Mrschimpf, Mrsponge, Mrstonky, Mrx9898, Msm, Muffins4989, Mupplan, Murasaki Seiko, Murderbike, Mushroom, Musicmanrak, Muslimpride009, Mysdaao, N. Harmonik, NFAN3, NFK!, NGMan62, NHJG, Nakhila9228, Nakon, Namine001, Naninuneno, NapHit, Napoleon Dynamite42, Narco, Narnia2514, Nathan Laing, Nathen, NawlinWiki, Ncboy2010, Ncmvocalist, Nehrams2020, Neier, Neilbeach, Neiljt, Neji255, Nelson2510, Nemo24, Neomerge, Neorser1336, Net1360, Netsnipe, NewEnglandYankee, NewYork483, Nick4545, Nickelodeon745, Nickelodeonfan2007, Nicktoonwild580, Nico357, Nicoli4000, Niduzzi, Night Gyr, Nights Not End, Nimrod 14, Ninja XLR, Ninjawarriordex, Ninnnu, Nintendoman01, Nitsud.efif, Nitweet, Nlu, Nmzanie, Nn123645, No Guru, Noha307, Noirish, NoseNuggets, Nosebutton, Not a winner, Not so big chris, Not-just-yeti, Notdedyet, Nothingofwater, Notshane, Ntay, Nufc, Numbo3, Nutter86, O p e t h, OOODDD, Obaidz96, Oddparents5000, Of, Ogen Mc, Oh babe, Oh my lantern, Ohconfucius, Ohnoitsjamie, Oklonia, OlEnglish, Old Guard, Oliviamaggie, Omicronpersei8, Onepiece226, OrangeDog, Ordbok, OregonD00d, Orfen, Original Username, Orioneight, Orizon, Ortensia, Oscarthecat, Oscinis, Osmium4, OverlordQ, Owen4004, Oxguy3, P24F, PAntoni, PGSONIC, PMDrive1061, Pablomartinez, Paganpoetry005, Paintballkidd07, Pajo1 1, PakiboyCDN, Panic! It's Emma, Paolo144, Papachu, Paper Luigi, Paradocks2, Paradocks5, Parhamr, Park70, Pascal.Tesson, Patrickrox11, Patstuart, Patton 3, Paul A, Paul Barlow, Paul the greatest, PaulMottley, Paxsimius, Peanut M&M, Peanut136, Pediagoof, Pedro thy master, Persian Poet Gal, Peruvianllama, Peter, Peter M Dodge, Pfalstad, Phantomsnake, PhattyFatt, Phil A. Fry, Phil1988, Phil21, Philip Trueman, Philipderby, Philwelch, Phuntsok2000, Pichu8boy, Pickleownsyou, Pictureuploader, Pieman93, Pienator, Piet Delport, Pig de Wig, Pikachuperson24, Pikawil, Pillow2011, Pilotguy, PimRijkee, Pinkalfonzochief19, Pittsburgh Poet, Pittsfordljb, Pizza1016, Pizza365, Pjdt1, Plainnym, Planecrazy20, Planetary Chaos, Plarter, Player2896, Plop, Plophole, Poli-Psy, Pongeboob Pooppants, Pooptown, Pop73, Porchcorpter, Portofinopost, PorygonX, Posidon09, Ppk01, Pranai, Premkudva, PrestonH, Princess Clown, Princess sunny, PrincessRosada, Producercunningham, Prolog, Pronoun, Protozoic Waste, ProveIt, Pruzman, PseudoSudo, Psycho Kirby, Pubaquoc, Puccafan920, Puchiko, Pur31337n355, PureRED, Purple Paint, Pômgut, QuasyBoy, Quendus, Quesodelpoodelpoo, Quibik, Quidam65, Quirk, Qwyrxian, Qxz, R, R-HIT, RPH, Rabbitfromanimalstudios, Radio Guy, Raghav273, Railer-man, Ral315, Randallrobinstine, RandomEcho, Randyfx, Raneman25, Rangermups, Ransack, Rapturerocks, Rard, Rat235478683, Rattis1, RattleMan, Raven23, Ravenpi, Ravster1993, Razorflame, Rcj442, Reach Out to the Truth, Readersmenu, Red Director, Redvans, Redyka94, Remember the dot, RememberMe?, Remurmur, Repetition, Res2216firestar, Resutas, Retiono Virginian, Reverter5000, RexNL, ReyBrujo, Rezashah4, Rgoodermote, Ric36, Riccosimba6, Rich Farmbrough, Richard4barnsley, Richard959, Richhoncho, Rickjr36, Rickyu22, Rikimaru, Ring2011, Rivemont, Rjfost, Rjwilmsi, Roadrunner3000, RobJ1981, Robbingdog, Robby Robertsun, RobertG, Robofish, Rocknroll47, Rockskeeper, Rodimus Rhyme, Rofl, Roman300, Ronbo76, Rorschach, Rory096, RoyBoy, Royboy193456, Royboycrashfan, Rrburke, Rsm99833, Rtreynor, Rudjek, Russ is the sex, Rutherfordjigsaw, Ryan Holloway, Ryan Postlethwaite, RyanGerbil10, Ryangibsonstewart, Ryanincro, Ryulong, SFGiants, SJP, SL93, SQL, Sabretooth, Sailboat12345, Saint Invective, Salmonofdoubt2, Sam916, Samlowry, Sammythesnake4, Sammywand365, Sampi, Sampo Sheep, Sanatluri, Sandmaster, Sango123, Sarkie, Sauc1343, Sb2007, Schavira, Schmiteye, SchmuckyTheCat, Scohoust, ScottMHoward, ScrapMetal, Scy1192, Sd31415, Secret Saturdays, Sedef1322, Seraphimblade, Seresin, Seritinajii, Sgt. R.K. Blue, Shadoman, Shadow El, Shadow-sama, Shadow1, Shanel, Shanes, Shark96z, Sharkdude95, SheepNotGoats, Shepard, Shermlindcastle, Shoeofdeath, ShortShadow, Showtimepg, Shuhao, SigKauffman, Signalizing, SilentBob88, Simmysimsim, Simpol Kyzel, Simpsons2010, Singerboi22, Singyouranthem, Sintonak.X, Sipi1230, Siriusblack902, Sivazh, Sjakkalle, Sjones23, Skarebo, Skiddyjim, Skomorokh, Skytvfreak, Slapjaw1, Slaryn, Slayerm10, Slof, Slon02, Slysplace, Smash, Smgold92, Smijes08, SnappingTurtle, Soangry, Socks 01, Sokoru, Sollywon, Solver, Some P. Erson, Someguy1221, Son of Kong, Sonic567, SonicBlue, Sonicxtreme, Sooner Dave, Southsydney, SpOnGeFaN818, SpaceChimp1992,

Spacepiratedude, Sparky the Seventh Chaos, SparrowsWing, Speciate, Speeda psx, Spettro9, Spiffyxd, SpigotMap, Spike Wilbury, SpikeMolec, SpikeTorontoRCP, Spittlespat, Spkonner, Splash, Splat5572, Sponge1987, Sponge3000, Sponge4000, Sponge67, Sponge8485, SpongeBobDude, SpongeBobRocksMan, SpongeJustin4, SpongeMcFly2015, SpongePappy, SpongeSebastian, SpongeZac, Spongebob1, Spongebobhannah, Spongeman537, Spongerulz67, Spongesquid, Spongeyfan, SpuriousQ, Sputnikcccp, Spyguy41, Squidward2602, Squirepants101, Ssilvers, StanBrinkerhoff, Star500, Starbucks95905, Starionwolf, Steel, Stelios7, Stephen Bain, Steve4961, StevenMario, Stevencho, Stevenrasnick, Steveo2, Stickjustin, Stone, StonedChipmunk, Stormbay, Stretchyrubberbands, StuartDouglas, Stwalkerster, Suduser85, Sue Rangell, SummaBritt, SummerPhD, Sundeuce98, Sunnybanks, SuperDude115, SuperFlash101, SuperKoala100, SuperSaiyaMan, Supermariofan13, Swagger28, Swalley, SweetPinkCandy, Swimboy814, Swimm212, Swotboy2000, Sylverstone, Symplectic Map, TBH, TFX, TGilmour, TH6944, TMBLover, TPIRFanSteve, TSO1D, TV IS GREAT!, TVfanatic2K, Taarten, Tabletop, Tad Lincoln, Tae1988, Tai112, Takua X, Tall Midget, TangoTizerWolfstone, Tardlink, Tassedethe, Tawker, Tbhotch, Tbone2001, Tbsdy lives, Tdoozle2005, Team Rocket agent, Tedder, Teen hippy, Teh Squonkz, TehBrandon, Tehkiddie, Teles, Tellyaddict, Teman13, Tennekis, Tensai, Terminator50, Terrx, Tesi1700, Tfine80, Thardin12, The 888th Avatar, The Arc of Fame, The Ed Master 10, The Gerg, The JPS, The Man 16, The Man in Question, The Movie King!, The PainKiller 666, The Rogue Penguin, The Runescape Junkie, The Shadow-Fighter, The Thing That Should Not Be, The Utahraptor, The chuck, The unknown clone trooper, The wub, TheAdventMaster, TheAznSensation, TheBlueFlamingo, TheGuitarHero, TheLoverofLove, TheRanger, TheRealFennShysa, TheRyk, TheSterTube, TheValentineBros, Thebigfan, Thebigfan2, Thegreat100, ThegreatWakkorati, Thekid959, Them23, Theman818, Themasterofwiki, Thenoblenew, Theodork, Therealinformer46, Therius, Theshywillraindeath, Thewiseeye3400, Thief Lord, Think outside the box, Thistheman, Thomas75, Thunderboltz, Tiamy, Tibrox, Tide rolls, Tinton5, Tiria, Tmisch64, Tmstarlac, Tony Fox, Tony1, Tonypizzaguy, Tornvmax, Touchface1, Transity, TrapStilton, Travelbird, TravisAF, Treebark, Tregoweth, Trenntsux, Tressif, Trevor MacInnis, Trivialist, Trogga, Troped, Trusilver, Tschow, Tsears, Tshill9, TurboBoostMan, Tuxedobob, Twofourd, Twooars, Tyler775, Tyrdium, UBracter, UK Bakosi, UberScienceNerd, Ultimateguy9999, Ultrapasty, Unionhawk, UnitedStatesian, Unreal7, Unused0025, Uranium grenade, Uturnaroun, Uzzo2, V4R, VG Cats Tipe 2, VP44444, Vaiol123, Valerius Myotis, Valientherox, Valley2city, Vampire31, Vbartilucci, Veemon12, Venerated, Vic201401, Victorirupp, Vidpro23, Vilerage, Vincelord, Vinhchaule, Volcanictelephone, Volt4ire, Voltorb, Vostok5, Vrray people1000, Vrrayman7000, Vulcanstar6, Vulian, WAvegetarian, WPjcm, WTRiker, WUTANG, Wafir, Waggers, Wahkeenah, Wakawakadis, WalshFan1, Waluigi Freak 99, Wangi, Ward3001, WarioWare, Warlordwolf, Warmpuppy2, WarthogDemon, Washedwithblood7, Wayne Slam, Wayward, We are the champions, Wearefictional, Weaselpie, Websurfer246, Weemer, WeezleBeezle, Welsh, Wengero, WereSpielChequers, Wertdunk999, Wgreaseball3, Whee-boy, WhisperToMe, Whispering, Whopper1987, WikHead, Wiki RoxMySox, Wiki alf, Wiki0709, WikiDoody17, WikiEditor44, WikiIvan, WikiKatie4, WikiMaster500, WikiPediaAid, WikiRigby, WikiSpector, Wikialexdx, Wikiaway, Wikier9, Wikipe-tan, Wikipediarules2221, Wikipediatrix, Wile e2005, Will Beback, Will122194, Wimt, Wingedsubmariner, Winter 2007, Wknight94, Wmplayer, Wondercat88, Wongshunyik, Woohookitty, Wouldyoulikeacookie, Wtfdontkill, Wtmitchell, Wuhwuzdat, Wwagner, Wxxvi, Wyatt Riot, Wynneruth, X-lostprophets-x, X06, XXAtreyuXx, Xaosflux, Xcentaur, Xenon54, Xeokym, Xezbeth, Xis10ce, Xmu, Xom55, XxAvalanchexX, Yamamoto Ichiro, Yamanbaiia, Yamiblaze, Yankeesman312, Ycchon, Ycolonna@cox.net, Yeyosmoka21, YgoFan90, Ylndgomez, Yoguy11, You're The Man Now Dog, Yowee, Yskyflyer, ZACHVega, Zacefron52, ZacheryWanzer, Zaiise, Zanimum, Zany zacky, Zaphody3k, Zasderfght, Zatbofhbq, Zenlax, Zepheus, Zephyr103, Zephyr2k, Zhouf12, Zidane tribal, Ziggurat, Zilog Jones, Zoe, Zone46, ZooFari, ZookPS3, Zozomormoraazozo, Zurishaddai, Zutzitzitzah, Zuwairi, Zwesomehandz, Zxombie, Zzuuzz, A, Мурад 97, 立足东方, 3800 anonymous edits

Alan Carr: Chatty Man *Source*: http://en.wikipedia.org/w/index.php?oldid=465289116 *Contributors*: 12345abcxyz20082009, After Midnight, AnOddName, Andremp0, BRUTE, Bearcat, Bencey, Bkonrad, Breakinguptheguy, Chrisjonsson14, Crystal Linux, DBuddy, David Rush, Davidglyngriffiths, Drilnoth, ELNO Checking, Gearoidm09, HearnyIchiban, January2007, Jennie--x, Jim Michael, Jim1138, Jimbo888, Jkaharper, Jlaws1994, John of Reading, Jonnyt 123, Katieh5584, Ksood91, Leszek Jańczuk, MC32, Magnius, McGeddon, Moozipan Cheese, Nick Number, NickJonasBeMine, Panel Guy, Rambo's Revenge, RememberDecember91, Rian19, Rian2011, Rich Farmbrough, Rui78901, Salavat, Sam-842, Sash 1990, Shokuwarrior, Sllewellyn7, Soophie, Stephenb, TBloemink, Tassedethe, The wub, TheDr2o10, Thealex1996, Theog101, Tim1357, Trushnakhatri, TylerGaRyan, 418 anonymous edits

Happy Feet Two *Source*: http://en.wikipedia.org/w/index.php?oldid=465534950 *Contributors*: 4twenty42o, Ahmedfarhat, Akcarver, AnmaFinotera, Arjayay, Art1991, Asaraullo05, Avadavat, Avenue X at Cicero, BKMastah, BRUTE, BarrettM82, Barry Wom, Bender235, Bilbo571, Blazes, Bluesilas, Bovineboy2008, Bt8257, C.Fred, Carniolus, Cineplex, Ckatz, CodyTheMaverick, Corey.7.11.1992, DailyEditor, Dan arndt, Danielj 08, De728631, December21st2012Freak, Denisarona, Dhabolt, Dravecky, Easy4me, Eippol, Erik, Esanchez7587, F-Yeah-Robin-Hollywood, Faster2010, FollowGuard, Freaky Face Films, Fredinandus, Gabrielkat, GoingBatty, Gran2, Grindor, Halil marx07, I hate a lot of bad movies, ILoveScratte2, Imagine Wizard, In the shining light, InfamousPrince, JBsupreme, JForget, Jasonbres, Jebus989, Jedi94, Jeff G., Jmac2681, JohnI, Jside, JustAGal, Kevin Canzanello, Krazycev13, LDEJRuff, Lakeyboy, Lava100100, Leonard^Bloom, Lionkingfan3, Logarkh, Lord Oblivion, Lupers, MarcoAurelio, Materialscientist, Mateusz5500, Mephistophelian, Mika1h, MikeAllen, MikeyMouse10, Millahnna, Monkeys 9711, Mrschimpf, Ndboy, New World Man, NiTenIchiRyu, Nymf, Ocaasi, Ottawa4ever, PMDrive1061, Philip Trueman, Phoenix1304, RegentsPark, Revrant, Rflores0915, RidgeRacerFan, Ring2011, Rjwilmsi, Sausage077, ScratteLover3, SeoMac, Sesu Prime, ShellyLover, Shoy, Sjones23, Skier Dude, SkyWalker, Skywatcher68, Sonicyouth86, Spongefrog, Sreejithk2000, Stevethecrayon, SummerPhD, Superghost987, Tastes like lead, Tbhotch, TehDogfather, The Mark of the Beast, Thegreat100, Unscented, VernoWhitney, Visokor, WhatGuy, Yos233, 794 anonymous edits

Image Sources, Licenses and Contributors

File:Williams, Robin (USGov) crop.jpg *Source*: http://en.wikipedia.org/w/index.php?title=File:Williams,_Robin_(USGov)_crop.jpg *License*: Public Domain *Contributors*: John J. Kruzel/American Forces Press Service

File:Robin Williams 2008.jpg *Source*: http://en.wikipedia.org/w/index.php?title=File:Robin_Williams_2008.jpg *License*: Creative Commons Attribution 2.0 *Contributors*: Steve Jurvetson from Menlo Park, USA

File:Robin williams uso.jpg *Source*: http://en.wikipedia.org/w/index.php?title=File:Robin_williams_uso.jpg *License*: Public Domain *Contributors*: United States Army

File:Star full.svg *Source*: http://en.wikipedia.org/w/index.php?title=File:Star_full.svg *License*: Public Domain *Contributors*: User:Conti from the original images by User:RedHotHeat

File:Star empty.svg *Source*: http://en.wikipedia.org/w/index.php?title=File:Star_empty.svg *License*: Creative Commons Attribution-Sharealike 2.5 *Contributors*: User:Conti from the original images by User:RedHotHeat

File:Flag of the United States.svg *Source*: http://en.wikipedia.org/w/index.php?title=File:Flag_of_the_United_States.svg *License*: Public Domain *Contributors*: Anomie

Image:Wheelchair symbol.svg *Source*: http://en.wikipedia.org/w/index.php?title=File:Wheelchair_symbol.svg *License*: Public Domain *Contributors*: ALE!, David Levy, Dream out loud, Ktims, Lensovet, NE2, Sarang, Stifle, Wst, 2 anonymous edits

Image:GuentherZ 2006-12-27 Palmenhaus 1334.jpg *Source*: http://en.wikipedia.org/w/index.php?title=File:GuentherZ_2006-12-27_Palmenhaus_1334.jpg *License*: GNU Free Documentation License *Contributors*: GuentherZ

File:Gnome globe current event.svg *Source*: http://en.wikipedia.org/w/index.php?title=File:Gnome_globe_current_event.svg *License*: GNU Lesser General Public License *Contributors*: David Vignoni (globe, clock face/ring), Anomie (clock hands), David Göthberg (making the clock red, shadows). Anomie and David G (putting all the parts together).

File:Jonas Brothers KCA.jpg *Source*: http://en.wikipedia.org/w/index.php?title=File:Jonas_Brothers_KCA.jpg *License*: Creative Commons Attribution-Sharealike 3.0 *Contributors*: Ucla90024

Image:2009 KCA Orange Carpet.jpg *Source*: http://en.wikipedia.org/w/index.php?title=File:2009_KCA_Orange_Carpet.jpg *License*: Creative Commons Attribution-Sharealike 3.0 *Contributors*: Ucla90024

File:Final Slime a.jpg *Source*: http://en.wikipedia.org/w/index.php?title=File:Final_Slime_a.jpg *License*: Creative Commons Attribution-Sharealike 3.0 *Contributors*: Socalphoto

File:Teddy bear from Aritificial Intelligence.jpeg *Source*: http://en.wikipedia.org/w/index.php?title=File:Teddy_bear_from_Aritificial_Intelligence.jpeg *License*: unknown *Contributors*: Courcelles, Monty845, Skier Dude

Image:First Congregational United Church of Christ copyright Kaihsu Tai 20080203.jpg *Source*: http://en.wikipedia.org/w/index.php?title=File:First_Congregational_United_Church_of_Christ_copyright_Kaihsu_Tai_20080203.jpg *License*: GNU Free Documentation License *Contributors*: Kaihsu Tai

File:Lockheed Vega 5b Smithsonian.jpg *Source*: http://en.wikipedia.org/w/index.php?title=File:Lockheed_Vega_5b_Smithsonian.jpg *License*: GNU Free Documentation License *Contributors*: Sergio Caltagirone

File:WilsonAdamsStillerMay09.jpg *Source*: http://en.wikipedia.org/w/index.php?title=File:WilsonAdamsStillerMay09.jpg *License*: Creative Commons Attribution 3.0 *Contributors*: cranberries at http://www.flickr.com/photos/51531384@N00/

File:Night at the museum label.JPG *Source*: http://en.wikipedia.org/w/index.php?title=File:Night_at_the_museum_label.JPG *License*: Creative Commons Attribution-Sharealike 3.0 *Contributors*: RadioFan (talk)

Image:MorkMindyHouse.jpg *Source*: http://en.wikipedia.org/w/index.php?title=File:MorkMindyHouse.jpg *License*: Public domain *Contributors*: JamesReyes at en.wikipedia

Image:BikiniLigging.PNG *Source*: http://en.wikipedia.org/w/index.php?title=File:BikiniLigging.PNG *License*: GNU Free Documentation License *Contributors*: Original uploader was Cars en travel at nl.wikipedia

File:Cal Arts entrance.jpg *Source*: http://en.wikipedia.org/w/index.php?title=File:Cal_Arts_entrance.jpg *License*: GNU Free Documentation License *Contributors*: Coolcaesar at en.wikipedia

License

SIA information can be obtained at www.ICGtesting.com
nted in the USA
OW09s1813101114
2906LV00009B/124/P

9 781743 382646